INFLATION RATE
(GDP Deflator)

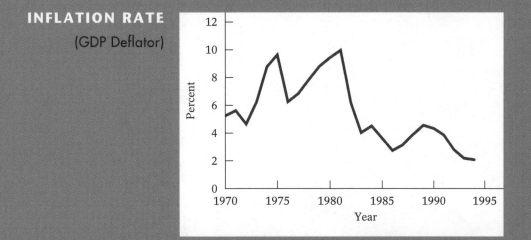

NOMINAL INTEREST RATE
(Three-Month Treasury Bills)

MACROECONOMICS

MACROECONOMICS

● ● ● ● ● ● ● ● ● ● ●

Third Edition

N. Gregory Mankiw

Harvard University

WORTH PUBLISHERS

Macroeconomics, Third Edition

Copyright © 1997, 1994, 1992 by Worth Publishers, Inc.

All rights reserved

Manufactured in the United States of America

Library of Congress Catalog Card Number: 96–060597

ISBN: 1–57259–141–2

Printing: 1 2 3 4 5–01 00 99 98 97

Development editors: Paul Shensa and Marjorie Anderson

Design: Malcolm Grear Designers

Art Director: George Touloumes

Production editor: Timothy C. Prairie

Production supervisor: Lou Capaldo

Line art: Academy Artworks, Inc.

Composition and prepress: Monotype Composition Company, Inc.

Printing and binding: Rand McNally Book Services

Photo Credit: p. v © Ingrid Kannel, Wellesley, MA.

Cover: Malcolm Grear Designers

Worth Publishers

33 Irving Place

New York, New York 10003

About the Author

N. Gregory Mankiw is Professor of Economics at Harvard University. He began his study of economics at Princeton University, where in 1980 he received an A.B. *summa cum laude*. After earning a Ph.D. in economics from MIT, he began teaching at Harvard in 1985 and was promoted to full professor in 1987. Today, he regularly teaches both undergraduate and graduate courses in macroeconomics.

Professor Mankiw is a prolific writer and a regular contributor to scholarly journals. His research ranges across many fields within economics and includes work on price adjustment, consumer behavior, financial markets, housing, monetary and fiscal policy, and economic growth. In addition to his duties at Harvard, he serves as Director of the Monetary Economics Program of the National Bureau of Economic Research, a nonprofit think tank in Cambridge, Massachusetts. He is also an adviser to the Federal Reserve Bank of Boston and the Congressional Budget Office.

Professor Mankiw lives in Wellesley, Massachusetts, with his wife Deborah and their two children Catherine and Nicholas. In his free time, he plays with his border terrier, Keynes.

To Deborah

Those branches of politics, or of the laws of social life, in which there exists a collection of facts sufficiently sifted and methodized to form the beginning of a science should be taught *ex professo*. Among the chief of these is Political Economy, the sources and conditions of wealth and material prosperity for aggregate bodies of human beings. . . .

The same persons who cry down Logic will generally warn you against Political Economy. It is unfeeling, they will tell you. It recognises unpleasant facts. For my part, the most unfeeling thing I know of is the law of gravitation: it breaks the neck of the best and most amiable person without scruple, if he forgets for a single moment to give heed to it. The winds and waves too are very unfeeling. Would you advise those who go to sea to deny the winds and waves—or to make use of them, and find the means of guarding against their dangers? My advice to you is to study the great writers on Political Economy, and hold firmly by whatever in them you find true; and depend upon it that if you are not selfish or hard-hearted already, Political Economy will not make you so.

John Stuart Mill
1867

Brief Table of Contents

Table of Contents

Part *Two*

The Economy in the Long Run 43

Chapter *3*

National Income: Its Production, Distribution, and Allocation 45

Chapter 5 . . .
. . . .
Unemployment 123

Chapter *6*
• • • • • • • • • • •
Money and Inflation 146

Part *Three*
. . . .
The Economy in the Short Run 225

Chapter *8*
. . . .
Introduction to Economic Fluctuations 227

Chapter *11*
Aggregate Demand in the Open Economy 299

Chapter *12*
• • • • • • • • • • •
Aggregate Supply 332

Chapter *13*
· · · · · · · · · · · ·
The Macroeconomic Policy Debate 361

Chapter *14*
· · · · · · · · · · · ·
Recent Developments in the Theory of Economic Fluctuations 385

Part *Four*
. . . .
More on the Microeconomics Behind Macroeconomics 401

Chapter *15*
. . . .
Consumption 403

Epilogue
· · · · · · · · · · · ·
What We Know, What We Don't 496

List of Case Studies

Preface

• • • • • • • • • • • •

Although poets may get pleasure from the sheer act of writing poetry, textbook authors are pleased only if their work is read, understood, and enjoyed by students. I have, therefore, been heartened by the response to the first two editions of this book. Professors at hundreds of schools in dozens of countries have chosen to use it in their courses. Student reaction, as reported in course evaluations and letters students have sent me, was as enthusiastic as I ever could have hoped.

In the first edition, I pointed out that this book differs markedly from those I used as a student both in its organization and its emphasis. In subsequent editions, I have refined the content of the book while preserving the features that make it distinctive. Let me begin this third edition by recapping four of my objectives for this book.

First, I offer a balance between short-run and long-run issues in macroeconomics. Courses in macroeconomics will always present the theory of short-run economic fluctuations, because it provides the basis for understanding most discussions of monetary and fiscal policy. Yet if students are to understand fully the implications of public policies, courses must give ample attention to long-run topics as well, including economic growth, the natural rate of unemployment, persistent inflation, and government debt. As if we needed reminding, recent years have highlighted the importance of understanding the effects of policies at all time horizons: any intelligent discussion of continuing budget deficits requires balancing short-run and long-run concerns.

Second, I integrate the insights of both Keynesian and classical economics. The prominent role of the Keynesian approach to economic fluctuations in this and most other textbooks is a testament to the influence and importance of Keynes's *General Theory*. Yet, in the aftermath of the Keynesian revolution, too many economists forgot that classical economics provides the right answers to many fundamental questions. In this book I incorporate many of the contributions of the classical economists before Keynes and the new classical economists of the past two decades. Substantial coverage is given, for example, to the loanable-funds theory of the interest rate, the quantity theory of money, and the problem of time inconsistency. At the same time, however, I recognize that many of the ideas of Keynes and the new Keynesians are necessary for understanding economic fluctuations. Substantial coverage is given also to the *IS-LM* model of aggregate demand, the short-run tradeoff between inflation and unemployment, and modern theories of wage and price rigidity.

Third, I present macroeconomics using a variety of simple models. Instead of pretending that there is one model that is complete enough to explain all facets of the economy, I encourage students to learn how to use and compare a set of prominent models. This approach has the pedagogical value that each model can be kept relatively simple and can be presented within one or two chapters. More important, this approach asks students to think like economists, who always keep various models in mind when analyzing economic events or public policies.

Fourth, I emphasize that macroeconomics is an empirical discipline, motivated and guided by a wide array of experience. This book contains 77 case studies that use macroeconomic theory to shed light on real-world data or events. To highlight the broad applicability of the basic theory, I have drawn the case studies both from current issues facing the world's economies and from dramatic historical episodes. The case studies analyze the policies of Alan Greenspan, George Bush, Henry Ford, and Alexander Hamilton. They teach the reader how to apply economic principles to issues from fourteenth-century Europe, the island of Yap, the land of Oz, and today's newspaper.

What's New in the Third Edition?

I have improved this book in its third edition in several ways. Most obviously, the book has been updated to incorporate new events, data, and ideas. Since the second edition was written, the Commerce Department introduced new chain-weighted measures of economic activity, Congress raised doubts about the accuracy of the consumer price index, the Clinton administration pushed for an increase in the minimum wage, Europe announced the name of its planned common currency, and capital flight forced the Mexican peso to collapse. As always, new research has refined our understanding of economic growth and fluctuations. Although the basics of macroeconomic theory are much the same as they were three years ago, enough has changed in the details and practice of macroeconomics to warrant putting out a new edition.

In addition, the book's pedagogy has been further refined. Although the overall organization remains the same, some material has been rearranged and rewritten. The Mundell-Fleming model, for instance, is now presented in Chapter 11, immediately after its cousin, the *IS-LM* model. Chapter 14, now called "Recent Developments in the Theory of Economic Fluctuations," presents a more intuitive description of real-business-cycle theory, as well as a discussion of new Keynesian economics. Chapter 6 presents a simpler and more complete discussion of the causes and effects of hyperinflation. Throughout the book, new case studies have been added, and some old ones have been omitted or revised. Dozens of new problems have been added at the ends of chapters. Together with various editors and students, I have scrutinized each sentence of the book to see whether it can be made clearer.

Finally, all the changes that I made, and the many others that I considered, were evaluated keeping in mind the benefits of brevity. From my own experience as a student, I know that long books are less likely to be read. My goal in this book is to offer the clearest, most up-to-date, most accessible course in macroeconomics in the fewest words possible.

The Arrangement of Topics

This new edition maintains the strategy of first examining the long run when prices are flexible and then examining the short run when prices are sticky. That is, it begins with classical models of the economy and explains fully the long-run equilibrium before discussing deviations from that equilibrium. This strategy has several advantages:

- Because the classical dichotomy permits the separation of real and monetary issues, the long-run material is easier for students to understand.

- When students begin studying short-run fluctuations, they understand fully the long-run equilibrium around which the economy is fluctuating.

- Beginning with market-clearing models makes clearer the link between macroeconomics and microeconomics.

- Students learn first the material that is less controversial among macroeconomists.

When I proposed this organizational strategy in the first edition, some instructors were skeptical about making such a major change in their courses. With time and experience, however, the skepticism has faded. Many instructors have reported to me that this organization greatly simplifies the teaching of macroeconomics.

I move now from strategy to tactics. What follows is a whirlwind tour of the book.

Part One: Introduction

The introductory material in Part One is brief so that students can get to the core topics quickly. Chapter 1 discusses the broad questions that macroeconomists address and the economist's approach of building models to explain the world. Chapter 2 introduces the key data of macroeconomics, emphasizing gross domestic product, the consumer price index, and the unemployment rate.

Part Two: The Economy in the Long Run

Part Two examines the long run over which prices are flexible. Chapter 3 presents the basic classical model of national income. In this model, the factors of production and the production technology determine the level of income, and the marginal products of the factors determine its distribution to households. In addition, the model shows how fiscal policy influences the allocation of the economy's resources among consumption, investment, and government purchases, and it highlights how the real interest rate equilibrates the supply and demand for goods and services.

Chapter 4 makes the classical analysis of the economy dynamic. It uses the Solow growth model to examine the evolution of the economy over time. The Solow model provides the basis for discussing why the standard of living varies so widely across countries and how public policies influence the level and growth of the standard of living.

Chapter 5 relaxes the assumption of full employment by discussing the dynamics of the labor market and the natural rate of unemployment. It examines various causes of unemployment, including job search, minimum-wage laws, union power, and efficiency wages. It also presents some important facts about patterns of unemployment.

Money and the price level are introduced in Chapter 6. Because prices are assumed to be fully flexible, the chapter presents the prominent ideas of classical monetary theory: the quantity theory of money, the inflation tax, the Fisher effect, the social costs of inflation, and the causes and costs of hyperinflation.

The study of open-economy macroeconomics begins in Chapter 7. Maintaining the assumption of full employment, this chapter presents models to explain the trade balance and the exchange rate. Various policy issues are addressed: the relationship between the budget deficit and the trade deficit, the macroeconomic impact of protectionist trade policies, and the effect of monetary policy on the value of a currency in the market for foreign exchange.

Part Three: The Economy in the Short Run

Part Three examines the short run when prices are sticky. It begins in Chapter 8 by introducing the model of aggregate supply and aggregate demand as well as the role of stabilization policy. Subsequent chapters refine the ideas introduced here.

Chapters 9 and 10 look more closely at aggregate demand. Chapter 9 presents the Keynesian cross and the theory of liquidity preference and uses these models as building blocks for developing the *IS-LM* model. Chapter 10 uses the *IS-LM* model to explain economic fluctuations and the aggregate demand curve. It concludes with an extended case study of the Great Depression.

The study of open-economy macroeconomics continues in Chapter 11, which focuses on short-run fluctuations in an open economy. This chapter presents the Mundell-Fleming model and shows how monetary and fiscal policies affect the economy under floating and fixed exchange-rate systems. It also discusses the debate over whether exchange rates should be floating or fixed.

Chapter 12 looks more closely at aggregate supply. It examines various approaches to explaining the short-run aggregate supply curve and discusses the short-run tradeoff between inflation and unemployment.

After the model of aggregate supply and aggregate demand has been fully developed, Chapter 13 turns to the debate over how this model should be applied to economic policy. It emphasizes two broad questions. Should monetary and fiscal policy be active or passive? Should policy be conducted by rule or by discretion? The chapter presents arguments on both sides of these questions.

Chapter 14 discusses recent developments in the theory of economic fluctuations. First, it presents the theory of real business cycles as an alternative way to view economic fluctuations. It discusses the basic elements of this new classical approach and the arguments advanced by its advocates and its critics. Second, it covers some new Keynesian developments in the theory of aggregate supply.

Part Four: More on the Microeconomics Behind Macroeconomics

After developing the long-run and short-run models, the book discusses several topics that refine our understanding of the economy by analyzing more fully the microeconomics behind macroeconomics. Chapter 15 presents the various theories of consumer behavior, including the Keynesian consumption function, Fisher's model of intertemporal choice, Modigliani's life-cycle hypothesis, and Friedman's permanent-income hypothesis. Chapter 16 focuses on the various debates over government debt, including the debate over Ricardian equivalence; it emphasizes that these debates arise largely because economists have different views of consumer behavior. Chapter 17 examines the theory behind the investment function. Chapter 18 provides additional material on the money market, including the role of the banking system in determining the money supply and the Baumol-Tobin model of money demand.

Epilogue
The book ends with a brief epilogue that reviews the broad lessons about which most macroeconomists would agree and some of the most important unresolved questions. This capstone chapter reminds students how the many models and themes of macroeconomics relate to one another. Here and throughout the book, I emphasize that despite the disagreements among macroeconomists, there is much that we know about how the economy works.

Alternative Syllabus

Instructors differ in the emphasis they place on various topics and in the sequence of topics they prefer. I have, therefore, tried to make this book as flexible as possible. Many of the chapters are self-contained. Instructors can change the emphases of their courses by rearranging chapters or by omitting some chapters entirely.

One example of an alternative syllabus is presented here. This syllabus maintains the strategy of first examining output and prices in the long run when prices are flexible, but it introduces sticky prices and short-run fluctuations earlier in the course. It defers all open-economy macroeconomics until after the study of fluctuations, and it defers the study of economic growth and the natural rate of unemployment until the end of the course.

Introduction
1. The Science of Macroeconomics
2. The Data of Macroeconomics

Income and Prices
3. National Income: Its Production, Distribution, and Allocation
6. Money and Inflation
8. Introduction to Economic Fluctuations
9. Aggregate Demand I
10. Aggregate Demand II
12. Aggregate Supply
13. The Macroeconomic Policy Debate
14. Recent Developments in the Theory of Economic Fluctuations

Open-Economy Macroeconomics

More on the Microeconomics Behind Macroeconomics

Learning Tools

I am pleased that students have found the previous editions of this book user-friendly. I have tried to make this third edition even more so.

Case Studies
Economics comes to life when it is applied to understanding actual events. Therefore, the 77 case studies (many new or revised in this edition) are an important learning tool. The frequency with which these case studies occur ensures that a student does not have to grapple with an overdose of theory before seeing the theory applied. Students report that the case studies are their favorite part of the book.

FYI Boxes
These boxes present ancillary material "for your information." I use these boxes to clarify difficult concepts, to provide additional information about the tools of economics, and to show how economics relates to our daily lives. Several are new or revised in this edition.

Comment Boxes
In this edition I have added comment boxes within many of the figures. The comment boxes describe briefly and draw attention to important points that the figures illustrate. They should help students both learn and review the material.

Mathematical Notes
I use occasional mathematical footnotes to keep more difficult material out of the body of the text. These notes make an argument more rigorous or present a proof of a mathematical result. They can easily be skipped by those students who have not been introduced to the necessary mathematical tools.

Chapter Summaries
Every chapter ends with a brief, nontechnical summary of its major lessons. Students can use the summaries to place the material in perspective and to review for exams.

Key Concepts
Learning the language of a field is a major part of any course. Within the chapter, each key concept is in **boldface** when it is introduced. At the end of the chapter, the key concepts are listed for review.

Questions for Review
After studying a chapter, students can immediately test their understanding of its basic lessons by answering the Questions for Review.

Problems and Applications
Every chapter includes Problems and Applications designed for homework assignments. Some of these are numerical applications of the theory in the chapter. Others encourage the student to go beyond the material in the chapter by addressing new issues that are closely related to the chapter topics. Some users of the second edition requested that more problems be added, and this third edition includes dozens of new ones.

Chapter Appendixes
Seven chapters include appendixes that offer additional material, sometimes at a higher level of mathematical sophistication. These are designed so that professors can cover certain topics in greater depth if they wish. The appendixes can be skipped altogether without loss of continuity.

Glossary
To help students become familiar with the language of macroeconomics, a glossary of more than 250 terms is provided at the back of the book.

Supplements for Students

Worth Publishers and I have been delighted at the positive feedback we have received on the supplements that accompany the book. There are two supplements for students that instructors can order to use in their courses.

Student Guide and Workbook
Roger Kaufman (Smith College) has revised his superb study guide for students. This guide offers various ways for students to learn the material in the text and assess their understanding.

- *Fill-in Questions* give students the opportunity to review and check their knowledge of the key terms and concepts in the chapter.
- *Multiple-Choice Questions* allow students to test themselves on the chapter material.
- *Exercises* guide students step by step through the various models using graphs and numerical examples.
- *Problems* ask students to apply the models on their own.

- *Data Questions* ask students to obtain and learn about readily available economic data.

- *Questions to Think About* require critical thinking as well as economic analysis.

MacroBytes

David Weil (Brown University) has updated his innovative software package for students. *MacroBytes* provides a range of activities to aid and motivate the student throughout the course.

- *Self-Tests.* Students can test their knowledge of the material in the book by taking multiple-choice tests on any chapter or combination of chapters. After the student responds, the program explains the answer and directs the student to specific sections in the book for additional study.

- *Data Plotter.* Students can explore macroeconomic data with time-series graphs and scatterplots.

- *Macro Models.* These modules provide simulations of the models presented in the book. Students can change the exogenous variables and see the outcomes in terms of shifting curves and recalculated numerical values of the endogenous variables. Each module contains exercises that instructors can assign as homework.

- *2001: A Game for Macroeconomists.* The game allows students to become President of the United States in the year 2001 and to make macroeconomic policy decisions based on news events, economic statistics, and approval ratings. It gives students a sense of the complex interconnections that influence the economy. It is also fun to play.

MacroBytes is available for the IBM PC in Windows format.

Supplements for Instructors

Additional supplements are available from Worth Publishers to help instructors enhance their courses.

Instructor's Resources

Andrew John (University of Virginia) and Patricia Pollard (Federal Reserve Bank) have revised this impressive resource manual for instructors. For each chapter of this book, the manual contains notes to the instructor, a detailed lecture outline, additional case studies, and coverage of advanced topics. Instructors can use the manual to prepare their lectures, and they can reproduce whatever pages they choose as handouts for students.

Solutions Manual

John Fernald (Federal Reserve Board) and Jason Furman (Harvard University) have updated the solutions manual for all of the Questions for Review and Problems and Applications. The manual also contains the answers to selected questions from the *Student Guide and Workbook* and the answers to the software exercises.

Test Bank
Nancy Jianakoplos (Colorado State University) has updated the test bank so that it now includes over 1000 multiple-choice questions to accompany the text. Several short numerical problems are also provided for each chapter. The Test Bank is available both as a printed book and on disks. The disks include a test-generation program and are available for the IBM PC and Apple Macintosh.

Transparency Masters
Instructors can obtain enlarged master copies of all the figures in the text to prepare overhead transparencies for use in lecture.

Translations

The English-language version of this book has been used in dozens of countries. To make the book more accessible for students around the world, editions are now (or will soon be) available in nine other languages: Armenian, French, German, Italian, Japanese, Mandarin, Portuguese, Russian, and Spanish. Instructors who would like information about these translations should contact Worth Publishers.

Acknowledgments

When writing and revising this book, I benefitted from the input of many reviewers and colleagues. I would like to thank each of those who, for this or previous editions, gave up their scarce time to help me improve the economics or pedagogy of this text:

Francis Ahking
University of Connecticut

Steven Allen
North Carolina State University

Laurence Ball
Johns Hopkins University

Robert Barry
College of William and Mary

Robert Barsky
University of Michigan

Susanto Basu
University of Michigan

Charles Bischoff
Binghamton University

Dwight M. Blood
Brigham Young University

Ronald Bodkin
University of Ottawa

Kathleen Brook
New Mexico State University

John Campbell
Harvard University

Niko Canner
McKinsey and Company

Vanessa Craft
Bentley College

Charles DeLorme, Jr.
University of Georgia

Paula DeMasi
International Monetary Fund

William Dickens
University of California at Berkeley

John Driscoll
Brown University

Donald Dutkowsky
Syracuse University

Karen Dynan
Federal Reserve Board

Douglas Elmendorf
Federal Reserve Board

Gerald Epstein
University of Massachusetts

Antonio Fatas
INSEAD

John Fernald
Federal Reserve Board

Peter Frevert
University of Kansas

Michelle R. Garfinkel
University of California at Irvine

Edward Gramlich
University of Michigan

Chris Hanes
University of Pennsylvania

Daniel Himarios
University of Texas at Arlington

Steven Holland
University of Kentucky

Dennis Jansen
Texas A&M University

Nancy Jianakoplos
Colorado State University

Andrew John
University of Virginia

Klaus Dieter John
Chemnitz University of Technology

David Johnson
Harvard University

Roger Kaufman
Smith College

Manfried Keil
Northeastern University

David C. Klingaman
Ohio University

Kenneth Koelln
University of North Texas

John Laitner
University of Michigan

John Lapp
North Carolina State University

Emily C. Lawrance
Denison University

Daniel Levy
Emory University

Bill Maloney
University of Illinois at Urbana-Champaign

Deborah Mankiw
NBER

W. Douglas McMillin
Louisiana State University

Starr McMullen
Oregon State University

David Meinster
Formerly Temple University

Andrew Metrick
Harvard University

Jeffrey Miron
Boston University

Egon Neuberger
State University of New York at Stony Brook

Neil Niman
University of New Hampshire

Stefan Oppers
International Monetary Fund

David Parsley
Vanderbilt University

Thomas Pogue
University of Iowa

Uri M. Possen
Cornell University

Michael Rashes
Harvard University

David Rearden
University of Kansas

Changyong Rhee
Seoul National University

Joseph Ritter
St. Louis Federal Reserve

David Romer
University of California at Berkeley

Bennett Rushkoff
Federal Trade Commission

Amy Salsbury
Harvard University

Laurence S. Seidman
University of Delaware

Matthew Shapiro
University of Michigan

Boris Simkovich
Harvard University

David Spencer
Brigham Young University

David Tabak
NERA

Lowell Taylor
Carnegie-Mellon University

Anne Villamil
University of Illinois at Urbana-Champaign

Ping Wang
Pennsylvania State University

David Weil
Brown University

Jeffrey Zax
University of Colorado at Boulder

I would like to thank those instructors who sent me their old exams, from which I culled dozens of new problems to add to this edition: Laurence Ball (Johns Hopkins University), Susanto Basu (University of Michigan), John Driscoll (Brown University), Rachel Friedberg (Brown University), David Romer (University of California at Berkeley), and David Weil (Brown University).

The people at Worth Publishers have continued to be congenial and dedicated. I am grateful to Marjorie Anderson, Lou Capaldo, Timothy Prairie, Paul Shensa, George Touloumes, and Demetrios Zangos. Alexandra Nickerson once again did a great job preparing the index.

I am also grateful to Yvonne Zinfon, my secretary at Harvard, for her reliability, patience, and good cheer.

Finally, I would like to thank my four-year-old daughter Catherine and one-year-old son Nicholas. They helped immensely with this revision—both by providing a pleasant distraction and by reminding me that textbooks are written for the next generation.

N. Gregory Mankiw

Cambridge, Massachusetts
May 1996

MACROECONOMICS

Introduction

Part One introduces you to the study of macroeconomics. Chapter 1 discusses why macroeconomics is an exciting and important subject, it explains the tools that economists use to analyze the economy, and it outlines the plan of this book. Chapter 2 discusses the types of data that economists and policymakers use to monitor the economy.

The Science of Macroeconomics

The whole of science is nothing more than the refinement of everyday thinking.

Albert Einstein

1-1 Why Study Macroeconomics?

Why are incomes higher today than they were in 1950, and why were they higher in 1950 than in 1900? Why do some countries have high rates of inflation while others maintain stable prices? What causes recessions and depressions—recurrent periods of falling incomes and rising unemployment—and how can public policy be used to reduce their frequency and severity? **Macroeconomics**, the study of the economy as a whole, attempts to answer these and many related questions.

To appreciate the importance of macroeconomics, you need only read the newspaper or listen to the news. The media report macroeconomic developments daily. Headlines such as PERSONAL INCOME RISES 4 PERCENT, FEDERAL RESERVE MOVES TO COMBAT INFLATION, or STOCKS FALL AMID FEARS OF RECESSION are routine.

Macroeconomic events touch all of our lives. Business executives forecasting the demand for their products must guess how fast consumers' incomes will grow. Senior citizens living on fixed incomes wonder how fast prices will rise. Unemployed workers looking for jobs hope that the economy will boom and that firms will be hiring. All are affected by the state of the economy.

It is no surprise that macroeconomic issues play a central role in political debate. In the 1970s, Presidents Richard Nixon, Gerald Ford, and Jimmy Carter all wrestled unsuccessfully with a rising rate of inflation. In the 1980s, Presidents Ronald Reagan and George Bush presided over large federal budget deficits. In 1993, President Bill Clinton moved into the Oval Office committed to reducing the deficit and increasing economic growth. The popularity of the incumbent president rises during booms and falls during recessions. Voters are keenly aware of macroeconomic events, and politicians are equally aware of the importance of macroeconomic policy.

The influence of economic events on politics is most apparent during presidential elections. Economic policy is a prime topic of debate for the candidates, and the state of the economy has a powerful influence on the outcome of the election. During the election of 1992, Clinton's chief strategist wanted to keep the campaign focused on the key issue. He kept a sign in his office that read, "The economy, stupid."

Macroeconomic issues also influence international relations. Over the past fifteen years, the United States has imported many more goods and services from other countries than it has exported to them. These imports have been financed by borrowing heavily from other countries, especially Japan. Such international economic developments are a frequent source of tension among world leaders. While Japan and the United States remain close political allies, the two countries often squabble over differences in economic policy.

Macroeconomists are the scientists who try to explain the workings of the economy as a whole. They collect data on incomes, prices, unemployment, and many other economic variables from different periods of time and from different countries. They then attempt to formulate general theories that help to explain these data.

Like astronomers studying the evolution of stars or biologists studying the evolution of species, macroeconomists cannot conduct controlled experiments—experimenting with the economy would be too costly. Instead, they rely on natural experiments. Macroeconomists observe that economies differ from one another and that they change over time. These observations provide both the motivation for developing macroeconomic theories and the data for testing them.

To be sure, macroeconomics is a young and imperfect science. The macroeconomist's ability to predict the future course of economic events is no better than the meteorologist's ability to predict next month's weather. But, as you will see, macroeconomists do know quite a lot about how the economy works.

Our goal in studying macroeconomics, however, is not just to explain economic events but also to improve economic policy. The monetary and fiscal tools of government can influence the economy in powerful ways—both for good and for ill—and macroeconomics helps policymakers evaluate alternative policies. Macroeconomists are asked to explain the economic world as it is and to consider what it could be.

Case Study *1-1*

● ● ● ● ● ● ● ● ● ● ● ●

The Historical Performance of the U.S. Economy

Economists use many types of data to measure the performance of an economy. Three macroeconomic variables are particularly important: real gross domestic product (GDP), the inflation rate, and the unemployment rate. **Real GDP** measures the total income of everyone in the economy (adjusted for the level of prices). The **inflation rate** measures how quickly prices are rising. The **unemployment rate** measures the fraction of the labor force that is out of work. Macroeconomists study how these variables are determined, why they change over time, and how they interact with one another.

Figure 1-1

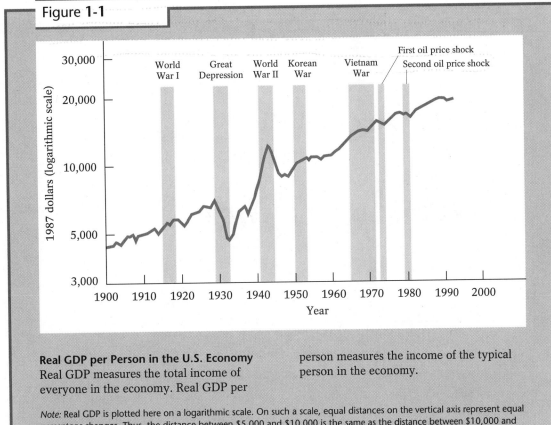

Real GDP per Person in the U.S. Economy
Real GDP measures the total income of everyone in the economy. Real GDP per person measures the income of the typical person in the economy.

Note: Real GDP is plotted here on a logarithmic scale. On such a scale, equal distances on the vertical axis represent equal *percentage* changes. Thus, the distance between $5,000 and $10,000 is the same as the distance between $10,000 and $20,000.

Source: U.S. Bureau of the Census (*Historical Statistics of the United States: Colonial Times to 1970*) and U.S. Department of Commerce.

Figure 1-1 shows real GDP per person for the U.S. economy. Two aspects of this figure are noteworthy. First, real GDP grows over time. Real GDP per person is today about five times its level in 1900. Second, growth in real GDP is not steady. There are repeated periods during which real GDP is falling, the most dramatic instance being the early 1930s. Such periods are called **recessions** if they are mild and **depressions** if they are more severe.

Figure 1-2 shows the U.S. inflation rate. You can see that inflation varies substantially. In the first half of the twentieth century, the inflation rate averaged about zero. Periods of falling prices, called **deflation**, were almost as common as periods of rising prices. In more recent history, inflation has been the norm. The inflation problem became most severe during the late 1970s, when prices rose persistently at a rate of almost 10 percent per year.

Figure 1-2

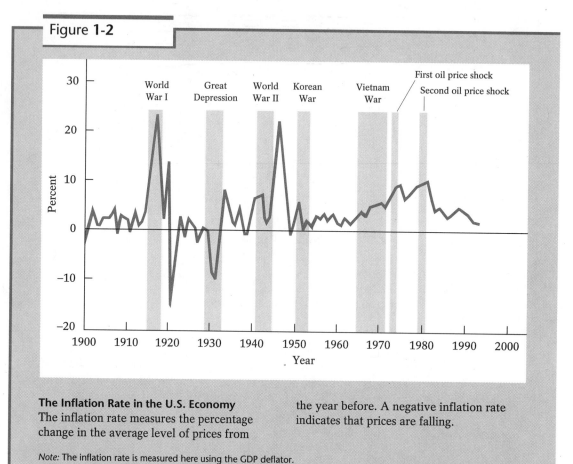

The Inflation Rate in the U.S. Economy
The inflation rate measures the percentage change in the average level of prices from the year before. A negative inflation rate indicates that prices are falling.

Note: The inflation rate is measured here using the GDP deflator.

Source: U.S. Bureau of the Census (*Historical Statistics of the United States: Colonial Times to 1970*) and U.S. Department of Commerce.

Figure 1-3 shows the U.S. unemployment rate. Notice that there is always some unemployment and that the amount varies from year to year. Although there is no pronounced long-term trend, unemployment since 1970 has been higher on average than unemployment during the 1950s and 1960s. Recessions and depressions are associated with unusually high unemployment. The highest rates of unemployment were reached during the Great Depression of the 1930s.

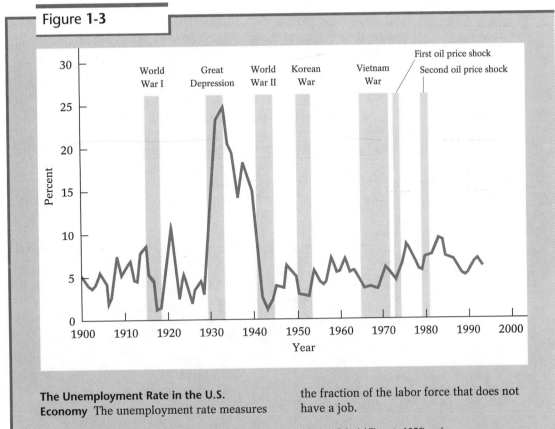

Figure 1-3

The Unemployment Rate in the U.S. Economy The unemployment rate measures the fraction of the labor force that does not have a job.

Source: U.S. Bureau of the Census (*Historical Statistics of the United States: Colonial Times to 1970*) and U.S. Department of Commerce.

These three figures offer a glimpse at the history of the U.S. economy. In the chapters that follow, we first discuss how these variables are measured and then develop theories to explain how they behave.

1-2 How Economists Think

Economists try to address the issues they study—even those that are politically charged—with a scientist's objectivity. Like any science, economics has its own set of tools: terminology, data, and a way of thinking. These tools can seem foreign and arcane to the uninitiated. The best way to become familiar with them is to practice using them. This book will afford you ample opportunity to do so. To make these tools less forbidding, however, let's discuss a few of them here.

Economic Models

Economists use **models** to understand the economy. Models are theories that summarize, often in mathematical terms, the relationships among economic variables. Models are useful because they help us to dispense with irrelevant details and to focus on important economic connections more clearly.

Models have two kinds of variables: exogenous variables and endogenous variables. **Exogenous variables** come from outside the model—they are the inputs into the model. **Endogenous variables** come from inside the model—they are the model's output. In other words, exogenous variables are fixed at the moment they enter the model, whereas endogenous variables are determined within the model. As Figure 1-4 illustrates, the purpose of a model is to show how the exogenous variables affect the endogenous variables.

Figure 1-4

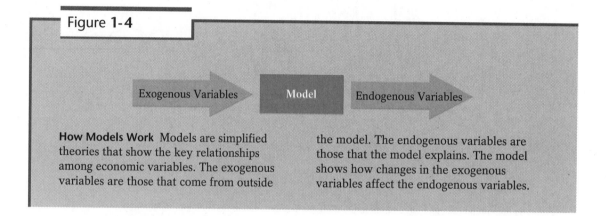

Exogenous Variables → Model → Endogenous Variables

How Models Work Models are simplified theories that show the key relationships among economic variables. The exogenous variables are those that come from outside the model. The endogenous variables are those that the model explains. The model shows how changes in the exogenous variables affect the endogenous variables.

For example, consider how an economist might develop a model of the market for pizza. The economist supposes that the quantity of pizza demanded by consumers Q^d depends on the price of pizza P_p and on aggregate income Y. This relationship is expressed in the equation

$$Q^d = D(P_p, Y),$$

where $D(\ )$ represents the demand function. Similarly, the economist supposes that the quantity of pizza supplied by pizzerias Q^s depends on the price of pizza P_p and on the price of cheese P_c because cheese is used to make pizza. This relationship is expressed as

$$Q^s = S(P_p, P_c),$$

where $S(\ )$ represents the supply function. Finally, the economist assumes that the price of pizza adjusts to equilibrate supply and demand:

$$Q^s = Q^d.$$

These three equations compose a model of the market for pizza.

The economist illustrates the model with a supply-and-demand diagram, as in Figure 1-5. The demand curve shows the relationship between the quantity of pizza demanded and the price of pizza, while holding aggregate income constant. The demand curve slopes downward because the higher the price of pizza, the more consumers switch to other foods and the less pizza they buy. The supply curve shows the relationship between the quantity of pizza supplied and the price of pizza, while holding the price of cheese constant. The supply curve slopes upward because the higher the price of pizza, the more pizza pizzerias produce. The equilibrium for the market is the price and quantity at which the supply and demand curves intersect. At the equilibrium price, consumers choose to buy exactly the amount of pizza that pizzerias choose to produce.

Figure 1-5

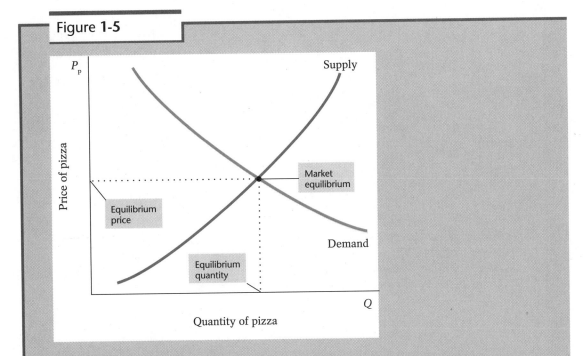

The Model of Supply and Demand The most famous economic model is that of supply and demand for a good or service—in this case, pizza. The demand curve is a downward-sloping curve relating the price of pizza to the quantity of pizza that consumers demand. The supply curve is an upward-sloping curve relating the price of pizza to the quantity of pizza that pizzerias supply. The price of pizza adjusts until the quantity supplied equals the quantity demanded. The point where the two curves cross is the market equilibrium, which shows the equilibrium price of pizza and the equilibrium quantity of pizza.

This model of the pizza market has two exogenous variables and two endogenous variables. The exogenous variables are aggregate income and the price of cheese. The model does not attempt to explain them but takes them as already determined (perhaps to be explained by another model). The endogenous variables are the price of pizza and the quantity of pizza exchanged. These are the variables that the model attempts to explain.

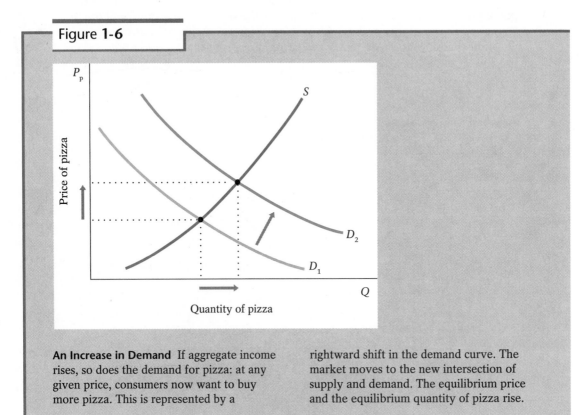

Figure 1-6

An Increase in Demand If aggregate income rises, so does the demand for pizza: at any given price, consumers now want to buy more pizza. This is represented by a rightward shift in the demand curve. The market moves to the new intersection of supply and demand. The equilibrium price and the equilibrium quantity of pizza rise.

The model shows how a change in one of the exogenous variables affects both endogenous variables. For example, if aggregate income increases, then the demand for pizza increases, as illustrated in Figure 1-6. The model shows that both the equilibrium price and the equilibrium quantity of pizza rise. Similarly, if the price of cheese increases, then the supply of pizza decreases, as illustrated in Figure 1-7. The model shows that in this case the equilibrium price of pizza rises and the equilibrium quantity of pizza falls. Thus, the model shows how changes in aggregate income or in the price of cheese affect the market for pizza.

Figure 1-7

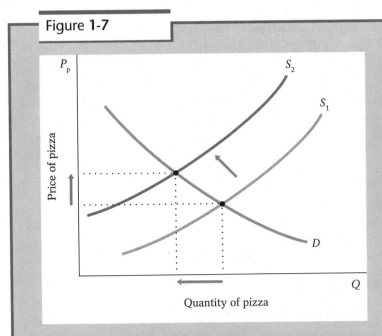

A Decrease in Supply If the price of cheese rises, the supply of pizza falls: at any given price, pizzerias find that the sale of pizza is less profitable and therefore choose to produce less pizza. This is represented by a leftward shift in the supply curve. The market moves to the new intersection of supply and demand. The equilibrium price rises, and the equilibrium quantity falls.

Like all models, this model of the pizza market makes many simplifying assumptions. The model does not take into account, for example, that every pizzeria is in a different location. For each customer, one pizzeria is more convenient than the others, and thus pizzerias have some ability to set their own prices. Although the model assumes that there is a single price for pizza, in fact there could be a different price at every pizzeria.

How should we react to the model's lack of realism? Should we discard the simple model of pizza supply and pizza demand? Should we attempt to build a more complex model that allows for diverse pizza prices? The answers to these questions depend on our purpose. On the one hand, if our goal is to explain how the price of cheese affects the average price of pizza and the amount of pizza sold, then the diversity of pizza prices is probably not important. The simple model of the pizza market does a good job of addressing that issue. On the other hand, if our goal is to explain why towns with three pizzerias have lower pizza prices than towns with one pizzeria, the simple model is less useful.

Using Functions to Express Relationships Among Variables

All economic models express relationships among economic variables. Often, these relationships are expressed as functions. A *function* is a mathematical concept that shows how one variable depends on a set of other variables. For example, in the model of the pizza market, we said that the quantity of pizza demanded depends on the price of pizza and on aggregate income. To express this, we use functional notation to write

$$Q^d = D(P_p, Y).$$

This equation says that the quantity of pizza demanded Q^d is a function of the price of pizza P_p and aggregate income Y. In functional notation, the variable preceding the parentheses denotes the function. In this case, $D(\ )$ is the function expressing how the variables in parentheses determine the quantity of pizza demanded.

If we knew more about the pizza market, we could give a numerical formula for the quantity of pizza demanded. We might be able to write

$$Q^d = 60 - 10P_p + 2Y.$$

In this case, the demand function is

$$D(P_p, Y) = 60 - 10P_p + 2Y.$$

For any price of pizza and aggregate income, this demand function gives the corresponding quantity of pizza demanded. For example, if aggregate income is $10 and the price of pizza is $2, then the quantity of pizza demanded is 60 pies; if the price of pizza rises to $3, the quantity of pizza demanded falls to 50 pies.

Functional notation allows us to express a relationship among variables even when the precise numerical relationship is unknown. For example, we might know that the quantity of pizza demanded falls when the price rises from $2 to $3, but we might not know by how much it falls. In this case, functional notation is useful: as long as we know that a relationship among the variables exists, we can express it using functional notation.

The art in economics is in judging when an assumption is clarifying and when it is misleading. Any model constructed to be completely realistic would be too complicated for anyone to understand. Simplification is a necessary part of building a useful model. Yet models lead to incorrect conclusions when they ignore crucial features of the economy. Economic modeling therefore requires care and common sense.

Eclectic Macroeconomics

Macroeconomists address many different questions. For example, they examine the influence of fiscal policy on national saving, the impact of unemployment insurance on the unemployment rate, and the role of monetary policy in maintaining stable prices. Macroeconomics is as diverse as the economy.

Because no single model can answer all questions, macroeconomists use many different models. An important and difficult task for students of macroeconomics is to keep in mind that there is no single "correct" model. Instead, there are many models—each of which is useful for a different purpose.

This book therefore presents many different models that address different questions and that make different assumptions. Remember that a model is only as good as its assumptions and that an assumption that is useful for some purposes may be misleading for others. When using a model to address a question, the economist must keep in mind the underlying assumptions and judge whether these assumptions are reasonable for the matter at hand.

Prices: Flexible versus Sticky

One crucial assumption of macroeconomic models is the speed with which wages and prices adjust. Economists normally presume that the price of a good or a service moves quickly to equilibrate supply and demand. In other words, they assume that, at the going price, demanders have bought all they want and suppliers have sold all they want. This assumption is called **market clearing** and is central to the model of the pizza market discussed earlier. For answering most questions, economists use market-clearing models.

But the assumption of *continuous* market clearing is not entirely realistic. For markets to clear continuously, prices must adjust instantly to changes in supply and demand. In fact, however, many wages and prices adjust slowly. Labor contracts often set wages for up to three years. Many firms leave their product prices the same for long periods of time—for example, magazine publishers change their newsstand prices only every three or four years. Although market-clearing models assume that all wages and prices are **flexible**, in the real world some wages and prices are **sticky**.

The apparent stickiness of prices does not necessarily make market-clearing models useless. After all, prices are not stuck forever; eventually, they do adjust to changes in supply and demand. Market-clearing models might not describe the economy at every instant, but they do describe the equilibrium toward which the economy slowly gravitates. Therefore, most macroeconomists believe that price flexibility is a good assumption for studying long-run issues, such as the economic growth we observe from decade to decade.

For studying short-run issues, such as year-to-year economic fluctuations, the assumption of price flexibility is less plausible. Over short periods, many prices are fixed at predetermined levels. Therefore, most macroeconomists believe that price stickiness is a better assumption for studying the behavior of the economy in the short run.

The Role of Microeconomics in Macroeconomics

Microeconomics, the study of the economy in the small, examines the activities of individual units in the economy. Microeconomists study how households and firms make decisions and how these decisionmakers interact in the marketplace. A central principle of microeconomics is that households and firms *optimize*— they do the best they can given their objectives and the constraints they face. In microeconomic models, households choose their purchases to maximize their level of satisfaction, which economists call *utility*, and firms make production decisions to maximize profit.

Because economy-wide events arise from the interaction of many households and many firms, macroeconomics and microeconomics are inextricably linked. When we study the economy as a whole, we must consider the decisions of individual economic actors. For example, to understand what determines total consumer spending, we must think about a family deciding how much to spend today and how much to save for the future. To understand what determines total investment spending, we must think about a firm deciding whether to build a new factory. Because aggregate variables are simply the sum of the variables describing many individual decisions, macroeconomics is inevitably tied to microeconomics.

Although microeconomic decisions always underlie economic models, in many models the optimizing behavior of households and firms is implicit rather than explicit. The model of the pizza market we discussed earlier is an example. Households' decisions about how much pizza to buy underlie the demand for pizza, and pizzerias' decisions about how much pizza to produce underlie the supply of pizza. Presumably, households make their decisions to maximize utility, and pizzerias make their decisions to maximize profit. Yet the model did not focus on these microeconomic decisions; it left them in the background. Similarly, in much of macroeconomics, the optimizing behavior of households and firms is left implicit.

1-3 How This Book Proceeds

This book has four parts. This chapter and the next make up Part One, the Introduction. Chapter 2 discusses how economists measure economic variables, such as aggregate income, the inflation rate, and the unemployment rate.

Part Two, The Economy in the Long Run, presents the classical model of the economy. The key assumption of the classical model is that prices adjust to equilibrate markets. That is, with only a few exceptions, the classical model assumes market clearing. For the reasons we have discussed, this assumption is best viewed as describing the economy in the long run.

Part Three, The Economy in the Short Run, examines the behavior of the economy when prices are sticky. It presents a non-market-clearing model of the economy and shows how the conclusions of the classical model change when the stickiness of prices is taken into account. This model with sticky prices is designed to analyze short-run issues, such as the reasons for economic fluctuations and the role of monetary and fiscal policy in stabilizing the economy.

Part Four, More on the Microeconomics Behind Macroeconomics, examines some of the microeconomic models that are useful for analyzing macroeconomic issues. For example, it examines the household's decisions regarding how much to consume and how much money to hold and the firm's decision regarding how much to invest. These individual decisions together form the larger macroeconomic picture. The goal of studying these microeconomic decisions in detail is to refine our understanding of the aggregate economy.

Summary

1. Macroeconomics is the study of the economy as a whole—including growth in incomes, changes in prices, and the rate of unemployment. Macroeconomists attempt both to explain economic events and to devise policies to improve economic performance.

2. To understand the economy, economists use models—theories that simplify reality in order to reveal how exogenous variables influence endogenous variables. The art in economics is in judging whether a model usefully captures the important economic relationships. Because no single model can answer all questions, macroeconomists use different models for different purposes.

3. Whether prices are flexible or sticky is a crucial assumption for a macroeconomic model. Most macroeconomists believe that market-clearing models describe the economy in the long run, but that prices are sticky in the short run.

4. Microeconomics is the study of how firms and individuals make decisions and how these decisionmakers interact. Since macroeconomic events arise from many microeconomic interactions, macroeconomists use many of the tools of microeconomics.

KEY CONCEPTS

Macroeconomics	Models
Real GDP	Exogenous variables
Inflation and deflation	Endogenous variables
Unemployment	Market clearing
Recession	Flexible and sticky prices
Depression	Microeconomics

QUESTIONS FOR REVIEW

1. Explain the difference between macroeconomics and microeconomics. How are these two fields related?

2. Why do economists build models?

3. What is a market-clearing model? When is the assumption of market clearing appropriate?

PROBLEMS AND APPLICATIONS

1. What macroeconomic issues have been in the news lately?

2. What do you think are the defining characteristics of a science? Does the study of the economy have these characteristics? Do you think macroeconomics should be called a science? Why or why not?

3. Use the model of supply and demand to explain how a fall in the price of frozen yogurt would affect the price of ice cream and the quantity of ice cream sold. In your explanation, identify the exogenous and the endogenous variables.

4. How often does the price you pay for a haircut change? What does your answer imply about the usefulness of market-clearing models for analyzing the market for haircuts?

The Data of Macroeconomics

Chapter 2

Data! Data! Data! I can't make bricks without clay.

Sherlock Holmes

Like all scientists, economists rely on both theory and observation. Since our goal is to understand how the economy works, observing the economy provides the basis for our theories. Once we have developed these theories, we turn again to observation to test them. This chapter discusses the types of observations that macroeconomists use to create and test their theories.

Casual observation provides one source of information about the economy. When you go shopping, you see how fast prices are rising. When you look for a job, you learn whether firms are hiring. Because you are a participant in the economy, you get some sense of economic conditions as you go about your life.

Economic statistics are a more systematic and objective source of information. The government regularly surveys households and firms to learn about their economic activity—how much they are earning, what they are buying, what prices they are charging, and so on. From these surveys, various statistics are computed that summarize the state of the economy. These statistics are the data that economists use to study the economy. They also help policymakers monitor economic developments and formulate appropriate policies.

This chapter focuses on the three economic statistics that economists and policymakers use most often. **Gross domestic product**, or **GDP**, tells us the nation's total income and the total expenditure on its output of goods and services. The **consumer price index**, or **CPI**, measures the level of prices. The **unemployment rate** tells us the fraction of workers who are unemployed. We see below how these statistics are computed and what they tell us about the economy.

2-1 Measuring the Value of Economic Activity: Gross Domestic Product

Gross domestic product is often considered the best measure of how well the economy is performing. This statistic is computed every three months by the Bureau of Economic Analysis, which is one part of the U.S. Department of

Commerce. It attempts to summarize in a single number the dollar value of economic activity. More precisely, GDP equals both

- The total income of everyone in the economy, and
- The total expenditure on the economy's output of goods and services.

From the standpoint of either income or expenditure, it is clear why GDP is a gauge of economic performance. GDP measures something people care about— their incomes. Similarly, an economy with a large output of goods and services can better satisfy the demands of households, firms, and the government.

How can GDP measure both the economy's income and the expenditure on its output? The reason is that these two quantities are really the same: for the economy as a whole, income must equal expenditure. To see why this is so, we turn to **national income accounting**, the accounting system used to measure GDP and many related statistics.

Income, Expenditure, and the Circular Flow

Imagine an economy that produces a single good, bread, from a single input, labor. Figure 2-1 illustrates all the economic transactions that occur between households and firms in this economy.

The inner loop in Figure 2-1 represents the flows of bread and labor. The households sell their labor to the firms. The firms use the labor of their workers to produce bread, which the firms in turn sell to the households. Hence, labor flows from households to firms, and bread flows from firms to households.

The outer loop in Figure 2-1 represents the corresponding flow of dollars. The households buy bread from the firms. The firms use some of the revenue from these sales to pay the wages of their workers, and the remainder is the profit belonging to the owners of the firms (who themselves are part of the household sector). Hence, expenditure on bread flows from households to firms, and income in the form of wages and profit flows from firms to households.

GDP measures the flow of dollars in this economy. We can compute it in two ways. GDP is the total income from the production of bread, which equals the sum of wages and profit—the top half of the circular flow of dollars. GDP is also the total expenditure on purchases of bread—the bottom half of the circular flow of dollars. Thus, we can look at the flow of dollars from firms to households or at the flow of dollars from households to firms.

The economy's total expenditure and its total income must be equal because every transaction has two sides—a buyer and a seller. The expenditure of buyers on purchases of products is, by the rules of accounting, income to the sellers of the products. Therefore, every transaction that affects expenditure must affect income, and every transaction that affects income must affect expenditure. For example, suppose that a firm produces and sells one more loaf of bread to a household. Clearly this transaction raises total expenditure on bread, but it also has an equal effect on total income. If the firm produces the extra loaf without hiring any more labor (such as by making the production

Figure 2-1

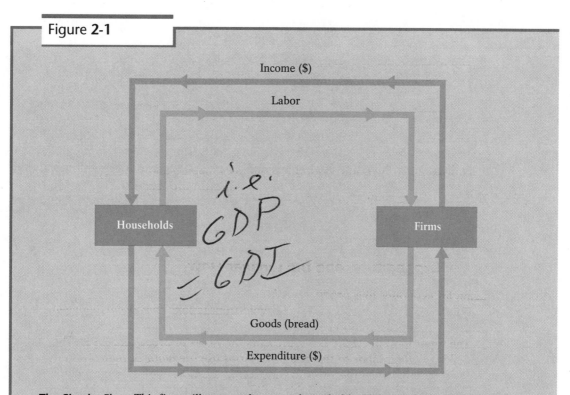

The Circular Flow This figure illustrates the flows between firms and households in an economy that produces one good, bread, from one input, labor. The inner loop represents the flows of labor and bread: households sell their labor to firms, and the firms sell the bread they produce to households. The outer loop represents the corresponding flows of dollars: households pay the firms for the bread, and the firms pay wages and profit to the households. In this economy, GDP is both the total expenditure on bread and the total income from the production of bread.

process more efficient), then profit increases. If the firm produces the extra loaf by hiring more labor, then wages increase. In both cases, expenditure and income increase equally.

Some Rules for Computing GDP

In the hypothetical economy that produces only bread, we can compute GDP simply by adding up the total expenditure on bread. A nation's economy, however, includes the production and sale of a vast number of diverse goods and services. To interpret correctly what GDP measures, we must understand some of the rules that govern its construction.

Stocks and Flows

Many economic variables measure a quantity of something—a quantity of money, a quantity of goods, and so on. Economists distinguish between two types of quantity variables: stocks and flows. A **stock** is a quantity measured at a given point in time, whereas a **flow** is a quantity measured per unit of time.

The bathtub, shown in Figure 2-2, is the classic example used to illustrate stocks and flows. The amount of water in the tub is a stock: it is the quantity of water in the tub at a given point in time. The amount of water coming out of the faucet is a flow: it is the quantity of water being added to the tub per unit of time. Note that we measure stocks and flows in different units. We say that the bathtub contains 50 *gallons* of water, but that water is coming out of the faucet at 5 *gallons per minute*.

Flow   Stock

Figure 2-2

Stocks and Flows The amount of water in a bathtub is a stock; it is a quantity measured at a given moment in time. The amount of water coming out of the faucet is a flow: it is a quantity measured per unit of time.

Stocks and flows are often related. In the bathtub example, these relationships are clear. The stock of water in the tub represents the accumulation of the flow out of the faucet, and the flow of water represents the change in the stock. When building theories to explain economic variables, it is often useful to determine whether the variables are stocks or flows and whether any relationships link them.

Here are some examples of related stocks and flows that we study in future chapters:

- A person's wealth is a stock; his income and expenditure are flows.

- The number of unemployed people is a stock; the number of people losing their jobs is a flow.

- The amount of capital in the economy is a stock; the amount of investment is a flow.

- The government debt is a stock; the government budget deficit is a flow.

The Treatment of Inventories Suppose that a firm in our one-good economy hires workers to produce more bread, pays their wages, and then fails to sell the additional bread. How does this transaction affect GDP?

The answer depends on what happens to the unsold bread. If the bread spoils, then profit is reduced by the amount that wages are increased—the firm has paid the workers more wages but has not received any benefit from doing so. Because the transaction affects neither expenditure nor income, it leaves GDP unaltered (although more is distributed as wages and less as profit). By contrast, if the bread is put into inventory to be sold later, the transaction is treated differently. In this case, profit is not reduced, and the owners of the firm are assumed to have "purchased" the bread for the firm's inventory. Because the higher wages raise total income, and greater inventory accumulation raises total expenditure, GDP rises.

The general rule is that when a firm increases its inventory of goods, this investment in inventory is counted both as part of expenditure and as part of income. Thus, production for inventory increases GDP just as much as production for final sale.

Adding Apples and Oranges We have been discussing GDP as if bread were the only item produced. Yet man does not live by bread alone. The U.S. economy produces many different goods and services—bread, beef, cars, cruises, and so on. GDP combines the value of these goods and services into one summary measure. The diversity of products in the economy complicates the calculation of GDP because different products have different values.

Suppose, for example, that the economy produces four apples and three oranges. How do we compute GDP? We could simply add apples and oranges and conclude that GDP equals seven pieces of fruit. But this makes sense only if apples and oranges have equal value, which is generally not true. (This would be even clearer if the economy had produced four watermelons and three grapes.)

To compute the total value of different goods and services, we use the market price as the measure of value. The market price is used because it reflects how much people are willing to pay for a good or service. Thus, if apples cost $0.50 each and oranges cost $1.00 each, GDP would be

$$\text{GDP} = (\text{Price of Apples} \times \text{Quantity of Apples})$$
$$+ (\text{Price of Oranges} \times \text{Quantity of Oranges})$$
$$= (\$0.50 \times 4) + (\$1.00 \times 3)$$
$$= \$5.00.$$

GDP equals $5.00—the value of all the apples, $2.00, plus the value of all the oranges, $3.00.

Intermediate Goods and Value-Added Many goods are produced in stages: raw materials are processed into intermediate goods by one firm and then sold to another firm for final processing. How should we treat such products when computing GDP? For example, suppose a cattle rancher sells one-quarter pound of meat to McDonald's for $0.50, and then McDonald's sells you a hamburger for $1.50. Should GDP include both the meat and the hamburger (a total of $2.00), or just the hamburger ($1.50)?

The answer is that GDP includes only the value of final goods. Thus, the hamburger is included in GDP but the meat is not: GDP increases by $1.50, not by $2.00. The reason is that the value of intermediate goods is already included as part of the price of the final goods. To add the intermediate goods to the final goods would be double-counting—that is, the meat would be counted twice. Hence, GDP is the total value of final goods and services produced.

One way to compute the value of all final goods and services is to sum the value-added at each stage of production. The **value-added** of a firm equals the value of the firm's output less the value of the intermediate goods that the firm purchases. In the case of the hamburger, the value-added of the rancher is $0.50 (assuming the rancher bought no intermediate goods), and the value-added of McDonald's is $1.50 − $0.50, or $1.00. Total value-added is $0.50 + $1.00, which equals $1.50. For the economy as a whole, the sum of all value-added must equal the value of all final goods and services. Hence, GDP is also the total value-added of all firms in the economy.

Housing Services and Other Imputations Although most goods and services are valued at their market prices when computing GDP, some are not sold in the marketplace and therefore do not have market prices. If GDP is to include the value of these goods and services, we must use an estimate of their value. Such an estimate is called an **imputed value**.

Imputations are especially important for determining the value of housing. A person who rents a house is buying housing services and is providing income for the landlord; the rent is part of GDP, both as expenditure by the renter and as income for the landlord. Many people, however, live in their own homes. Although they do not pay rent to a landlord, they are enjoying housing services similar to those that renters purchase. To take account of the housing services enjoyed by homeowners, GDP includes the "rent" that these home-owners "pay" to themselves. Of course, homeowners do not in fact pay themselves this rent. The Department of Commerce estimates what the market rent for a house would be if it were rented and includes that imputed rent as part of GDP. This imputed rent is included both in the homeowner's expenditure and in the homeowner's income.

Imputations also arise in valuing government services. For example, police officers, fire fighters, and senators provide services to the public. Measuring the value of these services is difficult because they are not sold in a market-place and therefore do not have a market price. The national income accounts include these services in GDP by valuing them at their cost. That is, the wages of these public servants are used as a measure of the value of their output.

In many cases, an imputation is called for in principle but, to keep things simple, is not made in practice. Since GDP includes the imputed rent on owner-occupied houses, one might expect it also to include the imputed rent on cars, lawn mowers, jewelry, and other durable goods owned by households. Yet the value of these services is left out of GDP. In addition, some of the output of the economy is produced and consumed at home and never enters the market-place. For example, meals cooked at home are similar to meals cooked at a restaurant, yet the value-added in meals at home is left out of GDP.

Finally, no imputation is made for the value of goods and services sold in the *underground economy*. The underground economy is the part of the economy that people hide from the government either because they wish to evade taxation or because the activity is illegal. Domestic workers paid "off the books" is one example. The illegal drug trade is another.

Since the imputations necessary for computing GDP are only approximate, and since the value of many goods and services is left out altogether, GDP is an imperfect measure of economic activity. These imperfections are most problematic when comparing standards of living across countries. The size of the underground economy, for instance, varies from country to country. Yet as long as the magnitude of these imperfections remains fairly constant over time, GDP is useful for comparing economic activity from year to year.

Real GDP versus Nominal GDP

Using the rules just described, economists compute GDP, which values the economy's total output of goods and services. But is GDP a good measure of economic well-being? Consider once again the economy that produces only apples and oranges. In this economy GDP is the sum of the value of all the apples produced and the value of all the oranges produced. That is,

$$GDP = (\text{Price of Apples} \times \text{Quantity of Apples})$$
$$+ (\text{Price of Oranges} \times \text{Quantity of Oranges}).$$

GDP can increase either because prices rise or because quantities rise.

GDP computed this way is not a good measure of economic well-being. That is, it does not accurately reflect how well the economy can satisfy the demands of households, firms, and the government. If all prices doubled without any change in quantities, GDP would double. Yet it would be misleading to say that the economy's ability to satisfy demands has doubled, because the quantity of every good produced remains the same. Economists call the value of goods and services measured at current prices **nominal GDP.**

A better measure of economic well-being would tally the economy's output of goods and services and would not be influenced by changes in prices. For this purpose, economists use **real GDP,** which is the value of goods and services measured at constant prices. To compute real GDP, a base year is chosen—say, 1992. Goods and services are then added up using 1992 prices to value the different goods. In our apple-and-orange economy, real GDP for 1996 would be

$$\text{Real GDP} = (1992 \text{ Price of Apples} \times 1996 \text{ Quantity of Apples})$$
$$+ (1992 \text{ Price of Oranges} \times 1996 \text{ Quantity of Oranges}).$$

Similarly, real GDP in 1997 would be

$$\text{Real GDP} = (1992 \text{ Price of Apples} \times 1997 \text{ Quantity of Apples})$$
$$+ (1992 \text{ Price of Oranges} \times 1997 \text{ Quantity of Oranges}).$$

The New, Chain-Weighted Measures of Real GDP

We have been discussing real GDP as if the prices used to compute this measure never change from their base-year values. If this were truly the case, over time the prices would become more and more dated. For instance, the price of computers has fallen substantially in recent years, while the price of a year at college has risen. When valuing the production of computers and education, it would be misleading to use the prices that prevailed ten or twenty years ago.

To solve this problem, the Bureau of Economic Analysis has periodically updated the prices used to compute real GDP. About every five years, a new base year is chosen. The prices are then held fixed and used to measure year-to-year changes in the production of goods and services until the base year is updated once again.

In 1995, the Bureau announced a new policy for dealing with changes in the base year. In particular, it will now emphasize *chain-weighted* measures of real GDP. With these new measures, the base year changes continuously over time. In essence, prices in 1995 are used to measure real growth from 1995 to 1996; prices in 1996 are used to measure real growth from 1996 to 1997; and so on. These various year-to-year growth rates are then put together to form a "chain" that can be used to compare the output of goods and services in any two years.

This new chain-weighted measure of real GDP is better than the more traditional measure because it ensures that the prices used to compute real GDP are never far out of date. For most purposes, however, the differences are not important. It turns out that the two measures of real GDP are highly correlated with each other. The reason is that most relative prices change slowly over time. Thus, both measures of real GDP reflect the same thing: economy-wide changes in the production of goods and services.

Because the prices are held constant, real GDP varies from year to year only if the quantities produced vary. Thus, real GDP summarizes the output of the economy, measured in base-year (in this case, 1992) dollars. Because a society's ability to provide economic satisfaction for its members ultimately depends on the quantities of goods and services produced, real GDP provides a better measure of economic well-being than nominal GDP.

The GDP Deflator

From nominal GDP and real GDP we can compute a third statistic: the GDP deflator. The **GDP deflator**, also called the implicit price deflator for GDP, is defined as

$$\text{GDP Deflator} = \frac{\text{Nominal GDP}}{\text{Real GDP}}.$$

The GDP deflator is the ratio of nominal GDP to real GDP.

To better understand nominal GDP, real GDP, and the GDP deflator, consider again an economy with only one good, bread. In any year, nominal GDP is the total number of dollars spent on bread in that year. Real GDP is the number of loaves of bread produced in that year times the price of bread in some base year. The GDP deflator is the price of bread in that year relative to the price of bread in the base year.

Actual economies, however, produce many goods. Nominal GDP, real GDP, and the GDP deflator aggregate the many different prices and quantities. Consider an economy that produces only apples and oranges. Letting P denote the price of a good, Q the quantity, and a superscript "92" the base year 1992, the GDP deflator would be

$$\text{GDP Deflator} = \frac{(P_{\text{apples}} \times Q_{\text{apples}}) + (P_{\text{oranges}} \times Q_{\text{oranges}})}{(P^{92}_{\text{apples}} \times Q_{\text{apples}}) + (P^{92}_{\text{oranges}} \times Q_{\text{oranges}})}.$$

The numerator of this expression equals nominal GDP, and the denominator equals real GDP. Both nominal GDP and real GDP can be viewed as the price of a basket of goods; in this case, the basket consists of the quantities of apples and oranges currently produced. The GDP deflator compares the current price of this basket to the price of the same basket in the base year.

The definition of the GDP deflator allows us to separate nominal GDP into two parts: one part measures quantities, and the other measures prices. That is,

$$\text{Nominal GDP} = \text{Real GDP} \times \text{GDP Deflator}.$$

Nominal GDP measures the dollar value of the output of the economy. Real GDP measures the amount of output—that is, output valued at constant (base-year) prices. The GDP deflator measures the price of the typical unit of output relative to its price in the base year.

The Components of Expenditure

Economists and policymakers care not only about the economy's total output of goods and services but also about the allocation of this output among alternative uses. The national income accounts divide GDP into four broad categories:

- Consumption (C)
- Investment (I)
- Government purchases (G)
- Net exports (NX).

Thus, letting Y stand for GDP,

$$Y = C + I + G + NX.$$

GDP is the sum of consumption, investment, government purchases, and net exports. Each dollar of GDP falls into one of these categories. This equation is

Two Arithmetic Tricks for Working with Percentage Changes

For manipulating many relationships in economics, there is an arithmetic trick that is useful to know: *The percentage change of a product of two variables is approximately the sum of the percentage changes in each of the variables.*

To see how this trick works, consider an example. Let P denote the GDP deflator and Y denote real GDP. Nominal GDP is $P \times Y$. The trick states that

$$\text{Percentage Change in } (P \times Y) \approx (\text{Percentage Change in } P)$$
$$+ (\text{Percentage Change in } Y).$$

For instance, suppose that in one year, real GDP is 100 and the GDP deflator is 2; the next year, real GDP is 103 and the GDP deflator is 2.1. We can calculate that real GDP rose by 3 percent and that the GDP deflator rose by 5 percent. Nominal GDP rose from 200 the first year to 216.3 the second year, an increase of 8.15 percent. Notice that the growth in nominal GDP (8.15 percent) is approximately the sum of the growth in the GDP deflator (5 percent) and the growth in real GDP (3 percent).

A second arithmetic trick follows as a corollary to the first: *The percentage change of a ratio is approximately the percentage change in the numerator minus the percentage change in the denominator.* Again, consider an example. Let Y denote GDP and L denote the population, so that Y/L is GDP per person. The second trick states

$$\text{Percentage Change in } (Y/L) \approx (\text{Percentage Change in } Y)$$
$$- (\text{Percentage Change in } L).$$

For instance, suppose that in the first year, Y is 100,000 and L is 100, so Y/L is 1,000; in the second year, Y is 110,000 and L is 103, so Y/L is 1,068. Notice that the growth in GDP per person (6.8 percent) is approximately the growth in income (10 percent) minus the growth in population (3 percent).

an *identity*—an equation that must hold because of the way the variables are defined. It is called the **national income accounts identity**.

Consumption consists of the goods and services bought by households. It is divided into three subcategories: nondurable goods, durable goods, and services. Nondurable goods are goods that last only a short time, such as food and clothing. Durable goods are goods that last a long time, such as cars and TVs. Services include the work done for consumers by individuals and firms, such as haircuts and doctor visits.

Investment consists of goods bought for future use. Investment is also divided into three subcategories: business fixed investment, residential fixed investment, and inventory investment. Business fixed investment is the purchase of new plants and equipment by firms. Residential investment is the purchase of new housing by households and landlords. Inventory investment is the in-

What Is Investment?

The term "investment" sometimes creates confusion for newcomers to macroeconomics. The confusion arises because what looks like investment for an individual may not be investment for the economy as a whole.

Suppose we observe these two events:

- Smith buys for himself a 100-year-old Victorian house.

- Jones builds for herself a brand-new contemporary house.

What is total investment here? Two houses, one house, or zero?

A macroeconomist seeing these two transactions counts only the Jones house as investment. Smith's transaction has not created new housing for the economy; it has merely reallocated existing housing. Smith's purchase is investment for Smith, but it is disinvestment for the person selling the house. By contrast, Jones has added new housing to the economy; her new house is counted as investment.

Similarly, consider these two events:

- Merrill buys $5 million in IBM stock from Lynch on the New York Stock Exchange.

- General Motors sells $10 million in stock to the public and uses the proceeds to build a new car factory.

Here, investment is $10 million. In the first transaction, Merrill is investing in IBM stock, and Lynch is disinvesting; there is no investment for the economy. By contrast, General Motors is using some of the economy's output of goods and services to add to its stock of capital; hence, its new factory is counted as investment.

The general rule is that purchases that reallocate existing assets among different individuals are not investment for the economy. Investment, as macroeconomists use the term, creates new capital.

crease in firms' inventory of goods (if the inventory is falling, inventory investment is negative).

Government purchases are the goods and services bought by federal, state, and local governments. This category includes such items as military equipment, highways, and the services that government workers provide. It does not include transfer payments to individuals, such as Social Security and welfare. Because transfer payments merely reallocate existing income and are not made in exchange for goods and services, they are not part of GDP.

The last category, **net exports,** takes into account trade with other countries. Net exports are the value of all goods and services exported to other countries minus the value of all goods and services that foreigners provide us. Net exports represent the net expenditure from abroad for our goods and services, which provides income for domestic producers.

Case Study *2-1*

● ● ● ● ● ● ● ● ● ● ● ● ●

GDP and Its Components

In 1994 the GDP of the United States totaled almost $7 trillion. This number is so large that it is almost impossible to comprehend. We can make it easier to understand by dividing it by the 1994 U.S. population of 261 million. In this way, we obtain GDP per person—the amount of expenditure for the average American—which equaled $25,852 in 1994.

How did we use this GDP? Table 2-1 shows that about two-thirds of it, or $17,757 per person, was spent on consumption. Investment was $3,963 per person. Government purchases were $4,509 per person, $1,121 of which was spent by the federal government on national defense.

Table 2-1

GDP and the Components of Expenditure: 1994

	Total (billions of dollars)	Per Person (dollars)
Gross Domestic Product	**$6,738.4**	**$25,852**
Consumption	**4,628.4**	**17,757**
Nondurable goods	1,394.3	5,349
Durable goods	591.5	2,269
Services	2,642.7	10,139
Investment	**1,032.9**	**3,963**
Nonresidential fixed investment	697.6	2,676
Residential fixed investment	283.0	1,086
Inventory investment	52.2	200
Government Purchases	**1,175.3**	**4,509**
Federal	437.3	1,678
Defense	292.3	1,121
Nondefense	145.0	556
State and local	738.0	2,831
Net Exports	**−98.2**	**−377**
Exports	718.7	2,757
Imports	816.9	3,134

Source: U.S. Department of Commerce.

The average person bought $3,134 of goods imported from abroad and produced $2,757 of goods that were exported to other countries. Thus, net exports were negative. Since we earned less from selling to foreigners than we spent on foreign goods, we must have financed the difference by taking out loans from foreigners (or, equivalently, by selling them some of our assets). Thus, the average American borrowed $377 from abroad in 1994.

● ● ● ● ● ● ● ● ● ● ● ● ●

GDP versus GNP

Gross domestic product measures the total income of everyone in the economy. But who exactly is included in this "everyone"? Americans working abroad? Foreigners working here?

To answer these questions, we should compare gross domestic product with a closely related statistic—gross national product. Here is the distinction:

- *Gross domestic product (GDP)* is total income earned *domestically*. It includes income earned domestically by foreigners, but it does not include income earned by domestic residents on foreign ground.

- *Gross national product (GNP)* is total income earned by *nationals* (that is, by residents of a nation). It includes the income that nationals earn abroad, but it does not include the income earned within a country by foreigners.

These two measures of income differ because a person can earn income and reside in different countries.

To understand the difference between GDP and GNP, consider several examples. Suppose a Mexican resident comes temporarily to the United States to work. The income he earns in the United States is part of U.S. GDP because it is earned domestically. But the income is not part of U.S. GNP because the worker is not a U.S. national. Similarly, if a U.S. resident works in Mexico, her income is part of U.S. GNP, but it is not part of U.S. GDP.

As another example, suppose a Japanese resident owns an apartment building in New York. The rent he earns is part of U.S. GDP because this income is earned domestically. But the rent is not part of U.S. GNP, because the landlord is not a U.S. national. Similarly, if a U.S. resident owns a factory in Haiti, the profit she makes is part of U.S. GNP, but it is not part of U.S. GDP.

For most purposes, the distinction between GDP and GNP is not crucial. Because most people earn most of their income in their home country, GDP and GNP move closely together. This book follows the conventional practice of focussing on GDP as the primary measure of the economy's income.

Other Measures of Income

The national income accounts include other measures of income that differ slightly in definition from GDP and GNP. It is important to be aware of the various measures, because economists and the press often refer to them.

To see how the alternative measures of income relate to one another, we start with GNP and subtract various quantities. To obtain *net national product (NNP)*, we subtract the depreciation of capital—the amount of the economy's stock of plants, equipment, and residential structures that wears out during the year:

$$NNP = GNP - \text{Depreciation.}$$

In the national income accounts, depreciation is called the *consumption of fixed capital.* It equals about 10 percent of GNP. Since the depreciation of capital is a cost of producing the output of the economy, subtracting depreciation shows the net result of economic activity. For this reason, some economists believe that NNP is a better measure of economic well-being than GNP or GDP.

The next adjustment in the national income accounts is for indirect business taxes, such as sales taxes. These taxes, which make up about 10 percent of NNP, place a wedge between the price that consumers pay for a good and the price that firms receive. Because firms never receive this tax wedge, it is not part of their income. Once we subtract indirect business taxes from NNP, we obtain a measure called *national income*:

$$\text{National Income } = \text{ NNP } - \text{ Indirect Business Taxes.}$$

National income measures how much everyone in the economy has earned.

The national income accounts divide national income into five components, depending on the way the income is earned. The five categories, and the percentage of national income that each comprises, are

- *Compensation of employees* (73.4%). The wages and fringe benefits earned by workers.

- *Proprietors' income* (8.7%). The income of noncorporate businesses, such as small farms, mom-and-pop stores, and law partnerships.

- *Rental income* (0.5%). The income that landlords receive, including the imputed rent that homeowners "pay" to themselves, less expenses, such as depreciation.

- *Corporate profits* (9.9%). The income of corporations after payments to their workers and creditors.

- *Net interest* (7.5%). The interest domestic businesses pay minus the interest they receive, plus interest earned from foreigners.

A series of adjustments takes us from national income to *personal income*, the amount of income that households and noncorporate businesses receive. Three of these adjustments are most important. First, we reduce national income by the amount that corporations earn but do not pay out, either because the corporations are retaining earnings or because they are paying taxes to the government. This adjustment is made by subtracting corporate profits (which equals the sum of corporate taxes, dividends, and retained earnings) and adding back dividends. Second, we increase national income by the net amount the government pays out in transfer payments. This adjustment equals government transfers to individuals minus social insurance contributions paid to the government. Third, we adjust national income to include the interest that households earn rather than the interest that businesses pay. This adjustment is made by adding personal interest income and subtracting net interest. (The difference between personal interest and net interest arises in part from the interest on the government debt.) Thus, personal income is

$$\text{Personal Income} = \text{National Income}$$
$$- \text{ Corporate Profits}$$
$$- \text{ Social Insurance Contributions}$$
$$- \text{ Net Interest}$$
$$+ \text{ Dividends}$$
$$+ \text{ Government Transfers to Individuals}$$
$$+ \text{ Personal Interest Income.}$$

Next, if we subtract personal tax payments and certain nontax payments to the government (such as parking tickets), we obtain *disposable personal income*:

$$\text{Disposable Personal Income} = \text{Personal Income}$$
$$- \text{ Personal Tax and Nontax Payments.}$$

Disposable personal income is the amount households and noncorporate businesses have available to spend after satisfying their tax obligations to the government.

Case Study *2-2*

• • • • • • • • • • • • • •

The Seasonal Cycle and Seasonal Adjustment

If we look at what happens to real GDP and other measures of income over the year, we find a regular seasonal pattern. The output of the economy rises during the year, reaching a peak in the fourth quarter (October, November, and December), and then falling in the first quarter (January, February, and March) of the next year. These regular seasonal changes are substantial. From the fourth quarter to the first quarter, real GDP falls on average about 8 percent.[1]

It is not surprising that real GDP follows a seasonal cycle. Some of these changes are attributable to changes in our ability to produce: for example, building homes is more difficult during the cold weather of winter than during other seasons. In addition, people have seasonal tastes: they have preferred times for such activities as vacations and Christmas shopping.

When economists study fluctuations in real GDP and other economic variables, they often want to eliminate the portion of fluctuations attributable to predictable seasonal changes. You will find that most of the economic statistics reported in the newspaper are *seasonally adjusted*—that is, statisticians have adjusted the data to remove the regular seasonal fluctuations. Therefore, when you observe a change in real GDP or any other data series, you must look beyond the seasonal cycle to explain the change.

• • • • • • • • • • • • • •

[1] Robert B. Barsky and Jeffrey A. Miron, "The Seasonal Cycle and the Business Cycle," *Journal of Political Economy* 97 (June 1989): 503–534.

2-2   Measuring the Cost of Living: The Consumer Price Index

A dollar today doesn't buy as much as it did twenty years ago. The cost of almost everything has gone up. This increase in the overall level of prices is called *inflation*, and it is one of the primary concerns of economists and policymakers. In later chapters we examine in detail the causes and effects of inflation. Here we discuss how economists measure changes in the cost of living.

The Price of a Basket of Goods

The most commonly used measure of the level of prices is the **consumer price index (CPI)**. The Bureau of Labor Statistics, which is part of the U.S. Department of Labor, has the job of computing the CPI. It begins by collecting the prices of thousands of goods and services. Just as GDP turns the quantities of many goods and services into a single number measuring the value of production, the CPI turns the prices of many goods and services into a single index measuring the overall level of prices.

How should economists aggregate the many prices in the economy into a single index that reliably measures the price level? They could simply compute an average of all prices. Yet this approach would treat all goods and services equally. Since people buy more chicken than caviar, the price of chicken should have a greater weight in the CPI than the price of caviar. The Bureau of Labor Statistics weights different items by computing the price of a basket of goods and services purchased by a typical consumer. The CPI is the price of this basket of goods and services relative to the price of the same basket in some base year.

For example, suppose that the typical consumer buys 5 apples and 2 oranges every month. That is, the basket of goods consists of 5 apples and 2 oranges. The CPI is

$$CPI = \frac{(5 \times \text{Current Price of Apples}) + (2 \times \text{Current Price of Oranges})}{(5 \times \text{1992 Price of Apples}) + (2 \times \text{1992 Price of Oranges})}.$$

In this CPI, 1992 is the base year. The index tells us how much it costs now to buy 5 apples and 2 oranges relative to how much it cost to buy the same basket of fruit in 1992.

The consumer price index is the most closely watched price index, but it is not the only one. Another is the producer price index, which measures the price of a typical basket of goods bought by firms rather than consumers. In addition to these overall price indices, the Bureau of Labor Statistics computes price indices for specific types of goods, such as food, housing, and energy.

The CPI versus the GDP Deflator

Earlier in this chapter we saw another measure of prices—the implicit price deflator for GDP, which is the ratio of nominal GDP to real GDP. The GDP deflator and the CPI give somewhat different information about the overall level of prices in the economy. There are three key differences between the two measures.

The first difference is that the GDP deflator measures the prices of all goods and services produced, whereas the CPI measures the prices of only the goods and services bought by consumers. Thus, an increase in the price of goods bought by firms or the government will show up in the GDP deflator but not in the CPI.

The second difference is that the GDP deflator includes only those goods produced domestically. Imported goods are not part of GDP and do not show up in the GDP deflator. Hence, an increase in the price of a Toyota made in Japan and sold in this country affects the CPI, because the Toyota is bought by consumers, but it does not affect the GDP deflator.

The third and most subtle difference results from the way the two measures aggregate the many prices in the economy. The CPI assigns fixed weights to the prices of different goods, whereas the GDP deflator assigns changing weights. In other words, the CPI is computed using a fixed basket of goods, whereas the GDP deflator allows the basket of goods to change over time as the composition of GDP changes. To see how this works, consider an economy that produces and consumes only apples and oranges. The GDP deflator is

$$\text{GDP Deflator} = \frac{\text{Nominal GDP}}{\text{Real GDP}}$$

$$= \frac{(P_{\text{apples}} \times Q_{\text{apples}}) + (P_{\text{oranges}} \times Q_{\text{oranges}})}{(P^{92}_{\text{apples}} \times Q_{\text{apples}}) + (P^{92}_{\text{oranges}} \times Q_{\text{oranges}})}.$$

The CPI is

$$\text{CPI} = \frac{(P_{\text{apples}} \times Q^{92}_{\text{apples}}) + (P_{\text{oranges}} \times Q^{92}_{\text{oranges}})}{(P^{92}_{\text{apples}} \times Q^{92}_{\text{apples}}) + (P^{92}_{\text{oranges}} \times Q^{92}_{\text{oranges}})}.$$

These equations show that both the CPI and the GDP deflator compare the cost of a basket of goods today with the cost of that same basket in the base year. The difference between the two measures is whether the basket changes over time. The CPI uses a fixed basket (base-year quantities), whereas the GDP deflator uses a changing basket (current quantities).

The following example shows how these approaches differ. Suppose that major frosts destroy the nation's orange crop. The quantity of oranges produced falls to zero, and the price of the few oranges that remain on grocers' shelves is driven sky-high. Because oranges are no longer part of GDP, the increase in the price of oranges does not show up in the GDP deflator. But because the CPI is computed with a fixed basket of goods that includes oranges, the increase in the price of oranges causes a substantial rise in the CPI.

Economists call a price index with a fixed basket of goods a *Laspeyres index* and a price index with a changing basket a *Paasche index*. Economic theorists have studied the properties of these different types of price indices to determine which is better. The answer, it turns out, is that neither is clearly superior.

The purpose of any price index is to measure the cost of living—that is, how much it costs to maintain a given standard of living. When prices of different goods are changing by different amounts, a Laspeyres index tends to overstate the increase in the cost of living, whereas a Paasche index tends to understate it. A Laspeyres index uses a fixed basket and thus does not take into account that consumers have the opportunity to substitute less expensive goods for more expensive ones. By contrast, a Paasche index accounts for the substitution of alternative goods, but it does not reflect the reduction in consumers' welfare that may result from such substitutions.

The example of the destroyed orange crop shows the problems with Laspeyres and Paasche price indices. Because the CPI is a Laspeyres index, it overstates the impact of the increase in orange prices on consumers: by using a fixed basket of goods, it ignores consumers' ability to substitute apples for oranges. By contrast, because the GDP deflator is a Paasche index, it understates the impact on consumers: the GDP deflator shows no rise in prices, yet surely the high price of oranges makes consumers worse off.

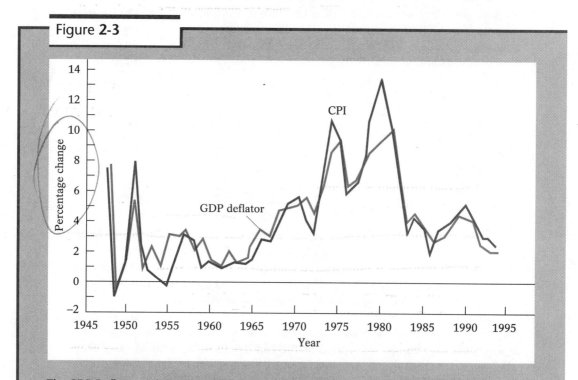

Figure 2-3

The GDP Deflator and the CPI This figure shows the percentage change in the GDP deflator and in the CPI for every year since 1948. Although these two measures of prices diverge at times, they usually tell the same story about how quickly prices are rising. Both the CPI and the GDP deflator show that prices rose slowly in most of the 1950s and 1960s, that they rose much more quickly in the 1970s, and that they rose slowly again in the 1980s and early 1990s.

Source: GDP deflator: U.S. Department of Commerce; CPI: U.S. Department of Labor.

Luckily, the difference between the GDP deflator and the CPI is usually not large in practice. Figure 2-3 shows the percentage change in the GDP deflator and the percentage change in the CPI for each year since 1948. Both measures usually tell the same story about how quickly prices are rising.

Case Study *2-3*

Does the CPI Overstate Inflation?

The consumer price index is a closely watched measure of inflation. Policymakers in the Federal Reserve monitor the CPI when choosing monetary policy. In addition, many laws and private contracts have cost-of-living allowances, called *COLAs*, which use the CPI to adjust for changes in the price level. For instance, Social Security benefits are adjusted automatically every year so that inflation will not erode the living standard of the elderly.

Because so much depends on the CPI, it is important to ensure that this measure of the price level is accurate. Many economists believe that the CPI tends to overstate inflation. There are various problems working in concert.

One problem is the substitution bias we have already discussed. Because the CPI measures the price of a fixed basket of goods, it does not reflect the ability of consumers to substitute toward goods whose relative prices have fallen. Thus, when relative prices change, the true cost of living rises less rapidly than the CPI.

A second problem is the introduction of new goods. When a new good is introduced into the marketplace, consumers are better off, because they have more products from which to choose. In effect, the introduction of new goods increases the purchasing power of the dollar. Yet this increase in purchasing power is not reflected in a lower CPI.

A third problem is unmeasured changes in quality. When a firm changes the quality of a good it sells, not all of the good's price change reflects a change in the cost of living. The Bureau of Economic Analysis does its best to account for changes in the quality of goods over time. For example, if Ford increases the horsepower of a particular car model from one year to the next, the CPI will reflect the change: the quality-adjusted price of the car will not rise as fast as the unadjusted price. Yet many changes in quality, such as comfort or safety, are hard to measure. If unmeasured quality improvement (rather than unmeasured quality deterioration) is typical, then the measured CPI rises faster than it should.

Because of these measurement problems, some economists have suggested reducing the indexation written into laws. For example, Social Security benefits could be indexed to CPI inflation minus 1 percent. Such a change would provide a rough way of offsetting these measurement problems. At the same time, it would automatically slow the growth in government spending.

In 1995, the Senate Finance Committee appointed a panel of five noted economists—Michael Boskin, Ellen Dulberger, Robert Gordon, Zvi Griliches, and Dale Jorgenson—to study the magnitude of the measurement error in the CPI. According to the panel's interim report, the CPI is biased upward by 0.7 to 2.0 percentage points per year, with their "best estimate" being 1.0 percentage point. This finding has important implications for policy, for correcting this measurement error would reduce the federal government's budget deficit by $634 billion over 10 years.[2]

2-3 Measuring Joblessness: The Unemployment Rate

One aspect of economic performance is how well an economy uses its resources. Since an economy's workers are its chief resource, keeping workers employed is a paramount concern of economic policymakers. The unemployment rate is the statistic that measures the percentage of those people wanting to work who do not have jobs.

Every month the U.S. Bureau of Labor Statistics computes the unemployment rate and many other statistics that economists and policymakers use to monitor developments in the labor market. These statistics come from a survey of about 60,000 households. Based on the responses to survey questions, each person in each household is placed into one of three categories: employed, unemployed, or not in the labor force. A person is employed if he or she spent most of the previous week working at a job, as opposed to keeping house, going to school, or doing something else. A person is unemployed if he or she is not

"Well, so long Eddie, the recession's over."

employed and is waiting for the start date of a new job, is on temporary layoff, or has been looking for a job. A person who fits into neither of the first two categories, such as a student or retiree, is not in the labor force. A person who wants a job but has given up looking—a *discouraged worker*—is counted as not in the labor force.

2 "Panel Sees a Corrected Price Index as Deficit-Cutter," *New York Times*, September 15, 1995, A30.

The **labor force** is defined as the sum of the employed and unemployed, and the **unemployment rate** is defined as the percentage of the labor force that is unemployed. That is,

$$\text{Labor Force} = \text{Number of Employed} + \text{Number of Unemployed},$$

and

$$\text{Unemployment Rate} = \frac{\text{Number of Unemployed}}{\text{Labor Force}} \times 100.$$

A related statistic is the **labor-force participation rate**, the percentage of the adult population that is in the labor force:

$$\text{Labor-Force Participation Rate} = \frac{\text{Labor Force}}{\text{Adult Population}} \times 100.$$

The Bureau of Labor Statistics computes these statistics for the overall population and for groups within the population: men and women, whites and blacks, teenagers and prime-age workers.

Figure 2-4 shows the breakdown of the population into the three categories for 1994. The statistics broke down as follows:

$$\text{Labor Force} = 123.1 + 8.0 = 131.1 \text{ million.}$$

$$\text{Unemployment Rate} = (8.0/131.1) \times 100 = 6.1\%.$$

$$\text{Labor-Force Participation Rate} = (131.1/196.8) \times 100 = 66.6\%.$$

Hence, about two-thirds of the adult population was in the labor force, and about 6 percent of those in the labor force did not have a job.

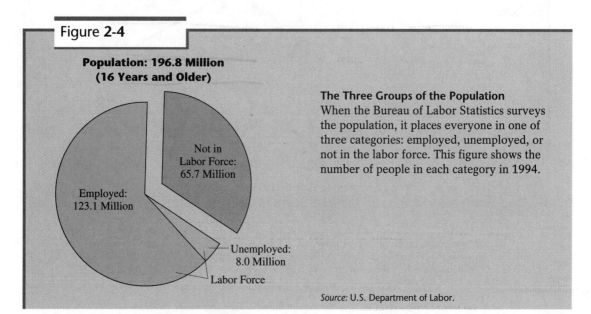

Figure 2-4

Population: 196.8 Million (16 Years and Older)

Not in Labor Force: 65.7 Million

Employed: 123.1 Million

Unemployed: 8.0 Million

Labor Force

The Three Groups of the Population
When the Bureau of Labor Statistics surveys the population, it places everyone in one of three categories: employed, unemployed, or not in the labor force. This figure shows the number of people in each category in 1994.

Source: U.S. Department of Labor.

Case Study *2-4*

• • • • • • • • • • • •

Unemployment, GDP, and Okun's Law

What relationship should we expect to find between unemployment and real GDP? Since employed workers help to produce goods and services and unemployed workers do not, increases in the unemployment rate should be associated with decreases in real GDP. This negative relationship between unemployment and GDP is called **Okun's law**, after Arthur Okun, the economist who first studied it.[3]

Figure 2-5 uses annual data for the United States to illustrate Okun's law.

Figure **2-5**

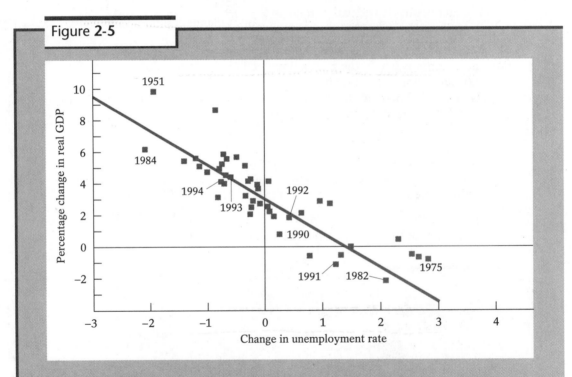

Okun's Law This figure is a scatterplot of the change in the unemployment rate on the horizontal axis and the percentage change in real GDP on the vertical axis. Each point represents one year. The negative correlation between these variables shows that increases in unemployment tend to be associated with decreases in real GDP.

Source: U.S. Department of Commerce and U.S. Department of Labor

[3] Arthur M. Okun, "Potential GNP: Its Measurement and Significance," in *Proceedings of the Business and Economics Statistics Section, American Statistical Association* (Washington, D.C.: American Statistical Association, 1962), 98–103; reprinted in Arthur M. Okun, *Economics for Policymaking* (Cambridge, Mass.: MIT Press, 1983), 145–158.

This figure is a scatterplot—a scatter of points where each point represents one observation (in this case, the data for a particular year). The horizontal axis represents the change in the unemployment rate from the previous year, and the vertical axis represents the percentage change in GDP. This figure shows clearly that year-to-year changes in the unemployment rate are closely associated with year-to-year changes in real GDP.

We can be more precise about the magnitude of the Okun's law relationship. The line drawn through the scatter of points tells us that

$$\text{Percentage Change in Real GDP} = 3\% - 2 \times \text{Change in the Unemployment Rate.}$$

If the unemployment rate remains the same, real GDP grows by about 3 percent; this normal growth is due to population growth, capital accumulation, and technological progress. In addition, for every percentage point the unemployment rate rises, real GDP growth typically falls by 2 percent. Hence, if the unemployment rate rises from 6 to 8 percent, then real GDP growth would be

$$\text{Percentage Change in Real GDP} = 3\% - 2 \times (8\% - 6\%)$$
$$= -1\%.$$

In this case, Okun's law says that GDP would fall by 1 percent, indicating that the economy is in a recession.

● ● ● ● ● ● ● ● ● ● ● ● ● ●

2-4 Conclusion: From Economic Statistics to Economic Models

The three statistics discussed in this chapter—gross domestic product, the consumer price index, and the unemployment rate—quantify the performance of the economy. Public and private decisionmakers use these statistics to monitor changes in the economy and to formulate appropriate policies. Economists use these statistics to develop and test theories about how the economy works.

In the chapters that follow, we examine some of these theories. Chapters 3 and 4 study GDP, Chapter 5 studies unemployment, and Chapter 6 studies inflation. We build models to help us understand how these variables are determined and how economic policy affects them. Having learned how to measure economic performance, we now learn how to explain it.

Summary

1. Gross domestic product (GDP) measures both the income of everyone in the economy and the total expenditure on the economy's output of goods and services.

2. Nominal GDP values goods and services at current prices. Real GDP values goods and services at constant prices. Real GDP rises only when the amount of goods and services has increased, whereas nominal GDP can rise either because output has increased or because prices have increased.

3. GDP is the sum of four categories of expenditure: consumption, investment, government purchases, and net exports.

4. The consumer price index (CPI) measures the price of a fixed basket of goods and services purchased by a typical consumer. Like the GDP deflator, which is the ratio of nominal GDP to real GDP, the CPI measures the overall level of prices.

5. The unemployment rate shows what fraction of those who would like to work do not have a job. Increases in the unemployment rate are typically associated with decreases in real GDP.

KEY CONCEPTS

Gross domestic product (GDP)	Investment
National income accounting	Government purchases
Stocks and flows	Net exports
Value-added	Consumer price index (CPI)
Imputed value	Labor force
Nominal versus real GDP	Unemployment rate
GDP deflator	Labor-force participation rate
National income accounts identity	Okun's law
Consumption	

QUESTIONS FOR REVIEW

1. List the two things that GDP measures. How can GDP measure two things at once?

2. What does the consumer price index measure?

3. List the three categories used by the Bureau of Labor Statistics to classify everyone in the economy. How does the Bureau compute the unemployment rate?

4. Explain Okun's law.

PROBLEMS AND APPLICATIONS

1. Look at the newspapers for the past few days. What new economic statistics have been released? How do you interpret these statistics?

2. A farmer grows a bushel of wheat and sells it to a miller for $1.00. The miller turns the wheat into flour and then sells the flour to a baker for $3.00. The baker uses the flour to make bread and sells the bread to an engineer for $6.00. The engineer eats the bread. What is the value-added by each person? What is GDP?

3. Suppose that a woman marries her butler. After they are married, her husband continues to wait on her as before, and she continues to support him as before (but as a husband rather than as a wage earner). How do you think the marriage affects GDP? How should it affect GDP?

4. Place each of the following transactions in one of the four components of expenditure: consumption, investment, government purchases, and net exports.

   a. Boeing sells an airplane to the Air Force.

   b. Boeing sells an airplane to American Airlines.

   c. Boeing sells an airplane to Air France.

   d. Boeing sells an airplane to Amelia Earhart.

   e. Boeing builds an airplane to be sold next year.

5. Find data on GDP and its components, and compute the percentage of GDP for the following components for 1950, 1970, and 1990.

   a. Personal consumption expenditures

   b. Gross private domestic investment

   c. Government purchases

   d. Net exports

   e. National defense purchases

   f. State and local purchases

   g. Imports

Do you see any stable relationships in the data? Do you see any trends? (*Hint*: A good place to look for data is the statistical appendices of the *Economic Report of the President*, which is written each year by the Council of Economic Advisers.)

6. Consider an economy that produces and consumes bread and automobiles. In the table below are data for two different years.

	Year 2000	Year 2010
Price of an automobile	$50,000	$60,000
Price of a loaf of bread	$10	$20
Number of automobiles produced	100	120
Number of loaves of bread produced	500,000	400,000

   a. Using the year 2000 as the base year, compute the following statistics for each year: nominal GDP, real GDP, the implicit price deflator for GDP, and a fixed-weight price index such as the CPI.

   b. How much have prices risen between year 2000 and year 2010? Compare the answers given by the Laspeyres and Paasche price indices. Explain the difference.

   c. Suppose you are a senator writing a bill to index Social Security and federal pensions. That is, your bill will adjust these benefits to offset changes in the cost of living. Will you use the GDP deflator or the CPI? Why?

7. Abby consumes only apples. In year 1, red apples cost $1 each, green apples cost $2 each, and Abby buys 10 red apples. In year 2, red apples cost $2, green apples cost $1, and Abby buys 10 green apples.

a. Using year 1 as the base year, compute a consumer price index for apples for each year. How does your index change from year 1 to year 2?

b. Compute Abby's nominal spending on apples in each year. How does it change from year 1 to year 2?

c. Using year 1 as the base year, compute Abby's real spending on apples in each year. How does it change from year 1 to year 2?

d. Defining the implicit price deflator as nominal spending divided by real spending, compute the deflator for each year. How does the deflator change from year 1 to year 2?

e. Suppose that Abby is equally happy eating red or green apples. How much has the true cost of living increased for Abby? Compare this answer to your answers to parts (a) and (d). What does this example tell you about Laspeyres and Paasche price indexes?

8. Consider how each of the following events is likely to affect real GDP. Do you think the change in real GDP reflects a similar change in economic well-being?

a. A hurricane in Florida forces Disney World to shut down for a month.

b. The discovery of a new, easy-to-grow strain of wheat increases farm harvests.

c. Increased hostility between unions and management sparks a rash of strikes.

d. Firms throughout the economy experience falling demand, causing them to lay off workers.

e. Congress passes new environmental laws that prohibit firms from using production methods that emit large quantities of pollution.

f. More high-school students drop out of school to take jobs mowing lawns.

g. Fathers around the country reduce their workweeks to spend more time with their children.

9. In a speech that Senator Robert Kennedy gave when he was running for president in 1968, he said the following about GDP:

[It] does not allow for the health of our children, the quality of their education, or the joy of their play. It does not include the beauty of our poetry or the strength of our marriages, the intelligence of our public debate or the integrity of our public officials. It measures neither our courage, nor our wisdom, nor our devotion to our country. It measures everything, in short, except that which makes life worthwhile, and it can tell us everything about America except why we are proud that we are Americans.

Was Robert Kennedy right? If so, why do we care about GDP?

The Economy in the Long Run

Chapters 3, 4, 5, 6, 7

We are now ready to build models to explain how the economy works. In this part of the book we examine *classical* models of the economy. The key assumption of classical models is that prices are flexible. Most economists agree that this assumption describes how the economy behaves in the long run.

We proceed as follows. Chapter 3 builds the most basic classical model, which provides the foundation for many of the models in later chapters. It discusses how much the economy produces, who gets the income from production, and how the economy's resources are allocated among alternative uses.

Whereas Chapter 3 assumes that the inputs into production—capital and labor—are fixed, Chapters 4 and 5 look at the factors of production more closely. Chapter 4 discusses the very long run over which the economy's stock of capital can change. Chapter 5 examines the labor market in order to explain what determines the natural rate of unemployment.

Chapter 6 introduces the concept of money and discusses a key macroeconomic variable—the inflation rate. As we will see, the classical model and its assumption of price flexibility give a simple link between monetary policy and inflation.

Chapter 7 extends the classical model to describe the behavior of an economy as it interacts with the economies of other nations. It discusses exports and imports, international borrowing and lending, and the exchange rate between different currencies. Our goal is to understand how various government policies affect an open economy.

Chapter 3

National Income: Its Production, Distribution, and Allocation

A large income is the best recipe for happiness I ever heard of.

Jane Austen

The macroeconomic variables introduced in Chapter 2 allow economists and policymakers to measure and compare economic performance from year to year and from country to country. Our goal, however, is not merely to measure economic performance but also to explain it. That is, we want to build economic models that help us to understand the behavior of the economy, the relationships among economic variables, and the effects of economic policy.

Perhaps the most important economic variable is gross domestic product (GDP), which measures both a nation's output of goods and services and its income. This chapter addresses four groups of questions about the sources and uses of GDP:

- How much do the firms in the economy produce? What determines a nation's total income?

- Who gets the income from production? How much goes to compensate workers, and how much goes to compensate owners of capital?

- Who buys the output of the economy? How much do households purchase for consumption, how much do households and firms purchase for investment, and how much does the government buy for public purposes?

- What equilibrates the demand for and supply of goods and services? What ensures that the sum of consumption, investment, and government purchases equals the level of production?

To answer these questions, we must examine how the various parts of the economy interact.

A good place to start is the circular flow diagram. In Chapter 2 we traced the circular flow of dollars in a hypothetical economy that produced one

45

Figure 3-1

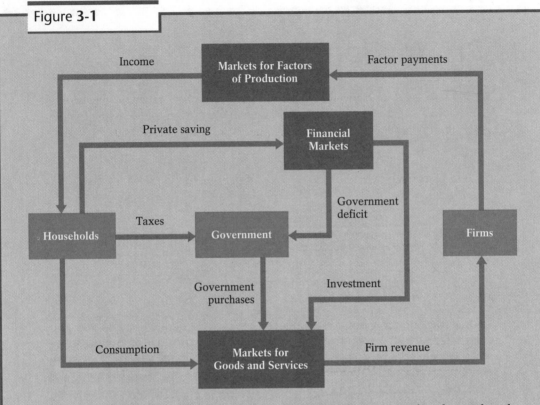

The Circular Flow of Dollars Through the Economy This figure is a more realistic version of the circular flow diagram found in Chapter 2. Each red box represents an economic actor—households, firms, and the government. Each blue box represents a type of market—the markets for goods and services, the markets for the factors of production, and financial markets. The arrows show the flow of dollars among the economic actors through the three types of markets.

product, bread, from labor services. Figure 3-1 more accurately reflects how real economies function. It shows the linkages among the economic actors—households, firms, and the government—and how dollars flow among them through the various markets in the economy.

Let's look at the flow of dollars from the viewpoints of these economic actors. Households receive income and use it to pay taxes to the government, to consume goods and services, and to save through the financial markets. Firms receive revenue from the sale of goods and services and use it to pay for the factors of production. Both households and firms borrow in financial markets to buy investment goods, such as housing, plant, and equipment. The government receives revenue from taxes, uses it to pay for government purchases, and, if it spends more than it receives, borrows in the financial markets to cover the deficit.

In this chapter we develop a basic classical model to explain the economic interactions depicted in Figure 3-1. We begin with firms. We look at what determines their level of production, which equals the level of national income. Then we examine how the markets for the factors of production distribute this income to households. Next, we consider how much of this income households consume and how much they save. In addition to discussing the demand for goods and services arising from the consumption of households, we discuss the demand arising from investment and government purchases. Finally, we come full circle and examine how the demand for goods and services (the sum of consumption, investment, and government purchases) and the supply of goods and services (the level of production) are brought into balance.

3-1 The Production of Goods and Services

An economy's output of goods and services—its GDP—depends on (1) its quantity of inputs, called the factors of production, and (2) its ability to turn inputs into output, as represented by the production function. We discuss each of these in turn.

The Factors of Production

Factors of production are the inputs used to produce goods and services. The two most important factors of production are capital and labor. Capital is the set of tools that workers use: the construction worker's crane, the accountant's calculator, and this author's personal computer. Labor is the time people spend working. We use the symbol K to denote the amount of capital and the symbol L to denote the amount of labor.

In this chapter we take the economy's factors of production as given. In other words, we assume that the economy has a fixed amount of capital and a fixed amount of labor. We write

$$K = \overline{K}.$$
$$L = \overline{L}.$$

The overbar means that each variable is fixed at some level. In Chapter 4 we examine what happens when the factors of production change over time, as they do in the real world. For now, to keep our analysis simple, we assume fixed amounts of capital and labor.

We also assume here that the factors of production are fully utilized—that is, that no resources are wasted. Again, in the real world, part of the labor force is unemployed, and some capital lies idle. In Chapter 5 we examine the reasons for unemployment, but for now we assume that both capital and labor are fully employed.

2 · The Production Function

The available production technology determines how much output is produced from given amounts of capital and labor. Economists express the available technology using a **production function**, which shows how the factors of production determine the amount of output produced. Letting Y denote the amount of output, we write the production function as

$$Y = F(K, L).$$

This equation states that output is a function of the amount of capital and the amount of labor.

The production function reflects the available technology. That is, the available technology is implicit in the way this function turns capital and labor into output. If someone invents a better way to produce a good, the result is more output from the same amounts of capital and labor. Thus, technological change alters the production function.

Many production functions exhibit **constant returns to scale**. A production function has constant returns to scale if an increase of an equal percentage in all factors of production causes an increase in output of the same percentage. If the production function has constant returns to scale, then we get 10 percent more output when we increase both capital and labor by 10 percent. Mathematically, a production function has constant returns to scale if

$$zY = F(zK, zL)$$

for any positive number z. This equation says that if we multiply both the amount of capital and the amount of labor by some factor z, output is also multiplied by z. We see in the next section that the assumption of constant returns to scale has an important implication for how the income from production is distributed.

As an example of a production function, consider production at a bakery. The kitchen and its equipment are the bakery's capital, the workers hired to make the bread are its labor, and the loaves of bread are its output. The bakery's production function shows that the number of loaves produced depends on the amount of equipment and the number of workers. If the production function has constant returns to scale, then we double the amount of bread produced when we double the amount of equipment and double the number of workers.

3 · The Fixed Supply of Goods and Services

We can now see that the factors of production and the production function together determine the supply of goods and services, which equals the economy's output. To express this mathematically, we write

$$Y = F(\overline{K}, \overline{L})$$
$$= \overline{Y}.$$

At any point in time, the output of the economy is fixed because the supplies of capital and labor and the technology for turning capital and labor into goods and services are fixed. Over time, output changes when factor supplies change or when technology changes. The greater the amount of capital or the amount of labor, the greater the output. The better the available technology as summarized in the production function, the greater the output.

3-2 Distributing National Income to the Factors of Production

As we discussed in Chapter 2, the total output of an economy equals its total income. Because the factors of production and the production function together determine the total output of goods and services, they also determine national income. The circular flow diagram in Figure 3-1 shows that this national income flows from firms to households through the markets for the factors of production.

In this section we discuss how these factor markets work. Economists have long studied factor markets in order to understand the distribution of income. (For example, Karl Marx, the noted nineteenth-century economist, spent much time trying to explain the incomes of capital and labor. The political philosophy of communism was in part based on Marx's now-discredited theory.) Here we examine the modern theory of how national income is divided among the factors of production. This theory, called the *neoclassical theory of distribution*, is accepted by most economists today.

Factor Prices

The distribution of national income is determined by factor prices. **Factor prices** are the amounts paid to the factors of production—the wage workers earn and the rent the owners of capital collect. As Figure 3-2 illustrates, the price each factor of production receives for its services is in turn determined by

Figure 3-2

Factor price (y-axis)
Quantity of factor (x-axis)

Factor supply

Factor demand

Equilibrium factor price

How a Factor of Production Is Compensated The price paid to any factor of production depends on the supply and demand for that factor's services. Because we have assumed that supply is fixed, the supply curve is vertical. The demand curve is downward sloping. The intersection of supply and demand determines the equilibrium factor price.

the supply and demand for that factor. Because we have assumed that the economy's factors of production are fixed, the factor supply curve in Figure 3-2 is vertical. The intersection of the downward-sloping factor demand curve and the vertical supply curve determines the equilibrium factor price.

To understand factor prices and the distribution of income, we must examine the demand for the factors of production. Factor demand arises from the thousands of firms that use capital and labor. We now look at the decisions faced by a typical firm.

The Problem Facing the Competitive Firm

The simplest assumption to make about a typical firm is that it is competitive. A competitive firm is small relative to the markets in which it trades, so it has little influence on market prices. For example, our firm produces a good and sells it at the market price. Because many firms produce this good, our firm can sell as much as it wants without causing the price of the good to fall, or it can stop selling altogether without causing the price of the good to rise. Nor can our firm have much effect on the wages of the workers it employs, because many other local firms also employ workers. The firm has no reason to pay more than the market wage, and if it tried to pay less, its workers would take jobs elsewhere. Therefore, the competitive firm takes prices—both of its output and of its inputs—as given.

To make its product, the firm needs two factors of production, capital and labor. As we did for the aggregate economy, we represent the firm's production technology by the production function

$$Y = F(K, L),$$

where Y is the number of units produced (the firm's output), K the number of machines used (the amount of capital), and L the number of hours worked by the firm's employees (the amount of labor). The firm produces more output if it has more machines or if its employees work more hours.

The firm sells its output at a price P, hires workers at a wage W, and rents capital at a rate R. Notice that when we speak of firms renting capital, we are assuming that households own the economy's stock of capital. In this analysis, households rent out their capital, just as they sell their labor. The firm obtains both factors of production from the households that own them.[1]

The goal of the firm is to maximize profit. *Profit* is revenue minus costs—it is what the owners of the firm keep after paying for the costs of production. Revenue equals $P \times Y$, the selling price of the good P multiplied by the amount of the good the firm produces Y. Costs include both labor costs and capital costs. Labor costs equal $W \times L$, the wage W times the amount of labor

---

[1]   This is a simplification. In the real world, the ownership of capital is indirect, because firms own capital and households own the firms. That is, real firms have two functions: owning capital and producing output. To help us understand how the factors of production are compensated, however, we assume that firms only produce output and that households own capital directly.

L. Capital costs equal $R \times K$, the rental price of capital R times the amount of capital K. We can write

$$\text{Profit} = \text{Revenue} - \text{Labor Costs} - \text{Capital Costs}$$
$$= PY - WL - RK.$$

To see how profit depends on the factors of production, we use the production function $Y = F(K, L)$ to substitute for Y in this equation to obtain

$$\text{Profit} = PF(K, L) - WL - RK.$$

The equation shows that profit depends on the product price P, the factor prices W and R, and the factor quantities L and K. The competitive firm takes the product price and the factor prices as given and chooses the amounts of labor and capital that maximize profit.

The Firm's Demand for Factors

We can now see how this firm decides how much labor to hire and how much capital to rent.

The Marginal Product of Labor   The more labor the firm employs, the more output it produces. The **marginal product of labor (MPL)** is the extra amount of output the firm gets from one extra unit of labor. In other words, if the firm hires an additional hour of labor, its production increases by MPL units. We can express this using the production function:

$$MPL = F(K, L + 1) - F(K, L).$$

The first term on the right-hand side is the amount of output produced with K units of capital and $L + 1$ units of labor; the second term is the amount of output produced with K units of capital and L units of labor. This equation states that the marginal product of labor is the difference between the amount of output produced with $L + 1$ units of labor and the amount produced with only L units of labor.

Most production functions have the property of **diminishing marginal product**: holding the amount of capital fixed, the marginal product of labor decreases as the amount of labor increases. For example, consider again the production of bread at a bakery. As a bakery hires more labor, it produces more bread. The MPL is the amount of extra bread produced when an extra unit of labor is hired. With each additional unit of labor, however, the MPL is smaller. Fewer additional loaves are produced because workers are less productive when the kitchen is more crowded. In other words, holding the size of the kitchen fixed, each additional unit of labor adds fewer loaves of bread to the bakery's output.

Figure 3-3 graphs the production function. It illustrates what happens to the amount of output when we hold the amount of capital constant and vary the amount of labor. This figure shows that the marginal product of labor is the slope of the production function. As the amount of labor increases, the production function becomes flatter, indicating diminishing marginal product.

Figure 3-3

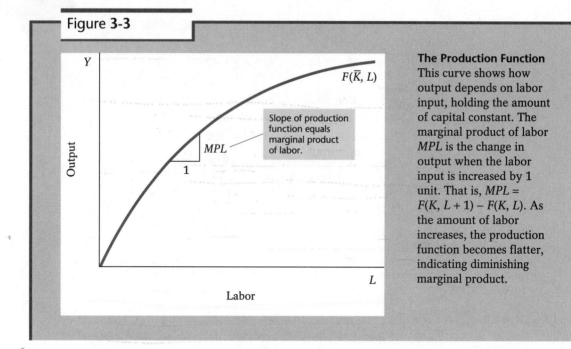

The Production Function This curve shows how output depends on labor input, holding the amount of capital constant. The marginal product of labor MPL is the change in output when the labor input is increased by 1 unit. That is, $MPL = F(K, L + 1) - F(K, L)$. As the amount of labor increases, the production function becomes flatter, indicating diminishing marginal product.

From the Marginal Product of Labor to Labor Demand When the competitive, profit-maximizing firm is deciding whether to hire an additional unit of labor, it considers how that decision affects profits. It therefore compares the extra revenue from the increased production that results from the added labor to the extra cost of a higher wage bill. The increase in revenue from an additional unit of labor depends on both the marginal product of labor and the price of the output. Because an extra unit of labor produces MPL units of output, and each unit of output sells for P dollars, the extra revenue is $P \times MPL$. The extra cost of hiring one more unit of labor is the wage W. Thus, the change in profit from hiring an additional unit of labor is

$$\Delta\text{Profit} = \Delta\text{Revenue} - \Delta\text{Cost}$$
$$= (P \times MPL) - W.$$

The symbol Δ (called *delta*) denotes the change in a variable.

We can now answer the question we asked at the beginning of this section: How much labor does the firm hire? The firm's manager knows that if the extra revenue $P \times MPL$ exceeds the wage W, an extra unit of labor increases profit. Therefore, the manager continues to hire labor until the next unit would no longer be profitable—that is, until the MPL falls to the point where the extra revenue equals the wage. The firm's demand for labor is determined by

$$P \times MPL = W.$$

We can write this as

$$MPL = W/P.$$

W/P is the **real wage**, the return to labor measured in units of output rather than in dollars. The real wage is the amount of purchasing power—measured as a quantity of goods and services—that the firm pays for each unit of labor. To maximize profit, the firm hires up to the point at which the marginal product of labor equals the real wage.

For example, again consider a bakery. Suppose the price of bread *P* is $2 per loaf, and a worker earns a wage *W* of $20 per hour. The real wage *W/P* is 10 loaves per hour. In this example, the firm keeps hiring workers until an additional worker would increase output by only 10 loaves per hour.

Figure 3-4 shows how the marginal product of labor depends on the amount of labor employed (holding the firm's capital stock constant). That is, this figure graphs the *MPL* schedule. Because the *MPL* diminishes as the amount of labor increases, this curve slopes downward. For any given real wage, the firm hires up to the point at which the *MPL* equals the real wage. Hence, the *MPL* schedule is the firm's labor demand curve.

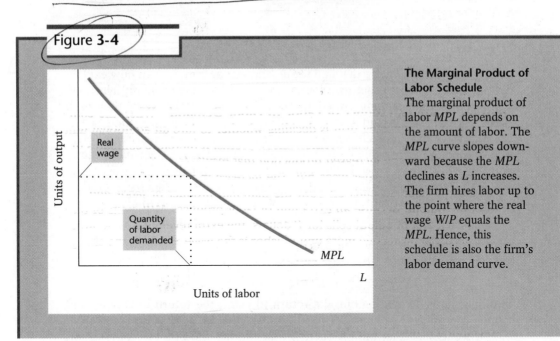

Figure 3-4

The Marginal Product of Labor Schedule
The marginal product of labor *MPL* depends on the amount of labor. The *MPL* curve slopes downward because the *MPL* declines as *L* increases. The firm hires labor up to the point where the real wage *W/P* equals the *MPL*. Hence, this schedule is also the firm's labor demand curve.

The Marginal Product of Capital and Capital Demand   The firm decides how much capital to rent in the same way it decides how much labor to hire. The **marginal product of capital** *(MPK)* is the amount of extra output the firm gets from an extra unit of capital,

$$MPK = F(K + 1, L) - F(K, L).$$

Thus, the marginal product of capital is the difference between the amount of output produced with $K + 1$ units of capital and that produced with only K units of capital. Like labor, capital is subject to diminishing marginal product.

The increase in profit from renting an additional machine is the extra revenue from selling the output of that machine minus the machine's rental price:

$$\Delta\text{Profit} = \Delta\text{Revenue} - \Delta\text{Cost}$$
$$= (P \times MPK) - R.$$

To maximize profit, the firm continues to rent more capital until the MPK falls to equal the real rental price:

$$MPK = R/P.$$

The **real rental price of capital** is the rental price measured in units of goods rather than in dollars.

To sum up, the competitive, profit-maximizing firm follows a simple rule about how much labor to hire and how much capital to rent. *The firm demands each factor of production until that factor's marginal product falls to equal its real factor price.*

The Division of National Income

Having analyzed the factor demand for the individual firm, we can now explain how the markets for the factors of production distribute the economy's income. If all firms in the economy are competitive and profit-maximizing, then each factor of production is paid its marginal contribution to the production process. The real wage paid to each worker equals the MPL, and the real rental price paid to each owner of capital equals the MPK. The total real wage bill is therefore MPL × L, and the total real return to capital owners is MPK × K.

The income that remains after the firms have paid the factors of production is the **economic profit** of the owners of the firms. Real economic profit is

$$\text{Economic Profit} = Y - (MPL \times L) - (MPK \times K).$$

Since we want to examine the distribution of national income, we rearrange the terms as follows:

$$Y = (MPL \times L) + (MPK \times K) + \text{Economic Profit}.$$

Total income is divided among the return to labor, the return to capital, and economic profit.

If we assume that the production function has the property of constant returns to scale, however, economic profit must be zero. That is, nothing is left after the factors of production are paid. This surprising conclusion follows from a famous mathematical result called *Euler's theorem*,[2] which states that if the production function has constant returns to scale, then

$$F(K, L) = (MPK \times K) + (MPL \times L).$$

If each factor of production is paid its marginal product, then the sum of these factor payments equals total output. That is, constant returns to scale, profit maximization, and competition together imply that economic profit is zero.

If economic profit is zero, how can we explain the existence of "profit" in

[2] *Mathematical Note:* To prove Euler's theorem, begin with the definition of constant returns to scale: $zY = F(zK, zL)$. Now differentiate with respect to z and then evaluate at $z = 1$.

the economy? The answer is that the term "profit" as normally used is different from economic profit. We have been assuming that there are three types of agents: workers, owners of capital, and owners of firms. Total income is divided among wages, return to capital, and economic profit. In the real world, however, most firms own rather than rent the capital they use. Hence, the owners of firms also own the capital. The term "profit" usually includes both economic profit and the return to capital. If we call this alternative definition **accounting profit**, we can say that

$$\text{Accounting Profit} = \text{Economic Profit} + (MPK \times K).$$

Under our assumptions—constant returns to scale, profit maximization, and competition—economic profit is zero. If these assumptions approximately describe the world, then the "profit" in the national income accounts must be mostly the return to capital.

We can now answer the question posed at the beginning of this chapter about how the income of the economy is distributed from firms to households. Each factor of production is paid its marginal product, and these factor payments exhaust total output. *Total output is divided between the payments to capital and the payments to labor, depending on their marginal productivities.*

Case Study 3-1

The Black Death and Factor Prices

According to the neoclassical theory of distribution, factor prices equal the marginal products of the factors of production. Because the marginal products depend on the quantities of the factors, a change in the quantity of any one factor alters the marginal products of all the factors. Therefore, a change in the supply of a factor alters equilibrium factor prices.

Fourteenth-century Europe provides a vivid example of how factor quantities affect factor prices. The outbreak of the bubonic plague—the Black Death—in 1348 reduced the population of Europe by about one-third within a few years. Because the marginal product of labor increases as the amount of labor falls, this massive reduction in the labor force raised the marginal product of labor. (The economy moved to the left along the curves in Figures 3-3 and 3-4.) Real wages increased substantially—doubling, by some estimates. The peasants who were fortunate enough to survive the plague enjoyed economic prosperity.

The reduction in the labor force caused by the plague also affected the return to land, the other major factor of production in medieval Europe. With fewer workers available to farm the land, an additional unit of land produced less additional output. This fall in the marginal product of land led to a decline in real rents of 50 percent or more. While the peasant classes prospered, the landed classes suffered reduced incomes.[3]

---

[3] Carlo M. Cipolla, *Before the Industrial Revolution: European Society and Economy, 1000–1700,* 2d ed. (New York: Norton, 1980), 200–202.

3-3   The Demand for Goods and Services

We have seen what determines the level of production and how the income from production is divided between workers and owners of capital. We now continue our tour of the circular flow diagram, Figure 3-1, and examine how the output from production is used.

In Chapter 2 we identified the four components of GDP:

- Consumption (C)
- Investment (I)
- Government purchases (G)
- Net exports (NX).

The circular flow diagram contains only the first three components. For now, to simplify the analysis, we assume a *closed economy*—a country that does not trade with other countries. Thus, net exports are always zero. We examine the macroeconomics of *open economies* in Chapter 7.

A closed economy has three uses for the goods and services it produces. These three components of GDP are expressed in the national income accounts identity:

$$Y = C + I + G.$$

Households consume some of the economy's output; firms and households use some of the output for investment; and the government buys some of the output for public purposes. We want to see how GDP is allocated among these three uses.

Consumption

When we eat food, wear clothing, or go to a movie, we are consuming some of the output of the economy. All forms of consumption together make up two-thirds of GDP. Since consumption is so large, macroeconomists have devoted much energy to studying how households decide how much to consume. Chapter 15 examines this work in detail. Here we consider the simplest story of consumer behavior.

Households receive income from their labor and their ownership of capital, pay taxes to the government, and then decide how much of their after-tax income to consume and how much to save. As we discussed in Section 3-2, the income that households receive equals the output of the economy Y. The government then taxes households an amount T. (Although the government imposes many kinds of taxes, such as personal and corporate income taxes and sales taxes, for our purposes we can lump all these taxes together.) We define income after the payment of all taxes, $Y - T$, as **disposable income**. Households divide their disposable income between consumption and saving.

We assume that the level of consumption depends directly on the level of disposable income. The higher is disposable income, the greater is consumption. Thus,

$$C = C(Y - T).$$

This equation states that consumption is a function of disposable income. The relationship between consumption and disposable income is called the consumption function.

The **marginal propensity to consume** *(MPC)* is the amount by which consumption changes when disposable income increases by one dollar. The *MPC* is between zero and one: an extra dollar of income increases consumption, but by less than one dollar. Thus, if households obtain an extra dollar of income, they save a portion of it. For example, if the *MPC* is 0.7, then households spend 70 cents of each additional dollar of disposable income on consumer goods and services and save 30 cents.

Figure 3-5 illustrates the consumption function. The slope of the consumption function tells us how much consumption increases when disposable income increases by one dollar. That is, the slope of the consumption function is the *MPC*.

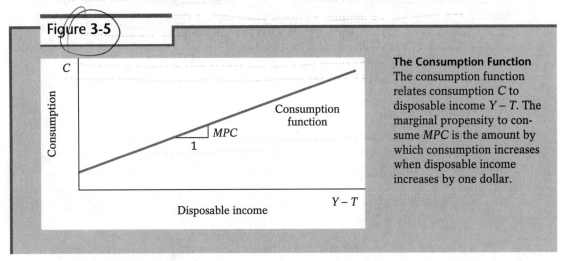

Figure 3-5

The Consumption Function
The consumption function relates consumption *C* to disposable income *Y* – *T*. The marginal propensity to consume *MPC* is the amount by which consumption increases when disposable income increases by one dollar.

Investment

Both firms and households purchase investment goods. Firms buy investment goods to add to their stock of capital and to replace existing capital as it wears out. Households buy new houses, which are also part of investment. Total investment in the United States averages about 15 percent of GDP.

The quantity of investment goods demanded depends on the interest rate. For an investment project to be profitable, its return must exceed its cost. Because the interest rate measures the cost of funds to finance investment, an increase in the interest rate results in fewer investment projects being profitable and, therefore, a decrease in the demand for investment goods.

For example, suppose that a firm is considering whether it should build a $1 million factory that would yield a return of $100,000 per year, or 10 percent. The firm compares this return to the cost of borrowing the $1 million. If the interest rate is below 10 percent, the firm borrows the money in financial markets and makes the investment. If the interest rate is above 10 percent, the firm forgoes the opportunity and does not build the factory.

The Many Different Interest Rates

If you look in the business section of a newspaper, you will find many different interest rates reported. By contrast, throughout this book, we will talk about "the" interest rate, as if there were only one interest rate in the economy. The only distinction we will make is between the nominal interest rate (which is not corrected for inflation) and the real interest rate (which is corrected for inflation). All the interest rates reported in the newspaper are nominal.

Why does the newspaper report so many interest rates? The various interest rates differ in three ways:

- *Term.* Some loans in the economy are for short periods of time, even as short as overnight. Other loans are for as long as thirty years. The interest rate on a loan depends on its term. Long-term interest rates are usually, but not always, higher than short-term interest rates.

- *Credit risk.* In deciding whether to make a loan, a lender must take into account the probability that the borrower will repay. The law allows borrowers to default on their loans by declaring bankruptcy. The higher the perceived probability of default, the higher the interest rate. The safest credit risk is the government, and so government bonds tend to pay a low interest rate. At the other extreme, financially shaky corporations can raise funds only by issuing *junk bonds*, which pay a high interest rate to compensate for the high risk of default.

- *Tax treatment.* The interest on different types of bonds is taxed differently. Most important, when state and local governments issue bonds, called *municipal bonds*, the holders of the bonds do not pay federal income tax on the interest income. Because of this tax advantage, municipal bonds pay a lower interest rate.

When you see two different interest rates in the newspaper, you can almost always explain the difference by considering the term, the credit risk, and the tax treatment of the loan.

Although there are many different interest rates in the economy, macroeconomists can usually ignore these distinctions. The various interest rates tend to move up and down together. The assumption that there is only one interest rate is, for our purposes, a useful simplification.

The firm makes the same investment decision even if it already has the $1 million. The firm can always deposit the money in a bank and earn interest on it. Building the factory is more profitable than a bank deposit if and only if the interest rate is less than the 10 percent return on the factory.

A person wanting to buy a new house faces a similar decision. The higher the interest rate, the greater the cost of carrying a mortgage. A $100,000 mortgage costs $8,000 per year if the interest rate is 8 percent and $10,000 per year if the interest rate is 10 percent. As the interest rate rises, the cost of owning a home rises, and the demand for new homes falls.

Economists distinguish between the nominal interest rate and the real interest rate. This distinction arises during periods of inflation or deflation—that is, when prices are not stable. The **nominal interest rate** is the interest rate as the term is normally used: it is the rate of interest that investors pay to borrow money. The **real interest rate** is the nominal interest rate corrected for the effects of inflation.

To see how nominal and real interest rates differ, consider a firm that decides to build a new factory and borrows the money from a bank at an interest rate of 8 percent. The nominal interest rate is therefore 8 percent—that is, the amount the firm owes to the bank grows by 8 percent per year. But if prices are rising, say by 5 percent per year, the dollars with which the firm will repay the bank are losing 5 percent of their value per year. Each year the firm owes 8 percent more dollars, but the dollars are worth 5 percent less. The real interest rate is 3 percent, the difference between the nominal interest rate and the rate of inflation.

In Chapter 6 we discuss the relation between nominal and real interest rates in more detail. Here it is sufficient to note that the real interest rate measures the true cost of borrowing. We therefore expect investment to depend on the real, rather than the nominal, interest rate.

The link between the real interest rate r and investment I can be expressed as

$$I = I(r).$$

This equation states that investment depends on the interest rate. Figure 3-6 shows this investment function. It slopes downward, because as the interest rate rises, the quantity of investment demanded falls.

Figure 3-6

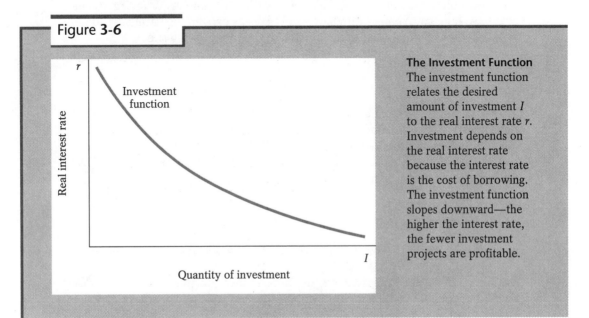

The Investment Function The investment function relates the desired amount of investment I to the real interest rate r. Investment depends on the real interest rate because the interest rate is the cost of borrowing. The investment function slopes downward—the higher the interest rate, the fewer investment projects are profitable.

Government Purchases

Government purchases are the third component of the demand for goods and services. The federal government buys guns, missiles, and the services of government employees. Local governments buy library books, build schools, and hire teachers. Governments at all levels build roads and other public works. All these transactions make up government purchases of goods and services, which account for about 20 percent of GDP in the United States.

These purchases are only one type of government spending. The other type is transfer payments to households, such as welfare for the poor and Social Security payments for the elderly. Unlike government purchases, transfer payments do not directly use the economy's output of goods and services. Therefore, they are not included in the variable G.

Transfer payments do affect the demand for goods and services indirectly. Transfer payments are the opposite of taxes: they increase households' disposable income, just as taxes reduce disposable income. Thus, an increase in transfer payments financed by an increase in taxes leaves disposable income unchanged. We can now revise our definition of T to equal taxes minus transfer payments. Disposable income, $Y - T$, includes both the negative impact of taxes and the positive impact of transfer payments.

If government purchases equal taxes minus transfers, then $G = T$, and the government has a *balanced budget*. If G exceeds T, the government runs a *budget deficit*, which it funds by issuing government debt—that is, by borrowing in the financial markets. If G is less than T, the government runs a *budget surplus*, which it can use to repay some of its outstanding loans and reduce its debt.

Here we do not try to explain the political process that leads to a particular fiscal policy—that is, to the level of government purchases and taxes. Instead, we take government purchases and taxes as exogenous variables. To denote that these variables are fixed outside of the model, we write

$$G = \overline{G}.$$
$$T = \overline{T}.$$

We do, however, want to examine the impact of fiscal policy on the variables determined within the model, the endogenous variables. The endogenous variables here are consumption, investment, and the interest rate.

To see how the exogenous variables affect the endogenous variables, we must solve our model. This is the subject of the next section.

3-4   Equilibrium and the Interest Rate

We have now come full circle in the circular flow diagram, Figure 3-1. We began by examining the supply of goods and services, and we have just discussed the demand for them.

How can we be certain that all these flows balance? In other words, what ensures that the sum of consumption, investment, and government purchases equals the amount of output produced? We will see that the interest rate has the crucial role of equilibrating supply and demand.

Equilibrium in the Market for Goods and Services: The Supply and Demand for the Economy's Output

The following equations summarize the discussion in Section 3-3 of the demand for goods and services:

$$Y = C + I + G$$
$$C = C(Y - T)$$
$$I = I(r)$$
$$G = \overline{G}$$
$$T = \overline{T}.$$

The demand for the economy's output comes from consumption, investment, and government purchases. Consumption depends on disposable income; investment depends on the real interest rate; and government purchases and taxes are the exogenous fiscal policy variables.

In addition to the demand for goods and services, we now consider the supply. As we discussed in Section 3-1, the factors of production and the production function determine the amount of output:

$$Y = F(\overline{K}, \overline{L})$$
$$= \overline{Y}.$$

Now let's combine these equations describing the supply and demand for output. If we substitute the consumption function and the investment function into the national income accounts identity, we obtain

$$Y = C(Y - T) + I(r) + G.$$

Since the variables G and T are fixed by policy, and the level of output Y is fixed by the factors of production and the production function, we can write

$$\overline{Y} = C(\overline{Y} - \overline{T}) + I(r) + \overline{G}.$$

This equation states that the supply of output equals its demand, which is the sum of consumption, investment, and government purchases.

Now you can see why the interest rate r plays a key role: it must adjust to ensure that the demand for goods equals the supply. The greater the interest rate, the lower the level of investment, and thus the lower the demand for goods and services, $C + I + G$. If the interest rate is too high, investment is too low, and the demand for output falls short of the supply. If the interest rate is too low, investment is too high, and the demand exceeds the supply. *At the equilibrium interest rate, the demand for goods and services equals the supply.*

Equilibrium in the Financial Markets: The Supply and Demand for Loanable Funds

Because the interest rate is the cost of borrowing and the return to lending in financial markets, we can better understand the role of the interest rate by thinking about the financial markets. To do this, rewrite the national income accounts identity as

$$Y - C - G = I.$$

The term $Y - C - G$ is the output that remains after the demands of consumers and the government have been satisfied; it is called **national saving** or simply **saving** (S). In this form, the national income accounts identity shows that saving equals investment.

We can split national saving into two parts to separate the saving of households from that of the government:

$$(Y - T - C) + (T - G) = I.$$

The term $(Y - T - C)$ is disposable income minus consumption, which is **private saving**. The term $(T - G)$ is government revenue minus government spending, which is **public saving**. (If government spending exceeds government revenue, the government runs a budget deficit, and public saving is negative.) National saving is the sum of private and public saving. The circular flow diagram in Figure 3-1 reveals an interpretation of this equation: this equation states that the flows into and out of the financial markets must balance.

To see the role of the interest rate in equilibrating financial markets, substitute the consumption function and the investment function into the national income accounts identity:

$$Y - C(Y - T) - G = I(r).$$

Next, make G and T fixed by policy and Y fixed by the factors of production and the production function:

$$\overline{Y} - C(\overline{Y} - \overline{T}) - \overline{G} = I(r)$$
$$\overline{S} = I(r).$$

The left-hand side of this equation shows that national saving depends on income Y and the fiscal policy variables G and T. For fixed values of Y, G, and T, national saving S is also fixed. The right-hand side of the equation shows that investment depends on the interest rate.

Figure 3-7 is a graph of both saving and investment as a function of the interest rate. The saving function is a vertical line, because in this model saving does not depend on the interest rate (although we relax this assumption later). The investment function slopes downward: the higher the interest rate, the fewer investment projects are profitable.

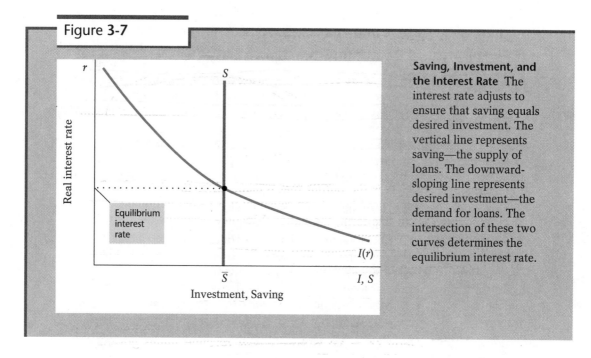

Figure 3-7

Saving, Investment, and the Interest Rate The interest rate adjusts to ensure that saving equals desired investment. The vertical line represents saving—the supply of loans. The downward-sloping line represents desired investment—the demand for loans. The intersection of these two curves determines the equilibrium interest rate.

From a quick glance at Figure 3-7, one might think it was a supply and demand diagram for a particular good. In fact, saving and investment can be interpreted in terms of supply and demand. In this case, the "good" is **loanable funds**, and its "price" is the interest rate. Saving is the supply of loans—individuals lend their saving to investors, or they deposit their saving in a bank that makes the loans for them. Investment is the demand for loans—investors borrow from the public directly by selling bonds or indirectly by borrowing from banks. Since investment depends on the interest rate, the demand for these loans also depends on the interest rate.

The interest rate adjusts until investment equals saving. If the interest rate is too low, investors want more of the economy's output than individuals want to save. Equivalently, the demand for loans exceeds the supply. When this happens, the interest rate rises. Conversely, if the interest rate is too high, saving exceeds investment; because the supply of loans is greater than the demand, the interest rate falls. The equilibrium interest rate is found where the two curves cross. *At the equilibrium interest rate, saving equals investment, and the supply of loans equals the demand.*

Changes in Saving: The Effects of Fiscal Policy

We can use our model to show how fiscal policy—changes in government purchases or taxes—affects the economy. Fiscal policy has a direct impact on the demand for the economy's output of goods and services. It thereby alters national saving, investment, and the equilibrium interest rate.

An Increase in Government Purchases   Consider first the effects of an increase in government purchases of an amount ΔG. The immediate impact is to increase the demand for goods and services by ΔG. But since total output is fixed by the factors of production, the increase in government purchases must be met by a decrease in some other category of demand. Since disposable income $Y - T$ is unchanged, consumption C is unchanged. The increase in government purchases must be met by an equal decrease in investment.

To induce investment to fall, the interest rate must rise. Hence, the increase in government purchases causes the interest rate to increase and investment to decrease. Government purchases are said to **crowd out** investment.

To grasp the effects of an increase in government purchases, consider the impact on the market for loanable funds. Since the increase in government purchases is not accompanied by an increase in taxes, the government finances the additional spending by borrowing—that is, by reducing public saving. Since private saving is unchanged, this government borrowing reduces national saving. As Figure 3-8 shows, a reduction in national saving is represented by a leftward shift in the supply of loanable funds available for investment. At the initial interest rate, the demand for loans exceeds the supply. The equilibrium interest rate rises to the point where the investment schedule crosses the new saving schedule. Thus, an increase in government purchases causes the interest rate to rise.

Figure 3-8

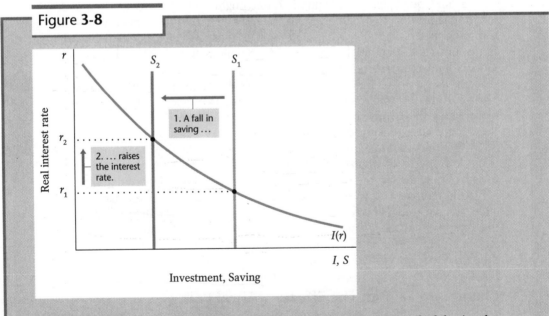

A Reduction in Saving A reduction in saving, possibly the result of a change in fiscal policy, shifts the vertical saving schedule to the left. The new equilibrium is the point at which the new saving schedule crosses the investment schedule. A reduction in saving lowers the amount of investment and raises the interest rate. Fiscal-policy actions that reduce saving crowd out investment.

Case Study *3-2*

● ● ● ● ● ● ● ● ● ● ● ● ● ●

Wars and Interest Rates in the United Kingdom, 1730–1920

Wars are traumatic—both for those who fight them and for a nation's economy. Because the economic changes accompanying them are often large, wars provide a natural experiment with which economists can test their theories. We can learn about the economy by seeing how in wartime the endogenous variables respond to the major changes in the exogenous variables.

One exogenous variable that changes substantially in wartime is the level of government purchases. Figure 3-9 shows military spending as a percentage of GDP for the United Kingdom from 1730 to 1919. This graph shows, as one

Figure 3-9

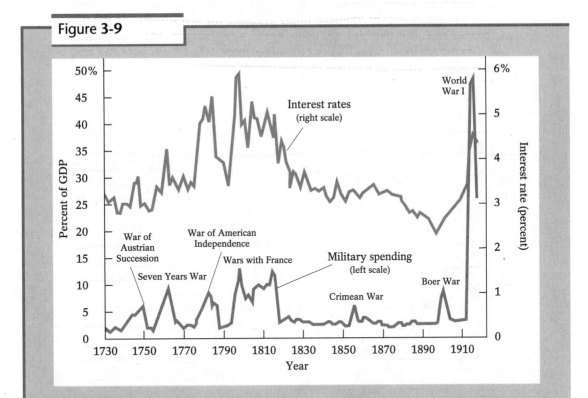

Military Spending and the Interest Rate in the United Kingdom This figure shows military spending as a percentage of GDP in the United Kingdom from 1730 to 1919. Not surprisingly, military spending rose substantially during each of the eight wars of this period. This figure also shows that the interest rate (here the rate on a government bond called a *consol*) tended to rise when military spending rose.

Source: Series constructed from various sources described in Robert J. Barro, "Government Spending, Interest Rates, Prices, and Budget Deficits in the United Kingdom, 1701–1918," *Journal of Monetary Economics* 20 (September 1987): 221–248.

would expect, that government purchases rose suddenly and dramatically during the eight wars of this period.

Our model predicts that this wartime increase in government purchases—and the increase in government borrowing to finance the wars—should have raised the demand for goods and services, reduced the supply of loanable funds, and raised the interest rate. To test this prediction, Figure 3-9 also shows the interest rate on long-term government bonds, called *consols* in the United Kingdom. A positive association between military purchases and interest rates is apparent in this figure. These data support the model's prediction: interest rates do tend to rise when government purchases increase.[4]

One problem with using wars to test theories is that many economic changes may be occurring at the same time. For example, in World War II, while government purchases increased dramatically, rationing also restricted consumption of many goods. In addition, the risk of defeat in the war and default by the government on its debt presumably increases the interest rate the government must pay. Economic models predict what happens when one exogenous variable changes and all the other exogenous variables remain constant. In the real world, however, many exogenous variables may change at once. Unlike controlled laboratory experiments, the natural experiments on which economists must rely are not always easy to interpret.

• • • • • • • • • • • • • •

A Decrease in Taxes   Now consider a reduction in taxes of ΔT. The immediate impact of the tax cut is to raise disposable income and thus to raise consumption. Disposable income rises by ΔT, and consumption rises by an amount equal to ΔT times the marginal propensity to consume *MPC*. The higher the *MPC*, the greater the impact of the tax cut on consumption.

Since the economy's output is fixed by the factors of production and the level of government purchases is fixed by the government, the increase in consumption must be met by a decrease in investment. For investment to fall, the interest rate must rise. Hence, a reduction in taxes, like an increase in government purchases, crowds out investment and raises the interest rate.

We can also analyze the effect of a tax cut by looking at saving and investment. Since the tax cut raises disposable income by ΔT, consumption goes up by $MPC \times \Delta T$. National saving S, which equals $Y - C - G$, falls by the same amount as consumption rises. As in Figure 3-8, the reduction in saving shifts the supply of loanable funds to the left, which increases the equilibrium interest rate and crowds out investment.

4   Daniel K. Benjamin and Levis A. Kochin, "War, Prices, and Interest Rates: A Martial Solution to Gibson's Paradox," in M. D. Bordo and A. J. Schwartz, eds., *A Retrospective on the Classical Gold Standard, 1821–1931* (Chicago: University of Chicago Press, 1984), 587–612; Robert J. Barro, "Government Spending, Interest Rates, Prices, and Budget Deficits in the United Kingdom, 1701–1918," *Journal of Monetary Economics* 20 (September 1987): 221–248.

Case Study 3-3

$r = R - i\omega$

. . . .

Fiscal Policy in the 1980s

One of the most dramatic economic events in recent history was the large change in U.S. fiscal policy in 1981. In 1980 Ronald Reagan was elected president on a platform to raise military spending and reduce taxes. The result of this combination of policies was, not surprisingly, a large imbalance between government spending and revenue. The federal budget went from a small surplus in the 1970s to a large deficit in the 1980s. In the 1980s the government borrowed at a rate unprecedented in peacetime.[5]

As our model predicts, this change in fiscal policy led to higher interest rates and lower national saving. The real interest rate (as measured by the yield on government bonds minus the inflation rate) rose from 0.4 percent in the 1970s to 5.7 percent in the 1980s. Gross national saving as a percentage of GDP fell from 16.7 percent in the 1970s to 14.1 percent in the 1980s. The change in fiscal policy in the 1980s had the effects that our simple model of the economy would predict.

. . . .

Changes in Investment Demand

So far, we have discussed how fiscal policy can change national saving. We can also use the model to examine the other side of the market—the demand for investment. In this section we look at the causes and effects of changes in investment demand.

One reason investment demand might increase is technological innovation. Suppose, for example, that someone invents a new technology, such as the railroad or the computer. Before a firm or household can use the innovation, it must buy investment goods. The invention of the railroad had no value until railroad cars were produced and tracks were laid. The idea of the computer was not productive until computers were manufactured. Thus, technological innovation leads to an increase in investment demand.

Investment demand may also change because the government encourages or discourages investment through the tax laws. For example, suppose that the government increases personal income taxes and uses the extra revenue to provide tax cuts for those who invest in new capital. Such a change in the tax laws makes more investment projects profitable and, like a technological innovation, increases the demand for investment goods.

[5] The figures for the budget deficit discussed here differ from official government figures by correcting for the effects of inflation. In government accounting practices, the nominal interest paid on the government debt is counted as expenditure. In these figures, and in the deficit figures used in the rest of this book, only the real interest on the government debt is counted as expenditure. Chapter 16 discusses this correction and other measurement issues regarding the budget deficit.

Figure 3-10 shows the effects of an increase in investment demand. At any given interest rate, the demand for investment goods (and also for loans) is higher. This increase in demand is represented by a shift in the investment schedule to the right. The economy moves from the old equilibrium, point A, to the new equilibrium, point B.

Figure 3-10

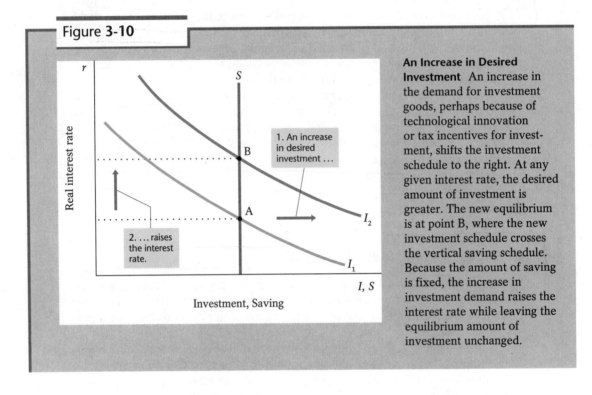

An Increase in Desired Investment An increase in the demand for investment goods, perhaps because of technological innovation or tax incentives for investment, shifts the investment schedule to the right. At any given interest rate, the desired amount of investment is greater. The new equilibrium is at point B, where the new investment schedule crosses the vertical saving schedule. Because the amount of saving is fixed, the increase in investment demand raises the interest rate while leaving the equilibrium amount of investment unchanged.

The surprising implication of Figure 3-10 is that the equilibrium amount of investment is unchanged. Under our assumptions, the fixed level of saving determines the amount of investment; in other words, there is a fixed supply of loans. An increase in investment demand merely raises the equilibrium interest rate.

We would reach a different conclusion, however, if we modified our simple consumption function and allowed consumption to depend on the interest rate. Since the interest rate is the return to saving (as well as the cost of borrowing), a higher interest rate might reduce consumption and increase saving. If so, the saving schedule would be upward sloping, as it is in Figure 3-11, rather than vertical.

With an upward-sloping saving schedule, an increase in investment demand would raise both the equilibrium interest rate and the equilibrium quantity of investment. Figure 3-12 shows such a change. The increase in the interest rate causes households to consume less and save more. The decrease in consumption frees resources for investment.

Figure 3-11

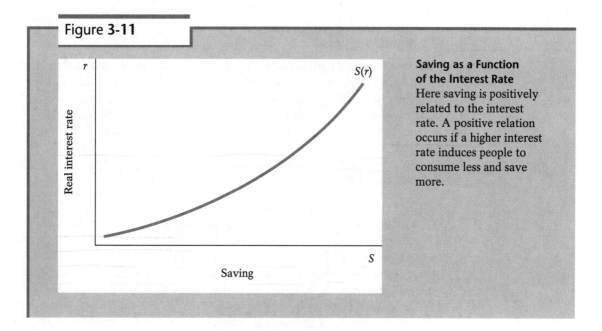

Saving as a Function of the Interest Rate Here saving is positively related to the interest rate. A positive relation occurs if a higher interest rate induces people to consume less and save more.

Figure 3-12

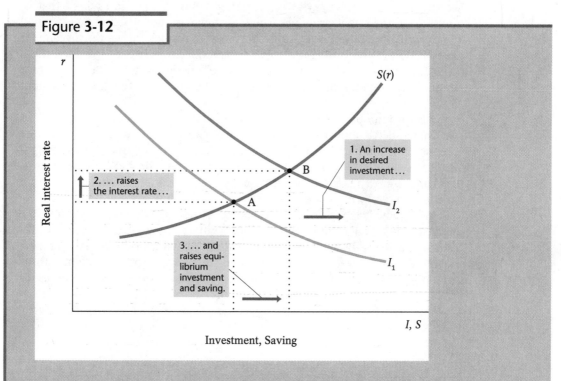

An Increase in Desired Investment When Saving Depends on the Interest Rate If saving depends on the interest rate, then a rightward shift in the investment schedule increases the interest rate and the amount of investment. The higher interest rate induces people to increase saving, which in turn allows investment to increase.

The Identification Problem

In our model, investment depends on the interest rate. The higher the interest rate, the fewer investment projects are profitable. The investment schedule therefore slopes downward.

Economists who look at macroeconomic data, however, usually fail to find an obvious association between investment and interest rates. In years when interest rates are high, investment is not always low. In years when interest rates are low, investment is not always high.

How do we interpret this finding? Does it mean that investment does not depend on the interest rate? Does it suggest that our model of the economy is inconsistent with how the economy actually functions?

Luckily, we do not have to discard our model. The inability to find an empirical relationship between investment and interest rates is an example of the *identification problem*. The identification problem arises when variables are related in more than one way. When we look at data, we are observing a combination of these different relationships, and it is difficult to "identify" any one of them.

To understand this problem more concretely, consider the relationships among saving, investment, and the interest rate. Suppose, on the one hand, that all changes in the interest rate resulted from changes in saving—that is, from shifts in the saving schedule. Then, as shown in the left-hand side of panel (a) in Figure 3-13, all changes would represent movement along the investment schedule. We would observe a negative relationship between investment and interest rates. As the right-hand side of panel (a) shows, the data would trace out the investment schedule; that is, we would "identify" the investment schedule.

Suppose, on the other hand, that all changes in the interest rate resulted from technological innovations—that is, from shifts in the investment schedule. Then, as shown in panel (b), all changes would represent movements in the investment schedule. We would observe a positive relationship between investment and interest rates. As the right-hand side of panel (b) shows, when we plot the data, we would "identify" the saving schedule.

More realistically, interest rates change sometimes because of shifts in the saving schedule and sometimes because of shifts in the investment schedule. In this mixed case, as shown in panel (c), a plot of the data would reveal no recognizable relation between interest rates and the quantity of investment, just as economists observe in actual data. The moral of the story is simple and is applicable to many other situations: The empirical relationship we expect to observe depends crucially on which exogenous variables we think are changing.

Figure 3-13

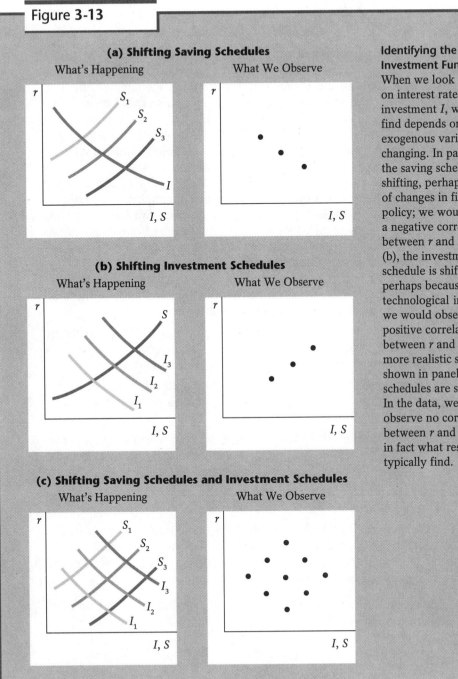

(a) Shifting Saving Schedules

What's Happening

What We Observe

(b) Shifting Investment Schedules

What's Happening

What We Observe

(c) Shifting Saving Schedules and Investment Schedules

What's Happening

What We Observe

Identifying the Investment Function When we look at data on interest rates r and investment I, what we find depends on which exogenous variables are changing. In panel (a), the saving schedule is shifting, perhaps because of changes in fiscal policy; we would observe a negative correlation between r and I. In panel (b), the investment schedule is shifting, perhaps because of technological innovations; we would observe a positive correlation between r and I. In the more realistic situation shown in panel (c), both schedules are shifting. In the data, we would observe no correlation between r and I, which is in fact what researchers typically find.

3-5 Conclusion

In this chapter we have developed a model that explains the production, distribution, and allocation of the economy's output of goods and services. Because the model incorporates all the interactions illustrated in the circular flow diagram in Figure 3-1, it is sometimes called a *general equilibrium model*. The model emphasizes how prices adjust to equilibrate supply and demand. Factor prices equilibrate factor markets. The interest rate equilibrates the supply and demand for goods and services (or, equivalently, the supply and demand for loanable funds).

Throughout the chapter, we have discussed various applications of the model. The model can explain how income is divided among the factors of production and how factor prices depend on factor supplies. We have also used the model to discuss how fiscal policy alters the allocation of output among its alternative uses—consumption, investment, and government purchases—and how it affects the equilibrium interest rate.

At this point it is useful to review some of the simplifying assumptions we have made in this chapter. In the following chapters we relax some of these assumptions in order to address a greater range of questions.

- We have assumed that the capital stock, the labor force, and the production technology are fixed. In Chapter 4 we see how changes over time in each of these lead to growth in the economy's output of goods and services.

- We have assumed that the labor force is fully employed. In Chapter 5 we examine the reasons for unemployment, and we see how public policy influences the level of unemployment.

- We have ignored the role of money, the asset with which goods and services are bought and sold. In Chapter 6 we discuss how money affects the economy and the influence of monetary policy.

- We have assumed that there is no trade with other countries. In Chapter 7 we consider how international interactions affect our conclusions.

- We have ignored the role of short-run sticky prices. In Chapters 8 through 12, we develop a model of short-run fluctuations that includes sticky prices. We then discuss how the model of short-run fluctuations relates to the model of national income developed in this chapter.

Before going on to these chapters, go back to the beginning of this one and make sure you can answer the four groups of questions about national income that begin the chapter.

Summary

1. The factors of production and the production technology determine the economy's output of goods and services. An increase in one of the factors of production or a technological advance raises output.

2. Competitive, profit-maximizing firms hire labor until the marginal product of labor equals the real wage. Similarly, these firms rent capital until the marginal product of capital equals the real rental price. Therefore, each factor of production is paid its marginal product. If the production function has constant returns to scale, all output is used to compensate the inputs.

3. The economy's output is used for consumption, investment, and government purchases. Consumption depends positively on disposable income. Investment depends negatively on the real interest rate. Government purchases and taxes are the exogenous variables of fiscal policy.

4. The real interest rate adjusts to equilibrate the supply and demand for the economy's output—or, equivalently, to equilibrate the supply of loanable funds (saving) and the demand for loanable funds (investment). A decrease in national saving, perhaps because of an increase in government purchases or a decrease in taxes, reduces the equilibrium amount of investment and raises the interest rate. An increase in investment demand, perhaps because of a technological innovation or a tax incentive for investment, also raises the interest rate. An increase in investment demand increases the quantity of investment only if higher interest rates stimulate additional saving.

KEY CONCEPTS

Factors of production

Production function

Constant returns to scale

Factor prices

Competition

Marginal product of labor (MPL)

Diminishing marginal product

Real wage

Marginal product of capital (MPK)

Real rental price of capital

Economic profit versus accounting profit

Disposable income

Consumption function

Marginal propensity to consume (MPC)

Nominal interest rate

Real interest rate

National saving (Saving)

Private saving

Public saving

Loanable funds

Crowding out

QUESTIONS FOR REVIEW

1. What determines the amount of output an economy produces?

2. Explain how a competitive, profit-maximizing firm decides how much of each factor of production to demand.

3. What is the role of constant returns to scale in the distribution of income?

4. What determines consumption and investment?

5. Explain the difference between government purchases and transfer payments. Give two examples of each.

6. What makes the demand for the economy's output of goods and services equal the supply?

7. Explain what happens to consumption, investment, and the interest rate when the government increases taxes.

PROBLEMS AND APPLICATIONS

1. Use the neoclassical theory of distribution to predict the impact on the real wage and the real rental price of capital of each of the following events:

   a. A wave of immigration increases the labor force.

   b. An earthquake destroys some of the capital stock.

   c. A technological advance improves the production function.

2. If a 10 percent increase in both capital and labor causes output to increase by less than 10 percent, the production function is said to exhibit *decreasing returns to scale*. If it causes output to increase by more than 10 percent, the production function is said to exhibit *increasing returns to scale*. Why might a production function exhibit decreasing or increasing returns to scale?

3. According to the neoclassical theory of distribution, the real wage earned by any worker equals that worker's marginal productivity. Let's use this insight to examine the incomes of two groups of workers: farmers and barbers.

   a. Over the past century, the productivity of farmers has risen substantially because of technological progress. According to the neoclassical theory, what should have happened to their real wage?

   b. In what units is the real wage discussed in part (a) measured?

   c. Over the same period, the productivity of barbers has remained constant. What should have happened to their real wage?

   d. In what units is the real wage in part (c) measured?

   e. Suppose workers can move freely between being farmers and being barbers. What does this mobility imply for the wages of farmers and barbers?

   f. What do your previous answers imply for the price of haircuts relative to the price of food?

   g. Who benefits from technological progress in farming—farmers or barbers?

4. The government raises taxes by $100 billion. If the marginal propensity to

consume is 0.6, what happens to the following?

a. Public saving.

b. Private saving.

c. National saving.

d. Investment.

5. Suppose that an increase in consumer confidence raises consumers' expectations of future income and thus the amount they want to consume today. This might be interpreted as an upward shift in the consumption function. How does this shift affect investment and the interest rate?

6. Consider an economy described by the following equations:

$$Y = C + I + G$$
$$Y = 5,000$$
$$G = 1,000$$
$$T = 1,000$$
$$C = 250 + 0.75(Y - T)$$
$$I = 1,000 - 50r.$$

a. In this economy, compute private saving, public saving, and national saving.

b. Find the equilibrium interest rate.

c. Now suppose that G rises to 1,250. Compute private saving, public saving, and national saving.

d. Find the new equilibrium interest rate.

7. Suppose that the government increases taxes and government purchases by equal amounts. What happens to the interest rate and investment in response to this balanced budget change? Does your answer depend on the marginal propensity to consume?

8. When the government subsidizes investment, such as with an investment tax credit, the subsidy often applies to only some types of investment. This question asks you to consider the effect of such a change. Suppose there are two types of investment in the economy: business investment and residential investment. And suppose that the government institutes an investment tax credit only for business investment.

a. How does this policy affect the demand curve for business investment? The demand curve for residential investment?

b. Draw the economy's supply and demand for loanable funds. How does this policy affect the supply and demand for loans? What happens to the equilibrium interest rate?

c. Compare the old and the new equilibrium. How does this policy affect the total quantity of investment? The quantity of business investment? The quantity of residential investment?

9. If consumption depended on the interest rate, how would that affect the conclusions reached in this chapter about the effects of fiscal policy?

Appendix

The Cobb-Douglas Production Function

What production function describes how actual economies turn capital and labor into GDP? The answer to this question came from a historic collaboration between a U.S. senator and a mathematician.

Paul Douglas was a U.S. senator from Illinois from 1949 to 1966. In 1927, however, when he was still a professor of economics, he noticed a surprising fact: The division of national income between capital and labor had been roughly constant over a long period. In other words, as the economy grew more prosperous over time, the income of workers and the income of capital owners grew at almost exactly the same rate. This observation caused Douglas to wonder what conditions lead to constant factor shares.

Douglas asked Charles Cobb, a mathematician, what production function, if any, would produce constant factor shares if factors always earned their marginal products. The production function would need to have the property that

$$\text{Capital Income} = MPK \times K = \alpha Y,$$

and

$$\text{Labor Income} = MPL \times L = (1 - \alpha)Y,$$

where α is a constant between zero and one that measures capital's share of income. That is, α determines what share of income goes to capital and what share goes to labor. Cobb showed that the function with this property is

$$Y = F(K, L) = AK^{\alpha}L^{1-\alpha},$$

where A is a parameter greater than zero that measures the productivity of the available technology. This function became known as the *Cobb-Douglas production function.*

Let's take a closer look at some of the properties of this production function. First, the Cobb-Douglas production function has constant returns to scale. That is, if capital and labor are increased by the same proportion, then output increases by that proportion as well.[6]

---

[6] *Mathematical Note*: To prove that the Cobb-Douglas production function has constant returns to scale, examine what happens when we multiply capital and labor by a constant z:

$$F(zK, zL) = A(zK)^{\alpha}(zL)^{1-\alpha}.$$

Expanding terms on the right,

$$F(zK, zL) = Az^{\alpha}K^{\alpha}z^{1-\alpha}L^{1-\alpha}.$$

Rearranging to bring like terms together, we get

$$F(zK, zL) = z^{\alpha}z^{1-\alpha}AK^{\alpha}L^{1-\alpha}.$$

Since $z^{\alpha}z^{1-\alpha} = z$, our function becomes

$$F(zK, zL) = zAK^{\alpha}L^{1-\alpha}.$$

But $AK^{\alpha}L^{1-\alpha} = F(K, L)$. Thus,

$$F(zK, zL) = zF(K, L) = zY.$$

Hence, the amount of output Y increases by the same factor z, which implies that this production function has constant returns to scale.

Next, consider the marginal products for the Cobb-Douglas production function. The marginal product of labor is[7]

$$MPL = (1 - \alpha)AK^{\alpha}L^{-\alpha},$$

and the marginal product of capital is

$$MPK = \alpha AK^{\alpha-1}L^{1-\alpha}.$$

From these equations, recalling that α is between zero and one, we can see what causes the marginal products of the two factors to change. An increase in the amount of capital raises the *MPL* and reduces the *MPK*. Similarly, an increase in the amount of labor reduces the *MPL* and raises the *MPK*. A technological advance that increases the parameter A raises the marginal product of both factors proportionately.

The marginal products for the Cobb-Douglas production function can also be written as[8]

$$MPL = (1 - \alpha)Y/L$$
$$MPK = \alpha Y/K.$$

The *MPL* is proportional to output per worker, and the *MPK* is proportional to output per unit of capital. *Y/L* is called *average labor productivity*, and *Y/K* is called *average capital productivity*. If the production function is Cobb-Douglas, then the marginal productivity of a factor is proportional to its average productivity.

We can now verify that if factors earn their marginal products, then the parameter α indeed tells us how much income goes to labor and how much goes to capital. The total wage bill, which we have seen is *MPL* $\times$ *L*, is simply $(1 - \alpha)Y$. Therefore, $(1 - \alpha)$ is labor's share of output. Similarly, the total return to capital, *MPK* $\times$ *K*, is αY, and α is capital's share of output. The ratio of labor income to capital income is a constant, $(1 - \alpha)/\alpha$, just as Douglas observed. The factor shares depend only on the parameter α, not on the amounts of capital or labor or on the state of technology as measured by the parameter A.

More recent data are also consistent with the Cobb-Douglas production function. Figure 3-14 shows the ratio of labor income to total income in the United States from 1946 to 1994. Despite the many changes in the economy over the past four decades, this ratio has remained about 0.7. This division of income is easily explained by a Cobb-Douglas production function in which the parameter α is about 0.3.

---

[7] *Mathematical Note*: Obtaining the formulas for the marginal products from the production function requires a bit of calculus. To find the *MPL*, differentiate the production function with respect to *L*. This is done by multiplying by the exponent $(1 - \alpha)$, and then subtracting 1 from the old exponent to obtain the new exponent, $-\alpha$. Similarly, to obtain the *MPK*, differentiate the production function with respect to *K*.

[8] *Mathematical Note*: To check these expressions for the marginal products, substitute in the production function for *Y* to show that these expressions are equivalent to the earlier formulas for the marginal products.

Figure 3-14

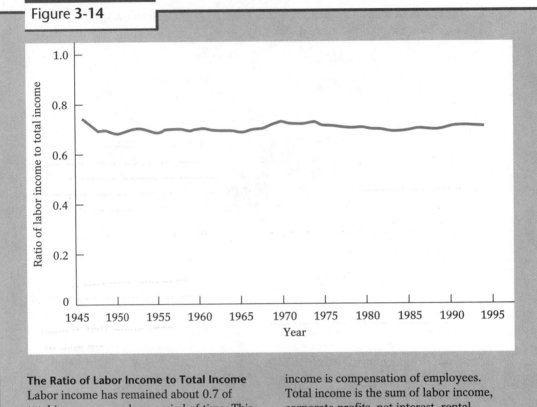

The Ratio of Labor Income to Total Income
Labor income has remained about 0.7 of
total income over a long period of time. This
approximate constancy of factor shares is
evidence for the Cobb-Douglas production
function. (This figure is produced from U.S.
national income accounts data. Labor
income is compensation of employees.
Total income is the sum of labor income,
corporate profits, net interest, rental
income, and depreciation. Proprietors'
income is excluded from these calculations,
because it is a combination of labor income
and capital income.)

Source: U.S. Department of Commerce.

MORE PROBLEMS AND APPLICATIONS

1. Suppose that the production function
is Cobb-Douglas with parameter α =
0.3.

   a. What fractions of income do capital and labor receive?

   b. Suppose that immigration raises
the labor force by 10 percent. What
happens to total output (in percent)?
The rental price of capital? The real
wage?

   c. Suppose that a gift of capital from
abroad raises the capital stock by 10
percent. What happens to total output
(in percent)? The rental price of capital? The real wage?

   d. Suppose that a technological advance raises the value of the parameter A by 10 percent. What happens to
total output (in percent)? The rental
price of capital? The real wage?

2. (This problem requires the use of calculus.) Consider a Cobb-Douglas production function with three inputs. K is capital (the number of machines), L is labor (the number of workers), and H is human capital (the number of college degrees among the workers). The production function is

$$Y = K^{1/3}L^{1/3}H^{1/3}.$$

a. Derive an expression for the marginal product of labor. How does an increase in the amount of human capital affect the marginal product of labor?

b. Derive an expression for the marginal product of human capital. How does an increase in the amount of human capital affect the marginal product of human capital?

c. What is the income share paid to labor? What is the income share paid to human capital? In the national income accounts of this economy, what share of total income do you think workers would appear to receive? (*Hint*: Consider where the return to human capital shows up.)

d. An unskilled worker earns the marginal product of labor, whereas a skilled worker earns the marginal product of labor plus the marginal product of human capital. Using your answers to (a) and (b), find the ratio of the skilled wage to the unskilled wage. How does an increase in the amount of human capital affect this ratio? Explain.

e. Some people advocate government funding of college scholarships as a way of creating a more egalitarian society. Others argue that scholarships help only those who are able to go to college. Do your answers to the above questions shed light on this debate?

Economic Growth

Is there some action a government of India could take that would lead the Indian economy to grow like Indonesia's or Egypt's? If so, what, exactly? If not, what is it about the "nature of India" that makes it so? The consequences for human welfare involved in questions like these are simply staggering: Once one starts to think about them, it is hard to think about anything else.

Robert E. Lucas, Jr.

Over the past century, most countries in the world have enjoyed substantial economic growth. Real incomes have risen from generation to generation, and these higher incomes have allowed people to consume greater quantities of goods and services than their ancestors. Higher levels of consumption have led to a higher standard of living.

To measure economic growth, economists use data on gross domestic product, which measures the total income of everyone in the economy. The real GDP of the United States today is more than three times its 1950 level, and real GDP per person is more than twice its 1950 level. In any given year, we can also observe large differences in the standard of living among countries. Table 4-1 shows income per person in 1992 of the world's 12 most populous countries. The United States tops the list with an income of $23,571 per person. Nigeria has an income per person of only $1,285—about 5 percent of the figure for the United States.

Our goal in this chapter is to understand these differences in income over time and across countries. In Chapter 3 we identified the factors of production—capital and labor—and the production technology as the sources of the economy's output and, thus, of its income. Differences in income must come from differences in capital, labor, and technology.

Our primary task is to develop a model of economic growth called the **Solow growth model**. Our analysis in Chapter 3 enabled us to describe the production, distribution, and allocation of the economy's output at a point in time. The analysis was static—a snapshot of the economy. To explain rising living standards, we must refine our analysis so that it describes changes in the economy over time. We want to make our analysis dynamic, so that it is more like a movie than a photograph. The Solow growth model shows how saving, population growth, and technological progress affect the growth of output over time.

Table 4-1	
International Differences in the Standard of Living, 1992	
Country	Income per Person (in U.S. dollars)
United States	$23,571
Japan	19,840
West Germany	19,320
Soviet Union (1989)	10,168
Mexico	8,213
Brazil	5,099
Indonesia	2,761
Bangladesh	1,983
China	1,961
Pakistan	1,881
India	1,683
Nigeria	1,285

Note: Many analysts believe that faulty reporting of data in the Soviet Union and China render the statistics from those countries unreliable, and that actual income per person is much lower than reported.

Source: Robert Summers and Alan Heston, Supplement (Mark 5.6) to "The Penn World Table (Mark 5): An Expanded Set of International Comparisons 1950–1988," *Quarterly Journal of Economics* (May 1991): 327–368.

The model also identifies some of the reasons that countries vary so widely in their standards of living.[1]

Our second task is to examine how economic policy can influence the level and growth of the standard of living. Our model provides a framework we can use to address one of the most important questions in economics: How much of the economy's output should be consumed today, and how much should be saved for the future? Since an economy's saving equals its investment, saving determines the amount of capital an economy will have for future production. National saving is influenced directly and indirectly by government policies. Evaluating these policies requires an understanding of the costs and benefits to society of alternative rates of saving.

4-1   The Accumulation of Capital

The Solow growth model shows how growth in the capital stock, growth in the labor force, and advances in technology interact, and how they affect output. As our first step in building the model, we examine how the supply and demand for goods determine the accumulation of capital. To do this, we hold the labor force and technology fixed. Later, we relax these assumptions, first by introducing changes in the labor force and then by introducing changes in technology.

[1] The Solow growth model is named after economist Robert Solow and was developed in the 1950s and 1960s. In 1987 Solow won the Nobel Prize in Economics for his work in economic growth. The model was introduced in Robert M. Solow, "A Contribution to the Theory of Economic Growth," *Quarterly Journal of Economics* (February 1956): 65–94.

The Supply and Demand for Goods

The supply and demand for goods plays a central role in the Solow model, just as it did in our static model of the economy. As in Chapter 3, the supply of goods determines how much output is produced at any given point in time, and the demand determines how this output is allocated among alternative uses.

The Supply of Goods and the Production Function   The supply of goods in the Solow model is based on the now familiar production function:

$$Y = F(K, L).$$

Output depends on the capital stock and the labor force. The Solow growth model assumes that the production function has constant returns to scale. Recall that a production function has constant returns to scale if

$$zY = F(zK, zL)$$

for any positive number z. That is, if we multiply both capital and labor by z, we also multiply the amount of output by z.

To keep the analysis simple, we express all quantities relative to the size of the labor force. Production functions with constant returns to scale are convenient for this purpose because output per worker depends only on the amount of capital per worker. To see that this is true, set $z = 1/L$ in the equation above to obtain

$$Y/L = F(K/L, 1).$$

This equation shows that output per worker Y/L is a function of capital per worker K/L.

We use lowercase letters to denote quantities per worker. Thus, $y = Y/L$ is output per worker, and $k = K/L$ is capital per worker. We can write the production function as

$$y = f(k),$$

where we define $f(k) = F(k, 1)$. It is more convenient to analyze the economy using this production function relating capital per worker to output per worker. Figure 4-1 illustrates the production function.

The slope of this production function shows how much extra output per worker is produced from an extra unit of capital per worker. This amount is the marginal product of capital MPK. Mathematically, we write

$$MPK = f(k + 1) - f(k).$$

Note that in Figure 4-1, as the amount of capital increases, the production function becomes flatter. The production function exhibits diminishing marginal product of capital: each incremental unit of capital produces less output than did the preceding unit. When there is only a little capital, an extra unit of capital is very useful and produces much additional output. When there is a lot of capital, an extra unit is less useful and produces less additional output.

Figure 4-1

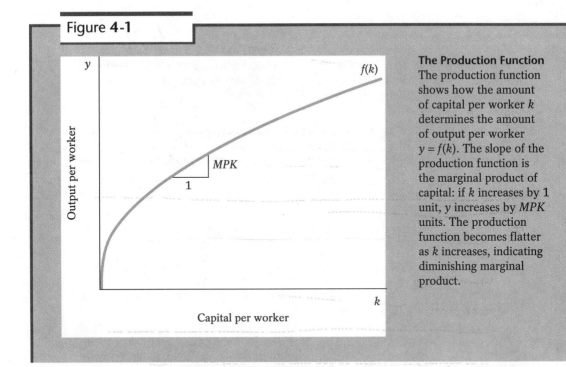

The Production Function
The production function shows how the amount of capital per worker k determines the amount of output per worker $y = f(k)$. The slope of the production function is the marginal product of capital: if k increases by 1 unit, y increases by MPK units. The production function becomes flatter as k increases, indicating diminishing marginal product.

The Demand for Goods and the Consumption Function   The demand for goods in the Solow model comes from consumption and investment. In other words, output per worker y is divided between consumption per worker c and investment per worker i:

$$y = c + i.$$

This equation is the national income accounts identity for the economy. It differs slightly from the identity in Chapter 3 because it omits government purchases (which for present purposes we can ignore) and because it expresses y, c, and i as quantities per worker.

The Solow model assumes that the consumption function takes the simple form

$$c = (1 - s)y,$$

where s, the saving rate, is a number between zero and one. This consumption function states that consumption is proportional to income. Each year, a fraction $(1 - s)$ of income is consumed and a fraction s is saved.

To see what this consumption function implies, substitute $(1 - s)y$ for c in the national income accounts identity:

$$y = (1 - s)y + i.$$

Rearrange the terms to obtain

$$i = sy.$$

This equation shows that investment, like consumption, is proportional to income. Since investment equals saving, the rate of saving s is also the fraction of output devoted to investment.

The Evolution of Capital and the Steady State

Having introduced the two main ingredients of the Solow model—the production function and the consumption function—we can now examine how increases in the capital stock over time result in economic growth. Two forces cause the capital stock to change:

- *Investment*: The capital stock rises as firms buy new plants and equipment.

- *Depreciation*: The capital stock falls as some of the old capital wears out.

To understand how the capital stock changes, we must understand the determinants of investment and depreciation.

We noted previously that investment per worker is a fraction of output per worker sy. By substituting the production function for y, we can express investment per worker as a function of the capital stock per worker:

$$i = sf(k).$$

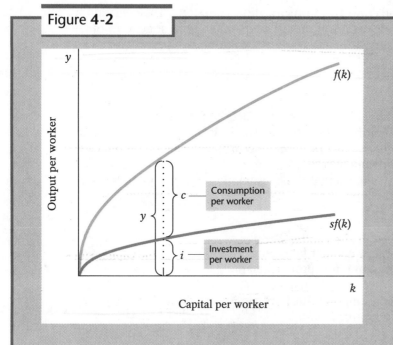

Figure 4-2

Output, Consumption, and Investment The saving rate s determines the allocation of output between consumption and investment. At any level of capital k, output is $f(k)$, investment is $sf(k)$, and consumption is $f(k) - sf(k)$.

The higher the level of capital k, the greater the levels of output $f(k)$ and investment i. This equation, which incorporates both the production and consumption functions, relates the existing stock of capital k to the accumulation of new capital i. Figure 4-2 shows how the saving rate determines the allocation of output between consumption and investment for every value of k.

To incorporate depreciation into the model, we assume that a certain fraction δ of the capital stock wears out each year. We call δ the *depreciation rate*. For example, if capital lasts an average of 25 years, then the depreciation rate is 4 percent per year ($\delta = 0.04$). The amount of capital that depreciates each year is δk. Figure 4-3 shows how depreciation depends on the capital stock.

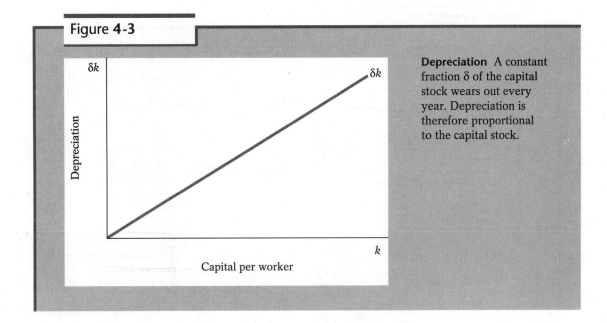

Figure 4-3

Depreciation A constant fraction δ of the capital stock wears out every year. Depreciation is therefore proportional to the capital stock.

We can express the impact of investment and depreciation on the capital stock with this adjustment equation:

$$\text{Change in Capital Stock} = \text{Investment} - \text{Depreciation}$$
$$\Delta k \quad\quad = \quad i \quad - \quad \delta k,$$

where Δk is the change in the capital stock between one year and the next. Because investment equals saving, we can write the change in the capital stock as

$$\Delta k = sf(k) - \delta k.$$

This equation states that the change in the capital stock equals investment $sf(k)$ minus the depreciation of existing capital δk.

Figure 4-4 graphs investment and depreciation for different levels of the capital stock k. The higher the capital stock, the greater the amounts of output and investment. Yet the higher the capital stock, the greater also the amount of depreciation.

Figure 4-4 shows that there is a single capital stock at which the amount of investment equals the amount of depreciation. If the economy has this capital stock, the capital stock will not change over time because the two forces acting to change it—investment and depreciation—just balance. That is, at this level of the capital stock, $\Delta k = 0$. We call this the **steady-state** level of capital and designate it as k^*.

Figure 4-4

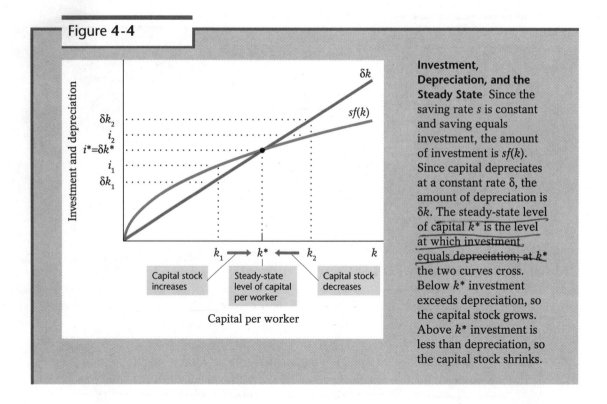

Investment, Depreciation, and the Steady State Since the saving rate s is constant and saving equals investment, the amount of investment is $sf(k)$. Since capital depreciates at a constant rate δ, the amount of depreciation is δk. The steady-state level of capital k^* is the level at which investment equals depreciation; at k^* the two curves cross. Below k^* investment exceeds depreciation, so the capital stock grows. Above k^* investment is less than depreciation, so the capital stock shrinks.

Approaching the Steady State

The steady state represents the long-run equilibrium of the economy. The economy ends up with the steady-state level of capital, regardless of the level of capital with which it begins.

Suppose that the economy starts with less than the steady-state level of capital, such as level k_1 in Figure 4-4. In this case, the level of investment exceeds the amount of depreciation. Over time, the capital stock will rise and will continue to rise—along with output—until it approaches the steady state k^*.

Similarly, suppose that the economy starts with more than the steady-state level of capital, such as level k_2. In this case, investment is less than depreciation: capital is wearing out faster than it is being replaced. The capital stock will fall, again approaching the steady-state level. Once the capital stock reaches the steady state, investment equals depreciation, and the capital stock neither increases nor decreases.

Approaching the Steady State: A Numerical Example

Let's use a numerical example to see how the Solow model works and how the economy approaches the steady state. For this example, we assume that the production function is[2]

$$Y = K^{1/2}L^{1/2}.$$

To derive the per-worker production function $f(k)$, divide both sides of the production function by L:

$$\frac{Y}{L} = \frac{K^{1/2}L^{1/2}}{L}.$$

Rearrange to obtain

$$\frac{Y}{L} = \left(\frac{K}{L}\right)^{1/2}.$$

Since $y = Y/L$ and $k = K/L$, this becomes

$$y = k^{1/2}.$$

This equation can also be written as

$$y = \sqrt{k}.$$

Output per worker is equal to the square root of the amount of capital per worker.

To complete the example, we assume that 30 percent of output is saved ($s = 0.3$), that 10 percent of the capital stock depreciates every year ($\delta = 0.1$), and that the economy starts off with 4 units of capital per worker ($k = 4$). We can now examine what happens to this economy over time.

We begin by looking at the production and allocation of output in the first year. According to the production function, the 4 units of capital per worker produce 2 units of output per worker. Since 70 percent of output is consumed and 30 percent is saved and invested, $c = 1.4$ and $i = 0.6$. Also, since 10 percent of the capital stock depreciates, $\delta k = 0.4$. With investment of 0.6 and depreciation of 0.4, the change in the capital stock is $\Delta k = 0.2$. The second year begins with 4.2 units of capital per worker.

---

[2] If you read the appendix to Chapter 3, you will recognize this as the Cobb-Douglas production function with the parameter α equal to 1/2.

Table 4-2

Approaching the Steady State: A Numerical Example

Assumptions: $y = \sqrt{k}$ $s = 0.3$ $\delta = 0.1$ Initial $k = 4.0$

Year	k	y	c	i	δk	Δk
1	4.000	2.000	1.400	0.600	0.400	0.200
2	4.200	2.049	1.435	0.615	0.420	0.195
3	4.395	2.096	1.467	0.629	0.440	0.189
4	4.584	2.141	1.499	0.642	0.458	0.184
5	4.768	2.184	1.529	0.655	0.477	0.178
.						
.						
.						
10	5.602	2.367	1.657	0.710	0.560	0.150
.						
.						
.						
25	7.321	2.706	1.894	0.812	0.732	0.080
.						
.						
.						
100	8.962	2.994	2.096	0.898	0.896	0.002
.						
.						
.						
∞	9.000	3.000	2.100	0.900	0.900	0.000

Table 4-2 shows how the economy progresses year by year. Every year, new capital is added and output grows. Over many years, the economy approaches a steady state with 9 units of capital per worker. In this steady state, investment of 0.9 exactly offsets depreciation of 0.9, so that the capital stock and output are no longer growing.

Following the progress of the economy for many years is one way to find the steady-state capital stock, but another way requires fewer calculations. Recall that

$$\Delta k = sf(k) - \delta k.$$

This equation shows how k evolves over time. Since $\Delta k = 0$ in the steady state, we know that

$$0 = sf(k^*) - \delta k^*,$$

or, equivalently,

$$\frac{k^*}{f(k^*)} = \frac{s}{\delta}.$$

This equation provides a way of finding the steady-state level of capital per worker, k^*. Substituting in our example, we obtain

$$\frac{k^*}{\sqrt{k^*}} = \frac{0.3}{0.1}.$$

Now square both sides of this equation to find

$$k^* = 9.$$

The steady-state capital stock is 9 units per worker. This result confirms the calculation of the steady state in Table 4-2.

Case Study *4-1*

· · · · · · · · · · · · ·

The Miracle of Japanese and German Growth

Japan and Germany are two success stories of economic growth. Although today they are economic superpowers, in 1945 the economies of both countries were in shambles. World War II had destroyed much of their capital stocks. In the decades after the war, however, these two countries experienced some of the most rapid growth rates on record. Between 1948 and 1972, output per person grew at 8.2 percent per year in Japan and 5.7 percent per year in Germany, compared to only 2.2 percent per year in the United States.

Are the postwar experiences of Japan and Germany so surprising from the standpoint of the Solow growth model? Consider an economy in steady state. Now suppose that a war destroys some of the capital stock. (That is, suppose the capital stock drops from k^* to k_1 in Figure 4-4.) Not surprisingly, the level of output immediately falls. But if the saving rate—the fraction of output devoted to saving and investment—is unchanged, the economy will then experience a period of high growth. Output grows because, at the lower capital stock, more capital is added by investment than is removed by depreciation. This high growth continues until the economy approaches its former steady state. Hence, although destroying part of the capital stock immediately reduces output, it is followed by higher than normal growth. The "miracle" of rapid growth in Japan and Germany, as it is often described in the business press, is what the Solow model predicts for countries in which war has greatly reduced the capital stock.

The explanation of Japanese and German growth is not this simple, however. There is another important difference between these countries and the United States that is key to their economic performance. Both Japan and Germany save and invest a higher fraction of their output than does the United States. They are, therefore, approaching a different steady state. To understand more fully the differences among countries, we must consider the effects of different saving rates.

· · · · · · · · · · · · ·

Changes in the Saving Rate

Consider what happens to an economy when the saving rate increases. Figure 4-5 shows such a change. We assume that the economy begins in a steady state with saving rate s_1 and capital stock k_1^*. The saving rate then increases from s_1 to s_2, causing an upward shift in the $sf(k)$ curve. At the initial saving rate s_1 and the initial capital stock k_1^*, the amount of investment just offsets the amount of depreciation. The moment after the saving rate rises, investment is higher, but the capital stock and depreciation are unchanged. Therefore, investment exceeds depreciation. The capital stock will gradually rise until the economy reaches the new steady state k_2^*, which has a higher capital stock and a higher level of output than the old steady state.

Figure 4-5

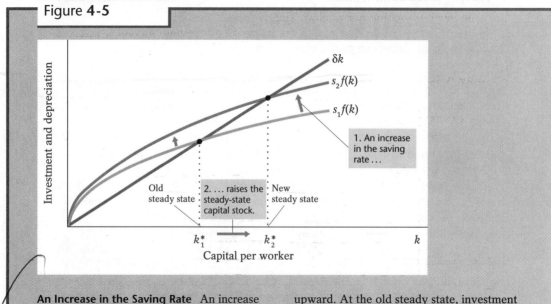

An Increase in the Saving Rate An increase in the saving rate s implies that the amount of investment for any given capital stock is higher. It therefore shifts the saving function upward. At the old steady state, investment now exceeds depreciation. The capital stock rises until the economy reaches a new steady state with more capital and output.

The Solow model shows that the saving rate is a key determinant of the steady-state capital stock. If the saving rate is high, the economy will have a large capital stock and a high level of output. If the saving rate is low, the economy will have a small capital stock and a low level of output.

What is the relationship between saving and economic growth? Higher saving leads to faster growth, but only temporarily. An increase in the rate of saving raises growth until the economy reaches the new steady state. If the economy maintains a high saving rate, it will also maintain a large capital stock and a high level of output, but it will not maintain a high rate of growth forever.

Case Study *4-2*

• • • • • • • • • • • • •

Saving and Investment Around the World

According to the Solow model, if a nation devotes a large fraction of its income to saving and investment, it will have a high steady-state capital stock and a high level of income. This theoretical conclusion has important practical implications. Indeed, it can help explain the large international variation in standards of living.

Figure 4-6 is a scatterplot of data from 84 countries. The figure includes most of the world's economies. (It excludes major oil-producing countries and countries that were communist during the period 1960-1992.) The data show a positive relationship between the fraction of output devoted to investment and the level of income per person. That is, countries with high rates of investment, such as the United States and Japan, usually have high incomes, whereas

Figure 4-6

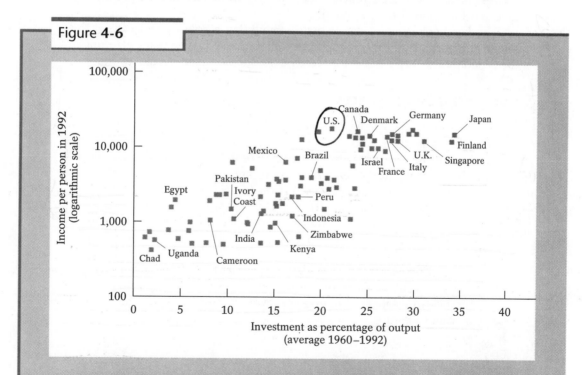

International Evidence on Investment Rates and Income per Person This scatterplot shows the experience of 84 countries, each represented by a single point. The horizontal axis shows the country's rate of investment, and the vertical axis shows the country's income per person. High investment is associated with high income per person, as the Solow model predicts.

Source: Robert Summers and Alan Heston, Supplement (Mark 5.6) to "The Penn World Table (Mark 5): An Expanded Set of International Comparisons 1950–1988," *Quarterly Journal of Economics* (May 1991): 327–368.

countries with low rates of investment, such as Uganda and Chad, have low incomes. As the Solow model suggests, the investment rate is a key determinant of whether a country is rich or poor.

Although the association in this figure is strong, it is not perfect. There must be other determinants of income per person beyond saving and investment. We return to the international differences later in the chapter to see what other variables enter the picture.

• • • • • • • • • • • • • •

4-2   The Golden Rule Level of Capital

Now that we have examined the link between the rate of saving and the steady-state levels of capital and income, we can discuss what amount of capital accumulation is optimal. Later, in Section 4-5, we describe how government policies influence a nation's saving rate. But first, in this section, we present the theory behind these policy decisions.

To keep our analysis simple, let's assume that a policymaker can set the saving rate at any level. By setting the saving rate, the policymaker determines the economy's steady state. What steady state should the policymaker choose?

Comparing Steady States

When choosing a steady state, the policymaker's goal is to maximize the well-being of the individuals who make up the society. Individuals themselves do not care about the amount of capital in the economy, or even the amount of output. They care about the amount of goods and services they can consume. Thus, a benevolent policymaker would want to choose the steady state with the highest level of consumption. The steady state with the highest consumption is called the **Golden Rule level of capital accumulation** and is denoted k^*_{gold}.[3]

How can we tell whether an economy is at the Golden Rule level? To answer this question, we must first determine steady-state consumption per worker. Then we can see which steady state provides the most consumption.

To find steady-state consumption per worker, we begin with the national income accounts identity

$$y = c + i$$

and rearrange it as

$$c = y - i.$$

Consumption is simply output minus investment. Since we want to find steady-state consumption, we substitute steady-state values for output and investment. Steady-state output per worker is $f(k^*)$, where k^* is the steady-state

---

[3] Edmund Phelps, "The Golden Rule of Accumulation: A Fable for Growthmen," *American Economic Review* 51 (September 1961): 638–643.

capital stock per worker. Furthermore, since the capital stock is not changing in the steady state, investment is equal to depreciation δk^*. Substituting $f(k^*)$ for y and δk^* for i, we can write steady-state consumption per worker as

$$c^* = f(k^*) - \delta k^*.$$

According to this equation, steady-state consumption is the difference between steady-state output and steady-state depreciation. It shows that increased capital has two effects on steady-state consumption: it causes greater output, but more output must be used to replace depreciating capital.

Figure 4-7 graphs steady-state output and steady-state depreciation as a function of the steady-state capital stock. Steady-state consumption is the gap between output and depreciation. This figure shows that there is one level of the capital stock—the Golden Rule level k^*_{gold}—that maximizes consumption.

When we compare steady states, we must acknowledge that higher levels of capital affect both output and depreciation. If the capital stock is below the Golden Rule level, an increase in the capital stock raises output more than depreciation, so that consumption rises. In this case, the production function is steeper than the δk^* line, so the gap between these two curves—which equals consumption—grows as k^* rises. By contrast, if the capital stock is above the Golden Rule level, an increase in the capital stock reduces consumption, since the increase in output is smaller than the increase in depreciation. In this case, the production function is flatter than the δk^* line, so the gap between the curves—consumption—shrinks as k^* rises. At the Golden Rule level of capital, the production function and the δk^* line have the same slope, and consumption is at its greatest level.

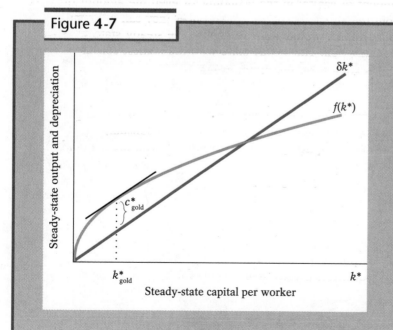

Figure 4-7

Steady-State Consumption The economy's output is used for consumption or investment. In the steady state, investment equals depreciation. Therefore, steady-state consumption is the difference between output $f(k^*)$ and depreciation δk^*. Steady-state consumption is maximized at the Golden Rule steady state. The Golden Rule capital stock is denoted k^*_{gold} and the Golden Rule consumption is denoted c^*_{gold}.

To make the point somewhat differently, suppose that the economy starts at some capital stock $k*$ and that the policymaker is considering increasing the capital stock to $k* + 1$. The amount of extra output would then be $f(k* + 1) - f(k*)$, which is the marginal product of capital MPK. The amount of extra depreciation from having 1 more unit of capital is the depreciation rate δ. The net effect of this extra unit of capital on consumption is then $MPK - \delta$, which is the marginal product of capital less the depreciation rate. If the steady-state capital stock is below the Golden Rule level, increases in capital increase consumption because the marginal product of capital is greater than the depreciation rate. If the steady-state capital stock exceeds the Golden Rule level, increases in capital reduce consumption because the marginal product of capital is less than the depreciation rate. Therefore, the following condition describes the Golden Rule:

$$MPK = \delta.$$

At the Golden Rule level of capital, the marginal product of capital equals the rate of depreciation. In other words, at the Golden Rule, the marginal product net of depreciation, $MPK - \delta$, equals zero.

Keep in mind that the economy does not automatically gravitate toward the Golden Rule steady state. The choice of a particular steady-state capital stock, such as the Golden Rule, implies a choice of a particular saving rate. Figure 4-8 shows the steady state if the saving rate is set to produce the Golden Rule level of capital. If the saving rate is higher than the one used in this figure, the steady-state capital stock will be too high. If the saving rate is lower, the steady-state capital stock will be too low.

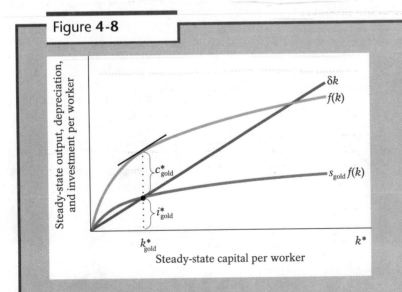

Figure 4-8

The Saving Rate and the Golden Rule There is one saving rate that produces the Golden Rule level of capital k^*_{gold}. A change in the saving rate would shift the $sf(k)$ curve, which would move the economy to a steady state with a lower level of consumption.

Steady-state output, depreciation, and investment per worker

δk
$f(k)$
c^*_{gold}
$s_{\text{gold}}f(k)$
i^*_{gold}
k^*_{gold}
k^*
Steady-state capital per worker

2.

Comparing Steady States: A Numerical Example

Consider the decision of a policymaker choosing a steady state in the following
economy. The production function is the same as in our earlier example:

$$y = \sqrt{k}.$$

$y/_L = \sqrt{K/_L}$

Output per worker is the square root of capital per worker. Depreciation is
again 10 percent of capital. This time, the policymaker chooses the saving rate
s and thus the economy's steady state.

To see the outcomes available to the policymaker, recall that the following equation holds in the steady state:

$$\frac{k^*}{f(k^*)} = \frac{s}{\delta}.$$

$\delta = .10$

$s = $ SAVINGS RATE.

In this economy, this equation becomes

$$\frac{k^*}{\sqrt{k^*}} = \frac{s}{0.1}.$$

Squaring both sides of this equation yields a solution for the steady-state capital stock. We find

$$k^* = 100s^2.$$

Using this result, we can compute the steady-state capital stock for any saving
rate.

Table 4-3 presents calculations showing the steady states that result from
various saving rates. We see that higher saving leads to higher capital, which in
turn leads to higher output and higher depreciation. Steady-state consumption,
the difference between output and depreciation, first rises with higher saving
rates and then declines. Consumption is highest when the saving rate is 0.5.
Hence, a saving rate of 0.5 produces the Golden Rule steady state.

Table 4-3

Comparing Steady States: A Numerical Example

Assumptions: $y = \sqrt{k}$ $\delta = 0.1$

s	k*	y*	δk*	c*	MPK	MPK − δ
0.0	0.0	0.0	0.0	0.0	∞	∞
0.1	1.0	1.0	0.1	0.9	0.500	0.400
0.2	4.0	2.0	0.4	1.6	0.250	0.150
0.3	9.0	3.0	0.9	2.1	0.167	0.067
0.4	16.0	4.0	1.6	2.4	0.125	0.025
0.5	25.0	5.0	2.5	2.5	0.100	0.000
0.6	36.0	6.0	3.6	2.4	0.083	−0.017
0.7	49.0	7.0	4.9	2.1	0.071	−0.029
0.8	64.0	8.0	6.4	1.6	0.062	−0.038
0.9	81.0	9.0	8.1	0.9	0.056	−0.044
1.0	100.0	10.0	10.0	0.0	0.050	−0.050

Another way to identify the Golden Rule steady state is from the marginal product of capital. For this production function, the marginal product is[4]

$$MPK = \frac{1}{2\sqrt{k}}.$$

Using this formula, the last two columns of Table 4-3 present the value of $MPK - \delta$ in the different steady states. Note again that in the Golden Rule steady state, the marginal product of capital net of depreciation equals zero.

The Transition to the Golden Rule Steady State

Let's now make our policymaker's problem more realistic. So far, we have been assuming that the policymaker can simply choose the economy's steady state. In this case, the policymaker would choose the steady state with highest consumption—the Golden Rule steady state. But now suppose that the economy has reached a steady state other than the Golden Rule. What happens to consumption, investment, and capital when the economy makes the transition between steady states? Might the impact of the transition deter the policymaker from trying to achieve the Golden Rule?

We must consider two cases: the economy might begin either with more capital than in the Golden Rule steady state, or with less. The second case—too little capital—presents far greater difficulties; it forces the policymaker to evaluate the benefits of current consumption relative to future consumption. As we see in Section 4-5, this situation describes actual economies, including that of the United States.

Starting With Too Much Capital   We first consider the case in which the economy begins with more capital than it would have in the Golden Rule steady state. In this case, the policymaker should pursue policies aimed at reducing the rate of saving in order to reduce the steady-state capital stock. Suppose that these policies succeed and that at some point in time—call it t_0—the saving rate falls to the level that will eventually lead to the Golden Rule steady state.

Figure 4-9 shows what happens to output, consumption, and investment when the saving rate falls. The reduction in the saving rate causes an immediate increase in the level of consumption and a decrease in the level of investment. Investment is now less than depreciation, so the economy is no longer in a steady state. Gradually, as the capital stock falls, output, consumption, and investment also fall to the new steady state. Because the new steady state is the Golden Rule steady state, we know that the level of consumption is now higher than it was before the change in the saving rate, even though output and investment are lower.

[4]   *Mathematical Note*: To derive this formula, note that the marginal product of capital is the derivative of the production function with respect to k.

Note that, compared to the old steady state, consumption is higher not just in the new steady state but also along the entire path to it. When the capital stock exceeds the Golden Rule level, reducing saving is clearly a good policy, for it increases consumption at every point in time.

Figure 4-9

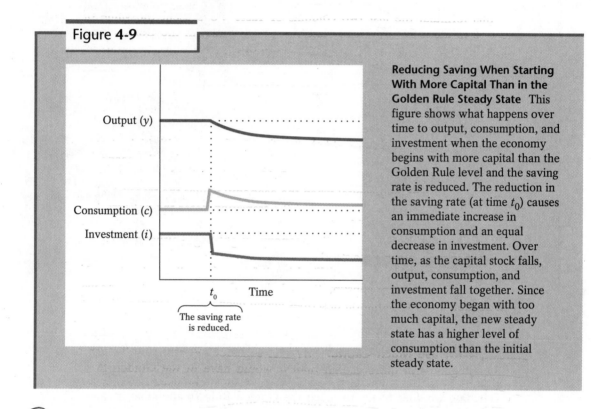

Output (*y*)

Consumption (*c*)

Investment (*i*)

t_0 Time

The saving rate
is reduced.

Reducing Saving When Starting With More Capital Than in the Golden Rule Steady State This figure shows what happens over time to output, consumption, and investment when the economy begins with more capital than the Golden Rule level and the saving rate is reduced. The reduction in the saving rate (at time t_0) causes an immediate increase in consumption and an equal decrease in investment. Over time, as the capital stock falls, output, consumption, and investment fall together. Since the economy began with too much capital, the new steady state has a higher level of consumption than the initial steady state.

Starting With Too Little Capital   When the economy begins with less capital than in the Golden Rule steady state, the policymaker must raise the saving rate to reach the Golden Rule. Figure 4-10 shows what happens. The increase in the saving rate at time t_0 causes an immediate fall in consumption and a rise in investment. Over time, higher investment causes the capital stock to rise. As capital accumulates, output, consumption, and investment gradually increase, eventually approaching the new steady-state levels. Because the initial steady state was below the Golden Rule, the increase in saving eventually leads to a higher level of consumption than that which prevailed initially.

Does the increase in saving that leads to the Golden Rule steady state raise economic welfare? Eventually it does, because the steady-state level of consumption is higher. But achieving that new steady state requires an initial period of reduced consumption. Note the contrast to the case in which the economy begins above the Golden Rule. *When the economy begins above the*

Figure 4-10

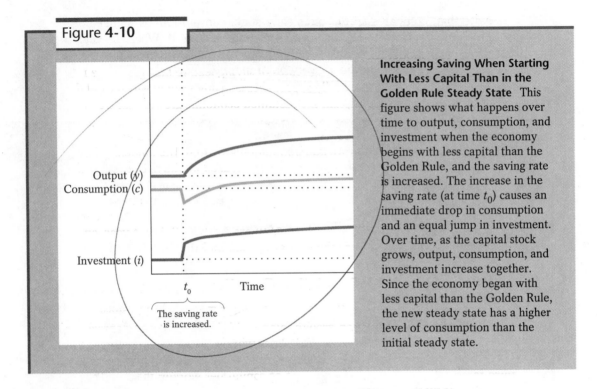

Increasing Saving When Starting With Less Capital Than in the Golden Rule Steady State This figure shows what happens over time to output, consumption, and investment when the economy begins with less capital than the Golden Rule, and the saving rate is increased. The increase in the saving rate (at time t_0) causes an immediate drop in consumption and an equal jump in investment. Over time, as the capital stock grows, output, consumption, and investment increase together. Since the economy began with less capital than the Golden Rule, the new steady state has a higher level of consumption than the initial steady state.

Golden Rule, reaching the Golden Rule produces higher consumption at all points in time. When the economy begins below the Golden Rule, reaching the Golden Rule requires reducing consumption today to increase consumption in the future.

Deciding whether to try to reach the Golden Rule steady state is especially difficult because the population of consumers changes over time. Reaching the Golden Rule achieves the highest steady-state level of consumption and thus benefits future generations. But when the economy is below the Golden Rule, reaching the Golden Rule requires raising investment and thus lowering the consumption of current generations.

When choosing whether to increase capital accumulation, the policymaker faces a tradeoff among the welfare of different generations. A policymaker who cares more about current generations than about future generations may decide not to pursue policies to reach the Golden Rule steady state. By contrast, a policymaker who cares about all generations equally will choose to reach the Golden Rule. Even though current generations will consume less, an infinite number of future generations will benefit by moving to the Golden Rule.

Thus, optimal capital accumulation depends crucially on how we weigh the interests of current and future generations. The biblical Golden Rule tells us, "do unto others as you would have them do unto you." If we heed this advice, we give all generations equal weight. In this case, it is optimal to reach the Golden Rule level of capital—which is why it is called the "Golden Rule."

4-3 Population Growth

The basic Solow model shows that capital accumulation, by itself, cannot explain sustained economic growth. High rates of saving lead to high growth temporarily, but the economy eventually approaches a steady state in which capital and output are constant. To explain the sustained economic growth that we observe in most parts of the world, we must expand the Solow model to incorporate the other two sources of economic growth: population growth and technological progress. In this section we add population growth to the model.

Instead of assuming that the population is fixed, as we did in Sections 4-1 and 4-2, we now suppose that the population and the labor force grow at a constant rate n. For example, in the United States, the population grows about 1 percent per year, so $n = 0.01$. This means that if 150 million people are working one year, then 151.5 million (1.01 × 150) are working the next year, and 153.015 million (1.01 × 151.5) the year after that, and so on.

The Steady State With Population Growth

Labor force growth, 1%/year = n

How does population growth affect the steady state? To answer this question, we must discuss how population growth, along with investment and depreciation, influences the accumulation of capital per worker. As we noted before, investment raises the capital stock, and depreciation reduces it. But now there is a third force acting to change the amount of capital per worker: the growth in the number of workers causes capital per worker to fall.

We continue to let lowercase letters stand for quantities per worker. Thus, $k = K/L$ is capital per worker, and $y = Y/L$ is output per worker. Keep in mind, however, that the number of workers is growing over time.

The change in the capital stock per worker is

$$\Delta k = i - (\delta + n)k.$$

This equation shows how new investment, depreciation, and population growth influence the per-worker capital stock. New investment increases k, whereas depreciation and population growth decrease k. We have seen this equation before in the special case of a constant population ($n = 0$).

We can think of the term $(\delta + n)k$ as *break-even investment*: the amount of investment necessary to keep the capital stock per worker constant. Break-even investment includes the depreciation of existing capital, which equals δk. It also includes the amount of investment necessary to provide new workers with capital. The amount of investment necessary for this purpose is nk, because there are n new workers for each existing worker, and because k is the amount of capital for each worker. The equation shows that population growth reduces the accumulation of capital per worker much the way depreciation does. Depreciation reduces k by wearing out the capital stock, whereas population growth reduces k by spreading the capital stock more thinly among a larger population of workers.

To make use of this equation, substitute $sf(k)$ for i. The equation can then be written as

$$\Delta k = sf(k) - (\delta + n)k.$$

Figure 4-11

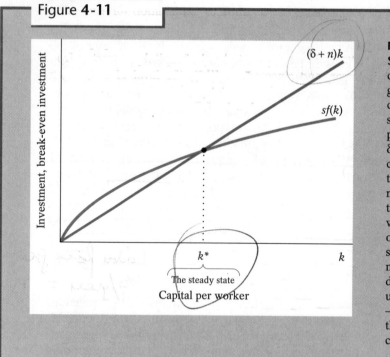

Population Growth in the Solow Model Like depreciation, population growth is one reason the capital stock per worker shrinks. If n is the rate of population growth and δ is the rate of depreciation, then $(\delta + n)k$ is the amount of investment necessary to keep constant the capital stock per worker k. For the economy to be in a steady state, investment $sf(k)$ must offset the effects of depreciation and population growth $(\delta + n)k$ —this is represented by the crossing of the two curves.

To see what determines the steady-state level of capital per worker, we use Figure 4-11, which extends the analysis of Figure 4-4 to include the effects of population growth. An economy is in a steady state if capital per worker k is unchanging. We designate the steady-state value of k as k^*. If k is less than k^*, investment is greater than break-even investment, so k rises. If k is greater than k^*, investment is less than break-even investment, so k falls.

In the steady state, the positive effect of investment on the capital stock per worker just balances the negative effects of depreciation and population growth. That is, at k^*, $\Delta k = 0$ and $i^* = \delta k^* + nk^*$. Once the economy is in the steady state, investment has two purposes. Some of it (δk^*) replaces the depreciated capital, and the rest (nk^*) provides the new workers with the steady-state amount of capital.

The Effects of Population Growth

Population growth alters the basic Solow model in three ways. First, it brings us closer to explaining sustained economic growth. In the steady state with population growth, capital per worker and output per worker are unchanging. Because the number of workers is growing at rate n, total capital and total output are also growing at the rate n. Hence, population growth cannot explain sustained growth in standards of living, because output per worker is constant in the steady state. But population growth can explain sustained growth in total output.

Second, population growth gives us another explanation for why some countries are rich and others are poor. Consider the effects of an increase in population growth. Figure 4-12 shows that an increase in the rate of population growth from n_1 to n_2 reduces the steady-state level of capital per worker from k_1^* to k_2^*. Since k^* is lower, and since $y^* = f(k^*)$, the level of output per worker y^* is also lower. Thus, the Solow model predicts that countries with higher population growth will have lower levels of GDP per person.

Figure 4-12

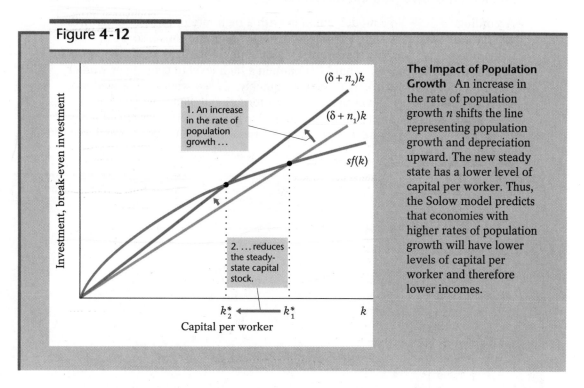

The Impact of Population Growth An increase in the rate of population growth n shifts the line representing population growth and depreciation upward. The new steady state has a lower level of capital per worker. Thus, the Solow model predicts that economies with higher rates of population growth will have lower levels of capital per worker and therefore lower incomes.

Finally, population growth affects our criterion for determining the Golden Rule level of capital accumulation. To see how this criterion changes, we proceed as we did previously. Consumption per worker is

$$c = y - i.$$

Since steady-state output is $f(k^*)$ and steady-state investment is $(\delta + n)k^*$, we can express steady-state consumption as

$$c^* = f(k^*) - (\delta + n)k^*.$$

Using an argument largely the same as before, we conclude that the level of k^* that maximizes consumption is the one at which

$$MPK = \delta + n,$$

or equivalently,

$$MPK - \delta = n.$$

In the Golden Rule steady state, the marginal product of capital net of depreciation equals the rate of population growth.

Case Study *4-3*

● ● ● ● ● ● ● ● ● ● ● ● ●

Population Growth Around the World

According to the Solow model, a nation with a high rate of population growth will have a low steady-state capital stock per worker and thus also a low level of income per worker. In other words, high population growth tends to impoverish a country, because it is hard to maintain a high level of capital per worker when the number of workers is growing quickly. To see whether the evidence supports this conclusion, we again turn to international data.

Figure 4-13 is a scatterplot of data for the same 84 countries examined in Case Study 4-2. The figure shows that countries with high rates of population

Figure 4-13

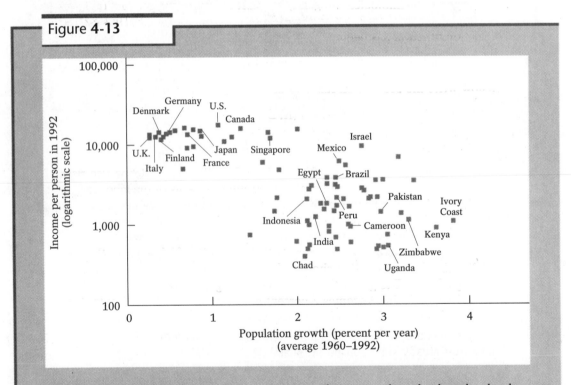

International Evidence on Population Growth and Income per Person This figure is a scatterplot of data from 84 countries. It shows that countries with high rates of population growth tend to have low levels of income per person, as the Solow model predicts.

Source: Robert Summers and Alan Heston, Supplement (Mark 5.6) to "The Penn World Table (Mark 5): An Expanded Set of International Comparisons 1950–1988," *Quarterly Journal of Economics* (May 1991): 327–368.

growth tend to have low levels of income per person. The international evidence is consistent with the Solow model's prediction that the rate of population growth is one determinant of a country's standard of living.

4-4 Technological Progress

We now incorporate technological progress, the third source of economic growth, into the Solow model. So far, our model has assumed an unchanging relationship between the inputs of capital and labor and the output of goods and services. Yet the model can be modified to allow for exogenous increases in society's ability to produce.

The Efficiency of Labor

To incorporate technological progress, we must return to the production function that relates total capital K and total labor L to total output Y. Thus far, the production function has been

$$Y = F(K, L).$$

We now write the production function as

$$Y = F(K, L \times E),$$

where E is a new variable called the **efficiency of labor**. The efficiency of labor reflects society's knowledge about production methods: as the available technology improves, the efficiency of labor rises. The efficiency of labor also rises if there are improvements in the health, education, or skills of the labor force.

The term $L \times E$ is the labor force measured in **efficiency units**. It takes into account the number of workers L and the efficiency of each worker E. This new production function states that total output Y depends on the number of units of capital K and on the number of efficiency units of labor, $L \times E$.

The simplest assumption about technological progress is that it causes the efficiency of labor E to grow at some constant rate g. For example, if $g = 0.02$, then each unit of labor becomes 2 percent more efficient each year: output increases as if the labor force had increased by an additional 2 percent. This form of technological progress is called labor-augmenting, and g is called the rate of **labor-augmenting technological progress**. Since the labor force L is growing at rate n, and the efficiency of each unit of labor E is growing at rate g, the number of efficiency units of labor $L \times E$ is growing at rate $n + g$.

The Steady State With Technological Progress

Expressing technological progress as labor-augmenting makes it analogous to population growth. In Section 4-3 we analyzed the economy in terms of quantities per worker and allowed the number of workers to rise over time. Now we analyze the economy in terms of quantities per efficiency unit of labor and allow the number of efficiency units to rise.

To do this, we need to reconsider our notation. We now let $k = K/(L \times E)$ stand for capital per efficiency unit, and $y = Y/(L \times E)$ stand for output per efficiency unit. With these definitions, we can again write $y = f(k)$.

This notation is not really as new as it seems. If we hold the efficiency of labor E constant at the arbitrary value of 1, as we have implicitly been doing all along, then these new definitions of k and y reduce to our old ones. When the efficiency of labor is growing, however, we must keep in mind that k and y now refer to quantities per efficiency unit of labor (not per worker).

Our analysis of the economy proceeds just as it did when we examined population growth. The equation showing the evolution of k over time now changes to

$$\Delta k = sf(k) - (\delta + n + g)k.$$

The new term involving g, the rate of technological progress, arises because k is the amount of capital per efficiency unit of labor. If g is high, then the number of efficiency units is growing quickly, and the amount of capital per efficiency unit tends to fall.

As shown in Figure 4-14, the inclusion of technological progress does not substantially alter our analysis of the steady state. There is one level of k, denoted k^*, at which capital per efficiency unit and output per efficiency unit are constant. This steady state represents the long-run equilibrium of the economy.

Figure 4-14

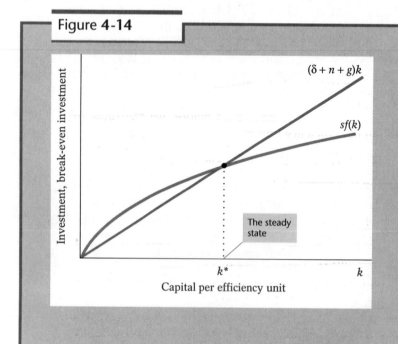

Introducing Technological Progress Including labor-augmenting technological progress at rate g affects our analysis in much the same way as did population growth. Now that k is defined as the amount of capital per efficiency unit of labor, increases in the number of efficiency units because of technological progress tend to decrease k. In the steady state, investment $sf(k)$ offsets the reductions in k due to depreciation, population growth, and technological progress.

The Effects of Technological Progress

Table 4-4 shows how four key variables behave in the steady state with techno-logical progress. As we have just seen, capital per efficiency unit k is constant in the steady state. Since $y = f(k)$, output per efficiency unit is also constant. Remember, though, that the number of efficiency units per worker is growing at rate g. Hence, output per worker ($Y/L = y \times E$) also grows at rate g. Total output [$Y = y \times (E \times L)$] grows at rate $n + g$.

Table 4-4	Steady-State Growth Rates in the Solow Model With Technological Progress	
Variable	Symbol	Steady-State Growth Rate
Capital per efficiency unit	$k = K/(E \times L)$	0
Output per efficiency unit	$y = Y/(E \times L) = f(k)$	0
Output per worker	$Y/L = y \times E$	g
Total output	$Y = y \times (E \times L)$	$n + g$

With the addition of technological progress, our model can finally explain the sustained increases in standards of living that we observe. That is, we have shown that technological progress can lead to sustained growth in output per worker. By contrast, a high rate of saving leads to a high rate of growth only until the steady state is reached. Once the economy is in steady state, the rate of growth of output per worker depends only on the rate of technological progress. *The Solow model shows that only technological progress can explain persistently rising living standards.*

The introduction of technological progress also modifies the criterion for the Golden Rule. The Golden Rule level of capital accumulation is now defined as the steady state that maximizes consumption per efficiency unit of labor. Following the same arguments that we have used before, we can show that steady-state consumption per efficiency unit is

$$c^* = f(k^*) - (\delta + n + g)k^*.$$

Steady-state consumption is maximized if

$$MPK = \delta + n + g,$$

or

$$MPK - \delta = n + g.$$

That is, at the Golden Rule level of capital, the net marginal product of capital, $MPK - \delta$, equals the rate of growth of total output, $n + g$. Because actual economies experience both population growth and technological progress, we must use this criterion to evaluate whether they have more or less capital than at the Golden Rule steady state.

Case Study *4-4*

● ● ● ● ● ● ● ● ● ● ● ● ● ● ●

Steady-State Growth in the United States

Now that we have introduced technological progress into the Solow model and explained sustained growth in standards of living, we should ask how well our theory fits the facts. According to the Solow model, technological progress will cause the values of many variables to rise together. In the steady state, output per worker and the capital stock per worker both grow at the rate of technological progress. Data for the United States over the past 40 years show that output per worker and the capital stock per worker have in fact grown at approximately the same rate—about 2 percent per year.

Technological progress also affects factor prices. Problem 8(d) at the end of the chapter asks you to show that in the steady state, the real wage grows at the rate of technological progress. The real rental price of capital, however, is constant over time. Again, these predictions hold true for the United States. Over the past 40 years, the real wage has increased about 2 percent per year; it has increased about the same amount as real GDP per worker. Yet the real rental price of capital (measured as real capital income divided by the capital stock) has remained about the same.

The Solow model's prediction about factor prices—and the success of this prediction—is especially noteworthy when contrasted with Karl Marx's theory of the development of capitalist economies. Marx predicted that the return to capital would decline over time and that this would lead to economic and political crisis. Economic history has not supported Marx's prediction, which partly explains why we now study Solow's theory of growth rather than Marx's.

● ● ● ● ● ● ● ● ● ● ● ● ● ●

Case Study *4-5*

● ● ● ● ● ● ● ● ● ● ● ● ● ●

Will the World's Economies Converge?

If you travel around the world, you will see tremendous variation in living standards. The world's poor countries have levels of income per person that are less than one-tenth the levels in the world's rich countries. These differences in income are reflected in every measure of the quality of life—from the number of televisions and telephones per household to the infant mortality rate and life expectancy.

Much research has been devoted to the question of whether economies converge over time. That is, do economies that start off poor subsequently grow faster than economies that start off rich? If they do, then the world's poor economies will tend to catch up with the world's rich economies. If not, then income disparities will persist.

As a matter of theory, whether economies converge depends on why they differed in the first place. On the one hand, if two economies with the same steady state start off with different capital stocks, then we should expect them to converge. The economy with the smaller capital stock will naturally grow more quickly. (In Case Study 4-1, we applied this logic to explain rapid growth in Germany and Japan after World War II.) On the other hand, if two economies have different steady states, perhaps because the economies have different rates of saving, then we should not expect convergence. Instead, each economy will approach its own steady state.

Experience is consistent with this analysis. In samples of economies with similar populations and policies, studies find that economies converge to one another at a rate of about 2 percent per year. That is, the gap between rich and poor economies closes by about 2 percent each year. An example is the economies of U.S. states. For historical reasons, such as the Civil War of the 1860s, income levels varied greatly among states a century ago. Yet these differences have slowly disappeared over time.

In international data, a more complex picture emerges. When researchers examine only data on income per person, they find little evidence of convergence: countries that start off poor do not grow faster on average than countries that start off rich. This finding suggests that different countries have different steady states. If statistical techniques are used to control for some of the determinants of the steady state, such as saving rates, population growth rates, and educational attainment, then once again the data show convergence at a rate of about 2 percent per year. In other words, the economies of the world exhibit *conditional convergence*: they appear to be converging to their own steady states, which in turn are determined by saving, population growth, and education.[5]

• • • • • • • • • • • • •

4-5 Policies to Promote Growth

Having used the Solow model to uncover the relationships among the different sources of economic growth, we can now use the theory to help guide our thinking about economic policy. Here we address four policy questions:

- Should our society save more or save less?

- How can policy influence the rate of saving?

- Are there some types of investment that policy should especially encourage?

- How can policy increase the rate of technological progress?

[5] Robert Barro and Xavier Sala-i-Martin, "Convergence across States and Regions," *Brookings Papers on Economic Activity* 1991, no. 1: 107–182; N. Gregory Mankiw, David Romer, and David N. Weil, "A Contribution to the Empirics of Economic Growth," *Quarterly Journal of Economics* (May 1992): 407–437.

Evaluating the Rate of Saving

The Solow growth model shows how the saving rate determines the steady-state levels of capital and output. One particular saving rate produces the Golden Rule steady state, which maximizes consumption per worker and thus economic well-being. These results help us address the first question for economic policy: Is the rate of saving in the economy too low, too high, or about right?

If the marginal product of capital net of depreciation is greater than the growth rate of output, the economy is operating with less capital than in the Golden Rule steady state. In this case, increasing the rate of saving will eventually lead to a steady state with higher consumption. On the other hand, if the net marginal product of capital is below the growth rate of output, the economy is operating with too much capital, and the rate of saving should be reduced. To evaluate a nation's rate of capital accumulation, one needs to compare the growth rate and the net return to capital.

This comparison requires an estimate of the growth rate, $n + g$, and an estimate of the net marginal product of capital, $MPK - \delta$. Real GDP in the United States grows an average of 3 percent per year, so $n + g = 0.03$. We can estimate the net marginal product of capital from the following three facts:

1. The capital stock is about 2.5 times one year's GDP.

2. Depreciation of capital is about 10 percent of GDP.

3. Capital's share in output is about 30 percent.

According to fact 1, $k = 2.5y$, and according to fact 2, $\delta k = 0.1y$. Therefore,

$$\delta = (\delta k)/k$$
$$= (0.1y)/(2.5y)$$
$$= 0.04.$$

That is, about 4 percent of the capital stock depreciates each year. To obtain the marginal product of capital from facts 1 and 3, recall our conclusion in Chapter 3 that capital is paid its marginal product. Therefore,

$$\text{Capital's Share} = (MPK \times K)/Y$$
$$= MPK \times (K/Y).$$

Now substitute the numbers from facts 1 and 3 into this equation:

$$0.30 = MPK \times 2.5.$$

This implies that

$$MPK = 0.30/2.5 = 0.12.$$

Thus, the marginal product of capital is about 12 percent per year. The net marginal product of capital, $MPK - \delta$, is about 8 percent per year, well in excess of the average growth rate of 3 percent per year.

The high return to capital implies that the capital stock in the U.S. economy is well below the Golden Rule level. This finding suggests that policymakers should want to increase the rate of saving and investment. In fact, for many years, increasing capital formation has been a high priority of economic policy.

Changing the Rate of Saving

Public policy influences national saving in two ways: directly through public saving, and indirectly through the incentives it gives for private saving.

Public saving is the difference between government revenue and government spending. If the government spends more than it raises in revenue, it runs a budget deficit, which represents negative saving. As we saw in Chapter 3, the budget deficit crowds out investment. The reduced capital stock that results is part of the burden of the national debt on future generations. On the other hand, if the government spends less than it raises in revenue, it runs a budget surplus. It can then retire some of the national debt and stimulate investment.

Private saving is affected by various government policies. Although not included in the Solow model, the saving decisions of households depend on the rate of return; the greater the return to saving, the more attractive saving becomes. High tax rates on capital income discourage private saving by reducing the rate of return. Various tax provisions, such as tax-exempt retirement accounts, are designed to raise the rate of return and encourage private saving. Economists differ in their views about how much private saving responds to these incentives.

Allocating the Economy's Investment

The Solow model makes the simplifying assumption that there is only one type of capital. In the world, of course, there are many types. Private businesses invest in traditional types of capital, such as bulldozers and steel plants, and newer types of capital, such as computers and robots. The government invests in various forms of public capital, called *infrastructure*, such as roads, bridges, and sewer systems.

In addition, there is *human capital*—the knowledge and skills that workers acquire through education, from early childhood programs such as Head Start to on-the-job training for adults in the labor force. Although the basic Solow model includes only physical capital and does not try to explain the efficiency of labor, in many ways human capital is analogous to physical capital. Like physical capital, human capital raises our ability to produce goods and services. Raising the level of human capital requires investment in the form of teachers, libraries, and student time. Recent research on economic growth has emphasized that human capital is at least as important as physical capital in explaining international differences in standards of living.[6]

---

[6] Robert E. Lucas, Jr., "On the Mechanics of Economic Development," *Journal of Monetary Economics* 22 (1988): 3–42; N. Gregory Mankiw, David Romer, and David N. Weil, "A Contribution to the Empirics of Economic Growth," *Quarterly Journal of Economics* (May 1992): 407–437.

Policymakers trying to stimulate economic growth must confront the issue of what kinds of capital the economy needs most. In other words, what kinds of capital yield the highest marginal products? To a large extent, policymakers can rely on the marketplace to allocate the pool of saving to alternative types of investment. Those industries with the highest marginal products of capital will naturally be most willing to borrow at market interest rates to finance new investment. Many economists advocate that the government should merely create a "level playing field" for different types of capital—for example, by ensuring that the tax system treats all forms of capital equally. The government can then rely on the market to allocate capital efficiently.

Other economists have suggested that the government should actively encourage particular forms of capital. They argue that technological advance occurs as a beneficial by-product of certain economic activities. Such a by-product is called an *externality*. For example, new and improved production processes may be devised during the process of accumulating capital. If this speculation is correct, then the benefits of capital accumulation to society may be greater than the Solow model suggests.[7] Moreover, some types of capital accumulation may yield greater externalities than others. If, for example, installing robots yields greater technological externalities than building a new steel mill, then perhaps the government should use the tax laws to encourage investment in robots. The success of such a *technology policy,* as it is called, requires that the government be able to measure the externalities of different economic activities. Most economists are skeptical about such policies because the measurement problem is so difficult.

One type of capital that necessarily requires the government is public capital. Local, state, and federal governments are always deciding whether to borrow to finance new roads, bridges, and transit systems. During the presidential campaign of 1992, Bill Clinton argued that the United States had been investing too little in infrastructure. He claimed that a higher level of infrastructure investment would make the economy substantially more productive. Among economists, this claim had both defenders and critics. Yet all of them agree that measuring the marginal product of public capital is difficult. Private capital generates an easily measured rate of profit for the firm owning the capital, whereas the benefits of public capital are more diffuse.

Encouraging Technological Progress

The Solow model shows that sustained growth in income per worker must come from technological progress. The Solow model, however, takes technological progress as exogenous; it does not explain it. Unfortunately, the determinants of technological progress are not well understood.

Despite this limited understanding, many public policies are designed to stimulate technological progress. Most of these policies encourage the private sector to devote resources to technological innovation. For example, the patent system gives a temporary monopoly to inventors of new products; the tax code

[7]   Paul Romer, "Crazy Explanations for the Productivity Slowdown," *NBER Macroeconomics Annual 2* (1987): 163–201.

offers tax breaks for firms engaging in research and development; and government agencies such as the National Science Foundation directly subsidize basic research in universities. In addition, as discussed above, proponents of technology policy argue that the government should take a more active role in promoting specific industries that are key for rapid technological progress.

Case Study 4-6

The Worldwide Slowdown in Economic Growth

One of the most perplexing problems that policymakers have faced over the past 20 years is the worldwide slowdown in economic growth that began in the early 1970s. Table 4-5 presents data on the growth in real GDP per person for the seven major world economies. Growth in the United States fell from 2.2 percent to 1.5 percent. Other countries experienced similar or more severe declines.

Table 4-5

The Slowdown in Growth Around the World

Country	Growth in Output Per Person (percent per year)	
	1948–1972	1972–1992
Canada	2.9	2.1
France	4.3	2.0
West Germany	5.7	2.1
Italy	4.9	2.8
Japan	8.2	3.4
United Kingdom	2.4	1.8
United States	2.2	1.5

Source: Angus Maddison, *Phases of Capitalist Development* (Oxford: Oxford University Press, 1982); *International Financial Statistics.*

Studies have shown that the slowdown in growth is attributable to a slowdown in the rate at which the production function is improving over time. The appendix to this chapter explains how economists measure changes in the production function with a variable called *total factor productivity*, which is closely related to the efficiency of labor in the Solow model. Accumulated over many years, even a small change in productivity growth has a large effect on economic welfare. Real income in the United States today is more than 20 percent lower than it would have been had productivity growth remained at its previous level.

Many economists have attempted to explain this adverse change. Here are some of their explanations:

- The composition of the labor force has been changing. The entrance of the younger baby-boom generation into the labor force beginning in the 1970s lowered the average level of experience and, therefore, the productivity of labor.

- An increase in government regulations, such as those to protect the environment, requires firms to use less productive production methods. The regulations reduce growth in productivity and incomes (even if the policy is socially desirable).

- Large changes in oil prices in the 1970s caused by OPEC, the oil cartel, made some of the capital stock prematurely obsolete. Firms may have retired some of their machinery that was heavily dependent on fuel.

- The world has started to run out of new ideas about how to produce. We have entered an age of slower technological progress.

Which of these suspects is the culprit? All of them are plausible, but it is difficult to prove beyond a reasonable doubt that any one of them is guilty. The worldwide slowdown in economic growth largely remains a mystery.[8]

4-6 Conclusion: Beyond the Solow Model

Although the Solow model provides the best framework with which to start studying economic growth, it is only a beginning. The model simplifies many aspects of the world, and it omits many others altogether. Economists who study economic growth try to build more sophisticated models that allow them to address a broader range of questions.

These advanced models usually turn one of the exogenous variables in the Solow model into an endogenous variable. For example, the Solow model takes the rate of saving as exogenous. As we see in Chapter 15, consumption arises from the decisions of households about how much to consume today and how much to save for the future. More sophisticated growth models replace the consumption function of the Solow model with an explicit theory of household behavior.

Perhaps most important, economists have tried to build models to explain the level and growth of the efficiency of labor. The Solow model shows that sustained growth in standards of living can arise only from technological progress. Our understanding of economic growth will not be complete until we understand how private decisions and public policy affect technological progress. This is one of the greatest challenges facing economists today.

---

[8] For various views on the growth slowdown, see "Symposium: The Slowdown in Productivity Growth," *The Journal of Economic Perspectives* 2 (Fall 1988): 3–98.

Summary

1. The Solow growth model shows that in the long run, an economy's rate of saving determines the size of its capital stock and thus its level of production. The higher the rate of saving, the higher the stock of capital and the higher the level of output.

2. An increase in the rate of saving causes a period of high growth until the new steady state is reached. In the long run, the saving rate does not affect the growth rate. Sustained growth of output per worker depends on technological progress.

3. The level of capital that maximizes consumption is called the Golden Rule level. At this level, the net marginal product of capital equals the growth rate of output. Estimates for actual economies, such as the United States, suggest that the capital stock is well below the Golden Rule level. To reach the Golden Rule requires increased investment and thus lower consumption for current generations.

4. Economic policymakers often claim that the rate of capital accumulation should be increased. Increased public saving and tax incentives for private saving are two ways to encourage capital accumulation.

5. The Solow model shows that an economy's rate of population growth is another long-run determinant of the standard of living. The higher the rate of population growth, the lower the level of output per worker.

6. In the early 1970s, the rate of growth fell substantially in most industrialized countries. The cause of this slowdown is not well understood.

KEY CONCEPTS

Solow growth model

Steady state

Golden Rule level of capital accumulation

Efficiency of labor

Efficiency units of labor

Labor-augmenting technological progress

QUESTIONS FOR REVIEW

1. In the Solow model, how does the saving rate affect the steady-state level of income? How does it affect the steady-state rate of growth?

2. Why might an economic policymaker choose the Golden Rule level of capital?

3. Might a policymaker choose a steady state with more capital than in the Golden Rule steady state? With less capital than in the Golden Rule steady state? Explain your answers.

4. In the Solow model, how does the rate of population growth affect the steady-state level of income? How does it affect the steady-state rate of growth?

5. What determines the steady-state rate of growth of income per worker?

6. How can economic policy influence the saving rate?

7. What has happened to the rate of growth over the past 40 years? How might you explain this phenomenon?

PROBLEMS AND APPLICATIONS

1. Country A and country B both have the production function

$$Y = F(K, L) = K^{1/2}L^{1/2}.$$

a. Does this production function have constant returns to scale? Explain.

b. What is the per-worker production function, $y = f(k)$?

c. Assume that neither country experiences population growth or technological progress and that 5 percent of capital depreciates each year. Assume further that country A saves 10 percent of output each year and country B saves 20 percent of output each year. Using your answer from part (b) and the steady-state condition that investment equals depreciation, find the steady-state level of capital per worker for each country. Then find the steady-state levels of income per worker and consumption per worker.

d. Suppose both countries start off with a capital stock per worker of 2. What are the levels of income per worker and consumption per worker? Remembering that the change in the capital stock is investment less depreciation, use a calculator to show how the capital stock per worker will evolve over time in both countries. For each year, calculate income per worker and consumption per worker.

How many years will it be before the consumption in country B is higher than the consumption in country A?

2. In the discussion of German and Japanese postwar growth, the text describes what happens when part of the capital stock is destroyed in a war. By contrast, suppose that a war does not directly affect the capital stock, but that casualties reduce the labor force.

a. What is the immediate impact on total output and on output per person?

b. Assuming that the saving rate is unchanged and that the economy was in a steady state before the war, what happens subsequently to output per worker in the postwar economy? Is the growth rate of output per worker after the war smaller or greater than normal?

3. The 1983 *Economic Report of the President* contained the following statement: "Devoting a larger share of national output to investment would help restore rapid productivity growth and rising living standards." Do you agree with this claim? Explain.

4. Suppose the production function is

$$y = \sqrt{k}.$$

a. Solve for the steady-state value of y as a function of s, n, g, and δ.

b. A developed country has a saving rate of 28 percent and a population growth rate of 1 percent per year. A less-developed country has a saving rate of 10 percent and a population growth rate of 4 percent per year. In both countries, $g = 0.02$ and $\delta = 0.04$. Find the steady-state value of y for each country.

c. What policies might the less-developed country pursue to raise its level of income?

5. In the United States, the capital share of GDP is about 30 percent; the average growth in output is about 3 percent per year; the depreciation rate is about 4 percent per year; and the capital–output ratio is about 2.5. Suppose that the production function is Cobb-Douglas, so that the capital share in output is constant, and that the United States has been in a steady state. (For a discussion of the Cobb-Douglas production function, see the appendix to Chapter 3.)

a. What must the saving rate be in the initial steady state? [*Hint*: Use the steady-state relationship, $sy = (\delta + n + g)k$.]

b. What is the marginal product of capital in the initial steady state?

c. Suppose that public policy raises the saving rate so that the economy reaches the Golden Rule level of capital. What will the marginal product of capital be at the Golden Rule steady state? Compare the marginal product at the Golden Rule steady state to the marginal product in the initial steady state. Explain.

d. What will the capital–output ratio be at the Golden Rule steady state? (*Hint*: For the Cobb-Douglas production function, the capital–output ratio

is simply related to the marginal product of capital.)

e. What must the saving rate be to reach the Golden Rule steady state?

6. One view of the consumption function, sometimes advocated by Marxist economists, is that workers have high propensities to consume and capitalists have low propensities to consume. To explore the implications of this view, suppose that an economy consumes all wage income and saves all capital income. Show that if the factors of production earn their marginal product, this economy reaches the Golden Rule level of capital accumulation. (*Hint*: Begin with the identity that saving equals investment. Then use the steady-state condition that investment is just enough to keep up with depreciation, population growth, and technological progress, and the fact that saving equals capital income in this economy.)

7. Many demographers predict that the United States will have zero population growth in the twenty-first century, in contrast to average population growth of about 1 percent per year in the twentieth century. Use the Solow model to forecast the effect of this slowdown in population growth on the growth of total output and the growth of output per person. Consider the effects both in the steady state and in the transition between steady states.

8. Prove each of the following statements about the steady state with population growth and technological progress.

a. The capital–output ratio is constant.

b. The capital and labor shares of income are constant. [*Hint*: Recall the definition $MPK = f(k + 1) - f(k)$.]

c. Total capital income and total labor income both grow at the rate of population growth plus the rate of technological progress, $n + g$.

d. The real rental price of capital is constant, and the real wage grows at the rate of technological progress g. (*Hint*: The real rental price of capital equals total capital income divided by the capital stock, and the real wage equals total labor income divided by the labor force.)

9. The amount of education the typical person receives varies substantially among countries. Suppose you were to compare a country with a highly educated labor force and a country with a less educated labor force. Assume that the countries are otherwise the same: they have the same saving rate, the same depreciation rate, the same population growth rate, and the same rate of technological progress. Also assume that both countries are in their steady states. Using the Solow model, what would you predict for the following variables?

a. The rate of growth of total income.

b. The level of income per worker.

c. The real rental price of capital.

d. The real wage.

10. In the Solow model, population growth leads to growth in total output, but not in output per worker. Do you think this would still be true if the production function exhibited increasing or decreasing returns to scale? Explain. (For the definitions of increasing and decreasing returns to scale, see Chapter 3, "Problems and Applications," Problem 2.)

11. Suppose that the production function does not exhibit diminishing marginal product of capital and that, instead, the production function is

$$y = Ak,$$

where A is a positive constant.

a. Show that this production function implies that the marginal product of capital is constant.

b. Show that, in this case, a higher saving rate leads to a permanently higher growth rate. (Remember that growth in a variable X is defined to be $\Delta X / X$.)

c. Why does this conclusion differ from that in the Solow model?

d. Do you think this production function is reasonable? Explain.

Appendix

Accounting for the Sources of Economic Growth

Real GDP in the United States has grown an average of 3 percent per year over the past 40 years. What accounts for this growth? In Chapter 3 we linked the output of the economy to the factors of production—capital and labor—and to the production technology. Here we divide the growth in output into three different sources: increases in capital, increases in labor, and advances in technology. This breakdown provides us with a measure of the rate of technological change.

Increases in the Factors of Production

We first examine how increases in the factors of production contribute to increases in output. We assume there is no technological change. Therefore, the production function relating output Y to capital K and labor L does not change over time:

$$Y = F(K, L).$$

In this case, the amount of output changes only because the amount of capital or labor changes.

Increases in Capital   First, consider changes in capital. If the amount of capital increases by ΔK units, by how much does the amount of output increase? To answer this question, we need to recall the definition of the marginal product of capital MPK:

$$MPK = F(K + 1, L) - F(K, L).$$

The marginal product of capital tells us how much output increases when capital increases by 1 unit. Therefore, when capital increases by ΔK units, output increases by approximately $MPK \times \Delta K$.[9]

For example, suppose that the marginal product of capital is 1/5; that is, an additional unit of capital increases the amount of output produced by

---

[9] Note the word "approximately" here. This answer is only an approximation because the marginal product of capital varies: it falls as the amount of capital increases. An exact answer would take into account that each unit of capital has a different marginal product. If the change in K is not too large, however, the approximation of a constant marginal product is very accurate.

one-fifth of a unit. If we increase the amount of capital by 10 units, we can compute the amount of additional output as follows:

$$\Delta Y = MPK \times \Delta K$$

$$= 1/5 \frac{\text{Output}}{\text{Capital}} \times 10 \text{ Units of Capital}$$

$$= 2 \text{ Units of Output.}$$

By increasing capital by 10 units, we obtain 2 more units of output. Thus, we use the marginal product of capital to convert changes in capital into changes in output.

Increases in Labor   Next, consider changes in labor. If the amount of labor increases by ΔL units, by how much does output increase? We answer this question the same way we answered the question about capital. The marginal product of labor *MPL* tells us how much output changes when labor increases by 1 unit—that is,

$$MPL = F(K, L + 1) - F(K, L).$$

Therefore, when the amount of labor increases by ΔL units, output increases by approximately $MPL \times \Delta L$.

For example, suppose that the marginal product of labor is 2; that is, an additional unit of labor increases the amount of output produced by 2 units. If we increase the amount of labor by 10 units, we can compute the amount of additional output as follows:

$$\Delta Y = MPL \times \Delta L$$

$$= 2 \frac{\text{Output}}{\text{Labor}} \times 10 \text{ Units of Labor}$$

$$= 20 \text{ Units of Output.}$$

By increasing labor by 10 units, we obtain 20 more units of output. Thus, we use the marginal product of labor to convert changes in labor into changes in output.

Increases in Capital and Labor   Finally, let's consider the more realistic case in which both factors of production change. Suppose that the amount of capital increases by ΔK and the amount of labor increases by ΔL. The increase in output then comes from two sources: more capital and more labor. We can divide this increase into the two sources using the marginal products of the two inputs:

$$\Delta Y = (MPK \times \Delta K) + (MPL \times \Delta L).$$

The first term in parentheses is the increase in output resulting from the increase in capital, and the second term in parentheses is the increase in output resulting from the increase in labor. This equation shows us how to attribute growth to each factor of production.

We now want to convert this last equation into a form that is easier to interpret and apply to the available data. First, with some algebraic rearrangement, the equation becomes[10]

$$\frac{\Delta Y}{Y} = \left(\frac{MPK \times K}{Y}\right)\frac{\Delta K}{K} + \left(\frac{MPL \times L}{Y}\right)\frac{\Delta L}{L}.$$

This form of the equation relates the growth rate of output, $\Delta Y/Y$, to the growth rate of capital, $\Delta K/K$, and the growth rate of labor, $\Delta L/L$.

Next, we need to find some way to measure the terms in parentheses in the last equation. In Chapter 3 we showed that the marginal product of capital equals its real rental price. Therefore, $MPK \times K$ is the total return to capital, and $(MPK \times K)/Y$ is capital's share of output. Similarly, the marginal product of labor equals the real wage. Therefore, $MPL \times L$ is the total compensation that labor receives, and $(MPL \times L)/Y$ is labor's share of output. Under the assumption that the production function has constant returns to scale, Euler's theorem tells us that these two shares sum to 1. In this case, we can write

$$\frac{\Delta Y}{Y} = \alpha\frac{\Delta K}{K} + (1 - \alpha)\frac{\Delta L}{L},$$

where α is capital's share and $(1 - \alpha)$ is labor's share.

This last equation gives us a simple formula for showing how changes in inputs lead to changes in output. In particular, we must weight the growth rates of the inputs by the factor shares. As we discussed in the appendix to Chapter 3, capital's share in the United States is about 30 percent—that is, $\alpha = 0.30$. Therefore, a 10 percent increase in the amount of capital ($\Delta K/K = 0.10$) leads to a 3 percent increase in the amount of output ($\Delta Y/Y = 0.03$). Similarly, a 10 percent increase in the amount of labor ($\Delta L/L = 0.10$) leads to a 7 percent increase in the amount of output ($\Delta Y/Y = 0.07$).

Technological Progress

So far in our analysis of the sources of growth, we have been assuming that the production function does not change over time. In practice, of course, technological progress improves the production function. For the same amount of inputs, we get more output today than we did in the past. We now extend the analysis to allow for technological progress.

We include the effects of the changing technology by writing the production function as

$$Y = AF(K, L),$$

where A is a measure of the current level of technology called *total factor productivity*. Output now increases not only because of increases in capital and labor but also because of increases in total factor productivity. If total factor productivity increases by 1 percent and if the inputs are unchanged, then output increases by 1 percent.

---

[10] *Mathematical Note*: To see that this is equivalent to the previous equation, note that we can multiply both sides of this equation by Y and thereby cancel Y from three places. We can cancel the K in the top and bottom of the first term on the right-hand side and the L in the top and bottom of the second term on the right-hand side. These algebraic manipulations turn this equation into the previous one.

Allowing for a changing technology adds another term to our equation accounting for economic growth:

$$\frac{\Delta Y}{Y} = \alpha\frac{\Delta K}{K} + (1 - \alpha)\frac{\Delta L}{L} + \frac{\Delta A}{A}$$

$$\begin{matrix} \text{Growth in} \\ \text{Output} \end{matrix} = \begin{matrix} \text{Contribution} \\ \text{of Capital} \end{matrix} + \begin{matrix} \text{Contribution} \\ \text{of Labor} \end{matrix} + \begin{matrix} \text{Growth in Total} \\ \text{Factor Productivity.} \end{matrix}$$

This is the key equation of growth accounting. It identifies and allows us to measure the three sources of growth: changes in the amount of capital, changes in the amount of labor, and changes in total factor productivity.

Because total factor productivity is not observable directly, it is measured indirectly. We have data on the growth in output, capital, and labor; we also have data on capital's share of output. From these data and from the growth-accounting equation, we can compute the growth in total factor productivity to make sure that everything adds up:

$$\frac{\Delta A}{A} = \frac{\Delta Y}{Y} - \alpha\frac{\Delta K}{K} - (1 - \alpha)\frac{\Delta L}{L}.$$

$\Delta A/A$ is the change in output that cannot be explained by changes in inputs. Thus, the growth in total factor productivity is computed as a residual—that is, as the amount of output growth that remains after we have accounted for the determinants of growth that we can measure. Indeed, $\Delta A/A$ is sometimes called the *Solow residual*, after Robert Solow, who first showed how to compute it.[11]

Total factor productivity can change for many reasons. Changes most often arise because of increased knowledge about production methods. The Solow residual is often used as a measure of technological progress. Yet other factors, such as education and government regulation, can affect total factor productivity as well. For example, if higher public spending raises the quality of education, then workers may become more productive and output may rise, which implies higher total factor productivity. As another example, if government regulations require firms to purchase capital to reduce pollution or increase worker safety, then the capital stock may rise without any increase in measured output, which implies lower total factor productivity. *Total factor productivity captures anything that changes the relation between measured inputs and measured output.*

The Sources of Growth in the United States

Having learned how to measure the sources of economic growth, we now look at the data. Table 4A-1 uses U.S. data to measure the contributions of the three sources of growth between 1950 and 1994.

[11] Robert M. Solow, "Technical Change and the Aggregate Production Function," *Review of Economics and Statistics* 39 (1957): 312–320. It is natural to ask how growth in labor efficiency E relates to growth in total factor productivity. One can show that $\Delta A/A = (1 - \alpha)\Delta E/E$, where α is capital's share. Thus, technological change as measured by growth in the efficiency of labor is proportional to technological change as measured by the Solow residual.

Table 4A-1					
Accounting for Economic Growth in the United States					
			Source of Growth		
Years	Output Growth $\Delta Y/Y$	$=$	Capital $\alpha\Delta K/K$	Labor $(1-\alpha)\Delta L/L$	Total Factor Productivity $\Delta A/A$
		(average percent increase per year)		+	+
1950–1959	4.0		0.4	0.5	3.1
1960–1969	4.1		0.9	1.2	2.0
1970–1979	2.9		1.1	1.5	0.3
1980–1989	2.5		0.9	1.3	0.3
1990–1994	2.0		0.6	0.6	0.9
1950–1994	3.2		0.8	1.0	1.4

Source: U.S. Department of Commerce, U.S. Department of Labor, and the author's calculations. The parameter α is set to equal 0.3.

This table shows that real GDP has grown an average of 3.2 percent per year since 1950. Of this 3.2 percent, 0.8 percent is attributable to increases in the capital stock, 1.0 percent to increases in total hours worked, and 1.4 percent to increases in total factor productivity. These data show that increases in capital, labor, and productivity have contributed almost equally to economic growth in the United States.

Table 4A-1 also shows that the growth in total factor productivity slowed substantially around 1970. In Case Study 4-6 we discussed some hypotheses to explain this productivity slowdown.

Case Study *4-7*

• • • • • • • • • • • • •

Growth in the East Asian Tigers

Perhaps the most spectacular growth experiences in recent history have been those of the "Tigers" of East Asia: Hong Kong, Singapore, South Korea, and Taiwan. From 1966 to 1990, real income per person grew more than 7 percent per year in each of these countries, compared to about 2 percent per year in the United States. In 25 years, these countries went from being among the world's poorest economies to being among the richest.

What accounts for this success? Some commentators have argued that the success of these four countries is due to their ability to imitate foreign technologies. By adopting technology developed abroad, the argument goes, these countries managed to improve their production functions substantially. If this argument is correct, these countries should have experienced unusually rapid growth in total factor productivity.

One recent study shed light on this issue by examining in detail the data from these four countries. The study found that their exceptional growth can be traced to large increases in measured factor inputs: increases in labor-force participation, increases in the capital stock, and increases in educational attainment. In South Korea, for example, the investment–GDP ratio rose from about 5 percent in the 1950s to about 30 percent in the 1980s; the percentage of the working population with at least a high-school education went from 26 percent in 1966 to 75 percent in 1991.

Once we account for growth in labor, capital, and human capital, little of the growth in output is left to explain. None of these four countries experienced unusually rapid growth in total factor productivity. Indeed, the average growth in total factor productivity in the East Asian Tigers was almost exactly the same as growth in total factor productivity in the United States.[12]

● ● ● ● ● ● ● ● ● ● ● ● ●

MORE PROBLEMS AND APPLICATIONS

1. In the economy of Solovia, the owners of capital get two-thirds of national income, and the workers receive one-third.

a. The men of Solovia stay at home performing household chores, while the women work in factories. If some of the men started working outside the home so that the labor force increased by 5 percent, what would happen to the measured output of the economy? Does labor productivity—defined as output per worker—increase, decrease, or stay the same? Does total factor productivity increase, decrease, or stay the same?

b. In year 1, the capital stock was 6, the labor input was 3, and output was 12. In year 2, the capital stock was 7, the labor input was 4, and output was 14. What happened to total factor productivity between the two years?

2. Labor productivity is defined as Y/L, the amount of output divided by the amount of labor input. Start with the growth-accounting equation and show that the growth in labor productivity depends on growth in total factor productivity and growth in the capital–labor ratio. In particular, show that

$$\frac{\Delta(Y/L)}{Y/L} = \frac{\Delta A}{A} + \alpha \frac{\Delta(K/L)}{K/L}.$$

Hint: You may find the following mathematical trick helpful. If $z = wx$, then the growth rate of z is approximately the growth rate of w plus the growth rate of x. That is,

$$\Delta z/z \approx \Delta w/w + \Delta x/x.$$

3. Suppose an economy described by the Solow model is in a steady state with population growth n of 1.0 percent per year and technological progress g of 2.0 percent per year. Total output and total capital grow at 3.0 percent per year. Suppose further that the capital share of output is 0.3. If you used the growth-accounting equation to divide output growth into three sources—capital, labor, and total factor productivity—how much would you attribute to each source? Compare your results to the figures we found for the United States in Table 4A-1.

[12] Alwyn Young, "The Tyranny of Numbers: Confronting the Statistical Realities of the East Asian Growth Experience," *Quarterly Journal of Economics* 101 (August 1995): 641–680.

Unemployment

Chapter 5

Unemployed labor means human want in the midst of plenty.
This is the most challenging paradox of modern times.

Henry Wallace

Unemployment is the macroeconomic problem that affects individuals most directly and severely. For most people, the loss of a job means a reduced living standard and psychological distress. It is therefore no surprise that unemployment is a frequent topic of political debate. Many politicians have used the "misery index"—the sum of the inflation and unemployment rates—to measure the health of the economy and the success or failure of economic policies.

Economists study unemployment to identify its causes and to help improve the public policies that affect the unemployed. Some of these policies, such as job-training programs, assist people in regaining employment. Others, such as unemployment insurance, alleviate some of the economic hardships that the unemployed face. Still other policies affect the prevalence of unemployment inadvertently. For example, most economists believe that laws prescribing a high minimum wage lead to greater unemployment. By pointing out a policy's unintended side effects, economists can help policymakers evaluate the various options.

In our previous discussion of the labor market, we ignored unemployment. In our study of national income in Chapter 3 and economic growth in Chapter 4, we assumed that the economy reaches full employment. In reality, of course, not everyone in the labor force has a job all the time: all free-market economies experience some unemployment.

Figure 5-1 shows the rate of unemployment—the percentage of the labor force unemployed—in the United States since 1948. Notice that there is always some unemployment, although the amount fluctuates from year to year. In this chapter we begin our study of unemployment by discussing why there is unemployment and what determines its level. We do not study the year-to-year fluctuations in the rate of unemployment until Part Three of this book, which examines short-run economic fluctuations. Here we examine the determinants of the **natural rate of unemployment**—the average rate of unemployment around which the economy fluctuates.

Figure 5-1

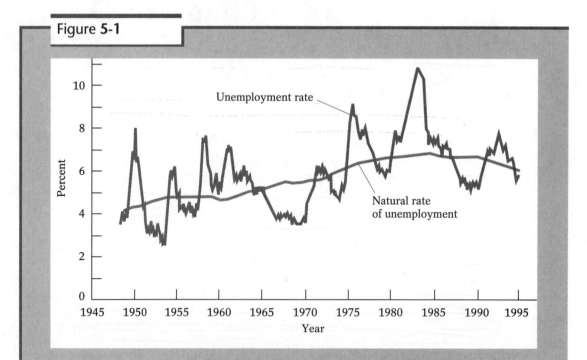

The Unemployment Rate and the Natural Rate of Unemployment in the United States There is always some unemployment. The natural rate of unemployment is the average level around which the unemployment rate fluctuates. (The natural rate of unemployment for any particular year is estimated here by averaging all the unemployment rates from ten years earlier to ten years later. Future unemployment rates are set at 6 percent.)

Source: U.S. Department of Labor.

5-1 Job Loss, Job Finding, and the Natural Rate of Unemployment

Every day some workers lose or quit their jobs, and some unemployed workers are hired. This perpetual ebb and flow determines the fraction of the labor force that is unemployed. In this section we develop a model of labor-force dynamics that shows what determines the natural rate of unemployment.[1]

Let L denote the labor force, E the number of employed workers, and U the number of unemployed workers. Because every worker is either employed or unemployed,

$$L = E + U.$$

The labor force is the sum of the employed and the unemployed. The rate of unemployment is U/L.

---

[1] Robert E. Hall, "A Theory of the Natural Rate of Unemployment and the Duration of Unemployment," *Journal of Monetary Economics* 5 (April 1979): 153–169.

To focus on the determinants of unemployment, we assume that the size of the labor force is fixed. The transition of individuals between employment and unemployment is illustrated in Figure 5-2. Let s denote the rate of job separation, the fraction of employed individuals who lose their job each month. Let f denote the rate of job finding, the fraction of unemployed individuals who find a job each month. We assume that both these rates are constant, and we see how together they determine the rate of unemployment.

Figure 5-2

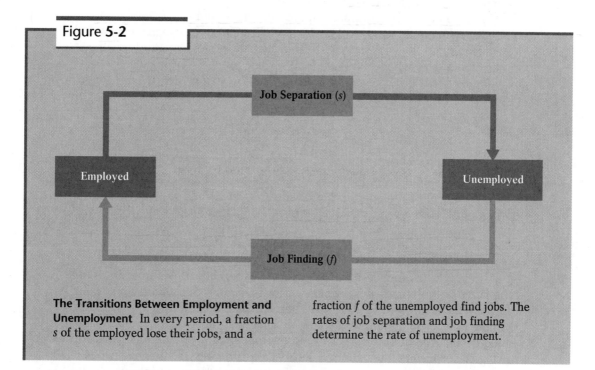

The Transitions Between Employment and Unemployment In every period, a fraction s of the employed lose their jobs, and a fraction f of the unemployed find jobs. The rates of job separation and job finding determine the rate of unemployment.

If the rate of unemployment is neither rising nor falling—that is, if the labor market is in a steady state—then the number of people finding jobs must equal the number of people losing jobs. Because fU is the number of people finding jobs and sE the number of people losing jobs, these two values must be equal:

$$fU = sE.$$

We can rearrange this equation to find the steady-state unemployment rate. Note that $E = L - U$; that is, the number of employed equals the labor force minus the number of unemployed. This implies that

$$fU = s(L - U).$$

Divide both sides of this equation by L to obtain

$$f\frac{U}{L} = s\left(1 - \frac{U}{L}\right).$$

Then solve for U/L to find

$$\frac{U}{L} = \frac{s}{s + f}.$$

This equation shows that the steady-state rate of unemployment U/L depends on the rates of job separation s and job finding f. The higher the rate of job separation, the higher the unemployment rate. The higher the rate of job finding, the lower the unemployment rate.

Here's a numerical example. Suppose that 1 percent of the employed lose their jobs each month ($s = 0.01$), which implies that the average job lasts 100 months, or about 8 years. Suppose further that about 20 percent of the unemployed find a job each month ($f = 0.20$), which implies that the average spell of unemployment lasts 5 months. In this case, the steady-state rate of unemployment is

$$\frac{U}{L} = \frac{0.01}{0.01 + 0.20}$$
$$= 0.0476.$$

The rate of unemployment in this example is about 5 percent.

This model of the natural rate of unemployment has an obvious but important implication for public policy. *Any policy aimed at lowering the natural rate of unemployment must either reduce the rate of job separation or increase the rate of job finding. Similarly, any policy that affects the rate of job separation or job finding also changes the natural rate of unemployment.*

Although this model is useful in relating the unemployment rate to job separation and job finding, it does not answer a central question: Why is there unemployment in the first place? If a person could always find a job quickly, then the rate of job finding would be very high, and the rate of unemployment would be near zero. This model of the unemployment rate assumes that job finding is not instantaneous, but it fails to explain why. In the next two sections, we examine two underlying reasons for unemployment: job search and wage rigidity.

5-2 Job Search and Frictional Unemployment

One reason for unemployment is that it takes time to match workers and jobs. The equilibrium model of the aggregate labor market discussed in Chapter 3 assumes that all workers and all jobs are identical, and therefore that all workers are equally well suited for all jobs. If this were really true and the labor market were in equilibrium, then a job loss would not cause unemployment: a laid-off worker would immediately find a new job at the market wage.

In fact, workers have different preferences and abilities, and jobs have different attributes. Furthermore, the flow of information about job candidates and job vacancies is imperfect, and the geographic mobility of workers is not instantaneous. Searching for an appropriate job takes time and effort. Indeed, because different jobs require different skills and pay different wages, unemployed workers may not accept the first job offer they receive. The unemployment caused by the time it takes workers to search for a job is called **frictional unemployment**.

Some frictional unemployment is inevitable in a changing economy. For many reasons, the types of goods that firms and households demand vary over time. As the demand for goods shifts, so does the demand for the labor that produces those goods. The invention of the personal computer, for example, reduced the demand for typewriters and, as a result, for labor by typewriter manufacturers. At the same time, it increased the demand for labor in the electronics industry. Similarly, because different regions produce different goods, the demand for labor may be rising in one part of the country while it is falling in another. An increase in the price of oil may cause the demand for labor to rise in oil-producing states such as Texas and fall in auto-producing states such as Michigan. Economists call such a change in the composition of demand among industries or regions a **sectoral shift**. Because sectoral shifts are always occurring, and because it takes time for workers to change sectors, there is always frictional unemployment.

Sectoral shifts are not the only cause of job separation and frictional unemployment. In addition, workers find themselves unexpectedly out of work when their firm fails, when their job performance is deemed unacceptable, or when their particular skills are no longer needed. Workers also may quit their jobs to change careers or to move to different parts of the country. As long as the supply and demand for labor among firms is changing, frictional unemployment is unavoidable.

Public Policy and Frictional Unemployment

Many public policies seek to decrease the natural rate of unemployment by reducing frictional unemployment. Government employment agencies disseminate information about job vacancies in order to match jobs and workers more efficiently. Public retraining programs are designed to ease the transition of workers from declining to growing industries. To the extent that these various programs increase the rate of job finding, they decrease the natural rate of unemployment.

Other government programs inadvertently increase the amount of frictional unemployment. One of these is **unemployment insurance**. Under this program, unemployed workers can collect a fraction of their wages for a certain period after losing their jobs. Although the precise terms of the program differ from year to year and from state to state, a typical worker covered by unemployment insurance in the United States receives 50 percent of his or her former wages for 26 weeks. In many European countries, unemployment-insurance programs are even more generous.

By softening the economic hardship of unemployment, unemployment insurance increases the amount of frictional unemployment and raises the natural rate. The unemployed who receive unemployment-insurance benefits are less pressed to search for new employment, and they are more likely to turn down unattractive job offers. This reduces the rate of job finding. In addition, when negotiating employment agreements, workers are less likely to seek guarantees of job security, because they know that unemployment insurance will partially protect their incomes. This raises the rate of job separation.

That unemployment insurance raises the natural rate of unemployment does not necessarily imply that the policy is undesirable. The program has the benefit of reducing workers' uncertainty about their incomes. Moreover, inducing workers to reject unattractive job offers may lead to a better matching between workers and jobs. Evaluating the costs and benefits of different systems of unemployment insurance is a difficult task that continues to be a topic of much research.

Economists who study unemployment insurance often propose ways to reform the system in order to reduce the amount of unemployment. One common proposal is to require a firm that lays off a worker to pay for that worker's unemployment benefits in full. Such a system is called *100 percent experience rated*, because the rate that each firm pays for unemployment insurance fully reflects the unemployment experience of its own workers. Most current programs are *partially experience rated*. Under this system, when a firm lays off a worker, it is charged only part of the worker's unemployment benefits; the remainder comes from the program's general revenue. Because a firm pays only a fraction of the cost of the unemployment it causes, it has an incentive to lay off workers when its demand for labor is temporarily low. By reducing that incentive, the proposed reform may reduce the prevalence of temporary layoffs.

Case Study 5-1

• • • • • • • • • • • • •

Unemployment Insurance and the Rate of Job Finding

Many studies have examined the effect of unemployment insurance on job search. The most persuasive studies use data on the experiences of unemployed individuals, rather than economy-wide rates of unemployment. Individual data often yield sharp results that are open to few alternative explanations.

One study followed the experience of individual workers as they used up their eligibility for unemployment-insurance benefits. It found that when unemployed workers become ineligible for benefits, they are more likely to find new jobs. In particular, the probability of a person finding a new job more than doubles when his or her benefits run out. This result suggests that an absence of benefits greatly increases the search effort of unemployed workers.[2]

Additional evidence on how economic incentives affect job search comes from an experiment that the state of Illinois ran in 1985. Randomly selected new claimants for unemployment insurance were each offered a $500 bonus if they found employment within 11 weeks. The subsequent experience of this

[2] Lawrence F. Katz and Bruce D. Meyer, "Unemployment Insurance, Recall Expectations, and Unemployment Outcomes," *Quarterly Journal of Economics* 105 (November 1990): 973–1002.

group was compared to that of a control group not offered the incentive. The average duration of unemployment for the group offered the $500 bonus was 17.0 weeks, compared to 18.3 weeks for the control group. Thus, the bonus reduced the average spell of unemployment by 7 percent, suggesting that more effort was devoted to job search. This experiment shows clearly that the incentives provided by the unemployment-insurance system affect the rate of job finding.[3]

5-3   Real-Wage Rigidity and Wait Unemployment

A second reason for unemployment is **wage rigidity**—the failure of wages to adjust until labor supply equals labor demand. In the equilibrium model of the labor market, as outlined in Chapter 3, the real wage adjusts to equilibrate supply and demand. Yet wages are not always flexible. Sometimes the real wage is stuck above the market-clearing level.

Figure 5-3 shows why wage rigidity leads to unemployment. When the real wage is above the level that equilibrates supply and demand, the quantity of labor supplied exceeds the quantity demanded. Firms must in some way ration the scarce jobs among workers. Real-wage rigidity reduces the rate of job finding and raises the level of unemployment.

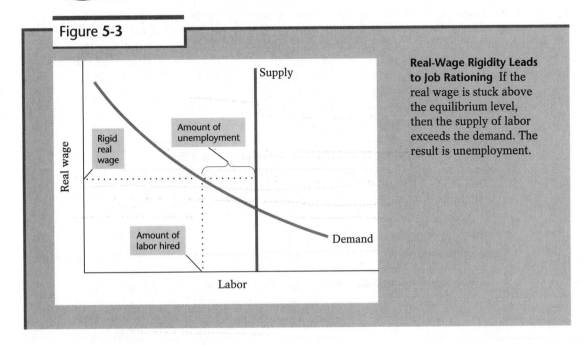

Figure 5-3

Real-Wage Rigidity Leads to Job Rationing If the real wage is stuck above the equilibrium level, then the supply of labor exceeds the demand. The result is unemployment.

---

[3] Stephen A. Woodbury and Robert G. Spiegelman, "Bonuses to Workers and Employers to Reduce Unemployment: Randomized Trials in Illinois," *American Economic Review* 77 (September 1987): 513–530.

The unemployment resulting from wage rigidity and job rationing is called **wait unemployment**. Workers are unemployed not because they are actively searching for the jobs that best suit their individual skills but because, at the going wage, the supply of labor exceeds the demand. These workers are simply waiting for jobs to become available.

To understand wage rigidity and wait unemployment, we must examine why the labor market does not clear. When the real wage exceeds the equilibrium level and the supply of workers exceeds the demand, we might expect firms to lower the wages they pay. Wait unemployment arises because firms fail to reduce wages despite an excess supply of labor. We now turn to three causes of this wage rigidity: minimum-wage laws, the monopoly power of unions, and efficiency wages.

Minimum-Wage Laws

The government causes wage rigidity when it prevents wages from falling to equilibrium levels. Minimum-wage laws set a legal minimum on the wages that firms pay their employees. Since the passage of the Fair Labor Standards Act of 1938, the U.S. federal government has enforced a minimum wage that usually has been between 30 and 50 percent of the average wage in manufacturing. For most workers, this minimum wage is not binding, because they earn well above the minimum. Yet for some workers, especially the unskilled and inexperienced, the minimum wage raises their wage above its equilibrium level. It therefore reduces the quantity of their labor that firms demand.

Economists believe that the minimum wage has its greatest impact on teenage unemployment. The equilibrium wages of teenagers tend to be low for two reasons. First, because teenagers are among the least skilled and least experienced members of the labor force, they tend to have low marginal productivity. Second, teenagers often take some of their "compensation" in the form of on-the-job training rather than direct pay. An apprenticeship is a classic example of training offered in place of wages. For both these reasons, the wage at which the supply of teenage workers equals the demand is low. The minimum wage is therefore more often binding for teenagers than for others in the labor force.

Many economists have studied the impact of the minimum wage on teenage employment. These researchers compare the variation in the minimum wage over time with the variation in the number of teenagers with jobs. These studies find that a 10 percent increase in the minimum wage reduces teenage employment by 1 to 3 percent.[4]

The minimum wage is a perennial source of political debate. Advocates of a higher minimum wage view it as a means of raising the income of the working poor. Certainly, the minimum wage provides only a meager standard of living. In 1994, when the minimum wage was $4.25 per hour, two adults working full time would just exceed the official poverty level of $15,141 for a family of four.

---

[4] Charles Brown, "Minimum Wage Laws: Are They Overrated?" *Journal of Economic Perspectives* 2 (Summer 1988): 133–146.

Opponents of a higher minimum wage argue that it is not the best way to help the working poor. They contend not only that the increased labor costs would raise unemployment, but also that the minimum wage is poorly targeted. Many minimum-wage earners are teenagers from middle-class homes working for discretionary spending money. Of the approximately 3 million workers who earn the minimum wage, more than one-third are teenagers.

To mitigate the effects on teenage unemployment, some economists and policymakers have long advocated exempting young workers from the regular minimum wage. This would permit a lower wage for teenagers, thereby reducing their unemployment and enabling them to get training and job experience. Opponents of this exemption argue that it gives firms an incentive to substitute teenagers for unskilled adults, thereby raising unemployment among that group. A limited exemption of this kind was tried from 1991 to 1993. Because of many restrictions on its use, however, it had only limited effect and, therefore, was not renewed by Congress.

Many economists and policymakers believe that tax credits are a better way to help the working poor. The *earned income tax credit* is an amount that poor working families are allowed to subtract from the taxes they owe. For a family with very low income, the credit exceeds its taxes, and the family receives a payment from the government. Unlike the minimum wage, the earned income tax credit does not raise labor costs to firms and, therefore, does not reduce the quantity of labor that firms demand. It has the disadvantage, however, of reducing the government's tax revenue.

Case Study 5-2

• • • • • • • • • • • • •

A Revisionist View of the Minimum Wage

Although most economists believe that increases in the minimum wage reduce employment among workers with little skill and experience, some recent studies question this conclusion. Three widely respected labor economists—David Card, Lawrence Katz, and Alan Krueger—examined several instances of minimum-wage changes in order to determine the magnitude of the employment response. What they found was startling.

One study examined hiring by fast-food restaurants in New Jersey when New Jersey raised the state minimum wage. Fast-food restaurants are a natural type of firm to examine because they employ many low-wage workers. To control for other effects, such as overall economic conditions, the New Jersey restaurants were compared to similar restaurants across the river in Pennsylvania. Pennsylvania did not raise its minimum wage at the same time. According to standard theory, employment in New Jersey restaurants should have fallen relative to employment in Pennsylvania restaurants. In contrast to this hypothesis, the data showed that employment *rose* in the New Jersey restaurants.

How is this seemingly perverse result possible? One explanation is that firms have some market power in the labor market. As you may have learned in courses in microeconomics, a monopsony firm buys less labor at a lower wage than a competitive firm would. In essence, the firm reduces employment in order to depress the wage it has to pay. A minimum wage prevents the monopsony firm from following this strategy and so (up to a point) can increase employment.

This new view of the minimum wage is controversial. Critics have questioned the reliability of the data used in the New Jersey study. Some studies using other data sources have reached the traditional conclusion that the minimum wage depresses employment. Moreover, most economists are skeptical of the monopsony explanation, since most firms compete with many other firms for workers. Yet this new view has directly affected the policy debate. Lawrence Katz was the first chief economist in the Department of Labor during the Clinton Administration. He was followed in this job by Alan Krueger. It is therefore not surprising that President Clinton has repeatedly advocated increases in the national minimum wage.[5]

Unions and Collective Bargaining

A second cause of wage rigidity is the monopoly power of unions. Table 5-1 shows the importance of unions in 12 major countries. In the United States, only 16 percent of workers belong to unions. In most European countries, unions play a greater role.

Table 5-1

Union Membership as a Percentage of Employment

Sweden	84
Denmark	75
Italy	47
United Kingdom	41
Australia	34
Canada	33
Germany	33
Netherlands	28
Switzerland	28
Japan	26
United States	16
France	11

Source: Clara Chang and Constance Sorrentino, "Union Membership Statistics in 12 Countries," *Monthly Labor Review* (December 1991): 46–53.

[5] To read more about this new view of the minimum wage, see David Card and Alan Krueger, *Myth and Measurement: The New Economics of the Minimum Wage* (Princeton, N.J.: Princeton University Press, 1995); Lawrence Katz and Alan Krueger, "The Effect of the Minimum Wage on the Fast-Food Industry," *Industrial and Labor Relations Review* 46 (October 1992): 6–21.

The wages of unionized workers are determined not by the equilibrium of supply and demand but by collective bargaining between union leaders and firm management. Often, the final agreement raises the wage above the equilibrium level and allows the firm to decide how many workers to employ. The result is a reduction in the number of workers hired and an increase in wait unemployment.

Unions can also influence the wages paid by firms whose work forces are not unionized because the threat of unionization can keep wages above the equilibrium level. Most firms dislike unions. Unions not only raise wages but also increase the bargaining power of labor on many other issues, such as hours of employment and working conditions. A firm may choose to pay its workers high wages to keep them happy in order to discourage them from forming a union.

The unemployment caused by unions and by the threat of unionization is an instance of conflict between different groups of workers—**insiders** and **outsiders**. Those workers already employed by a firm, the insiders, typically try to keep their firm's wages high. The unemployed, the outsiders, bear part of the cost of higher wages because at a lower wage they might be hired. These two groups inevitably have conflicting interests. The effect of any bargaining process on wages and employment depends crucially on the relative influence of each group.

Case Study 5-3

• • • • • • • • • • • • •

Unionization and Unemployment in the United States and Canada

Throughout the 1960s the United States and Canada had similar labor markets. The rates of unemployment in the two countries were about the same on average, and they fluctuated together. In the mid-1970s, the experiences of the two countries began to diverge. Unemployment became much more prevalent in Canada than in the United States. Over the past decade, the Canadian unemployment rate has been about 2 to 3 percentage points above the U.S. unemployment rate.

The changing roles of unions in the two countries is one possible explanation for this divergence. In the 1960s, about 30 percent of the labor force was unionized in each country. But Canadian labor laws did more to foster unionization than U.S. laws did. Unionization rose in Canada while it fell in the United States.

As one might have predicted, changes in real wages accompanied the change in unionization. The real wage in Canada increased by about 30 percent relative to the real wage in the United States. This evidence suggests that unions in Canada pushed the real wage further above the equilibrium level, leading to more wait unemployment.

The divergence in the two unemployment rates may also be attributable to the increase in the availability of unemployment-insurance benefits in Canada.

Not only does unemployment insurance raise search times and the amount of frictional unemployment, but it also interacts with the effects of unionization in two ways. First, unemployment insurance makes unemployed workers more willing to wait for a high-wage job in a unionized firm rather than take a lower-wage job in a nonunion firm. Second, since unemployment insurance partially protects the incomes of unemployed workers, it makes unions more willing to press for high wages at the expense of lower employment.[6]

Efficiency Wages

Efficiency-wage theories propose a third cause of wage rigidity in addition to minimum-wage laws and unionization. These theories hold that high wages make workers more productive. The influence of wages on worker efficiency may explain the failure of firms to cut wages despite an excess supply of labor. Even though a wage reduction would lower a firm's wage bill, it would also—if these theories are correct—lower worker productivity and the firm's profits.

Economists have proposed various theories to explain how wages affect worker productivity. One efficiency-wage theory, which is applied mostly to poorer countries, holds that wages influence nutrition. Better-paid workers can afford a more nutritious diet, and healthier workers are more productive. A firm may decide to pay a wage above the equilibrium level to maintain a healthy work force. Obviously, this consideration is not important for employers in wealthy countries, such as the United States and most of Europe, since the equilibrium wage is well above the level necessary to maintain good health.

A second efficiency-wage theory, which is more relevant for developed countries, holds that high wages reduce labor turnover. Workers quit jobs for many reasons—to accept better positions at other firms, to change careers, or to move to other parts of the country. The more a firm pays its workers, the greater their incentive to stay with the firm. By paying a high wage, a firm reduces the frequency of quits, thereby decreasing the time spent hiring and training new workers.

A third efficiency-wage theory holds that the average quality of a firm's work force depends on the wage it pays its employees. If a firm reduces its wage, the best employees may take jobs elsewhere, leaving the firm with inferior employees who have fewer alternative opportunities. Economists call this unfavorable sorting *adverse selection*. By paying a wage above the equilibrium level, the firm may reduce adverse selection, improve the average quality of its work force, and thereby increase productivity.

A fourth efficiency-wage theory holds that a high wage improves worker effort. This theory posits that firms cannot perfectly monitor their employees' work effort, and that employees must themselves decide how hard to work. Workers can choose to work hard, or they can choose to shirk and risk getting caught and fired. Economists call this possibility of dishonest behavior *moral*

---

[6] Herbert G. Grubel, "Drifting Apart: Canadian and U.S. Labor Markets," *Contemporary Policy Issues* 6 (January 1988): 39–55; also in *Journal of Economic and Monetary Affairs* 2 (Winter 1988): 59–75.

hazard. The firm can reduce the problem of moral hazard by paying a high wage. The higher the wage, the greater the cost to the worker of getting fired. By paying a higher wage, a firm induces more of its employees not to shirk and thus increases their productivity.

All these efficiency-wage theories share the theme that the firm operates more efficiently if it pays its workers a high wage. These theories imply that it is sometimes in the firm's interest to keep wages above the equilibrium level. The result of this wage rigidity is wait unemployment.[7]

Case Study *5-4*

● ● ● ● ● ● ● ● ● ● ● ●

Henry Ford's $5 Workday

In 1914 the Ford Motor Company started paying its workers $5 per day. Since the prevailing wage at the time was between $2 and $3 per day, Ford's wage was well above the equilibrium level. Not surprisingly, long lines of job seekers waited outside the Ford plant gates hoping for a chance to earn this high wage.

What was Ford's motive? Henry Ford later wrote, "We wanted to pay these wages so that the business would be on a lasting foundation. We were building for the future. A low wage business is always insecure. . . . The payment of five dollars a day for an eight hour day was one of the finest cost cutting moves we ever made."

From the standpoint of traditional economic theory, Ford's explanation seems peculiar. He was suggesting that *high* wages imply *low* costs. But perhaps Ford had discovered efficiency-wage theory. Perhaps he was using the high wage to increase worker productivity.

Evidence suggests that paying such a high wage did benefit the company. According to an engineering report written at the time, "The Ford high wage does away with all the inertia and living force resistance. . . . The workingmen are absolutely docile, and it is safe to say that since the last day of 1913, every single day has seen major reductions in Ford shops' labor costs." Absenteeism fell by 75 percent, suggesting a large increase in worker effort. Alan Nevins, a historian who studied the early Ford Motor Company, wrote, "Ford and his associates freely declared on many occasions that the high wage policy had turned out to be good business. By this they meant that it had improved the discipline of the workers, given them a more loyal interest in the institution, and raised their personal efficiency."[8]

● ● ● ● ● ● ● ● ● ● ●

---

[7] For more extended discussions of efficiency wages, see Janet Yellen, "Efficiency Wage Models of Unemployment," *American Economic Review Papers and Proceedings* (May 1984): 200–205; and Lawrence Katz, "Efficiency Wages: A Partial Evaluation," *NBER Macroeconomics Annual* (1986): 235–276.

[8] Jeremy I. Bulow and Lawrence H. Summers, "A Theory of Dual Labor Markets With Application to Industrial Policy, Discrimination, and Keynesian Unemployment," *Journal of Labor Economics* 4 (July 1986): 376–414; Daniel M. G. Raff and Lawrence H. Summers, "Did Henry Ford Pay Efficiency Wages?" *Journal of Labor Economics* 5 (October 1987, Part 2): S57–S86.

5-4   Patterns of Unemployment

We now turn to some additional facts about unemployment. These facts will help us to evaluate our theories of unemployment and assess public policies aimed at reducing it.

The Duration of Unemployment

When a person becomes unemployed, is the spell of unemployment likely to be short or long? The answer to this question is important because it indicates the reasons for the unemployment and what policy response is appropriate. On the one hand, if most unemployment is short-term, one might argue that it is frictional and perhaps unavoidable. Unemployed workers may need some time to search for the job that is best suited to their skills and tastes. On the other hand, long-term unemployment cannot easily be attributed to the time it takes to match jobs and workers: we would not expect this matching process to take many months. Long-term unemployment is more likely to be wait unemployment. Thus, data on the duration of unemployment can affect our view about the reasons for unemployment.

The answer to our question turns out to be subtle. The data show that most spells of unemployment are short, but that most weeks of unemployment are attributable to the long-term unemployed. Consider the data for a typical year, 1974, during which the unemployment rate was 5.6 percent. In that year, 60 percent of the spells of unemployment ended within one month, yet 69 percent of the weeks of unemployment occurred in spells that lasted two or more months.[9]

To see how both these facts can be true, consider the following example. Suppose that 10 people are unemployed for part of a given year. Of these 10 people, 8 are unemployed for 1 month, and 2 are unemployed for 12 months, totaling 32 months of unemployment. In this example, most spells of unemployment are short: 8 of the 10 unemployment spells, or 80 percent, end in 1 month. Yet most months of unemployment are attributable to the long-term unemployed: 24 of the 32 months of unemployment, or 75 percent, are experienced by the 2 workers who are unemployed for 12 months. Depending on whether we look at spells of unemployment or months of unemployment, most unemployment can appear to be short-term or long-term.

This evidence on the duration of unemployment has an important implication for public policy. If the goal is to lower substantially the rate of unemployment, policies must aim at the long-term unemployed, because these individuals account for a large amount of unemployment. Yet policies must be carefully targeted, because the long-term unemployed constitute a small minority of those who become unemployed. Most people who become unemployed find work within a short time.

---

[9] Kim B. Clark and Lawrence H. Summers, "Labor Market Dynamics and Unemployment: A Reconsideration," *Brookings Papers on Economic Activity* (1979:1): 13–72.

Variation in the Unemployment Rate Across Demographic Groups

The rate of unemployment varies substantially across different groups within the population. Table 5-2 presents the U.S. unemployment rates for different demographic groups for 1994, when the overall rate was 6.1 percent.

Table 5-2	Unemployment Rate by Demographic Group: 1994			
Age	White Male	White Female	Black Male	Black Female
16–19	16.3	13.8	37.6	32.6
20 and over	4.8	4.6	10.3	9.8

Source: U.S. Department of Labor.

This table shows that younger workers have much higher unemployment rates than older ones. To explain this difference, recall our model of the natural rate of unemployment. The model isolates two possible causes for a high rate of unemployment: a low rate of job finding, or a high rate of job separation. When economists study data on the transition of individuals between employment and unemployment, they find that those groups with high unemployment tend to have high rates of job separation. They find less variation across groups in the rate of job finding. For example, an employed white male is four times more likely to become unemployed if he is a teenager than if he is middle-aged; once unemployed, his rate of job finding is not closely related to his age.

These findings help explain the higher unemployment rates for younger workers. Younger workers have only recently entered the labor market, and they are often uncertain about their career plans. It may be best for them to try different types of jobs before making a long-term commitment to a specific occupation. If so, we should expect a higher rate of job separation and a higher rate of frictional unemployment for this group.

Another fact that stands out from Table 5-2 is that unemployment rates are much higher for blacks than for whites. This phenomenon is not well understood. Data on transitions between employment and unemployment show that the higher unemployment rates for blacks, and especially for black teenagers, arise because of both higher rates of job separation and lower rates of job finding. Possible reasons for the lower rates of job finding include less access to informal job-finding networks and discrimination by employers.

The Upward Drift in Unemployment

Over the past 40 years, the rate of unemployment in the United States has drifted upward. As Figure 5-4 shows, unemployment averaged well below 5 percent in the 1950s and 1960s, and well over 6 percent in the 1970s, 1980s, and early 1990s. Although economists do not have a conclusive explanation for this change, they have proposed various hypotheses.

Figure 5-4

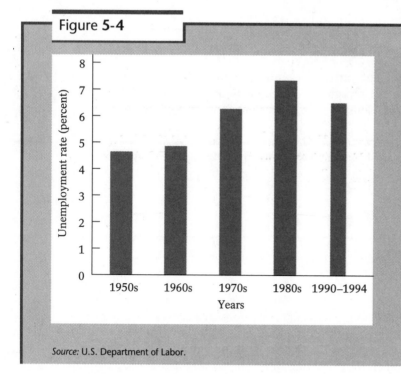

The Upward Drift in the Unemployment Rate The rate of unemployment in the United States has gradually drifted upward: the average in each decade since 1950 has exceeded that in the previous decade. The trend appears to have reversed in the 1990s.

Source: U.S. Department of Labor.

One explanation stresses the changing composition of the U.S. labor force. After World War II, birth rates rose dramatically, producing a baby-boom generation that began entering the labor force around 1970. Because younger workers have higher unemployment rates, this influx of baby-boomers into the labor force increased the average level of unemployment. At roughly the same time, the participation of women in the labor force was also increasing significantly. In 1960 women made up 33 percent of the labor force; by 1980 this proportion had risen to 43 percent. Since women historically have had higher unemployment rates than men (a difference that has disappeared in recent years), the increasing proportion of women in the labor force may have raised the average unemployment rate.

These two demographic changes, however, cannot fully explain the upward trend in unemployment because the trend was also apparent for fixed demographic groups. For example, for men between the ages of 25 and 54, the average unemployment rate rose from 3.2 percent in the 1950s and 1960s to 5.8 percent in the 1980s and early 1990s.

A second explanation is that the increase in women's labor-force participation, by increasing the number of two-income households, also increased the unemployment rate for men. Unemployed men with working wives may be more likely to turn down unattractive job offers than are men who are the sole breadwinners. If so, the resulting decrease in the rate of job finding by men would increase their unemployment rate.

Though plausible, this explanation is hard to reconcile with the evidence. Contrary to what one might expect, men with working wives have lower unemployment rates than men whose wives do not work.[10] Moreover, the unemployment rate for single men has also drifted upward. Thus, the increasing prevalence of two-income households cannot fully explain the upward drift in overall unemployment.

A third possible explanation for the upward trend in unemployment is that sectoral shifts have become more prevalent. The greater the amount of sectoral reallocation, the greater the rate of job separation and the higher the level of frictional unemployment.[11] One source of sectoral shifts has been the volatility in oil prices caused by the international oil cartel, OPEC. As shown in Figure 5-5, the relative price of oil was stable until the early 1970s. The large

Figure 5-5

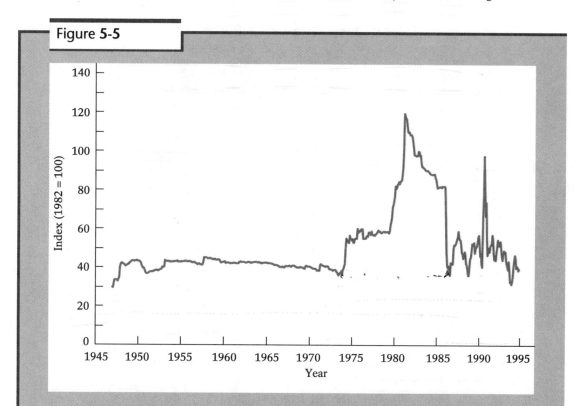

The Relative Price of Oil: A Source of Sectoral Shifts This figure shows the relative price of oil, as measured by the producer price index for crude petroleum divided by the producer price index for all commodities. It shows that, since the early 1970s, the relative price of oil has been highly volatile. Changes in this relative price are a possible source of sectoral shifts and therefore may help to explain the increase in the unemployment rate over time.

Source: U.S. Department of Labor.

[10] Kevin M. Murphy and Robert H. Topel, "The Evolution of Unemployment in the United States: 1968–1985," *NBER Macroeconomics Annual* (1987): 11–68.

[11] David M. Lilien, "Sectoral Shifts and Cyclical Unemployment," *Journal of Political Economy* 90 (August 1982): 777–793.

changes in oil prices since 1972 may have required reallocating labor between more-energy-intensive and less-energy-intensive sectors. If so, oil-price volatility may have increased the rate of unemployment. This explanation has been hard to evaluate. It is, however, consistent with recent developments: in the 1990s, oil prices have become more stable, and the average level of unemployment has fallen somewhat.

In the end, the upward drift in the unemployment rate remains a mystery. Some of the proposed explanations are plausible, but none seems conclusive. Perhaps there is no single answer. The upward drift in the unemployment rate may be the result of several unrelated developments.

Transitions Into and Out of the Labor Force

So far we have been ignoring an important aspect of labor-market dynamics: the movement of individuals into and out of the labor force. Our model of the natural rate of unemployment assumes that the labor force is fixed. In this case, the sole reason for unemployment is job separation, and the sole reason for leaving unemployment is job finding.

In fact, changes in the labor force are important. About one-third of the unemployed have only recently entered the labor force. Some of these entrants are young workers still looking for their first jobs; the others have worked before but had temporarily left the labor force. In addition, not all unemployment ends with job finding: almost half of all spells of unemployment end in the unemployed person's withdrawal from the labor market.

These individuals entering and leaving the labor force make unemployment statistics more difficult to interpret. On the one hand, some individuals calling themselves unemployed may not be seriously looking for a job and perhaps should best be viewed as out of the labor force. Their "unemployment" may not represent a social problem. On the other hand, some individuals may want a job but, after an unsuccessful search, have given up looking. These **discouraged workers** are counted as being out of the labor force and do not show up in unemployment statistics. Even though their joblessness is unmeasured, it may nonetheless be a social problem.

The Rise in European Unemployment

Although our discussion has focused primarily on unemployment in the United States, one puzzling question about unemployment concerns recent developments in Europe. Figure 5-6 shows the rate of unemployment in the countries that make up the European Community—Austria, Belgium, Denmark, Finland, France, Germany, Greece, Ireland, Italy, Luxembourg, Netherlands, Portugal, Spain, Sweden, and the United Kingdom. As you can see, the rate of unemployment has risen substantially in recent years. It averaged 4.1 percent from 1970 to 1980 and 9.8 percent from 1984 to 1994. This adverse development has been given its own name—*Eurosclerosis*.

What is the cause of rising European unemployment? No one knows for sure, but there is a leading theory. Many economists believe that the problem

Figure 5-6

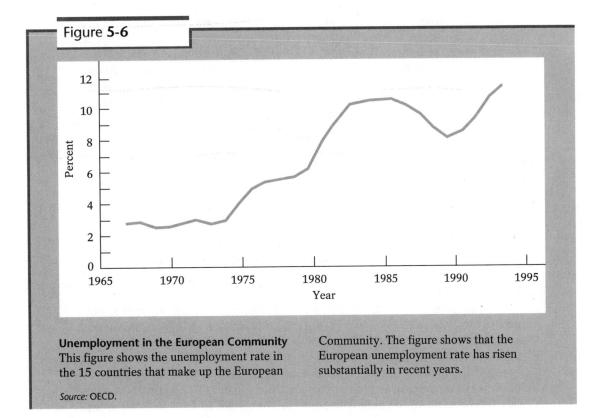

Unemployment in the European Community
This figure shows the unemployment rate in the 15 countries that make up the European Community. The figure shows that the European unemployment rate has risen substantially in recent years.

Source: OECD.

can be traced to generous benefits for unemployed workers, coupled with a technologically driven fall in the demand for unskilled workers relative to skilled workers.

There is no question that most European countries have generous programs for those without jobs. These programs go by various names: social insurance, the welfare state, or simply the dole. Many countries allow the unemployed to collect benefits indefinitely, rather than for only a short period of time as in the United States. Studies have shown that countries with more generous benefits tend to have higher rates of unemployment. In some sense, those living on the dole are really out of the labor force: given the employment opportunities available, taking a job is less attractive than remaining without work. Yet these people are often counted as unemployed in government statistics.

There is also no question that the demand for unskilled workers has fallen relative to the demand for skilled workers. This change in demand is probably due to changes in technology: computers, for example, increase the demand for workers who can use them while reducing the demand for those who cannot. In the United States, this change in demand has been reflected in wages rather than unemployment. Over the past two decades, the wages of unskilled workers have fallen relative to the wages of skilled workers. In Europe, however, the welfare state provides unskilled workers with an alternative to working for low wages. As the wages of unskilled workers fall, more workers view the dole as the best available option. The result is higher unemployment.

This diagnosis of Eurosclerosis does not suggest an easy remedy. Reducing the magnitude of government benefits would encourage workers to get off the dole and accept low-wage jobs. But it would also exacerbate economic inequality—the very problem that welfare-state policies were designed to address.[12]

5-5   Conclusion

Unemployment represents wasted resources. Unemployed workers have the potential to contribute to national income but are not doing so. Those searching for jobs to suit their skills are happy when the search is over, and those waiting for jobs in firms that pay above-equilibrium wages are happy when positions open up.

Unfortunately, neither search unemployment nor wait unemployment can be easily reduced. The government cannot make job search instantaneous, nor can it easily bring wages closer to equilibrium levels. Zero unemployment is not a plausible goal for free-market economies.

Yet public policy is not powerless in the fight to reduce unemployment. Job-training programs, the unemployment-insurance system, the minimum wage, and the laws governing collective bargaining are often topics of political debate. The policies we choose are likely to have important effects on the prevalence of unemployment.

Summary

1. The natural rate of unemployment is the steady-state rate of unemployment. It depends on the rate of job separation and the rate of job finding.

2. Because it takes time for workers to search for the job that best suits their individual skills and tastes, some frictional unemployment is inevitable. Various government policies, such as unemployment insurance, alter the amount of frictional unemployment.

3. Wait unemployment results when the real wage remains above the level that equilibrates labor supply and labor demand. Minimum-wage legislation is one cause of wage rigidity. Another cause is unions and the threat of unionization.

---

[12] For more discussion of these issues, see Paul Krugman, "Past and Prospective Causes of High Unemployment," in *Reducing Unemployment: Current Issues and Policy Options*, Federal Reserve Bank of Kansas City, August 1994.

Finally, efficiency-wage theories suggest that, for various reasons, firms may find it profitable to keep wages high despite an excess supply of labor.

4. Whether we conclude that most unemployment is short-term or long-term depends on how we look at the data. Most spells of unemployment are short. Yet most weeks of unemployment are attributable to the small number of long-term unemployed.

5. The unemployment rates among demographic groups differ substantially. In particular, the unemployment rates for younger workers are much higher than for older workers. This results from a difference in the rate of job separation rather than from a difference in the rate of job finding.

6. The unemployment rate has gradually drifted upward over the past 40 years. Various explanations have been proposed, including the changing demographic composition of the labor force, the increase in the number of two-earner households, and an increase in sectoral shifts.

7. Individuals who have recently entered the labor force, including both new entrants and reentrants, make up about one-third of the unemployed. Transitions into and out of the labor force make unemployment statistics more difficult to interpret.

KEY CONCEPTS

Natural rate of unemployment

Frictional unemployment

Sectoral shift

Unemployment insurance

Wage rigidity

Wait unemployment

Insiders versus outsiders

Efficiency wages

Discouraged workers

QUESTIONS FOR REVIEW

1. What determines the natural rate of unemployment?

2. Describe the difference between frictional unemployment and wait unemployment.

3. Give three explanations for a real wage above the level that equilibrates labor supply and labor demand.

4. Is most unemployment long-term or short-term? Explain your answer.

5. How do economists explain the upward drift in the rate of unemployment over the past 40 years?

PROBLEMS AND APPLICATIONS

1. Answer the following questions about your own experience in the labor force:

   a. When you or one of your friends is looking for a part-time job, how many weeks does it typically take? After you find a job, how many weeks does it typically last?

   b. From your estimates, calculate (in a rate per week) your rate of job finding f and your rate of job separation s. (*Hint*: If f is the rate of job finding, then the average spell of unemployment is $1/f$.)

   c. What is the natural rate of unemployment for the population you represent?

2. In this chapter we saw that the steady-state rate of unemployment is $U/L = s/(s + f)$. Suppose that the unemployment rate does not begin at this level. Show that unemployment will evolve over time and reach this steady state. (*Hint*: Express the change in the number of unemployed as a function of s, f, and U. Then show that if unemployment is above the natural rate, unemployment falls, and if unemployment is below the natural rate, unemployment rises.)

3. The residents of a certain dormitory have collected the following data: People who live in the dorm can be classified as either involved in a relationship or uninvolved. Among involved people, 10 percent experience a breakup of their relationship every month. Among uninvolved people, 5 percent will enter into a relationship every month. What is the steady-state fraction of residents who are uninvolved?

4. Suppose that Congress passes legislation making it more difficult for firms to fire workers. (An example is a law requiring severance pay for fired workers.) If this legislation reduces the rate of job separation without affecting the rate of job finding, how would the natural rate of unemployment change? Do you think that it is plausible that the legislation would not affect the rate of job finding? Why or why not?

5. Consider an economy with the following Cobb-Douglas production function:

$$Y = K^{1/3}L^{2/3}.$$

   The economy has 1,000 units of capital and a labor force of 1,000 workers.

   a. What is the equation describing the demand for labor in this economy? (*Hint*: Review the appendix to Chapter 3.)

   b. If the real wage can adjust to equilibrate labor supply and labor demand, what is the real wage? In this equilibrium, what is employment, output, and the total amount earned by workers?

   c. Now suppose that Congress, concerned about the welfare of the working class, passes a law requiring firms to pay workers a real wage of 1 unit of output. How does this wage compare to the equilibrium wage?

   d. Congress cannot dictate how many workers firms hire at the mandated wage. Given this fact, what are the effects of this law? Specifically, what happens to employment, output, and the total amount earned by workers?

   e. Will Congress succeed in its goal of helping the working class? Explain.

f. Do you think that this analysis provides a good way of thinking about a minimum-wage law? Why or why not?

6. Suppose that a country experiences a reduction in productivity—that is, an adverse shock to the production function.

a. What happens to the labor demand curve?

b. How would this change in productivity affect the labor market—that is, employment, unemployment, and real wages—if the labor market were always in equilibrium?

c. How would this change in productivity affect the labor market if unions prevented real wages from falling?

7. In any city at any time, some of the stock of usable office space is vacant. This vacant office space is unemployed capital. How would you explain this phenomenon? Is it a social problem?

8. Consider how unemployment would affect the Solow growth model of Chapter 4. Suppose that output is produced according to the production function

$$Y = K^{\alpha}[(1 - u^*)L]^{1-\alpha},$$

where K is capital, L is the labor force, and u^* is the natural rate of unemployment. The national saving rate is s, the labor force grows at rate n, and capital depreciates at rate δ. There is no technological progress.

a. Express output per worker ($y = Y/L$) as a function of capital per worker ($k = K/L$) and the natural rate of unemployment. Describe the steady state of this economy.

b. Suppose that some change in government policy reduces the natural rate of unemployment. Describe how this change affects output both immediately and over time. Is the steady-state effect on output larger or smaller than the immediate effect? Explain.

Chapter 6

Money and Inflation

*Lenin is said to have declared that the best way to destroy the
Capitalist System was to debauch the currency. . . . Lenin was
certainly right. There is no subtler, no surer means of overturning
the existing basis of society than to debauch the currency. The
process engages all the hidden forces of economic law on the side of
destruction, and does it in a manner which not one man in a million
is able to diagnose.*

John Maynard Keynes

In 1970 the *New York Times* cost 15 cents, the median price of a single-family
home was $23,000, and the average wage in manufacturing was $3.35 per
hour. In 1993 the *Times* cost 50 cents, the price of a home was $106,800, and
the average wage was $11.76 per hour. This overall increase in prices is called
inflation, and it is the subject of this chapter.

The rate of inflation—the percentage change in the overall level of
prices—varies substantially over time and across countries. In the United
States, prices rose an average of 2.7 percent per year in the 1960s, 7.1 percent
per year in the 1970s, and 4.9 percent per year in the 1980s. U.S. inflation has,
by international standards, been moderate. In Israel in the early 1980s, prices
increased over 100 percent every year. In Germany between December 1922
and December 1923, prices rose an average of 500 percent per month. Such an
episode of extraordinarily high inflation is called a **hyperinflation**.

Many people consider inflation a major social problem. Certainly economic policymakers monitor inflation closely. In the 1970s President Gerald
Ford declared inflation "public enemy number one," and in the 1980s President Ronald Reagan called inflation "the cruelest tax." Opinion polls show that
the general public also views inflation as pernicious.

In this chapter we examine the causes, effects, and social costs of inflation. Because inflation is the increase in the price level, we begin our study by
examining how prices are determined. A price is the rate at which money is exchanged for a good or a service. To understand prices, we must understand
money—what it is, what affects its supply and demand, and what influence it

has on the economy. This chapter is an introduction to a branch of economics called *monetary economics*.

The "hidden forces of economic law" that lead to inflation are not as mysterious as suggested in the quotation that opens this chapter. Section 6-1 begins our analysis of inflation by discussing the economist's concept of "money" and how, in most modern economies, the government controls the number of dollars in the hands of the public. Section 6-2 shows that the quantity of money determines the price level, and that the rate of growth in the quantity of money determines the rate of inflation.

Inflation in turn has numerous effects of its own on the economy. Section 6-3 discusses the revenue that the government raises by printing money, sometimes called the *inflation tax*. Section 6-4 examines how inflation affects the nominal interest rate. Section 6-5 discusses how the nominal interest rate in turn affects the quantity of money people wish to hold and, thereby, the price level.

After completing our analysis of the causes and effects of inflation, in Section 6-6 we address what is perhaps the most important question about inflation: Is it a major social problem? Does inflation really amount to "overturning the existing basis of society"?

Finally, in Section 6-7, we discuss the extreme case of hyperinflation. Hyperinflations are interesting to examine, for they show clearly the forces of monetary economics. Just as a seismologist can learn much by studying an earthquake, monetary economists can learn much by studying how hyperinflations begin and end.

6-1 What Is Money?

When we say that a person has a lot of money, we usually mean that he or she is wealthy. By contrast, economists use the term **money** in a more specialized way. To an economist, money does not refer to all wealth but only to one type of it. *Money is the stock of assets that can be readily used to make transactions.* Roughly speaking, the dollars in the hands of the public make up the nation's stock of money.

The Functions of Money

Money has three purposes. It is a store of value, a unit of account, and a medium of exchange.

As a **store of value**, money is a way to transfer purchasing power from the present to the future. If I work today and earn $100, I can hold the money and spend it tomorrow, next week, or next month. Of course, money is an imperfect store of value: if prices are rising, the real value of money is falling. Even so, people hold money because they can trade the money for goods and services at some time in the future.

As a **unit of account**, money provides the terms in which prices are quoted and debts are recorded. Microeconomics teaches us that resources are allocated according to relative prices—the prices of goods relative to other goods—yet stores post their prices in dollars and cents. A car dealer tells you that a car costs $12,000, not 400 shirts (even though it may amount to the same thing). Similarly, most debts require the debtor to deliver a specified number of dollars in the future, not a specified amount of some commodity. Money is the yardstick with which we measure economic transactions.

As a **medium of exchange**, money is what we use to buy goods and services. "This note is legal tender for all debts, public and private" is printed on the U.S. dollar. When we walk into stores, we are confident that the shopkeepers will accept our money in exchange for the items they are selling.

To better understand the functions of money, try to imagine an economy without it: a barter economy. In such a world, trade requires the **double coincidence of wants**—the unlikely happenstance of two people each having a good that the other wants at the right time and place to make an exchange. A barter economy permits only simple transactions.

Money makes more indirect transactions possible. A professor uses her salary to buy books; the book publisher uses its revenue from the sale of books to buy paper; the paper company uses its revenue from the sale of paper to pay the lumberjack; the lumberjack uses his income to send his child to college; and the college uses its tuition receipts to pay the salary of the professor. In a complex, modern economy, trade is usually indirect and requires the use of money.

The Types of Money

Money takes many forms. In the U.S. economy we make transactions with an item whose sole function is to act as money: dollar bills. These pieces of green paper with small portraits of famous Americans would have little value if they were not widely accepted as money. Money that has no intrinsic value is called **fiat money**, since it is established as money by government decree.

Although fiat money is the norm in most economies today, historically most societies have used for money a commodity with some intrinsic value. Money of this sort is called **commodity money**.

Gold is the most widespread example of commodity money. An economy in which gold serves as money is said to be on a **gold standard**. Gold is a form of commodity money because it can be used for various purposes—jewelry, dental fillings, and so on—as well as for transactions. The gold standard was common throughout the world during the late nineteenth century.

"And how would you like your funny money?"

Drawing by Bernard Schoenbaum; © 1979
The New Yorker Magazine Inc.

Case Study *6-1*

• • • • • • • • • • • • •

Money in a POW Camp

An unusual form of commodity money developed in the Nazi prisoner of war (POW) camps during World War II. The Red Cross supplied the prisoners with various goods—food, clothing, cigarettes, and so on. Yet these rations were allocated without close attention to personal preferences, so naturally the allocations were often inefficient. One prisoner may have preferred chocolate, while another may have preferred cheese, and a third may have wanted a new shirt. The differing tastes and endowments of the prisoners led them to trade with one another.

Barter proved to be an inconvenient way to allocate these resources, however, because it required the double coincidence of wants. In other words, a barter system was not the easiest way to ensure that each prisoner received the goods he valued most. Even the limited economy of the POW camp needed some form of money to facilitate transactions.

Eventually, cigarettes became the established "currency" in which prices were quoted and with which trades were made. A shirt, for example, cost about 80 cigarettes. Services were also quoted in cigarettes: some prisoners offered to do other prisoners' laundry for 2 cigarettes per garment. Even non-smokers were happy to accept cigarettes in exchange, knowing they could trade the cigarettes in the future for some good they did enjoy. Within the POW camp the cigarette became the store of value, the unit of account, and the medium of exchange.[1]

• • • • • • • • • • • • •

How Fiat Money Evolves

It is not surprising that some form of commodity money arises to facilitate exchange: people are willing to accept a commodity currency such as gold because it has intrinsic value. The development of fiat money, however, is more perplexing. What would make people begin to value something that is intrinsically useless?

To understand how the evolution from commodity money to fiat money takes place, imagine an economy in which people carry around bags of gold. When a purchase is made, the buyer measures out the appropriate amount of gold. If the seller is convinced that the weight and purity of the gold are right, the buyer and seller make the exchange.

The government first intervenes to reduce transaction costs. Using raw gold as money is costly because it takes time to verify the purity of the gold and to measure the correct quantity. To help reduce these costs, the government

---

[1] R.A. Radford, "The Economic Organisation of a P.O.W. Camp," *Economica* (November 1945): 189–201. The use of cigarettes as money is not limited to this example. In the Soviet Union in the late 1980s, packs of Marlboros were preferred to the ruble in the large underground economy.

mints gold coins of known purity and weight. The coins are easier to use than gold bullion because their values are widely recognized.

The next step is for the government to issue gold certificates—pieces of paper that can be redeemed for a certain quantity of gold. If people believe the government's promise to pay, these bills are just as valuable as the gold itself. In addition, because the bills are lighter than the gold, they are easier to use in transactions. Eventually, no one carries gold around at all, and these gold-backed government bills become the monetary standard.

Finally, the gold backing becomes irrelevant. If no one ever bothers to redeem the bills for gold, no one cares if the option is abandoned. As long as everyone continues to accept the paper bills in exchange, they will have value and serve as money. Thus, the system of commodity money evolves into a system of fiat money.

Case Study *6-2*

● ● ● ● ● ● ● ● ● ● ● ● ● ●

Money on the Island of Yap

The economy of Yap, a small island in the Pacific, once had a type of money that was something between commodity and fiat money. The traditional medium of exchange in Yap was *fei*, stone wheels up to 12 feet in diameter. These stones had holes in the center so that they could be carried on poles and used for exchange.

Large stone wheels are not a convenient form of money. The stones were heavy, so it took substantial effort for a new owner to take his *fei* home after completing a bargain. Although the monetary system facilitated exchange, it did so at great cost.

Eventually, it became common practice for the new owner of the *fei* not to bother to take physical possession of the stone. Instead, the new owner merely accepted a claim to the *fei* without moving it. In future bargains, he traded this claim for goods that he wanted. Having physical possession of the stone became less important than having legal claim to it.

This practice was put to a test when an extremely valuable stone was lost at sea during a storm. Because the owner lost his money by accident rather than through negligence, it was universally agreed that his claim to the *fei* remained valid. Even generations later, when no one alive had ever seen this stone, the claim to this *fei* was still valued in exchange.[2]

● ● ● ● ● ● ● ● ● ● ● ● ● ●

How the Quantity of Money Is Controlled

The quantity of money available is called the **money supply**. In an economy that uses commodity money, the money supply is the quantity of that commodity. In an economy that uses fiat money, such as most economies today, the

---

[2] Norman Angell, *The Story of Money* (New York: Frederick A. Stokes Company, 1929), 88–89.

government controls the supply of money: legal restrictions give the government a monopoly on the printing of money. Just as the level of taxation and the level of government purchases are policy instruments of the government, so is the supply of money.

In the United States and many other countries, the control of the money supply is delegated to a partially independent institution called the **central bank**. The central bank of the United States is the Federal Reserve—often called the Fed. If you look at a U.S. dollar bill, you will see that it is called a Federal Reserve Note. The members of the Federal Reserve Board, who are appointed by the president and confirmed by Congress, together decide on the money supply. The control of the money supply is called **monetary policy**.

The primary way in which the Fed controls the supply of money is through **open-market operations**—the purchase and sale of government bonds. To increase the supply of money, the Fed uses dollars to buy government bonds from the public. This purchase increases the quantity of dollars in circulation. To decrease the supply of money, the Fed sells some of its government bonds. This open-market sale of bonds takes some dollars out of the hands of the public.

In Chapter 18 we discuss in detail how the Fed controls the supply of money. For our current discussion, these details are not crucial. It is sufficient to assume that the Fed directly controls the supply of money.

How the Quantity of Money Is Measured

One of the goals of this chapter is to determine how the money supply affects the economy; we turn to that problem in the next section. As a background for that analysis, let's first discuss how economists measure the quantity of money.

Because money is the stock of assets used for transactions, the quantity of money is the quantity of those assets. In simple economies, this quantity is easily measured. In the POW camp, the quantity of money was the quantity of cigarettes in the camp. But how can we measure the quantity of money in more complex economies such as ours? The answer is not obvious, because no single asset is used for all transactions. People can use various assets to make transactions, although some assets are more convenient than others. This ambiguity leads to numerous measures of the quantity of money.

The most obvious asset to include in the quantity of money is **currency**, the sum of outstanding paper money and coins. Most day-to-day transactions use currency as the medium of exchange.

A second type of asset used for transactions is **demand deposits**, the funds people hold in their checking accounts. If most sellers accept personal checks, assets in a checking account are almost as convenient as currency. In both cases, the assets are in a form ready to facilitate a transaction. Demand deposits are therefore added to currency when measuring the quantity of money.

Once we admit the logic of including demand deposits in the measured money stock, many other assets become candidates for inclusion. Funds in savings accounts, for example, can be easily transferred into checking accounts; these assets are almost as convenient for transactions. Money market mutual funds allow investors to write checks against their accounts, although restrictions often apply with regard to the size of the check or the number of checks written. Because these assets can be easily used for transactions, they should arguably be included in the quantity of money.

Since it is unclear exactly which assets should be included in the money stock, various measures are available. Table 6-1 presents the five measures of the money stock that the Federal Reserve calculates for the U.S. economy, together with a list of which assets are included in each measure. From the smallest to the largest, they are designated C, $M1$, $M2$, $M3$, and L. The most commonly used measures for studying the effects of money on the economy are $M1$ and $M2$. There is no consensus, however, about which measure of the money stock is best. Disagreements about monetary policy sometimes arise because different measures of money are moving in different directions. Luckily, the different measures normally move together and so tell the same story about whether the quantity of money is growing quickly or slowly.

Table 6-1

The Measures of Money

Symbol	Assets Included	Amount in March 1995 (billions of dollars)
C	Currency	$ 363
$M1$	Sum of currency, demand deposits, traveler's checks, and other checkable deposits	1,148
$M2$	Sum of $M1$ and overnight repurchase agreements, Eurodollars, money market deposit accounts, money market mutual fund shares, and savings and small time deposits	3,630
$M3$	Sum of $M2$ and large time deposits and term repurchase agreements	4,357
L	Sum of M3 and savings bonds, short-term Treasury securities, and other liquid assets	5,426

Source: Federal Reserve.

6-2 The Quantity Theory of Money

Having defined what money is and described how it is controlled and measured, we can now examine how the quantity of money affects the economy. To do this, we must see how the quantity of money is related to other economic variables.

Transactions and the Quantity Equation

People hold money to buy goods and services. The more money they need for such transactions, the more money they hold. Thus, the quantity of money in the economy is closely related to the number of dollars exchanged in transactions.

The link between transactions and money is expressed in the following equation, called the **quantity equation**:

$$\text{Money} \times \text{Velocity} = \text{Price} \times \text{Transactions}$$
$$M \times V = P \times T.$$

Let's examine each of the four variables in this equation.

The right-hand side of the quantity equation tells us about transactions. T represents the total number of transactions during some period of time, say, a year. In other words, T is the number of times in a year that goods or services are exchanged for money. P is the price of a typical transaction—the number of dollars exchanged. The product of the price of a transaction and the number of transactions, PT, equals the number of dollars exchanged in a year.

The left-hand side of the quantity equation tells us about the money used to make the transactions. M is the quantity of money. V is called the **transactions velocity of money** and measures the rate at which money circulates in the economy. In other words, velocity tells us the number of times a dollar bill changes hands in a given period of time.

For example, suppose that 60 loaves of bread are sold in a given year at $0.50 per loaf. Then T equals 60 loaves per year, and P equals $0.50 per loaf. The total number of dollars exchanged is

$$PT = \$0.50/\text{loaf} \times 60 \text{ loaves/year} = \$30/\text{year}.$$

The right-hand side of the quantity equation equals $30 per year, which is the dollar value of all transactions.

Suppose further that the quantity of money in the economy is $10. Then we can compute velocity as

$$V = PT/M$$
$$= (\$30/\text{year})/(\$10)$$
$$= 3 \text{ times per year.}$$

That is, for $30 of transactions per year to take place with $10 of money, each dollar must change hands 3 times per year.

The quantity equation is an *identity*: the definitions of the four variables make it true. The equation is useful because it shows that if one of the variables changes, one or more of the others must also change to maintain the equality. For example, if the quantity of money increases and the velocity of money stays unchanged, then either the price or the number of transactions must rise.

From Transactions to Income

Economists usually use a slightly different version of the quantity equation than the one just introduced. The problem with the first equation is that the number of transactions is difficult to measure. To solve this problem, the number of transactions T is replaced by the total output of the economy Y.

Transactions and output are closely related, because the more the economy produces, the more goods are bought and sold. They are not the same, however. When one person sells a used car to another person, for example, they make a transaction using money, even though the used car is not part of current output. Nonetheless, the dollar value of transactions is roughly proportional to the dollar value of output.

If Y denotes the amount of output and P denotes the price of one unit of output, then the dollar value of output is PY. We encountered measures for these variables when we discussed the national income accounts in Chapter 2: Y is real GDP, P the GDP deflator, and PY nominal GDP. The quantity equation becomes

$$\text{Money} \times \text{Velocity} = \text{Price} \times \text{Output}$$
$$M \times V = P \times Y.$$

Because Y is also total income, V in this version of the quantity equation is called the **income velocity of money**. The income velocity of money tells us the number of times a dollar bill enters someone's income in a given period of time. This version of the quantity equation is the most common, and it is the one we use from now on.

The Money Demand Function and the Quantity Equation

When we analyze how money affects the economy, it is often convenient to express the quantity of money in terms of the quantity of goods and services it can buy. This amount is M/P and is called **real money balances**.

Real money balances measure the purchasing power of the stock of money. For example, consider an economy that produces only bread. If the quantity of money is $10, and the price of a loaf is $0.50, then real money balances are 20 loaves of bread. That is, the stock of money in the economy is able to buy 20 loaves at current prices.

A **money demand function** is an equation that shows what determines the quantity of real money balances people wish to hold. A simple money demand function is

$$(M/P)^d = kY,$$

where k is a constant. This equation states that the quantity of real money balances demanded is proportional to real income.

The money demand function is like the demand function for a particular good. Here the "good" is the convenience of holding real money balances. Just as owning an automobile makes it easier for a person to travel, holding money makes it easier to make transactions. Therefore, just as higher income leads to a greater demand for automobiles, higher income also leads to a greater demand for real money balances.

From this money demand function, we can derive the quantity equation. To do so we add the condition that the demand for real money balances $(M/P)^d$ must equal the supply M/P. Therefore,

$$M/P = kY.$$

A simple rearrangement of terms changes this equation into

$$M(1/k) = PY,$$

which can be written as

$$MV = PY,$$

where $V = 1/k$. Hence, when we use the quantity equation, we are assuming that the supply of real money balances equals the demand, and that the demand is proportional to income.

The Assumption of Constant Velocity

We can view the quantity equation as merely defining velocity as the ratio of nominal GDP to the quantity of money. Yet we can turn the equation into a useful theory—called the **quantity theory of money**—by making the additional assumption that velocity is constant.

As with many of the assumptions in economics, we can justify the assumption of constant velocity only as an approximation. Velocity does change if the money demand function changes. For example, the introduction of the automatic teller machine allows people to reduce their average money holdings, which reduces the money demand parameter k; the machines raise the rate at which money circulates in the economy, which implies greater velocity V. Nonetheless, the assumption of constant velocity provides a good approximation in many situations. Let's therefore assume that velocity is constant and see what this assumption implies about the effects of the money supply on the economy.

Once we assume that velocity is constant, the quantity equation can be seen as a theory of nominal GDP. The quantity equation says

$$M\overline{V} = PY,$$

where the bar over V means that velocity is fixed. Therefore, a change in the quantity of money (M) must cause a proportionate change in nominal GDP (PY). That is, the quantity of money determines the dollar value of the economy's output.

Money, Prices, and Inflation

We now have a theory to explain what determines the economy's overall level of prices. The theory has three building blocks:

1. The factors of production and the production function determine the level of output Y. We borrow this conclusion from Chapter 3.

2. The money supply determines the nominal value of output PY. This conclusion follows from the quantity equation and the assumption that the velocity of money is fixed.

3. The price level P is then the ratio of the nominal value of output PY to the level of output Y.

In other words, the productive capability of the economy determines real GDP, the quantity of money determines nominal GDP, and the GDP deflator is the ratio of nominal GDP to real GDP.

This theory explains what happens when the Fed changes the supply of money. Because velocity is fixed, any change in the supply of money leads to a proportionate change in nominal GDP. Because the factors of production and the production function have already determined real GDP, the change in nominal GDP must represent a change in the price level. Hence, the quantity theory implies that the price level is proportional to the money supply.

Because the inflation rate is the percentage change in the price level, this theory of the price level is also a theory of the inflation rate. The quantity equation, written in percentage-change form, is

$$\text{\% Change in } M \; + \; \text{\% Change in } V \; = \; \text{\% Change in } P \; + \; \text{\% Change in } Y.$$

Consider each of these four terms. First, the percentage change in the quantity of money M is under the control of the central bank. Second, the percentage change in velocity V reflects shifts in money demand; we have assumed velocity is constant, so the percentage change in velocity is zero. Third, the percentage change in the price level P is the rate of inflation; this is the variable in the equation that we would like to explain. Fourth, the percentage change in output Y depends on growth in the factors of production and on technological progress, which for our present purposes we can take as given. This analysis tells us that (except for a constant that depends on exogenous growth in output) the growth in the money supply determines the rate of inflation.

Thus, the quantity theory of money states that the central bank, which controls the money supply, has the ultimate control over the rate of inflation. If the central bank keeps the money supply stable, the price level will be stable. If the central bank increases the money supply quickly, the price level will rise quickly.

Case Study 6-3

● ● ● ● ● ● ● ● ● ● ● ● ● ●

Inflation and Money Growth

"Inflation is always and everywhere a monetary phenomenon." So wrote Milton Friedman, the great monetary economist who won the Nobel Prize for economics in 1976. The quantity theory of money leads us to agree that the growth in the quantity of money is the primary determinant of the inflation rate. Yet Friedman's claim is empirical, not theoretical. To evaluate his claim, and to judge the usefulness of our theory, we need to look at data on money and prices.

Friedman, together with fellow economist Anna Schwartz, wrote two treatises on monetary history that documented the sources and effects of changes in the quantity of money over the past century. Figure 6-1 uses some of their data and plots the average rate of money growth and the average rate

Figure 6-1

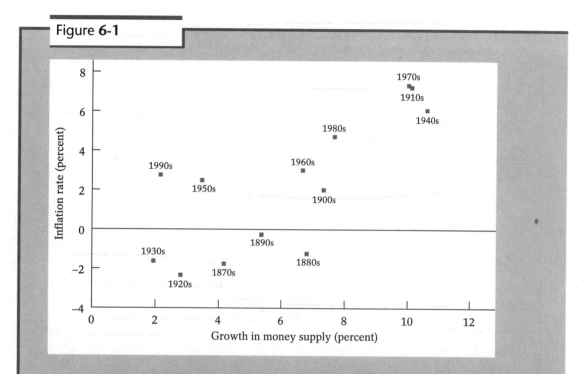

Historical Data on Inflation and Money Growth In this scatterplot of money growth and inflation, each point represents a decade. The horizontal axis shows the average growth in the money supply (as measured by *M*2) over the decade, and the vertical axis shows the average rate of inflation (as measured by the GDP deflator). The positive correlation between money growth and inflation is evidence for the quantity theory's prediction that high money growth leads to high inflation.

Source: For the data through the 1960s: Milton Friedman and Anna J. Schwartz, *Monetary Trends in the United States and the United Kingdom: Their Relation to Income, Prices, and Interest Rates 1867–1975* (Chicago: University of Chicago Press, 1982). For recent data: U.S. Department of Commerce, Federal Reserve Board.

of inflation in the United States over each decade since the 1870s. The data verify the link between growth in the quantity of money and inflation. Decades with high money growth tend to have high inflation, and decades with low money growth tend to have low inflation.[3]

Figure 6-2 examines the same question with international data. It shows the average rate of inflation and the average rate of money growth in the decade of the 1980s in 34 countries. Again, the link between money growth and inflation is clear. Countries with high money growth tend to have high inflation, and countries with low money growth tend to have low inflation.

---

[3] Milton Friedman and Anna J. Schwartz, *A Monetary History of the United States, 1867–1960* (Princeton, N.J.: Princeton University Press, 1963); Milton Friedman and Anna J. Schwartz, *Monetary Trends in the United States and the United Kingdom: Their Relation to Income, Prices, and Interest Rates, 1867–1975* (Chicago: University of Chicago Press, 1982).

Figure 6-2

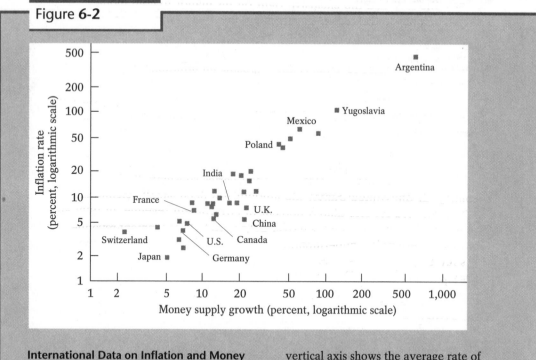

International Data on Inflation and Money Growth In this scatterplot, each point represents a country. The horizontal axis shows the average growth in the money supply (as measured by currency plus demand deposits) during the 1980s, and the vertical axis shows the average rate of inflation (as measured by the GDP deflator). Once again, the positive correlation is evidence for the quantity theory's prediction that high money growth leads to high inflation.

Source: International Financial Statistics.

If we looked at monthly data on money growth and inflation, rather than decadal data, we would not see as close a connection between these two variables. This theory of inflation works best in the long run, not in the short run. We examine the short-run impact of changes in the quantity of money when we turn to economic fluctuations in Part Three of this book.

6-3 Seigniorage: The Revenue From Printing Money

The government can finance its spending in three ways. First, it can raise revenue through taxes, such as personal and corporate income taxes. Second, it can borrow from the public. Third, it can simply print money.

~~The revenue raised through the printing of money is called **seigniorage**.~~ The term comes from *seigneur*, the French word for "feudal lord." In the Middle Ages, the lord had the exclusive right on his manor to coin money. Today this right belongs to the central government, and it is one source of revenue.

When the government prints money to finance expenditure, it increases the money supply. The increase in the money supply, in turn, causes inflation. Printing money to raise revenue is like imposing an *inflation tax*.

At first it may not be obvious that inflation can be viewed as a tax. After all, no one receives a bill for this tax—the government merely prints the money it needs. Who then pays the inflation tax? The answer is the holders of money. As prices rise, the real value of the money in your wallet falls. When the government prints new money for its use, it makes the old money in the hands of the public less valuable. Thus, inflation is a tax on holding money.

The amount raised by printing money varies substantially from country to country. In the United States, the amount has been small: seigniorage has usually accounted for less than 3 percent of government revenue. In Italy and Greece, seigniorage has often been over 10 percent of government revenue.[4] In countries experiencing hyperinflation, seigniorage is often the government's chief source of revenue—indeed, the need to print money to finance expenditure is a primary cause of hyperinflation.

Case Study *6-4*

● ● ● ● ● ● ● ● ● ● ● ● ● ●

Paying for the American Revolution

Although seigniorage has not been a major source of revenue for the U.S. government in recent history, the situation was very different two centuries ago. Beginning in 1775 the Continental Congress needed to find a way to finance the Revolution, but it had limited ability to raise revenue through taxation. It therefore relied heavily on the printing of fiat money to help pay for the war.

The Continental Congress's reliance on seigniorage increased over time. In 1775 new issues of continental currency were approximately $6 million. This amount increased to $19 million in 1776, $13 million in 1777, $63 million in 1778, and $125 million in 1779.

Not surprisingly, this rapid growth in the money supply led to massive inflation. At the war's end, the price of gold in continental dollars was more than 100 times its level of only a few years earlier. The large quantity of the continental currency made the continental dollar nearly worthless. Even today the expression "not worth a continental" means that something has little real value.

● ● ● ● ● ● ● ● ● ● ● ● ●

6-4 **Inflation and Interest Rates**

So far we have examined the link between money growth and inflation. We now discuss the link between inflation and interest rates.

---

[4] Stanley Fischer, "Seigniorage and the Case for a National Money," *Journal of Political Economy* 90 (April 1982): 295–313.

Two Interest Rates: Real and Nominal

Suppose you deposit your savings in a bank account that pays 8 percent interest annually. Next year, you withdraw your savings and the accumulated interest. Are you 8 percent richer than you were when you made the deposit a year earlier?

The answer depends on what "richer" means. Certainly, you have 8 percent more dollars than you had before. But if prices have risen, so that each dollar buys less, then your purchasing power has not risen by 8 percent. If the inflation rate was 5 percent, then the amount of goods you can buy has increased by only 3 percent. And if the inflation rate was 10 percent, then your purchasing power actually fell by 2 percent.

Economists call the interest rate that the bank pays the **nominal interest rate** and the increase in your purchasing power the **real interest rate.** If i denotes the nominal interest rate, r the real interest rate, and π the rate of inflation, then the relationship among these three variables can be written as

$$r = i - \pi.$$

The real interest rate is the difference between the nominal interest rate and the rate of inflation.

The Fisher Effect

Rearranging terms in our equation for the real interest rate, we can show that the nominal interest rate is the sum of the real interest rate and the inflation rate:

$$i = r + \pi.$$

The equation written in this way is called the **Fisher equation**, after economist Irving Fisher (1867–1947). It shows that the nominal interest rate can change for two reasons: because the real interest rate changes or because the inflation rate changes.

Once we separate the nominal interest rate into these two parts, we can use this equation to develop a theory of the nominal interest rate. Chapter 3 showed that the real interest rate adjusts to equilibrate saving and investment. The quantity theory of money shows that the rate of money growth determines the rate of inflation. The Fisher equation then tells us to add the real interest rate and the inflation rate together to determine the nominal interest rate.

The quantity theory and the Fisher equation together tell us how money growth affects the nominal interest rate. According to the quantity theory, an increase in the rate of money growth of 1 percent causes a 1 percent increase in the rate of inflation. According to the Fisher equation, a 1 percent increase in the rate of inflation in turn causes a 1 percent increase in the nominal interest rate. The one-for-one relation between the inflation rate and the nominal interest rate is called the **Fisher effect**.

Case Study 6-5

• • • • • • • • • • • • • •

Inflation and Nominal Interest Rates

How useful is the Fisher effect in explaining interest rates? To answer this question we look at two types of data on inflation and nominal interest rates.

Figure 6-3 shows the variation over time in the nominal interest rate and the inflation rate in the United States. You can see that, over the past forty years, the Fisher effect has worked fairly well. When inflation is high, nominal interest rates also tend to be high.

Figure 6-3

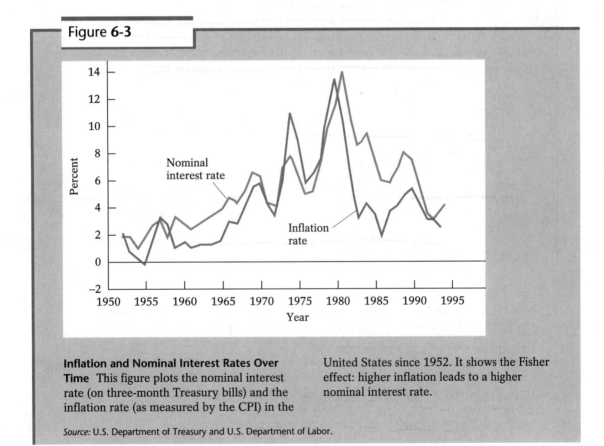

Inflation and Nominal Interest Rates Over Time This figure plots the nominal interest rate (on three-month Treasury bills) and the inflation rate (as measured by the CPI) in the United States since 1952. It shows the Fisher effect: higher inflation leads to a higher nominal interest rate.

Source: U.S. Department of Treasury and U.S. Department of Labor.

Figure 6-4 examines the variation across countries in the nominal interest rate and the inflation rate at a single point in time. Once again, the inflation rate and nominal interest rate are closely related. Countries with high inflation tend to have high nominal interest rates as well.

The link between inflation and interest rates is well known to Wall Street investment firms. Since bond prices move inversely with interest rates, one can

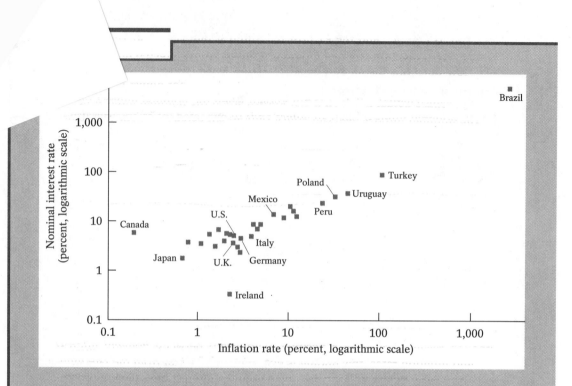

Inflation and Nominal Interest Rates Across Countries This scatterplot exhibits the three-month nominal interest rate and the inflation rate (during the previous year) in 30 countries in 1994. The positive correlation between the inflation rate and the nominal interest rate is evidence for the Fisher effect.

Source: International Financial Statistics.

get rich by predicting correctly the direction in which interest rates will move. Many Wall Street firms hire *Fed watchers* to monitor monetary policy and news about inflation in order to anticipate changes in interest rates.

• • • • • • • • • • • • •

Two Real Interest Rates: *Ex Ante* and *Ex Post*

When a borrower and lender agree on a nominal interest rate, they do not know what the inflation rate over the term of the loan will be. Therefore, we must distinguish between two concepts of the real interest rate: the real interest rate the borrower and lender expect when the loan is made, called the *ex ante* **real interest rate**, and the real interest rate actually realized, called the *ex post* **real interest rate**.

Although borrowers and lenders cannot predict future inflation with certainty, they do have some expectation of the inflation rate. Let π denote actual future inflation and π^e the expectation of future inflation. The *ex ante* real interest rate is $i - \pi^e$, and the *ex post* real interest rate is $i - \pi$. The two real interest rates differ when actual inflation π differs from expected inflation π^e.

How does this distinction between actual and expected inflation modify the Fisher effect? Clearly, the nominal interest rate cannot adjust to actual inflation, because actual inflation is not known when the nominal interest rate is set. The nominal interest rate can adjust only to expected inflation. The Fisher effect is more precisely written as

$$i = r + \pi^e.$$

Nominal i = real + π^e   *Fisher effect*

The *ex ante* real interest rate r is determined by equilibrium in the market for goods and services, as described by the model in Chapter 3. The nominal interest rate i moves one-for-one with changes in expected inflation π^e.

Case Study 6-6

Nominal Interest Rates in the Nineteenth Century

Although recent data show a positive relationship between nominal interest rates and inflation rates, this finding is not universal. In data from the late nineteenth and early twentieth centuries, high nominal interest rates did not accompany high inflation. The apparent absence of any Fisher effect during this time puzzled Irving Fisher. He suggested that inflation "caught merchants napping."

How should we interpret the absence of an apparent Fisher effect in nineteenth-century data? Does this period of history provide evidence against the adjustment of nominal interest rates to inflation? Recent research suggests that this period has little to tell us about the validity of the Fisher effect. The reason is that the Fisher effect relates the nominal interest rate to expected inflation and, according to this research, inflation at this time was largely unexpected.

Although expectations are not directly observable, we can draw inferences about them by examining the persistence of inflation. In recent experience, inflation has been highly persistent: when it is high one year, it tends to be high the next year as well. Therefore, when people have observed high inflation, it has been rational for them to expect high inflation in the future. By contrast, during the nineteenth century, when the gold standard was in effect, inflation had little persistence. High inflation in one year was just as likely to be followed the next year by low inflation as by high inflation. Therefore, high inflation did not imply high expected inflation and did not lead to high nominal interest rates. So, in a sense, Fisher was right to say that inflation "caught merchants napping."[5]

---

[5] Robert B. Barsky, "The Fisher Effect and the Forecastability and Persistence of Inflation," *Journal of Monetary Economics* 19 (January 1987): 3–24.

6-5   The Nominal Interest Rate and the Demand for Money

The quantity theory is based on a simple money demand function: it assumes that the demand for real money balances is proportional to income. Although the quantity theory is a good place to start when analyzing the role of money, it is not the whole story. Here we add another determinant of the quantity of money demanded—the nominal interest rate.

The Cost of Holding Money

The money you hold in your wallet does not earn interest. If instead of holding that money you used it to buy government bonds or deposited it in a savings account, you would earn the nominal interest rate. The nominal interest rate is what you give up by holding money rather than bonds: it is the opportunity cost of holding money.

Another way to see that the cost of holding money equals the nominal interest rate is by comparing the real returns on alternative assets. Assets other than money, such as government bonds, earn the real return r. Money earns an expected real return of $-\pi^e$, since its real value declines at the rate of inflation. When you hold money, you give up the difference between these two returns. Thus, the cost of holding money is $r - (-\pi^e)$, which the Fisher equation tells us is the nominal interest rate i.

Just as the quantity of bread demanded depends on the price of bread, the quantity of money demanded depends on the price of holding money. Hence, the demand for real money balances depends both on the level of income and on the nominal interest rate. We write the general money demand function as

$$(M/P)^d = L(i, Y).$$

The letter L is used to denote money demand because money is the liquid asset—the asset most easily used to make transactions. This equation states that the demand for the liquidity of real money balances is a function of income and the nominal interest rate. The higher the level of income Y, the greater the demand for real money balances. The higher the nominal interest rate i, the lower the demand for real money balances.

Future Money and Current Prices

Money, prices, and interest rates are now related in several ways. Figure 6-5 illustrates the linkages we have discussed. As the quantity theory of money explains, money supply and money demand together determine the equilibrium price level. Changes in the price level are, by definition, the rate of inflation. Inflation, in turn, affects the nominal interest rate through the Fisher effect. But

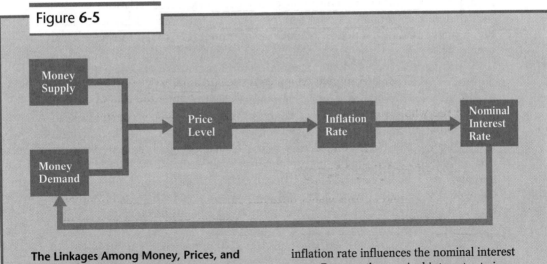

Figure 6-5

The Linkages Among Money, Prices, and Interest Rates This figure provides a schematic illustration of the relationships among money, prices, and interest rates. Money supply and money demand determine the price level. Changes in the price level determine the inflation rate. The inflation rate influences the nominal interest rate. Because the nominal interest rate is the cost of holding money, it may affect money demand. This last link (shown as a green line) is omitted from the basic quantity theory of money.

now, since the nominal interest rate is the cost of holding money, the nominal interest rate feeds back to affect the demand for money.

Consider how the introduction of this last link affects our theory of the price level. First, equate the supply of real money balances M/P to the demand $L(i, Y)$:

$$M/P = L(i, Y).$$

Next, use the Fisher equation to write the nominal interest rate as the sum of the real interest rate and expected inflation:

$$M/P = L(r + \pi^e, Y).$$

This equation states that the level of real money balances depends on the expected rate of inflation.

The last equation tells a more sophisticated story than the quantity theory about the determination of the price level. The quantity theory of money says that today's money supply determines today's price level. This conclusion remains partly true: if the nominal interest rate and the level of output are held constant, the price level moves proportionally with the money supply. Yet the nominal interest rate is not constant; it depends on expected inflation, which in turn depends on money growth. The presence of the nominal interest rate in the money demand function yields an additional channel through which money supply affects the price level.

This general money-demand equation implies that the price level depends not just on today's money supply but also on the money supply expected in the future. To see why, suppose the Fed announces that it will raise the money supply in the future, but it does not change the money supply today. This announcement causes people to expect higher money growth and higher inflation. Through the Fisher effect, this increase in expected inflation raises the nominal interest rate. The higher nominal interest rate immediately reduces the demand for real money balances. Because the quantity of money has not changed, the reduced demand for real money balances leads to a higher price level. Hence, higher expected money growth in the future leads to a higher price level today.

The effect of money on prices is fairly complex. The appendix to this chapter works out the mathematics relating the price level to current and future money. The conclusion of the analysis is that the price level depends on a weighted average of the current money supply and the money supply expected to prevail in the future.

6-6   The Social Costs of Inflation

Our discussion of the causes and effects of inflation does not tell us much about the social problems that result from inflation. We turn to those problems now.

If you ask the average person why inflation is a social problem, he will probably answer that inflation makes him poorer. "Each year my boss gives me a raise, but prices go up and that takes some of my raise away from me." The implicit assumption in this statement is that if there were no inflation, he would get the same raise and be able to buy more goods.

This complaint about inflation is a common fallacy. From Chapters 3 and 4, we know that increases in the purchasing power of labor come from capital accumulation and technological progress. In particular, the real wage does not depend on how much money the government chooses to print. If the government slowed the rate of money growth, prices would not rise as quickly. But workers would not see their real wage increasing more rapidly. Instead, when inflation slowed, they would get smaller raises each year.

Why, then, is inflation a social problem? It turns out that the costs of inflation are subtle. Indeed, economists disagree about the size of the social costs. To the surprise of many laymen, some economists argue that the costs of inflation are small—at least for the moderate rates of inflation that most countries have experienced in recent years.[6]

---

[6] See, for example, Chapter 2 of Alan Blinder, *Hard Heads, Soft Hearts: Tough-Minded Economics for a Just Society* (Reading, Mass.: Addison Wesley, 1987).

Expected Inflation

Consider first the case of expected inflation. Suppose that every month the price level rose by 1 percent. What would be the social costs of such a steady and predictable 12 percent annual inflation?

One cost is the distortion of the inflation tax on the amount of money people hold. As we have already discussed, a higher inflation rate leads to a higher nominal interest rate, which in turn leads to lower real money balances. If people are to hold lower money balances on average, they must make more frequent trips to the bank to withdraw money—for example, they might withdraw $50 twice a week rather than $100 once a week. The inconvenience of reducing money holding is metaphorically called the **shoeleather cost of** inflation, because walking to the bank more often causes one's shoes to wear out more quickly.

A second cost of inflation arises because high inflation induces firms to change their posted prices more often. Changing prices is sometimes costly: for example, it may require printing and distributing a new catalog. These costs are called **menu costs**, because the higher the rate of inflation, the more often restaurants have to print new menus.

A third cost of inflation arises because firms facing menu costs change prices infrequently; therefore, the higher the rate of inflation, the greater the variability in relative prices. For example, suppose a firm issues a new catalog every January. If there is no inflation, then the firm's prices relative to the overall price level are constant over the year. Yet if inflation is 1 percent per month, then from the beginning to the end of the year the firm's relative prices fall by 12 percent. Thus, inflation induces variability in relative prices. Since market economies rely on relative prices to allocate resources efficiently, inflation leads to microeconomic inefficiencies.

A fourth cost of inflation results from the tax laws. Many provisions of the tax code do not take into account the effects of inflation. Inflation can alter individuals' tax liability, often in ways that lawmakers did not intend.

One example of the failure of the tax code to deal with inflation is the tax treatment of capital gains. Suppose you buy some stock today and sell it a year from now at the same real price. It would seem reasonable for the government not to levy a tax, since you have earned no real income from this investment. Indeed, if there is no inflation, a zero tax liability would be the outcome. But suppose the rate of inflation is 12 percent and you initially paid $100 per share for the stock; for the real price to be the same a year later, you must sell the stock for $112 per share. In this case the tax code, which ignores the effects of inflation, says that you have earned $12 per share in income, and the government taxes you on this capital gain. The problem, of course, is that the tax code measures income as the nominal rather than the real capital gain. In this example, and in many others, inflation distorts how taxes are levied.

A fifth cost of inflation is the inconvenience of living in a world with a changing price level. Money is the yardstick with which we measure economic transactions. When there is inflation, that yardstick is changing in length. To continue the analogy, suppose that Congress passed a law specifying that a yard would equal 36 inches in 1997, 35 inches in 1998, 34 inches in 1999, and so on. Although the law would result in no ambiguity, it would be highly in-convenient. When someone measured a distance in yards, it would be neces-sary to specify whether the measurement was in 1997 yards or 1998 yards; to compare distances measured in different years, one would need to make an "inflation" correction. Similarly, the dollar is a less useful measure when its value is always changing.

For example, a changing price level complicates personal financial plan-ning. One important decision that all households face is how much of their in-come to consume today and how much to save for retirement. A dollar saved today and invested at a fixed nominal interest rate will yield a fixed dollar amount in the future. Yet the real value of that dollar amount— which will de-termine the retiree's living standard—depends on the future price level. Decid-ing how much to save would be much simpler if people could count on the price level in 30 years being similar to its level today.

Unexpected Inflation

Unexpected inflation has an effect that is more pernicious than any of the costs of steady, anticipated inflation: it arbitrarily redistributes wealth among indi-viduals. You can see how this works by examining long-term loans. Loan agree-ments typically specify a nominal interest rate, which is based on the expected rate of inflation. If inflation turns out differently from what was expected, the *ex post* real return that the debtor pays to the creditor differs from what both parties anticipated. On the one hand, if inflation turns out to be higher than ex-pected, the debtor wins and the creditor loses because the debtor repays the loan with less valuable dollars. On the other hand, if inflation turns out to be lower than expected, the creditor wins and the debtor loses because the repay-ment is worth more than the two parties anticipated.

Consider, for example, a person taking out a mortgage in 1960. At the time, a 30-year mortgage had an interest rate of about 6 percent per year. This rate was based on a low rate of expected inflation—inflation over the previous decade had averaged only 2.5 percent. The creditor probably expected to re-ceive a real return of about 3.5 percent, and the debtor expected to pay this real return. In fact, over the life of the mortgage, the inflation rate averaged 5 percent, so the *ex post* real return was only 1 percent. This unanticipated infla-tion benefited the debtor at the expense of the creditor.

Unanticipated inflation also hurts individuals on fixed pensions. Workers and firms often agree on a fixed nominal pension when the worker retires (or even earlier). Since the pension is deferred earnings, the worker is essentially providing the firm a loan: the worker provides labor services to the firm while young but does not get fully paid until old age. Like any creditor, the worker is hurt when inflation is higher than anticipated. Like any debtor, the firm is hurt when inflation is lower than anticipated.

These situations provide a clear argument against highly variable infla-tion. The more variable the rate of inflation, the greater the uncertainty that both debtors and creditors face. Since most people are *risk averse*—they dis-like uncertainty—the unpredictability caused by highly variable inflation hurts almost everyone.

Given these effects of inflation uncertainty, it is puzzling that nominal contracts are so prevalent. One might expect debtors and creditors to protect themselves from this uncertainty by writing contracts in real terms—that is, by indexing to some measure of the price level. In economies with extremely high and variable inflation, indexation is often widespread; sometimes this indexation takes the form of writing contracts using a more stable foreign currency. In economies with moderate inflation, such as the United States, indexation is less common. Yet even in the United States, some long-term obligations are indexed: for example, Social Security benefits for the elderly are adjusted annually in response to changes in the consumer price index.

Finally, in thinking about the costs of inflation, it is important to note a widely documented but little understood fact: high inflation is variable inflation. That is, countries with high average inflation also tend to have inflation rates that change greatly from year to year. The implication is that if a country decides to pursue a high-inflation monetary policy, it will likely have to accept highly variable inflation as well. As we have just discussed, highly variable inflation increases uncertainty for both creditors and debtors by subjecting them to arbitrary and potentially large redistributions of wealth.

Case Study *6-7*

• • • • • • • • • • • • •

The Free Silver Movement, the Election of 1896, and the Wizard of Oz

The redistributions of wealth caused by unexpected changes in the price level are often a source of political turmoil, as evidenced by the Free Silver movement in the late nineteenth century. From 1880 to 1896 the price level in the United States fell 23 percent. This deflation was good for creditors, the bankers of the Northeast, but it was bad for debtors, the farmers of the South and West. One proposed solution to this problem was to replace the gold standard with a bimetallic standard, under which both gold and silver could be minted into coin. The move to a bimetallic standard would increase the money supply and stop the deflation.

The silver issue dominated the presidential election of 1896. William McKinley, the Republican nominee, campaigned on a platform of preserving the gold standard. William Jennings Bryan, the Democratic nominee, supported the bimetallic standard. In a famous speech, Bryan proclaimed, "You shall not press down upon the brow of labor this crown of thorns, you shall not crucify mankind upon a cross of gold." Not surprisingly, McKinley was the candidate of the conservative eastern establishment, while Bryan was the candidate of the southern and western populists.

This debate over silver found its most memorable expression in a children's book, *The Wizard of Oz*. Written by a midwestern journalist, L. Frank Baum, just after the 1896 election, it tells the story of Dorothy, a girl lost in a strange land far from her home in Kansas. Dorothy (representing traditional American values) makes three friends: a scarecrow (the farmer), a tin woodman (the industrial worker), and a lion whose roar exceeds his might (William

Jennings Bryan). Together, the four of them make their way along a perilous yellow brick road (the gold standard), hoping to find the Wizard who will help Dorothy return home. Eventually they arrive in Oz (Washington), where everyone sees the world through green glasses (money). The Wizard (William McKinley) tries to be all things to all people but turns out to be a fraud. Dorothy's problem is solved only when she learns about the magical power of her silver slippers.[7]

Although the Republicans won the election of 1896 and the United States stayed on a gold standard, the Free Silver advocates got what they ultimately wanted: inflation. Around the time of the election, gold was discovered in Alaska, Australia, and South Africa. In addition, gold refiners devised the cyanide process, which facilitated the extraction of gold from ore. These developments led to increases in the money supply and in prices. From 1896 to 1910 the price level rose 35 percent.

• • • • • • • • • • • • • • •

6-7   Hyperinflation

Hyperinflation is often defined as inflation that exceeds 50 percent per month, which is just over 1 percent per day. Compounded over many months, this rate of inflation leads to very large increases in the price level. An inflation rate of 50 percent per month implies a more than 100-fold increase over a year, and a more than 2-million-fold increase over three years. Here we consider the costs and causes of such extreme inflation.

The Costs of Hyperinflation

Although economists debate whether the costs of moderate inflation are large or small, no one doubts that hyperinflation imposes a high toll on society. The costs are qualitatively the same as those we discussed earlier. When inflation reaches extreme levels, however, these costs are more apparent because they are so severe.

The shoeleather costs associated with reduced money holding, for instance, are serious under hyperinflation. Business executives devote much time and energy to cash management when cash loses its value quickly. By diverting this time and energy from more valuable activities, such as production and investment decisions, hyperinflation makes the economy run less efficiently.

Menu costs also become larger under hyperinflation. Firms have to change prices so often that normal business practices, such as printing and distributing catalogs with fixed prices, become impossible. In one restaurant during the German hyperinflation of the 1920s, a waiter would stand up on a table every 30 minutes to call out the new prices.

---

[7] The movie made forty years later hid much of the allegory by changing Dorothy's slippers from silver to ruby. For more on this topic, see Henry M. Littlefield, "The Wizard of Oz: Parable on Populism," *American Quarterly* 16 (Spring 1964): 47–58; and Hugh Rockoff, "The Wizard of Oz as a Monetary Allegory," *Journal of Political Economy* 98 (August 1990): 739–760.

Similarly, relative prices do not do a good job of reflecting true scarcity during hyperinflations. When prices change frequently by large amounts, it is hard for customers to shop around for the best price. Highly volatile and rapidly rising prices can alter behavior in many ways. According to one report, when patrons entered a pub during the German hyperinflation, they would often buy two pitchers of beer. Although the second pitcher would lose value by getting warm over time, it would lose value less rapidly than the money left sitting in the patron's wallet.

Tax systems are also distorted by hyperinflation—but in ways that are quite different than under moderate inflation. In most tax systems there is a delay between the time when a tax is levied and the time when the tax is paid to the government. In the United States, for example, taxpayers are required to make estimated income tax payments every three months. This short delay does not matter much under low inflation. By contrast, during hyperinflation, even a short delay greatly reduces real tax revenue. By the time the government gets the money it is due, the money has fallen in value. The result is that, once hyperinflations start, the real tax revenue of the government often falls substantially.

Finally, no one should underestimate the sheer inconvenience of living with hyperinflation. When carrying money to the grocery store is as burdensome as carrying the groceries back home, the monetary system is not doing its best to facilitate exchange. The government tries to overcome this problem by adding more and more zeros to the paper currency, but often it cannot keep up with the exploding price level.

Eventually, these costs of hyperinflation become intolerable. Over time, money loses its role as a store of value, unit of account, and medium of exchange. Barter becomes more common. And more stable unofficial monies—cigarettes or the U.S. dollar—naturally start to replace the official money.

Case Study *6-8*

• • • • • • • • • • • •

Life During the Bolivian Hyperinflation

The following article from the Wall Street Journal shows what life was like during the hyperinflation in Bolivia in 1985. What costs of inflation does this article emphasize? Does the Bolivian experience conform to the assessment by Lenin and Keynes in the quotation that began this chapter?

Precarious Peso—Amid Wild Inflation, Bolivians Concentrate on Swapping Currency

LA PAZ, Bolivia—When Edgar Miranda gets his monthly teacher's pay of 25 million pesos, he hasn't a moment to lose. Every hour, pesos drop in value. So, while his wife rushes to market to lay in a month's supply of rice and noodles, he is off with the rest of the pesos to change them into black-market dollars.

Mr. Miranda is practicing the First Rule of Survival amid the most out-of-control inflation in the world today. Bolivia is a case study of how runaway inflation undermines a society. Price increases are so huge that the figures build up almost beyond comprehension. In one six-month period, for example, prices soared at an annual rate of 38,000%. By official count, however, last year's inflation reached 2,000%, and this year's is expected to hit 8,000%—though other estimates range many times higher. In any event, Bolivia's rate dwarfs Israel's 370% and Argentina's 1,100%—two other cases of severe inflation.

It is easier to comprehend what happens to the 38-year-old Mr. Miranda's pay if he doesn't quickly change it into dollars. The day he was paid 25 million pesos, a dollar cost 500,000 pesos. So he received $50. Just days later, with the rate at 900,000 pesos, he would have received $27.

"We think only about today and converting every peso into dollars," says Ronald MacLean, the manager of a gold-mining firm. "We have become myopic."

And intent on survival. Civil servants won't hand out a form without a bribe. Lawyers, accountants, hairdressers, even prostitutes have almost given up working to become money-changers in the streets. Workers stage repeated strikes and steal from their bosses. The bosses smuggle production abroad, take out phony loans, duck taxes—anything to get dollars for speculation.

The production at the state mines, for example, dropped to 12,000 tons last year from 18,000. The miners pad their wages by smuggling out the richest ore in their lunch pails, and the ore goes by a contraband network into neighboring Peru. Without a major tin mine, Peru now exports some 4,000 metric tons of tin a year.

"We don't produce anything. We are all currency speculators," a heavy-equipment dealer in La Paz says. "People don't know what's good and bad anymore. We have become an amoral society. . . ."

It is an open secret that practically all of the black-market dollars come from the illegal cocaine trade with the U.S. Cocaine traffickers earn an estimated $1 billion a year. . . .

But meanwhile the country is suffering from inflation largely because the government's revenues cover a mere 15% of its expenditures and its deficit has widened to nearly 25% of the country's total annual output. The revenues are hurt by a lag in tax payments, and taxes aren't being collected largely because of widespread theft and bribery.

Source: Reprinted by permission of the *Wall Street Journal,* © August 13, 1985, page 1, Dow Jones & Company, Inc. All Rights Reserved Worldwide.

● ● ● ● ● ● ● ● ● ● ● ● ● ● ●

The Causes of Hyperinflation

Why do hyperinflations start, and how do they end? This question can be answered at different levels.

The most obvious answer is that hyperinflations are due to excessive growth in the supply of money. When the central bank prints money, the price level rises. When it prints money rapidly enough, the result is hyperinflation.

To stop the hyperinflation, the central bank must simply reduce the rate of money growth.

This answer is incomplete, however, for it leaves open the question of why central banks in hyperinflating economies choose to print so much money. To address this deeper question, we must turn our attention from monetary to fiscal policy. Most hyperinflations begin when the government has inadequate tax revenue to pay for its spending. Although the government might prefer to finance this budget deficit by issuing debt, it may find itself unable to borrow, perhaps because lenders view the government as a bad credit risk. To cover the deficit, the government turns to the only mechanism at its disposal—the printing press. The result is rapid money growth and hyperinflation.

Once the hyperinflation is under way, the fiscal problems become even more severe. Because of the delay in collecting tax payments, real tax revenue falls as inflation rises. Thus, the government's need to rely on seigniorage is self-reinforcing. Rapid money creation leads to hyperinflation, which leads to a larger budget deficit, which leads to even more rapid money creation.

The ends of hyperinflations almost always coincide with fiscal reforms. Once the magnitude of the problem becomes apparent, the government finally musters the political will to reduce government spending and increase taxes. These fiscal reforms reduce the need for seigniorage, which allows a reduction in money growth. Hence, even if inflation is always and everywhere a monetary phenomenon, the end of hyperinflation is usually a fiscal phenomenon as well.[8]

Case Study *6-9*

• • • • • • • • • • • • • •

Hyperinflation in Interwar Germany

After World War I, Germany experienced one of history's most spectacular examples of hyperinflation. At the war's end, the Allies demanded that Germany pay substantial reparations. These payments led to fiscal deficits in Germany, which the German government eventually financed by printing large quantities of money.

Figure 6-6 shows the quantity of money and the general price level in Germany from January 1922 to December 1924. During this period both money and prices rose at an amazing rate. For example, the price of a daily newspaper rose from 0.30 marks in January 1921 to 1 mark in May 1922, to 8 marks in October 1922, to 100 marks in February 1923, and to 1,000 marks in September 1923. Then, in the fall of 1923, prices really took off: the newspaper sold for 2,000 marks on October 1, 20,000 marks on October 15, 1 million marks on October 29, 15 million marks on November 9, and 70 million marks

---

[8] For more on these issues, see Thomas J. Sargent, "The End of Four Big Inflations," in Robert Hall, ed., *Inflation* (Chicago: University of Chicago Press, 1983), 41–98; and Rudiger Dornbusch and Stanley Fischer, "Stopping Hyperinflations: Past and Present," *Weltwirtschaftliches Archiv* 122 (April 1986): 1–47.

on November 17. In December 1923 the money supply and prices abruptly stabilized.[9]

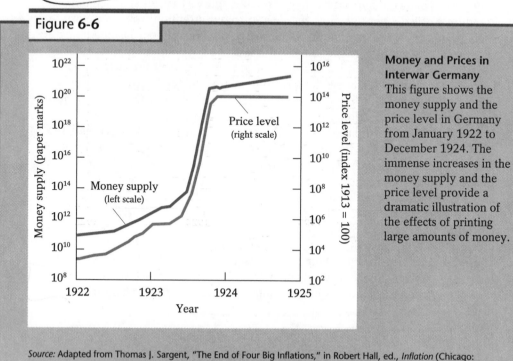

Figure 6-6

Money and Prices in Interwar Germany This figure shows the money supply and the price level in Germany from January 1922 to December 1924. The immense increases in the money supply and the price level provide a dramatic illustration of the effects of printing large amounts of money.

Source: Adapted from Thomas J. Sargent, "The End of Four Big Inflations," in Robert Hall, ed., *Inflation* (Chicago: University of Chicago Press, 1983): 41–98.

Just as fiscal problems caused the German hyperinflation, a fiscal reform ended it. At the end of 1923, the number of government employees was cut by one-third, and the reparations payments were temporarily suspended and eventually reduced. At the same time, a new central bank, the Rentenbank, replaced the old central bank, the Reichsbank. The Rentenbank was committed to not financing the government by printing money.

According to our theoretical analysis of money demand, an end to a hyperinflation should lead to an increase in real money balances, for the cost of holding money falls. Figure 6-7 shows that real money balances in Germany did fall as inflation increased, and then increased again as inflation fell. Yet the increase in real money balances was not immediate. Perhaps the adjustment of real money balances to the cost of holding money is a gradual process. Or perhaps it took time for people in Germany to believe that the inflation had really ended, so that expected inflation fell more gradually than actual inflation.

---

[9]   The data on newspaper prices are from Michael Mussa, "Sticky Individual Prices and the Dynamics of the General Price Level," *Carnegie-Rochester Conference on Public Policy* 15 (Autumn 1981): 261–296.

Figure 6-7

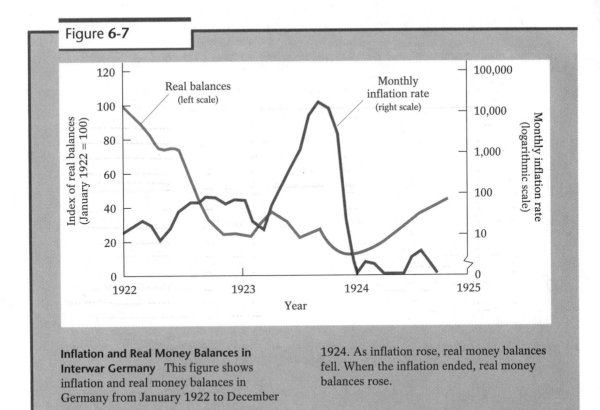

Inflation and Real Money Balances in Interwar Germany This figure shows inflation and real money balances in Germany from January 1922 to December 1924. As inflation rose, real money balances fell. When the inflation ended, real money balances rose.

Source: Adapted from Thomas J. Sargent, "The End of Four Big Inflations," in Robert Hall, ed., *Inflation* (Chicago: University of Chicago Press, 1983): 41–93.

● ● ● ● ● ● ● ● ● ● ● ● ●

6-8 Conclusion: The Classical Dichotomy

We have finished our discussion of money and inflation. Let's now step back and examine a key assumption that has been implicit in our discussion.

In Chapters 3, 4, and 5, we explained many macroeconomic variables, such as real GDP, the capital stock, the real wage, and the real interest rate. These variables fall into two categories. The first category is *quantities*. For example, real GDP is the quantity of goods produced in a given year; the capital stock is the amount of capital available at a given time. The second category is *relative prices*. For example, the real wage is the relative price of consumption and leisure; the real interest rate is the price of output today relative to output tomorrow. Together these two categories—quantities and relative prices—are called **real variables**.

In this chapter we examined **nominal variables**. Nominal variables are expressed in terms of money. There are many nominal variables: the price level, the inflation rate, the wage a person earns (the number of dollars received for working).

At first it may seem surprising that we were able to explain real variables without introducing nominal variables or the existence of money. In previous chapters we studied the level and allocation of the economy's output without mentioning the rate of inflation. Our theory of the labor market explained the real wage without explaining the nominal wage.

Economists call this theoretical separation of real and nominal variables the classical dichotomy. It is the hallmark of classical macroeconomic theory. The classical dichotomy is an important insight, because it greatly simplifies economic theory. In particular, it allows us to examine real variables, as we have done, while ignoring nominal variables. The classical dichotomy arises because, in classical theory, changes in the money supply do not influence real variables. This irrelevance of money for real variables is called **monetary neutrality**. For many purposes—in particular for studying long-run issues—monetary neutrality is approximately correct.

Yet monetary neutrality does not fully describe the world in which we live. Beginning in Chapter 8, we discuss departures from the classical model and monetary neutrality. These departures are crucial for understanding many macroeconomic phenomena, such as short-run economic fluctuations.

Summary

1. Money is the stock of assets used for transactions. It serves as a store of value, a unit of account, and a medium of exchange. Different sorts of assets are used as money: commodity money systems use an asset with intrinsic value, whereas fiat money systems use an asset whose sole function is to serve as money. In modern economies, a central bank such as the Federal Reserve has the responsibility for controlling the supply of money.

2. The quantity theory of money states that nominal GDP is proportional to the stock of money. Because the factors of production and the production function determine real GDP, the quantity theory implies that the price level is proportional to the quantity of money. Therefore, the rate of growth in the quantity of money determines the inflation rate.

3. Seigniorage is the revenue that the government raises by printing money. It is a tax on money holding. Although seigniorage is quantitatively small in most economies, it is often a major source of government revenue in economies experiencing hyperinflation.

4. The nominal interest rate is the sum of the real interest rate and the inflation rate. The Fisher effect says that the nominal interest rate moves one-for-one with expected inflation.

5. The nominal interest rate is the cost of holding money. Thus, one might expect the demand for money to depend on the nominal interest rate. If it does, then the price level depends on both the current quantity of money and the quantities of money expected in the future.

6. The costs of expected inflation include shoeleather costs, menu costs, the cost of relative price variability, tax distortions, and the inconvenience of making inflation corrections. The cost of unexpected inflation is the arbitrary redistribution of wealth between debtors and creditors.

7. During hyperinflations, most of the costs of inflation become severe. Hyperinflations begin when governments finance large budget deficits by printing money. They end when fiscal reforms eliminate the need for seigniorage.

8. According to classical economic theory, money is neutral: the money supply does not affect real variables. Therefore, classical theory allows us to study how real variables are determined without any reference to the money supply. The equilibrium in the money market then determines the price level and, as a result, all other nominal variables. This theoretical separation of real and nominal variables is called the classical dichotomy.

KEY CONCEPTS

Inflation

Hyperinflation

Money

Store of value

Unit of account

Medium of exchange

Double coincidence of wants

Fiat money

Commodity money

Gold standard

Money supply

Central bank

Federal Reserve

Monetary policy

Open-market operations

Currency

Demand deposits

Quantity equation

Transactions velocity of money

Income velocity of money

Real money balances

Money demand function

Quantity theory of money

Seigniorage

Nominal and real interest rates

Fisher equation and Fisher effect

Ex ante and ex post real interest rates

Shoeleather costs

Menu costs

Real and nominal variables

Classical dichotomy

Monetary neutrality

QUESTIONS FOR REVIEW

1. Describe the functions of money.

2. What is fiat money? What is commodity money?

3. Who controls the money supply and how?

4. Write the quantity equation and explain it.

5. What does the assumption of constant velocity imply?

6. Who pays the inflation tax?

7. If inflation rises from 6 to 8 percent, what happens to real and nominal interest rates according to the Fisher effect?

8. List all the costs of inflation you can think of, and rank them according to how important you think they are.

9. Explain the roles of monetary and fiscal policy in causing and ending hyperinflations.

PROBLEMS AND APPLICATIONS

1. What are the three functions of money? Which of the functions do the following items satisfy? Which do they not satisfy?

    a. A credit card

    b. A painting by Rembrandt

    c. A subway token

2. In the country of Wiknam, the velocity of money is constant. Real GDP grows by 5 percent per year, the money stock grows by 14 percent per year, and the nominal interest rate is 11 percent. What is the real interest rate?

3. In 1994, a newspaper article written by the Associated Press reported that the U.S. economy was experiencing a low rate of inflation. It said that "low inflation has a downside: 45 million recipients of Social Security and other benefits will see their checks go up by just 2.8 percent next year."

    a. Why does inflation affect the increase in Social Security and other benefits?

    b. Is this effect a cost of inflation, as the article suggests? Why or why not?

4. Suppose you are advising a small country (such as Bermuda) on whether to print its own money or to use the money of its larger neighbor (such as the United States). What are the costs and benefits of a national money? Does the relative political stability of the two countries have any role in this decision?

5. During World War II, both Germany and England had plans for a paper weapon: they each printed the other's currency, with the intention of dropping large quantities by airplane. Why might this have been an effective weapon?

6. Calvin Coolidge once said that "inflation is repudiation." What might he have meant by this? Do you agree? Why or why not? Does it matter whether the inflation is expected or unexpected?

7. Some economic historians have noted that during the period of the gold standard, gold discoveries were most likely to occur after a long deflation. (The discoveries of 1896 are an example.) Why might this be true?

8. Suppose that consumption depends on the level of real money balances (on

the grounds that real money balances are part of wealth). Show that if real money balances depend on the nominal interest rate, then an increase in the rate of money growth affects consumption, investment, and the real interest rate. Does the nominal interest rate adjust more than one-for-one or less than one-for-one to expected inflation?

This deviation from the classical dichotomy and the Fisher effect is called the *Mundell-Tobin effect*. How might you decide whether the Mundell-Tobin effect is important in practice?

Appendix

The Impact of Current and Future Money on the Price Level

In this chapter we showed that if the quantity of real money balances demanded depends on the cost of holding money, the price level depends on both the current money supply and the future money supply. We now examine more explicitly how this works.

To keep the math as simple as possible, we posit a money demand function that is linear in the natural logarithms of all the variables. The money demand function is

$$m_t - p_t = -\gamma(p_{t+1} - p_t), \tag{A1}$$

where m_t is the log of the quantity of money at time t, p_t is the log of the price level at time t, and γ is a parameter that governs the sensitivity of money demand to the rate of inflation. By the property of logarithms, $m_t - p_t$ is the log of real money balances, and $p_{t+1} - p_t$ is the inflation rate between period t and period $t + 1$. This equation states that if inflation goes up by 1 percentage point, real money balances fall by γ percent.

We have made a number of assumptions in writing the money demand function in this way. First, by excluding the level of output as a determinant of money demand, we are implicitly assuming that it is constant. Second, by including the rate of inflation rather than the nominal interest rate, we are assuming that the real interest rate is constant. Third, by including actual inflation rather than expected inflation, we are assuming perfect foresight. All of these assumptions are for simplification.

We want to solve Equation A1 to express the price level as a function of current and future money. To do this, note that Equation A1 can be rewritten as

$$p_t = \left(\frac{1}{1 + \gamma}\right) m_t + \left(\frac{\gamma}{1 + \gamma}\right) p_{t+1}. \tag{A2}$$

This equation states that the current price level is a weighted average of the current money supply and the next period's price level. The next period's price level will be determined the same way as this period's price level:

$$p_{t+1} = \left(\frac{1}{1 + \gamma}\right) m_{t+1} + \left(\frac{\gamma}{1 + \gamma}\right) p_{t+2}. \tag{A3}$$

Use Equation A3 to substitute for p_{t+1} in Equation A2 to obtain

$$p_t = \frac{1}{1 + \gamma} m_t + \frac{\gamma}{(1 + \gamma)^2} m_{t+1} + \frac{\gamma^2}{(1 + \gamma)^2} p_{t+2}. \qquad (A4)$$

Equation A4 states that the current price level is a weighted average of the current money supply, the next period's money supply, and the following period's price level. Once again, the price level in $t + 2$ is determined as in Equation A2:

$$p_{t+2} = \left(\frac{1}{1 + \gamma}\right) m_{t+2} + \left(\frac{\gamma}{1 + \gamma}\right) p_{t+3}. \qquad (A5)$$

Now use Equation A5 to substitute into Equation A4 to obtain

$$p_t = \frac{1}{1 + \gamma} m_t + \frac{\gamma}{(1 + \gamma)^2} m_{t+1} + \frac{\gamma^2}{(1 + \gamma)^3} m_{t+2} + \frac{\gamma^3}{(1 + \gamma)^3} p_{t+3}. \qquad (A6)$$

By now you see the pattern. We can continue to use Equation A2 to substitute for the future price level. If we do this an infinite number of times, we find

$$p_t = \left(\frac{1}{1 + \gamma}\right)\left[m_t + \left(\frac{\gamma}{1 + \gamma}\right) m_{t+1} + \left(\frac{\gamma}{1 + \gamma}\right)^2 m_{t+2}\right.$$
$$\left. + \left(\frac{\gamma}{1 + \gamma}\right)^3 m_{t+3} + \ldots \right], \qquad (A7)$$

where "..." indicates an infinite number of analogous terms. According to Equation A7, the current price level is a weighted average of the current money supply and all future money supplies.

Note the importance of γ, the parameter governing the sensitivity of real money balances to inflation. The weights on the future money supplies decline geometrically at rate $\gamma/(1 + \gamma)$. If γ is small, then $\gamma/(1 + \gamma)$ is small, and the weights decline quickly. In this case, the current money supply is the primary determinant of the price level. (Indeed, if γ equals zero, then we obtain the quantity theory of money: the price level is proportional to the current money supply, and the future money supplies do not matter at all.) If γ is large, then $\gamma/(1 + \gamma)$ is close to 1, and the weights decline slowly. In this case, the future money supplies play a key role in determining today's price level.

Finally, let's relax the assumption of perfect foresight. If the future is not known with certainty, then we should write the money demand function as

$$m_t - p_t = -\gamma(Ep_{t+1} - p_t), \qquad (A8)$$

where Ep_{t+1} is the expected price level. Equation A8 states that real money balances depend on expected inflation. By following steps similar to those above, we can show that

$$p_t = \left(\frac{1}{1 + \gamma}\right)\left[m_t + \left(\frac{\gamma}{1 + \gamma}\right) Em_{t+1} + \left(\frac{\gamma}{1 + \gamma}\right)^2 Em_{t+2}\right.$$
$$\left. + \left(\frac{\gamma}{1 + \gamma}\right)^3 Em_{t+3} + \ldots \right]. \qquad (A9)$$

Equation A9 states that the price level depends on the current money supply and expected future money supplies.

Some economists use this model to argue that *credibility* is important for ending hyperinflation. Because the price level depends on both current and expected future money, inflation depends on both current and expected future money growth. Therefore, to end high inflation, both money growth and expected money growth must fall. Expectations, in turn, depend on credibility—the perception that the central bank is truly committed to a new, more stable policy.

How can a central bank achieve credibility in the midst of hyperinflation? Credibility is often achieved by removing the underlying cause of the hyperinflation—the need for seigniorage. Thus, a credible fiscal reform is often necessary for a credible change in monetary policy. This fiscal reform might take the form of reduced government spending and increased political independence of the central bank. Reduced spending decreases the need for seigniorage in the present. Increased independence allows the central bank to resist government demands for seigniorage in the future.

Chapter 7

The Open Economy

No nation was ever ruined by trade.

Benjamin Franklin

Many of the goods and services we enjoy are produced abroad. We eat Norwegian salmon as well as Texas beef, drive cars made in Japan as well as Michigan, and vacation in Mexico as well as Florida. The freedom to import and export benefits the citizens of all countries. Trade allows each country to specialize in what it produces best, and it provides everyone with a greater variety of goods and services.

Over the past four decades the volume of international trade has been increasing, making the economies of the world more interdependent. Figure 7-1

Figure 7-1

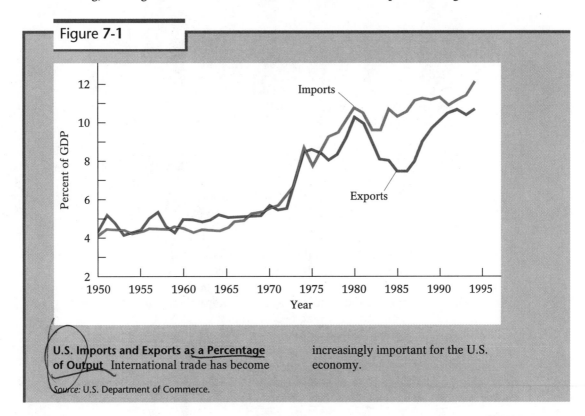

U.S. Imports and Exports as a Percentage of Output International trade has become increasingly important for the U.S. economy.

Source: U.S. Department of Commerce.

displays imports and exports as a percentage of GDP for the United States. It shows clearly the upward trend in international trade. In the 1950s imports were less than 5 percent of GDP; today they are over 10 percent.

While international trade is important for the United States, it is vital for many other countries. Figure 7-2 shows imports and exports as a percentage of GDP for seven major industrial countries. In Canada and the United Kingdom, for example, imports are about 25 percent of GDP. In these countries, international trade is central to analyzing economic developments and formulating economic policies.

Figure 7-2

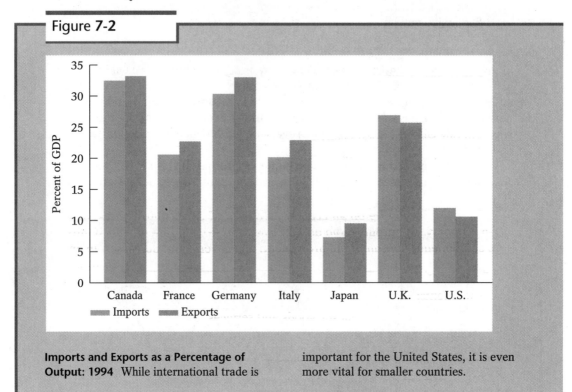

Imports and Exports as a Percentage of Output: 1994 While international trade is important for the United States, it is even more vital for smaller countries.

Source: International Financial Statistics.

In previous chapters we simplified our analysis by assuming that the economy does not trade internationally. That is, we assumed a closed economy. As we have just seen, however, actual economies export goods and services abroad, and they import goods and services from abroad. In this chapter we begin our study of open-economy macroeconomics.

We begin in Section 7-1 with questions of measurement. To understand how the open economy works, we must understand the key macroeconomic variables that measure the interactions among countries. Accounting identities reveal a key insight: the flow of goods and services across national borders is always matched by an equivalent flow of funds to finance capital accumulation.

In Section 7-2 we examine the determinants of these international flows. We develop a model of the small open economy that corresponds to our model of the closed economy in Chapter 3. The model shows what determines whether a country is a borrower or a lender in world markets, and how policies at home and abroad affect the flows of capital and goods.

In Section 7-3 we extend the model to discuss the prices at which a country makes exchanges in world markets. We examine what determines the price of domestic goods relative to foreign goods. We also examine what determines the rate at which the domestic currency trades for foreign currencies. Our model shows how protectionist trade policies—policies designed to protect domestic industries from foreign competition—influence the amount of international trade and the rate of exchange.

7-1 The International Flows of Capital and Goods

We begin our study of open-economy macroeconomics by taking another look at national income accounting, which we first discussed in Chapter 2.

The Role of Net Exports

Consider the expenditure on an economy's output of goods and services. In a closed economy, all output is sold domestically, and expenditure is divided into three components: consumption, investment, and government purchases. In an open economy, some output is sold domestically, and some is exported to be sold abroad. We can divide expenditure on an open economy's output Y into four components:

- C^d, consumption of domestic goods and services
- I^d, investment in domestic goods and services
- G^d, government purchases of domestic goods and services
- EX, exports of domestic goods and services.

The division of expenditure into these components is expressed in the identity

$$Y = C^d + I^d + G^d + EX.$$

The sum of the first three terms, $C^d + I^d + G^d$, is domestic spending on domestic goods and services. The fourth term, EX, is foreign spending on domestic goods and services.

We now want to make this identity more useful. To do this, note that domestic spending on all goods and services is the sum of domestic spending on domestic goods and services and on foreign goods and services. Hence, total consumption C equals consumption of domestic goods and services C^d plus consumption of foreign goods and services C^f; total investment I equals investment in domestic goods and services I^d plus investment in foreign goods and services I^f; and total government purchases G equals government purchases of domestic goods and services G^d plus government purchases of foreign goods and services G^f. Thus,

$$C = C^d + C^f$$
$$I = I^d + I^f$$
$$G = G^d + G^f.$$

We substitute these three equations into the identity above:

$$Y = (C - C^f) + (I - I^f) + (G - G^f) + EX.$$

We can rearrange to obtain

$$Y = C + I + G + EX - (C^f + I^f + G^f).$$

The sum of domestic spending on foreign goods and services $(C^f + I^f + G^f)$ is expenditure on imports (IM). We can thus write the national income accounts identity as

$$Y = C + I + G + EX - IM.$$

Because spending on imports is included in domestic spending $(C + I + G)$, and because goods and services imported from abroad are not part of a country's output, this equation subtracts spending on imports. Defining **net exports** to be exports minus imports ($NX = EX - IM$), the identity becomes

$$Y = C + I + G + NX.$$

This equation states that expenditure on domestic output is the sum of consumption, investment, government purchases, and net exports. This form of the national income accounts identity is the most common; it should be familiar from Chapter 2.

The national income accounts identity shows how domestic output, domestic spending, and net exports are related. In particular,

$$NX = Y - (C + I + G)$$
$$\text{Net Exports} = \text{Output} - \text{Domestic Spending}.$$

If output exceeds domestic spending, we export the difference: net exports are positive. If output falls short of domestic spending, we import the difference: net exports are negative.

Net Foreign Investment and the Trade Balance

In an open economy, as in the closed economy we discussed in Chapter 3, financial markets and goods markets are closely related. To see the relationship, we must rewrite the national income accounts identity in terms of saving and investment. Begin with the identity

$$Y = C + I + G + NX.$$

Subtract C and G from both sides to obtain

$$Y - C - G = I + NX.$$

Recall from Chapter 3 that $Y - C - G$ is national saving S, the sum of private saving, $Y - T - C$, and public saving, $T - G$. Therefore,

$$S = I + NX.$$

Subtracting I from both sides of the equation, we can write the national income accounts identity as

$$S - I = NX.$$

SAVING − INV = net X

This form of the national income accounts identity shows the relationship between the international flow of funds for capital accumulation, $S - I$, and the international flow of goods and services, NX.

Let's look more closely at each part of this identity. The value $S - I$ is called **net foreign investment**. Net foreign investment is the excess of domestic saving over domestic investment; it is equal to the amount that domestic residents are lending abroad minus the amount that foreigners are lending to us. The second part of this identity, NX, is called the **trade balance**. The trade balance is another name for our net export of goods and services.

The national income accounts identity shows that net foreign investment always equals the trade balance. That is,

Net Foreign Investment = Trade Balance
$$S - I \qquad = \qquad NX.$$

If $S - I$ and NX are positive, we have a **trade surplus**. In this case, we are net lenders in world financial markets, and we are exporting more goods than we are importing. If $S - I$ and NX are negative, we have a **trade deficit**. In this case, we are net borrowers in world financial markets, and we are importing more goods than we are exporting.

The national income accounts identity shows that the international flow of funds to finance capital accumulation and the international flow of goods and services are two sides of the same coin. On the one hand, if our saving exceeds our investment, the saving that is not invested domestically is used to make loans to foreigners. Foreigners require these loans because we are providing them with more goods and services than they are providing us. That is, we are running a trade surplus. On the other hand, if our investment exceeds our saving, the extra investment must be financed by borrowing from abroad. These foreign loans enable us to import more goods and services than we export. That is, we are running a trade deficit.

Note that the international flow of capital can take many forms. It is easiest to assume—as we have done so far—that when we run a trade deficit, foreigners make loans to us. This happens, for example, when the Japanese buy the debt issued by U.S. corporations or by the U.S. government. But, equivalently, the flow of capital can take the form of foreigners buying domestic assets. For example, when Japanese investors bought Rockefeller Center in New York, that transaction reduced U.S. net foreign investment. In both the case of foreigners buying domestically issued debt and the case of foreigners buying domestically owned assets, foreigners are obtaining a claim to the future returns to domestic capital. In other words, in both cases, foreigners end up owning some of the domestic capital stock.

7-2 Saving and Investment in a Small Open Economy

So far in our discussion of the international flows of goods and capital, we have merely rearranged accounting identities. That is, we have defined some of the variables that measure transactions in an open economy, and we have shown the links among these variables that follow from their definitions. Our next step is to develop a model that explains the behavior of these variables. We can then use the model to answer questions such as how the trade balance responds to changes in policy.

Here we present a model of the international flows of capital and goods. Since net foreign investment is domestic saving minus domestic investment, our model explains net foreign investment by explaining these two variables. The model also explains the trade balance, because the trade balance must equal net foreign investment.

To develop this model, we use some of the elements of the model of national income in Chapter 3. In contrast to the model in Chapter 3, however, we do not assume that the real interest rate equilibrates saving and investment. Instead, we allow the economy to run a trade deficit and borrow from other countries, or to run a trade surplus and lend to other countries.

If the real interest rate does not equilibrate saving and investment in this model, what does determine the real interest rate? We answer this question here by considering the simple case of a **small open economy** with perfect capital mobility. By "small" we mean that this economy is a small part of the world market and thus, by itself, can have only a negligible effect on the world interest rate. By "perfect capital mobility" we mean that residents of the country have full access to world financial markets. In particular, the government does not impede international borrowing or lending. Thus, the interest rate in a small open economy equals the **world interest rate** r^*, the real interest rate prevailing in world financial markets. We write

$$r = r^*.$$

The small open economy takes the world real interest rate as given.

Let us discuss for a moment what determines the world real interest rate. In a closed economy, the equilibrium of saving and investment determines the interest rate. Surely, the world economy—barring interplanetary trade—is a closed economy. Therefore, the equilibrium of world saving and world investment determines the world interest rate. Our small open economy has a negligible effect on the world real interest rate because, being a small part of the world, it has a negligible effect on world saving and world investment.

The Model

To build the model of the small open economy, we take three assumptions from Chapter 3:

- The output of the economy Y is fixed by the factors of production and the production function. We write this as

$$Y = \overline{Y} = F(\overline{K}, \overline{L}).$$

- Consumption C is positively related to disposable income $Y - T$. We write the consumption function as

$$C = C(Y - T).$$

- Investment I is negatively related to the real interest rate r. We write the investment function as

$$I = I(r).$$

These are the three key parts of our model. If you do not understand these relationships, review Chapter 3 before continuing.

We can now return to the accounting identity and write it as

$$NX = (Y - C - G) - I$$
$$NX = \qquad S \qquad - I.$$

Substituting our three assumptions from Chapter 3 and the condition that the interest rate equals the world interest rate, we obtain

$$NX = [\overline{Y} - C(\overline{Y} - T) - G] - I(r^*)$$
$$= \qquad \overline{S} \qquad - I(r^*).$$

This equation shows what determines saving S and investment I—and thus the trade balance NX. Remember that saving depends on fiscal policy: lower government purchases G or higher taxes T raise national saving. Investment depends on the world real interest rate r^*: high interest rates make some investment projects unprofitable. Therefore, the trade balance depends on these variables as well.

In Chapter 3 we graphed saving and investment as in Figure 7-3. In the closed economy studied there, the real interest rate adjusts to equilibrate saving and investment—that is, the real interest rate is found where the saving and investment curves cross. In the small open economy, however, the real interest rate equals the world real interest rate. The trade balance is determined by the difference between saving and investment at the world interest rate.

At this point, you might wonder about the mechanism that causes the trade balance to equal net foreign investment. The determinants of net foreign investment are easy to understand. When domestic saving falls short of domestic investment, investors borrow from abroad; when saving exceeds investment, the excess is lent to other countries. But what causes those who import and export to behave in a way that ensures that the international flow of goods exactly balances this international flow of capital? For now we leave this question unanswered, but we return to it in Section 7-3 when we discuss the determination of exchange rates.

Figure 7-3

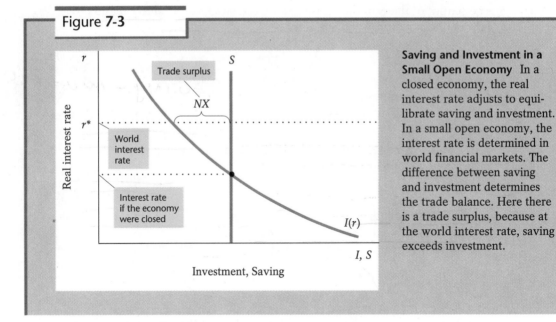

Saving and Investment in a Small Open Economy In a closed economy, the real interest rate adjusts to equilibrate saving and investment. In a small open economy, the interest rate is determined in world financial markets. The difference between saving and investment determines the trade balance. Here there is a trade surplus, because at the world interest rate, saving exceeds investment.

How Policies Influence the Trade Balance

Suppose that the economy begins in a position of balanced trade. That is, at first, its exports exactly balance its imports, so net exports NX equal zero, and investment I equals saving S. Let's use our model to predict the effects of government policies at home and abroad.

Fiscal Policy at Home   Consider first what happens to the small open economy if the government expands domestic spending by increasing government purchases. The increase in G reduces national saving, because $S = Y - C - G$. With an unchanged world real interest rate, investment remains the same. Therefore, saving falls below investment, and some investment must now be financed by borrowing from abroad. Since $NX = S - I$, the fall in S implies a fall in NX. The economy now runs a trade deficit.

The same logic applies to a decrease in taxes. A tax cut lowers T, raises disposable income $Y - T$, stimulates consumption, and reduces national saving. (Even though some of the tax cut finds its way into private saving, public saving falls by the full amount of the tax cut; in total, saving falls.) Since $NX = S - I$, the reduction in national saving in turn lowers NX.

Figure 7-4 illustrates these effects. A fiscal policy change that increases private consumption C or public consumption G reduces national saving ($Y - C - G$) and, therefore, shifts to the left the vertical line that represents saving. Because NX is the distance between the saving schedule and the investment schedule at the world interest rate, this shift reduces NX. *Hence, starting from balanced trade, a change in fiscal policy that reduces national saving leads to a trade deficit.*

Figure 7-4

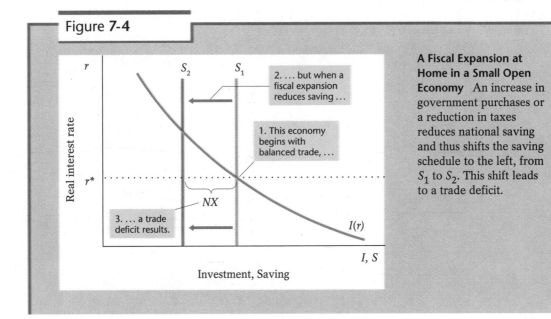

1. This economy begins with balanced trade, ...

2. ... but when a fiscal expansion reduces saving ...

3. ... a trade deficit results.

A Fiscal Expansion at Home in a Small Open Economy An increase in government purchases or a reduction in taxes reduces national saving and thus shifts the saving schedule to the left, from S_1 to S_2. This shift leads to a trade deficit.

Case Study 7-1

The Twin Deficits

The United States has experienced an unusual episode of expansionary fiscal policy since the early 1980s. With the support of President Ronald Reagan, the Congress passed legislation in 1981 that substantially cut personal income taxes over the next three years. Because these tax cuts were not met with equal cuts in government spending, the federal budget went into deficit. These budget deficits continued not only through Reagan's two terms in office but also through the terms of George Bush and Bill Clinton.

According to our model, such a policy should reduce national saving, thereby causing a trade deficit. And, in fact, that is exactly what happened. Figure 7-5 shows national saving, investment, the trade balance, and the federal budget balance as a percentage of GDP since 1960. Before 1980, the federal budget was, on average, roughly in balance. Budget surpluses were common, as the debt used to finance World War II was gradually being paid off. During this time, the trade balance also averaged a small surplus. Americans were saving more than they were investing at home, and the difference was invested abroad.

The situation changed dramatically around 1981. At that time, the federal government started to run a budget deficit of a size unprecedented in peacetime. This policy reduced national saving, leading to a large trade deficit. That is, since U.S. saving was no longer sufficient to finance U.S. investment, other countries started lending to the United States. In 1981, the U.S. stock of net

Not True! [handwritten annotation]

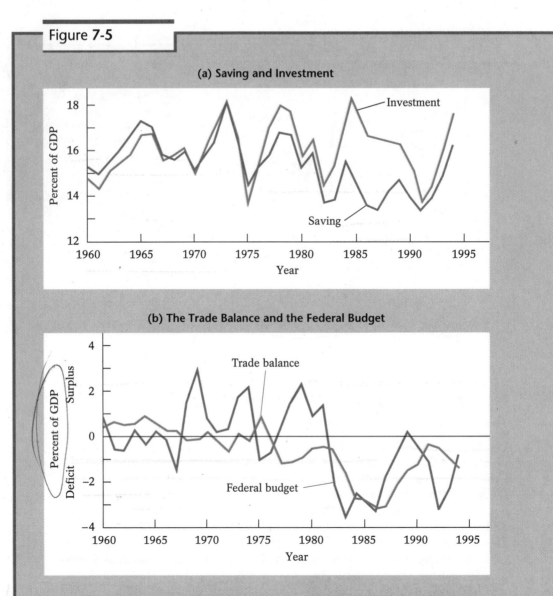

Figure 7-5

(a) Saving and Investment

(b) The Trade Balance and the Federal Budget

Saving, Investment, the Trade Balance, and the Budget Deficit: The U.S. Experience Panel (a) shows national saving and investment as a percentage of GDP since 1960. The trade balance equals saving minus investment. Panel (b) shows the trade balance and the federal budget balance as a percentage of GDP. Positive numbers represent a surplus, and negative numbers represent a deficit. Note that in the early 1980s, the federal government began running large budget deficits, which reduced national saving and led to large trade deficits.

Note: The numbers for the budget deficit are corrected for the effects of inflation: only the real interest on the debt is counted as expenditure. For a discussion of this correction, see Chapter 16. The numbers for the trade balance are net exports in current dollars from the national income accounts.

Source: U.S. Department of Commerce.

foreign assets was about 12.3 percent of GDP; in 1993 it was *negative* 8.8 percent. The United States went from being the world's largest creditor to being the world's largest debtor.

Fiscal Policy Abroad Consider now what happens to a small open economy when foreign governments increase their government purchases. If these foreign countries are a small part of the world economy, then their fiscal change has a negligible impact on other countries. But if these foreign countries are a large part of the world economy, their increase in government purchases reduces world saving and causes the world interest rate to rise.

The increase in the world interest rate raises the cost of borrowing and, thus, reduces investment in our small open economy. Because there has been no change in domestic saving, saving S now exceeds investment I. Some of our saving begins to flow abroad. Since $NX = S - I$, the reduction in I must also increase NX. Hence, reduced saving abroad leads to a trade surplus at home.

Figure 7-6 illustrates how a small open economy starting from balanced trade responds to a foreign fiscal expansion. Because the policy change is occurring abroad, the domestic saving and investment schedules remain the same. The only change is an increase in the world interest rate. Since the trade balance is the difference between the two schedules, the increase in the interest rate leads to a trade surplus. *Hence, an increase in the world interest rate due to a fiscal expansion abroad leads to a trade surplus.*

i.e. capital outflow = − on KAB = surplus on CAB

Figure 7-6

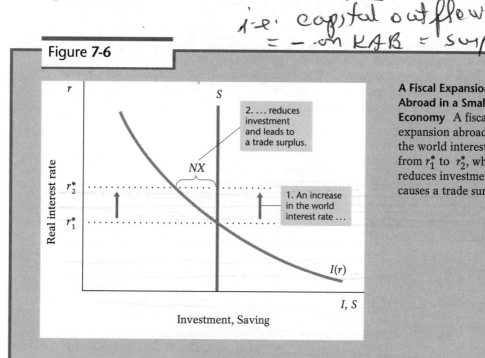

2. ... reduces investment and leads to a trade surplus.

NX

1. An increase in the world interest rate ...

$I(r)$

r

S

Real interest rate

r_2^*

r_1^*

I, S

Investment, Saving

A Fiscal Expansion Abroad in a Small Open Economy A fiscal expansion abroad raises the world interest rate from r_1^* to r_2^*, which reduces investment and causes a trade surplus.

Figure 7-7

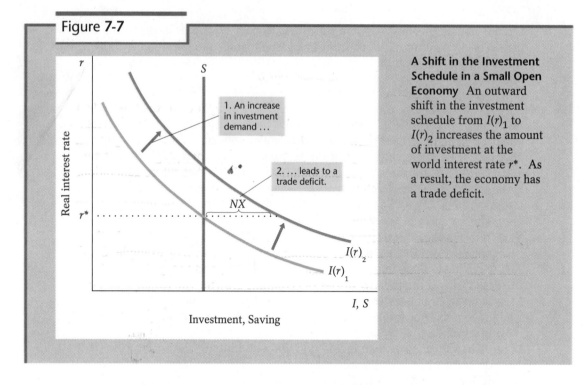

A Shift in the Investment Schedule in a Small Open Economy An outward shift in the investment schedule from $I(r)_1$ to $I(r)_2$ increases the amount of investment at the world interest rate r^*. As a result, the economy has a trade deficit.

1. An increase in investment demand ...

2. ... leads to a trade deficit.

Shifts in Investment Demand Consider what happens to our small open economy if its investment schedule shifts outward. This shift would occur if, for example, the government changed the tax laws to encourage domestic investment by providing an investment tax credit. Figure 7-7 illustrates the impact of a shift in the investment schedule. At a given world interest rate, investment is now higher. Because saving is unchanged, some investment must now be financed by borrowing from abroad. Of course, $NX = S - I$, so the increase in I implies a decrease in NX. Hence, *an outward shift in the investment schedule causes a trade deficit.*

Evaluating Economic Policy

Our model of the open economy shows that the flow of goods and services measured by the trade balance is inextricably connected to the flow of funds for capital accumulation measured by net foreign investment. Net foreign investment is the difference between domestic saving and domestic investment. Thus, the impact of economic policies on the trade balance can always be found by examining their impact on saving and investment. Policies that increase investment or decrease saving tend to cause a trade deficit, and policies that decrease investment or increase saving tend to cause a trade surplus.

Our analysis of the open economy has been positive, not normative. That is, our analysis of how economic policies influence the international flows of capital and goods has not told us whether these policies are desirable. Evaluating economic policies and their impact on the open economy is a frequent topic of debate among economists and policymakers.

When a country runs a trade deficit, as the United States did throughout the 1980s and early 1990s, policymakers must confront the question of whether the trade deficit represents a national problem. Most economists view a trade deficit not as a problem in itself, but perhaps as a symptom of a problem. The U.S. trade deficits of the 1980s and early 1990s reflected a low saving rate. A low saving rate means that we are putting away less for the future. In a closed economy, low saving leads to low investment and a smaller future capital stock. In an open economy, low saving leads to a trade deficit and a growing foreign debt, which eventually must be repaid. In both cases, high current consumption leads to lower future consumption, implying that future generations bear the burden of low national saving.

Yet trade deficits are not always a reflection of economic malady. When poor rural economies develop into modern industrial economies, they sometimes finance their high levels of investment with foreign borrowing. In these cases, trade deficits are a sign of economic development. For example, South Korea ran large trade deficits throughout the 1970s, and today the country is viewed as one of the success stories of economic growth. The lesson is that one cannot judge economic performance from the trade balance alone. Instead, one must look at the underlying causes of the international flows.

7-3 Exchange Rates

Having examined the international flows of capital and of goods and services, we now extend the analysis by considering the prices that apply to these transactions. The *exchange rate* between two countries is the price at which exchanges between them take place. In this section we first examine precisely what the exchange rate measures, and we then discuss how exchange rates are determined.

Nominal and Real Exchange Rates

Economists distinguish between two exchange rates: the nominal exchange rate and the real exchange rate. Let's discuss each and see how they are related.

The Nominal Exchange Rate The **nominal exchange rate** is the relative price of the currency of two countries. For example, if the exchange rate between the U.S. dollar and the Japanese yen is 120 yen per dollar, then you can exchange one dollar for 120 yen in world markets for foreign currency. A Japanese who wants to obtain dollars would pay 120 yen for each dollar he bought. An American who wants to obtain yen would get 120 yen for each dollar he paid. When people refer to "the exchange rate" between two countries, they usually mean the nominal exchange rate.

The Real Exchange Rate The **real exchange rate** is the relative price of the goods of two countries. That is, the real exchange rate tells us the rate at which we can trade the goods of one country for the goods of another. The real exchange rate is sometimes called the *terms of trade*.

How Newspapers Report the Exchange Rate

You can find exchange rates reported daily in many newspapers. Here's how they are reported in the *Wall Street Journal*:

CURRENCY TRADING

EXCHANGE RATES

Thursday, January 4, 1996

The New York foreign exchange selling rates below apply to trading among banks in amounts of $1 million and more, as quoted at 3 p.m. Eastern time by Bankers Trust Co., Dow Jones Telerate Inc. and other sources. Retail transactions provide fewer units of foreign currency per dollar.

Country	U.S. $ equiv. Thu	U.S. $ equiv. Wed	Currency per U.S. $ Thu	Currency per U.S. $ Wed
Argentina (Peso)	1.0007	1.0007	.9993	.9993
Australia (Dollar)	.7459	.7480	1.3407	1.3369
Austria (Schilling)	.09800	.09870	10.204	10.132
Bahrain (Dinar)	2.6532	2.6525	.3769	.3770
Belgium (Franc)	.03350	.03370	29.851	29.674
Brazil (Real)	1.0288	1.0288	.9720	.9720
Britain (Pound)	1.5523	1.5520	.6442	.6443
30-Day Forward	1.5483	1.5508	.6459	.6448
90-Day Forward	1.5462	1.5485	.6467	.6458
180-Day Forward	1.5456	1.5450	.6470	.6472
Canada (Dollar)	.7378	.7389	1.3554	1.3533
30-Day Forward	.7400	.7392	1.3514	1.3528
90-Day Forward	.7400	.7392	1.3514	1.3529
180-Day Forward	.7382	.7386	1.3547	1.3540
Chile (Peso)	.002460	.002460	406.50	406.50
China (Renminbi)	.1206	.1206	8.2919	8.2919
Colombia (Peso)	.001010	.001010	990.10	990.10
Czech. Rep. (Koruna) .				
Commercial rate	.03728	.03747	26.821	26.688
Denmark (Krone)	.1782	.1794	5.6117	5.5741
Ecuador (Sucre)	....	....	....	....
Floating rate	.0003430	.0003430	2915.45	2915.45
Finland (Markka)	.2290	.2308	4.3668	4.3328
France (Franc)	.2030	.2027	4.9265	4.9335
30-Day Forward	.2031	.2028	4.9228	4.9299
90-Day Forward	.2033	.2031	4.9177	4.9242
180-Day Forward	.2036	.2033	4.9127	4.9193
Germany (Mark)	.6932	.6916	1.4425	1.4460
30-Day Forward	.6903	.6929	1.4486	1.4432
90-Day Forward	.6924	.6951	1.4443	1.4386
180-Day Forward	.6994	.6978	1.4297	1.4331
Greece (Drachma)	.004193	.004209	238.49	237.59
Hong Kong (Dollar)	.1293	.1292	7.7340	7.7399
Hungary (Forint)	.007130	.007158	140.25	139.70
India (Rupee)	.02840	.02840	35.211	35.211
Indonesia (Rupiah)	.0004360	.0004360	2293.58	2293.58
Ireland (Punt)	1.5947	1.6005	.6271	.6248
Israel (Shekel)	.3177	.3177	3.1476	3.1476
Italy (Lira)	.0006341	.0006347	1577.00	1575.50
Japan (Yen)	.009501	.009536	105.25	104.87
30-Day Forward	.009467	.009580	105.63	104.38
90-Day Forward	.009546	.009660	104.76	103.52
180-Day Forward	.009738	.009772	102.69	102.33
Jordan (Dinar)	1.4104	1.4104	.7090	.7090
Kuwait (Dinar)	3.3395	3.3389	.2994	.2995
Lebanon (Pound)	.0006260	.0006260	1597.44	1597.44
Malaysia (Ringgit)	.3909	.3928	2.5582	2.5458
Malta (Lira)	2.8289	2.8365	.3535	.3525
Mexico (Peso)	....	....	....	....
Floating rate	.1325	.1322	7.5450	7.5650
Netherland (Guilder)	.6194	.6177	1.6145	1.6188
New Zealand (Dollar)	.6548	.6542	1.5272	1.5286
Norway (Krone)	.1563	.1575	6.3980	6.3492
Pakistan (Rupee)	.02920	.02920	34.247	34.247
Peru (new Sol)	.4292	.4292	2.3299	2.3299
Philippines (Peso)	.03820	.03820	26.178	26.178
Poland (Zloty)	.4045	.4045	2.4722	2.4722
Portugal (Escudo)	.006632	.006659	150.78	150.17
Russia (Ruble) (a)	.0002145	.0002155	4661.00	4640.00
Saudi Arabia (Riyal)	.2667	.2667	3.7495	3.7495
Singapore (Dollar)	.7000	.7053	1.4286	1.4178
Slovak Rep. (Koruna)	.03368	.03368	29.690	29.690
South Africa (Rand)	.2754	.2752	3.6307	3.6332
South Korea (Won)	.001270	.001285	787.40	778.21
Spain (Peseta)	.008197	.008239	122.00	121.37
Sweden (Krona)	.1509	.1516	6.6269	6.5963
Switzerland (Franc)	.8605	.8583	1.1621	1.1651
30-Day Forward	.8560	.8611	1.1682	1.1613
90-Day Forward	.8616	.8668	1.1606	1.1537
180-Day Forward	.8765	.8740	1.1410	1.1441
Taiwan (Dollar)	.03660	.03670	27.322	27.248
Thailand (Baht)	.03971	.03971	25.183	25.183
Turkey (Lira)	.00001688	.00001667	59237.50	59986.50
United Arab (Dirham)	.2723	.2723	3.6724	3.6724
Uruguay (New Peso) ..				
Financial	.1404	.1404	7.1225	7.1225
Venezuela (Bolivar)	.003448	.003448	290.00	290.00
	....	....		
SDR	1.4743	1.4818	.6783	.6749
ECU	1.2810	1.2810		

Special Drawing Rights (SDR) are based on exchange rates for the U.S., German, British, French, and Japanese currencies. Source: International Monetary Fund.

European Currency Unit (ECU) is based on a basket of community currencies.

a-fixing, Moscow Interbank Currency Exchange

Notice that each exchange rate is reported in two ways. On this Thursday, 1 dollar bought 105.25 yen, and 1 yen bought 0.009501 dollars. We can say the exchange rate is 105.25 yen per dollar, or we can say the exchange rate is 0.009501 dollars per yen. Since 0.009501 equals 1/105.25, these two ways of expressing the exchange rate are equivalent. This book always expresses the exchange rate in units of foreign currency per dollar.

The exchange rate on this Thursday of 105.25 yen per dollar was up from 104.87 yen per dollar on Wednesday. Such a rise in the exchange rate is called an *appreciation* of the dollar; a fall in the exchange rate is called a *depreciation*.

To see the relation between the real and nominal exchange rates, consider a single good produced in many countries: cars. Suppose an American car costs $10,000 and a similar Japanese car costs 2,400,000 yen. To compare the prices of the two cars, we must convert them into a common currency. If a dollar is worth 120 yen, then the American car costs 1,200,000 yen. Comparing the price of the American car (1,200,000 yen) and the price of the Japanese car (2,400,000 yen), we conclude that the American car costs one-half of what the Japanese car costs. In other words, at current prices, we can exchange 2 American cars for 1 Japanese car.

We can summarize our calculation above as follows:

$$\text{Real Exchange Rate} = \frac{(120 \text{ yen/dollar}) \times (10,000 \text{ dollars/American Car})}{(2,400,000 \text{ yen/Japanese Car})}$$

$$= 0.5 \frac{\text{Japanese Car}}{\text{American Car}}.$$

At these prices and this exchange rate, we obtain one-half of a Japanese car per American car. More generally, we can write this calculation as

$$\text{Real Exchange Rate} = \frac{\text{Nominal Exchange Rate} \times \text{Price of Domestic Good}}{\text{Price of Foreign Good}}$$

The rate at which we exchange foreign and domestic goods depends on the prices of the goods in the local currencies and on the rate at which the currencies are exchanged.

This calculation of the real exchange rate for a single good suggests how we should define the real exchange rate for a broader basket of goods. Let e be the nominal exchange rate (the number of yen per dollar), P be the price level in the United States (measured in dollars), and P^* be the price level in Japan (measured in yen). Then the real exchange rate ε is

$$
\begin{array}{ccccc}
\text{Real} & & \text{Nominal} & & \text{Ratio of} \\
\text{Exchange} & = & \text{Exchange} & \times & \text{Price} \\
\text{Rate} & & \text{Rate} & & \text{Levels} \\
\varepsilon & = & e & \times & (P/P^*).
\end{array}
$$

The real exchange rate between two countries is computed from the nominal exchange rate and the price levels in the two countries. *If the real exchange rate is high, foreign goods are relatively cheap, and domestic goods are relatively expensive. If the real exchange rate is low, foreign goods are relatively expensive, and domestic goods are relatively cheap.*

The Real Exchange Rate and Net Exports

Just as the price of bread affects the demand for bread, the relative price of domestic and foreign goods affects the demand for these goods. If the real exchange rate is low so that domestic goods are relatively cheap, domestic residents will purchase few imported goods: they will buy Fords rather than Toyotas, drink Coors rather than Heineken, and vacation in Florida rather than

Europe. For the same reason, foreigners will buy many of our goods. Therefore, our net exports will be high.

The opposite occurs if the real exchange rate is high and, therefore, domestic goods are expensive relative to foreign goods. Domestic residents will buy many imported goods, and foreigners will buy few of our goods. Therefore, our net exports will be low.

We write this relationship between the real exchange rate and net exports as

$$NX = NX(\varepsilon).$$

"How about Nebraska? The dollar's still strong in Nebraska."

This equation states that net exports are a function of the real exchange rate. Figure 7-8 illustrates this negative relationship between the trade balance and the real exchange rate.

Figure 7-8

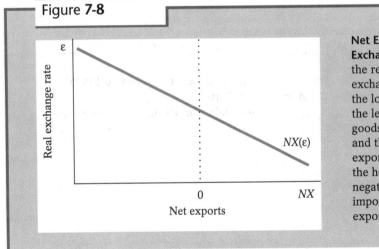

Net Exports and the Real Exchange Rate   The figure shows the relationship between the real exchange rate and net exports: the lower the real exchange rate, the less expensive are domestic goods relative to foreign goods, and thus the greater are our net exports. Note that a portion of the horizontal axis measures negative values of *NX*: because imports can exceed exports, net exports can be less than zero.

Case Study 7-2

• • • • • • • • • • • • •

How Businesses Respond to the Exchange Rate

Companies engaged in international trade monitor the exchange rate closely. The following article from the *New York Times* shows how some industries responded in early 1993 to a fall in the real exchange rate. According to the article, net exports do respond to changes in the exchange rate, but the response may take some time.

No Quick Gain from Stronger Yen

The Clinton Administration is proclaiming the dollar's latest plunge against the yen as a windfall for America—one that should finally shrink the nation's painful trade deficit with Japan. "The stronger yen is the best single thing that could have happened to the trade deficit," a senior Administration official said last week.

But improvement is not likely to come quickly, even though a stronger yen pushes up the price of Japanese goods sold in the United States while enabling American products to be sold for less in Japan. Indeed, the yen might have to stay strong for two years or more, many experts say, to have much impact on American-Japanese trade. The reason is that American and Japanese companies are resisting any adjustment in prices to reflect the changing values of their currencies.

Cooper Industries, for example, exports spark plugs and crankshafts to Japan, but as with many American companies, Cooper says it will not cut the yen prices of its products. . . .

But the stronger yen and weaker dollar certainly give American companies a pricing advantage in their competition with the Japanese, if the companies want to use it. In two months, the dollar has fallen 11 percent against the yen, to 110 yen to the dollar, compared with 124 in February. At 110, the level is the lowest since World War II. That means that an American-made spark plug sold in Japan for 124 yen now brings the manufacturer $1.11, rather than $1 collected in February. That leaves room to cut the yen price, which could increase sales in Japan.

The Japanese, conversely, must raise dollar prices in the United States to collect the same number of yen once the dollars are exchanged for the Japanese currency. A few companies, including Honda and Nissan, announced price increases this month. . . .

The Clinton Administration is counting on the yen's strength to shrink the trade deficit. . . . Administration officials even cite a trade theory that says that for every 1 percent increase in the value of the yen, the trade deficit with Japan will eventually shrink by $5 billion.

The Boeing Company's transactions with Japan tend to support this theory. Boeing prices the planes it sells to Japan in dollars, not yen. So the fall in the value of the dollar means that the Japanese can spend less in yen to buy the dollars to buy the planes.

"We sell planes under long-term negotiated contracts, and we don't expect any impact on prices from the latest currency changes," said Paul Binder, a Boeing spokesman. Boeing, the nation's single biggest exporter, sold the Japanese $2.5 billion in commercial airliners last year, or 5 percent of the total American exports to Japan in 1992. The shipment to Japan will be similarly large this year—and less costly to the Japanese in yen, which could encourage them to buy more planes.

Source: The *New York Times*, April 26, 1993, p. D1.

ts of the Real Exchange Rate

el of the real exchange rate, we combine the relationship be-
and the real exchange rate with our model of the trade bal-
t two forces determine the real exchange rate:

xchange rate is related to net exports. The lower the real ex-
ate, the less expensive domestic goods are relative to foreign
nd the greater is the demand for net exports.

ide balance must equal net foreign investment, which implies that
net exports equal saving minus investment. Saving is fixed by the consumption function and fiscal policy; investment is fixed by the investment
function and the world interest rate.

Figure 7-9 illustrates these two conditions. The line showing the relationship
between net exports and the real exchange rate slopes downward because a
low real exchange rate makes domestic goods relatively inexpensive. The line
representing the excess of saving over investment, $S - I$, is vertical because
neither saving nor investment depends on the real exchange rate. The crossing
of these two lines determines the equilibrium exchange rate.

Figure 7-9 looks like an ordinary supply-and-demand diagram. In fact,
you can think of this diagram as representing the supply and demand for
foreign-currency exchange. The vertical line, $S - I$, represents the excess of
domestic saving over domestic investment, and thus the supply of dollars to be
exchanged into foreign currency and invested abroad. The downward-sloping
line, NX, represents the net demand for dollars coming from foreigners who
want dollars to buy our goods. *At the equilibrium real exchange rate, the supply of dollars available for net foreign investment balances the demand for
dollars by foreigners buying our net exports.*

Figure 7-9

**How the Real Exchange Rate
Is Determined** The real
exchange rate is determined
by the crossing of the vertical
line representing saving minus
investment and the downward-
sloping net-exports schedule. At
this intersection, the quantity of
dollars supplied for net foreign
investment equals the quantity
of dollars demanded for the net
export of goods and services.

How Policies Influence the Real Exchange Rate

We can use this model to show how the changes in economic policy we discussed earlier affect the real exchange rate.

Fiscal Policy at Home   What happens to the real exchange rate if the government reduces national saving by increasing government purchases or cutting taxes? As we discussed earlier, this reduction in saving lowers $S - I$ and thus NX. That is, the reduction in saving causes a trade deficit.

Figure 7-10 shows how the equilibrium real exchange rate adjusts to ensure that NX falls. The change in policy shifts the vertical $S - I$ line to the left, lowering the supply of dollars to be invested abroad. The lower supply causes the equilibrium real exchange rate to rise from ε_1 to ε_2—that is, the dollar becomes more valuable. Because of the rise in the value of the dollar, domestic goods become more expensive relative to foreign goods, which causes exports to fall and imports to rise.

Figure 7-10

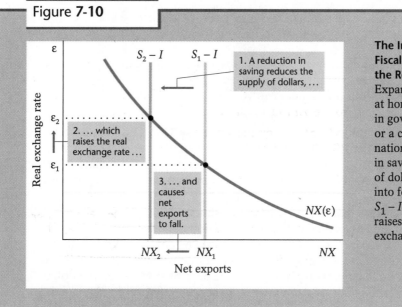

The Impact of Expansionary Fiscal Policy at Home on the Real Exchange Rate Expansionary fiscal policy at home, such as an increase in government purchases or a cut in taxes, reduces national saving. The fall in saving reduces the supply of dollars to be exchanged into foreign currency, from $S_1 - I$ to $S_2 - I$. This shift raises the equilibrium real exchange rate from ε_1 to ε_2.

Fiscal Policy Abroad   What happens to the real exchange rate if foreign governments increase government purchases or cut taxes? This change in fiscal policy reduces world saving and raises the world interest rate. The increase in the world interest rate reduces domestic investment I, which raises $S - I$ and thus NX. That is, the increase in the world interest rate causes a trade surplus.

Figure 7-11 shows that this change in policy shifts the vertical $S - I$ line to the right, raising the supply of dollars to be invested abroad. The equilibrium

Figure 7-11

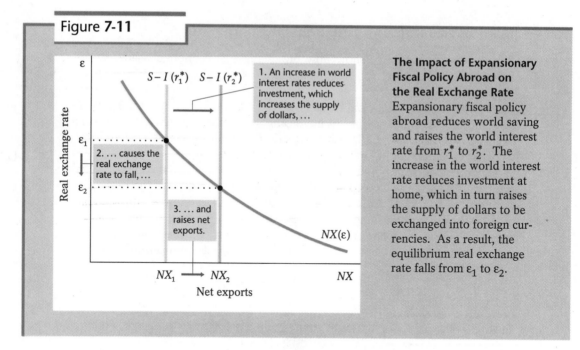

1. An increase in world interest rates reduces investment, which increases the supply of dollars, ...

2. ... causes the real exchange rate to fall, ...

3. ... and raises net exports.

$NX(\varepsilon)$

$NX_1 \longrightarrow NX_2$

NX

Net exports

The Impact of Expansionary Fiscal Policy Abroad on the Real Exchange Rate Expansionary fiscal policy abroad reduces world saving and raises the world interest rate from r_1^* to r_2^*. The increase in the world interest rate reduces investment at home, which in turn raises the supply of dollars to be exchanged into foreign currencies. As a result, the equilibrium real exchange rate falls from ε_1 to ε_2.

real exchange rate falls. That is, the dollar becomes less valuable, and domestic goods become less expensive relative to foreign goods.

Shifts in Investment Demand   What happens to the real exchange rate if investment demand at home increases, perhaps because Congress passes an investment tax credit? At the given world interest rate, the increase in investment demand leads to higher investment. A higher value of I means lower values of $S - I$ and NX. That is, the increase in investment demand causes a trade deficit.

Figure 7-12 shows that the increase in investment demand shifts the vertical $S - I$ line to the left, reducing the supply of dollars to be invested abroad. The equilibrium real exchange rate rises. Hence, when the investment tax credit makes investing in the United States more attractive, it also increases the value of the U.S. dollars necessary to make these investments. When the dollar appreciates, domestic goods become more expensive relative to foreign goods, and net exports fall.

The Effects of Trade Policies

Now that we have a model that explains the trade balance and the real exchange rate, we have the tools to examine the macroeconomic effects of trade policies. Trade policies, broadly defined, are policies designed to influence directly the amount of goods and services exported or imported. Most often, trade policies take the form of protecting domestic industries from foreign competition—either by placing a tax on foreign imports (a tariff) or by restricting the amount of goods and services that can be imported (a quota).

Figure 7-12

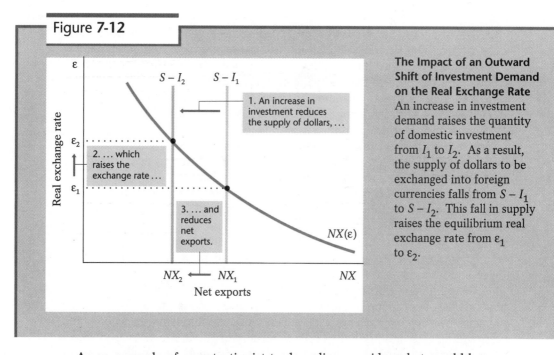

The Impact of an Outward Shift of Investment Demand on the Real Exchange Rate An increase in investment demand raises the quantity of domestic investment from I_1 to I_2. As a result, the supply of dollars to be exchanged into foreign currencies falls from $S - I_1$ to $S - I_2$. This fall in supply raises the equilibrium real exchange rate from ε_1 to ε_2.

As an example of a protectionist trade policy, consider what would happen if the government prohibited the import of foreign cars. For any given real exchange rate, imports would now be lower, implying that net exports (exports minus imports) would be higher. Thus, the net-exports schedule shifts outward, as in Figure 7-13. To see the effects of the policy, we compare the old equilibrium and the new equilibrium. In the new equilibrium, the real exchange rate is higher, and net exports are unchanged. That is, despite the shift in the net-exports schedule, the equilibrium level of net exports remain the same.

Figure 7-13

The Impact of Protectionist Trade Policies on the Real Exchange Rate A protectionist trade policy, such as a ban on imported cars, raises the demand for net exports from $NX(\varepsilon)_1$ to $NX(\varepsilon)_2$. This shift raises the real exchange rate from ε_1 to ε_2. Notice that, despite the shift in the net-exports schedule, the equilibrium level of net exports is unchanged.

This analysis shows that protectionist trade policies do not affect the trade balance. This surprising conclusion is often overlooked in the popular debate over trade policies. Since a trade deficit reflects an excess of imports over exports, one might guess that reducing imports—such as by prohibiting the import of foreign cars—would reduce a trade deficit. Yet our model shows that protectionist policies lead only to an appreciation of the real exchange rate. The increase in the price of domestic goods relative to foreign goods tends to lower net exports, offsetting the increase in net exports that is directly attributable to the trade restriction. Because protectionist policies do not alter either investment or saving, they cannot alter the trade balance.

Protectionist policies do affect the amount of trade, however. As we have seen, because the real exchange rate appreciates, the goods and services we produce become more expensive relative to foreign goods and services. We therefore export less in the new equilibrium. Since net exports are unchanged, we must import less as well. Thus, protectionist policies reduce both the quantity of imports and the quantity of exports.

This reduction in the total amount of trade is the reason economists almost always oppose protectionist policies. International trade benefits all countries by allowing each country to specialize in what it produces best and by providing each country with a greater variety of goods and services. Protectionist policies diminish these gains from trade. Although these policies benefit certain groups within society—for example, a ban on imported cars helps domestic car producers—society on average is worse off when policies reduce the amount of international trade.

The Determinants of the Nominal Exchange Rate

We now turn our attention from the real exchange rate to the nominal exchange rate—the rate at which the currencies of two countries trade. Recall the relationship between the real and the nominal exchange rate:

$$\text{Real Exchange Rate} = \text{Nominal Exchange Rate} \times \text{Ratio of Price Levels}$$

$$\varepsilon = e \times (P/P^*).$$

We can write the nominal exchange rate as

$$e = \varepsilon \times (P^*/P).$$

This equation shows that the nominal exchange rate depends on the real exchange rate and the price levels in the two countries. If the domestic price level P rises, then the nominal exchange rate e will fall: because a dollar is worth less, a dollar will buy fewer yen. On the other hand, if the Japanese price level P^* rises, then the nominal exchange rate will increase: because the yen is worth less, a dollar will buy more yen.

It is instructive to consider changes in exchange rates over time. The exchange rate equation can be written

% Change in e = % Change in ε + % Change in P^* − % Change in P.

The percentage change in ε is the change in the real exchange rate. The percentage change in P is our inflation rate π, and the percentage change in P^* is the foreign country's inflation rate π^*. Thus, the percentage change in the nominal exchange rate is

% Change in e = % Change in ε + $(\pi^* - \pi)$

$$\begin{array}{ccc} \text{Percentage Change in} & = & \text{Percentage Change in} & + & \text{Difference in} \\ \text{Nominal Exchange Rate} & & \text{Real Exchange Rate} & & \text{Inflation Rates.} \end{array}$$

This equation states that the percentage change in the nominal exchange rate between the currencies of two countries equals the percentage change in the real exchange rate plus the difference in their inflation rates. *If a country has a high rate of inflation relative to the United States, a dollar will buy an increasing amount of the foreign currency over time. If a country has a low rate of inflation relative to the United States, a dollar will buy a decreasing amount of the foreign currency over time.*

This analysis shows how monetary policy affects the nominal exchange rate. We know from Chapter 6 that high growth in the money supply leads to high inflation. One consequence of high inflation is a depreciating currency: high π implies falling e. In other words, just as growth in the amount of money raises the price of goods measured in terms of money, it also tends to raise the price of foreign currencies measured in terms of the domestic currency.

Case Study *7-3*

• • • • • • • • • • • • •

Inflation and Nominal Exchange Rates

If we look at data on exchange rates and price levels of different countries, we quickly see the importance of inflation for explaining changes in the nominal exchange rate. The most dramatic examples come from periods of very high inflation. For example, the price level in Mexico rose by 2,300 percent from 1983 to 1988. Because of this inflation, the number of pesos a person could buy with a U.S. dollar rose from 144 in 1983 to 2,281 in 1988.

The same relationship holds true for countries with more moderate inflation. Figure 7-14 is a scatterplot showing the relationship between inflation and the exchange rate for 11 countries. On the horizontal axis is the difference between each country's average inflation rate and the average inflation rate of the United States. On the vertical axis is the average percentage change in the exchange rate between each country's currency and the U.S. dollar. The positive relationship between these two variables is clear in this figure. Countries with relatively high inflation tend to have depreciating currencies, and countries with relatively low inflation tend to have appreciating currencies.

As an example, consider the exchange rate between German marks and U.S. dollars. Both Germany and the United States have experienced inflation over the past twenty years, so both the mark and the dollar buy fewer goods than they once did. But, as Figure 7-14 shows, inflation in Germany has been

Figure 7-14

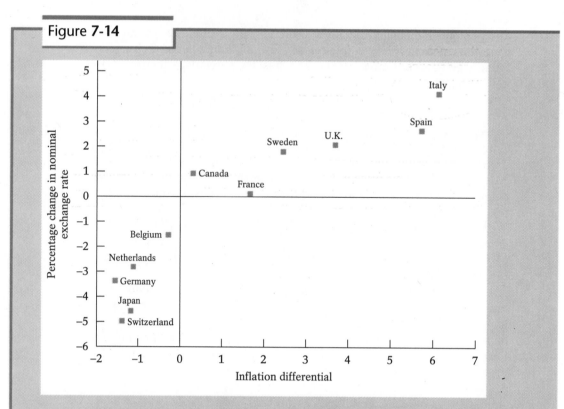

Inflation Differentials and the Exchange Rate This scatterplot shows the relationship between inflation and the nominal exchange rate. The horizontal axis shows the country's average inflation rate minus the U.S. average inflation rate over the period 1970–1994. The vertical axis is the average percentage change in the country's exchange rate (per U.S. dollar) over that period. This figure shows that countries with relatively high inflation tend to have depreciating currencies, and that countries with relatively low inflation tend to have appreciating currencies.

Source: International Financial Statistics.

lower than inflation in the United States. This means that the value of the mark has fallen less than the value of the dollar. Therefore, the number of German marks you can buy with a U.S. dollar has been falling over time.

● ● ● ● ● ● ● ● ● ● ● ● ● ● ●

The Special Case of Purchasing-Power Parity

A basic tenet in economics, called the *law of one price*, says that the same good cannot sell for different prices in different locations at the same time. If a bushel of wheat sold for less in New York than in Chicago, it would be profitable to buy wheat in New York and then sell it in Chicago. Always ready to take advantage of such opportunities, astute arbitrageurs would increase the demand for wheat in New York and increase the supply in Chicago. This would drive the price up in New York and down in Chicago—thereby ensuring that prices are equalized in the two markets.

The law of one price applied to the international marketplace is called **purchasing-power parity**. It states that if international arbitrage is possible, then a dollar (or any other currency) must have the same purchasing power in every country. The argument goes as follows. If a dollar could buy more wheat domestically than abroad, there would be opportunities to profit by buying wheat domestically and selling it abroad. Profit-seeking arbitrageurs would drive up the domestic price of wheat relative to the foreign price. Similarly, if a dollar could buy more wheat abroad than domestically, the arbitrageurs would buy wheat abroad and sell it domestically, driving down the domestic price relative to the foreign price. Thus, profit-seeking by international arbitrageurs causes wheat prices to be the same in all countries.

We can interpret the doctrine of purchasing-power parity using our model of the real exchange rate. The quick action of these international arbitrageurs implies that net exports are highly sensitive to small movements in the real exchange rate. A small decrease in the price of domestic goods relative to foreign goods—that is, a small decrease in the real exchange rate—causes arbitrageurs to buy goods domestically and sell them abroad. Similarly, a small increase in the relative price of domestic goods causes arbitrageurs to import goods from abroad. Therefore, as in Figure 7-15, the net-exports schedule is very flat at the real exchange rate that equalizes purchasing power among countries: any small movement in the real exchange rate leads to a large change in net exports. This extreme sensitivity of net exports guarantees that the equilibrium real exchange rate is always close to the level that ensures purchasing-power parity.

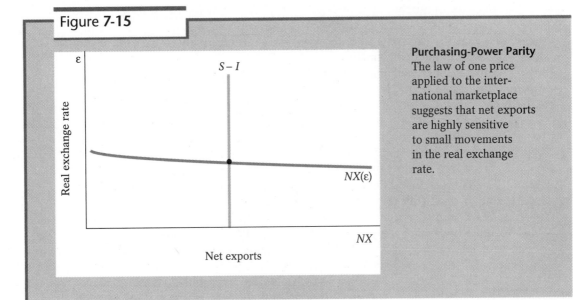

Figure 7-15

Purchasing-Power Parity The law of one price applied to the international marketplace suggests that net exports are highly sensitive to small movements in the real exchange rate.

Purchasing-power parity has two important implications. First, since the net-exports schedule is flat, changes in saving or investment do not influence the real or nominal exchange rate. Second, since the real exchange rate is fixed, all changes in the nominal exchange rate result from changes in price levels.

Is this doctrine of purchasing-power parity realistic? Most economists believe that, despite its appealing logic, purchasing-power parity does not provide a completely accurate description of the world. First, many goods are not easily traded. A haircut can be more expensive in Tokyo than in New York, yet there is no room for international arbitrage since it is impossible to transport haircuts. Second, even tradeable goods are not always perfect substitutes. Some consumers prefer Toyotas, and others prefer Fords. Thus, the relative price of Toyotas and Fords can vary to some extent without leaving any profit opportunities. For these reasons, real exchange rates do in fact vary over time.

Although the doctrine of purchasing-power parity does not describe the world perfectly, it does provide a reason to expect limited movement in the real exchange rate. There is much validity to its underlying logic: the farther the real exchange rate drifts from the level predicted by purchasing-power parity, the greater the incentive for individuals to engage in international arbitrage in goods. Although we cannot rely on purchasing-power parity to eliminate all movements in the real exchange rate, this doctrine does provide a reason to expect that movements in the real exchange rate will typically be small or temporary.

Case Study 7-4

• • • • • • • • • • • • •

The Big Mac Around the World

The doctrine of purchasing-power parity says that after we adjust for exchange rates, we should find that goods sell for the same price everywhere. Conversely, it says that the exchange rate between two currencies should depend on the price levels in the two countries.

To see how well this doctrine works, *The Economist*, an international newsmagazine, regularly collects data on the price of a good sold in many countries: the McDonald's Big Mac hamburger. According to purchasing-power parity, the price of a Big Mac should be closely related to the country's nominal exchange rate. The higher the price of a Big Mac in the local currency, the higher the exchange rate (measured per U.S. dollar) should be.

Table 7-1 presents the international prices in 1993, when a Big Mac sold for $2.28 in the United States. With these data we can use the doctrine of purchasing-power parity to predict nominal exchange rates. For example, since a Big Mac cost 391 yen in Japan, we would predict that the exchange rate between the dollar and the yen was 391/2.28, or 171, yen per dollar. At this exchange rate, a Big Mac would have cost the same in Japan and the United States.

Table 7-1 shows the predicted and actual exchange rates for 24 countries. You can see that the evidence on purchasing-power parity is mixed. In some

Table 7-1

Big Mac Prices and the Exchange Rate: An Application of Purchasing-Power Parity

Country	Currency	Price of a Big Mac	Exchange Rate (per U.S. dollar) Predicted	Exchange Rate (per U.S. dollar) Actual
Argentina	Peso	3.60	1.58	1.00
Australia	Dollar	2.45	1.07	1.39
Belgium	Franc	109.00	47.81	32.45
Brazil	Cruzeiro	77,000.00	33,772.00	27,521.00
Britain	Pound	1.79	0.79	0.64
Canada	Dollar	2.76	1.21	1.26
China	Yuan	8.50	3.73	5.68
Denmark	Crown	25.75	11.29	6.06
France	Franc	18.50	8.11	5.34
Germany	Mark	4.60	2.02	1.58
Hong Kong	Dollar	9.00	3.95	7.73
Hungary	Forint	157.00	68.86	88.18
Ireland	Pound	1.48	0.65	0.65
Italy	Lira	4,500.00	1,974.00	1,523.00
Japan	Yen	391.00	171.00	113.00
Malaysia	Ringgit	3.35	1.47	2.58
Mexico	Peso	7.09	3.11	3.10
Netherlands	Guilder	5.45	2.39	1.77
Russia	Ruble	780.00	342.00	686.00
South Korea	Won	2,300.00	1,009.00	796.00
Spain	Peseta	325.00	143.00	114.00
Sweden	Crown	25.50	11.18	7.43
Switzerland	Franc	5.70	2.50	1.45
Thailand	Baht	48.00	21.05	25.16
United States	Dollar	2.28	1.00	1.00

Note: The predicted exchange rate is the exchange rate that would make the price of a Big Mac in that country equal to its price in the United States.

Source: The Economist, April 17, 1993, p. 79.

cases, the predicted and actual exchange rates differed substantially. For example, the predicted exchange rate of 171 yen per dollar was quite different from the actual rate of 113 yen per dollar. Yet, for most countries, the predicted and actual exchange rates were in the same ballpark. In some cases, such as the U.S. neighbors of Canada and Mexico, the predicted and actual exchange rates were very close. Although not exact, purchasing-power parity does provide a rough guide to the level of exchange rates.

• • • • • • • • • • • • • •

7-4   Conclusion: The United States as a Large Open Economy

In this chapter we have seen how a small open economy works. We have examined the determinants of the international flow of funds for capital accumulation and the international flow of goods and services. We have also examined the determinants of a country's real and nominal exchange rates. Our analysis shows how various policies—monetary policies, fiscal policies, and trade policies—affect the trade balance and the exchange rate.

The economy we have studied is "small" in the sense that its interest rate is fixed by world financial markets. That is, we have assumed that this economy does not affect the world interest rate, and that the economy can borrow and lend at the world interest rate in unlimited amounts. This assumption contrasts with the assumption we made when we studied the closed economy in Chapter 3. In the closed economy, the domestic interest rate equilibrates domestic saving and domestic investment, implying that policies that influence saving or investment alter the equilibrium interest rate.

Which of these analyses should we apply to an economy like the United States? The answer is a little of both. On the one hand, the United States is not so large or so isolated that it is immune to developments occurring abroad. The large trade deficits of the 1980s and 1990s show the importance of international financial markets for funding U.S. investment. Hence, the closed-economy analysis of Chapter 3 cannot by itself fully explain the impact of policies on the U.S. economy.

On the other hand, the U.S. economy is not so small and so open that the analysis of this chapter applies perfectly either. First, the United States is large enough that it can influence world financial markets. Indeed, U.S. fiscal policy was blamed for the high real interest rates that prevailed throughout the world in the 1980s. Second, capital may not be perfectly mobile among countries. If individuals prefer holding their wealth in domestic rather than foreign assets, funds for capital accumulation will not flow freely to equate interest rates in all countries. For these two reasons, we cannot directly apply our model of the small open economy to the United States.

When analyzing policy for a country like the United States, we need to combine the closed-economy logic of Chapter 3 and the small-open-economy logic of this chapter. The appendix to this chapter builds a model of an economy between these two extremes. In this intermediate case, there is international borrowing and lending, but the interest rate is not fixed by world financial markets. Instead, the more the economy borrows from abroad, the higher the interest rate it must offer foreign investors. The results, not surprisingly, are a mixture of the two polar cases we have already examined.

Consider, for example, a reduction in national saving due to a fiscal expansion. As in the closed economy, this policy raises the interest rate and crowds out investment. As in the small open economy, it also causes a trade deficit and an appreciation of the exchange rate. Hence, although the model of the small open economy examined here does not precisely describe an economy like the United States, it does provide approximately the right answer to how policies affect the trade balance and the exchange rate.

Summary

1. Net exports are the difference between exports and imports. They are equal to the difference between what we produce and what we demand for consumption, investment, and government purchases.

2. Net foreign investment is the excess of domestic saving over domestic investment. The trade balance is the amount received for our net exports of goods and services. The national income accounts identity shows that net foreign investment always equals the trade balance.

3. The impact of any policy on the trade balance can be determined by examining its impact on saving and investment. Policies that raise saving or lower investment lead to a trade surplus, and policies that lower saving or raise investment lead to a trade deficit.

4. The nominal exchange rate is the rate at which people trade the currency of one country for the currency of another country. The real exchange rate is the rate at which people trade the goods produced by the two countries. The real exchange rate equals the nominal exchange rate multiplied by the ratio of the price levels in the two countries.

5. The higher our real exchange rate, the lower the demand for our net exports. The equilibrium real exchange rate is the rate at which the quantity of net exports demanded equals net foreign investment.

6. The nominal exchange rate is determined by the real exchange rate and the price levels in the two countries. Other things equal, a high rate of inflation leads to a depreciating currency.

KEY CONCEPTS

Net exports

Net foreign investment

Trade balance

Trade surplus and trade deficit

Small open economy

World interest rate

Nominal exchange rate

Real exchange rate

Purchasing-power parity

QUESTIONS FOR REVIEW

1. What are net foreign investment and the trade balance? Explain how they are related.

2. Define the nominal exchange rate and the real exchange rate.

3. If a small open economy cuts defense spending, what happens to saving, investment, the trade balance, the interest rate, and the exchange rate?

4. If a small open economy bans the import of Japanese VCRs, what happens to saving, investment, the trade balance, the interest rate, and the exchange rate?

5. If Germany has low inflation and Italy has high inflation, what will happen to the exchange rate between the German mark and the Italian lira?

PROBLEMS AND APPLICATIONS

1. Use the model of the small open economy to predict what would happen to the trade balance, the real exchange rate, and the nominal exchange rate in response to each of the following events.

   a. A fall in consumer confidence about the future induces consumers to spend less and save more.

   b. The introduction of a stylish line of Toyotas makes some consumers prefer foreign cars over domestic cars.

   c. The introduction of automatic teller machines reduces the demand for money.

2. Consider an economy described by the following equations:

$$Y = C + I + G + NX$$
$$Y = 5,000$$
$$G = 1,000$$
$$T = 1,000$$
$$C = 250 + 0.75(Y - T)$$
$$I = 1,000 - 50\,r$$
$$NX = 500 - 500\,\varepsilon$$
$$r = r^* = 5$$

   a. In this economy, solve for national saving, investment, the trade balance, and the equilibrium exchange rate.

   b. Suppose now that G rises to 1,250. Solve for national saving, investment, the trade balance, and the equilibrium exchange rate. Explain what you find.

   c. Now suppose that the world interest rate rises from 5 to 10 percent. (G is again 1,000.) Solve for national saving, investment, the trade balance, and the equilibrium exchange rate. Explain what you find.

3. The country of Leverett is a small open economy. Suddenly, a change in world fashions makes the exports of Leverett unpopular.

   a. What happens in Leverett to saving, investment, net exports, the interest rate, and the exchange rate?

   b. The citizens of Leverett like to travel abroad. How will this change in the exchange rate affect them?

   c. The fiscal policymakers of Leverett want to adjust taxes to maintain the exchange rate at its previous level.

What should they do? If they do this, what are the overall effects on saving, investment, net exports, and the interest rate?

4. What will happen to the trade balance and the real exchange rate of a small open economy when government purchases increase, such as during a war? Does your answer depend on whether this is a local war or a world war?

5. In 1995, President Clinton considered placing a 100 percent tariff on the import of Japanese luxury cars. Discuss the economics and politics of such a policy. In particular, how would the policy affect the U.S. trade deficit? How would it affect the exchange rate? Who would be hurt by such a policy? Who would benefit?

6. Suppose that some foreign countries begin to subsidize investment by instituting an investment tax credit.

    a. What happens to world investment demand as a function of the world interest rate?

    b. What happens to the world interest rate?

    c. What happens to investment in our small open economy?

    d. What happens to our trade balance?

    e. What happens to our real exchange rate?

7. "Traveling in Italy is much cheaper now than it was ten years ago," says a friend. "Ten years ago, a dollar bought 1,000 lire; this year, a dollar buys 1,500 lire."

Is your friend right or wrong? Given that total inflation over this period was 25 percent in the United States and 100 percent in Italy, has it become more or less expensive to travel in Italy? Write your answer using a concrete example—like a cup of American coffee versus a cup of Italian espresso—that will convince your friend.

8. The newspaper reports that the nominal interest rate is 12 percent per year in Canada and 8 percent per year in the United States. Suppose that the real interest rates are equalized in the two countries and that purchasing-power parity holds.

    a. Using the Fisher equation, which was discussed in Chapter 6, what can you infer about expected inflation in Canada and in the United States?

    b. What can you infer about the expected change in the exchange rate between the Canadian dollar and the U.S. dollar?

    c. A friend proposes a get-rich-quick scheme: borrow from a U.S. bank at 8 percent, deposit the money in a Canadian bank at 12 percent, and make a 4 percent profit. What's wrong with this scheme?

The Large Open Economy

When analyzing policy for a country like the United States, we need to combine the closed-economy logic of Chapter 3 and the small-open-economy logic of this chapter. In this appendix we build a model of an economy between these two extremes, called the *large open economy*.

Net Foreign Investment

The key difference between the small and large open economies is the behavior of net foreign investment. In the model of the small open economy, capital flows freely into or out of the economy at a fixed world interest rate r^*. The model of the large open economy makes a different assumption about international capital flows. To understand that assumption, keep in mind that net foreign investment is the amount that domestic investors lend abroad minus the amount that foreign investors lend here.

Imagine that you are a domestic investor—such as the portfolio manager of a university endowment—deciding where to invest your funds. You could invest domestically (by, for example, making loans to U.S. companies), or you could invest abroad (by making loans to foreign companies). Many factors may affect your decision, but surely one of them is the interest rate you can earn. The higher the interest rate you can earn domestically, the less attractive you would find foreign investment.

Investors abroad face a similar decision. They have a choice between investing in their home country, or lending to the United States. The higher the interest rate in the United States, the more willing foreigners are to lend to U.S. companies and to buy U.S. assets.

Thus, because of the behavior of both domestic and foreign investors, net foreign investment NFI is negatively related to the domestic interest rate r. As the interest rate rises, less of our saving flows abroad, and more funds for capital accumulation flow in from other countries. We write this as

$$NFI = NFI(r).$$

This equation states that net foreign investment is a function of the domestic interest rate. Figure 7-16 illustrates this relationship. Notice that NFI can be either positive or negative, depending on whether the economy is a lender or borrower in world financial markets.

To see how this NFI function relates to our previous models, consider Figure 7-17. This figure shows two special cases: a vertical NFI function and a horizontal NFI function.

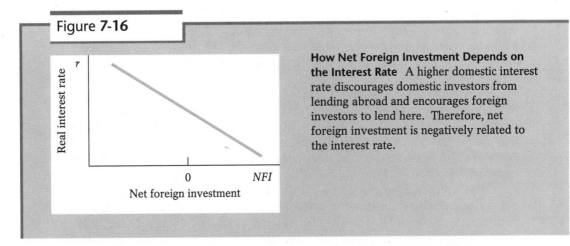

Figure 7-16

How Net Foreign Investment Depends on the Interest Rate A higher domestic interest rate discourages domestic investors from lending abroad and encourages foreign investors to lend here. Therefore, net foreign investment is negatively related to the interest rate.

The closed economy is the special case shown in panel (a) of Figure 7-17. In the closed economy, $NFI = 0$ at all interest rates. This situation would arise if investors here and abroad were unwilling to hold foreign assets, regardless of the return. It might also arise if the government prohibited its citizens from transacting in foreign financial markets, as some governments do. In the closed economy, there is no international borrowing or lending, and the interest rate adjusts to equilibrate domestic saving and investment.

The small open economy with perfect capital mobility is the special case shown in panel (b) of Figure 7-17. In this case, capital flows freely into and out of the country at the fixed world interest rate r^*. This situation would arise if

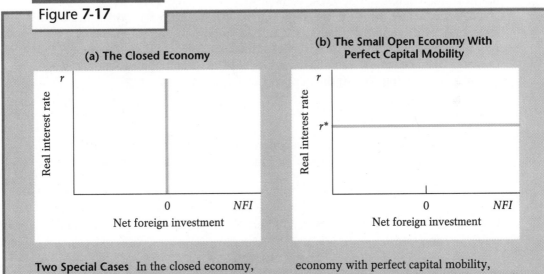

Figure 7-17

Two Special Cases In the closed economy, shown in panel (a), net foreign investment is zero for all interest rates. In the small open economy with perfect capital mobility, shown in panel (b), net foreign investment is perfectly elastic at the world interest rate r^*.

investors here and abroad bought whatever asset yielded the highest return, and if this economy were too small to affect the world interest rate. The economy's interest rate would be fixed at the interest rate prevailing in world financial markets.

Why isn't the interest rate of a large open economy like the United States fixed by the world interest rate? There are two reasons. The first is that the United States is large enough to influence world financial markets. The more the United States lends abroad, the greater is the supply of loans in the world economy, and the lower interest rates become around the world. The more the United States borrows from abroad (that is, the more negative *NFI* becomes), the higher are world interest rates. We use the label "large open economy" because this model applies to an economy large enough to affect world interest rates.

There is, however, a second reason that the interest rate in an economy may not be fixed by the world interest rate: capital may not be perfectly mobile. That is, investors here and abroad prefer holding their wealth in domestic rather than foreign assets. Such a preference for domestic assets could arise because of imperfect information about foreign assets or because of government impediments to international borrowing and lending. In either case, funds for capital accumulation will not flow freely to equalize interest rates in all countries. Instead, net foreign investment will depend on domestic interest rates relative to foreign interest rates. U.S. investors will lend abroad only if U.S. interest rates are comparatively low, and foreign investors will lend in the United States only if U.S. interest rates are comparatively high. The large-open-economy model, therefore, may apply even to a small economy if capital does not flow freely into and out of the economy.

Hence, either because the large open economy affects world interest rates, or because capital is imperfectly mobile, or perhaps for both reasons, the *NFI* function slopes downward. Except for this new *NFI* function, the model of the large open economy resembles the model of the small open economy. We put all the pieces together in the next section.

The Model

To understand how the large open economy works, we need to consider two key markets: the market for loanable funds and the market for foreign exchange.

The Market for Loanable Funds   An open economy's saving S is used in two ways: to finance domestic investment I and to finance net foreign investment *NFI*. We can write

$$S = I + NFI.$$

Consider how these three variables are determined. National saving is fixed by the level of output, fiscal policy, and the consumption function. Investment and net foreign investment both depend on the interest rate. We can write

$$\overline{S} = I(r) + NFI(r).$$

Figure 7-18

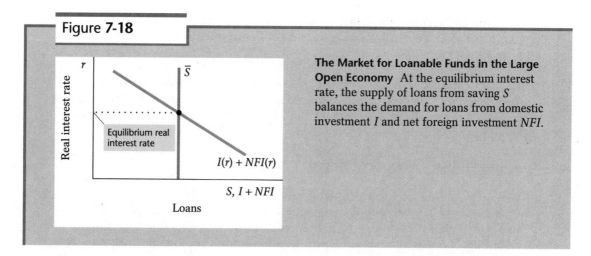

The Market for Loanable Funds in the Large Open Economy At the equilibrium interest rate, the supply of loans from saving S balances the demand for loans from domestic investment I and net foreign investment NFI.

Figure 7-18 shows the market for loanable funds. The supply of loans is national saving. The demand for loans is the sum of the demand for domestic investment and the demand for net foreign investment. The interest rate adjusts to equilibrate supply and demand.

The Market for Foreign Exchange Next, consider the relationship between net foreign investment and the trade balance. The national income accounts identity tells us

$$NX = S - I.$$

Since NX is a function of the exchange rate, and since $NFI = S - I$, we can write

$$NX(\varepsilon) = NFI.$$

Figure 7-19 shows the equilibrium in the market for foreign exchange. Once again, the real exchange rate is the price that equilibrates the trade balance and net foreign investment.

Figure 7-19

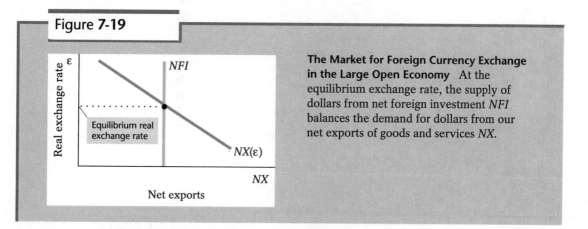

The Market for Foreign Currency Exchange in the Large Open Economy At the equilibrium exchange rate, the supply of dollars from net foreign investment NFI balances the demand for dollars from our net exports of goods and services NX.

The last variable we should consider is the nominal exchange rate. As before, the nominal exchange rate is the real exchange rate times the ratio of the price levels:

$$e = \varepsilon \times (P^*/P).$$

The real exchange rate is determined as in Figure 7-19, and the price levels are determined by monetary policies here and abroad, as we discussed in Chapter 6. Forces that move the real exchange rate or the price levels also move the nominal exchange rate.

Policies in the Large Open Economy

We can now consider how economic policies influence the large open economy. Figure 7-20 shows the three diagrams we need for the analysis. Panel (a) shows the equilibrium in the market for loanable funds; panel (b) shows the relationship between the equilibrium interest rate and net foreign investment; and panel (c) shows the equilibrium in the market for foreign exchange.

Figure 7-20

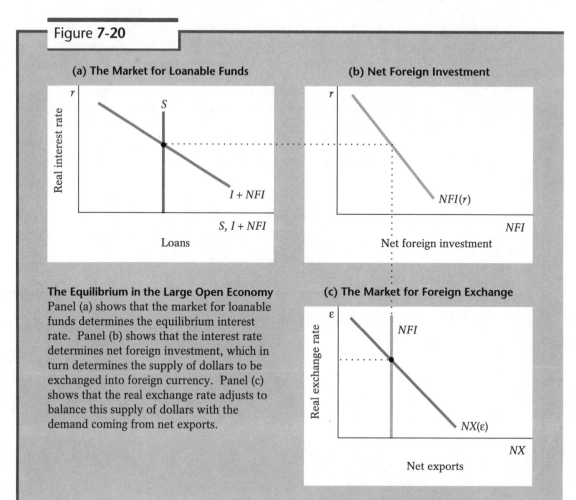

(a) The Market for Loanable Funds

(b) Net Foreign Investment

The Equilibrium in the Large Open Economy
Panel (a) shows that the market for loanable funds determines the equilibrium interest rate. Panel (b) shows that the interest rate determines net foreign investment, which in turn determines the supply of dollars to be exchanged into foreign currency. Panel (c) shows that the real exchange rate adjusts to balance this supply of dollars with the demand coming from net exports.

(c) The Market for Foreign Exchange

Fiscal Policy at Home   Consider the effects of expansionary fiscal policy—an increase in government purchases or a decrease in taxes. Figure 7-21 shows what happens. The policy reduces national saving S, thereby reducing the supply of loans and raising the equilibrium interest rate r. The higher interest rate reduces both domestic investment I and net foreign investment NFI. The fall in net foreign investment reduces the supply of dollars to be exchanged into foreign currency. The exchange rate appreciates, and net exports fall.

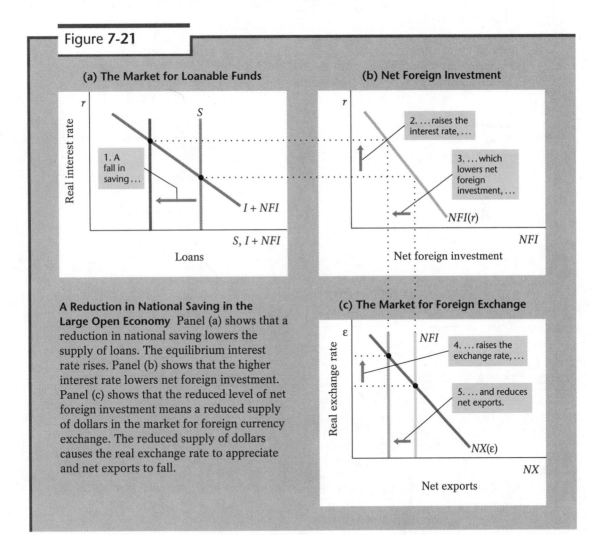

Figure 7-21

(a) The Market for Loanable Funds

(b) Net Foreign Investment

1. A fall in saving...

2. ...raises the interest rate, ...

3. ...which lowers net foreign investment, ...

A Reduction in National Saving in the Large Open Economy Panel (a) shows that a reduction in national saving lowers the supply of loans. The equilibrium interest rate rises. Panel (b) shows that the higher interest rate lowers net foreign investment. Panel (c) shows that the reduced level of net foreign investment means a reduced supply of dollars in the market for foreign currency exchange. The reduced supply of dollars causes the real exchange rate to appreciate and net exports to fall.

(c) The Market for Foreign Exchange

4. ...raises the exchange rate, ...

5. ...and reduces net exports.

Note that the impact of fiscal policy in this model combines its impact in the closed economy and its impact in the small open economy. As in the closed economy, a fiscal expansion in a large open economy raises the interest rate and crowds out investment. As in the small open economy, a fiscal expansion causes a trade deficit and an appreciation in the exchange rate.

One way to see how the three types of economy are related is to consider the identity

$$S = I + NX.$$

In all three cases, expansionary fiscal policy reduces national saving S. In the closed economy, the fall in S coincides with an equal fall in I, and NX stays constant at zero. In the small open economy, the fall in S coincides with an equal fall in NX, and I remains constant at the level fixed by the world interest rate. The large open economy is the intermediate case: both I and NX fall, each by less than the fall in S.

Shifts in Investment Demand   Suppose that the investment demand schedule shifts outward, perhaps because Congress passes an investment tax credit. Figure 7-22 shows the effect. The demand for loans rises, raising the equilib-

Figure 7-22

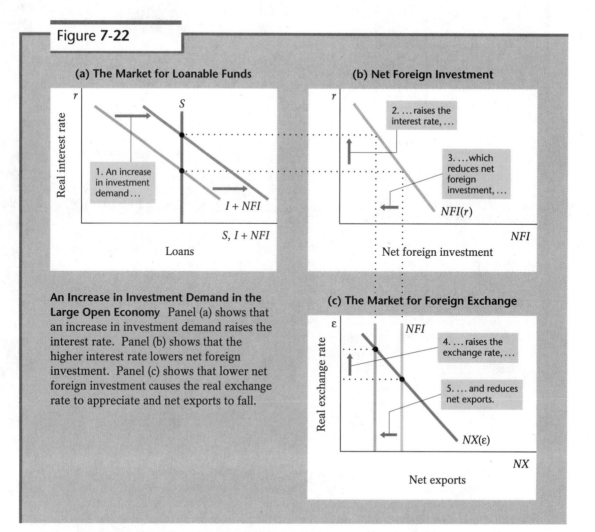

(a) The Market for Loanable Funds

(b) Net Foreign Investment

1. An increase in investment demand...

2. ...raises the interest rate, ...

3. ...which reduces net foreign investment, ...

(c) The Market for Foreign Exchange

4. ...raises the exchange rate, ...

5. ...and reduces net exports.

An Increase in Investment Demand in the Large Open Economy   Panel (a) shows that an increase in investment demand raises the interest rate. Panel (b) shows that the higher interest rate lowers net foreign investment. Panel (c) shows that lower net foreign investment causes the real exchange rate to appreciate and net exports to fall.

rium interest rate. The higher interest rate reduces net foreign investment: Americans make fewer loans abroad, and foreigners make more loans here. The fall in net foreign investment reduces the supply of dollars in the market for foreign exchange. The exchange rate appreciates, and net exports fall.

Trade Policies   Figure 7-23 shows the effect of a trade restriction, such as an import quota. The reduced demand for imports shifts the net exports schedule outward. Since nothing has changed in the market for loanable funds, the interest rate remains the same, which in turn implies that net foreign investment remains the same. The shift in the net exports schedule causes the exchange rate to appreciate. The rise in the exchange rate makes U.S. goods expensive relative to foreign goods, which depresses exports and stimulates imports. In the end, the trade restriction does not affect the trade balance.

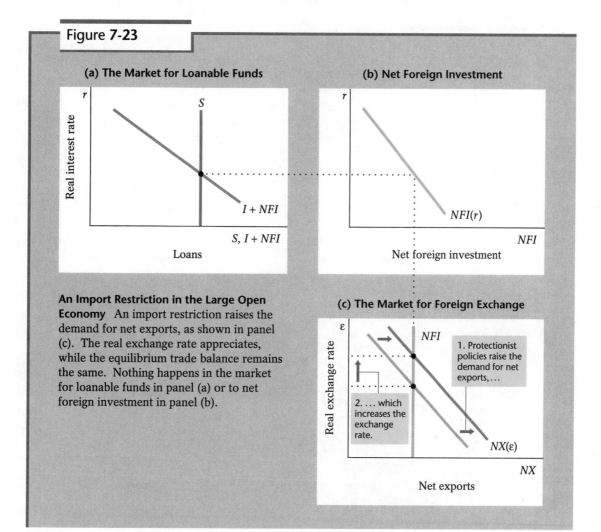

Figure 7-23

(a) The Market for Loanable Funds

(b) Net Foreign Investment

An Import Restriction in the Large Open Economy   An import restriction raises the demand for net exports, as shown in panel (c). The real exchange rate appreciates, while the equilibrium trade balance remains the same. Nothing happens in the market for loanable funds in panel (a) or to net foreign investment in panel (b).

(c) The Market for Foreign Exchange

1. Protectionist policies raise the demand for net exports, ...

2. ... which increases the exchange rate.

Shifts in Net Foreign Investment   There are various reasons that the *NFI* schedule might shift. One reason is fiscal policy abroad. For example, suppose that Germany pursues a fiscal policy that raises German saving. This policy reduces the German interest rate. The lower German interest rate discourages American investors from lending in Germany and encourages German investors to lend in the United States. For any given U.S. interest rate, U.S. net foreign investment falls.

Another reason the *NFI* schedule might shift is political instability abroad. Suppose that a war or revolution breaks out in another country. Investors around the world will try to withdraw their assets from that country and seek a "safe haven" in a stable country such as the United States. The result is a reduction in U.S. net foreign investment.

Figure 7-24 shows the impact of a shift in the *NFI* schedule. The reduced demand for loans lowers the equilibrium interest rate. The lower interest rate

Figure 7-24

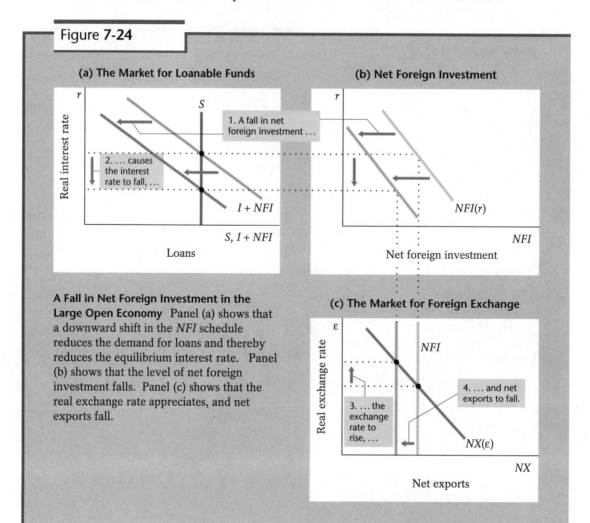

(a) The Market for Loanable Funds

1. A fall in net foreign investment . . .

2. . . . causes the interest rate to fall, . . .

$I + NFI$

$S, I + NFI$

Loans

(b) Net Foreign Investment

$NFI(r)$

NFI

Net foreign investment

A Fall in Net Foreign Investment in the Large Open Economy Panel (a) shows that a downward shift in the *NFI* schedule reduces the demand for loans and thereby reduces the equilibrium interest rate. Panel (b) shows that the level of net foreign investment falls. Panel (c) shows that the real exchange rate appreciates, and net exports fall.

(c) The Market for Foreign Exchange

NFI

3. . . . the exchange rate to rise, . . .

4. . . . and net exports to fall.

$NX(\varepsilon)$

NX

Net exports

tends to raise net foreign investment, but this only partly mitigates the shift in the *NFI* schedule. The reduced level of net foreign investment reduces the supply of dollars in the market for foreign exchange. The exchange rate appreciates, and net exports fall.

Conclusion

How different are large and small open economies? Certainly, policies affect the interest rate in a large open economy, unlike in a small open economy. But, in other ways, the two models yield similar conclusions. In both large and small open economies, policies that raise saving or lower investment lead to trade surpluses. Similarly, policies that lower saving or raise investment lead to trade deficits. In both economies, protectionist trade policies cause the exchange rate to appreciate and do not influence the trade balance. Because the results are so similar, for most questions one can use the simpler model of the small open economy, even if the economy being examined is not really small.

MORE PROBLEMS AND APPLICATIONS

1. If a war broke out abroad, it would affect the U.S. economy in many ways. Use the model of the large open economy to examine each of the following effects of such a war. What happens in the United States to saving, investment, the trade balance, the interest rate, and the exchange rate? (To keep things simple, consider each of the following effects separately.)

a. The U.S. government, fearing it may need to enter the war, increases its purchases of military equipment.

b. Other countries raise their demand for high-tech weapons, a major export of the United States.

c. The war makes U.S. firms uncertain about the future, and the firms delay some investment projects.

d. The war makes U.S. consumers uncertain about the future, and the consumers save more in response.

e. Americans become apprehensive about traveling abroad, so more of them spend their vacations in the United States.

f. Foreign investors seek a safe haven for their portfolios in the United States.

2. On September 21, 1995, "House Speaker Newt Gingrich threatened to send the United States into default on its debt for the first time in the nation's history, to force the Clinton Administration to balance the budget on Republican terms" (*New York Times*, September 22, 1995, p. A1). That same day, the interest rate on 30-year U.S. government bonds rose from 6.46 to 6.55 percent, and the dollar fell in value from 102.7 to 99.0 yen. Use the model of the large open economy to explain this event.

Part Three

The Economy in the Short Run

In Part Two we developed theories to explain how the economy behaves in the long run. Those theories were based on the classical dichotomy—the premise that real variables such as output and employment are independent of nominal variables such as the money supply and the price level. Classical theories are useful for explaining long-run trends, including the economic growth we observe from decade to decade. Yet most economists believe that the classical dichotomy does not hold in the short run and, therefore, that classical theories cannot explain year-to-year fluctuations in output and employment. Here, in Part Three, we see how economists explain short-run fluctuations.

Chapter 8 discusses the key differences between the long run and the short run, and it introduces the model of aggregate supply and aggregate demand. With this model we can show how shocks to the economy lead to short-run fluctuations in output and employment. We can also show how monetary policy can cause or cure those fluctuations.

The next four chapters develop more fully the model of aggregate supply and aggregate demand. Chapters 9 and 10 present the *IS-LM* model, which shows how monetary and fiscal policy affect the aggregate demand for goods and services. Chapter 11 presents the Mundell-Fleming model, which brings international issues into the analysis of aggregate demand. Chapter 12 discusses theories of aggregate supply and their implications.

In Chapter 13 we enter the debate over how policymakers should respond to short-run fluctuations. Should monetary and fiscal policy take an active or a passive role? Should policy be conducted by rule or by discretion?

The final chapter in Part Three, Chapter 14, presents some recent developments in the theory of short-run fluctuations. It discusses the avenues of research that economists are now exploring to improve our understanding of the economy, and it highlights the disagreements about which avenues are likely to prove most fruitful.

Introduction to Economic Fluctuations

The modern world regards business cycles much as the ancient Egyptians regarded the overflowing of the Nile. The phenomenon recurs at intervals, it is of great importance to everyone, and natural causes of it are not in sight.

John Bates Clark, 1898

Economic fluctuations present a recurring problem for economists and policy-makers. As you can see in Figure 8-1, the real GDP of the U.S. economy grows on average about 3 percent each year, but this growth is not at all smooth. Recessions—periods of falling incomes and rising unemployment—are frequent. In the recession of 1990, real GDP fell 2.2 percent from its peak to its trough, and the unemployment rate rose to 7.7 percent. Recessions are also associated with shorter workweeks: more workers have part-time jobs, and fewer workers work overtime.

Economists call these fluctuations in output and employment the *business cycle*. Although this term suggests that fluctuations in the economy are regular and predictable, neither is the case. Recessions are as irregular as they are common. Sometimes they are close together, such as the recessions of 1980 and 1982. Sometimes they are far apart, such as the recessions of 1982 and 1990.

In Part Two of this book, we developed models to identify the determinants of national income, unemployment, inflation, and other economic variables. Yet we did not examine why these variables fluctuate so much from year to year. Here in Part Three we develop a model to explain these short-run fluctuations. Because real GDP is the best single measure of economic well-being, it is the focus of our model.

Just as Egypt has attempted to stem the flooding of the Nile Valley with the Aswan Dam, modern society tries to control the business cycle with appropriate economic policies. The model we develop over the next several chapters shows how monetary and fiscal policies influence the business cycle. We will see that these policies can either stabilize or exacerbate economic fluctuations.

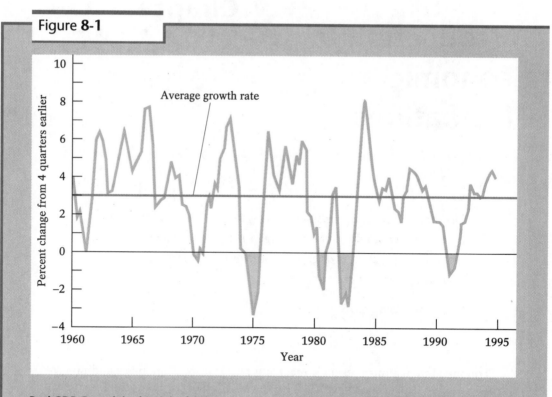

Figure 8-1

Real GDP Growth in the United States
Growth in real GDP averages about 3 percent per year, as indicated by the green line, but there are substantial fluctuations around this average. Recessions are periods when the production of goods and services is declining, represented here by negative growth in real GDP.

Source: U.S. Department of Commerce.

8-1 How the Short Run and Long Run Differ

To build a model of short-run fluctuations, we must first decide how that model will differ from the long-run classical model we developed in Chapters 3 through 7. Most macroeconomists believe that the key difference between the short run and the long run is the behavior of prices. *In the long run, prices are flexible and can respond to changes in supply or demand. In the short run, many prices are "stuck" at some predetermined level.* Because prices behave differently in the short run than in the long run, economic policies have different effects over different time horizons.

To see how the short run and the long run differ, consider the effects of a change in monetary policy. Suppose that the Federal Reserve suddenly reduced the money supply by 5 percent. According to the classical model, which almost all economists agree describes the economy in the long run, the money supply affects nominal variables—variables measured in terms of money—but not real variables. As we discussed in Chapter 6, this principle is known as the *classical dichotomy*. In the long run, a 5 percent reduction in the money supply lowers all prices (including nominal wages) by 5 percent while all real variables remain the same. Thus, in the long run, changes in the money supply do not cause fluctuations in output and employment.

In the short run, however, many prices do not respond to changes in monetary policy. A reduction in the money supply does not immediately cause all firms to cut the wages they pay, all stores to change the price tags on their goods, all mail-order firms to issue new catalogs, and all restaurants to print new menus. Instead, there is little immediate change in many prices; that is, many prices are sticky. This short-run price stickiness implies that the short-run impact of a change in the money supply is not the same as the long-run impact.

A model of economic fluctuations must take into account this short-run price stickiness. We will see that since prices do not adjust instantly to changes in the money supply, the classical dichotomy breaks down. The failure of prices to adjust to changes in the money supply implies that, in the short run, output and employment must do some of the adjusting instead. In other words, changes in the money supply can induce short-run fluctuations.

As a general principle, if prices are sticky, the amount of output produced can deviate from the level implied by the classical model. In the classical model, the amount of output depends on the economy's ability to *supply* goods and services, which in turn depends on the supplies of capital and labor and on the available technology. Here we will see that flexible prices are a crucial feature of the classical model: the model assumes that prices adjust to ensure that the quantity of output demanded equals the quantity supplied. By contrast, when prices are sticky, output also depends on the *demand* for goods and services. Demand in turn is influenced by monetary policy, fiscal policy, and various other factors. Thus, price stickiness provides a rationale for the usefulness of monetary and fiscal policy in stabilizing the economy in the short run.

In the remainder of this chapter we introduce a model that can explain short-run economic fluctuations. The model of supply and demand, which we used in Chapter 1 to discuss the market for pizza, offers some of the most fundamental insights in economics. This model shows how the supply and demand for any good jointly determine the good's price and the quantity sold, and how changes in exogenous variables affect the price and quantity. Here we present the "economy-size" version of this model—*the model of aggregate supply and aggregate demand*. This macroeconomic model allows us to study how the aggregate price level and the quantity of aggregate output are determined. It also provides a way to contrast how the economy behaves in the long run and how it behaves in the short run.

Although the model of aggregate supply and aggregate demand resembles the model of supply and demand for a single good, the analogy is not exact. The model of supply and demand for a single good considers only one good within a large economy. By contrast, the model of aggregate supply and aggregate demand is a sophisticated model that incorporates the interactions among many markets.

Case Study *8-1*

● ● ● ● ● ● ● ● ● ● ● ● ●

The Puzzle of Sticky Magazine Prices

How sticky are prices? The answer to this question depends on what price we consider. Some commodities, such as wheat, soybeans, and pork bellies, are traded on organized exchanges, and their prices change every minute. No one would call these prices sticky. Yet the prices of most goods and services change much less frequently. One survey found that 39 percent of firms change their prices once a year, and another 10 percent change their prices less than once a year.[1]

The reasons for price stickiness are not always apparent. Consider, for example, the market for magazines. A study has documented that magazines change their newsstand prices very infrequently. The typical magazine allows inflation to erode its real price by about 25 percent before it raises its nominal price. When inflation is 4 percent per year, the typical magazine changes its price about every 6 years.[2]

Why do magazines leave their prices unchanged for so long? Economists do not have a definitive answer. The question is puzzling because it would seem that for magazines, the cost of a price change is small. To change prices, a mail-order firm must issue a new catalog and a restaurant must print a new menu, but a magazine publisher can simply print a new price on the cover of the next issue. Perhaps the cost to the publisher of charging the wrong price is also not very great. Or maybe customers would find it inconvenient if the price of their favorite magazine changed every month.

Thus, it is often not easy to explain sticky prices at the microeconomic level. The cause of price stickiness is, therefore, an active area of research. In Chapter 12 and again in Chapter 14, we discuss some recent theories about why prices are sticky.

Although not yet fully explained, price stickiness is widely believed to be crucial for understanding economic fluctuations. In this chapter we begin to develop the link between sticky prices and economic fluctuations.

● ● ● ● ● ● ● ● ● ● ● ● ●

8-2   Aggregate Demand

Aggregate demand (*AD*) is the relationship between the quantity of output demanded and the aggregate price level. In other words, the aggregate demand curve tells us the quantity of goods and services people will buy at any given level of prices. We examine the theory of aggregate demand in detail in Chapters 9 through 11. Here we use the quantity theory of money to provide a very simple, although incomplete, derivation of the aggregate demand curve.

---

[1]   Alan S. Blinder, "On Sticky Prices: Academic Theories Meet the Real World," in N.G. Mankiw, ed., *Monetary Policy* (Chicago: University of Chicago Press, 1994): 117–154.

[2]   Stephen G. Cecchetti, "The Frequency of Price Adjustment: A Study of the Newsstand Prices of Magazines," *Journal of Econometrics* 31 (1986): 255–274.

The Quantity Equation as Aggregate Demand

Recall from Chapter 6 that the quantity theory says that

$$MV = PY,$$

where M is the money supply, V is the velocity of money (which for now we assume is constant), P is the price level, and Y is the amount of output. This equation states that the money supply determines the nominal value of output, which in turn is the product of the price level and the amount of output.

You might recall that the quantity equation can be rewritten in terms of the supply and demand for real money balances:

$$M/P = (M/P)^d = kY,$$

where $k = 1/V$. In this form, the quantity equation states that the supply of real money balances M/P equals the demand $(M/P)^d$ and that the demand is proportional to the amount of output Y.

For any fixed money supply, the quantity equation yields a negative relationship between the price level P and output Y. Figure 8-2 graphs the combinations of P and Y that satisfy the quantity equation holding the money supply constant. This is called the aggregate demand curve.

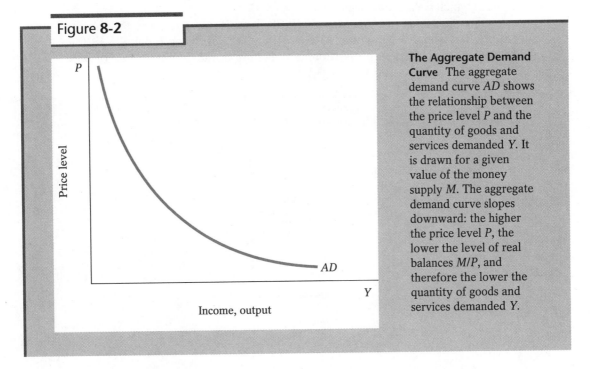

Figure 8-2

The Aggregate Demand Curve The aggregate demand curve AD shows the relationship between the price level P and the quantity of goods and services demanded Y. It is drawn for a given value of the money supply M. The aggregate demand curve slopes downward: the higher the price level P, the lower the level of real balances M/P, and therefore the lower the quantity of goods and services demanded Y.

Why the Aggregate Demand Curve Slopes Downward

The aggregate demand curve slopes downward. For any fixed money supply, the quantity equation fixes the nominal value of output PY. Therefore, if the price level P goes up, output Y must go down.

One way to understand the negative relationship between P and Y is to consider the link between money and transactions. Because we have assumed that the velocity of money is fixed, the money supply determines the dollar value of all transactions in the economy. If the price level rises, so that each transaction requires more dollars, the quantity of transactions and thus the quantity of goods and services purchased must fall.

Equivalently, we could look at the supply and demand for real money balances. If output is higher, people engage in more transactions and need higher real balances M/P. For a fixed money supply M, higher real balances imply a lower price level. Conversely, if the price level is lower, real money balances are higher; the higher level of real balances allows a greater volume of transactions and thus a higher level of output.

Shifts in the Aggregate Demand Curve

The aggregate demand curve is drawn for a fixed value of the money supply. In other words, it tells us the possible combinations of P and Y for a given value of M. If the money supply changes, then the possible combinations of P and Y change—that is, the aggregate demand curve shifts. Let's examine some situations in which a shift may occur.

First, consider what happens if the Federal Reserve reduces the money supply. The quantity equation, $MV = PY$, tells us that the reduction in the money supply leads to a proportionate reduction in the nominal value of out-

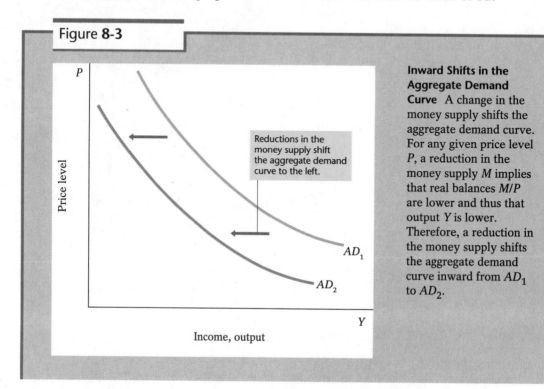

Figure 8-3

Inward Shifts in the Aggregate Demand Curve A change in the money supply shifts the aggregate demand curve. For any given price level P, a reduction in the money supply M implies that real balances M/P are lower and thus that output Y is lower. Therefore, a reduction in the money supply shifts the aggregate demand curve inward from AD_1 to AD_2.

Reductions in the money supply shift the aggregate demand curve to the left.

AD_1

AD_2

P

Price level

Y

Income, output

put PY. For any given price level, the amount of output is lower, and for any given amount of output, the price level is lower. As in Figure 8-3, the aggregate demand curve relating P and Y shifts inward.

Next, consider what happens if the Fed increases the money supply. The quantity equation tells us that there is an increase in PY. For any given price level, the amount of output is higher, and for any given amount of output, the price level is higher. As shown in Figure 8-4, the aggregate demand curve shifts outward.

Fluctuations in the money supply are not the only source of fluctuations in aggregate demand. Even if the money supply is held constant, the aggregate demand curve shifts because of changes in the velocity of money. When we study the aggregate demand curve more fully in the next three chapters, we consider many possible reasons that it might shift.

Figure 8-4

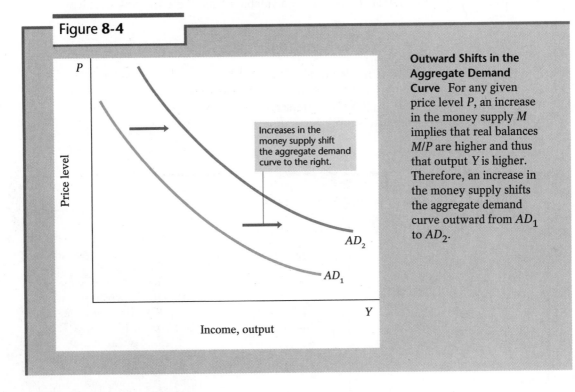

Increases in the money supply shift the aggregate demand curve to the right.

Outward Shifts in the Aggregate Demand Curve For any given price level P, an increase in the money supply M implies that real balances M/P are higher and thus that output Y is higher. Therefore, an increase in the money supply shifts the aggregate demand curve outward from AD_1 to AD_2.

8-3 Aggregate Supply

By itself, the aggregate demand curve does not tell us the price level or the amount of output; it merely gives a relationship between these two variables. To accompany the aggregate demand curve, we need another relationship between P and Y that crosses the aggregate demand curve—an aggregate supply curve. The aggregate demand curve and the aggregate supply curve together pin down the price level and the amount of output.

Aggregate supply (*AS*) is the relationship between the quantity of goods and services supplied and the price level. Because prices are flexible in the long run and sticky in the short run, this relationship depends on the time horizon under consideration. We need to discuss two different aggregate supply curves: the long-run aggregate supply curve *LRAS* and the short-run aggregate supply curve *SRAS*. We also need to discuss the transition from the short run to the long run.

The Long Run: The Vertical Aggregate Supply Curve

Since the classical model describes how the economy behaves in the long run, we derive the long-run aggregate supply curve from the classical model. Recall from Chapter 3 that the amount of output produced depends on the fixed amounts of capital and labor and on the available technology. To show this, we write

$$Y = F(\bar{K}, \bar{L})$$
$$= \bar{Y}.$$

According to the classical model, output does not depend on the price level. To show that output is the same for all price levels, we draw a vertical aggregate supply curve, as in Figure 8-5. The intersection of the aggregate demand curve with this vertical aggregate supply curve determines the price level.

Figure 8-5

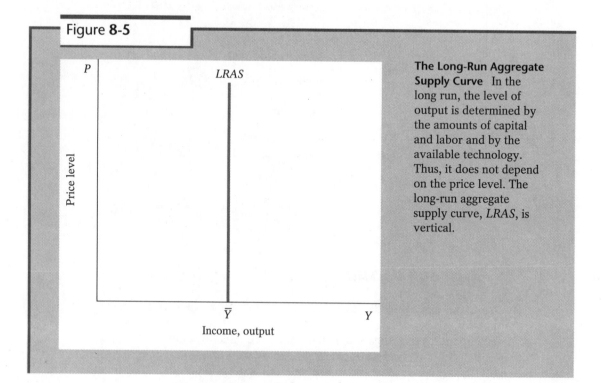

The Long-Run Aggregate Supply Curve   In the long run, the level of output is determined by the amounts of capital and labor and by the available technology. Thus, it does not depend on the price level. The long-run aggregate supply curve, *LRAS*, is vertical.

Figure **8-6**

Shifts in Aggregate Demand in the Long Run A reduction in the money supply shifts the aggregate demand curve downward from AD_1 to AD_2. The equilibrium for the economy moves from point A to point B. Since the aggregate supply curve is vertical in the long run, the reduction in aggregate demand affects the price level but not the level of output.

If the aggregate supply curve is vertical, then changes in aggregate demand affect prices but not output. For example, if the money supply falls, the aggregate demand curve shifts downward, as in Figure 8-6. The economy moves from the old intersection of aggregate supply and aggregate demand, point A, to the new intersection, point B. The shift in aggregate demand affects only prices.

The vertical aggregate supply curve satisfies the classical dichotomy, since it implies that the level of output is independent of the money supply. This long-run level of output, $\overline{Y}$, is called the *full-employment* or *natural* level of output. It is the level of output at which the economy's resources are fully employed or, more realistically, at which unemployment is at its natural rate.

The Short Run: The Horizontal Aggregate Supply Curve

The classical model and the vertical aggregate supply curve apply only in the long run. In the short run, some prices are sticky and, therefore, do not adjust to changes in demand. Because of this price stickiness, the short-run aggregate supply curve is not vertical.

As an extreme example, suppose that all firms have issued price catalogs and that it is costly for them to issue new ones. Thus, all prices are stuck at predetermined levels. At these prices, firms are willing to sell as much as their customers are willing to buy, and they hire just enough labor to produce the

The Short Run, the Long Run, and the Very Long Run

This book discusses numerous models of the economy, each with its own set of simplifying assumptions. One way to categorize the models is by the time horizon over which they apply. The models fall into three categories:

- *The Short Run*   This chapter and the following ones present the short-run theory of the economy. This theory assumes that prices are sticky and that, because of this price stickiness, capital and labor are sometimes not fully employed. Price stickiness is widely viewed as being important for explaining the economic fluctuations we observe from month to month or from year to year.

- *The Long Run*   Chapter 3 presented the basic long-run theory of the economy, called the classical model. Chapter 6 presented the classical theory of money, and Chapter 7 presented the classical theory of the open economy. These chapters assumed that prices are flexible and, therefore, that capital and labor are fully employed. These chapters also took as fixed the quantities of capital and labor, as well as the technology for turning capital and labor into output. These assumptions are best suited for a time horizon of several years. Over this period, prices can adjust to equilibrium levels, yet capital, labor, and technology are relatively constant.

- *The Very Long Run*   Chapter 4 presented the basic theory of economic growth, called the Solow model. This model analyzes the time horizon over which the capital stock, the labor force, and the available technology can change. This model is designed to explain how the economy works over a period of several decades.

When analyzing economic policies, it is important to keep in mind that they influence the economy over all time horizons. We must, therefore, draw on the insights of all these models.

---

amount demanded. Since the price level is fixed, we represent this situation in Figure 8-7 with a horizontal aggregate supply curve.

The short-run equilibrium of the economy is the intersection of the aggregate demand curve and this horizontal short-run aggregate supply curve. In this case, changes in aggregate demand do affect the level of output. For example, if the Fed suddenly reduces the money supply, the aggregate demand curve shifts inward, as in Figure 8-8. The economy moves from the old intersection of aggregate demand and aggregate supply, point A, to the new intersection, point B. Because the price level is fixed, the shift in aggregate demand causes output to fall.

A fall in aggregate demand reduces output in the short run because prices do not adjust instantly. After the sudden fall in aggregate demand, firms are stuck with prices that are too high. With demand low and prices high, firms sell less of their product, so they reduce employment and production. The economy experiences a recession.

Figure 8-7

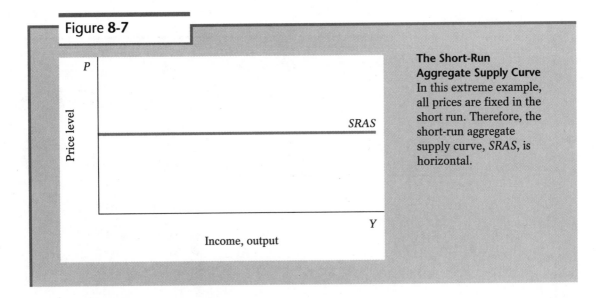

The Short-Run Aggregate Supply Curve In this extreme example, all prices are fixed in the short run. Therefore, the short-run aggregate supply curve, *SRAS*, is horizontal.

Figure 8-8

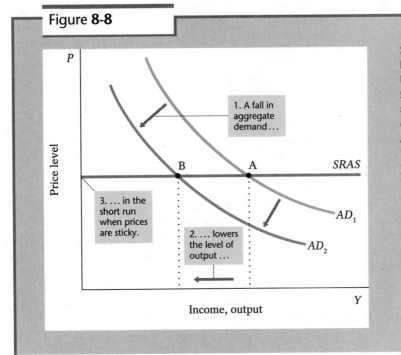

Shifts in Aggregate Demand in the Short Run A reduction in the money supply shifts the aggregate demand curve downward from AD_1 to AD_2. The equilibrium for the economy moves from point A to point B. Since the aggregate supply curve is horizontal in the short run, the reduction in aggregate demand reduces the level of output.

From the Short Run to the Long Run

We can summarize our analysis so far as follows: *Over short periods of time, prices are sticky, the aggregate supply curve is flat, and changes in aggregate demand affect the output of the economy. Over long periods of time, prices are flexible, the aggregate supply curve is vertical, and changes in aggregate*

Figure 8-9

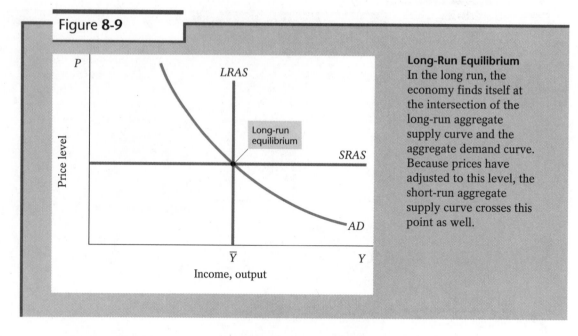

Long-Run Equilibrium
In the long run, the economy finds itself at the intersection of the long-run aggregate supply curve and the aggregate demand curve. Because prices have adjusted to this level, the short-run aggregate supply curve crosses this point as well.

demand affect only the price level. Thus, changes in aggregate demand have different effects over different time horizons.

Let's trace the effects over time of a fall in aggregate demand. Suppose that the economy begins in long-run equilibrium, as shown in Figure 8-9. In this figure, there are three curves: the aggregate demand curve, the long-run aggregate supply curve, and the short-run aggregate supply curve. The long-run equilibrium is the point at which aggregate demand crosses the long-run aggregate supply curve. Prices have adjusted to reach this equilibrium. Therefore, when the economy is in its long-run equilibrium, the short-run aggregate supply curve must cross this point as well.

Now suppose that the Fed reduces the money supply and the aggregate demand curve shifts downward, as in Figure 8-10. In the short run, prices are sticky, so the economy moves from point A to point B. Output and employment fall below their natural levels, which means the economy is in a recession. Over time, in response to the low demand, wages and prices fall. The gradual reduction in the price level moves the economy downward along the aggregate demand curve to point C, which is the new long-run equilibrium. In the new long-run equilibrium (point C), output and employment are back to their natural levels, but prices are lower than in the old long-run equilibrium (point A).

Case Study *8-2*

● ● ● ● ● ● ● ● ● ● ● ● ●

Gold, Greenbacks, and the Contraction of the 1870s

The aftermath of the Civil War in the United States provides a vivid example of how contractionary monetary policy affects the economy. Before the war,

Figure 8-10

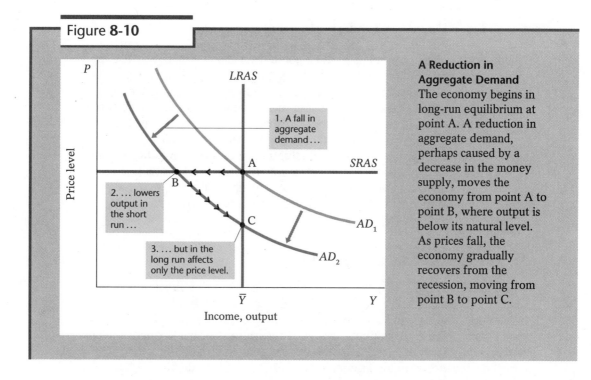

A Reduction in Aggregate Demand The economy begins in long-run equilibrium at point A. A reduction in aggregate demand, perhaps caused by a decrease in the money supply, moves the economy from point A to point B, where output is below its natural level. As prices fall, the economy gradually recovers from the recession, moving from point B to point C.

the United States was on a gold standard. Paper dollars were readily convertible into gold. Under this policy, the quantity of gold determined the money supply and the price level.

In 1862, after the Civil War broke out, the Treasury announced that it would no longer exchange gold for dollars. In essence, this act replaced the gold standard with a system of fiat money. Over the next few years, the government printed large quantities of paper currency—called *greenbacks* for their color—and used the seigniorage to finance wartime expenditure. Because of this increase in the money supply, the price level approximately doubled during the war.

When the war was over, much political debate centered on the question of whether to return to the gold standard. The Greenback Party was formed with the primary goal of maintaining the system of fiat money. Eventually, however, the Greenback Party lost the debate. Policymakers decided to retire the greenbacks over time in order to reinstate the gold standard at the rate of exchange between dollars and gold that had prevailed before the war. Their goal was to return the value of the dollar to its former level.

Returning to the gold standard in this way required reversing the wartime rise in prices, which meant a fall in aggregate demand. (To be more precise, the growth in aggregate demand needed to fall short of the growth in the natural rate of output.) As the price level fell, the economy experienced a recession from 1873 to 1879, the longest on record. By 1879, the price level was back to its level before the war, and the gold standard was reinstated.

8-4 Stabilization Policy

Fluctuations in the economy as a whole come from changes in aggregate supply or aggregate demand. Economists call exogenous changes in these curves **shocks** to the economy. Shocks disrupt economic well-being by pushing output and employment away from their natural rates. The model of aggregate supply and aggregate demand shows how shocks cause economic fluctuations.

The model is also useful for evaluating how macroeconomic policy can respond to shocks in order to dampen fluctuations. **Stabilization policy** is public policy aimed at keeping output and employment at their natural rates. Because the money supply has a powerful impact on aggregate demand, monetary policy is an important component of stabilization policy.

Shocks to Aggregate Demand

Consider an example of a shock to aggregate demand: the invention of automatic teller machines. These machines make cash easier to obtain and, therefore, reduce the demand for money. For example, suppose that before the introduction of teller machines, everyone went to the bank once a week, withdrew $100, and then spent the money gradually over the week; in this case, average money holdings equaled $50. After the introduction of teller machines, everyone goes to the bank twice a week and withdraws $50; now, average money holdings equal $25. In this example, money demand falls by one-half.

This reduction in money demand is equivalent to an increase in the velocity of money. To see this, remember that

$$M/P = kY,$$

where $k = 1/V$. A decrease in real money balances for any given amount of output implies a decrease in k and an increase in V. Because the introduction of automatic teller machines allows people to hold fewer dollars in their wallets, the dollars circulate more quickly. That is, because people obtain money more often, there is less time between when a dollar is received and when it is spent. Hence, velocity increases.

If the money supply is held constant, the increase in velocity causes nominal spending to rise and the aggregate demand curve to shift outward, as in Figure 8-11. In the short run, the increase in demand raises the output of the economy—it causes an economic boom. At the old prices, firms now sell more output. Therefore, they hire more workers, ask their existing workers to work longer hours, and make greater use of their factories and equipment.

Over time, the high level of aggregate demand pulls up wages and prices. As the price level rises, the quantity of output demanded declines, and the economy gradually approaches the natural rate of production. But during the transition to the higher price level, the economy's output is higher than the natural rate.

Figure 8-11

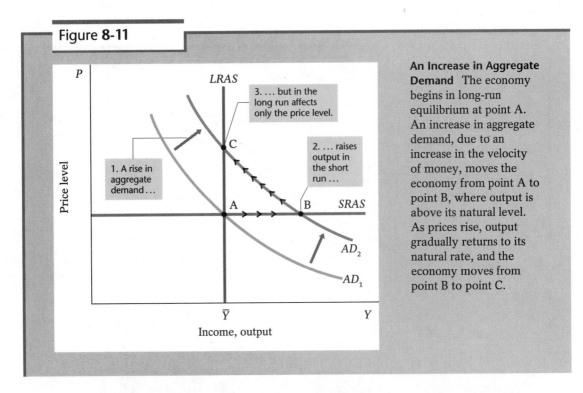

An Increase in Aggregate Demand The economy begins in long-run equilibrium at point A. An increase in aggregate demand, due to an increase in the velocity of money, moves the economy from point A to point B, where output is above its natural level. As prices rise, output gradually returns to its natural rate, and the economy moves from point B to point C.

What can the Fed do to dampen this boom and keep output closer to the natural rate? The Fed might reduce the money supply to offset the increase in velocity. Offsetting the change in velocity would stabilize aggregate demand. Thus, the Fed can reduce or even eliminate the impact of demand shocks on output and employment if it can skillfully control the money supply. Whether the Fed in fact has the necessary skill is a more difficult question, which we take up in Chapter 13.

Case Study *8-3*

• • • • • • • • • • • • •

Velocity and the 1982 Recession

Is the velocity of money steady, or is it highly volatile? The answer to this question influences how the Fed should conduct monetary policy. On the one hand, if velocity is steady, then it is easy to stabilize aggregate demand: the Fed needs only to keep the money supply constant, or growing at a steady rate. On the other hand, if velocity is highly volatile, then stabilizing aggregate demand requires adjusting the money supply frequently to offset the changes in velocity.

The deep recession that the United States experienced in 1982 is partly attributable to a large, unexpected, and still mostly unexplained decline in velocity. Figure 8-12 graphs velocity (measured here as nominal GDP divided by $M1$) since 1959. The figure shows that velocity rose steadily in the 1960s and

Figure **8-12**

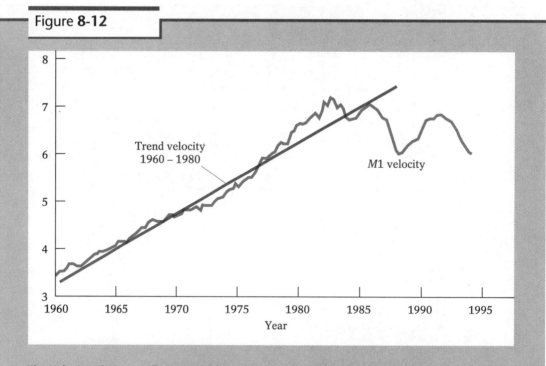

The Velocity of Money   For reasons that are still not fully understood, the velocity of money (nominal GDP divided by *M*1) fell in the early 1980s substantially below its previous upward trend. This fall contributed to a reduction in aggregate demand, which in turn led to the 1982 recession, one of the deepest in recent history.

Source: U.S. Department of Commerce and Federal Reserve.

1970s but then fell markedly after 1981. The experience of the early 1980s shows that the Fed cannot rely on the velocity of money remaining stable.

In 1982 the Fed could have offset the fall in velocity by raising the money supply. Containing inflation was the Fed's primary concern in the early 1980s, however, so it slowed the rate of money growth instead, further depressing aggregate demand. The combination of these two forces—falling velocity and anti-inflationary monetary policy—led to the deepest recession since the Great Depression of the 1930s.

How should we evaluate the Fed's actions? It attained its goal of lower inflation (even more quickly than it expected), but the cost was a substantial fall in output and employment. The 1982 recession highlights the conflicting goals of the Fed: maintaining full employment and keeping inflation under control. Stabilization policy often involves a tradeoff between these two objectives.[3]

[3]   For two views of what we learned about monetary policy from the experience of the 1980s, see Benjamin M. Friedman, "Lessons on Monetary Policy from the 1980s," *Journal of Economic Perspectives* 2 (Summer 1988): 51–72; and William Poole, "Monetary Policy Lessons of Recent Inflation and Disinflation," *Journal of Economic Perspectives* 2 (Summer 1988): 73–100.

Shocks to Aggregate Supply

Shocks to aggregate supply, as well as shocks to aggregate demand, can cause economic fluctuations. A *supply shock* is a shock to the economy that alters the cost of producing goods and services and, as a result, the prices that firms charge. Because supply shocks have a direct impact on the price level, they are sometimes called *price shocks*. Examples are:

- A drought that destroys crops. The reduction in food supply pushes up food prices.

- A new environmental protection law that requires firms to reduce their emissions of pollutants. Firms pass on the added costs to customers in the form of higher prices.

- An increase in union aggressiveness. This pushes up wages and the prices of the goods produced by union workers.

- The organization of an international oil cartel. By curtailing competition, the major oil producers can raise the world price of oil.

All these events are adverse supply shocks: they push up costs and prices. A favorable supply shock, such as the breakup of an international oil cartel, reduces costs and prices.

Figure 8-13 shows how an adverse supply shock affects the economy. The short-run aggregate supply curve shifts upward. (The supply shock may also lower the natural level of output and thus shift the long-run aggregate supply curve to the left, but we ignore that effect here.) If aggregate demand is held constant, the economy moves from point A to point B: the price level rises and the amount of output falls below the natural rate. An experience like this is

Figure 8-13

An Adverse Supply Shock
An adverse supply shock pushes up costs and thus prices. If aggregate demand is held constant, the economy moves from point A to point B, leading to stagflation—a combination of increasing prices and falling output. Eventually, as prices fall, the economy returns to the natural rate, point A.

called **stagflation**, because it combines stagnation (falling output) with inflation (rising prices).

Faced with an adverse supply shock, a policymaker controlling aggregate demand, such as the Fed, has a difficult choice between two options. The first option, implicit in Figure 8-13, is to hold aggregate demand constant. In this case, output and employment are lower than the natural rate. Eventually, prices will fall to restore full employment at the old price level (point A). But the cost of this process is a painful recession.

The second option, illustrated in Figure 8-14, is to expand aggregate demand to bring the economy toward the natural rate more quickly. If the increase in aggregate demand coincides with the shock to aggregate supply, the economy goes immediately from point A to point C. In this case, the Fed is said to *accommodate* the supply shock. The drawback of this option, of course, is that the price level is permanently higher. There is no way to adjust aggregate demand both to maintain full employment and to keep the price level stable.

Figure 8-14

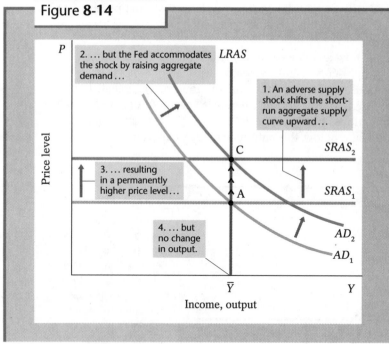

2. ... but the Fed accommodates the shock by raising aggregate demand ...

1. An adverse supply shock shifts the short-run aggregate supply curve upward ...

3. ... resulting in a permanently higher price level ...

4. ... but no change in output.

Accommodating an Adverse Supply Shock
In response to an adverse supply shock, the Fed can increase aggregate demand to prevent a reduction in output. The economy moves from point A to point C. The cost of this policy is a permanently higher level of prices.

Case Study *8-4*

How OPEC Helped Cause Stagflation in the 1970s and Euphoria in the 1980s

The most disruptive supply shocks in recent history were caused by OPEC, the Organization of Petroleum Exporting Countries. In the early 1970s, OPEC's coordinated reduction in the supply of oil nearly doubled the world price. This increase in oil prices caused stagflation in most industrial countries. These statistics show what happened in the United States:

Year	Change in Oil Prices	Inflation Rate (CPI)	Unemployment Rate
1973	11.0%	6.2%	4.9%
1974	68.0	11.0	5.6
1975	16.0	9.1	8.5
1976	3.3	5.8	7.7
1977	8.1	6.5	7.1

The 68 percent increase in the price of oil in 1974 was an adverse supply shock of major proportions. As one would have expected, it led to both higher inflation and higher unemployment.

A few years later, when the world economy had nearly recovered from the first OPEC recession, almost the same thing happened again. OPEC raised oil prices, causing further stagflation. Here are the statistics for the United States:

Year	Change in Oil Prices	Inflation Rate (CPI)	Unemployment Rate
1978	9.4%	7.7%	6.1%
1979	25.4	11.3	5.8
1980	47.8	13.5	7.0
1981	44.4	10.3	7.5
1982	−8.7	6.1	9.5

The increases in oil prices in 1979, 1980, and 1981 again led to double-digit inflation and higher unemployment.

In the mid-1980s, political turmoil among the Arab countries weakened OPEC's ability to restrain supplies of oil. Oil prices fell, reversing the stagflation of the 1970s and the early 1980s. Here's what happened:

Year	Changes in Oil Prices	Inflation Rate (CPI)	Unemployment Rate
1983	−7.1%	3.2%	9.5%
1984	−1.7	4.3	7.4
1985	−7.5	3.6	7.1
1986	−44.5	1.9	6.9
1987	18.3	3.6	6.1

In 1986 oil prices fell by nearly half. This favorable supply shock led to one of the lowest inflation rates experienced in recent U.S. history and to falling unemployment.

More recently, OPEC has not been a major cause of economic fluctuations. With the exception of a brief period after Iraq invaded Kuwait in the summer of 1990, the price of oil has been relatively stable. Yet the experience of the 1970s and 1980s could always repeat itself. Events in the Middle East are a potential source of shocks to economies around the world.[4]

8-5   Conclusion

This chapter has introduced a framework to study economic fluctuations: the model of aggregate supply and aggregate demand. The model is built on the assumption that prices are sticky in the short run and flexible in the long run. It shows how shocks to the economy cause output to deviate temporarily from the level implied by the classical model.

The model also highlights the role of monetary policy. Poor monetary policy can be a source of shocks to the economy. A well-run monetary policy can respond to shocks and stabilize the economy.

In the chapters that follow, we refine our understanding of this model and our analysis of stabilization policy. Chapters 9 through 11 go beyond the quantity equation to refine our theory of aggregate demand. This refinement shows that aggregate demand depends on fiscal policy as well as monetary policy. Chapter 12 examines aggregate supply in more detail and discusses why wages and prices are sticky. Chapter 13 examines the debate over the virtues and limits of stabilization policy.

Summary

1. The crucial difference between the long run and the short run is that prices are flexible in the long run but sticky in the short run. The model of aggregate supply and aggregate demand provides a framework to analyze economic fluctuations and see how the impact of policies varies over different time horizons.

2. The aggregate demand curve slopes downward. It tells us that the lower the price level, the greater the aggregate demand for goods and services.

3. In the long run, the aggregate supply curve is vertical: output is determined by the amounts of capital and labor and by the available technology. Therefore, shifts in aggregate demand affect the price level but not output or employment.

4. In the short run, the aggregate supply curve is horizontal, since wages and prices are predetermined. Therefore, shifts in aggregate demand affect output and employment.

5. Shocks to aggregate demand and aggregate supply cause economic fluctuations. Since the Fed can shift the aggregate demand curve, it can attempt to offset these shocks to maintain output and employment at their natural rates.

---

[4] Statistics used here are from the Bureau of Labor Statistics. Some economists have suggested that changes in oil prices played a major role in economic fluctuations even before the 1970s. See James D. Hamilton, "Oil and the Macroeconomy Since World War II," *Journal of Political Economy* 91 (April 1983): 228–248.

KEY CONCEPTS

Aggregate demand

Aggregate supply

Shocks

Stabilization policy

Stagflation

QUESTIONS FOR REVIEW

1. Give an example of a price that is sticky in the short run and flexible in the long run.

2. Why does the aggregate demand curve slope downward?

3. Explain the impact of an increase in the money supply in the short run and in the long run.

4. Why is it easier for the Fed to deal with demand shocks than with supply shocks?

PROBLEMS AND APPLICATIONS

1. Suppose that a change in government regulations allows banks to start paying interest on checking accounts. Recall that the money stock is the sum of currency and demand deposits, including checking accounts, so this regulatory change makes holding money more attractive.

   a. How does this change affect the demand for money?

   b. What happens to the velocity of money?

   c. If the Fed keeps the money supply constant, what will happen to output and prices in the short run and in the long run?

   d. Should the Fed keep the money supply constant in response to this regulatory change? Why or why not?

2. The Fed reduces the money supply by 5 percent.

   a. What happens to the aggregate demand curve?

   b. What happens to the level of out-put and the price level in the short run and in the long run?

   c. According to Okun's law, what happens to unemployment in the short run and in the long run? (*Hint:* Okun's law is the relationship between output and unemployment discussed in Chapter 2.)

   d. What happens to the real interest rate in the short run and in the long run? (*Hint:* Use the model of the real interest rate in Chapter 3 to see what happens when output changes.)

3. Let's examine how the goals of the Fed influence its response to shocks. Suppose Fed A cares only about keeping the price level stable, and Fed B cares only about keeping output and employment at their natural rates. Explain how each Fed would respond to

   a. An exogenous decrease in the velocity of money.

   b. An exogenous increase in the price of oil.

Aggregate Demand I

*I shall argue that the postulates of the classical theory are
applicable to a special case only and not to the general case. . . .
Moreover, the characteristics of the special case assumed by the
classical theory happen not to be those of the economic society in
which we actually live, with the result that its teaching is misleading
and disastrous if we attempt to apply it to the facts of experience.*

John Maynard Keynes, *The General Theory*

The most disruptive economic fluctuation in U.S. history was the Great Depression. In the 1930s the United States experienced massive unemployment and greatly reduced incomes. In the Depression's worst year, 1933, one-fourth of the U.S. labor force was unemployed, and real GDP was 30 percent below its 1929 level.

This devastating episode caused many economists to question the validity of classical economic theory—the theory we examined in Chapters 3 through 7. Classical theory seemed incapable of explaining the Depression. According to that theory, national income depends on factor supplies and the available technology, neither of which changed substantially from 1929 to 1933. After the onset of the Depression, many economists believed that a new model was needed to explain such a large and sudden economic downturn and to suggest government policies that might reduce the economic hardship so many people faced.

In 1936 the British economist John Maynard Keynes revolutionized economics with his book *The General Theory of Employment, Interest, and Money*. Keynes proposed a new way to analyze the economy, which he presented as an alternative to classical theory. His vision of how the economy works quickly became a center of controversy. Yet, as economists debated *The General Theory*, a new understanding of economic fluctuations gradually developed.

Keynes proposed that low aggregate demand is responsible for the low income and high unemployment that characterize economic downturns. He criticized classical theory for assuming that aggregate supply alone—capital, labor, and technology—determines national income. Economists today reconcile these two views with the model of aggregate demand and aggregate supply in-

Figure 9-1

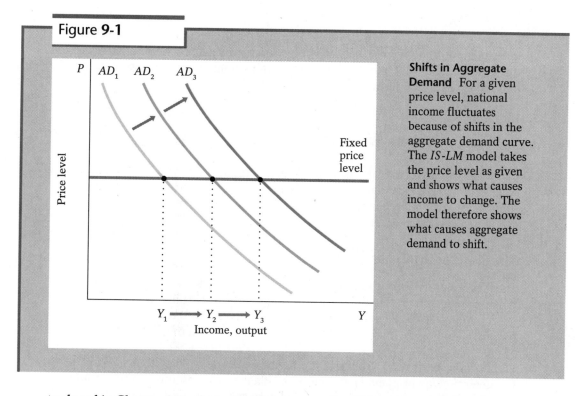

Shifts in Aggregate Demand For a given price level, national income fluctuates because of shifts in the aggregate demand curve. The *IS-LM* model takes the price level as given and shows what causes income to change. The model therefore shows what causes aggregate demand to shift.

troduced in Chapter 8. In the long run, prices are flexible, and aggregate supply determines income. But in the short run, prices are sticky, so changes in aggregate demand influence income.

In this chapter and the next one, we continue our study of economic fluctuations by looking more closely at aggregate demand. Our goal is to identify the variables that shift the aggregate demand curve, causing fluctuations in national income. We also examine more fully the tools policymakers can use to influence aggregate demand. In Chapter 8 we derived the aggregate demand curve from the quantity theory of money, and we showed that monetary policy can shift the aggregate demand curve. In this chapter we see that the government can influence aggregate demand with both monetary and fiscal policy.

The model of aggregate demand developed in this chapter, called the *IS-LM* **model**, is the leading interpretation of Keynes's theory. This model takes the price level as exogenous and then shows what determines national income. There are two ways to view the *IS-LM* model. We can view it as showing what causes income to change in the short run when the price level is fixed. Or we can view the *IS-LM* model as showing what causes the aggregate demand curve to shift. These two views of the model are equivalent: as Figure 9-1 shows, in the short run when the price level is fixed, changes in income result from shifts in the aggregate demand curve.

The two parts of the *IS-LM* model are, not surprisingly, the *IS* **curve** and the *LM* **curve**. *IS* stands for "investment" and "saving." The *IS* curve represents the market for goods and services we discussed in Chapter 3. *LM* stands for "liquidity" and "money." The *LM* curve represents the supply and demand for money we discussed in Chapter 6. Because the interest rate influences both investment and money demand, it is the variable that links the two halves of the *IS-LM* model. The model shows how interactions between these markets determine aggregate demand.[1]

9-1   The Goods Market and the *IS* Curve

The *IS* curve plots the relationship between the interest rate and the level of income that arises in the market for goods and services. To develop this relationship, we begin with a simple theory of the demand for goods and services, called the **Keynesian cross**.

The Keynesian Cross

The Keynesian cross is the simplest interpretation of Keynes's theory of national income and is a building block for the more complex and realistic *IS-LM* model. Many of the elements of the Keynesian cross should be familiar from our discussion of the market for goods and services in Chapter 3.

Planned Expenditure   To derive the Keynesian cross, we begin by looking at the determinants of planned expenditure. Planned expenditure is the amount households, firms, and the government plan to spend on goods and services.

The difference between actual and planned expenditure is unplanned inventory investment. When firms sell less of their product than they planned, their stock of inventories automatically rises. Conversely, when firms sell more than planned, their stock of inventories falls. Because these unplanned changes in inventory are counted as spending by firms, actual expenditure can be either above or below planned expenditure.

Assuming that the economy is closed, so that net exports are zero, we write planned expenditure E as the sum of consumption C, planned investment I, and government purchases G:

$$E = C + I + G.$$

To this equation, we add the consumption function

$$C = C(Y - T),$$

which states that consumption depends on disposable income $(Y - T)$. Disposable income is total income Y minus taxes T. In addition, we assume that planned investment is fixed,

$$I = \bar{I},$$

and that fiscal policy—the levels of government purchases and taxes—is fixed:

$$G = \bar{G}$$
$$T = \bar{T}.$$

[1] The *IS-LM* model was introduced in a classic article by the Nobel-prize-winning economist John R. Hicks, "Mr. Keynes and the Classics: A Suggested Interpretation," *Econometrica* 5 (1937): 147–159.

Combining these equations, we obtain

$$E = C(Y - \bar{T}) + \bar{I} + \bar{G}.$$

This equation shows that planned expenditure is a function of income Y, the exogenous level of planned investment $\bar{I}$, and the exogenous fiscal policy variables $\bar{G}$ and $\bar{T}$.

Figure 9-2 graphs planned expenditure as a function of the level of income. This line slopes upward because higher income leads to higher consumption and thus higher planned expenditure. The slope of this line is the marginal propensity to consume, the MPC: it shows how much planned expenditure increases when income rises by \$1.

Figure 9-2

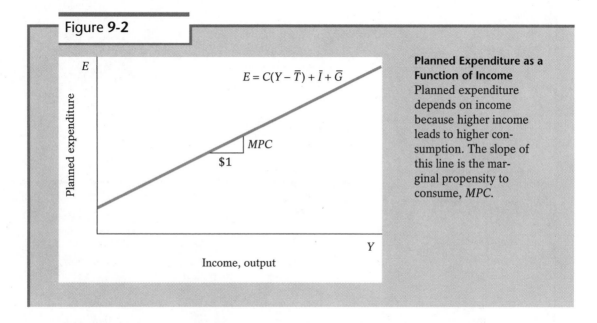

Planned Expenditure as a Function of Income Planned expenditure depends on income because higher income leads to higher consumption. The slope of this line is the marginal propensity to consume, MPC.

The Economy in Equilibrium   We now assume that the economy is in equilibrium when actual expenditure equals planned expenditure. Recall that Y equals not only total income but also actual expenditure on goods and services. We write the equilibrium condition as

$$\text{Actual Expenditure} = \text{Planned Expenditure}$$
$$Y = E.$$

The 45-degree line in Figure 9-3 plots the points where this condition holds. With the addition of the planned-expenditure function, this diagram becomes the Keynesian cross. The equilibrium of this economy is at point A, where the planned-expenditure function crosses the 45-degree line.

How does the economy get to the equilibrium? For many firms, inventories play an important role in the adjustment process. Unplanned changes in inventories induce firms to change production levels, and this in turn changes income and expenditure.

Figure 9-3

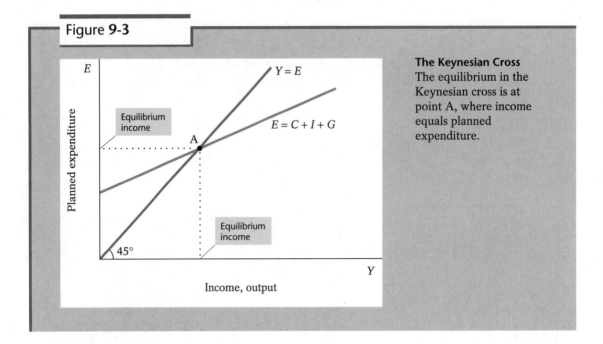

The Keynesian Cross
The equilibrium in the Keynesian cross is at point A, where income equals planned expenditure.

Figure 9-4

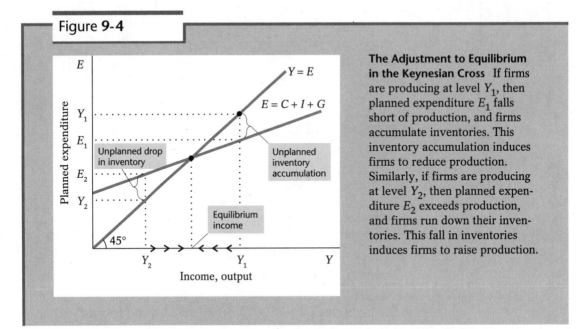

The Adjustment to Equilibrium in the Keynesian Cross If firms are producing at level Y_1, then planned expenditure E_1 falls short of production, and firms accumulate inventories. This inventory accumulation induces firms to reduce production. Similarly, if firms are producing at level Y_2, then planned expenditure E_2 exceeds production, and firms run down their inventories. This fall in inventories induces firms to raise production.

For example, suppose GDP is at a level greater than the equilibrium level, such as the level Y_1 in Figure 9-4. In this case, planned expenditure is E_1, which is less than Y_1. Because planned expenditure is less than production, firms are selling less than they produce. Firms add the unsold goods to their stock of inventories. This unplanned rise in inventories induces firms to lay off workers and reduce production, and these actions in turn reduce GDP. This process of unintended inventory accumulation and falling income continues until income falls to the equilibrium level. At the equilibrium, income equals planned expenditure.

Similarly, suppose GDP is at a level lower than the equilibrium level, such as the level Y_2 in Figure 9-4. In this case, planned expenditure is E_2, which is more than Y_2. Because planned expenditure exceeds production, firms are selling more than they are producing. As firms see their stock of inventories fall, they hire more workers and increase production. This process continues until income equals planned expenditure.

In summary, the Keynesian cross shows how income Y is determined for given levels of planned investment I and fiscal policy G and T. We can use this model to show how income changes when one of these exogenous variables changes.

Fiscal Policy and the Multiplier: Government Purchases   Consider how changes in government purchases affect the economy. Because government purchases are one component of expenditure, higher government purchases result in higher planned expenditure for any given level of income. If government purchases rise by ΔG, then the planned-expenditure schedule shifts upward by ΔG, as in Figure 9-5. The equilibrium of the economy moves from point A to point B.

Figure 9-5

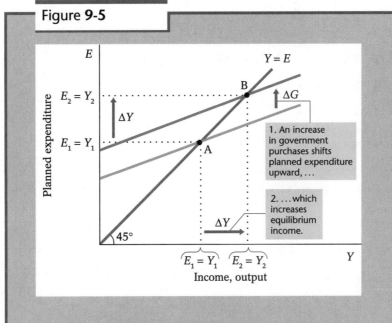

1. An increase in government purchases shifts planned expenditure upward, …

2. …which increases equilibrium income.

An Increase in Government Purchases in the Keynesian Cross An increase in government purchases of ΔG raises planned expenditure by that amount for any given level of income. The equilibrium moves from point A to point B, and income rises from Y_1 to Y_2. Note that the increase in income ΔY exceeds the increase in government purchases ΔG. Thus, fiscal policy has a multiplied effect on income.

This graph shows that an increase in government purchases leads to an even greater increase in income. That is, ΔY is larger than ΔG. The ratio $\Delta Y/\Delta G$ is called the **government-purchases multiplier**; it tells us how much income rises in response to a $1 increase in government purchases. An implication of the Keynesian cross is that the government-purchases multiplier is larger than 1.

Why does fiscal policy have a multiplied effect on income? The reason is that, according to the consumption function, higher income causes higher consumption. Because an increase in government purchases raises income, it also raises consumption, which further raises income, which further raises consumption, and so on. Therefore, in this model, an increase in government purchases causes a greater increase in income.

How big is the multiplier? To answer this question, we trace through each step of the change in income. The process begins when expenditure rises by ΔG, which implies that income rises by ΔG as well. This increase in income in turn raises consumption by $MPC \times \Delta G$, where MPC is the marginal propensity to consume. This increase in consumption raises expenditure and income once again. This second increase in income of $MPC \times \Delta G$ again raises consumption, this time by $MPC \times (MPC \times \Delta G)$, which again raises expenditure and income, and so on. This feedback from consumption to income to consumption continues indefinitely. The total effect on income is

Initial Change in Government Purchases	$=$		ΔG
First Change in Consumption		$= MPC$	$\times \Delta G$
Second Change in Consumption		$= MPC^2$	$\times \Delta G$
Third Change in Consumption		$= MPC^3$	$\times \Delta G$

$$\Delta Y = (1 + MPC + MPC^2 + MPC^3 + \ldots)\Delta G.$$

The government-purchases multiplier is

$$\Delta Y/\Delta G = 1 + MPC + MPC^2 + MPC^3 + \ldots.$$

This expression for the multiplier is an example of an *infinite geometric series*. A result from algebra allows us to write the multiplier as[2]

$$\Delta Y/\Delta G = 1/(1 - MPC).$$

---

[2] *Mathematical Note:* We prove this algebraic result as follows. Let

$$z = 1 + x + x^2 + \ldots.$$

Multiply both sides of this equation by x:

$$xz = x + x^2 + x^3 + \ldots.$$

Subtract the second equation from the first:

$$z - xz = 1.$$

Rearrange this last equation to obtain

$$z(1 - x) = 1,$$

which implies

$$z = 1/(1 - x).$$

This completes the proof.

For example, if the marginal propensity to consume is 0.6, the multiplier is

$$\Delta Y/\Delta G = 1 + 0.6 + 0.6^2 + 0.6^3 + \ldots$$
$$= 1/(1 - 0.6)$$
$$= 2.5.$$

In this case, a \$1.00 increase in government purchases raises equilibrium income by \$2.50.[3]

Fiscal Policy and the Multiplier: Taxes   Consider now how changes in taxes affect equilibrium income. A decrease in taxes of ΔT immediately raises disposable income $Y - T$ by ΔT and, therefore, increases consumption by $MPC \times \Delta T$. For any given level of income Y, planned expenditure is now higher. As Figure 9-6 shows, the planned-expenditure schedule shifts upward by $MPC \times \Delta T$. The equilibrium of the economy moves from point A to point B.

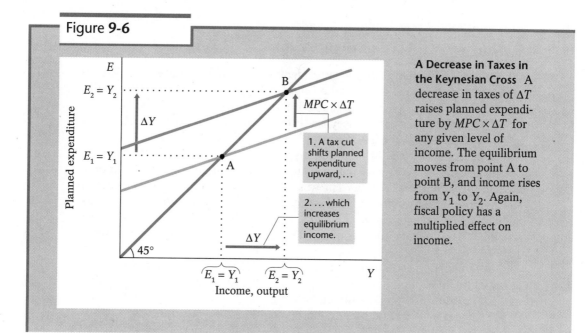

Figure 9-6

A Decrease in Taxes in the Keynesian Cross A decrease in taxes of ΔT raises planned expenditure by $MPC \times \Delta T$ for any given level of income. The equilibrium moves from point A to point B, and income rises from Y_1 to Y_2. Again, fiscal policy has a multiplied effect on income.

---

[3] *Mathematical Note:* The government-purchases multiplier is most easily derived using a little calculus. Begin with the equation

$$Y = C(Y - T) + I + G.$$

Differentiate to obtain

$$dY = C'dY + dG,$$

and then rearrange to find

$$dY/dG = 1/(1 - C').$$

This is the same as the equation in the text.

Just as an increase in government purchases has a multiplied effect on income, so does a decrease in taxes. As before, the initial change in expenditure is multiplied by $1/(1 - MPC)$. The overall effect on income of the change in taxes is

$$\Delta Y/\Delta T = -MPC/(1 - MPC).$$

This expression is the **tax multiplier**, the amount income changes in response to a \$1 change in taxes. For example, if the marginal propensity to consume is 0.6, then the tax multiplier is

$$\Delta Y/\Delta T = -0.6/(1 - 0.6) = -1.5.$$

In this example, a \$1.00 cut in taxes raises equilibrium income by \$1.50.[4]

Case Study 9-1

● ● ● ● ● ● ● ● ● ● ● ● ●

Kennedy, Keynes, and the 1964 Tax Cut

When John F. Kennedy became President of the United States in 1961, he brought to Washington some of the brightest young economists of the day to work on the Council of Economic Advisers. These economists, who had been schooled in the economics of Keynes, brought Keynesian ideas to discussions of economic policy at the highest level.

One of the Council's first proposals was to expand national income by reducing taxes. This eventually led to a substantial cut in personal and corporate income taxes in 1964. The tax cut was intended to stimulate expenditure on consumption and investment, leading to higher levels of income and employment. When a reporter asked Kennedy why he advocated a tax cut, Kennedy replied, "To stimulate the economy. Don't you remember your Economics 101?"

As Kennedy's economic advisers predicted, the passage of the tax cut was followed by an economic boom. Growth in real GDP was 5.3 percent in 1964 and 6.0 percent in 1965. The unemployment rate fell from 5.7 percent in 1963 to 5.2 percent in 1964 and then to 4.5 percent in 1965.

---

[4] *Mathematical Note:* As before, the multiplier is most easily derived using a little calculus. Begin with the equation

$$Y = C(Y - T) + I + G.$$

Differentiate to obtain

$$dY = C'(dY - dT),$$

and then rearrange to find

$$dY/dT = -C'/(1 - C').$$

This is the same as the equation in the text.

Economists continue to debate the source of this rapid growth in the early 1960s. A group called *supply-siders* argues that the economic boom resulted from the incentive effects of the cut in income tax rates. According to supply-siders, when workers are allowed to keep a higher fraction of their earnings, they supply substantially more labor and expand the aggregate supply of goods and services. Keynesians, however, emphasize the impact of tax cuts on aggregate demand. They view the 1964 tax cut as a successful experiment with expansionary fiscal policy and as a confirmation of Keynesian economics.[5]

• • • • • • • • • • • • • •

The Interest Rate, Investment, and the *IS* Curve

The Keynesian cross is only a steppingstone on our path to the *IS-LM* model. The Keynesian cross is useful because it shows what determines the economy's income for any given level of planned investment. Yet it makes the unrealistic assumption that the level of planned investment is fixed. As we discussed in Chapter 3, we can expect planned investment to depend on the interest rate.

To add this relationship between the interest rate and investment to our model, we write the level of planned investment as

$$I = I(r).$$

This investment function is graphed in panel (a) of Figure 9-7. Because the interest rate is the cost of borrowing to finance investment projects, an increase in the interest rate reduces planned investment. As a result, the investment function slopes downward.

We can combine the investment function with the Keynesian-cross diagram to determine how income changes when the interest rate changes. Because investment is inversely related to the interest rate, an increase in the interest rate from r_1 to r_2 reduces the quantity of investment from $I(r_1)$ to $I(r_2)$. The reduction in planned investment, in turn, shifts the planned-expenditure function downward, as in panel (b) of Figure 9-7. The shift in the planned-expenditure function causes the level of income to fall from Y_1 to Y_2. Hence, an increase in the interest rate lowers income.

The *IS* curve summarizes the relationship between the interest rate and the level of income that results from the investment function and the Keynesian cross. The higher the interest rate, the lower the level of planned investment, and thus the lower the level of income. For this reason, the *IS* curve slopes downward, as in panel (c) of Figure 9-7.

---

[5] For an analysis of the 1964 tax cut by one of Kennedy's economists, see Arthur Okun, "Measuring the Impact of the 1964 Tax Reduction," in W. W. Heller, ed., *Perspectives on Economic Growth* (New York: Random House, 1968); reprinted in Arthur M. Okun, *Economics for Policymaking* (Cambridge, Mass.: MIT Press, 1983), 405–423.

Figure 9-7

Deriving the *IS* Curve Panel (a) shows the investment function: an increase in the interest rate from r_1 to r_2 reduces planned investment from $I(r_1)$ to $I(r_2)$. Panel (b) shows the Keynesian cross: a decrease in planned investment from $I(r_1)$ to $I(r_2)$ reduces income from Y_1 to Y_2. Panel (c) shows the *IS* curve summarizing this relationship between the interest rate and income: the higher the interest rate, the lower the level of income.

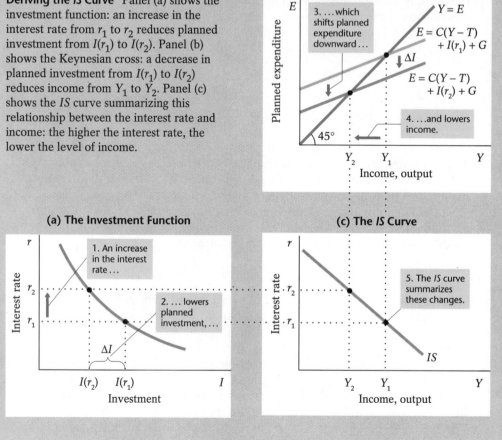

(b) The Keynesian Cross

(a) The Investment Function

(c) The *IS* Curve

How Fiscal Policy Shifts the *IS* Curve

The *IS* curve shows us the level of income for any given interest rate. As we learned from the Keynesian cross, the level of income also depends on fiscal policy. The *IS* curve is drawn for a given fiscal policy; that is, when we construct the *IS* curve, we hold G and T fixed. When fiscal policy changes, the *IS* curve shifts.

Figure 9-8 uses the Keynesian cross to show how an increase in government purchases from G_1 to G_2 shifts the *IS* curve. This figure is drawn for a given interest rate $\bar{r}$ and thus for a given level of planned investment. The Keynesian cross shows that this change in fiscal policy raises planned expenditure and thereby increases equilibrium income from Y_1 to Y_2. Therefore, an increase in government purchases shifts the *IS* curve outward.

Figure 9-8

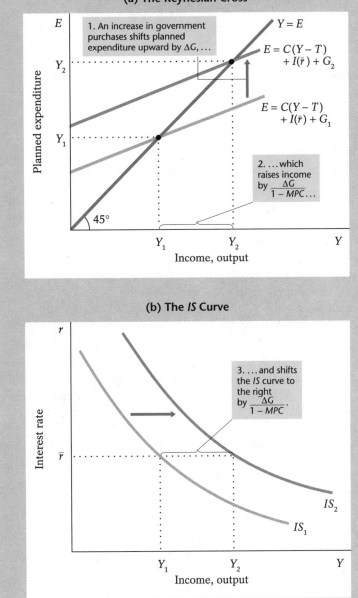

(a) The Keynesian Cross

1. An increase in government purchases shifts planned expenditure upward by ΔG, ...

$Y = E$

$E = C(Y - T) + I(\bar{r}) + G_2$

$E = C(Y - T) + I(\bar{r}) + G_1$

2. ... which raises income by $\dfrac{\Delta G}{1 - MPC}$ ...

$45°$

Planned expenditure

Income, output

(b) The *IS* Curve

3. ... and shifts the *IS* curve to the right by $\dfrac{\Delta G}{1 - MPC}$.

IS_2

IS_1

Interest rate

Income, output

An Increase in Government Purchases Shifts the *IS* Curve Outward Panel (a) shows that an increase in government purchases raises planned expenditure. For any given interest rate, the upward shift in planned expenditure of ΔG leads to an increase in income of $\Delta G/(1 - MPC)$. Therefore, in panel (b), the *IS* curve shifts to the right by this amount.

We can use the Keynesian cross to see how other changes in fiscal policy shift the *IS* curve. Because a decrease in taxes also expands expenditure and income, it too shifts the *IS* curve outward. A decrease in government purchases or an increase in taxes reduces income; therefore, such a change in fiscal policy shifts the *IS* curve inward.

In summary, the IS *curve shows the relationship between the interest rate and the level of income that arises from the market for goods and services. The* IS *curve is drawn for a given fiscal policy. Changes in fiscal policy that raise the demand for goods and services shift the* IS *curve to the right. Changes in fiscal policy that reduce the demand for goods and services shift the* IS *curve to the left.*

A Loanable-Funds Interpretation of the *IS* Curve

When we first studied the market for goods and services in Chapter 3, we noted an equivalence between the supply and demand for goods and services and the supply and demand for loanable funds. This equivalence provides another way to interpret the *IS* curve.

Recall that the national income accounts identity can be written as

$$Y - C - G = I$$
$$S = I.$$

The left-hand side of this equation is national saving S—the sum of private saving, $Y - T - C$, and public saving, $T - G$—and the right-hand side is investment I. National saving represents the supply of loanable funds, and investment represents the demand for these funds.

To see how the market for loanable funds produces the *IS* curve, substitute the consumption function for C and the investment function for I:

$$Y - C(Y - T) - G = I(r).$$

The left-hand side of this equation shows that the supply of loanable funds depends on income and fiscal policy. The right-hand side shows that the demand for loanable funds depends on the interest rate. The interest rate adjusts to equilibrate the supply and demand for loans.

As Figure 9-9 illustrates, we can interpret the *IS* curve as showing the interest rate that equilibrates the market for loanable funds for any given level of income. When income rises from Y_1 to Y_2, national saving, which equals $Y - C - G$, increases. (Consumption rises by less than income, because the marginal propensity to consume is less than 1.) The increased supply of loanable funds drives down the interest rate from r_1 to r_2. The *IS* curve summarizes this relationship: higher income implies higher saving, which in turn implies a lower equilibrium interest rate. For this reason, the *IS* curve slopes downward.

This alternative interpretation of the *IS* curve also explains why a change in fiscal policy shifts the *IS* curve. An increase in government purchases or a decrease in taxes reduces national saving for any given level of income. The reduced supply of loanable funds raises the interest rate that equilibrates the market. Because the interest rate is now higher for any given level of income, the *IS* curve shifts upward in response to the expansionary change in fiscal policy.

Finally, note that the *IS* curve does not determine either income Y or the interest rate r. Instead, the *IS* curve is a relationship between Y and r arising in

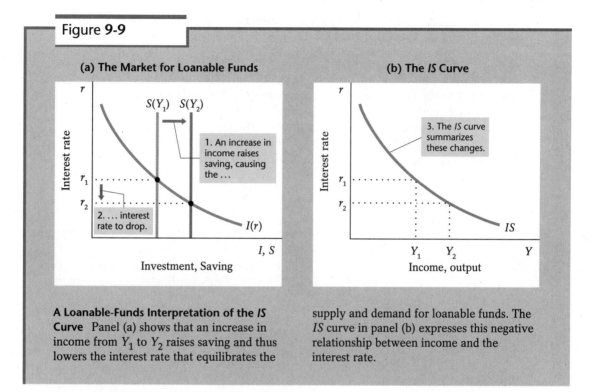

Figure 9-9

(a) The Market for Loanable Funds

(b) The *IS* Curve

A Loanable-Funds Interpretation of the *IS* Curve   Panel (a) shows that an increase in income from Y_1 to Y_2 raises saving and thus lowers the interest rate that equilibrates the supply and demand for loanable funds. The *IS* curve in panel (b) expresses this negative relationship between income and the interest rate.

the market for goods and services or, equivalently, the market for loanable funds. To determine the equilibrium of the economy, we need another relationship between these two variables, to which we now turn.

9-2   The Money Market and the *LM* Curve

The *LM* curve plots the relationship between the interest rate and the level of income that arises in the market for money balances. To understand this relationship, we begin by looking at a simple theory of the interest rate, called the **theory of liquidity preference**.

The Theory of Liquidity Preference

The theory of liquidity preference is the simplest interpretation of Keynes's theory of the interest rate. Just as the Keynesian cross is a building block for the *IS* curve, the theory of liquidity preference is a building block for the *LM* curve. The theory explains how the supply and demand for real money balances, which we studied in Chapter 6, determine the interest rate.

We begin with the supply of real money balances. If M stands for the supply of money and P stands for the price level, then M/P is the supply of real money balances. The theory of liquidity preference assumes there is a fixed supply of real balances. That is,

$$(M/P)^s = \overline{M}/\overline{P}.$$

The money supply M is an exogenous policy variable chosen by the central bank, such as the Federal Reserve. The price level P is also an exogenous variable in this model. (We take the price level as given because the *IS-LM* model—our ultimate goal in this chapter—explains the short run when the price level is fixed.) These assumptions imply that the supply of real balances is fixed and, in particular, does not depend on the interest rate. When we plot the supply of real money balances against the interest rate in Figure 9-10, we obtain a vertical supply curve.

Figure 9-10

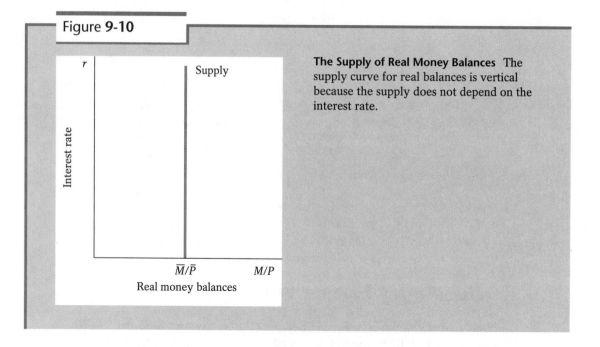

The Supply of Real Money Balances The supply curve for real balances is vertical because the supply does not depend on the interest rate.

Next, consider the demand for real money balances. People hold money because it is a "liquid" asset—that is, because it is easily used to make transactions. The theory of liquidity preference postulates that the quantity of real money balances demanded depends on the interest rate. The interest rate is the opportunity cost of holding money: it is what you forgo by holding money, which does not bear interest, instead of interest-bearing bank deposits or bonds. When the interest rate rises, people want to hold less of their wealth in the form of money.

We write the demand for real money balances as

$$(M/P)^d = L(r),$$

where the function $L(\ )$ denotes the demand for the liquid asset—money. This equation states that the quantity of real balances demanded is a function of the

Figure 9-11

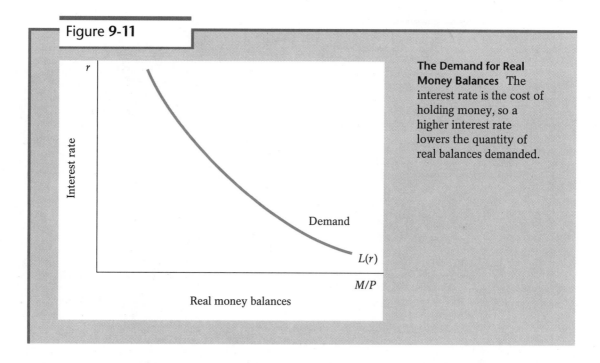

The Demand for Real Money Balances The interest rate is the cost of holding money, so a higher interest rate lowers the quantity of real balances demanded.

interest rate. Figure 9-11 shows the relationship between the interest rate and the quantity of real balances demanded. This demand curve slopes downward because higher interest rates reduce the quantity of real balances demanded.[6]

To explain what interest rate prevails in the economy, we combine the supply and demand for real money balances in Figure 9-12. According to the theory of liquidity preference, the interest rate adjusts to equilibrate the money market. At the equilibrium interest rate, the quantity of real balances demanded equals the quantity supplied.

The adjustment of the interest rate to this equilibrium of money supply and money demand occurs because people try to adjust their portfolios of assets if the interest rate is not at the equilibrium level. If the interest rate is too high, the quantity of real balances supplied exceeds the quantity demanded. Individuals holding the excess supply of money try to convert some of their non-interest-bearing money into interest-bearing bank deposits or bonds. Banks and bond issuers, who prefer to pay lower interest rates, respond to this excess supply of money by lowering the interest rates they offer. Conversely, if the interest rate is too low, so that the quantity of money demanded exceeds the quantity supplied, individuals try to obtain money by selling bonds or making bank withdrawals, which drives the interest rate up. At the equilibrium interest rate, people are content with their portfolios of monetary and non-monetary assets.

[6] Note that r is being used to denote the interest rate here, as it was in our discussion of the *IS* curve. More accurately, it is the nominal interest rate that determines money demand and the real interest rate that determines investment. To keep things simple, we are ignoring expected inflation, which creates the difference between the real and nominal interest rates. The role of expected inflation in the *IS-LM* model is explored in Chapter 10.

Figure 9-12

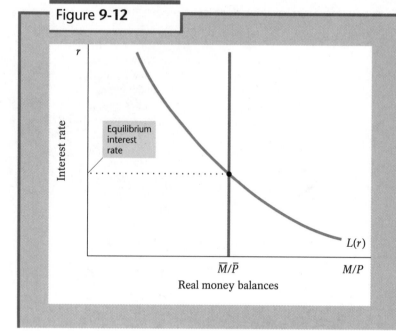

The Theory of Liquidity Preference The supply and demand for real money balances determine the interest rate. At the equilibrium interest rate, the quantity of real money balances demanded equals the quantity supplied.

Equilibrium interest rate

$L(r)$

$\overline{M}/\overline{P}$ M/P
Real money balances

Figure 9-13

A Reduction in the Money Supply in the Theory of Liquidity Preference If the price level is fixed, a reduction in the money supply from M_1 to M_2 reduces the supply of real balances. The equilibrium interest rate therefore rises from r_1 to r_2.

1. A fall in the money supply . . .

2. . . . raises the interest rate.

r_2

r_1

$L(r)$

$M_2/P \longleftarrow M_1/P$ M/P
Real money balances

According to the theory of liquidity preference, a decrease in the money supply raises the interest rate, and an increase in the money supply lowers the interest rate. To see why, suppose that the Fed decreases the money supply. A fall in M reduces M/P, since P is fixed in the model. The supply of real balances shifts to the left, as in Figure 9-13. The equilibrium interest rate rises from r_1 to r_2. The higher interest rate induces people to hold a smaller quantity of real money balances.

Case Study *9-2*

● ● ● ● ● ● ● ● ● ● ● ● ●

Paul Volcker, Tight Money, and Rising Interest Rates

The early 1980s saw the largest and quickest reduction in inflation in recent U.S. history. By the late 1970s inflation had reached the double-digit range; in 1979, consumer prices were rising at a rate of 11.3 percent per year. In October 1979, only two months after becoming the chairman of the Federal Reserve, Paul Volcker announced that monetary policy would aim to reduce the rate of inflation. This announcement began a period of tight money that, by 1983, brought the inflation rate down to about 3 percent.

How does such a monetary tightening influence interest rates? The answer depends on the time horizon. Our analysis of the Fisher effect in Chapter 6 suggests that Volcker's change in monetary policy would lower inflation, and this in turn would lead to lower nominal interest rates. Yet the theory of liquidity preference predicts that, in the short run when prices are sluggish, anti-inflationary monetary policy would lead to falling real balances and higher nominal interest rates.

Both conclusions are consistent with experience. Nominal interest rates did fall in the 1980s as inflation fell. But comparing the year before the October 1979 announcement and the year after, we find that real balances (M1 divided by the CPI) fell 8.3 percent and the nominal interest rate (on commercial paper) rose from 10.1 percent to 11.9 percent. Hence, although a monetary tightening leads to lower interest rates in the long run, it leads to higher interest rates in the short run.

● ● ● ● ● ● ● ● ● ● ● ● ●

Income, Money Demand, and the *LM* Curve

We now use the theory of liquidity preference to derive the *LM* curve. We see that the equilibrium interest rate—the interest rate that equilibrates money supply and money demand—depends on the level of income. The *LM* curve expresses this relationship between the level of income and the interest rate.

So far we have assumed that only the interest rate influences the quantity of real balances demanded. More realistically, the level of income Y also affects money demand. When income is high, expenditure is high, so people engage in more transactions that require the use of money. Thus, greater income implies greater money demand. We now write the money demand function as

$$(M/P)^d = L(r, Y).$$

The quantity of real money balances demanded is negatively related to the interest rate and positively related to income.

Using the theory of liquidity preference, we can see what happens to the interest rate when the level of income changes. For example, consider what happens in Figure 9-14 when income increases from Y_1 to Y_2. As panel (a) illustrates, this increase in income shifts the money demand curve to the right. To equilibrate the market for real money balances, the interest rate must rise from r_1 to r_2. Therefore, higher income leads to a higher interest rate.

Figure 9-14

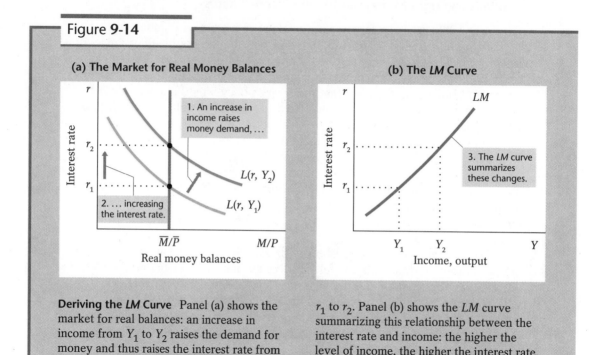

(a) The Market for Real Money Balances

1. An increase in income raises money demand, …

2. … increasing the interest rate.

$L(r, Y_2)$

$L(r, Y_1)$

Real money balances

(b) The LM Curve

3. The LM curve summarizes these changes.

Income, output

Deriving the LM Curve Panel (a) shows the market for real balances: an increase in income from Y_1 to Y_2 raises the demand for money and thus raises the interest rate from r_1 to r_2. Panel (b) shows the LM curve summarizing this relationship between the interest rate and income: the higher the level of income, the higher the interest rate.

The LM curve plots this relationship between the level of income and the interest rate. The higher the level of income, the higher the demand for real money balances, and the higher the equilibrium interest rate. For this reason, the LM curve slopes upward, as in panel (b) of Figure 9-14.

How Monetary Policy Shifts the LM Curve

The LM curve tells us the interest rate that equilibrates the money market for any given level of income. The theory of liquidity preference shows that the equilibrium interest rate depends on the supply of real balances. The LM curve is drawn for a given supply of real money balances. If real balances change—for example, if the Fed alters the money supply—the LM curve shifts.

We can use the theory of liquidity preference to understand how monetary policy shifts the *LM* curve. Suppose that the Fed decreases the money supply from M_1 to M_2, which causes the supply of real balances to fall from M_1/P to M_2/P. Figure 9-15 shows what happens. Holding constant the amount of income and thus the demand curve for real balances, we see that a reduction in the supply of real balances raises the interest rate that equilibrates the money market. Hence, a decrease in real balances shifts the *LM* curve upward.

Figure 9-15

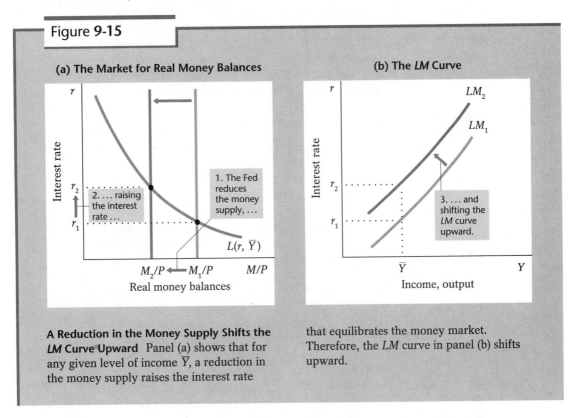

(a) The Market for Real Money Balances

(b) The *LM* Curve

A Reduction in the Money Supply Shifts the *LM* Curve Upward Panel (a) shows that for any given level of income $\overline{Y}$, a reduction in the money supply raises the interest rate that equilibrates the money market. Therefore, the *LM* curve in panel (b) shifts upward.

In summary, the LM curve shows the relationship between the interest rate and the level of income that arises in the market for real money balances. The LM curve is drawn for a given supply of real money balances. Decreases in the supply of real money balances shift the LM curve upward. Increases in the supply of real money balances shift the LM curve downward.

A Quantity-Equation Interpretation of the *LM* Curve

When we first discussed aggregate demand and the short-run determination of income in Chapter 8, we derived the aggregate demand curve from the quantity theory of money. We wrote the quantity equation,

$$MV = PY,$$

and assumed that velocity V is constant. This assumption implies that, for any given price level, the supply of money alone determines the level of income. Because this level of income does not depend on the interest rate, the quantity theory is equivalent to a vertical LM curve.

We can derive the more realistic upward-sloping LM curve from the quantity equation by relaxing the assumption that velocity is constant. The assumption of constant velocity is equivalent to the assumption that the demand for real money balances depends only on the level of income. In reality, the demand for real money balances also depends on the interest rate: a higher interest rate raises the cost of holding money and reduces money demand. As people respond to a higher interest rate by reducing the amount of money they hold, each dollar in the economy circulates from person to person more quickly—that is, the velocity of money increases. We can write this as

$$MV(r) = PY.$$

The velocity function $V(r)$ indicates that velocity is positively related to the interest rate.

This form of the quantity equation yields an LM curve that slopes upward. Because an increase in the interest rate raises the velocity of money, it raises the level of income for any given money supply and price level. The LM curve expresses this positive relationship between the interest rate and income.

This equation also shows why changes in the money supply shift the LM curve. For any given interest rate and price level, an increase in the money supply raises the level of income. Thus, increases in the money supply shift the LM curve to the right, and decreases in the money supply shift the LM curve to the left.

Keep in mind that the quantity equation is merely another way to express the theory behind the LM curve. This interpretation of the LM curve is substantively the same as that provided by the theory of liquidity preference. In both cases, the LM curve represents a positive relationship between income and the interest rate that arises from the money market.

Finally, remember that the LM curve by itself does not determine either income Y or the interest rate r. Like the IS curve, the LM curve is only a relationship between these two endogenous variables. The IS and LM curves together determine the equilibrium in the economy.

9-3   Conclusion: The Short-Run Equilibrium

We now have all the components of the IS-LM model. The two equations of this model are

$$Y = C(Y - T) + I(r) + G \qquad IS$$
$$M/P = L(r, Y). \qquad\qquad LM$$

The model takes fiscal policy, G and T, monetary policy M, and the price level P as exogenous. Given these exogenous variables, the IS curve provides the combinations of r and Y that satisfy the equation representing the goods market, and the LM curve provides the combinations of r and Y that satisfy the equation representing the money market. These two curves are shown together in Figure 9-16.

Figure 9-16

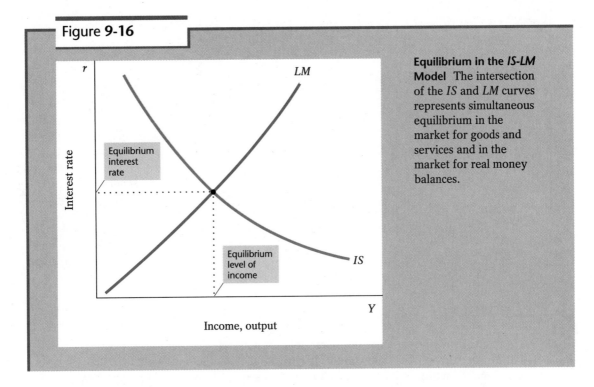

Equilibrium in the *IS-LM* Model The intersection of the *IS* and *LM* curves represents simultaneous equilibrium in the market for goods and services and in the market for real money balances.

The equilibrium of the economy is the point at which the IS curve and the LM curve cross. This point gives the interest rate r and the level of income Y that satisfy conditions for equilibrium in both the goods market and the money market. In other words, at this intersection, actual expenditure equals planned expenditure, and the demand for real money balances equals the supply.

As we conclude this chapter, let's recall that our ultimate goal in developing the IS-LM model is to analyze short-run fluctuations in economic activity. Figure 9-17 illustrates how the different pieces of our theory fit together. In this chapter we developed the Keynesian cross and the theory of liquidity preference as building blocks for the IS-LM model. As we will see more fully in the next chapter, the IS-LM model helps explain the position and slope of the aggregate demand curve. The aggregate demand curve, in turn, is a piece of the model of aggregate supply and aggregate demand, which economists use to explain the short-run effects of policy changes and other events on national income.

Figure 9-17

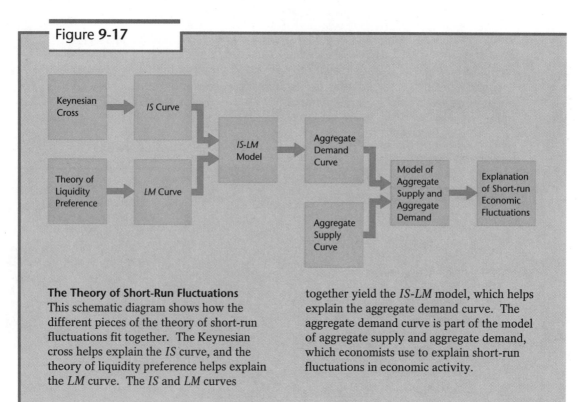

The Theory of Short-Run Fluctuations
This schematic diagram shows how the different pieces of the theory of short-run fluctuations fit together. The Keynesian cross helps explain the *IS* curve, and the theory of liquidity preference helps explain the *LM* curve. The *IS* and *LM* curves together yield the *IS-LM* model, which helps explain the aggregate demand curve. The aggregate demand curve is part of the model of aggregate supply and aggregate demand, which economists use to explain short-run fluctuations in economic activity.

Summary

1. The Keynesian cross is a simple model of income determination. It takes fiscal policy and planned investment as exogenous and then shows that there is one level of national income at which actual expenditure equals planned expenditure. It shows that changes in fiscal policy have a multiplied impact on income.

2. Once we allow planned investment to depend on the interest rate, the Keynesian cross yields a relationship between the interest rate and national income. A higher interest rate lowers planned investment, and this in turn lowers national income. The *IS* curve summarizes this negative relationship between the interest rate and income.

3. The theory of liquidity preference is a simple model of the determination of the interest rate. It takes the money supply and the price level as exogenous and assumes that the interest rate adjusts to equilibrate the supply and demand for real money balances. The theory implies that increases in the money supply lower the interest rate.

4. Once we allow the demand for real balances to depend on national income, the theory of liquidity preference yields a relationship between income and the interest rate. A higher level of income raises the demand for real balances, and

this in turn raises the interest rate. The *LM* curve summarizes this positive relationship between income and the interest rate.

5. The *IS-LM* model combines the elements of the Keynesian cross and the elements of the theory of liquidity preference. The intersection of the *IS* curve and the *LM* curve shows the interest rate and income that satisfy equilibrium both in the goods market and in the money market.

KEY CONCEPTS

IS-LM model

IS curve

LM curve

Keynesian cross

Government-purchases multiplier

Tax multiplier

Theory of liquidity preference

QUESTIONS FOR REVIEW

1. Use the Keynesian cross to explain why fiscal policy has a multiplied effect on national income.

2. Use the theory of liquidity preference to explain why an increase in the money supply lowers the interest rate. What

does this explanation assume about the price level?

3. Why does the *IS* curve slope downward?

4. Why does the *LM* curve slope upward?

PROBLEMS AND APPLICATIONS

1. Use the Keynesian cross to predict the impact of

   a. An increase in government purchases.

   b. An increase in taxes.

   c. An equal increase in government purchases and taxes.

2. In the Keynesian cross, assume that the consumption function is given by

$$C = 200 + 0.75 (Y - T).$$

   Planned investment is 100; government purchases and taxes are both 100.

   a. Graph planned expenditure as a function of income.

   b. What is the equilibrium level of income?

   c. If government purchases increase to 125, what is the new equilibrium income?

   d. What level of government purchases is needed to achieve an income of 1,600?

3. Although our development of the Keynesian cross in this chapter assumes that taxes are a fixed amount, in many countries taxes depend on income. Let's represent the tax system by writing tax revenue as

$$T = \overline{T} + tY,$$

where $\overline{T}$ and t are parameters of the tax code. The parameter t is the marginal tax rate: if income rises by \$1, taxes rise by t × \$1.

a. How does this tax system change the way consumption responds to changes in GDP?

b. In the Keynesian cross, how does this tax system alter the response of the economy to a change in government purchases?

c. In the *IS-LM* model, how does this tax system alter the slope of the *IS* curve?

4. Consider the impact of an increase in thriftiness in the Keynesian cross. Suppose the consumption function is

$$C = \overline{C} + c(Y - T),$$

where $\overline{C}$ is a parameter called *autonomous consumption* and c is the marginal propensity to consume.

a. What happens to equilibrium income when society becomes more thrifty, as represented by a decline in $\overline{C}$?

b. What happens to equilibrium saving?

c. Why do you suppose this result is called the *paradox of thrift*?

d. Does this paradox arise in the classical model of Chapter 3? Why or why not?

5. Suppose that the money demand function is

$$(M/P)^d = 1,000 - 100r,$$

where r is the interest rate in percent. The money supply M is 1,000 and the price level P is 2.

a. Graph the supply and demand for real money balances.

b. What is the equilibrium interest rate?

c. Assume that the price level is fixed. What happens to the equilibrium interest rate if the supply of money is raised from 1,000 to 1,200?

d. If the Fed wishes to raise the interest rate to 7 percent, what money supply should it set?

Chapter 10

Aggregate Demand II

Science is a parasite: the greater the patient population the better the advance in physiology and pathology; and out of pathology arises therapy. The year 1932 was the trough of the great depression, and from its rotten soil was belatedly begot a new subject that today we call macroeconomics.

Paul Samuelson

In Chapter 9 we assembled the pieces of the *IS-LM* model. We saw that the *IS* curve represents the equilibrium in the market for goods and services, that the *LM* curve represents the equilibrium in the market for real money balances, and that the *IS* and *LM* curves together determine national income in the short run when the price level is fixed. Now we turn our attention to applying the model. This chapter uses the *IS-LM* model to analyze three issues.

First, we examine the potential causes of fluctuations in national income. To be more precise, we use the *IS-LM* model to see how changes in the exogenous variables influence the endogenous variables. Because monetary and fiscal policy are among the exogenous variables, the *IS-LM* model shows how these policies influence the economy in the short run. The model also shows how various shocks to the money and goods markets influence the economy.

Second, we discuss how the *IS-LM* model fits into the model of aggregate supply and aggregate demand we developed in Chapter 8. In particular, we examine how the *IS-LM* model provides a theory of the aggregate demand curve. Here we relax the assumption that the price level is fixed, and we show that the *IS-LM* model implies a negative relationship between the price level and national income.

Third, we study the Great Depression, the episode that motivated Keynes to emphasize aggregate demand as a key determinant of national income. As the quotation at the beginning of this chapter indicates, the Great Depression is the event that gave birth to short-run macroeconomic theory. We can use the *IS-LM* model to discuss the various explanations of this traumatic economic downturn.

10-1   Explaining Fluctuations With the *IS-LM* Model

The intersection of the *IS* curve and the *LM* curve determines the level of national income. National income fluctuates when one of these curves shifts, changing the short-run equilibrium of the economy. In this section we examine how changes in policy and exogenous shocks to the economy can cause these curves to shift.

Changes in Fiscal Policy

We first examine the impact of changes in fiscal policy on the economy. Recall that changes in fiscal policy shift the *IS* curve. The *IS-LM* model shows how these shifts in the *IS* curve affect income and the interest rate.

   Consider the effect of an increase in government purchases of ΔG. The government-purchases multiplier in the Keynesian cross tells us that, at any given interest rate, this change in fiscal policy raises the level of income by $\Delta G/(1 - MPC)$. Therefore, as Figure 10-1 illustrates, the *IS* curve shifts to the right by this amount. The equilibrium of the economy moves from point A to point B. The increase in government purchases raises both income and the interest rate.

Figure 10-1

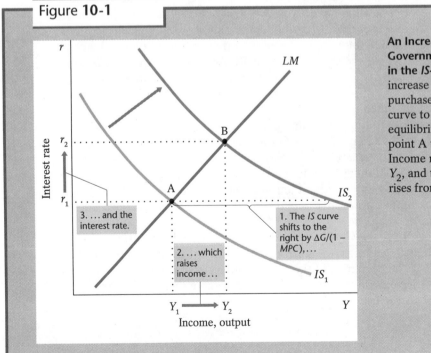

An Increase in Government Purchases in the *IS-LM* Model An increase in government purchases shifts the *IS* curve to the right. The equilibrium moves from point A to point B. Income rises from Y_1 to Y_2, and the interest rate rises from r_1 to r_2.

3. ...and the interest rate.

1. The *IS* curve shifts to the right by $\Delta G/(1 - MPC)$,...

2. ...which raises income...

Figure 10-2

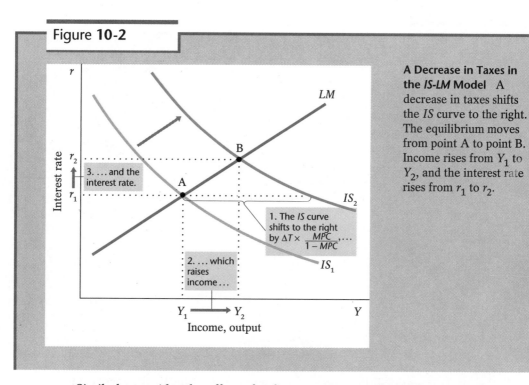

A Decrease in Taxes in the *IS-LM* Model A decrease in taxes shifts the *IS* curve to the right. The equilibrium moves from point A to point B. Income rises from Y_1 to Y_2, and the interest rate rises from r_1 to r_2.

Similarly, consider the effect of a decrease in taxes of ΔT. The tax multiplier in the Keynesian cross tells us that, at any given interest rate, this change in policy raises the level of income by $\Delta T \times MPC/(1 - MPC)$. Therefore, as Figure 10-2 illustrates, the *IS* curve shifts to the right by this amount. The equilibrium of the economy moves from point A to point B. The tax cut raises both income and the interest rate.

Note that the increase in income in response to a fiscal expansion is smaller in the *IS-LM* model than in the Keynesian cross. You can see this in Figures 10-1 and 10-2. The horizontal shift in the *IS* curve equals the rise in equilibrium income in the Keynesian cross. This amount is larger than the increase in equilibrium income here in the *IS-LM* model. The difference arises because the Keynesian cross assumes that investment is fixed, whereas the *IS-LM* model takes into account that investment falls when the interest rate rises. In the *IS-LM* model, a fiscal expansion raises the interest rate and crowds out investment.

Changes in Monetary Policy

We now examine the impact of a change in monetary policy. Recall that a change in monetary policy shifts the *LM* curve. The *IS-LM* model shows how a shift in the *LM* curve affects income and the interest rate.

Consider the impact of an increase in the money supply. An increase in M leads to an increase in M/P, since P is fixed. The theory of liquidity preference shows that for any given level of income, an increase in real money balances leads to a lower interest rate. Therefore, the *LM* curve shifts downward, as in

Figure 10-3

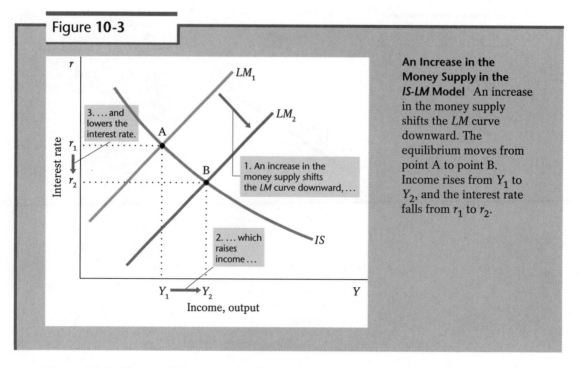

An Increase in the Money Supply in the *IS-LM* Model An increase in the money supply shifts the *LM* curve downward. The equilibrium moves from point A to point B. Income rises from Y_1 to Y_2, and the interest rate falls from r_1 to r_2.

Figure 10-3. The equilibrium moves from point A to point B. The increase in the money supply lowers the interest rate and raises the level of income.

Thus, the *IS-LM* model shows that monetary policy influences income by changing the interest rate. This conclusion sheds light on our analysis of monetary policy in Chapter 8. In that chapter we showed that in the short run, when prices are sticky, an expansion in the money supply raises income. But we did not discuss how a monetary expansion induces greater spending on goods and services—a process that is called the **monetary transmission mechanism**. The *IS-LM* model shows that an increase in the money supply lowers the interest rate, which stimulates investment and thereby expands the demand for goods and services.

The Interaction Between Monetary and Fiscal Policy

When analyzing any change in monetary or fiscal policy, it is important to keep in mind that these policies may not be independent of each other. A change in one may influence the other. This interdependence may alter the impact of a policy change.

For example, consider the plan proposed by President Clinton in 1993 to reduce the budget deficit by raising taxes. What effect should this policy have on the economy? According to the *IS-LM* model, the answer depends on how the Federal Reserve responds to the tax increase.

Figure 10-4 shows three of the many possible outcomes. In panel (a), the Fed holds the money supply constant. The tax increase shifts the *IS* curve to the left, reducing both income and the interest rate. In panel (b), the Fed wants to hold the interest rate constant. In this case, when the tax increase shifts the

Figure 10-4

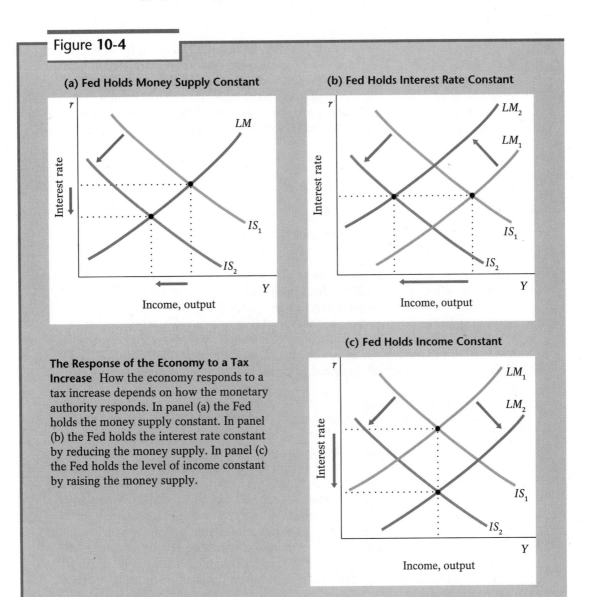

(a) Fed Holds Money Supply Constant

(b) Fed Holds Interest Rate Constant

(c) Fed Holds Income Constant

The Response of the Economy to a Tax Increase How the economy responds to a tax increase depends on how the monetary authority responds. In panel (a) the Fed holds the money supply constant. In panel (b) the Fed holds the interest rate constant by reducing the money supply. In panel (c) the Fed holds the level of income constant by raising the money supply.

IS curve to the left, the Fed must decrease the money supply to keep the interest rate at its original level. This shifts the *LM* curve upward. The interest rate does not fall, but income falls by a larger amount than if the Fed had held the money supply constant.

In panel (c), the Fed wants to prevent the tax increase from lowering income. It must, therefore, raise the money supply. In this case, the tax increase does not cause a recession, but it does cause a large fall in the interest rate. Although income is unchanged, the combination of a tax increase and a monetary expansion changes the allocation of the economy's resources. The higher taxes depress consumption, while the lower interest rate stimulates investment.

From this example we can see that the impact of a change in fiscal policy depends on the policy the Fed pursues—that is, on whether it holds the money supply, the interest rate, or the level of income constant. More generally, whenever analyzing a change in one policy, we must make an assumption about its effect on the other policy. What assumption is most appropriate depends on the case at hand and the many political considerations that lie behind economic policymaking.

Case Study *10-1*

• • • • • • • • • • • • • •

Policy Analysis With Macroeconometric Models

The *IS-LM* model shows how monetary and fiscal policy influence the equilibrium level of income. The predictions of the model, however, are qualitative, not quantitative. The *IS-LM* model shows that increases in government purchases raise GDP and that increases in taxes lower GDP. But when economists analyze specific policy proposals, they need to know not just the direction of the effect but the size as well. For example, if Congress increases taxes by $100 billion and if monetary policy is not altered, how much will GDP fall? To answer this question, economists need to go beyond the graphical representation of the *IS-LM* model.

Macroeconometric models of the economy provide one way to evaluate policy proposals. A **macroeconometric model** is a model that describes the economy quantitatively, rather than just qualitatively. Many of these models are essentially more complicated and more realistic versions of our *IS-LM* model. The economists who build macroeconometric models use historical data to estimate parameters such as the marginal propensity to consume, the sensitivity of investment to the interest rate, and the sensitivity of money demand to the interest rate. Once a model is built, economists can simulate the effects of alternative policies with the help of a computer.

Table 10-1 shows the fiscal-policy multipliers implied by one widely used macroeconometric model, the Data Resources Incorporated (DRI) model, named for the economic forecasting firm that developed it. The multipliers are given for two assumptions about how the Fed might respond to changes in fiscal policy.

Table **10-1**
The Fiscal-Policy Multipliers in the DRI Model

Assumption About Monetary Policy	$\Delta Y/\Delta G$	$\Delta Y/\Delta T$
Nominal interest rate held constant	1.93	−1.19
Money supply held constant	0.60	−0.26

Note: This table gives the fiscal-policy multipliers for a sustained change in government purchases or in personal income taxes. These multipliers are for the fourth quarter after the policy change is made.

Source: Otto Eckstein, *The DRI Model of the U.S. Economy* (New York: McGraw-Hill, 1983), 169.

One assumption about monetary policy is that the Fed keeps the nominal interest rate constant. That is, when fiscal policy shifts the *IS* curve to the right or to the left, the Fed adjusts the money supply to shift the *LM* curve in the same direction. Because there is no crowding out of investment due to a changing interest rate, the fiscal-policy multipliers are similar to those from the Keynesian cross. The DRI model indicates that, in this case, the government-purchases multiplier is 1.93, and the tax multiplier is −1.19. That is, a $100 billion increase in government purchases raises GDP by $193 billion, and a $100 billion increase in taxes lowers GDP by $119 billion.

The second assumption about monetary policy is that the Fed keeps the money supply constant so that the *LM* curve does not shift. In this case, there is substantial crowding out. The government-purchases multiplier is only 0.60, and the tax multiplier is only −0.26. That is, a $100 billion increase in government purchases raises GDP by $60 billion, and a $100 billion increase in taxes lowers GDP by $26 billion.

Table 10-1 shows that the fiscal-policy multipliers are very different under the two assumptions about monetary policy. The impact of any change in fiscal policy depends crucially on how the Fed responds to that change.

● ● ● ● ● ● ● ● ● ● ● ● ● ● ●

Shocks in the *IS-LM* Model

Because the *IS-LM* model shows how national income is determined in the short run, we can use the model to examine how various economic disturbances affect income. So far we have seen how changes in fiscal policy shift the *IS* curve and how changes in monetary policy shift the *LM* curve. Similarly, we can group other disturbances into two categories: shocks to the *IS* curve and shocks to the *LM* curve.

Shocks to the *IS* curve are exogenous changes in the demand for goods and services. Some economists, including Keynes, have emphasized that changes in demand can arise from investors' *animal spirits*—exogenous and perhaps self-fulfilling waves of optimism and pessimism. For example, suppose that firms become pessimistic about the future of the economy and that this pessimism causes them to build fewer new factories. This reduction in the demand

Calvin and Hobbes   by Bill Watterson

Calvin and Hobbes copyright 1992 Watterson. Dist. by Universal Press Syndicate.

for investment goods causes a contractionary shift in the investment function: at every interest rate, firms want to invest less. The fall in investment shifts the *IS* curve to the left, reducing income and employment. This fall in equilibrium income in part validates the firms' initial pessimism.

Shocks to the *IS* curve may also arise from changes in the demand for consumer goods. Suppose that a rise in consumer confidence in the economy induces consumers to save less for the future and consume more today. We can interpret this change as an upward shift in the consumption function. This shift in the consumption function causes the *IS* curve to shift to the right, raising income.

Shocks to the *LM* curve arise from exogenous changes in the demand for money. Suppose that the demand for money increases substantially, as it did in the early 1980s. An increase in money demand implies that for any given level of income and money supply, the interest rate necessary to equilibrate the money market is higher. Hence, an increase in money demand shifts the *LM* curve upward, which tends to raise the interest rate and depress income.

In summary, several kinds of events can cause economic fluctuations by shifting the *IS* curve or the *LM* curve. Remember, however, that such fluctuations are not inevitable. Monetary and fiscal policy can try to offset exogenous shocks. If changes in policy are well timed, shocks to the *IS* or *LM* curves will not lead to fluctuations in income or employment.

10-2   *IS-LM* as a Theory of Aggregate Demand

We have been using the *IS-LM* model to explain national income in the short run when the price level is fixed. To see how the *IS-LM* model fits into the model of aggregate supply and aggregate demand developed in Chapter 8, we now examine what happens in the *IS-LM* model as the price level changes. As was promised when we began our study of this model, the *IS-LM* model provides a theory to explain the position and slope of the aggregate demand curve.

From the *IS-LM* Model to the Aggregate Demand Curve

Recall from Chapter 8 that the aggregate demand curve is a relationship between the price level and the level of national income. In Chapter 8 this relationship was derived from the quantity theory of money. For a given money supply, a higher price level implies a lower level of income. Increases in the money supply shift the aggregate demand curve to the right, and decreases in the money supply shift the aggregate demand curve to the left.

We now use the *IS-LM* model, rather than the quantity theory, to derive the aggregate demand curve. First, we use the *IS-LM* model to show that national income falls as the price level rises; the downward-sloping aggregate demand curve expresses this relationship. Second, we examine what causes the aggregate demand curve to shift.

Figure 10-5

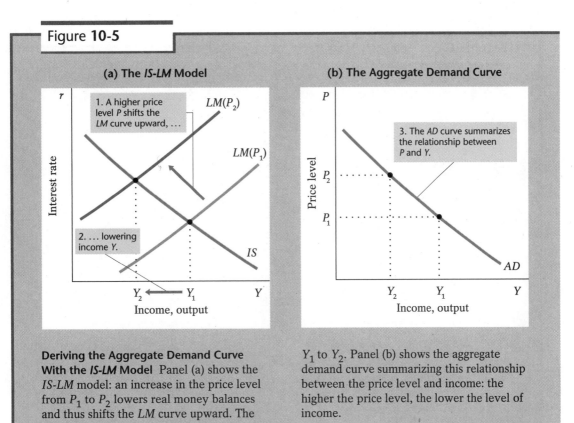

(a) The *IS-LM* Model

1. A higher price level P shifts the LM curve upward, ...

$LM(P_2)$

$LM(P_1)$

2. ... lowering income Y.

IS

$Y_2 \leftarrow Y_1$ Y

Income, output

Interest rate

r

(b) The Aggregate Demand Curve

3. The AD curve summarizes the relationship between P and Y.

P

P_2

P_1

AD

Y_2 Y_1 Y

Income, output

Price level

Deriving the Aggregate Demand Curve With the *IS-LM* Model Panel (a) shows the *IS-LM* model: an increase in the price level from P_1 to P_2 lowers real money balances and thus shifts the *LM* curve upward. The shift in the *LM* curve lowers income from Y_1 to Y_2. Panel (b) shows the aggregate demand curve summarizing this relationship between the price level and income: the higher the price level, the lower the level of income.

Why does the aggregate demand curve slope downward? To answer this question, we examine what happens in the *IS-LM* model when the price level changes. Figure 10-5 illustrates the impact of a changing price level. For any given money supply M, a higher price level P reduces the supply of real money balances M/P. A lower supply of real money balances shifts the *LM* curve upward, which raises the interest rate and lowers the equilibrium level of income, as shown in panel (a). Here the price level rises from P_1 to P_2, and national income falls from Y_1 to Y_2. The aggregate demand curve in panel (b) plots the negative relationship between national income and the price level that arises from the *IS-LM* model.

What causes the aggregate demand curve to shift? Because the aggregate demand curve summarizes the results of the *IS-LM* model for any given price level, shocks that shift the *IS* curve or the *LM* curve cause the aggregate demand curve to shift. Expansionary monetary or fiscal policy raises income in the *IS-LM* model and thus shifts the aggregate demand curve to the right, as in Figure 10-6. Similarly, contractionary monetary or fiscal policy lowers income in the *IS-LM* model and thus shifts the aggregate demand curve to the left.

We can summarize these results as follows. A change in income in the IS-LM *model resulting from a change in the price level represents a movement along the aggregate demand curve. A change in income in the* IS-LM *model for a fixed price level represents a shift in the aggregate demand curve.*

Figure **10-6**

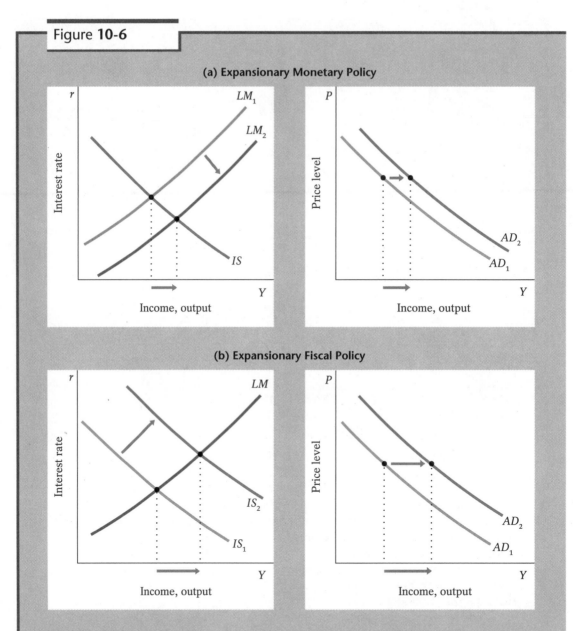

(a) Expansionary Monetary Policy

(b) Expansionary Fiscal Policy

How Monetary and Fiscal Policy Shift the Aggregate Demand Curve   Panel (a) shows a monetary expansion. For any given price level, an increase in the money supply raises real money balances, shifts the LM curve downward, and raises income. Hence, an increase in the money supply shifts the aggregate demand curve to the right. Panel (b) shows a fiscal expansion, such as an increase in government purchases or a decrease in taxes. The fiscal expansion shifts the IS curve to the right and, for any given price level, raises income. Hence, a fiscal expansion shifts the aggregate demand curve to the right.

The *IS-LM* Model in the Short Run and Long Run

The *IS-LM* model is designed to explain the economy in the short run when the price level is fixed. Yet, now that we have seen how a change in the price level influences the equilibrium, we can also use the *IS-LM* model to describe the economy in the long run when the price level adjusts to ensure that the economy produces at its natural rate. By using the *IS-LM* model to describe the long run, we can show clearly how the Keynesian model of national income differs from the classical model of Chapter 3.

Panel (a) of Figure 10-7 shows the three curves that are necessary for understanding the short-run and long-run equilibria: the *IS* curve, the *LM* curve, and the vertical line representing the natural rate of output $\overline{Y}$. The *LM* curve is, as always, drawn for a fixed price level, P_1. The short-run equilibrium of the economy is point K, where the *IS* curve crosses the *LM* curve.

Panel (b) of Figure 10-7 shows the same situation in the diagram of aggregate supply and aggregate demand. At the price level P_1, the quantity of output demanded is below the natural rate. In other words, at the existing price level, there is insufficient demand for goods and services to keep the economy at its natural rate.

In these two diagrams we can examine the short-run equilibrium at which the economy finds itself and the long-run equilibrium toward which the econ-

---

Figure 10-7

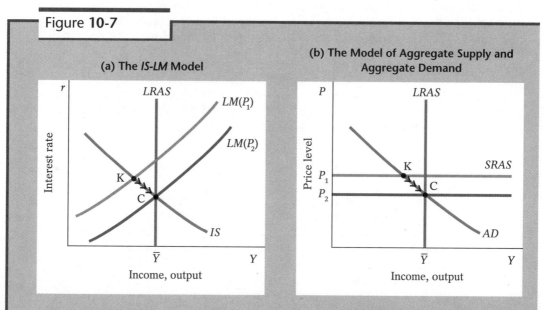

(a) The *IS-LM* Model

(b) The Model of Aggregate Supply and Aggregate Demand

The Short-Run and Long-Run Equilibria
We can compare the short-run and long-run equilibria using either the *IS-LM* diagram in panel (a) or the aggregate supply–aggregate demand diagram in panel (b). In the short run, the price level is stuck at P_1. The short-run equilibrium of the economy is therefore point K. In the long run, the price level adjusts so that the economy is at the natural rate. The long-run equilibrium is therefore point C.

omy gravitates. Point K describes the short-run equilibrium, because it assumes that the price level is stuck at P_1. Eventually, the low demand for goods and services causes prices to fall, and the economy moves back toward its natural rate. When the price level reaches P_2, the economy is at point C, the long-run equilibrium. The diagram of aggregate supply and aggregate demand shows that at point C, the quantity of goods and services demanded equals the natural rate of output. This long-run equilibrium is achieved in the *IS-LM* diagram by a shift in the *LM* curve: the fall in the price level raises real money balances and therefore shifts the *LM* curve to the right.

We can now see the key difference between Keynesian and classical approaches to the determination of national income. The Keynesian assumption (represented by point K) is that the price level is stuck. Depending on monetary policy, fiscal policy, and the other determinants of aggregate demand, output may deviate from the natural rate. The classical assumption (represented by point C) is that the price level is flexible. The price level adjusts to ensure that national income is always at the natural rate.

To make the same point somewhat differently, we can think of the economy as being described by three equations. The first two are the *IS* and *LM* equations:

$$Y = C(Y - T) + I(r) + G \qquad IS$$
$$M/P = L(r, Y). \qquad\qquad LM$$

The *IS* equation describes the goods market, and the *LM* equation describes the money market. These two equations contain three variables of interest: Y, P, and r. The Keynesian approach is to complete the model with the assumption of fixed prices, so the third equation is

$$P = P_1.$$

This assumption implies that r and Y must adjust to satisfy the *IS* and *LM* equations. The classical approach is to complete the model with the assumption that output reaches the natural rate, so the third equation is

$$Y = \overline{Y}.$$

This assumption implies that r and P must adjust in order to satisfy the *IS* and *LM* equations.

Which assumption is most appropriate? The answer depends on the time horizon. The classical assumption best describes the long run. Hence, our long-run analysis of national income in Chapter 3 and prices in Chapter 6 assumes that output equals the natural rate. The Keynesian assumption best describes the short run. Therefore, our analysis of economic fluctuations relies on the assumption of a fixed price level.

10-3   The Great Depression

Now that we have developed the model of aggregate demand, let's use it to address the question that originally motivated Keynes: what caused the Great Depression? Even today, more than half a century after the event, economists continue to debate the cause of this major economic downturn. The Great Depression provides an extended case study to show how economists use the *IS-LM* model to analyze economic fluctuations.[1]

Before turning to the explanations economists have proposed, look at Table 10-2, which presents some statistics regarding the Depression. These statistics are the battlefield on which debate about the Depression takes place. What do you think happened? An *IS* shift? An *LM* shift? Or something else?

The Spending Hypothesis: Shocks to the *IS* Curve

Because the decline in income in the early 1930s coincided with falling interest rates, some economists have suggested that the cause of the decline was a contractionary shift in the *IS* curve. This view is sometimes called the *spending hypothesis*, because it places primary blame for the Depression on an exogenous fall in spending on goods and services. Economists have attempted to explain this decline in spending in several ways.

Some argue that a downward shift in the consumption function caused the contractionary shift in the *IS* curve. The stock market crash of 1929 may have been partly responsible for this decline in consumption. By reducing wealth and increasing uncertainty about the future prospects of the U.S. economy, the crash may have induced consumers to save more of their income.

Others explain the decline in spending by pointing to the large drop in investment in housing. Some economists believe that the residential investment boom of the 1920s was excessive, and that once this "overbuilding" became apparent, the demand for residential investment declined drastically. Another possible explanation for the fall in residential investment is the reduction in immigration in the 1930s: a more slowly growing population demands less new housing.

Once the Depression began, several events occurred that could have reduced spending further. First, the widespread bank failures may have reduced investment. Banks play the crucial role of getting the funds available for investment to those households and firms that can best use them. The closing of many banks in the early 1930s may have prevented some businesses from getting the funds they needed for capital investment and, therefore, may have led to a further contractionary shift in the investment function.[2]

In addition, the fiscal policy of the 1930s caused a contractionary shift in the *IS* curve. Politicians at that time were more concerned with balancing the budget than with using fiscal policy to stimulate the economy. The Revenue Act of 1932 increased various taxes, especially those falling on lower- and middle-

[1] For a flavor of the debate, see Milton Friedman and Anna J. Schwartz, *A Monetary History of the United States, 1867–1960* (Princeton, N.J.: Princeton University Press, 1963); Peter Temin, *Did Monetary Forces Cause the Great Depression?* (New York: W. W. Norton, 1976); the essays in Karl Brunner, ed., *The Great Depression Revisited* (Boston: Martinus Nijhoff Publishing, 1981); and the symposium on the Great Depression in the Spring 1993 issue of the *Journal of Economic Perspectives*.

[2] Ben Bernanke, "Non-Monetary Effects of the Financial Crisis in the Propagation of the Great Depression," *American Economic Review* 73 (June 1983): 257–276.

Table 10-2	What Happened During the Great Depression?				
Year	Unemployment Rate	Real GNP	Consumption	Investment	Government Purchases
1929	3.2	203.6	139.6	40.4	22.0
1930	8.9	183.5	130.4	27.4	24.3
1931	16.3	169.5	126.1	16.8	25.4
1932	24.1	144.2	114.8	4.7	24.2
1933	25.2	141.5	112.8	5.3	23.3
1934	22.0	154.3	118.1	9.4	26.6
1935	20.3	169.5	125.5	18.0	27.0
1936	17.0	193.2	138.4	24.0	31.8
1937	14.3	203.2	143.1	29.9	30.8
1938	19.1	192.9	140.2	17.0	33.9
1939	17.2	209.4	148.2	24.7	35.2
1940	14.6	227.2	155.7	33.0	36.4

Source: Historical Statistics of the United States, Colonial Times to 1970, Parts I and II. U.S. Department of Commerce, Bureau of Census, 1975, Washington, D.C. The unemployment rate is series D9. Real GNP, consumption, investment, and government purchases are series F3, F48, F52, and F66, and are measured in billions of 1958 dollars. The interest rate is the prime Commercial Paper rate, 4–6 months, series x445.

income consumers.[3] The Democratic platform of that year expressed concern about the budget deficit and advocated an "immediate and drastic reduction of governmental expenditures." In the midst of historically high unemployment, policymakers searched for ways to raise taxes and reduce government spending.

There are, therefore, several ways to explain a contractionary shift in the *IS* curve. Keep in mind that these different views are not inconsistent with one another. There may be no single explanation for the decline in spending. It is possible that all of these changes coincided and that together they led to a major reduction in spending.

The Money Hypothesis: A Shock to the *LM* Curve

Table 10-2 shows that the money supply fell 25 percent from 1929 to 1933, during which time the unemployment rate rose from 3.2 percent to 25.2 percent. This fact provides the motivation and support for what is called the *money hypothesis*, which places primary blame for the Depression on the Federal Reserve for allowing the money supply to fall by such a large amount.[4] The best known advocates of this interpretation are Milton Friedman and Anna Schwartz, who

---

[3] E. Cary Brown, "Fiscal Policy in the 'Thirties: A Reappraisal," *American Economic Review* 46 (December 1956): 857–879.

[4] We discuss the reason for this large decrease in the money supply in Chapter 18, where we examine the money supply process in more detail. In particular, see Case Study 18-1.

Year	Nominal Interest Rate	Money Supply	Price Level	Inflation	Real Money Balances
1929	5.9	26.6	50.6	—	52.6
1930	3.6	25.8	49.3	− 2.6	52.3
1931	2.6	24.1	44.8	−10.1	54.5
1932	2.7	21.1	40.2	− 9.3	52.5
1933	1.7	19.9	39.3	− 2.2	50.7
1934	1.0	21.9	42.2	7.4	51.8
1935	0.8	25.9	42.6	0.9	60.8
1936	0.8	29.6	42.7	0.2	62.9
1937	0.9	30.9	44.5	4.2	69.5
1938	0.8	30.5	43.9	− 1.3	69.5
1939	0.6	34.2	43.2	− 1.6	79.1
1940	0.6	39.7	43.9	1.6	90.3

The money supply is series x414, currency plus demand deposits, measured in billions of dollars. The price level is the GNP deflator (1958 = 100), series E1. The inflation rate is the percent change in the price level series. Real money balances, calculated by dividing the money supply by the price level and multiplying by 100, are in billions of 1958 dollars.

defend it in their treatise on U.S. monetary history. Friedman and Schwartz argue that contractions in the money supply have caused most economic downturns and that the Great Depression is a particularly vivid example.

Using the *IS-LM* model, we might interpret the money hypothesis as explaining the Depression by a contractionary shift in the *LM* curve. Seen in this way, however, the money hypothesis runs into two problems.

The first problem is the behavior of real money balances. Monetary policy leads to a contractionary shift in the *LM* curve only if real money balances fall. Yet from 1929 to 1931 real money balances rose slightly, since the fall in the money supply was accompanied by an even greater fall in the price level. Although the monetary contraction may be responsible for the rise in unemployment from 1931 to 1933, when real money balances did fall, it probably should not be blamed for the initial downturn from 1929 to 1931.

The second problem for the money hypothesis is the behavior of interest rates. If a contractionary shift in the *LM* curve triggered the Depression, we should have observed higher interest rates. Yet nominal interest rates fell continuously from 1929 to 1933.

These two reasons appear sufficient to reject the view that the Depression was instigated by a contractionary shift in the *LM* curve. But was the fall in the money stock irrelevant? Next, we turn to another mechanism through which monetary policy might have been responsible for the severity of the Depression—the deflation of the 1930s.

The Money Hypothesis Again: The Effects of Falling Prices

From 1929 to 1933 the price level fell 25 percent. Many economists blame this deflation for the severity of the Great Depression. They argue that the deflation may have turned what in 1931 was a typical economic downturn into an unprecedented period of high unemployment and depressed income. If correct, this argument gives new life to the money hypothesis. Since the falling money supply was, plausibly, responsible for the falling price level, it could be responsible for the severity of the Depression. To evaluate this argument, we must discuss how changes in the price level affect income in the *IS-LM* model.

The Stabilizing Effects of Deflation   In the *IS-LM* model we have developed so far, falling prices raise income. For any given supply of money *M*, a lower price level implies higher real money balances *M/P*. An increase in real money balances causes an expansionary shift in the *LM* curve, which leads to higher income.

Another channel through which falling prices expand income is called the **Pigou effect**. Arthur Pigou, a prominent classical economist in the 1930s, pointed out that real money balances are part of households' wealth. As prices fall and real money balances rise, consumers should feel wealthier and spend more. This increase in consumer spending should cause an expansionary shift in the *IS* curve, also leading to higher income.

These two reasons led some economists in the 1930s to believe that falling prices would help the economy restore itself to full employment. Yet other economists were less confident in the economy's ability to correct itself. They pointed to other effects of falling prices, to which we now turn.

The Destabilizing Effects of Deflation   Economists have proposed two theories to explain how falling prices could depress income rather than raise it. The first, called the **debt-deflation theory**, describes the effects of unexpected falls in the price level. The second explains the effects of expected deflation.

The debt-deflation theory begins with an observation that should be familiar from Chapter 6: unanticipated changes in the price level redistribute wealth between debtors and creditors. If a debtor owes a creditor $1,000, then the real amount of this debt is $1,000/P$, where *P* is the price level. A fall in the price level raises the real amount of this debt—the amount of purchasing power the debtor must repay the creditor. Therefore, an unexpected deflation enriches creditors and impoverishes debtors.

The debt-deflation theory then posits that this redistribution of wealth affects spending on goods and services. In response to the redistribution from debtors to creditors, debtors spend less and creditors spend more. If these two groups have equal spending propensities, there is no aggregate impact. But it seems reasonable to assume that debtors have higher propensities to spend than creditors—perhaps that is why the debtors are in debt in the first place. In this case, debtors reduce their spending by more than creditors raise theirs. The net effect is a reduction in spending, a contractionary shift in the *IS* curve, and lower national income.

To understand how *expected* changes in prices can affect income, we need to add a new variable to the *IS-LM* model. Our discussion of the model so far has not distinguished between the nominal and real interest rates. Yet we know from previous chapters that investment depends on the real interest rate and that money demand depends on the nominal interest rate. If i is the nominal interest rate and π^e is expected inflation, then the *ex ante* real interest rate is $i - \pi^e$. We can now write the *IS-LM* model as

$$Y = C(Y - T) + I(i - \pi^e) + G \qquad IS$$
$$M/P = L(i, Y). \qquad LM$$

Expected inflation enters as a variable in the *IS* curve. Thus, changes in expected inflation shift the *IS* curve.

Let's use this extended *IS-LM* model to examine how changes in expected inflation influence the level of income. We begin by assuming that everyone expects the price level to remain the same. In this case, there is no expected inflation ($\pi^e = 0$), and these two equations produce the familiar *IS-LM* model. Figure 10-8 depicts this initial situation with the *LM* curve and the *IS* curve labeled IS_1. The intersection of these two curves determines the nominal and real interest rates, which for now are the same.

Now suppose that everyone suddenly expects that the price level will fall in the future, so that π^e becomes negative. The real interest rate is now higher at any given nominal interest rate. This increase in the real interest rate depresses planned investment spending, shifting the *IS* curve from IS_1 to IS_2.

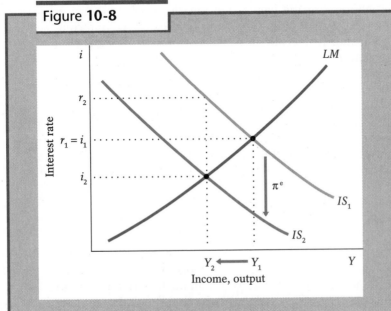

Figure 10-8

Expected Deflation in the IS-LM Model An expected deflation raises the real interest rate for any given nominal interest rate, reducing desired investment. The reduction in investment shifts the *IS* curve downward. The level of income falls from Y_1 to Y_2. The nominal interest rate falls from i_1 to i_2, and the real interest rate rises from r_1 to r_2.

Thus, an expected deflation leads to a reduction in national income from Y_1 to Y_2. The nominal interest rate falls from i_1 to i_2, while the real interest rate rises from r_1 to r_2.

Note that there is a common thread in these two stories of destabilizing deflation. In both, falling prices depress national income by causing a contractionary shift in the IS curve. Since a deflation of the size observed from 1929 to 1933 is unlikely except in the presence of a major contraction in the money supply, these two explanations give some of the responsibility for the Depression—especially its severity—to the Fed. In other words, if falling prices are destabilizing, then a contraction in the money supply can lead to a fall in income, even without a decrease in real money balances or a rise in nominal interest rates.

Could the Depression Happen Again?

Economists study the Depression both because of its intrinsic interest as a major economic event and to provide guidance to policymakers so that it will not happen again. To state with confidence whether this event could recur, we would need to know why it happened. Because there is not yet agreement on the causes of the Great Depression, it is impossible to rule out with certainty another depression of this magnitude.

Yet most economists believe that the mistakes that led to the Great Depression are unlikely to be repeated. The Fed seems unlikely to allow the money supply to fall by one-fourth. Many economists believe that the deflation of the early 1930s was responsible for the depth and length of the Depression. And it seems likely that such a prolonged deflation was possible only in the presence of a falling money supply.

The fiscal-policy mistakes of the Depression are also unlikely to be repeated. Fiscal policy in the 1930s not only failed to help but actually further depressed aggregate demand. Few economists today would advocate such a rigid adherence to a balanced budget in the face of massive unemployment.

In addition, there are many institutions today that would help prevent the events of the 1930s from recurring. The system of Federal Deposit Insurance makes widespread bank failures less likely. The income tax causes an automatic reduction in taxes when income falls, which stabilizes the economy. Finally, economists know more today than they did in the 1930s. Our knowledge of how the economy works, limited as it still is, should help policymakers formulate better policies to combat such widespread unemployment.

10-4　Conclusion

The purpose of this chapter and the previous one has been to deepen our understanding of aggregate demand. We now have the tools to analyze monetary and fiscal policy in the long run and in the short run. In the long run, prices are flexible, and we use the classical analysis of Part Two of this book. In the short run, prices are sticky, and we use the *IS-LM* model to examine how changes in policy influence the economy.

Although the model presented in this chapter provides the basic framework for analyzing aggregate demand, it is not the whole story. In later chapters, we examine in more detail the elements of this model and thereby refine our understanding of aggregate demand. In Chapter 15, for example, we study theories of consumption. Since the consumption function is a crucial piece of the *IS-LM* model, a change in our analysis of consumption may modify our view of the impact of monetary and fiscal policy on the economy. The simple *IS-LM* model presented in Chapters 9 and 10 provides the benchmark for this further analysis.

Summary

1. The *IS-LM* model is a general theory of aggregate demand. The exogenous variables in the model are fiscal policy, monetary policy, and the price level. The model explains two endogenous variables: the interest rate and the level of national income.

2. The *IS* curve represents the negative relationship between the interest rate and the level of income that arises from equilibrium in the market for goods and services. The *LM* curve represents a positive relationship between the interest rate and the level of income that arises from equilibrium in the market for real money balances. Equilibrium in the *IS-LM* model—the intersection of the *IS* and *LM* curves—represents simultaneous equilibrium in the market for goods and services and in the market for real money balances.

3. Expansionary fiscal policy—an increase in government purchases or a decrease in taxes—shifts the *IS* curve to the right. This shift in the *IS* curve increases the interest rate and income. The increase in income represents a rightward shift in the aggregate demand curve. Similarly, contractionary fiscal policy shifts the *IS* curve to the left, lowers the interest rate and income, and shifts the aggregate demand curve to the left.

4. Expansionary monetary policy shifts the *LM* curve downward. This shift in the *LM* curve lowers the interest rate and raises income. The increase in income represents a rightward shift of the aggregate demand curve. Similarly, contractionary monetary policy shifts the *LM* curve upward, raises the interest rate, lowers income, and shifts the aggregate demand curve to the left.

KEY CONCEPTS

Monetary transmission mechanism   Pigou effect

Macroeconometric model   Debt-deflation theory

QUESTIONS FOR REVIEW

1. Explain why the aggregate demand curve slopes downward.

2. What is the impact of an increase in taxes on the interest rate, income, consumption, and investment?

3. What is the impact of a decrease in the money supply on the interest rate, income, consumption, and investment?

4. Describe the possible effects of falling prices on equilibrium income.

PROBLEMS AND APPLICATIONS

1. According to the *IS-LM* model, what happens to the interest rate, income, consumption, and investment under the following circumstances?

   a. The central bank increases the money supply.

   b. The government increases government purchases.

   c. The government increases taxes.

   d. The government increases government purchases and taxes by equal amounts.

2. Use the *IS-LM* model to predict the effects of each of the following shocks on income, the interest rate, consumption, and investment. In each case, explain what the Fed should do in order to stabilize income.

   a. After the invention of a new high-speed computer chip, many firms decide to upgrade their computer systems.

   b. A wave of credit-card fraud increases the frequency with which people make transactions in cash.

   c. A best-seller titled "Retire Rich" convinces the public to increase the percentage of their income devoted to saving.

3. Consider the economy of Hicksonia.

   a. The consumption function is given by
   $$C = 200 + 0.75(Y - T).$$

The investment function is
   $$I = 200 - 25r.$$

Government purchases and taxes are both 100. For this economy, graph the *IS* curve for *r* ranging from 0 to 8.

   b. The money demand function in Hicksonia is
   $$(M/P)^d = Y - 100r.$$

The money supply *M* is 1,000 and the price level *P* is 2. For this economy, graph the *LM* curve for *r* ranging from 0 to 8.

   c. Find the equilibrium interest rate *r* and the equilibrium level of income *Y*.

   d. Suppose that government purchases are raised from 100 to 150. How much does the *IS* curve shift? What are the new equilibrium interest rate and level of income?

   e. Suppose instead that the money supply is raised from 1,000 to 1,200. How much does the *LM* curve shift? What are the new equilibrium interest rate and level of income?

   f. With the initial values for monetary and fiscal policy, suppose that the price level rises from 2 to 4. What happens? What are the new equilibrium interest rate and level of income?

g. Derive and graph an equation for the aggregate demand curve. What happens to this aggregate demand curve if fiscal or monetary policy changes, as in parts (d) and (e)?

4. Explain why each of the following statements is true. Discuss the impact of monetary and fiscal policy in each of these special cases.

a. If investment does not depend on the interest rate, the *IS* curve is vertical.

b. If money demand does not depend on the interest rate, the *LM* curve is vertical.

c. If money demand does not depend on income, the *LM* curve is horizontal.

d. If money demand is extremely sensitive to the interest rate, the *LM* curve is horizontal.

5. Suppose that the government wants to raise investment but keep output constant. In the *IS-LM* model, what mix of monetary and fiscal policy will achieve this goal? In the early 1980s, the U.S. government cut taxes and ran a budget deficit while the Fed pursued a tight monetary policy. What effect should this policy mix have?

6. Use the *IS-LM* diagram to describe the short-run and long-run effects of the following changes on national income, the price level, and the interest rate.

a. An increase in the money supply.

b. An increase in government purchases.

c. An increase in taxes.

7. The Fed is considering two alternative monetary policies:

• holding the money supply constant, or

• adjusting the money supply to hold the interest rate constant.

In the *IS-LM* model, which policy will better stabilize output under the following conditions?

a. All shocks to the economy arise from exogenous changes in the demand for goods and services.

b. All shocks to the economy arise from exogenous changes in the demand for money.

8. Suppose that the demand for real money balances depends on disposable income. That is, the money demand function is

$$M/P = L(r, Y - T).$$

Using the *IS-LM* model, discuss whether this change in the money demand function alters the following:

a. The analysis of changes in government purchases.

b. The analysis of changes in taxes.

Appendix

· · · · · · · · · · · · ·

The Simple Algebra of the *IS-LM* Model and the Aggregate Demand Curve

The chapter analyzes the *IS-LM* model with graphs of the *IS* and *LM* curves. Here we analyze the model algebraically rather than graphically. This alternative presentation offers additional insight into how monetary and fiscal policy influence aggregate demand.

The *IS* Curve

One way to think about the *IS* curve is that it describes the combinations of income Y and the interest rate r that satisfy an equation first seen in Chapter 3:

$$Y = C(Y - T) + I(r) + G.$$

This equation combines the national income accounts identity, the consumption function, and the investment function. It states that the quantity of goods produced, Y, must equal the quantity of goods demanded, $C + I + G$.

We can learn more about the *IS* curve by considering the special case in which the consumption function and investment function are linear. We begin with the national income accounts identity

$$Y = C + I + G.$$

Now suppose that the consumption function is

$$C = a + b(Y - T),$$

where a and b are numbers greater than zero, and the investment function is

$$I = c - dr,$$

where c and d also are numbers greater than zero. The parameter b is the marginal propensity to consume, so we expect b to be between zero and one. The parameter d determines how much investment responds to the interest rate; because investment rises when the interest rate falls, there is a minus sign in front of d.

From these three equations, we can derive an algebraic expression for the *IS* curve and see what influences the *IS* curve's position and slope. If we substitute the consumption and investment functions into the national income accounts identity, we obtain

$$Y = [a + b(Y - T)] + (c - dr) + G.$$

Note that Y shows up on both sides of this equation. We can simplify this equation by bringing all the Y terms to the left-hand side and rearranging the terms on the right-hand side:

$$Y - bY = (a + c) + (G - bT) - dr.$$

We solve for Y to get

$$Y = \frac{a + c}{1 - b} + \frac{1}{1 - b}G + \frac{-b}{1 - b}T + \frac{-d}{1 - b}r.$$

This equation expresses the *IS* curve algebraically. It tells us the level of income Y for any given interest rate r and fiscal policy G and T. Holding fiscal policy fixed, the equation gives us a relationship between the interest rate and the level of income: the higher the interest rate, the lower the level of income. The *IS* curve graphs this equation for different values of Y and r given fixed values of G and T.

Using this last equation, we can verify our previous conclusions about the *IS* curve. First, because the coefficient of the interest rate is negative, the *IS* curve slopes downward: higher interest rates reduce income. Second, because the coefficient of government purchases is positive, an increase in government purchases shifts the *IS* curve to the right. Third, because the coefficient of taxes is negative, an increase in taxes shifts the *IS* curve to the left.

The coefficient of the interest rate, $-d/(1 - b)$, tells us what determines whether the *IS* curve is steep or flat. If investment is highly sensitive to the interest rate, then d is large, and income is highly sensitive to the interest rate as well. In this case, small changes in the interest rate lead to large changes in income: the *IS* curve is relatively flat. Conversely, if investment is not very sensitive to the interest rate, then d is small, and income is also not very sensitive to the interest rate. In this case, large changes in interest rates lead to small changes in income: the *IS* curve is relatively steep.

Similarly, the slope of the *IS* curve depends on the marginal propensity to consume b. The larger the marginal propensity to consume, the larger the change in income resulting from a given change in the interest rate. The reason is that a large marginal propensity to consume leads to a large multiplier for changes in investment. The larger the multiplier, the larger the impact of a change in investment on income, and the flatter the *IS* curve.

The marginal propensity to consume b also determines how much changes in fiscal policy shift the *IS* curve. The coefficient of G, $1/(1 - b)$, is the government-purchases multiplier in the Keynesian cross. Similarly, the coefficient of T, $-b/(1 - b)$, is the tax multiplier in the Keynesian cross. The larger the marginal propensity to consume, the greater the multiplier, and thus the greater the shift in the IS curve that arises from a change in fiscal policy.

The *LM* Curve

The LM curve describes the combinations of income Y and the interest rate r that satisfy the money-market equilibrium condition

$$M/P = L(r, Y).$$

This equation simply equates money supply and money demand.

We can learn more about the LM curve by considering the case in which the money demand function is linear—that is,

$$L(r, Y) = eY - fr,$$

where e and f are numbers greater than zero. The value of e determines how much the demand for money rises when income rises. The value of f determines how much the demand for money falls when the interest rate rises. There is a minus sign in front of the interest rate term because money demand is inversely related to the interest rate.

The equilibrium in the money market is now described by

$$M/P = eY - fr.$$

To see what this equation implies, rearrange the terms so that r is on the left-hand side. We obtain

$$r = (e/f)Y - (1/f)M/P.$$

This equation gives us the interest rate that equilibrates the money market for any values of income and real money balances. The LM curve graphs this equation for different values of Y and r given a fixed value of M/P.

From this last equation, we can verify some of our conclusions about the LM curve. First, because the coefficient of income is positive, the LM curve slopes upward: higher income requires a higher interest rate to equilibrate the money market. Second, because the coefficient of real money balances is negative, decreases in real balances shift the LM curve upward, and increases in real balances shift the LM curve downward.

From the coefficient of income, e/f, we can see what determines whether the LM curve is steep or flat. If money demand is not very sensitive to the level of income, then e is small. In this case, only a small change in the interest rate is necessary to offset the small increase in money demand caused by a change in income: the LM curve is relatively flat. Similarly, if the quantity of money demanded is not very sensitive to the interest rate, then f is small. In this case, a shift in money demand due to a change in income leads to a large change in the equilibrium interest rate: the LM curve is relatively steep.

The Aggregate Demand Curve

To find the aggregate demand equation, we must find the level of income that satisfies both the *IS* equation and the *LM* equation. To do this, substitute the *LM* equation for the interest rate r into the *IS* equation to obtain

$$Y = \frac{a + c}{1 - b} + \frac{1}{1 - b}G + \frac{-b}{1 - b}T + \frac{-d}{1 - b}[(e/f)Y - (1/f)M/P].$$

With some algebraic manipulation, we can solve for Y. The final equation for Y is

$$Y = \frac{z(a + c)}{1 - b} + \frac{z}{1 - b}G + \frac{-zb}{1 - b}T + \frac{d}{(1 - b)[f + de/(1 - b)]}M/P,$$

where $z = f/[f + de/(1 - b)]$ is a composite of some of the parameters and is between zero and one.

This last equation expresses the aggregate demand curve algebraically. It says that income depends on fiscal policy, G and T, monetary policy M, and the price level P. The aggregate demand curve graphs this equation for different values of Y and P given fixed values of G, T, and M.

We can explain the slope and position of the aggregate demand curve with this equation. First, the aggregate demand curve slopes downward, since an increase in P lowers M/P and thus lowers Y. Second, increases in the money supply raise income and shift the aggregate demand curve to the right. Third, increases in government purchases or decreases in taxes also raise income and shift the aggregate demand curve to the right. Note that, because z is less than one, the multipliers for fiscal policy are smaller in the *IS-LM* model than in the Keynesian cross. Hence, the parameter z reflects the crowding out of investment discussed earlier.

Finally, this equation shows the relationship between the aggregate demand curve derived in this chapter from the *IS-LM* model and the aggregate demand curve derived in Chapter 8 from the quantity theory of money. The quantity theory assumes that the interest rate does not influence the quantity of real money balances demanded. Put differently, the quantity theory assumes that the parameter f equals zero. If f equals zero, then the composite parameter z also equals zero, so fiscal policy does not influence aggregate demand. Thus, the aggregate demand curve derived in Chapter 8 is a special case of the aggregate demand curve derived here.

Case Study *10-2*

● ● ● ● ● ● ● ● ● ● ● ● ●

The Effectiveness of Monetary and Fiscal Policy

Economists have long debated whether monetary or fiscal policy exerts a more powerful influence on aggregate demand. According to the *IS-LM* model, the answer to this question depends on the parameters of the *IS* and *LM* curves. Therefore, economists have spent much energy arguing about the size of these parameters. The most hotly contested parameters are those that describe the influence of the interest rate on economic decisions.

Those economists who believe that fiscal policy is more potent than monetary policy argue that the responsiveness of investment to the interest rate—measured by the parameter *d*—is small. If you look at the algebraic equation for aggregate demand, you will see that a small value of *d* implies a small effect of the money supply on income. The reason is that when *d* is small, the *IS* curve is nearly vertical, and shifts in the *LM* curve do not cause much of a change in income. In addition, a small value of *d* implies a large value of *z*, which in turn implies that fiscal policy has a large effect on income. The reason for this large effect is that when investment is not very responsive to the interest rate, there is little crowding out.

Those economists who believe that monetary policy is more potent than fiscal policy argue that the responsiveness of money demand to the interest rate—measured by the parameter *f*—is small. When *f* is small, *z* is small, and fiscal policy has a small effect on income; in this case, the *LM* curve is nearly vertical. In addition, when *f* is small, changes in the money supply have a large effect on income.

Most economists today do not endorse either of these extreme views. The evidence indicates that the interest rate affects both investment and money demand. This finding implies that both monetary and fiscal policy are important determinants of aggregate demand.

Chapter 11

Aggregate Demand in the Open Economy

We now extend our analysis of aggregate demand to include international trade and finance. As we first discussed in Chapter 7, the world's major economies are open. Open economies export some of the goods and services they produce, and they import some of the goods and services they consume. Open economies also borrow and lend in world financial markets.

In this chapter we discuss how open economies behave in the short run. Our primary goal is to understand how monetary and fiscal policies influence the aggregate income of an open economy. The model we develop in this chapter, called the **Mundell-Fleming model**, is an open-economy version of the *IS-LM* model. Both models assume that the price level is fixed and then show what causes fluctuations in aggregate income. Both also stress the interaction between the goods market and the money market. The key difference is that the *IS-LM* model assumes a closed economy, whereas the Mundell-Fleming model assumes a small open economy. The Mundell-Fleming model extends the short-run model of national income from Chapters 9 and 10 by including the effects of international trade and finance from Chapter 7.

One lesson of the Mundell-Fleming model is that the behavior of an economy depends on the exchange-rate system it has adopted. We begin by assuming a floating exchange rate. That is, we assume that the central bank allows the exchange rate to adjust to changing economic conditions. We then examine how the economy operates under a fixed exchange rate, and we discuss the debate over whether exchange rates should be floating or fixed.

11-1 The Mundell-Fleming Model

In this section we build the Mundell-Fleming model.[1] In the following sections we use the model to examine the impact of various policies under floating and fixed exchange rates.

---

[1] The Mundell-Fleming model was developed in the early 1960s. Mundell's contributions are collected in Robert A. Mundell, *International Economics* (New York: Macmillan, 1968). For Fleming's contribution, see J. Marcus Fleming, "Domestic Financial Policies under Fixed and under Floating Exchange Rates," *IMF Staff Papers 9* (November 1962): 369–379.

Components of the Model

The Mundell-Fleming model is built from components that should be familiar to you from previous chapters. We begin by presenting the three equations that make up the model:

$$Y = C(Y - T) + I(r) + G + NX(e) \qquad IS$$
$$M/P = L(r, Y) \qquad LM$$
$$r = r^*.$$

Before combining these equations into a short-run model of a small open economy, let's review each of them in turn.

The first equation describes the goods market. It tells us that aggregate income Y is the sum of consumption C, investment I, government purchases G, and net exports NX. Consumption depends positively on disposable income $Y - T$. Investment depends negatively on the interest rate r. Net exports depend negatively on the exchange rate e.

Recall that we define the exchange rate e as the amount of foreign currency per unit of domestic currency—for example, e might be 100 yen per dollar. For the purposes of the Mundell-Fleming model, we do not need to distinguish between the real and nominal exchange rates. In Chapter 7 we related net exports to the real exchange rate ε, which equals eP/P^*, where P is the domestic price level and P^* is the foreign price level. Because the Mundell-Fleming model assumes that prices are fixed, changes in the real exchange rate are proportional to changes in the nominal exchange rate. That is, when the nominal exchange rate rises, foreign goods become less expensive compared to domestic goods, so exports fall and imports rise.

The second equation describes the money market. It states that the supply of real money balances, M/P, equals the demand, $L(r, Y)$. The demand for real balances depends negatively on the interest rate and positively on income. The money supply M is an exogenous variable controlled by the central bank. Like the IS-LM model, the Mundell-Fleming model takes the price level P as an exogenous variable.

The third equation states that the world interest rate r^* determines the interest rate in this economy. This equation holds because we are examining a small open economy. That is, the economy is sufficiently small relative to the world economy that it can borrow or lend as much as it wants in world financial markets without affecting the world interest rate.

These three equations fully describe the Mundell-Fleming model. Our job is to examine the implications of these equations for short-run fluctuations in a small open economy. If you do not understand the equations, review Chapters 7 and 9 before continuing.

A Graphical Presentation

The Mundell-Fleming model is most easily analyzed graphically. The simplest way to depict the model is to use a graph in which income is on the horizontal axis and the exchange rate is on the vertical axis, as in Figure 11-1. This graph is drawn holding the interest rate constant at the world interest rate. The two equations in this figure are

$$Y = C(Y - T) + I(r^*) + G + NX(e) \qquad IS^*$$
$$M/P = L(r^*, Y). \qquad\qquad\qquad LM^*$$

We label these curves IS^* and LM^* to remind us that we are holding the interest rate constant at the world interest rate r^*. The equilibrium of the economy is found where the IS^* curve and the LM^* curve intersect. This intersection determines the exchange rate and the level of income.

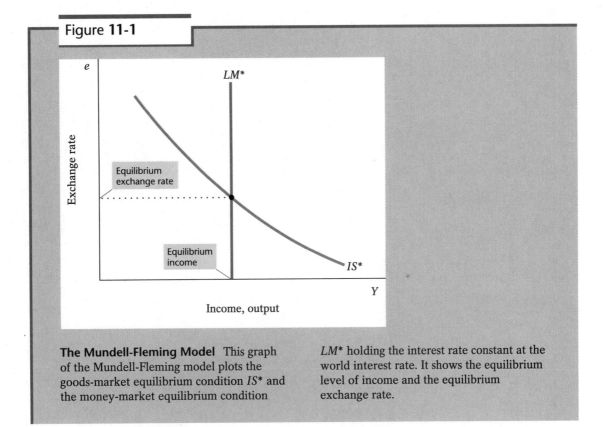

Figure 11-1

The Mundell-Fleming Model This graph of the Mundell-Fleming model plots the goods-market equilibrium condition IS^* and the money-market equilibrium condition LM^* holding the interest rate constant at the world interest rate. It shows the equilibrium level of income and the equilibrium exchange rate.

The LM^* curve is vertical because the exchange rate does not enter into the LM^* equation. Given the world interest rate, the LM^* equation determines aggregate income, regardless of the exchange rate. Figure 11-2 shows how the LM^* curve arises from the world interest rate and the LM curve, which relates the interest rate and income.

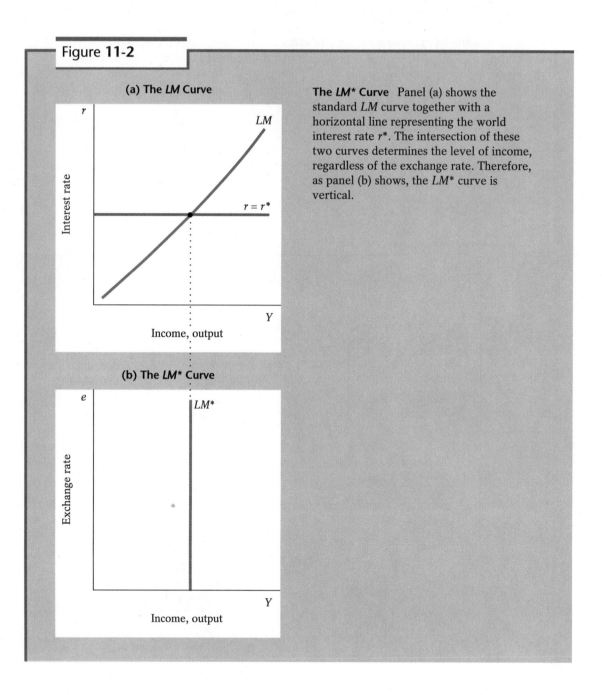

Figure 11-2

(a) The *LM* Curve

(b) The *LM** Curve

The *LM** Curve Panel (a) shows the standard *LM* curve together with a horizontal line representing the world interest rate r^*. The intersection of these two curves determines the level of income, regardless of the exchange rate. Therefore, as panel (b) shows, the *LM** curve is vertical.

The *IS** curve slopes downward because a higher exchange rate lowers net exports and thus lowers aggregate income. To show how this works, Figure 11-3 combines the net-exports schedule and the Keynesian cross diagram to derive the *IS** curve. An increase in the exchange rate from e_1 to e_2 lowers net

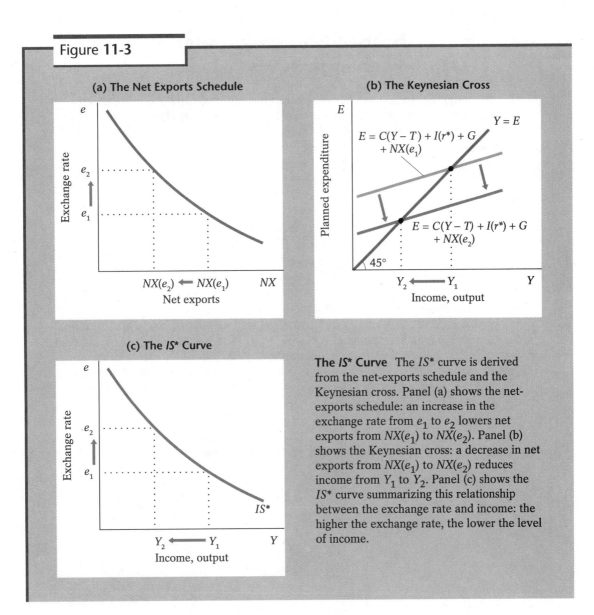

Figure 11-3

(a) The Net Exports Schedule

(b) The Keynesian Cross

(c) The IS* Curve

The IS* Curve The IS* curve is derived from the net-exports schedule and the Keynesian cross. Panel (a) shows the net-exports schedule: an increase in the exchange rate from e_1 to e_2 lowers net exports from $NX(e_1)$ to $NX(e_2)$. Panel (b) shows the Keynesian cross: a decrease in net exports from $NX(e_1)$ to $NX(e_2)$ reduces income from Y_1 to Y_2. Panel (c) shows the IS* curve summarizing this relationship between the exchange rate and income: the higher the exchange rate, the lower the level of income.

exports from $NX(e_1)$ to $NX(e_2)$. The reduction in net exports reduces planned expenditure and thus lowers income. Just as the standard IS curve combines the investment schedule and the Keynesian cross, the IS* curve combines the net-exports schedule and the Keynesian cross.

We can now use the diagram in Figure 11-1 for the Mundell-Fleming model to show how aggregate income Y and the exchange rate e respond to changes in policy.

11-2   **The Small Open Economy Under Floating Exchange Rates**

Before analyzing the impact of policies in an open economy, we must specify the international monetary system in which the country has chosen to operate. We start with the system relevant for most major economies today: **floating exchange rates**. Under floating exchange rates, the exchange rate is allowed to fluctuate freely in response to changing economic conditions.

Fiscal Policy

Suppose that the government stimulates domestic spending by increasing government purchases or by cutting taxes. This expansionary fiscal policy shifts the IS^* curve to the right, as in Figure 11-4. As a result, the exchange rate rises, while the level of income remains the same.

This conclusion about fiscal policy stands in stark contrast to the conclusion of the closed-economy IS-LM model. In a closed economy, a fiscal expansion raises income. In a small open economy with a floating exchange rate, a fiscal expansion leaves income at the same level. The reason for the difference is that, in an open economy, the reduction in national saving due to a fiscal expansion causes net foreign investment to fall and the exchange rate to appreciate. The appreciation of the exchange rate reduces net exports, offsetting the expansion in the domestic demand for goods and services.

Figure 11-4

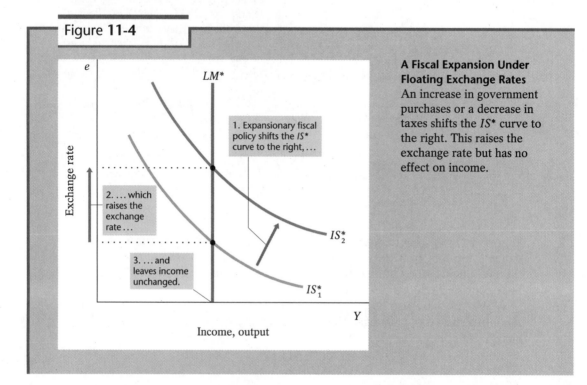

A Fiscal Expansion Under Floating Exchange Rates An increase in government purchases or a decrease in taxes shifts the IS^* curve to the right. This raises the exchange rate but has no effect on income.

To better understand the difference between the closed and open economies, consider the equation describing equilibrium in the money market:

$$M/P = L(r, Y).$$

The supply of real money balances M/P is fixed, and the demand must always equal this fixed supply. In a closed economy, a fiscal expansion causes the interest rate to rise, and this allows equilibrium income to rise. By contrast, in a small open economy, r is fixed at r^*, so there is only one level of income that can satisfy this equation. Hence, in a small open economy, the appreciation of the exchange rate and the fall in net exports must be exactly large enough to offset fully the expansionary impact of fiscal policy.

Monetary Policy

Suppose now that the central bank increases the money supply. Because the price level is assumed to be fixed, the increase in the money supply means an increase in real balances. The increase in real balances shifts the LM^* curve to the right, as in Figure 11-5. Hence, an increase in the money supply raises income and lowers the exchange rate.

Although monetary policy influences income in an open economy, as it does in a closed economy, the monetary transmission mechanism is different. Recall that in a closed economy an increase in the money supply lowers the interest rate and thus stimulates investment. In a small open economy, the interest rate is fixed by the world interest rate. As soon as an increase in the money

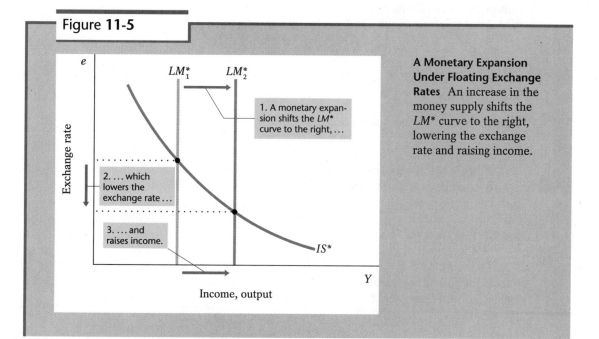

Figure 11-5

1. A monetary expansion shifts the LM^* curve to the right, ...

2. ... which lowers the exchange rate ...

3. ... and raises income.

A Monetary Expansion Under Floating Exchange Rates An increase in the money supply shifts the LM^* curve to the right, lowering the exchange rate and raising income.

supply puts downward pressure on the domestic interest rate, capital flows out of the economy, as investors seek a higher return elsewhere. This capital outflow prevents the domestic interest rate from falling. In addition, because the capital outflow increases the supply of the domestic currency in the market for foreign-currency exchange, the exchange rate depreciates. The fall in the exchange rate makes domestic goods inexpensive relative to foreign goods and, thereby, stimulates net exports. Hence, in a small open economy, monetary policy influences income by altering the exchange rate rather than the interest rate.

Case Study *11-1*

● ● ● ● ● ● ● ● ● ● ● ● ● ●

The Rise in the Dollar, 1979–1982

In the early 1980s the United States experienced an unusual combination of tight monetary policy and loose fiscal policy. The chief goal of Fed Chairman Paul Volcker was to reduce the high rate of inflation inherited from the 1970s. At the same time, President Ronald Reagan wanted to fulfill his electoral promise to cut taxes and raise defense spending.

The Mundell-Fleming model predicts that both policies would raise the value of the dollar. And, indeed, the dollar rose relative to all major currencies. In 1979 the dollar could buy 218 Japanese yen or 1.83 German marks. In 1982 the dollar was worth 248 yen or 2.42 marks. This rise in the value of the dollar made imported goods less expensive. U.S. firms competing against similar foreign companies, such as those in the auto industry, became less competitive. European vacations became more affordable, and many Americans took advantage of this opportunity to travel abroad.

● ● ● ● ● ● ● ● ● ● ● ● ● ●

Trade Policy

Suppose that the government reduces the demand for imported goods by imposing an import quota or a tariff. What happens to aggregate income and the exchange rate?

Since net exports equal exports minus imports, a reduction in imports means an increase in net exports. That is, the net-exports schedule shifts to the right, as in Figure 11-6. This shift in the net-exports schedule moves the IS^* curve to the right. Hence, the trade restriction raises the exchange rate and has no effect on income.

A stated goal of policies to restrict trade is often to alter the trade balance NX. Yet, as we first saw in Chapter 7, such policies do not necessarily have that effect. The same conclusion holds in the Mundell-Fleming model under floating exchange rates. Recall that

$$NX(e) = Y - C(Y - T) - I(r) - G.$$

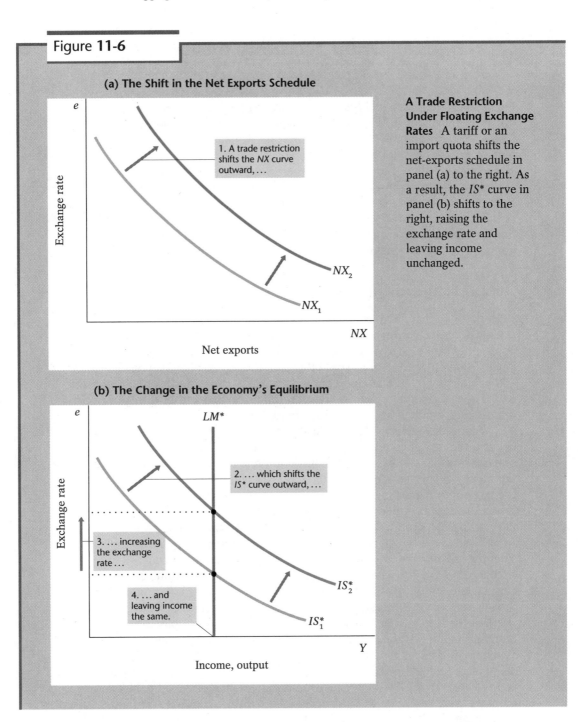

Figure 11-6

(a) The Shift in the Net Exports Schedule

1. A trade restriction shifts the NX curve outward, ...

NX_2

NX_1

Net exports

NX

e — Exchange rate

(b) The Change in the Economy's Equilibrium

LM*

2. ... which shifts the IS* curve outward, ...

3. ... increasing the exchange rate ...

4. ... and leaving income the same.

IS_2^*

IS_1^*

Income, output

Y

e — Exchange rate

A Trade Restriction Under Floating Exchange Rates   A tariff or an import quota shifts the net-exports schedule in panel (a) to the right. As a result, the IS* curve in panel (b) shifts to the right, raising the exchange rate and leaving income unchanged.

Because a trade restriction does not affect income, consumption, investment, or government purchases, it does not affect the trade balance. Although the shift in the net-exports schedule tends to raise NX, the increase in the exchange rate reduces NX by the same amount.

11-3 The Small Open Economy Under Fixed Exchange Rates

We now turn to the second type of exchange-rate system: **fixed exchange rates**. In the 1950s and 1960s, most of the world's major economies, including the United States, operated within the Bretton Woods system—an international monetary system under which most governments agreed to fix exchange rates. The world abandoned this system in the early 1970s, and exchange rates were allowed to float freely. Recently, many European countries have reinstated a system of fixed exchange rates among themselves, and some economists have advocated a return to a worldwide system of fixed exchange rates. In this section we discuss how such a system works, and we examine the impact of economic policies on an economy with a fixed exchange rate.

How a Fixed-Exchange-Rate System Works

Under a system of fixed exchange rates, a central bank stands ready to buy or sell the domestic currency for foreign currencies at a predetermined price. Suppose, for example, that the Fed announced that it was going to fix the exchange rate at 100 yen per dollar. It would then stand ready to give $1 in exchange for 100 yen or to give 100 yen in exchange for $1. To carry out this policy, the Fed would need a reserve of dollars (which it can print) and a reserve of yen (which it must have accumulated from past transactions).

Fixing the exchange rate dedicates monetary policy to the single goal of keeping the exchange rate at the announced level. In other words, the essence of a fixed-exchange-rate system is the commitment of the central bank to allow the money supply to adjust to whatever level will ensure that the equilibrium exchange rate equals the announced exchange rate. Moreover, as long as the central bank stands ready to buy or sell foreign currency at the fixed exchange rate, the money supply adjusts automatically to the necessary level.

To see how fixing the exchange rate determines the money supply, consider the following example. Suppose that the Fed announces that it will fix the exchange rate at 100 yen per dollar, but, in the current equilibrium with the current money supply, the exchange rate is 150 yen per dollar, 50 yen above the announced rate. This situation is illustrated in panel (a) of Figure 11-7. Notice that there is a profit opportunity: an arbitrageur could buy 300 yen in the marketplace for $2, and then sell the yen to the Fed for $3, making a $1 profit. When the Fed buys these yen from the arbitrageur, the dollars it pays automatically increase the money supply. The rise in the money supply shifts the LM^* curve to the right, lowering the equilibrium exchange rate. In this way, the money supply continues to rise until the equilibrium exchange rate falls to the announced level.

Conversely, suppose that when the Fed announces that it will fix the exchange rate at 100 yen per dollar, the equilibrium is 50 yen per dollar. Panel (b) of Figure 11-7 shows this situation. In this case, an arbitrageur could make a profit by buying 100 yen from the Fed for $1 and then selling the yen in the marketplace for $2. When the Fed sells these yen, the $1 it receives automati-

Figure 11-7

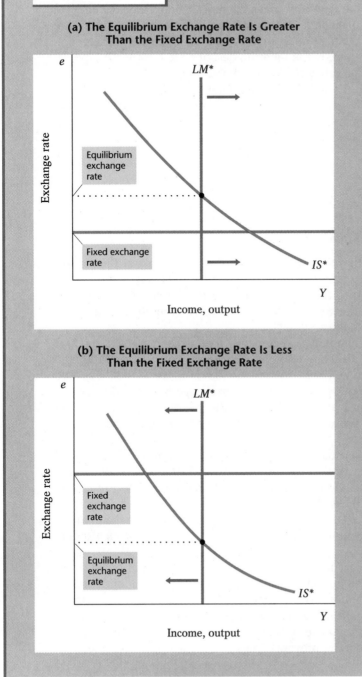

(a) The Equilibrium Exchange Rate Is Greater Than the Fixed Exchange Rate

e

LM*

Exchange rate

Equilibrium exchange rate

Fixed exchange rate

IS*

Y

Income, output

(b) The Equilibrium Exchange Rate Is Less Than the Fixed Exchange Rate

e

LM*

Exchange rate

Fixed exchange rate

Equilibrium exchange rate

IS*

Y

Income, output

How a Fixed Exchange Rate Governs the Money Supply In panel (a), the equilibrium exchange rate exceeds the fixed level. Arbitrageurs will buy foreign currency in foreign-exchange markets and sell it to the Fed for a profit. This process automatically increases the money supply, shifting the *LM** curve to the right and lowering the exchange rate. In panel (b), the equilibrium exchange rate is below the fixed level. Arbitrageurs will buy dollars in foreign-exchange markets and use them to buy foreign currency from the Fed. This process automatically reduces the money supply, shifting the *LM** curve to the left and raising the exchange rate.

cally reduces the money supply. The fall in the money supply shifts the *LM** curve to the left, raising the equilibrium exchange rate. The money supply continues to fall until the equilibrium exchange rate rises to the announced level.

It is important to understand that this exchange-rate system fixes the nominal exchange rate. Whether it also fixes the real exchange rate depends on the time horizon under consideration. If prices are flexible, as they are in the long run, then the real exchange rate can change even while the nominal exchange rate is fixed. Therefore, in the long run described in Chapter 7, a policy to fix the nominal exchange rate would not influence any real variable, including the real exchange rate. A fixed nominal exchange rate would influence only the money supply and the price level. Yet in the short run described by the Mundell-Fleming model, prices are fixed, so a fixed nominal exchange rate implies a fixed real exchange rate as well.

Case Study *11-2*

● ● ● ● ● ● ● ● ● ● ● ● ● ● ● ●

The International Gold Standard

During the late nineteenth and early twentieth centuries, most of the world's major economies operated under a gold standard. Each country maintained a reserve of gold and agreed to exchange one unit of its currency for a specified amount of gold. Through the gold standard, the world's economies maintained a system of fixed exchange rates.

To see how an international gold standard fixes exchange rates, suppose that the U.S. Treasury stands ready to buy or sell 1 ounce of gold for $100, and the Bank of England stands ready to buy or sell 1 ounce of gold for 100 pounds. Together, these policies fix the rate of exchange between dollars and pounds: $1 must trade for 1 pound. Otherwise, the law of one price would be violated, and it would be profitable to buy gold in one country and sell it in the other.

Suppose, for example, that the exchange rate were 2 pounds per dollar. In this case, an arbitrageur could buy 200 pounds for $100, use the pounds to buy 2 ounces of gold from the Bank of England, bring the gold to the United States, and sell it to the Treasury for $200—making a $100 profit. Moreover, by bringing the gold to the United States from England, the arbitrageur would increase the money supply in the United States and decrease the money supply in England.

Thus, during the era of the gold standard, the international transport of gold by arbitrageurs was an automatic mechanism adjusting the money supply and stabilizing exchange rates. This system did not completely fix exchange rates, because shipping gold across the Atlantic was costly. Yet the international gold standard did keep the exchange rate within a range dictated by transportation costs. It thereby prevented large and persistent movements in exchange rates.[2]

● ● ● ● ● ● ● ● ● ● ● ● ● ● ●

[2] For more on how the gold standard worked, see the essays in Barry Eichengreen, ed., *The Gold Standard in Theory and History* (New York: Methuen, 1985).

Fiscal Policy

Let's now examine how economic policies affect a small open economy with a fixed exchange rate. Suppose that the government stimulates domestic spending by increasing government purchases or by cutting taxes. This policy shifts the IS^* curve to the right, as in Figure 11-8, putting upward pressure on the exchange rate. But because the money supply adjusts to keep the exchange rate unchanged, the money supply must rise, shifting the LM^* curve to the right. In contrast to the situation under floating exchange rates, a fiscal expansion under fixed exchange rates raises aggregate income. The rise in income occurs because a fiscal expansion under a fixed-exchange-rate system causes an automatic monetary expansion.

Figure 11-8

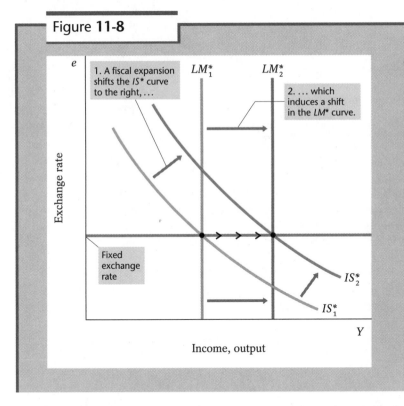

A Fiscal Expansion Under Fixed Exchange Rates
A fiscal expansion shifts the IS^* curve to the right. To maintain the fixed exchange rate, the Fed must increase the money supply, thereby shifting the LM^* curve to the right. Hence, in contrast to the case of floating exchange rates, under fixed exchange rates a fiscal expansion raises income.

Monetary Policy

What happens if the Fed tries to increase the money supply—for example, by buying bonds from the public? The initial impact of this policy is to shift the LM^* curve to the right, lowering the exchange rate, as in Figure 11-9. But, because the Fed is committed to buying and selling foreign currency at a fixed exchange rate, arbitrageurs quickly sell dollars to the Fed, causing the money supply and the LM^* curve to return to their initial positions. Hence, monetary policy as usually conducted is ineffectual under a fixed exchange rate. By

Figure 11-9

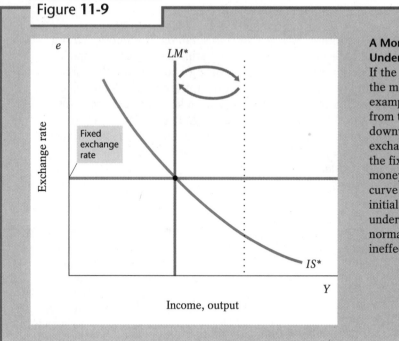

A Monetary Expansion Under Fixed Exchange Rates If the Fed tries to increase the money supply—for example, by buying bonds from the public—it will put downward pressure on the exchange rate. To maintain the fixed exchange rate, the money supply and the LM^* curve must return to their initial positions. Hence, under fixed exchange rates, normal monetary policy is ineffectual.

agreeing to fix the exchange rate, the Fed gives up its control over the money supply.

A country with a fixed exchange rate can, however, conduct a type of monetary policy: it can decide to change the level at which the exchange rate is fixed. A reduction in the value of the currency is called a **devaluation**, and an increase in its value is called a **revaluation**. In the Mundell-Fleming model, a devaluation shifts the LM^* curve to the right; it acts like an increase in the money supply under a floating exchange rate. A devaluation thus expands net exports and raises aggregate income. Conversely, a revaluation shifts the LM^* curve to the left, reduces net exports, and lowers aggregate income.

Case Study *11-3*

● ● ● ● ● ● ● ● ● ● ● ● ● ● ●

Devaluation and the Recovery from the Great Depression

The Great Depression of the 1930s was a global problem. Although events in the United States may have precipitated the downturn, all of the world's major economies experienced huge declines in production and employment. Yet not all governments responded to this calamity in the same way.

One key difference among governments was how committed they were to the fixed exchange rate set by the international gold standard. Some countries, such as France, Germany, Italy, and the Netherlands, maintained the old rate of exchange between gold and currency. Other countries, such as Denmark, Finland, Norway, Sweden, and the United Kingdom, reduced the amount of gold they would pay for each unit of currency by about 50 percent. By reducing the gold content of their currencies, these governments devalued their currencies relative to those of other countries.

The subsequent experience of these two groups of countries conforms to the prediction of the Mundell-Fleming model. Those countries that pursued a policy of devaluation recovered quickly from the Depression. The lower value of the currency raised the money supply, stimulated exports, and expanded production. By contrast, those countries that maintained the old exchange rate suffered longer with a depressed level of economic activity.[3]

Trade Policy

Suppose that the government reduces imports by imposing an import quota or a tariff. This policy shifts the net-exports schedule to the right and thus shifts the IS^* curve to the right, as in Figure 11-10. The shift in the IS^* curve tends to raise the exchange rate. To keep the exchange rate at the fixed level, the money supply must rise, shifting the LM^* curve to the right.

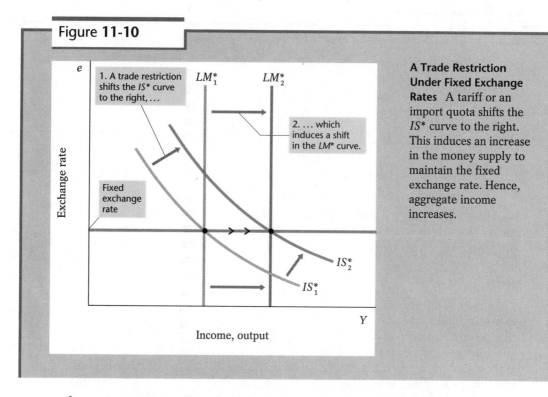

Figure 11-10

A Trade Restriction Under Fixed Exchange Rates A tariff or an import quota shifts the IS^* curve to the right. This induces an increase in the money supply to maintain the fixed exchange rate. Hence, aggregate income increases.

The result of a trade restriction under a fixed exchange rate is very different from that under a floating exchange rate. In both cases, a trade restriction shifts the net-exports schedule to the right, but only under a fixed exchange rate does a trade restriction increase net exports NX. The reason is that a trade restriction under a fixed exchange rate induces monetary expansion rather than an appreciation of the exchange rate. The monetary expansion, in turn, raises aggregate income. Recall the accounting identity

$$NX = S - I.$$

When income rises, saving also rises, implying an increase in net exports.

Policy in the Mundell-Fleming Model: A Summary

The Mundell-Fleming model shows that the effect of almost any economic policy on a small open economy depends on whether the exchange rate is floating or fixed. Table 11-1 summarizes our analysis of the effects of fiscal, monetary, and trade policies on income, the exchange rate, and the trade balance. What is most striking is that all of the results are different under floating and fixed exchange rates.

Table 11-1

The Mundell-Fleming Model: Summary of Policy Effects

	Floating			Fixed		
	Impact on:					
Policy	Y	e	NX	Y	e	NX
Fiscal expansion	0	↑	↓	↑	0	0
Monetary expansion	↑	↓	↑	0	0	0
Import restriction	0	↑	0	↑	0	↑

Note: This table shows the direction of impact of various economic policies on income Y, the exchange rate e, and the trade balance NX. A "↑" indicates that the variable increases; a "↓" indicates that it decreases; a "0" indicates no effect. Remember that the exchange rate is defined as the amount of foreign currency per unit of domestic currency (for example, 100 yen per dollar).

To be more specific, the Mundell-Fleming model shows that the power of monetary and fiscal policy to influence aggregate income depends on the exchange-rate regime. Under floating exchange rates, only monetary policy can affect income. The usual expansionary impact of fiscal policy is offset by a rise in the value of the currency. Under fixed exchange rates, only fiscal policy can affect income. The normal potency of monetary policy is lost because the money supply is dedicated to maintaining the exchange rate at the announced level.

11-4   Interest-Rate Differentials

So far, our analysis has assumed that the interest rate in a small open economy is equal to the world interest rate: $r = r^*$. To some extent, however, interest rates differ around the world. We now consider the causes and effects of international interest-rate differentials.

Country Risk and Expectations

When we assumed earlier that the interest rate is determined by the world interest rate, we were applying the law of one price. We reasoned that if the domestic interest rate were above the world interest rate, people from abroad would lend to that country, driving the domestic interest rate down. And if the domestic interest rate were below the world interest rate, domestic residents would lend abroad in order to earn a higher return, driving the domestic interest rate up. In the end, the domestic interest rate would equal the world interest rate.

Why doesn't this logic always apply? There are two reasons.

One reason is country risk. When investors buy U.S. government bonds or make loans to U.S. corporations, they are fairly confident that they will eventually get their principal and interest. By contrast, in some less developed countries, it is plausible to fear that a revolution or other political upheaval might prevent repayment of loans. Borrowers in such countries often have to pay higher interest rates to compensate lenders for this risk.

Another reason interest rates differ across countries is expected changes in the exchange rate. For example, suppose that people expect the French franc to fall in value relative to the U.S. dollar. Then loans made in francs will be repaid in a less valuable currency than loans made in dollars. To compensate for this expected fall in the French currency, the interest rate in France will be higher than the interest rate in the United States.

Thus, because of both country risk and expectations of future exchange-rate changes, the interest rate of a small open economy can differ from interest rates in other economies around the world. Let's now see how this fact affects our analysis.

Differentials in the Mundell-Fleming Model

To incorporate interest-rate differentials into the Mundell-Fleming model, we assume that the interest rate in our small open economy is determined by the world interest rate plus a risk premium θ:

$$r = r^* + \theta.$$

The risk premium is determined by perceived political risk of making loans in a country and the expected change in the real exchange rate. For our purposes here, we can take the risk premium as exogenous in order to examine how changes in the risk premium affect the economy.

The model is largely the same as before. The two equations are

$$Y = C(Y - T) + I(r^* + \theta) + G + NX(e) \qquad IS^*$$
$$M/P = L(r^* + \theta, Y). \qquad LM^*$$

For any given fiscal policy, monetary policy, price level, and risk premium, these two equations determine the level of output and exchange rate that equilibrate the goods market and the money market. For any given risk premium, monetary policy, fiscal policy, and trade policy work as we have already seen.

Now suppose that political turmoil causes the country's risk premium θ to rise. The most direct effect is that the domestic interest rate r rises. The higher interest rate, in turn, has two effects. First, the IS^* curve shifts to the left, because the higher interest rate reduces investment. Second, the LM^* curve shifts to the right, because the higher interest rate reduces the demand for money, and this allows a higher level of output for any given money supply. As Figure 11-11 shows, these shifts cause the currency to depreciate. This fall in the value of the currency, in turn, makes domestic goods and services less expensive, so exports rise and imports fall. Hence, even though higher interest rates depress investment, output rises because of a greater increase in net exports.

Figure 11-11

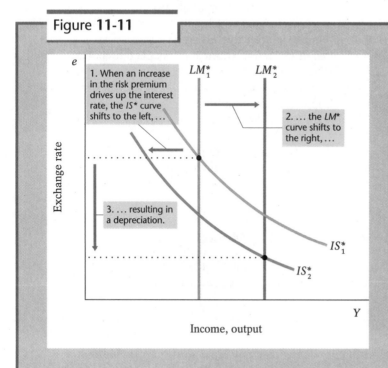

1. When an increase in the risk premium drives up the interest rate, the IS^* curve shifts to the left, …

2. … the LM^* curve shifts to the right, …

3. … resulting in a depreciation.

LM_1^* LM_2^* IS_1^* IS_2^*

e — Exchange rate

Y — Income, output

An Increase in the Risk Premium An increase in the risk premium associated with a country drives up the interest rate. Because the higher interest rate reduces investment, the IS^* curve shifts to the left. Because it also reduces money demand, the LM^* curve shifts to the right. Output rises, and the exchange rate depreciates.

This analysis has an important implication: expectations of the exchange rate are partially self-fulfilling. For example, suppose that people come to believe that the French franc will not be valuable in the future. Investors will place a larger risk premium on French assets: θ will rise in France. This expectation will drive up French interest rates and, as we have just seen, will drive down the value of the French currency. *Thus, the expectation that a currency will lose value in the future causes it to lose value today.*

Case Study *11-4*

● ● ● ● ● ● ● ● ● ● ● ● ●

Meltdown in Mexico

In August 1994, a Mexican peso was worth 30 cents. A year later, it was worth only 16 cents. What explains this massive fall in the value of the Mexican currency? Country risk is a large part of the story.

At the beginning of 1994, Mexico was a country on the rise. The recent passage of the North American Free Trade Agreement (NAFTA), which reduced trade barriers among the United States, Canada, and Mexico, made many confident in the future of the Mexican economy. Investors around the world were eager to make loans to the Mexican government and to Mexican corporations.

Political developments soon changed that perception. A violent uprising in the Chiapas region of Mexico made the political situation in Mexico seem precarious. Then Luis Donaldo Colosio, the leading presidential candidate, was assassinated. The political future looked less certain, and many investors started placing a larger risk premium on Mexican assets.

At first, the rising risk premium did not affect the value of the peso, for Mexico was operating with a fixed exchange rate. Under a fixed exchange rate, the central bank agrees to trade the domestic currency (pesos) for a foreign currency (dollars) at a predetermined rate. When an increase in the country risk premium puts downward pressure on the value of the currency, the central bank stands ready to accept pesos and pay out dollars at the fixed rate. This automatic exchange-market intervention contracts the money supply (shifting the LM^* curve to the left) when the currency might otherwise depreciate.

Yet Mexico's reserves of foreign currency were too small to maintain its fixed exchange rate. When Mexico ran out of dollars at the end of 1994, the Mexican government announced a devaluation of the peso. This choice had repercussions, however, because the government had repeatedly promised that it would not devalue. Investors became even more distrustful of Mexican policymakers and feared further Mexican devaluations.

Investors around the world (including those in Mexico) avoided buying Mexican assets. The country risk premium rose once again, adding to the upward pressure on interest rates and the downward pressure on the peso. The Mexican stock market plummeted. When the Mexican government needed to roll over some of its debt that was coming due, investors were unwilling to buy the new debt. Default appeared to be the government's only option. In just a few months, Mexico had gone from being a promising emerging economy to being a risky economy with a government on the verge of bankruptcy.

Then the United States stepped in. The U.S. government had three motives: to help its neighbor to the south, to prevent the massive illegal immigration that might follow government default and economic collapse, and to prevent the investor pessimism regarding Mexico from spreading to other developing countries. The U.S. government led an international effort to bail out the Mexican government. In particular, the United States provided loan guarantees for Mexican government debt, which allowed the Mexican government to refinance the debt that was coming due. These loan guarantees helped restore confidence in the Mexican economy, thereby reducing to some extent the country risk premium.

The Mexican meltdown of 1994–1995 had many facets, and the long-term ramifications are still uncertain. Yet one lesson is clear: changes in perceived country risk, often attributable to political instability, are an important determinant of interest rates and exchange rates in small open economies.

● ● ● ● ● ● ● ● ● ● ● ● ● ●

11-5 Should Exchange Rates Be Floating or Fixed?

Having analyzed how an economy works under floating and fixed exchange rates, we turn to the question of which exchange-rate regime is preferable. The international monetary system is often a topic of heated debate among international economists and policymakers. Historically, most economists have favored a system of floating exchange rates. Yet, in recent years, some have advocated a return to fixed exchange rates.

The primary argument for a floating exchange rate is that it allows monetary policy to be used for other purposes. Under fixed rates, monetary policy is committed to the single goal of maintaining the exchange rate at its announced level. Yet the exchange rate is only one of the many macroeconomic variables that monetary policy can influence. A system of floating exchange rates leaves monetary policymakers free to pursue other goals, such as stabilizing employment or prices.

Advocates of fixed exchange rates argue that exchange-rate uncertainty makes international trade more difficult. After the world abandoned the Bretton Woods system of fixed exchange rates in the early 1970s, both real and nominal exchange rates became more volatile than anyone had expected. Some economists attribute this volatility to irrational and destabilizing speculation by international investors. Business executives often claim that this volatility is harmful because it increases the uncertainty that accompanies international business transactions. Yet, despite this exchange-rate volatility, the amount of world trade has continued to rise under floating exchange rates.

Advocates of fixed exchange rates sometimes argue that a commitment to a fixed exchange rate is one way to discipline the monetary authority and prevent excessive growth in the money supply. Yet there are many other policy rules to which the central bank could be committed. In Chapter 13, for instance, we will discuss policy rules such as targets for nominal GDP or the price level. Fixing the exchange rate has the advantage of being simpler to implement than these other policy rules, since the money supply adjusts automatically, but this policy probably leads to greater instability in both income and employment.

In the end, the choice between floating and fixed rates is not as stark as it may seem at first. During periods of fixed exchange rates, countries can change the value of their currency if maintaining the exchange rate conflicts too severely with other goals. During periods of floating exchange rates, countries often use formal or informal targets for the exchange rate when deciding whether to expand or contract the money supply. We rarely observe exchange rates that are completely fixed or completely floating. Instead, under both systems, stability of the exchange rate is usually one among many of the central bank's objectives.

Case Study *11-5*

● ● ● ● ● ● ● ● ● ● ● ● ●

The European Monetary System

Since 1979, most European countries have participated in the *European Monetary System (EMS)*. The goal of the EMS is to limit fluctuations in the exchange rates among the member countries. Relative to currencies not included in the EMS, such as the U.S. dollar, these European currencies fluctuate together. An organization of countries like the EMS is called an **exchange-rate union**.

The EMS does not completely fix exchange rates. The central banks of the member countries allow their exchange rates to fluctuate within bands around specific targets. The exchange rate can float as long as it remains inside the band. But when the exchange rate approaches its upper or lower limit, the central bank is committed to intervene in the market for foreign exchange. That is, the central bank must adjust the money supply to keep the exchange rate within its band. Thus, members of the EMS lose some of their ability to conduct independent monetary policy.

When the efforts to maintain the targets cause other problems, the countries of the EMS sometimes do change the targets. Such a change is called a *realignment*. One goal of the EMS is to make realignments less necessary by coordinating monetary and fiscal policies among member countries.

In the views of many European policymakers, the EMS is the first step toward *monetary union*—a common currency for all of Europe. In December 1995 European leaders agreed to introduce by 2002 a common currency called the *euro*. Once the euro is introduced, a single central bank will conduct monetary policy for all of Europe. The German mark, the French franc, the Dutch guilder, and several other national monies will no longer be legal tender.

●   ●   ●   ●   ●   ●   ●   ●   ●   ●   ●   ●   ●   ●

11-6   The Mundell-Fleming Model with a Changing Price Level

So far we have been using the Mundell-Fleming model to study the small open economy in the short run when the price level is fixed. To see how this model relates to models we have examined previously, let's consider what happens when the price level changes.

To examine price adjustment in an open economy, we must distinguish between the nominal exchange rate e and the real exchange rate ε, which equals eP/P^*. We can write the Mundell-Fleming model as

$$Y = C(Y - T) + I(r^*) + G + NX(\varepsilon) \qquad IS^*$$
$$M/P = L(r^*, Y). \qquad\qquad\qquad\qquad LM^*$$

These equations should be familiar by now. The first equation describes the IS^* curve, and the second equation describes the LM^* curve. Note that net exports depend on the real exchange rate.

Figure 11-12 shows what happens when the price level falls. Because a lower price level raises the level of real money balances, the LM^* curve shifts to the right, as in panel (a) of Figure 11-12. The real exchange rate depreciates, and the equilibrium level of income rises.

The aggregate demand curve summarizes this negative relationship between the price level and the level of income, as shown in panel (b) of Figure 11-12. Thus, the aggregate demand curve that arises from the Mundell-Fleming model is similar to the one that arises from the IS-LM model. Policies that raise income in the Mundell-Fleming model shift the aggregate demand curve to the right; policies that lower income in the Mundell-Fleming model shift the aggregate demand curve to the left.

We can use this diagram to show how the short-run model in this chapter is related to the long-run model in Chapter 7. Figure 11-13 shows the short-run and long-run equilibria. In both panels of the figure, point K describes the short-run equilibrium, because it assumes a fixed price level. At this equilibrium, the demand for goods and services is too low to keep the economy producing at its natural rate. Over time, low demand causes the price level to fall. The fall in the price level raises real money balances, shifting the LM^* curve to the right. The real exchange rate depreciates, so net exports rise. Eventually,

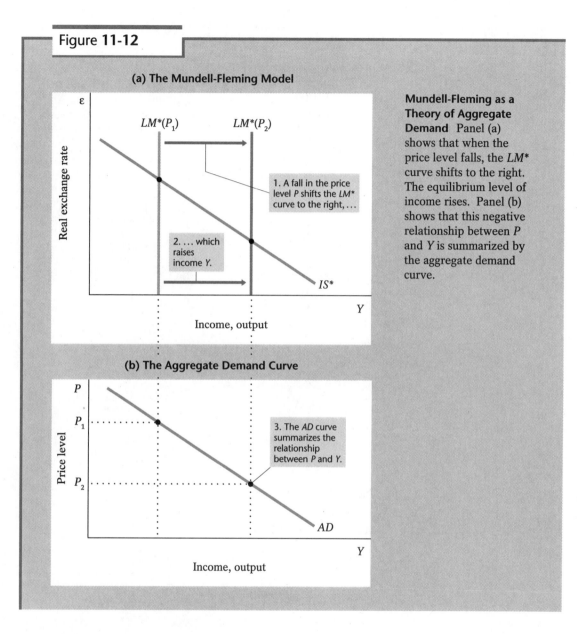

Figure 11-12

(a) The Mundell-Fleming Model

1. A fall in the price level P shifts the LM* curve to the right, ...

2. ... which raises income Y.

(b) The Aggregate Demand Curve

3. The AD curve summarizes the relationship between P and Y.

Mundell-Fleming as a Theory of Aggregate Demand Panel (a) shows that when the price level falls, the LM* curve shifts to the right. The equilibrium level of income rises. Panel (b) shows that this negative relationship between P and Y is summarized by the aggregate demand curve.

the economy reaches point C, the long-run equilibrium. The speed of transition between the short-run and long-run equilibria depends on how quickly the price level adjusts to restore the economy to the natural rate.

The levels of income at point K and point C are both of interest. Our central concern in this chapter has been how policy influences point K, the short-run equilibrium. In Chapter 7 we examined the determinants of point C, the long-run equilibrium. Whenever policymakers consider any change in policy, they need to consider both the short-run and long-run effects of their decision.

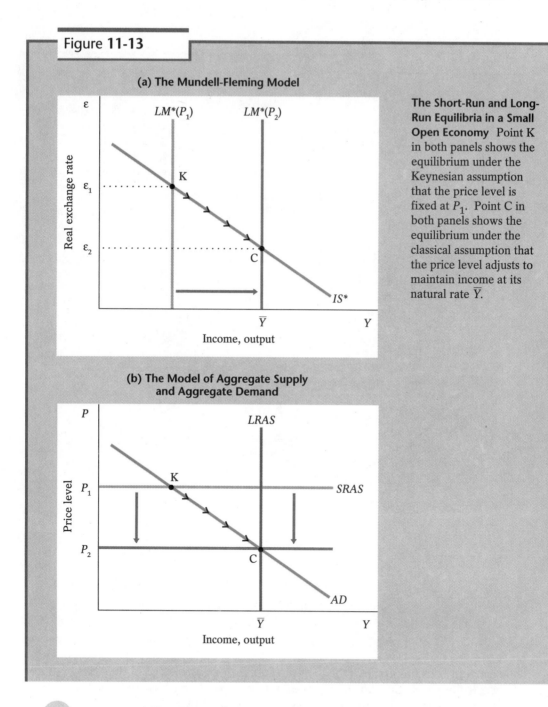

Figure 11-13

(a) The Mundell-Fleming Model

The Short-Run and Long-Run Equilibria in a Small Open Economy Point K in both panels shows the equilibrium under the Keynesian assumption that the price level is fixed at P_1. Point C in both panels shows the equilibrium under the classical assumption that the price level adjusts to maintain income at its natural rate $\overline{Y}$.

(b) The Model of Aggregate Supply and Aggregate Demand

11-7   A Concluding Reminder

In this chapter we have examined how a small open economy works in the short run when prices are sticky. We have seen how monetary and fiscal policy influence income and the exchange rate, and how the behavior of the economy depends on whether the exchange rate is floating or fixed. In closing, it is worth repeating a lesson from Chapter 7. Many countries, including the United States, are neither closed economies nor small open economies: they lie somewhere in between.

A large open economy like the United States combines the behavior of a closed economy and the behavior of a small open economy. When analyzing policies in a large open economy, we need to consider both the closed-economy logic of Chapter 10 and the open-economy logic developed in this chapter. The appendix to this chapter presents a model for the intermediate case of a large open economy. The results of that model are, as one would guess, a mixture of the two polar cases we have already examined.

To see how we can draw on the logic of both the closed and small open economies and apply these insights to the United States, consider how a monetary contraction affects the economy in the short run. In a closed economy, a monetary contraction raises the interest rate, lowers investment, and thus lowers aggregate income. In a small open economy with a floating exchange rate, a monetary contraction raises the exchange rate, lowers net exports, and thus lowers aggregate income. The interest rate is unaffected, however, because it is determined by world financial markets.

The U.S. economy contains elements of both cases. Because the United States is large enough to affect the world interest rate and because capital is not perfectly mobile across countries, a monetary contraction does raise the interest rate and depress investment. At the same time, a monetary contraction also raises the value of the dollar, thereby depressing net exports. Hence, although the Mundell-Fleming model does not precisely describe an economy like that of the United States, it does predict correctly what happens to international variables such as the exchange rate, and it shows how international interactions alter the effects of monetary and fiscal policies.

Summary

1. The Mundell-Fleming model is the *IS-LM* model for a small open economy. It takes the price level as given and then shows what causes fluctuations in income and the exchange rate.

2. The Mundell-Fleming model shows that fiscal policy does not influence aggregate income under floating exchange rates. A fiscal expansion causes the currency to appreciate, reducing net exports and offsetting the usual expansionary impact on aggregate income. Fiscal policy does influence aggregate income under fixed exchange rates.

3. The Mundell-Fleming model shows that monetary policy does not influence aggregate income under fixed exchange rates. Any attempt to expand the money supply is futile, because the money supply must adjust to ensure that the exchange rate stays at its announced level. Monetary policy does influence aggregate income under floating exchange rates.

4. If investors are wary of holding assets in a country, the interest rate in that country may exceed the world interest rate by some risk premium. According to the Mundell-Fleming model, an increase in the risk premium causes the interest rate to rise and the currency of that country to depreciate.

5. There are advantages to both floating and fixed exchange rates. Floating exchange rates leave monetary policymakers free to pursue objectives other than exchange rate stability. Fixed exchange rates reduce some of the uncertainty in international business transactions.

KEY CONCEPTS

Mundell-Fleming model

Floating exchange rates

Fixed exchange rates

Devaluation

Revaluation

Exchange-rate union

QUESTIONS FOR REVIEW

1. In the Mundell-Fleming model with floating exchange rates, explain what happens to aggregate income, the exchange rate, and the trade balance when taxes are raised. What would happen if exchange rates were fixed rather than floating?

2. In the Mundell-Fleming model with floating exchange rates, explain what happens to aggregate income, the exchange rate, and the trade balance when the money supply is reduced. What would happen if exchange rates were fixed rather than floating?

3. In the Mundell-Fleming model with floating exchange rates, explain what happens to aggregate income, the exchange rate, and the trade balance when a quota on imported cars is removed. What would happen if exchange rates were fixed rather than floating?

4. What are the advantages of floating exchange rates and fixed exchange rates?

PROBLEMS AND APPLICATIONS

1. Use the Mundell-Fleming model to predict what would happen to aggregate income, the exchange rate, and the trade balance under both floating and fixed exchange rates in response to each of the following shocks:

   a. A fall in consumer confidence about the future induces consumers to spend less and save more.

   b. The introduction of a stylish line of Toyotas makes some consumers prefer foreign cars over domestic cars.

   c. The introduction of automatic teller machines reduces the demand for money.

2. The Mundell-Fleming model takes the world interest rate r^* as an exogenous variable. Let's consider what happens when this variable changes.

   a. What might cause the world interest rate to rise?

   b. In the Mundell-Fleming model with a floating exchange rate, what happens to aggregate income, the exchange rate, and the trade balance when the world interest rate rises?

c. In the Mundell-Fleming model with a fixed exchange rate, what happens to aggregate income, the exchange rate, and the trade balance when the world interest rate rises?

3. Business executives and policymakers are often concerned about the "competitiveness" of American industry (the ability of U.S. industries to sell their goods profitably in world markets).

a. How would a change in the exchange rate affect competitiveness?

b. Suppose you wanted to make domestic industries more competitive but did not want to alter aggregate income. According to the Mundell-Fleming model, what combination of monetary and fiscal policies should you pursue?

4. Suppose that higher income implies higher imports and thus lower net exports. That is, the net exports function is

$$NX = NX(e, Y).$$

Examine the effects in a small open economy of a fiscal expansion on income and the trade balance under

a. A floating exchange rate.

b. A fixed exchange rate.

How does your answer compare to the results in Table 11-1?

5. Suppose that money demand depends on disposable income, so that the equation for the money market becomes

$$M/P = L(r, Y - T).$$

Analyze the impact of a tax cut in a small open economy on the exchange rate and income under both floating and fixed exchange rates.

6. Suppose that the price level relevant for money demand includes the price of imported goods and that the price of imported goods depends on the exchange rate. That is, the money market is described by

$$M/P = L(r, Y),$$

where

$$P = \lambda P_d + (1 - \lambda)P_f/e.$$

The parameter λ is the share of domestic goods in the price index P. Assume the price of domestic goods P_d and the price of foreign goods measured in foreign currency P_f are fixed.

a. Explain why in this model the LM^* curve is upward sloping rather than vertical.

b. What is the impact of expansionary fiscal policy under floating exchange rates in this model? Explain. Contrast with the standard Mundell-Fleming model.

c. The effect of the exchange rate on the price level is sometimes called an "endogenous supply shock." Why might it be called this?

7. Use the Mundell-Fleming model to answer the following questions about the state of California (a small open economy).

a. If California suffers from a recession, should the state government use monetary or fiscal policy to stimulate employment? Explain. (*Note:* For this question, assume that the state government can print dollar bills.)

b. If California prohibited the import of wines from the state of Washington, what would happen to output, the exchange rate, and the trade balance? Consider both the short-run and the long-run impacts.

A Short-Run Model of the Large Open Economy

Appendix

• • • • • • • • • • • • • •

When analyzing policies in an economy such as the United States, we need to combine the closed-economy logic of the *IS-LM* model and the small-open-economy logic of the Mundell-Fleming model. This appendix presents a model for the intermediate case of a large open economy.

As we discussed in the appendix to Chapter 7, a large open economy differs from a small open economy because its interest rate is not fixed by world financial markets. In a large open economy, we must consider the relationship between the interest rate and net foreign investment. Net foreign investment is the amount that domestic investors lend abroad minus the amount that foreign investors lend here. As the domestic interest rate falls, domestic investors find foreign lending more attractive, and foreign investors find lending here less attractive. Thus, net foreign investment is negatively related to the interest rate. Here we add this relationship to our short-run model of national income.

The three equations of the model are

$$Y = C(Y - T) + I(r) + G + NX(e)$$
$$M/P = L(r, Y)$$
$$NX(e) = NFI(r).$$

The first two equations are the same as those used in the Mundell-Fleming model of this chapter. The third equation, taken from the appendix to Chapter 7, states that the trade balance *NX* equals net foreign investment *NFI* and that net foreign investment depends on the domestic interest rate.

To see what this model implies, substitute the third equation into the first, so the model becomes

$$Y = C(Y - T) + I(r) + G + NFI(r) \qquad IS$$
$$M/P = L(r, Y). \qquad LM$$

These two equations are much like the two equations of the closed-economy *IS-LM* model. The only difference is that expenditure now depends on the interest rate for two reasons. As before, a higher interest rate reduces investment. But now, a higher interest rate also reduces net foreign investment and thus lowers net exports.

To analyze this model, we can use the three graphs in Figure 11-14. Panel (a) shows the *IS-LM* diagram. As in the closed-economy model in Chapters 9 and 10, the interest rate *r* is on the vertical axis, and income *Y* is on the horizontal axis. The *IS* and *LM* curves together determine the equilibrium level of income and the equilibrium interest rate.

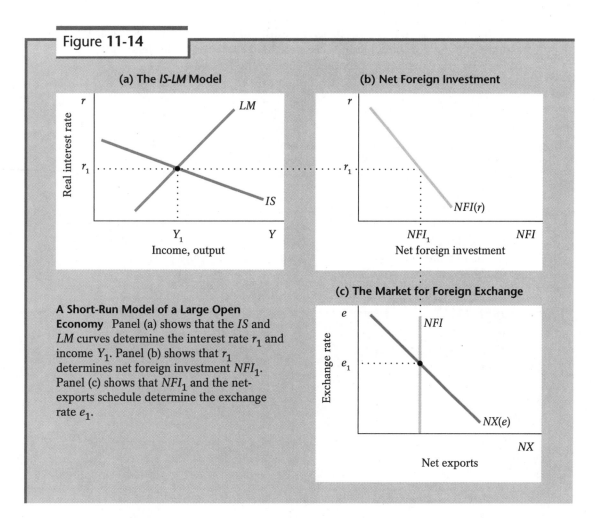

Figure 11-14

(a) The *IS-LM* Model

Real interest rate (r)

r_1

LM

IS

Y_1

Income, output (Y)

(b) Net Foreign Investment

r

r_1

$NFI(r)$

NFI_1 NFI

Net foreign investment

(c) The Market for Foreign Exchange

e

Exchange rate

e_1

NFI

$NX(e)$

NX

Net exports

A Short-Run Model of a Large Open Economy Panel (a) shows that the *IS* and *LM* curves determine the interest rate r_1 and income Y_1. Panel (b) shows that r_1 determines net foreign investment NFI_1. Panel (c) shows that NFI_1 and the net-exports schedule determine the exchange rate e_1.

The new net-foreign-investment term in the *IS* equation, $NFI(r)$, makes this *IS* curve flatter than it would be in a closed economy. The more responsive net foreign investment is to the interest rate, the flatter the *IS* curve is. You might recall from the Chapter 7 appendix that the small open economy represents the extreme case in which net foreign investment is infinitely elastic at the world interest rate. In this extreme case, the *IS* curve is completely flat. Hence, a small open economy would be depicted in this figure with a horizontal *IS* curve.

Panels (b) and (c) show how the equilibrium from the *IS-LM* model determines net foreign investment, the trade balance, and the exchange rate. In panel (b) we see that the interest rate determines net foreign investment. This curve slopes downward because a higher interest rate discourages domestic investors from lending abroad and encourages foreign investors to lend here. In panel (c) we see that the exchange rate adjusts to ensure that net exports of goods and services equal net foreign investment.

Now let's use this model to examine the impact of various policies. We assume that the economy has a floating exchange rate, since this assumption is correct for most large open economies such as the United States.

Fiscal Policy

Figure 11-15 examines the impact of a fiscal expansion. An increase in government purchases or a cut in taxes shifts the *IS* curve to the right. As panel (a) illustrates, this shift in the *IS* curve leads to an increase in the level of income and an increase in the interest rate. These two effects are similar to those in a closed economy.

Yet, in the large open economy, the higher interest rate reduces net foreign investment, as in panel (b). The fall in net foreign investment reduces the supply of dollars in the market for foreign exchange. The exchange rate appreciates, as in panel (c). Because domestic goods become more expensive relative to foreign goods, net exports fall.

Figure 11-15

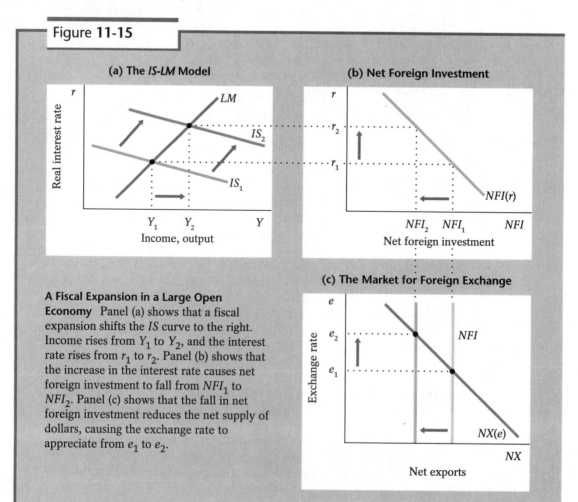

(a) The *IS-LM* Model

(b) Net Foreign Investment

(c) The Market for Foreign Exchange

A Fiscal Expansion in a Large Open Economy Panel (a) shows that a fiscal expansion shifts the *IS* curve to the right. Income rises from Y_1 to Y_2, and the interest rate rises from r_1 to r_2. Panel (b) shows that the increase in the interest rate causes net foreign investment to fall from NFI_1 to NFI_2. Panel (c) shows that the fall in net foreign investment reduces the net supply of dollars, causing the exchange rate to appreciate from e_1 to e_2.

Figure 11-15 shows that a fiscal expansion does raise income in the large open economy, unlike in a small open economy under a floating exchange rate. The impact on income, however, is smaller than in a closed economy. In a closed economy, the expansionary impact of fiscal policy is partially offset by the crowding out of investment: as the interest rate rises, investment falls, reducing the fiscal-policy multipliers. In a large open economy, there is yet another offsetting factor: as the interest rate rises, net foreign investment falls, the exchange rate appreciates, and net exports fall. Together these effects are not large enough to make fiscal policy powerless, as it is in a small open economy, but they do reduce fiscal policy's impact.

Monetary Policy

Figure 11-16 examines the effect of a monetary expansion. An increase in the money supply shifts the LM curve to the right, as in panel (a). The level of

Figure 11-16

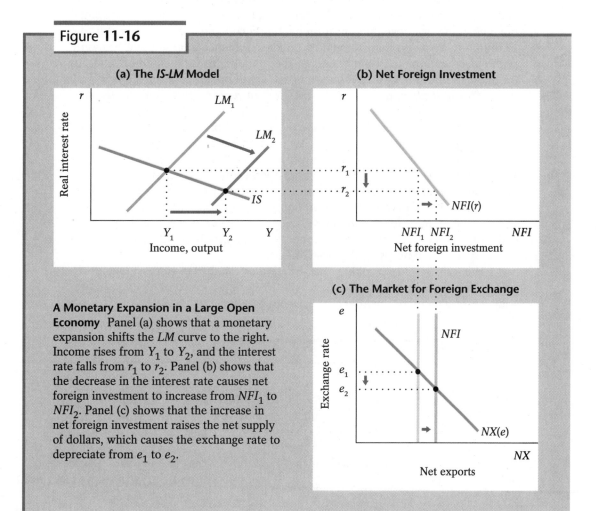

A Monetary Expansion in a Large Open Economy Panel (a) shows that a monetary expansion shifts the LM curve to the right. Income rises from Y_1 to Y_2, and the interest rate falls from r_1 to r_2. Panel (b) shows that the decrease in the interest rate causes net foreign investment to increase from NFI_1 to NFI_2. Panel (c) shows that the increase in net foreign investment raises the net supply of dollars, which causes the exchange rate to depreciate from e_1 to e_2.

income rises, and the interest rate falls. Once again, these effects are similar to those in a closed economy.

Yet, as panel (b) shows, the lower interest rate leads to higher net foreign investment. The increase in *NFI* raises the supply of dollars in the market for foreign exchange. The exchange rate depreciates, as in panel (c). As domestic goods become cheaper relative to foreign goods, net exports rise.

We can now see that the monetary transmission mechanism has two parts in a large open economy. As in a closed economy, a monetary expansion lowers the interest rate. As in a small open economy, a monetary expansion causes the currency to depreciate in the market for foreign exchange. The lower interest rate stimulates investment, and the lower exchange rate stimulates net exports.

A Rule of Thumb

This model of the large open economy describes well the U.S. economy today. Yet it is somewhat more complicated and cumbersome than the model of the closed economy we studied in Chapters 9 and 10 and the model of the small open economy we developed in this chapter. Fortunately, there is a useful rule of thumb to help you determine how policies influence a large open economy without remembering all the details of the model: *The large open economy is an average of the closed economy and the small open economy. To find how any policy will affect any variable, find the answer in the two extreme cases and take an average.*

For example, how does a monetary contraction affect the interest rate and investment in the short run? In a closed economy, the interest rate rises, and investment falls. In a small open economy, neither the interest rate nor investment changes. The effect in the large open economy is an average of these two cases: a monetary contraction raises the interest rate and reduces investment, but only somewhat. The fall in net foreign investment mitigates the rise in the interest rate and the fall in investment that would occur in a closed economy. But unlike in a small open economy, the international flow of capital is not so strong as to negate fully these effects.

This rule of thumb makes the simple models all the more valuable. Although they do not describe perfectly the world in which we live, they do provide a useful guide to the effects of economic policy.

MORE PROBLEMS AND APPLICATIONS

1. Imagine that you run the central bank in a large open economy. Your goal is to stabilize income. Under your policy, what happens to the money supply, the interest rate, the exchange rate, and the trade balance in response to each of the following shocks?

a. The president raises taxes to reduce the budget deficit.

b. The president restricts the import of Japanese cars.

2. Over the past several decades, investors around the world have become

more willing to take advantage of opportunities in other countries. Because of this increasing sophistication, economies are more open today than in the past. Consider how this development affects the ability of monetary policy to influence the economy.

a. If investors become more willing to substitute foreign and domestic assets, what happens to the slope of the *NFI* function?

b. If the *NFI* function changes in this way, what happens to the slope of the *IS* curve?

c. How does this change in the *IS* curve affect the Fed's ability to control the interest rate?

d. How does this change in the *IS* curve affect the Fed's ability to control national income?

3. The country of Markum is well described as a large open economy. Policymakers in Markum want to raise the level of investment without changing total output or the exchange rate.

a. Is there any combination of domestic monetary and fiscal policies that would achieve the policymakers' goal?

b. Is there any combination of domestic monetary, fiscal, and trade policies that would achieve this goal?

c. Is there any combination of monetary and fiscal policies at home and abroad that would achieve this goal?

4. Suppose that a large open economy has a fixed exchange rate.

a. Describe what happens in response to a fiscal contraction, such as a tax increase. Compare your answer to the case of a small open economy.

b. Describe what happens if the central bank expands the money supply by buying bonds from the public. Compare your answer to the case of a small open economy.

Aggregate Supply

> *There is always a temporary tradeoff between inflation and unemployment; there is no permanent tradeoff. The temporary tradeoff comes not from inflation per se, but from unanticipated inflation, which generally means, from a rising rate of inflation.*

Milton Friedman

We now turn our attention to aggregate supply. In the previous three chapters, we examined how changes in monetary and fiscal policy and shocks to the money and goods markets shift the aggregate demand curve. To see how shifts in aggregate demand affect the quantity of output and the level of prices, we must add aggregate supply to the analysis. In particular, we must understand what determines the position and slope of the aggregate supply curve. That is our goal in this chapter.

When we introduced the aggregate supply curve in Chapter 8, we established that aggregate supply behaves very differently in the short run than in the long run. In the long run, prices are flexible, and the aggregate supply curve is vertical. When the aggregate supply curve is vertical, shifts in the aggregate demand curve affect the price level, but the output of the economy remains at its natural rate. By contrast, in the short run, prices are sticky, and the aggregate supply curve is not vertical. In this case, shifts in aggregate demand do cause fluctuations in output. In Chapter 8 we took a simplified view of price stickiness by drawing the short-run aggregate supply curve as a horizontal line, representing the extreme situation in which all prices are fixed.

To refine our understanding of aggregate supply, we begin by looking more closely at explanations for the slope of the short-run aggregate supply curve. Because economists disagree about how best to explain aggregate supply, we examine four prominent models. Although different in some important details, these models share a common theme about what makes the short-run and long-run aggregate supply curves differ and a common conclusion that the short-run aggregate supply curve is upward sloping.

After examining the models, we see that the short-run aggregate supply curve implies a tradeoff between two measures of economic performance: inflation and unemployment. According to this tradeoff, to reduce the rate of inflation policymakers must temporarily raise unemployment, and to reduce unemployment they must accept higher inflation. As the quotation at the beginning of the chapter suggests, the tradeoff between inflation and unemployment holds only in the short run.

12-1 Four Models of Aggregate Supply

Here we present four prominent models of aggregate supply, roughly in the order of their development. In all the models, the short-run aggregate supply curve is not vertical, because of some market imperfection. As a result, shifts in the aggregate demand curve cause the level of output to deviate temporarily from the natural rate.

All four models yield an aggregate supply equation of the form

$$Y = \overline{Y} + \alpha(P - P^e) \qquad \alpha > 0,$$

where Y is output, $\overline{Y}$ is the natural rate of output, P is the price level, and P^e is the expected price level. This equation states that output deviates from its natural rate when the price level deviates from the expected price level. The parameter α indicates how much output responds to unexpected changes in the price level; $1/\alpha$ is the slope of the aggregate supply curve.

Each of the four models tells a different story about what lies behind this equation. In other words, each highlights a particular reason that unexpected price movements are associated with fluctuations in output.

The Sticky-Wage Model

To explain why the short-run aggregate supply curve is not vertical, many economists stress the sluggish behavior of nominal wages. In many industries, especially those that are unionized, nominal wages are set by long-term contracts, so wages cannot adjust quickly when economic conditions change. Even in industries not covered by formal contracts, implicit agreements between workers and firms may limit wage changes. Wages may also depend on social norms and notions of fairness that evolve slowly. For these reasons, many economists believe that nominal wages are sluggish, or "sticky," in the short run.

The **sticky-wage model** shows what a sticky nominal wage implies for aggregate supply. To preview the model, consider what happens to the amount of output produced when the price level rises.

1. When the nominal wage is stuck, a rise in the price level lowers the real wage, making labor cheaper.

2. The lower real wage induces firms to hire more labor.

3. The additional labor hired produces more output.

This positive relationship between the price level and the amount of output means that the aggregate supply curve slopes upward during the time when the nominal wage cannot adjust.

To develop this story of aggregate supply more formally, assume that workers and firms bargain over and agree on the nominal wage before they know what the price level will be when their agreement takes effect. The bargaining parties—the workers and the firms—have in mind a target real wage.

The target may be the real wage that equilibrates labor supply and demand. More likely, it also depends on other factors—union power, efficiency-wage considerations, and so on—that keep the real wage above the equilibrium level, as we discussed in Chapter 5.

The two parties set the nominal wage W based on the target real wage ω and on their expectation of the price level P^e. The nominal wage they set is

$$W \quad = \quad \omega \quad \times \quad P^e$$

Nominal Wage = Target Real Wage × Expected Price Level.

After the nominal wage has been set and before labor has been hired, firms learn the actual price level P. The real wage turns out to be

$$W/P \quad = \quad \omega \quad \times \quad (P^e/P)$$

$$\text{Real Wage} = \text{Target Real Wage} \times \frac{\text{Expected Price Level}}{\text{Actual Price Level}}.$$

This equation shows that the real wage deviates from its target if the actual price level differs from the expected price level. When the actual price level is greater than expected, the real wage is less than its target; when the actual price level is less than expected, the real wage is greater than its target.

The final assumption of the model is that employment is determined by the quantity of labor that firms demand. In other words, the bargain between the workers and the firms does not determine the level of employment in advance; instead, the workers agree to provide as much labor as the firms wish to buy at the predetermined wage. We describe the firms' hiring decisions by the labor demand function

$$L = L^d(W/P),$$

which states that the lower the real wage, the more labor firms hire. The labor demand curve is shown in panel (a) of Figure 12-1. Output is determined by the production function

$$Y = F(L),$$

which states that the more labor is hired, the more output is produced. This is shown in panel (b) of Figure 12-1.

Panel (c) of Figure 12-1 shows the resulting aggregate supply curve. Unexpected price changes move the real wage away from the target real wage. The change in the real wage in turn influences the amounts of labor hired and output produced. The aggregate supply curve can be written as

$$Y = \bar{Y} + \alpha(P - P^e).$$

Output deviates from its natural level when the price level deviates from the expected price level.[1]

[1]   For more on the sticky-wage model, see Jo Anna Gray, "Wage Indexation: A Macroeconomic Approach," *Journal of Monetary Economics* 2 (April 1976): 221–235; and Stanley Fischer, "Long-term Contracts, Rational Expectations, and the Optimal Money Supply Rule," *Journal of Political Economy* 85 (February 1977): 191–205.

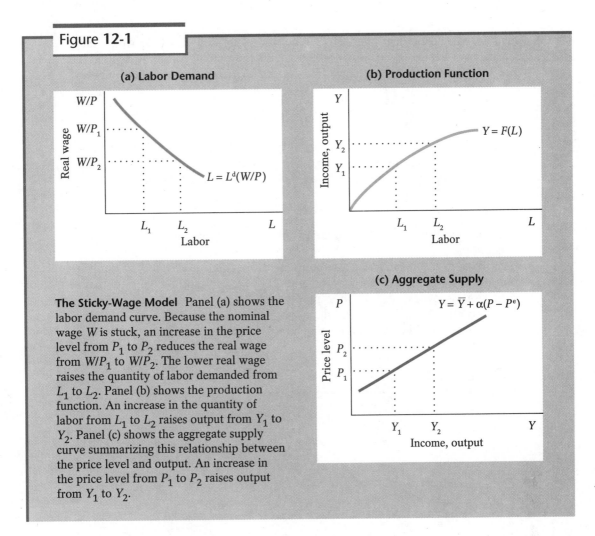

Figure 12-1

(a) Labor Demand

(b) Production Function

(c) Aggregate Supply

The Sticky-Wage Model Panel (a) shows the labor demand curve. Because the nominal wage W is stuck, an increase in the price level from P_1 to P_2 reduces the real wage from W/P_1 to W/P_2. The lower real wage raises the quantity of labor demanded from L_1 to L_2. Panel (b) shows the production function. An increase in the quantity of labor from L_1 to L_2 raises output from Y_1 to Y_2. Panel (c) shows the aggregate supply curve summarizing this relationship between the price level and output. An increase in the price level from P_1 to P_2 raises output from Y_1 to Y_2.

The Worker-Misperception Model

The next model of the short-run aggregate supply curve also focuses on the labor market. Yet, unlike the sticky-wage model, the **worker-misperception model** assumes that wages are free to equilibrate the supply and demand for labor. Its key assumption is that workers temporarily confuse real and nominal wages.

The two components of the worker-misperception model are labor supply and labor demand. As before, the quantity of labor demanded depends on the real wage:

$$L^d = L^d(W/P).$$

The labor supply curve is new:

$$L^s = L^s(W/P^e).$$

This equation states that the quantity of labor supplied depends on the real wage that workers expect. Workers know their nominal wage W, but they do not know the overall price level P. When deciding how much to work, they consider the expected real wage, which equals the nominal wage W divided by their expectation of the price level P^e. We can write the expected real wage as

$$\frac{W}{P^e} = \frac{W}{P} \times \frac{P}{P^e}.$$

The expected real wage is the product of the actual real wage W/P and worker misperception of the level of prices, as measured by P/P^e. To see what determines labor supply, we can substitute this expression for W/P^e and write

$$L^s = L^s(W/P \times P/P^e).$$

The quantity of labor supplied depends on the real wage and on worker misperceptions.

To see what this model says about aggregate supply, consider the equilibrium in the labor market, shown in Figure 12-2. As is usual, the labor demand curve slopes downward, the labor supply curve slopes upward, and the wage adjusts to equilibrate supply and demand. Note that the position of the labor supply curve and thus the equilibrium in the labor market depend on worker misperception P/P^e.

Figure 12-2

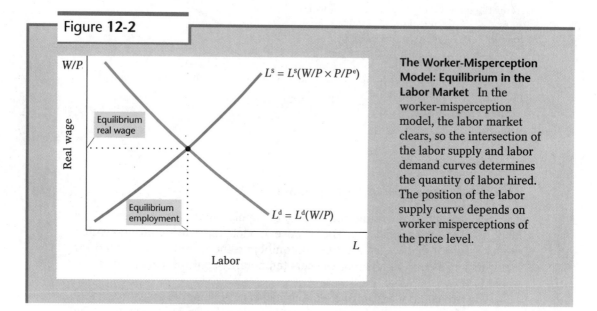

The Worker-Misperception Model: Equilibrium in the Labor Market In the worker-misperception model, the labor market clears, so the intersection of the labor supply and labor demand curves determines the quantity of labor hired. The position of the labor supply curve depends on worker misperceptions of the price level.

When the price level P rises, there are two possible reactions. If workers had anticipated the change, then P^e rises proportionately with P. In this case, neither labor supply nor labor demand changes. The real wage and the level of employment remain the same. The nominal wage rises by the same amount as prices.

By contrast, suppose that the price level rises without workers being aware of it. In this case, P^e remains the same. Then, at every real wage, workers are willing to supply more labor because they believe that their real wage is higher than it actually is. The increase in P/P^e shifts the labor supply curve to the right, as in Figure 12-3. This shift in labor supply lowers the real wage and raises the level of employment. In essence, the increase in the nominal wage caused by the rise in the price level leads workers to think that their real wage is higher, and this misperception induces them to supply more labor. In actuality, the nominal wage rises by less than the price level. Firms are assumed to be better informed than workers and to recognize the fall in the real wage, so they hire more labor and produce more output.

Figure 12-3

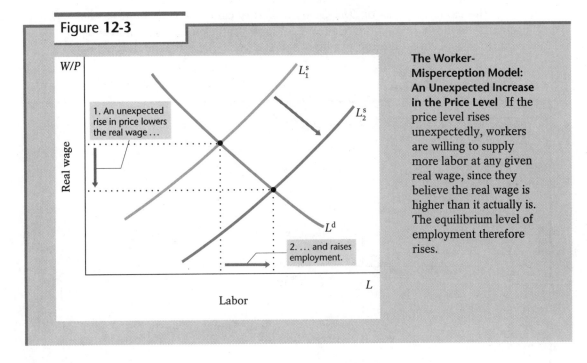

The Worker-Misperception Model: An Unexpected Increase in the Price Level If the price level rises unexpectedly, workers are willing to supply more labor at any given real wage, since they believe the real wage is higher than it actually is. The equilibrium level of employment therefore rises.

To sum up, the worker-misperception model says that deviations of prices from expected prices induce workers to alter their supply of labor. The model implies an aggregate supply curve of the same form as the sticky-wage model:

$$Y = \overline{Y} + \alpha(P - P^e).$$

Output deviates from the natural rate when the price level deviates from the expected price level.[2]

[2] The worker-misperception model as presented here comes from the classic article by Milton Friedman, "The Role of Monetary Policy," *American Economic Review* 58 (March 1968): 1–17.

Case Study *12-1*

• • • • • • • • • • • • •

The Cyclical Behavior of the Real Wage

In any model with an unchanging labor demand curve, such as the two models we just discussed, employment rises when the real wage falls. In the sticky-wage and worker-misperception models, an unexpected rise in the price level lowers the real wage and thereby raises the quantity of labor hired and the amount of output produced. The real wage should be *countercyclical*: it should fluctuate in the opposite direction from employment and output. Keynes himself wrote in *The General Theory* that "an increase in employment can only occur to the accompaniment of a decline in the rate of real wages."

The earliest attacks on *The General Theory* came from economists challenging Keynes's prediction. Figure 12-4 is a scatterplot of the percentage change in real compensation per hour and the percentage change in real GDP

Figure 12-4

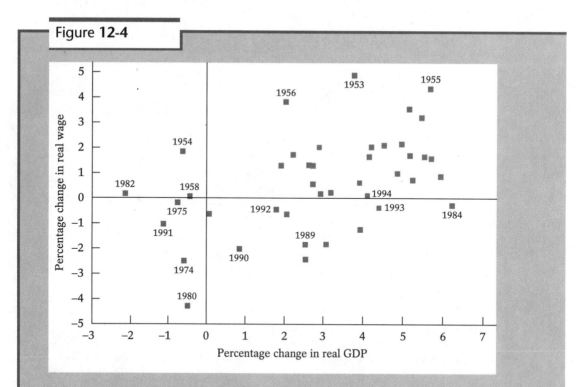

The Cyclical Behavior of the Real Wage
This scatterplot shows the percentage change in real GDP and the percentage change in the real wage (real compensation per hour). As output fluctuates, the real wage typically moves in the same direction. That is, the real wage is somewhat procyclical. This observation is inconsistent with the sticky-wage and worker-misperception models.

Source: U.S. Department of Commerce and U.S. Department of Labor.

using annual data for the U.S. economy. If Keynes's prediction were correct, this figure would show a negative relationship. Yet it shows only a weak correlation between the real wage and output. If the real wage is cyclical at all, it is slightly *procyclical*: the real wage tends to rise when output rises. Thus, abnormally high labor costs cannot explain the low employment and output observed in recessions.

How should we interpret this evidence? Most economists conclude that the sticky-wage and worker-misperception models cannot, by themselves, fully explain aggregate supply. They advocate models in which the labor demand curve shifts over the business cycle. These shifts may arise because firms have sticky prices and cannot sell all they want at those prices; we discuss this possibility below. Alternatively, the labor demand curve may shift because of shocks to technology, which alter labor productivity. The theory we discuss in Chapter 14, called the theory of real business cycles, gives a prominent role to technology shocks as a source of economic fluctuations.[3]

The Imperfect-Information Model

The third model of aggregate supply, the **imperfect-information model**, also assumes that markets clear and that the short-run and long-run aggregate supply curves differ because of short-run misperceptions about prices. But unlike the worker-misperception model, it does not assume that firms are better informed than their workers. In its simplest form, the model does not distinguish between workers and firms at all.

The imperfect-information model assumes that each supplier in the economy produces a single good and consumes many goods. Because the number of goods is so large, suppliers cannot observe all prices at all times. They monitor closely the prices of what they produce but less closely the prices of all the goods that they consume. Because of imperfect information, they sometimes confuse changes in the overall level of prices with changes in relative prices. This confusion influences decisions about how much to supply, and it leads to a short-run relationship between the price level and output.

Consider the decision facing a single supplier—a wheat farmer, for instance. Because the farmer earns income from selling wheat and uses this income to buy goods and services, the amount of wheat she chooses to produce depends on the price of wheat relative to the prices of other goods and services in the economy. If the relative price of wheat is high, the farmer is motivated to work hard and produce more wheat, because the reward is great. If the relative price of wheat is low, she prefers to enjoy more leisure and produce less wheat.

Unfortunately, when the farmer makes her production decision, she does not know the relative price of wheat. As a wheat producer, she monitors the

---

[3] For some of the recent work on this topic, see Mark J. Bils, "Real Wages over the Business Cycle: Evidence from Panel Data," *Journal of Political Economy* 93 (1985): 666–689; Scott Sumner and Stephen Silver, "Real Wages, Employment, and the Phillips Curve," *Journal of Political Economy* 97 (June 1989): 706–720; and Gary Solon, Robert Barsky, and Jonathan A. Parker, "Measuring the Cyclicality of Real Wages: How Important is Composition Bias?" *Quarterly Journal of Economics* 109 (February 1994): 1–25.

wheat market closely and always knows the nominal price of wheat. But she does not know the prices of all the other goods in the economy. She must, therefore, estimate the relative price of wheat using the nominal price of wheat and her expectation of the overall price level.

Consider how the farmer responds if all prices in the economy, including the price of wheat, increase. One possibility is that she expected this change in prices. When she observes an increase in the price of wheat, her estimate of its relative price is unchanged. She does not work any harder.

The other possibility is that the farmer did not expect the price level to increase (or to increase by this much). When she observes the increase in the price of wheat, she is not sure whether other prices have risen (in which case wheat's relative price is unchanged) or whether only the price of wheat has risen (in which case its relative price is higher). The rational inference is that some of each has happened. In other words, the farmer infers from the increase in the nominal price of wheat that its relative price has risen somewhat. She works harder and produces more.

Our wheat farmer is not unique. When the price level rises unexpectedly, all suppliers in the economy observe increases in the prices of the goods they produce. They all infer, rationally but mistakenly, that the relative prices of the goods they produce have risen. They work harder and produce more.

To sum up, the imperfect-information model says that when prices exceed expected prices, suppliers raise their output. The model implies an aggregate supply curve that is now familiar:

$$Y = \overline{Y} + \alpha(P - P^e).$$

Output deviates from the natural rate when the price level deviates from the expected price level.[4]

The Sticky-Price Model

Our fourth and final model of aggregate supply, the **sticky-price model**, emphasizes that firms do not instantly adjust the prices they charge in response to changes in demand. Sometimes prices are set by long-term contracts between firms and customers. Even without formal agreements, firms may hold prices steady in order not to annoy their regular customers with frequent price changes. Some prices are sticky because of the way markets are structured: once a firm has printed and distributed its catalog or price list, it is costly to alter prices.

To see how sticky prices can help explain aggregate supply, we must first consider the pricing decisions of individual firms. We can then add together the decisions of many firms to obtain the aggregate supply curve.

Consider the decision facing a single firm that has some monopoly control over the price it charges. The firm's desired price p depends on two macroeconomic variables:

[4] To read more on the imperfect-information model, see Robert E. Lucas, Jr., "Understanding Business Cycles," *Stabilization of the Domestic and International Economy*, vol. 5 of Carnegie-Rochester Conference on Public Policy (Amsterdam: North-Holland Publishing Company, 1977); reprinted in Robert E. Lucas, Jr., *Studies in Business Cycle Theory* (Cambridge, Mass.: MIT Press, 1981).

- The overall level of prices P. A higher price level implies that the firm's costs are higher. Hence, the higher the overall price level, the more the firm would like to charge for its product.

- The level of aggregate income Y. A higher level of income raises the demand for the firm's product. Because marginal cost increases at higher levels of production, the greater the demand, the higher the firm's desired price.

We write the firm's desired price as

$$p = P + a(Y - \overline{Y}),$$

where a is a parameter greater than zero. This equation says that the desired price p depends on the overall level of prices P and on the level of aggregate output relative to the natural rate $Y - \overline{Y}$.[5]

Now assume that there are two types of firms. Some have flexible prices: they always set their prices according to this equation. Others have sticky prices: they announce their prices in advance based on what they expect economic conditions to be. Firms with sticky prices set prices according to

$$p = P^e + a(Y^e - \overline{Y}^e),$$

where, as before, a superscript "e" represents the expected value of a variable. For simplicity, assume that these firms expect output to be at its natural rate, so that the last term, $a(Y^e - \overline{Y}^e)$, is zero. Then these firms set the price

$$p = P^e.$$

That is, firms with sticky prices set their prices based on what they expect other firms to charge.

We can use the pricing rules of the two groups of firms to derive the aggregate supply equation. To do this, we find the overall price level in the economy, which is the weighted average of the prices set by the two groups. If s is the fraction of firms with sticky prices and $1 - s$ the fraction with flexible prices, then the overall price level is

$$P = sP^e + (1 - s)[P + a(Y - \overline{Y})].$$

The first term is the price of the sticky-price firms weighted by their fraction in the economy, and the second term is the price of the flexible-price firms weighted by their fraction. Now subtract $(1 - s)P$ from both sides of this equation to obtain

$$sP = sP^e + (1 - s)[a(Y - \overline{Y})].$$

Divide both sides by s to solve for the overall price level:

$$P = P^e + [(1 - s)a/s](Y - \overline{Y}).$$

[5] *Mathematical note:* The firm cares most about its relative price, which is the ratio of its nominal price to the overall price level. If we interpret p and P as the logarithms of the firm's price and the price level, then this equation states that the desired relative price depends on the deviation of output from the natural rate.

The two terms in this equation are explained as follows:

- When firms expect a high price level, they expect high costs. Those firms that fix prices in advance set their prices high. These high prices cause the other firms to set high prices also. Hence, a high expected price level leads to a high actual price level.

- When output is high, the demand for goods is high. Those firms with flexible prices set their prices high, which leads to a high price level. The effect of output on the price level depends on the proportion of firms with flexible prices.

Hence, the overall price level depends on the expected price level and on the level of output.

Algebraic rearrangement puts this aggregate pricing equation into a more familiar form:

$$Y = \overline{Y} + \alpha(P - P^e),$$

where $\alpha = s/[(1 - s)a]$. Like the other models, the sticky-price model says that the deviation of output from the natural rate is associated with the deviation of the price level from the expected price level.

Although the sticky-price model emphasizes the goods market, consider briefly what is happening in the labor market. If a firm's price is stuck in the short run, then a reduction in aggregate demand reduces the amount that the firm is able to sell. The firm responds to the drop in sales by reducing its production and its demand for labor. Note the contrast to the sticky-wage and worker-misperception models. The firm here does not move along a fixed labor demand curve. Instead, fluctuations in output are associated with shifts in the labor demand curve. Because of these shifts in labor demand, employment, production, and the real wage can all move in the same direction. Thus, the real wage can be procyclical.[6]

Case Study *12-2*

• • • • • • • • • • • •

International Differences in the Aggregate Supply Curve

Although all countries experience economic fluctuations, these fluctuations are not exactly the same everywhere. International differences are intriguing puzzles in themselves, and they often provide a way to test alternative economic theories. Examining international differences has been especially fruitful in research on aggregate supply.

When economist Robert Lucas proposed the imperfect-information model, he noted that the slope of the aggregate supply curve should depend on

---

[6] For a more advanced development of the sticky-price model, see Julio Rotemberg, "Monopolistic Price Adjustment and Aggregate Output," *Review of Economic Studies* 49 (1982): 517–531; or Laurence Ball, N. Gregory Mankiw, and David Romer, "The New Keynesian Economics and the Output-Inflation Tradeoff," *Brookings Papers on Economic Activity* (1988:1): 1–65.

the variability of aggregate demand. In countries where aggregate demand fluctuates widely, the aggregate price level fluctuates widely as well. Because most movements in prices in these countries do not represent movements in relative prices, suppliers should have learned not to respond much to unexpected changes in the price level. Therefore, the aggregate supply curve should be relatively steep (that is, α will be small). Conversely, in countries where aggregate demand is relatively stable, suppliers should have learned that most price changes are relative price changes. Accordingly, in these countries, suppliers should be more responsive to unexpected price changes, making the aggregate supply curve relatively flat (that is, α will be large).

Lucas tested this prediction by examining international data on output and prices. He found that changes in aggregate demand have the biggest effect on output in those countries where aggregate demand and prices are most stable. Lucas concluded that the evidence supports the imperfect-information model.[7]

The sticky-price model also makes predictions about the slope of the short-run aggregate supply curve. In particular, it predicts that the average rate of inflation should influence the slope of the short-run aggregate supply curve. When the average rate of inflation is high, it is very costly for firms to keep prices fixed for long intervals. Thus, firms adjust prices more frequently. More frequent price adjustment in turn allows the overall price level to respond more quickly to shocks to aggregate demand. Hence, a high rate of inflation should make the short-run aggregate supply curve steeper.

International data support this prediction of the sticky-price model. In countries with low average inflation, the short-run aggregate supply curve is relatively flat: fluctuations in aggregate demand have large effects on output and are slowly reflected in prices. High-inflation countries have steep short-run aggregate supply curves. In other words, high inflation appears to erode the frictions that cause prices to be sticky.[8]

Note that the sticky-price model can also explain Lucas's finding that countries with variable aggregate demand have steep aggregate supply curves. If the price level is highly variable, few firms will commit to prices in advance (s will be small). Hence, the aggregate supply curve will be steep (α will be small).

● ● ● ● ● ● ● ● ● ● ● ● ● ●

Summary and Implications

Figure 12-5 lists the four models of aggregate supply and the market imperfection that each uses to explain why the short-run aggregate supply curve is not vertical. The figure divides the models according to two characteristics. The

---

[7] Robert E. Lucas, Jr., "Some International Evidence on Output-Inflation Tradeoffs," *American Economic Review* 63 (June 1973): 326–334; reprinted in Robert E. Lucas, Jr., *Studies in Business Cycle Theory* (Cambridge, Mass.: MIT Press, 1981).

[8] Laurence Ball, N. Gregory Mankiw, and David Romer, "The New Keynesian Economics and the Output-Inflation Tradeoff," *Brookings Papers on Economic Activity* (1988:1): 1–65.

Figure 12-5

Market With Imperfection

	Labor	Goods
Yes	**Worker-Misperception Model:** Workers confuse nominal wage changes with real wage changes.	**Imperfect-Information Model:** Suppliers confuse changes in the price level with changes in relative prices.
No	**Sticky-Wage Model:** Nominal wages adjust slowly.	**Sticky-Price Model:** The prices of goods and services adjust slowly.

Markets Clear?

Comparison of Models of Aggregate Supply The four models of aggregate supply differ in two characteristics: whether they assume that markets clear and whether the key market imperfection lies in the goods market or in the labor market.

first is whether the model assumes that markets clear—that is, whether wages and prices are free to equilibrate supply and demand. The second is whether the model emphasizes the labor or the goods market as the source of the market imperfection.

Keep in mind that these models of aggregate supply are not necessarily incompatible with one another. We need not accept one model and reject the others. The world may contain all four of these market imperfections, and all may contribute to the behavior of short-run aggregate supply.

Although the four models of aggregate supply differ in their assumptions and emphases, their implications for the economy are similar. All can be summarized by the equation

$$Y = \overline{Y} + \alpha(P - P^e).$$

This equation, plotted in Figure 12-6, relates deviations of output from the natural rate to deviations of the price level from the expected price level. *If the price level is higher than the expected price level, output exceeds its natural rate. If the price level is lower than the expected price level, output falls short of its natural rate.*

Figure 12-7 uses this aggregate supply equation to show how the economy responds to an unexpected increase in aggregate demand. In the short run, the equilibrium moves from point A to point B. The increase in aggregate demand raises the price level above the expected price level and raises output above the natural rate. In the long run, the expected price level rises, so the short-run aggregate supply curve shifts upward. As the expected price level rises, the equilibrium of the economy moves from point B to point C. The economy returns to the natural level of output, but with an even higher price level.

Figure 12-6

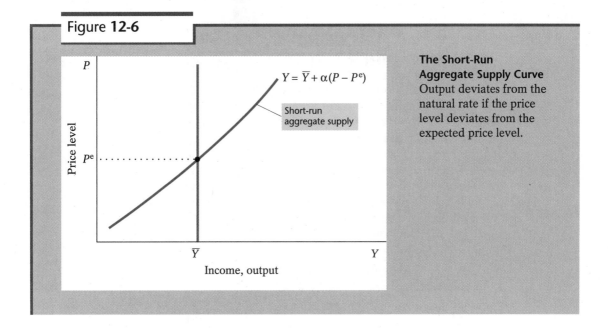

The Short-Run Aggregate Supply Curve Output deviates from the natural rate if the price level deviates from the expected price level.

Figure 12-7

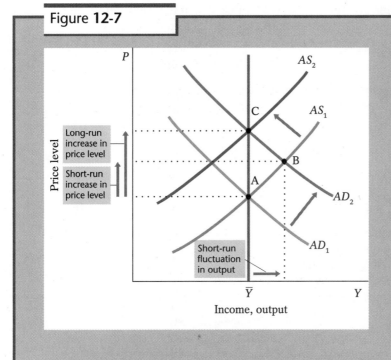

A Shift in Aggregate Demand When aggregate demand increases unexpectedly, the price level rises above the expected price level and output rises above the natural rate, moving the economy along the short-run aggregate supply curve from point A to point B. In the long run, the expected price level rises, the short-run aggregate supply curve shifts upward, and output returns to the natural rate at point C. In this way, shifts in the aggregate demand curve lead to fluctuations in output only in the short run.

12-2 Inflation, Unemployment, and the Phillips Curve

Two goals of economic policymakers are low inflation and low unemployment. Here we examine a relationship between inflation and unemployment called the **Phillips curve**. The Phillips curve is merely another way to express aggregate supply. The short-run aggregate supply curve shows a positive relationship between the price level and output. Since inflation is the rate of change in the price level, and since unemployment fluctuates inversely with output, a negative relationship between inflation and unemployment lies behind the aggregate supply curve. The Phillips curve expresses this negative relationship.

The Phillips curve posits that the inflation rate—the percentage change in the price level—depends on three forces:

- Expected inflation
- The deviation of unemployment from the natural rate, called *cyclical unemployment*
- Supply shocks, denoted here as ε.

These three forces are expressed in the following equation:

$$\pi \quad = \quad \pi^e \quad - \quad \beta(u - u^n) \quad + \quad \varepsilon$$

$$\text{Inflation} = \frac{\text{Expected}}{\text{Inflation}} - \left(\beta \times \frac{\text{Cyclical}}{\text{Unemployment}}\right) + \frac{\text{Supply}}{\text{Shock}}$$

where β is a parameter greater than zero. Notice the minus sign before the cyclical unemployment term: high unemployment tends to reduce inflation.

From Aggregate Supply to the Phillips Curve

To see that the Phillips curve and the aggregate supply curve express essentially the same relationship, write the aggregate supply equation as

$$P = P^e + (1/\alpha)(Y - \overline{Y}).$$

With one subtraction, one substitution, and one addition, we can derive the Phillips curve.

First, subtract last year's price level P_{-1} from both sides of the equation to obtain

$$(P - P_{-1}) = (P^e - P_{-1}) + (1/\alpha)(Y - \overline{Y}).$$

The term on the left-hand side, $P - P_{-1}$, is the difference between the current price level and last year's price level, which is inflation π.[9] The term on the right-hand side, $P^e - P_{-1}$, is the difference between the expected price level and last year's price level, which is expected inflation π^e. Therefore, we can replace $P - P_{-1}$ with π and $P^e - P_{-1}$ with π^e:

$$\pi = \pi^e + (1/\alpha)(Y - \overline{Y}).$$

[9] *Mathematical note:* This statement is not precise, because inflation is really the percentage change in the price level. To make the statement more precise, interpret P as the logarithm of the price level. By the properties of logarithms, the change in P is roughly the inflation rate. The reason is that $dP = d(\log \text{ price level}) = d(\text{price level})/\text{price level}$.

The History of the Modern Phillips Curve

The Phillips curve is named after British economist A. W. Phillips. In 1958 Phillips observed a negative relationship between the unemployment rate and the rate of wage inflation.[10] The Phillips curve that economists use today differs in three ways from the relationship Phillips examined.

First, the modern Phillips curve substitutes price inflation for wage inflation. This difference is not crucial, because price inflation and wage inflation are closely related. In periods when wages are rising quickly, prices are rising quickly as well.

Second, the modern Phillips curve includes expected inflation. This addition is due to the work of Milton Friedman and Edmund Phelps. In developing the worker-misperception model in the 1960s, these two economists emphasized the importance of expectations for aggregate supply.

Third, the modern Phillips curve includes supply shocks. Credit for this addition goes to OPEC, the Organization of Petroleum Exporting Countries. In the 1970s OPEC caused large increases in the world price of oil, which made economists more aware of the importance of shocks to aggregate supply.

Next, recall from Chapter 2 that Okun's law gives a relationship between output and unemployment. One version of Okun's law states that the deviation of output from its natural rate is inversely related to the deviation of unemployment from its natural rate; that is, when output is higher than the natural rate of output, unemployment is lower than the natural rate of unemployment. Using this relationship, we can substitute $-\beta(u - u^n)$ for $(1/\alpha)(Y - \bar{Y})$. The equation becomes

$$\pi = \pi^e - \beta(u - u^n).$$

Finally, add a supply shock ε to represent exogenous influences on prices, such as a change in oil prices, a change in the minimum wage, or the imposition of government controls on prices:

$$\pi = \pi^e - \beta(u - u^n) + \varepsilon.$$

Thus, we obtain the Phillips curve from the aggregate supply equation.

Now step back from this algebra. Notice that the Phillips curve retains the key feature of the short-run aggregate supply curve: a link between real and nominal variables that causes the classical dichotomy to fail. More precisely, the Phillips curve demonstrates the connection between real economic activity and unexpected changes in the price level. *The Phillips curve is merely a convenient way to express and analyze aggregate supply.*

[10]   A. W. Phillips, "The Relationship between Unemployment and the Rate of Change of Money Wages in the United Kingdom, 1861–1957," *Economica* 25 (November 1958): 283–299.

Expectations and Inflation Inertia

To make the Phillips curve useful for analyzing the choices facing policymakers, we need to say what determines expected inflation. A simple and often plausible assumption is that people form their expectations of inflation based on recently observed inflation. This assumption is called **adaptive expectations**. For example, suppose that people expect prices to rise this year at the same rate as they did last year. Then

$$\pi^e = \pi_{-1}.$$

In this case, we can write the Phillips curve as

$$\pi = \pi_{-1} - \beta(u - u^n) + \varepsilon,$$

which states that inflation depends on past inflation, cyclical unemployment, and a supply shock.

The first term in this form of the Phillips curve, π_{-1}, implies that inflation is inertial. If unemployment is at its natural rate and if there are no supply shocks, prices will continue to rise at the prevailing rate of inflation. This inertia arises because past inflation influences expectations of future inflation and because these expectations influence the wages and prices that people set. Robert Solow captured the concept of inflation inertia well when, during the high inflation of the 1970s, he wrote, "Why is our money ever less valuable? Perhaps it is simply that we have inflation because we expect inflation, and we expect inflation because we've had it."

In the model of aggregate supply and aggregate demand, inflation inertia is interpreted as persistent upward shifts in both the aggregate supply curve and the aggregate demand curve. Consider first aggregate supply. If prices have been rising quickly, people will expect them to continue to rise quickly. Because the position of the short-run aggregate supply curve depends on the expected price level, the short-run aggregate supply curve will shift upward over time. It will continue to shift upward until some event, such as a recession or a supply shock, changes inflation and thereby changes expectations of inflation.

The aggregate demand curve must also be shifting upward in order to confirm the expectations of inflation. Most often, the continued rise in aggregate demand is due to persistent growth in the money supply. If the Fed suddenly halted money growth, aggregate demand would stabilize, and the upward shift in aggregate supply would cause a recession. The high unemployment in the recession would reduce inflation and expected inflation, causing inflation inertia to subside.

The Two Causes of Rising and Falling Inflation

The second and third terms in the Phillips curve show the two forces that can change the rate of inflation.

The second term, $\beta(u - u^n)$, shows that cyclical unemployment—the deviation of unemployment from its natural rate—exerts upward or downward pressure on inflation. Low unemployment pulls the inflation rate up. This is called **demand-pull inflation** because high aggregate demand is responsible for this type of inflation. High unemployment pulls the inflation rate down. The parameter β measures how responsive inflation is to cyclical unemployment.

The third term, ε, shows that inflation also rises and falls because of supply shocks. An adverse supply shock, such as the rise in world oil prices in the 1970s, implies a positive value of ε and causes inflation to rise. This is called **cost-push inflation** because adverse supply shocks are typically events that push up the costs of production. A beneficial supply shock, such as the oil glut that led to a fall in oil prices in the 1980s, makes ε negative and causes inflation to fall.

Case Study *12-3*

• • • • • • • • • • • • •

Inflation and Unemployment in the United States

Because inflation and unemployment are such important measures of economic performance, macroeconomic developments are often viewed through the lens of the Phillips curve. Figure 12-8 displays the history of inflation and unemployment in the United States since 1961. In it we can trace the rises and falls in inflation over the past three decades.

Figure **12-8**

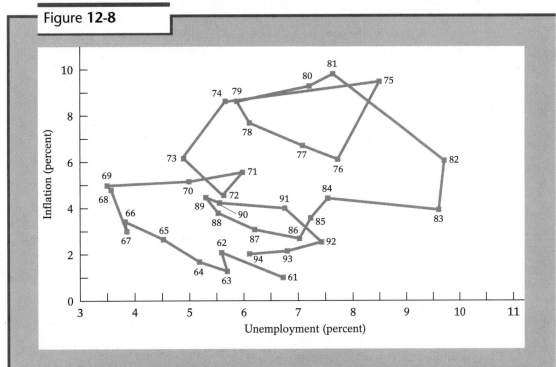

Inflation and Unemployment in the United States Since 1961 This figure uses annual data on the unemployment rate and the inflation rate (percentage change in the GDP deflator) to illustrate macroeconomic developments over the past three decades.

In the 1960s, expansionary policy lowered unemployment and raised inflation. The tax cut in 1964, together with expansionary monetary policy, pushed the unemployment rate below 5 percent. The continuing expansion of the economy in the late 1960s was a by-product of government spending for the Vietnam War. Unemployment fell lower and inflation rose higher than policymakers intended.

The 1970s were a period of economic turmoil. The decade began with policymakers trying to lower the inflation inherited from the 1960s. Temporary controls on wages and prices and a demand-induced recession reduced the inflation rate only slightly. The effects of wage and price controls ended when the controls were lifted, and the recession was too small to counteract the inflationary impact of the boom that had preceded it. By 1972 the unemployment rate was the same as a decade earlier, while inflation was 3 percentage points higher.

Beginning in 1973 policymakers had to cope with the large supply shocks caused by the Organization of Petroleum Exporting Countries (OPEC). OPEC first raised oil prices in the mid-1970s, pushing the inflation rate up to about 10 percent. A recession in 1975 reduced inflation somewhat, but further OPEC price hikes pushed inflation up again in the late 1970s.

The 1980s began with high inflation and high expectations of inflation. Under the leadership of Chairman Paul Volcker, the Federal Reserve doggedly pursued monetary policies aimed at reducing inflation. In 1982 and 1983 the unemployment rate reached its highest level in 40 years. High unemployment, aided by a fall in oil prices in 1986, pulled the inflation rate down from about 10 percent to about 3 percent. By 1987 the unemployment rate of about 6 percent was close to most estimates of the natural rate. Unemployment continued to fall, however, reaching a low of 5.2 percent in 1989 and beginning a new round of demand-pull inflation.

The decade of the 1990s began with a recession, which was caused by several contractionary shocks to aggregate demand. (See Case Study 13-1.) The unemployment rate rose to 7.3 percent in 1992. Inflation fell, but only slightly. Unlike in the previous recession, unemployment in the 1990 recession was never far above the natural rate, so the effect on inflation was small.

Thus, recent macroeconomic history exhibits the many causes of inflation. The 1960s and the 1980s show the two sides of demand-pull inflation: in the 1960s low unemployment pulled inflation up, and in the 1980s high unemployment pulled inflation down. The 1970s show the effects of cost-push inflation.

•   •   •   •   •   •   •   •   •   •   •   •   •   •

The Short-Run Tradeoff Between Inflation and Unemployment

Consider the options the Phillips curve gives to a policymaker who can influence aggregate demand with monetary or fiscal policy. At any moment, expected inflation and supply shocks are beyond the policymaker's immediate control. Yet, by changing aggregate demand, the policymaker can alter output, unemployment, and inflation. The policymaker can expand aggregate demand to lower unemployment and raise inflation. Or the policymaker can depress aggregate demand to raise unemployment and lower inflation.

Figure 12-9 plots the Phillips-curve equation and shows the short-run tradeoff between inflation and unemployment. The policymaker can manipulate aggregate demand to choose a combination of inflation and unemployment on this curve, called the *short-run Phillips curve*.

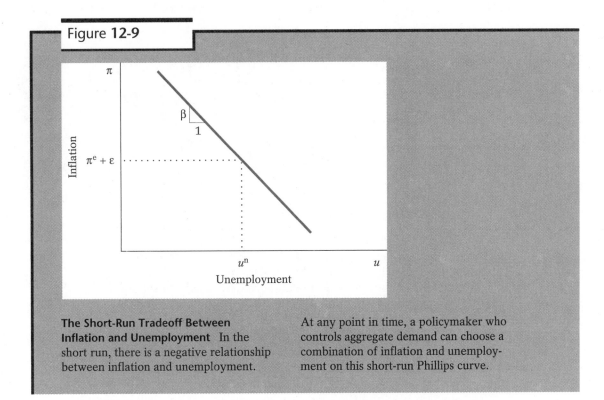

Figure 12-9

The Short-Run Tradeoff Between Inflation and Unemployment In the short run, there is a negative relationship between inflation and unemployment.

At any point in time, a policymaker who controls aggregate demand can choose a combination of inflation and unemployment on this short-run Phillips curve.

Notice that the short-run Phillips curve depends on expected inflation. If expected inflation rises, the curve shifts upward, and the policymaker's tradeoff becomes less favorable: inflation is higher for any level of unemployment. Figure 12-10 shows how the tradeoff depends on expected inflation.

Because people adjust their expectations of inflation over time, this tradeoff between inflation and unemployment holds only in the short run. The policymaker cannot keep inflation above expected inflation forever. Eventually, expectations adapt to whatever inflation rate the policymaker chooses. In the long run, the classical dichotomy holds, unemployment returns to its natural rate, and there is no tradeoff between inflation and unemployment.

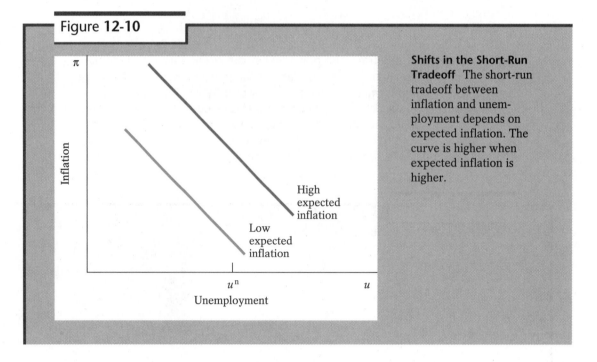

Figure 12-10

Shifts in the Short-Run Tradeoff The short-run tradeoff between inflation and unemployment depends on expected inflation. The curve is higher when expected inflation is higher.

Disinflation and the Sacrifice Ratio

Imagine an economy in which unemployment is at its natural rate and inflation is running at 6 percent. What would happen to unemployment and output if the central bank pursued a policy to reduce inflation from 6 to 2 percent?

The Phillips curve shows that in the absence of a beneficial supply shock, lowering inflation requires a period of high unemployment and reduced output. But by how much and for how long would unemployment need to rise above the natural rate? Before deciding whether to reduce inflation, policymakers must know how much output would be lost during the transition to lower inflation. This cost can then be compared with the benefits of lower inflation.

Much research has used the available data to examine the Phillips curve quantitatively. The results of these studies are often summarized in a number called the **sacrifice ratio**, the percentage of a year's real GDP that must be forgone to reduce inflation by 1 percentage point. Although estimates of the sacrifice ratio vary substantially, a typical estimate is about 5: for every percentage point that inflation is to fall, 5 percent of one year's GDP must be sacrificed.[11]

We can also express the sacrifice ratio in terms of unemployment. Okun's law says that a change of 1 percentage point in the unemployment rate translates into a change of 2 percentage points in GDP. So reducing inflation by 1 percentage point requires about 2.5 percentage points of cyclical unemployment.

[11] Arthur M. Okun, "Efficient Disinflationary Policies," *American Economic Review* 68 (May 1978): 348–352; Robert J. Gordon and Stephen R. King, "The Output Cost of Disinflation in Traditional and Vector Autoregressive Models," *Brookings Papers on Economic Activity* (1982:1): 205–245.

We can use the sacrifice ratio to estimate by how much and for how long unemployment must rise to reduce inflation. If reducing inflation by 1 percentage point requires a sacrifice of 5 percent of a year's GDP, reducing inflation by 4 percentage points requires a sacrifice of 20 percent of a year's GDP. Equivalently, this reduction in inflation requires a sacrifice of 10 percentage points of cyclical unemployment.

This disinflation could take various forms, each totaling the same sacrifice of 20 percent of a year's GDP. For example, a rapid disinflation would lower output by 10 percent for 2 years: this is sometimes called the *cold turkey* solution to inflation. A moderate disinflation would lower output by 5 percent for 4 years. An even more gradual disinflation would depress output by 2 percent for a decade.

Rational Expectations and Painless Disinflation

Because the expectation of inflation influences the short-run tradeoff between inflation and unemployment, a crucial question is, how do people form expectations? So far, we have been assuming that expected inflation depends on recently observed inflation. Although this assumption of adaptive expectations is plausible, it is probably too simple to be applicable in all circumstances.

An alternative approach is to assume that people have **rational expectations**. That is, we might assume that people optimally use all the available information, including information about current policies, to forecast the future. Because monetary and fiscal policies influence inflation, expected inflation should also depend on the monetary and fiscal policies in effect. According to the theory of rational expectations, a change in monetary or fiscal policy will change expectations, and an evaluation of any policy change must incorporate this effect on expectations. If people do form their expectations rationally, then inflation may be less inertial than it first appears.

Here is how Thomas Sargent, a prominent advocate of rational expectations, describes its implications for the Phillips curve:

> An alternative "rational expectations" view denies that there is any inherent momentum to the present process of inflation. This view maintains that firms and workers have now come to expect high rates of inflation in the future and that they strike inflationary bargains in light of these expectations. However, it is held that people expect high rates of inflation in the future precisely because the government's current and prospective monetary and fiscal policies warrant those expectations. . . . Thus inflation only seems to have a momentum of its own; it is actually the long-term government policy of persistently running large deficits and creating money at high rates which imparts the momentum to the inflation rate. An implication of this view is that inflation can be stopped much more quickly than advocates of the "momentum" view have indicated and that their estimates of the length of time and the costs of stopping inflation in terms of foregone output are erroneous. . . . [Stopping inflation] would require a change in the policy regime: there must be an abrupt change in the continuing government policy, or strategy, for setting deficits now and in the future that is sufficiently binding as to be widely believed. . . . How costly such a

move would be in terms of foregone output and how long it would be in taking effect would depend partly on how resolute and evident the government's commitment was.[12]

Thus, advocates of rational expectations argue that the short-run Phillips curve does not accurately represent the options available. They believe that if policymakers are credibly committed to reducing inflation, rational people will understand the commitment and quickly lower their expectations of inflation. According to the theory of rational expectations, traditional estimates of the sacrifice ratio are not useful for evaluating the impact of alternative policies. Under a credible policy, the costs of reducing inflation may be much lower than estimates of the sacrifice ratio suggest.

In the most extreme case, one can imagine reducing the rate of inflation without causing any recession at all. A painless disinflation has two requirements. First, the plan to reduce inflation must be announced before the workers and firms who set wages and prices have formed their expectations. Second, the workers and firms must believe the announcement; otherwise, they will not reduce their expectations of inflation. If both requirements are met, the announcement will immediately shift the short-run tradeoff between inflation and unemployment downward, permitting a lower rate of inflation without higher unemployment.

Although the rational-expectations approach remains controversial, almost all economists agree that expectations of inflation influence the short-run tradeoff between inflation and unemployment. The credibility of a policy to reduce inflation is therefore one determinant of how costly the policy will be. Unfortunately, it is often difficult to predict whether the public will view the announcement of a new policy as credible. The central role of expectations makes forecasting the results of alternative policies far more difficult.

Case Study *12-4*

● ● ● ● ● ● ● ● ● ● ● ● ●

The Sacrifice Ratio in Practice

The Phillips curve with adaptive expectations implies that reducing inflation requires a period of high unemployment and low output. By contrast, the rational-expectations approach suggests that reducing inflation can be much less costly. What happens during actual disinflations?

Consider the U.S. disinflation in the early 1980s. This decade began with some of the highest rates of inflation in U.S. history. Yet because of the tight monetary policies the Fed pursued under Chairman Paul Volcker, the rate of inflation fell substantially in the first few years of the decade. This episode provides a natural experiment with which to estimate how much output is lost during the process of disinflation.

---

[12] Thomas J. Sargent, "The Ends of Four Big Inflations," in Robert E. Hall, ed., *Inflation: Causes and Effects* (Chicago: University of Chicago Press, 1982).

The first question is, how much did inflation fall? As measured by the GDP deflator, inflation reached a peak of 9.7 percent in 1981. It is natural to end the episode in 1985 because oil prices plunged in 1986—a large, beneficial supply shock unrelated to Fed policy. In 1985, inflation was 3.0 percent, so we can estimate that the Fed engineered a reduction in inflation of 6.7 percentage points over four years.

The second question is, how much output was lost during this period? Table 12-1 shows the unemployment rate from 1982 to 1985. Assuming that the natural rate of unemployment was 6 percent, we can compute the amount of cyclical unemployment in each year. In total over this period, there were 9.5 percentage points of cyclical unemployment. Okun's law says that 1 percentage point of unemployment translates into 2 percentage points of GDP. Therefore, 19.0 percentage points of annual GDP were lost during the disinflation.

Table 12-1

Unemployment During the Volcker Disinflation

Year	Unemployment Rate	Natural Rate	Cyclical Unemployment
1982	9.5%	6.0%	3.5%
1983	9.5	6.0	3.5
1984	7.4	6.0	1.4
1985	7.1	6.0	1.1
			Total 9.5%

Now we can compute the sacrifice ratio for this episode. We know that 19.0 percentage points of GDP were lost and that inflation fell by 6.7 percentage points. Hence, 19.0/6.7, or 2.8, percentage points of GDP were lost for each percentage-point reduction in inflation. The estimate of the sacrifice ratio from the Volcker disinflation is 2.8.

This estimate of the sacrifice ratio is smaller than the estimates made before Volcker was appointed Fed chairman. In other words, Volcker reduced inflation at a smaller cost than many economists had predicted. One explanation is that Volcker's tough stand was credible enough to influence expectations of inflation directly. Yet the change in expectations was not large enough to make the disinflation painless: in 1982 unemployment reached its highest level since the Great Depression.

Although the Volcker disinflation is only one historical episode, this kind of analysis can be applied to other disinflations. A recent study documented the results of 65 disinflations in 19 countries. In almost all cases, the reduction in inflation came at the cost of temporarily lower output. Yet the size of the output loss varied from episode to episode. Rapid disinflations usually had smaller sacrifice ratios than slower ones. That is, in contrast to what the Phillips curve with adaptive expectations suggests, a cold turkey approach appears less costly than a gradual one. Moreover, countries with more flexible wage-setting institutions, such as shorter labor contracts, had smaller sacrifice ratios. These findings indicate that reducing inflation always has some cost, but that policies and institutions can affect its magnitude.[13]

• • • • • • • • • • • • • •

Hysteresis and the Challenge to the Natural-Rate Hypothesis

Our discussion of economic fluctuations in Chapters 8 through 12 has been based on an assumption called the **natural-rate hypothesis**, summarized in the following statement.

> *Fluctuations in aggregate demand affect output and employment only in the short run. In the long run, the economy returns to the levels of output, employment, and unemployment described by the classical model.*

The natural-rate hypothesis allows macroeconomists to study separately short-run and long-run developments in the economy.

Recently, some economists have challenged the natural-rate hypothesis by suggesting that aggregate demand may affect output and employment even in the long run. They have pointed out a number of mechanisms through which recessions might leave permanent scars on the economy by altering the natural rate of unemployment. **Hysteresis** is the term used to describe the long-lasting influence of history on the natural rate.

A recession can have permanent effects if it changes the people who become unemployed. For instance, workers might lose valuable job skills when unemployed, lowering their ability to find a job even after the recession ends. Alternatively, a long period of unemployment may change an individual's attitude toward work and reduce the desire to find employment. In either case, the recession permanently inhibits the process of job search and raises the amount of frictional unemployment.

Another way in which a recession can permanently affect the economy is by changing the process that determines wages. Those who become unemployed may lose their influence on the wage-setting process. Unemployed workers may lose their status as union members, for example. More generally, some of the *insiders* in the wage-setting process become *outsiders*. If the smaller group of insiders cares more about high real wages and less about high employment, then the recession may permanently push real wages further above the equilibrium level and raise the amount of wait unemployment.

Hysteresis remains a controversial topic. It is still not clear whether this phenomenon is significant, or why it might be more pronounced in some countries than in others. Yet the topic is important, because hysteresis greatly increases the cost of recessions. Put another way, hysteresis raises the sacrifice ratio, because output is lost even after the period of disinflation is over.

---

[13]   Laurence Ball, "What Determines the Sacrifice Ratio?" in *Monetary Policy*, edited by N. Gregory Mankiw (Chicago: University of Chicago Press, 1994).

Case Study *12-5*

• • • • • • • • • • • •

Unemployment in the United Kingdom in the 1980s

Doubts about the natural-rate hypothesis and interest in hysteresis arose largely in response to the experience in the 1980s of several European countries, especially the United Kingdom. In the 1970s U.K. unemployment averaged 3.4 percent, whereas in the 1980s it averaged 9.4 percent. This rise in unemployment presented a problem for policymakers and a puzzle for economists.

The rise in unemployment was caused in large part by the policies designed by the Thatcher government to reduce inflation. When the Conservative party won control and Margaret Thatcher became prime minister in 1979, inflation was running almost 18 percent per year. Contractionary monetary and fiscal policies caused the rate of unemployment to rise from 4.3 percent in 1979 to 11.1 percent in 1984. As the Phillips curve predicts, the rise in unemployment lowered inflation to less than 5 percent in 1984.

The puzzle is that unemployment remained high even after inflation had stabilized. Because this high unemployment did not lower inflation further, it appeared that the natural rate of unemployment had risen. Theories of hysteresis provide reasons why the recession might have raised the natural rate of unemployment.[14]

• • • • • • • • • • • •

12-3   Conclusion

In this chapter we discussed four models of aggregate supply and the resulting tradeoff between inflation and unemployment. We saw that the four models have similar predictions for the aggregate economy. We also saw that the Phillips curve, according to which inflation depends on expected inflation, cyclical unemployment, and supply shocks, provides a convenient way to express and analyze aggregate supply.

Keep in mind that not all economists endorse all the ideas discussed here. There is widespread disagreement, for instance, about the practical importance of rational expectations and the relevance of hysteresis. If you find it difficult to fit all the pieces together, you are not alone. The study of aggregate supply remains one of the most unsettled—and therefore one of the most exciting—research areas in macroeconomics.

---

[14]   Olivier J. Blanchard and Lawrence H. Summers, "Beyond the Natural Rate Hypothesis," *American Economic Review* 78 (May 1988): 182–187.

Summary

1. The four theories of aggregate supply—the sticky-wage, worker-misperception, imperfect-information, and sticky-price models—attribute deviations of output and employment from the natural rate to various market imperfections. According to all four theories, output rises above the natural rate when the price level exceeds the expected price level, and output falls below the natural rate when the price level is less than the expected price level.

2. Economists often express aggregate supply in a relationship called the Phillips curve. The Phillips curve says that inflation depends on expected inflation, the deviation of unemployment from its natural rate, and supply shocks. According to the Phillips curve, policymakers who control aggregate demand face a short-run tradeoff between inflation and unemployment.

3. If expected inflation depends on recently observed inflation, then inflation has inertia, which means that reducing inflation requires either a beneficial supply shock or a period of high unemployment and reduced output. If people have rational expectations, however, then a credible announcement of a change in policy might be able to influence expectations directly and, therefore, reduce inflation without causing a recession.

4. Most economists accept the natural-rate hypothesis, according to which fluctuations in aggregate demand have only short-run effects on output and unemployment. Some economists, however, have suggested ways in which recessions can leave permanent scars on the economy by raising the natural rate of unemployment.

KEY CONCEPTS

Sticky-wage model

Worker-misperception model

Imperfect-information model

Sticky-price model

Phillips curve

Adaptive expectations

Demand-pull inflation

Cost-push inflation

Sacrifice ratio

Rational expectations

Natural-rate hypothesis

Hysteresis

QUESTIONS FOR REVIEW

1. Explain the four theories of aggregate supply. On what market imperfection does each theory rely? What do the theories have in common?

2. How is the Phillips curve related to aggregate supply?

3. Why might inflation be inertial?

4. Explain the differences between demand-pull inflation and cost-push inflation.

5. Under what circumstances might it be possible to reduce inflation without causing a recession?

6. Explain two ways in which a recession might raise the natural rate of unemployment.

PROBLEMS AND APPLICATIONS

1. Consider the following changes in the sticky-wage model.

   a. Suppose that labor contracts specify that the nominal wage be fully indexed for inflation. That is, the nominal wage is to be adjusted to fully compensate for changes in the consumer price index. How does full indexation alter the aggregate supply curve in this model?

   b. Suppose now that indexation is only partial. That is, for every increase in the CPI, the nominal wage rises, but by a smaller percentage. How does partial indexation alter the aggregate supply curve in this model?

2. In the sticky-price model, describe the aggregate supply curve in the following special cases. How do these cases compare to the short-run aggregate supply curve we discussed in Chapter 8?

   a. No firms have flexible prices ($s = 1$).

   b. The desired price does not depend on aggregate output ($a = 0$).

3. Suppose that an economy has the Phillips curve

$$\pi = \pi_{-1} - 0.5(u - 0.06).$$

   a. What is the natural rate of unemployment?

   b. Graph the short-run and long-run relationships between inflation and unemployment.

   c. How much cyclical unemployment is necessary to reduce inflation by 5 percentage points? Using Okun's law, compute the sacrifice ratio.

   d. Inflation is running at 10 percent. The Fed wants to reduce it to 5 percent. Give two scenarios that will achieve that goal.

4. According to the rational-expectations approach, if everyone believes that policymakers are committed to reducing inflation, the cost of reducing inflation—the sacrifice ratio—will be lower than if the public is skeptical about the policymakers' intentions. Why might this be true? How might credibility be achieved?

5. Assume that people have rational expectations and that the economy is described by the sticky-wage or sticky-price model. Explain why each of the following propositions is true:

   a. Only unanticipated changes in the money supply affect real GDP. Changes in the money supply that were anticipated when wages and prices were set do not have any real effects.

   b. If the Fed chooses the money supply at the same time as people are setting wages and prices, so that everyone has the same information about the state of the economy, then monetary policy cannot be used systematically to stabilize output. Hence, a policy of keeping the money supply constant will have the same real effects as a policy of adjusting the money supply in response to the state of the economy. (This is called the *policy irrelevance proposition*.)

c. If the Fed sets the money supply well after people have set wages and prices, so the Fed has collected more information about the state of the economy, then monetary policy can be used systematically to stabilize output.

6. Suppose that an economy has the Phillips curve

$$\pi = \pi_{-1} - 0.5(u - u^n)$$

and that the natural rate of unemployment is given by an average of the past two years' unemployment:

$$u^n = 0.5(u_{-1} + u_{-2}).$$

a. Why might the natural rate of unemployment depend on recent unemployment (as is assumed in the above equation)?

b. Suppose that the Fed follows a policy to reduce permanently the inflation rate by 1 percentage point. What effect will that policy have on the unemployment rate over time?

c. What is the sacrifice ratio in this economy? Explain.

d. What do these equations imply about the short-run and long-run tradeoffs between inflation and unemployment?

7. Some economists believe that taxes have an important effect on labor supply.

They argue that higher taxes cause people to want to work less and that lower taxes cause them to want to work more. Consider how this effect alters the macroeconomic analysis of tax changes.

a. If this view is correct, how does a tax cut affect the natural rate of output?

b. How does a tax cut affect the aggregate demand curve? The long-run aggregate supply curve? The short-run aggregate supply curve?

c. What is the short-run impact of a tax cut on output and the price level? How does your answer differ from the case without the labor-supply effect?

d. What is the long-run impact of a tax cut on output and the price level? How does your answer differ from the case without the labor-supply effect?

8. Economist Alan Blinder, whom Bill Clinton appointed to be Vice Chairman of the Federal Reserve, once wrote the following:

The costs that attend the low and moderate inflation rates experienced in the United States and in other industrial countries appear to be quite modest—more like a bad cold than a cancer on society. . . . As rational individuals, we do not volunteer for a lobotomy to cure a head cold. Yet, as a collectivity, we routinely prescribe the economic equivalent of lobotomy (high unemployment) as a cure for the inflationary cold.[15]

What do you think Blinder meant by this? What are the policy implications of the viewpoint Blinder is advocating? Do you agree? Why or why not?

[15] Alan Blinder, *Hard Heads, Soft Hearts: Tough-Minded Economics for a Just Society* (Reading, Mass.: Addison-Wesley, 1987): 51.

Chapter 13

The Macroeconomic Policy Debate

The Federal Reserve's job is to take away the punch bowl just as the party gets going.

William McChesney Martin

What we need is not a skilled monetary driver of the economic vehicle continuously turning the steering wheel to adjust to the unexpected irregularities of the route, but some means of keeping the monetary passenger who is in the back seat as ballast from occasionally leaning over and giving the steering wheel a jerk that threatens to send the car off the road.

Milton Friedman

Economists argue most vehemently during discussions of economic policy. The two quotations above—the first from a former chairman of the Federal Reserve, the second from a prominent critic of the Fed—exemplify the diversity of opinion over how macroeconomic policy should be conducted.

Some economists, such as William McChesney Martin, view the economy as inherently unstable. They argue that the economy experiences frequent shocks to aggregate demand and aggregate supply. Unless policymakers use monetary and fiscal policy to stabilize the economy, these shocks will lead to unnecessary and inefficient fluctuations in output, unemployment, and inflation. According to the popular saying, macroeconomic policy should "lean against the wind," stimulating the economy when it is depressed and slowing the economy when it is overheated.

Other economists, such as Milton Friedman, view the economy as naturally stable. They blame bad economic policies for the large and inefficient fluctuations we have sometimes experienced. They argue that economic policy should not try to "fine-tune" the economy. Instead, economic policymakers should admit their limited abilities and be satisfied if they do no harm.

This debate has persisted for decades with numerous protagonists advancing various arguments for their positions. The fundamental issue is how policymakers should use the theory of economic fluctuations developed in the last five chapters. In this chapter we ask two questions that arise in this debate. First, should monetary and fiscal policy take an active role in trying to stabilize the economy, or should policy remain passive? Second, should policymakers be free to use their discretion in responding to changing economic conditions, or should they be committed to following a fixed policy rule?

13-1   Should Policy Be Active or Passive?

Policymakers in the federal government view economic stabilization as one of their primary responsibilities. The analysis of macroeconomic policy is a regular duty of the Council of Economic Advisers, the Congressional Budget Office, the Federal Reserve, and other government agencies. When Congress or the president is considering a major change in fiscal policy, or when the Federal Reserve is considering a major change in monetary policy, foremost in the discussion are whether the change will influence inflation and unemployment and whether aggregate demand needs to be stimulated or depressed.

Although the government has long conducted monetary and fiscal policy, the view that it should try to stabilize the economy is more recent. The Employment Act of 1946 was a key piece of legislation in which the government held itself accountable for macroeconomic performance. The act states that "it is the continuing policy and responsibility of the Federal Government to . . . promote full employment and production." This law was written when the memory of the Great Depression was still fresh. The lawmakers who wrote it believed, as many economists do, that in the absence of an active government role in the economy, events like the Great Depression could occur regularly.

To many economists the case for active government policy is clear and simple. Recessions are periods of high unemployment, low incomes, and reduced economic well-being. The model of aggregate demand and aggregate supply shows how shocks to the economy cause recessions. It also shows how monetary and fiscal policy can prevent recessions by responding to these shocks. These economists consider it wasteful not to use these policy instruments to stabilize the economy.

Other economists are critical of the government's attempts to stabilize the economy. They argue that the government should take a hands-off approach to macroeconomic policy. At first, this view might seem surprising. If our model shows how to prevent or reduce the severity of recessions, why do these critics want the government to refrain from using monetary and fiscal policy for economic stabilization? To find out, let's consider some of their arguments.

Lags in the Implementation and Effects of Policies

Economic stabilization would be easy if the effects of policy were immediate. Making policy would be like driving a car: policymakers would simply adjust their instruments to keep the economy on the desired path. Driving comes naturally to most people because a car changes direction almost immediately after the steering wheel is turned.

Making economic policy, however, is more similar to steering a large ship than to driving a car. Steering a ship is difficult because a ship changes course long after the pilot adjusts the rudder. And once the ship starts to turn, it continues long after the rudder is returned to normal. A novice is likely to oversteer and, after noticing the mistake, overreact by steering too much in the opposite direction. The result could be unstable, as the novice responds to previous mistakes by making larger and larger corrections.

Like a ship's pilot, economic policymakers face the problem of long lags. Indeed, the problem for policymakers is even more difficult, because the lengths of the lags are hard to predict. These long and variable lags greatly complicate the conduct of monetary and fiscal policy.

Economists distinguish between two lags in the conduct of stabilization policy: the inside lag and the outside lag. The **inside lag** is the time between a shock to the economy and the policy action responding to that shock. This lag arises because it takes time for policymakers first to recognize that a shock has occurred and then to put appropriate policies into effect. The **outside lag** is the time between a policy action and its influence on the economy. This lag arises because policies do not immediately influence spending, income, and employment.

Fiscal policy has a long inside lag. In the United States, changes in spending or taxes require the approval of the president and both houses of Congress. The legislative process is often slow and cumbersome. For example, the 1964 tax cut, which was designed to stimulate the economy, was first proposed by President Kennedy in 1962. These delays make fiscal policy an imprecise tool for stabilizing the economy.

Monetary policy has a long outside lag. Monetary policy works through interest rates, which in turn influence investment. But many firms make investment plans far in advance. Therefore, a change in monetary policy is thought not to affect economic activity until about six months after it is made.

The long and variable lags associated with monetary and fiscal policy certainly make stabilizing the economy more difficult. Advocates of passive policy argue that, because of these lags, successful stabilization policy is almost impossible. Indeed, attempts to stabilize the economy are all too often destabilizing. Suppose that the economy's condition changes between the time when a policy action begins and the time when the policy affects the economy. In this case, active policy may end up stimulating the economy when it is overheated or depressing the economy when it is cooling off. Advocates of active policy admit that such lags do require policymakers to be cautious. But, they argue, these lags do not necessarily mean that policy should be completely passive, especially in the face of a severe and protracted economic downturn.

Some policies, called **automatic stabilizers**, are designed to reduce the lags associated with stabilization policy. Automatic stabilizers are policies that stimulate or depress the economy when necessary without any deliberate policy change. For example, the system of income taxes automatically reduces taxes when the economy goes into a recession, without any change in the tax laws, because individuals and corporations pay less tax when their incomes fall. Similarly, the unemployment-insurance system and the welfare program automatically raise transfer payments when the economy moves into a recession, because more people apply for benefits. One can view these automatic stabilizers as fiscal policy without any inside lag.

Case Study *13-1*

● ● ● ● ● ● ● ● ● ● ● ● ● ●

The 1990 Recession

When President Clinton took office in 1993, the United States was recovering from a recent recession. The downturn in economic activity began in the middle of 1990. Unemployment rose from 5.1 percent in June 1990 to 7.7 percent in June 1992. Although not severe by historical standards, the recession was a cause of much concern among policymakers. High unemployment lingered throughout 1992, and the state of the economy became a central issue in the presidential campaign.

What caused this recession? It appears that there is no single culprit, but there is a group of likely suspects.

One early cause of the recession was a contractionary shift in the *LM* curve due to monetary policy. The low unemployment rate in the late 1980s was, by most estimates, below the natural rate, and inflation appeared to be heating up. This caused the Fed to slow the rate of money growth. Short-term interest rates rose from 6 percent in the middle of 1988 to almost 9 percent a year later.

Shortly after the Fed's tightening, two shocks to the *IS* curve appear to have contributed to the downturn. First, for various reasons (including inadequate previous regulation), many financial institutions such as the savings and loans found themselves at or near the point of bankruptcy. This made bankers and bank regulators more cautious in approving loans. The resulting "credit crunch" forced some firms to forgo investment projects, thereby reducing the demand for investment goods. Second, when Iraq invaded Kuwait in the summer of 1990, consumer confidence fell. The uncertainty caused by the Gulf War may have induced consumers to delay spending until the uncertainty was resolved.

Could the recession have been avoided? In retrospect, it is clear that a more expansionary monetary policy would have helped. The Fed did lower interest rates, but only gradually as the recession unfolded. Short-term interest rates fell to about 3 percent in 1992. Yet, at the same time, growth in some measures of the money supply was quite low. One interpretation of these events is that the Fed was unaware of the magnitude of the *IS* shocks. When the Fed saw falling interest rates, it might have misinterpreted this as evidence of expansionary shifts in the *LM* curve rather than contractionary shifts in the *IS* curve. Because data on income are available only after a lag, and because income responds to monetary policy with a lag, the Fed would have learned of its mistake after it was too late to prevent the recession.

The 1990 recession shows some of the difficulties in short-run stabiliza-

What's in the Index of Leading Economic Indicators?

Each month the Bureau of Economic Analysis, which is part of the U.S. Department of Commerce, announces the *index of leading economic indicators*. This index is made up from eleven data series that are often used to forecast changes in economic activity about six to nine months ahead. Here is a list of the eleven series. Can you explain why each of these might help predict changes in real GDP?

1. Average workweek of production workers in manufacturing.

2. Average initial weekly claims for state unemployment insurance. This series is inverted in computing the index, so that a decrease in the series raises the index.

3. New orders for consumer goods and materials, adjusted for inflation.

4. Vendor performance. This is a measure of the number of companies receiving slower deliveries from suppliers.

5. Contracts and orders for plant and equipment, adjusted for inflation.

6. New building permits issued.

7. Change in manufacturers' unfilled orders.

8. Change in sensitive materials prices.

9. Index of stock prices.

10. Money supply (*M2*), adjusted for inflation.

11. Index of consumer expectations.

tion policy. There are many sources of shocks to the economy, and the magnitudes of the shocks are not easily observed. Because policymakers can recognize and offset the shocks only after a substantial lag, their ability to stabilize the economy is limited.

● ● ● ● ● ● ● ● ● ● ● ● ●

The Difficult Job of Economic Forecasting

Because policy influences the economy after a substantial lag, successful stabilization policy requires the ability to predict accurately future economic conditions. If we cannot predict whether the economy will be in a boom or a recession in six months or a year, we cannot evaluate whether monetary and fiscal policy should now be trying to expand or contract aggregate demand. Unfortunately, economic developments are often unpredictable, at least given our current understanding of the economy.

One way forecasters try to look ahead is with **leading indicators**. A leading indicator is a data series that usually fluctuates in advance of the economy. A large fall in a leading indicator signals that a recession is more likely.

Another way forecasters look ahead is with models of the economy. Both government agencies and private forecasting firms maintain large-scale computer models. These models are made up of many equations, each representing a part of the economy. After making assumptions about the path of the exogenous variables, such as monetary policy, fiscal policy, and oil prices, these models yield predictions about unemployment, inflation, and other endogenous variables. Keep in mind, however, that the validity of these predictions is only as good as the model and the assumptions about the exogenous variables.

"It's true, Caesar. Rome is declining, but I expect it to pick up in the next quarter."

Case Study *13-2*

• • • • • • • • • • • • • •

Two Episodes in Economic Forecasting

Economic forecasting is a crucial input to private and public decisionmaking. Business executives rely on forecasts when deciding how much to produce and how much to invest in plant and equipment. Government policymakers also rely on them when developing economic policies.

How accurate is economic forecasting? We can answer this question by looking at how well forecasters have done in the past.

The most severe economic downturn in U.S. history, the Great Depression of the 1930s, caught economic forecasters by surprise. Even after the stock market crash of 1929, they remained confident that the economy would not suffer a substantial setback. In late 1931, when the economy was clearly in bad shape, the eminent economist Irving Fisher predicted that it would recover quickly. Subsequent events showed that these forecasts were much too optimistic.[1]

Figure 13-1 shows how economic forecasters did during the recession of 1982, the most severe economic downturn in the United States since the Great Depression. This figure shows the actual unemployment rate (in blue) and six attempts to predict it for the following five quarters (in red). You can see that the forecasters did well predicting unemployment one quarter ahead. The more distant forecasts, however, were often inaccurate. For example, in the second quarter of 1981, forecasters were predicting little change in the unemployment rate over the next five quarters; yet only two quarters later, unemployment began to rise sharply. The rise in unemployment to almost 11 percent in the fourth quarter of 1982 caught the forecasters by surprise. After the

[1] Kathryn M. Dominguez, Ray C. Fair, and Matthew D. Shapiro, "Forecasting the Depression: Harvard versus Yale," *American Economic Review* 78 (September 1988): 595–612. This article shows how badly economic forecasters did during the Great Depression, and it argues that they could not have done any better with the modern forecasting techniques available today.

Figure 13-1

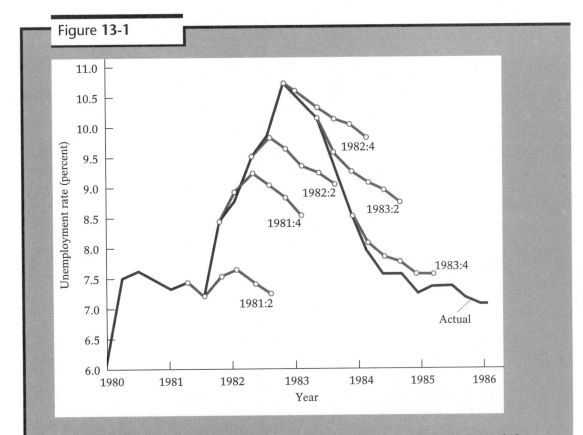

Forecasting the Recession of 1982 The blue line shows the actual unemployment rate from the first quarter of 1980 to the first quarter of 1986. The red lines show the unemployment rate predicted at six points in time: the second quarter of 1981, the fourth quarter of 1981, the second quarter of 1982, and so on. For each forecast, the symbols mark the current unemployment rate and the forecast for the subsequent five quarters. Notice that the forecasters missed both the rapid rise in the unemployment rate and the subsequent rapid decline.

Source: The unemployment rate is from the U.S. Department of Labor. The predicted unemployment rate is the median forecast of about 20 forecasters surveyed by the American Statistical Association and the National Bureau of Economic Research.

depth of the recession became apparent, the forecasters failed to predict how rapid the subsequent decline in unemployment would be.

These two episodes—the Great Depression and the recession of 1982— show that many of the most dramatic economic events are unpredictable. Although private and public decisionmakers have little choice but to rely on economic forecasts, they must always keep in mind that these forecasts come with a large margin of error.

Ignorance, Expectations, and the Lucas Critique

The prominent economist Robert Lucas once wrote, "As an advice-giving profession we are in way over our heads." Even many of those who advise policymakers would agree with this assessment. Economics is a young science, and there is still much that we do not know. Economists cannot be completely confident when they assess the effects of alternative policies. This ignorance suggests that economists should be cautious when offering policy advice.

Although there are many topics about which economists' knowledge is limited, Lucas has emphasized the issue of how people form expectations of the future. Expectations play a crucial role in the economy because they influence the behavior of consumers, investors, and other economic actors. People's expectations depend on many things, including the economic policies being pursued by the government. Thus, estimating the effect of a policy change requires knowing how people's expectations will respond to the policy change. Lucas has argued that traditional methods of policy evaluation do not adequately take into account this impact of policy on expectations. This criticism of traditional policy evaluation is known as the **Lucas critique**.[2]

We saw one example of the Lucas critique in Chapter 12 when we discussed the role of rational expectations in the cost of reducing inflation. Traditional estimates of the sacrifice ratio—the number of percentage points of GDP that must be forgone to reduce inflation by 1 percentage point—rely on the assumption of adaptive expectations. That is, they assume that expected inflation depends on past inflation. Advocates of the rational-expectations approach claim that reducing inflation can be much less costly because expectations will respond to a credible change in policy. In other words, they claim that traditional estimates of the sacrifice ratio are unreliable because they are subject to the Lucas critique.

The Historical Record

In judging whether government policy should play an active or passive role in the economy, we must consider the historical record. If the economy has experienced many large shocks to aggregate supply and aggregate demand, and if policy has successfully insulated the economy from these shocks, then the case for active policy should be clear. Conversely, if the economy has experienced few large shocks, and if the fluctuations we have observed can be traced to inept economic policy, then the case for passive policy should be clear. Thus, our view of stabilization policy should be influenced by whether policy has historically been stabilizing or destabilizing. For this reason, the debate over macroeconomic policy often turns into a debate over macroeconomic history.

Yet history does not settle the debate over stabilization policy. Disagreements over history arise because it is not easy to identify the sources of economic fluctuations. The historical record often permits more than one interpretation.

The Great Depression is a case in point. Economists' views on macroeco-

---

[2]　Robert E. Lucas, Jr., "Econometric Policy Evaluation: A Critique," *Carnegie Rochester Conference on Public Policy* 1 (Amsterdam: North-Holland Publishing Company, 1976), 19–46; reprinted in Robert E. Lucas, Jr., *Studies in Business Cycle Theory* (Cambridge, Mass.: MIT Press, 1981).

nomic policy are often related to their views on the cause of the Depression. Some economists believe that a large contractionary shock to private spending caused the Depression. They assert that policymakers should have responded by stimulating aggregate demand. Other economists believe that the large fall in the money supply caused the Depression. They assert that the Depression would have been avoided if the Fed had been pursuing a passive monetary policy of increasing the money supply at a steady rate. Hence, depending on one's beliefs about its cause, the Great Depression can be viewed either as an example of why active monetary and fiscal policy is necessary or as an example of why it is dangerous.

Case Study *13-3*

● ● ● ● ● ● ● ● ● ● ● ● ●

Is the Stabilization of the Economy a Figment of the Data?

Keynes wrote *The General Theory* in the 1930s, and in the wake of the Keynesian revolution, governments around the world began to view economic stabilization as a primary responsibility. Some economists believe that the development of Keynesian theory has had a profound influence on the behavior of the economy. Comparing data from before World War I and after World War II, they find that real GDP and unemployment have become much more stable. This, some Keynesians claim, is the best argument for active stabilization policy: it has worked.

In a series of provocative and influential papers, Christina Romer has challenged this assessment of the historical record. She argues that the measured reduction in volatility reflects not an improvement in economic policy and performance but rather an improvement in the economic data. The older data are much less accurate than the newer data. Romer claims that the higher volatility of unemployment and real GDP reported for the period before World War I is largely a figment of the data.

Romer uses various techniques to make her case. One is to construct more accurate data for the earlier period. This task is difficult because data sources are not readily available. A second way is to construct *less* accurate data for the recent period—that is, data that are comparable to the older data and thus suffer from the same imperfections. After constructing new "bad" data, Romer finds that the recent period appears much more volatile—indeed, almost as volatile as the early period—suggesting that the volatility of the early period may be largely an artifact of data construction.

Romer's work is an important part of the continuing debate over whether macroeconomic policy has improved the performance of the economy. Although her work remains controversial, most economists now believe that the economy is only slightly more stable than it was in the past.[3]

● ● ● ● ● ● ● ● ● ● ● ● ●

[3]   Christina D. Romer, "Spurious Volatility in Historical Unemployment Data," *Journal of Political Economy* 94 (February 1986): 1–37; Christina D. Romer, "Is the Stabilization of the Postwar Economy a Figment of the Data?" *American Economic Review* 76 (June 1986): 314–334.

13-2   Should Policy Be Conducted by Rule or by Discretion?

A second topic of debate among economists is whether economic policy should be conducted by rule or by discretion. Policy is conducted by rule if policymakers announce in advance how policy will respond to various situations and commit themselves to following through on this announcement. Policy is conducted by discretion if policymakers are free to size up the situation case by case and choose whatever policy seems appropriate at the time.

The debate over rules versus discretion is distinct from the debate over passive versus active policy. Policy can be conducted by rule and yet be either passive or active. For example, a passive policy rule might specify steady growth in the money supply of 3 percent per year. An active policy rule might specify that

$$\text{Money Growth} = 3\% + (\text{Unemployment Rate} - 6\%).$$

Under this rule, the money supply grows at 3 percent if the unemployment rate is 6 percent, but for every percentage point by which the unemployment rate exceeds 6 percent, money growth increases by an extra percentage point. This rule tries to stabilize the economy by raising money growth when the economy is in a recession.

We begin this section by discussing why policy might be improved by a commitment to a fixed policy rule. We then examine several possible policy rules.

Distrust of Policymakers and the Political Process

Some economists believe that economic policy is too important to be left to the discretion of policymakers. Although this view is more political than economic, evaluating it is central to how we judge the role of economic policy. If politicians are incompetent or opportunistic, then we may not want to give them the discretion to use the powerful tools of monetary and fiscal policy.

Incompetence in economic policy arises for several reasons. Some economists view the political process as erratic, perhaps because it reflects the shifting power of special interest groups. In addition, macroeconomics is complicated, and politicians often do not have sufficient knowledge of it to make informed judgments. This ignorance allows charlatans to propose incorrect but superficially appealing solutions to complex problems. The political process often cannot weed out the advice of charlatans from that of competent economists.

Opportunism in economic policy arises when the objectives of policymakers conflict with the well-being of the public. Some economists fear that politicians use macroeconomic policy to further their own electoral ends. If citizens vote on the basis of economic conditions prevailing at the time of the election, then politicians have an incentive to pursue policies that will make the economy look good during election years. A president might cause a recession soon after coming into office in order to lower inflation and then stimulate the economy as the next election approaches to lower unemployment; this would ensure that both inflation and unemployment are low on election day. Manipulation of the economy for electoral gain, called the **political business cycle**, has been the subject of extensive research by economists and political scientists.[4]

Distrust of the political process leads some economists to advocate placing economic policy outside the realm of politics. Some have proposed constitutional amendments, such as a balanced-budget amendment, that would tie the hands of legislators and insulate the economy from both incompetence and opportunism.

Case Study *13-4*

● ● ● ● ● ● ● ● ● ● ● ●

The Economy Under Republican and Democratic Presidents

How does the political party in power affect the economy? Researchers working at the boundary between economics and political science have been studying this question. One intriguing finding is that the two political parties in the United States appear to conduct systematically different macroeconomic policies.

Table 13-1 presents the growth in real GDP in each of the four years of the presidential terms since 1948. Notice that growth is usually low, and often negative, in the second year of Republican administrations. Six of the seven years in which real GDP fell are second or third years of Republican administrations. By contrast, the economy is usually booming in the second and third years of Democratic administrations.

One interpretation of this finding is that the two parties have different preferences regarding inflation and unemployment. That is, rather than viewing politicians as opportunistic, perhaps we should view them as merely partisan. Republicans seem to dislike inflation more than Democrats do. Therefore, Republicans pursue contractionary policies soon after coming into office and are willing to endure a recession in order to reduce inflation. Democrats pursue more expansionary policies to reduce unemployment and are willing to endure the higher inflation that results. Examining growth in the money supply shows that monetary policy is, in fact, less inflationary during Republican administrations. Thus, it seems that the two political parties pursue dramatically different policies, and that the political process is one source of economic fluctuations.

Even if we accept this interpretation of the evidence, it is not clear whether it argues for or against fixed policy rules. On the one hand, a policy rule would insulate the economy from these political shocks. Under a fixed rule, the Fed would be unable to alter monetary policy in response to the changing political climate. The economy might be more stable, and long-run economic performance might be improved. On the other hand, a fixed policy

---

4 William Nordhaus, "The Political Business Cycle," *Review of Economic Studies* 42 (1975): 169–190; Edward Tufte, *Political Control of the Economy* (Princeton, N. J.: Princeton University Press, 1978).

| Table **13-1** | **Real GDP Growth During Democratic and Republican Administrations** | | | |

Democratic Administrations

| President | Year of Term | | | |
	First	Second	Third	Fourth
Truman	0.4	8.7	9.9	4.3
Kennedy/Johnson	2.7	5.2	4.1	5.6
Johnson	5.5	5.9	2.6	4.2
Carter	4.5	4.8	2.5	−0.5
Clinton	3.1	4.0		
Average	3.2	5.7	4.8	3.4

Republican Administrations

| President | Year of Term | | | |
	First	Second	Third	Fourth
Eisenhower I	3.7	−0.7	5.6	2.0
Eisenhower II	1.9	−0.5	5.5	2.2
Nixon	2.7	0.0	2.9	5.1
Nixon/Ford	5.2	−0.6	−0.8	4.9
Reagan I	1.8	−2.2	3.9	6.2
Reagan II	3.2	2.9	3.1	3.9
Bush	2.5	1.2	−0.6	2.3
Average	3.0	0.0	2.8	3.8

Source: Department of Commerce, Bureau of Economic Analysis.

rule would reduce the voice of the electorate in influencing macroeconomic policy.[5]

• • • • • • • • • • • • • •

The Time Inconsistency of Discretionary Policy

If we assume that we can trust our policymakers, discretion at first glance appears superior to a fixed policy rule. Discretionary policy is, by its nature, flexible. As long as policymakers are intelligent and benevolent, there might appear to be little reason to deny them flexibility in responding to changing conditions.

Yet a case for rules over discretion arises from the problem of **time inconsistency** of policy. In some situations policymakers may want to announce in advance the policy they will follow in order to influence the expectations of private decisionmakers. But later, after the private decisionmakers have acted

[5] Alberto Alesina, "Macroeconomics and Politics," *NBER Macroeconomics Annual* 3 (1988): 13–52.

on the basis of their expectations, these policymakers may be tempted to re-nege on their announcement. Understanding that policymakers may be incon-sistent over time, private decisionmakers are led to distrust policy announce-ments. In this situation, to make their announcements credible, policymakers may want to make a commitment to a fixed policy rule.

Time inconsistency is illustrated most simply in a political rather than an economic example—specifically, public policy about negotiating with terrorists over the release of hostages. The announced policy of many nations is that they will not negotiate over hostages. Such an announcement is intended to deter terrorists: if there is nothing to be gained from kidnapping hostages, rational terrorists won't kidnap any. In other words, the purpose of the announcement is to influence the expectations of terrorists and thereby their behavior.

But, in fact, unless the policymakers are credibly committed to the policy, the announcement has little effect. Terrorists know that once hostages are taken, policymakers face an overwhelming temptation to make some conces-sion to obtain the hostages' release. The only way to deter rational terrorists is to take away the discretion of policymakers and commit them to a rule of never negotiating. If policymakers were truly unable to make concessions, the incen-tive for terrorists to take hostages would be largely eliminated.

The same problem arises less dramatically in the conduct of monetary policy. Consider the dilemma of a Federal Reserve that cares about both infla-tion and unemployment. According to the Phillips curve, the tradeoff between inflation and unemployment depends on expected inflation. The Fed would prefer everyone to expect low inflation so that it will face a favorable tradeoff. To reduce expected inflation, the Fed often announces that low inflation is the paramount goal of monetary policy.

But an announcement of a policy of low inflation is by itself not credible. Once households and firms have formed their expectations of inflation and acted on them, the Fed has an incentive to renege on its announcement and im-plement expansionary monetary policy in order to reduce unemployment. People understand the Fed's incentive to renege and therefore do not believe the announcement in the first place. Just as a president facing a hostage crisis is sorely tempted to negotiate their release, a Federal Reserve with discretion is sorely tempted to inflate in order to reduce unemployment. And just as terror-ists discount announced policies of never negotiating, households and firms discount announced policies of low inflation.

The surprising outcome of this analysis is that policymakers can some-times better achieve their goals by having their discretion taken away from them. In the case of rational terrorists, fewer hostages will be taken and killed if policymakers are committed to following the seemingly harsh rule of refus-ing to negotiate for hostages' freedom. In the case of monetary policy, there will be lower inflation without higher unemployment if the Fed is committed to a policy of zero inflation.

The time inconsistency of policy arises in many other contexts. Here are some examples:

- To encourage investment, the government announces that it will not tax income from capital. But after the capital is in place, the government is tempted to renege on its promise because the taxation of existing capital does not distort economic incentives.

- To encourage research, the government announces that it will give a temporary monopoly to companies that discover new drugs. But after a drug has been discovered, the government is tempted to revoke the patent or to regulate the price in order to make the drug more affordable.

- To encourage good behavior, a parent announces that he or she will punish a child whenever the child breaks a rule. But after the child has misbehaved, the parent is tempted to forgive this transgression, because punishment is unpleasant for the parent as well as for the child.

- To encourage you to work hard, your professor announces that this course will end with an exam. But after you have studied and learned all the material, the professor is tempted to cancel the exam so that he or she won't have to grade it.

In each case, rational agents understand the incentive for the policymaker to renege, and this expectation affects their behavior. And in each case, the solution is to take away the policymaker's discretion with a commitment to a fixed policy rule.[6]

Case Study *13-5*

● ● ● ● ● ● ● ● ● ● ● ● ● ● ●

Alexander Hamilton versus Time Inconsistency

Time inconsistency has long been a problem associated with discretionary policy. In fact, it was one of the first problems that confronted Alexander Hamilton when President George Washington appointed him the first U.S. Secretary of the Treasury in 1789.

Hamilton faced the question of how to deal with the debts that the new nation had accumulated as it fought for its independence from Britain. When the revolutionary government incurred the debts, it promised to honor them when the war was over. But after the war, many Americans advocated defaulting on the debt because repaying the creditors would require taxation, which is always costly and unpopular.

Hamilton opposed the time-inconsistent policy of repudiating the debt. He knew that the nation would likely need to borrow again sometime in the future. In his *First Report on the Public Credit*, which he presented to Congress in 1790, he wrote

> If the maintenance of public credit, then, be truly so important, the next inquiry which suggests itself is: By what means is it to be effected? The ready answer to

---

[6] The appendix to this chapter examines more analytically the time-inconsistency problem in monetary policy. For more on time inconsistency, see Finn E. Kydland and Edward C. Prescott, "Rules Rather Than Discretion: The Inconsistency of Optimal Plans," *Journal of Political Economy* 85 (June 1977): 473–492; and Robert J. Barro and David Gordon, "A Positive Theory of Monetary Policy in a Natural Rate Model," *Journal of Political Economy* 91 (August 1983): 589–610.

which question is, by good faith; by a punctual performance of contracts. States, like individuals, who observe their engagements are respected and trusted, while the reverse is the fate of those who pursue an opposite conduct.

Thus, Hamilton proposed that the nation make a commitment to the policy rule of honoring its debts.

The policy rule that Hamilton originally proposed has continued for over two centuries. Today, unlike in Hamilton's time, when Congress debates spending priorities, no one seriously proposes defaulting on the public debt as a way to reduce taxes. In the case of public debt, everyone now agrees that the government should be committed to a fixed policy rule.

● ● ● ● ● ● ● ● ● ● ● ● ●

Rules for Monetary Policy

Even if we are convinced that policy rules are superior to discretion, the debate over macroeconomic policy is not over. If the Fed were to commit to a rule for monetary policy, what rule should it choose? Let's discuss briefly three policy rules that various economists advocate.

Some economists, called **monetarists**, advocate that the Fed keep the money supply growing at a steady rate. The quotation at the beginning of this chapter from Milton Friedman—the most famous monetarist—exemplifies this view of monetary policy. Monetarists believe that fluctuations in the money supply are responsible for most large fluctuations in the economy. They argue that slow and steady growth in the money supply would yield stable output, employment, and prices.

Although a monetarist policy rule might have prevented many of the economic fluctuations we have experienced historically, most economists believe that it is not the best possible policy rule. Steady growth in the money supply stabilizes aggregate demand only if the velocity of money is stable. But the large fall in velocity in the early 1980s, which we discussed in Chapter 8, shows that velocity is sometimes unstable. Most economists believe that a policy rule needs to allow the money supply to adjust to various shocks to the economy.

A second policy rule that economists widely advocate is a nominal GDP target. Under this rule, the Fed announces a planned path for nominal GDP. If nominal GDP rises above the target, the Fed reduces money growth to dampen aggregate demand. If it falls below the target, the Fed raises money growth to stimulate aggregate demand. Since a nominal GDP target allows monetary policy to adjust to changes in the velocity of money, most economists believe it would lead to greater stability in output and prices than a monetarist policy rule.

A third policy rule that is often advocated is a target for the price level. Under this rule, the Fed announces a planned path for the price level and adjusts the money supply when the actual price level deviates from the target. Proponents of this rule usually believe that price stability should be the primary goal of monetary policy.

Notice that all these rules are expressed in terms of some nominal variable—the money supply, nominal GDP, or the price level. One can also imagine policy rules expressed in terms of real variables. For example, the Fed might try to target the unemployment rate at 5 percent. The problem with such a rule is that no one knows exactly what the natural rate of unemployment is. If the Fed chose a target for the unemployment rate below the natural rate, the result would be accelerating inflation. Conversely, if the Fed chose a target for the unemployment rate above the natural rate, the result would be accelerating deflation. For this reason, economists rarely advocate rules for monetary policy expressed solely in terms of real variables, even though real variables such as unemployment and real GDP are the best measures of economic performance.

Case Study *13-6*

• • • • • • • • • • • • • •

Central-Bank Independence

Suppose you were put in charge of writing the constitution and laws for a country. Would you give the president of the country authority over the policies of the central bank? Or would you allow the central bank to make decisions free from such political influence? In other words, assuming that monetary policy is made by discretion rather than by rule, who should exercise that discretion?

Countries vary greatly in how they choose to answer this question. In some countries, the central bank is one branch of the government; in other countries, the central bank is largely independent. In the United States, Fed governors are appointed for 14-year terms, and they cannot be recalled if the president is unhappy with their decisions. This institutional structure gives the Fed a degree of independence similar to that of the Supreme Court.

Many researchers have investigated the effects of constitutional design on monetary policy. They have examined the laws of different countries to construct an index of central-bank independence. This index is based on various characteristics, such as the length of term, the role of government officials on the bank board, and the frequency of contact between the government and the central bank. The researchers have then examined the correlation between central-bank independence and macroeconomic performance.

The results of these studies are striking: more independent central banks are strongly associated with lower and more stable inflation. Figure 13-2 shows a scatterplot of central-bank independence and average inflation. Countries with an independent central bank, such as Germany, Switzerland, and the United States, tend to have low average inflation. Countries whose central banks are not independent, such as New Zealand and Spain, tend to have higher average inflation.

Researchers have also found there is no relationship between central-bank independence and real economic activity. In particular, central-bank independence is not correlated with average unemployment, the volatility of unemployment, the average growth of real GDP, or the volatility of real GDP.

Figure 13-2

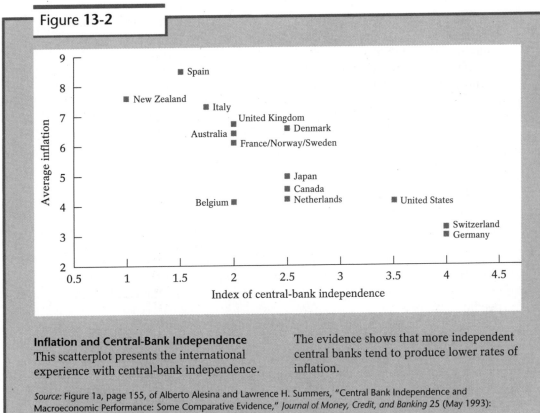

Inflation and Central-Bank Independence
This scatterplot presents the international experience with central-bank independence.

The evidence shows that more independent central banks tend to produce lower rates of inflation.

Source: Figure 1a, page 155, of Alberto Alesina and Lawrence H. Summers, "Central Bank Independence and Macroeconomic Performance: Some Comparative Evidence," *Journal of Money, Credit, and Banking* 25 (May 1993): 151–162. Average inflation is for the period 1955–1988.

Central-bank independence appears to offer countries a free lunch: it has the benefit of lower inflation without any apparent cost. This finding has led some countries, such as New Zealand, to rewrite their laws in order to give their central banks greater independence.[7]

Rules for Fiscal Policy

Although most discussion of policy rules centers on monetary policy, economists and politicians also frequently propose rules for fiscal policy. The rule that has received the most attention is the balanced-budget rule. Under a balanced-budget rule, the government would not be allowed to spend more than it receives in tax revenue. In the United States, many state governments operate under such a fiscal policy rule, since state constitutions often require a balanced budget. A recurring topic of political debate is whether the federal constitution should require a balanced budget for the federal government.

[7] For a more complete presentation of these findings and references to the large literature on central-bank independence, see Alberto Alesina and Lawrence H. Summers, "Central Bank Independence and Macroeconomic Performance: Some Comparative Evidence," *Journal of Money, Credit, and Banking* 25 (May 1993): 151–162.

Most economists oppose a strict rule requiring the government to balance its budget. There are three reasons to believe that a budget deficit or surplus is sometimes appropriate.

First, a budget deficit or surplus can help stabilize the economy. In essence, a balanced-budget rule would revoke the automatic stabilizing powers of the system of taxes and transfers. When the economy goes into a recession, taxes automatically fall, and transfers automatically rise. While these automatic responses help stabilize the economy, they push the budget into deficit. A strict balanced-budget rule would require that the government raise taxes or reduce spending in a recession, but these actions would further depress aggregate demand.

Second, a budget deficit or surplus can be used to reduce the distortion of incentives caused by the tax system. High tax rates impose a cost on society by discouraging economic activity. The higher the tax rates, the greater the social cost of taxes. The total social cost of taxes is minimized by keeping tax rates relatively stable rather than making them high in some years and low in others. Economists call this policy *tax smoothing*. To keep tax rates smooth, a deficit is necessary in years of unusually low income (recessions) and unusually high expenditure (wars).

Third, a budget deficit can be used to shift a tax burden from current to future generations. For example, some economists argue that if the current generation fights a war to maintain freedom, future generations benefit as well and should bear some of the burden. To pass on some of the war's costs, the current generation can finance the war with a budget deficit. The government can later retire the debt by levying taxes on the next generation.

These considerations lead most economists to reject a strict balanced-budget rule. At the very least, a rule for fiscal policy needs to take account of the recurring episodes, such as recessions and wars, during which a budget deficit is a reasonable policy response.

Case Study *13-7*

●　●　●　●　●　●　●　●　●　●　●　●　●　●

The Debt–GDP Ratio Over Two Hundred Years

If we look back over the course of U.S. history, we can see that the indebtedness of the federal government has varied substantially over time. Figure 13-3 shows the ratio of the federal debt to GDP since 1790. The government debt, relative to the size of the economy, varies from close to zero in the 1830s to a maximum of 129 percent of GDP in 1946.

Historically, the primary cause of increases in the government debt is war. The debt–GDP ratio rises sharply during major wars and falls slowly during peacetime. The notable exception is the 1980s and 1990s, when the federal government ran substantial budget deficits in peacetime.

Many economists think that this historical pattern is the appropriate way to run fiscal policy. For reasons of both tax smoothing and generational equity,

Figure **13-3**

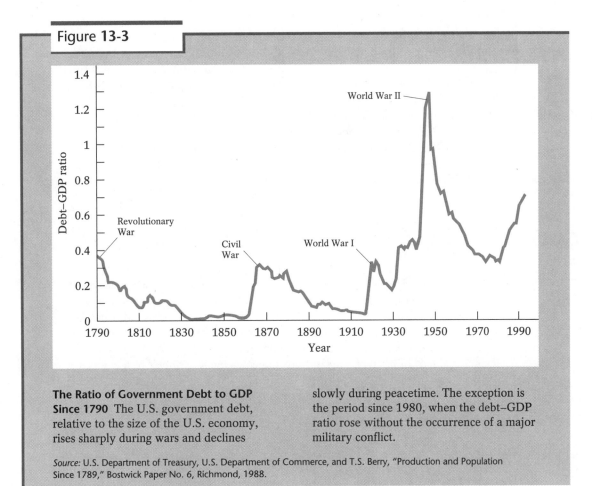

The Ratio of Government Debt to GDP Since 1790 The U.S. government debt, relative to the size of the U.S. economy, rises sharply during wars and declines slowly during peacetime. The exception is the period since 1980, when the debt–GDP ratio rose without the occurrence of a major military conflict.

Source: U.S. Department of Treasury, U.S. Department of Commerce, and T.S. Berry, "Production and Population Since 1789," Bostwick Paper No. 6, Richmond, 1988.

deficit financing of wars appears optimal. The recent deficits have been more controversial, however. Many economists have criticized these budget deficits as imposing an unjustifiable burden on future generations.[8]

13-3   Conclusion: Making Policy in an Uncertain World

In this chapter we have examined whether policy should take an active or passive role in responding to economic fluctuations and whether policy should be conducted by rule or by discretion. There are many arguments on both sides of

[8] For a critique of the deficits of the 1980s, see Benjamin M. Friedman, *Day of Reckoning: The Consequences of American Economic Policy Under Reagan and After* (New York: Random House, 1988).

these questions. Perhaps the only clear conclusion is that there is no simple and compelling case for any particular view of macroeconomic policy. In the end, you must weigh the various arguments, both economic and political, and decide for yourself what kind of role the government should play in trying to stabilize the economy.

For better or worse, economists play a key role in the formulation of economic policy. Because the economy is complex, this role is often difficult. Yet it is also inevitable. Economists cannot sit back and wait until our knowledge of the economy has been perfected before giving advice. In the meantime, someone must advise economic policymakers. That job, difficult as it sometimes is, falls to economists.

The role of economists in the policymaking process goes beyond giving advice to policymakers. Even economists cloistered in academia influence policy indirectly through their research and writing. In the conclusion of *The General Theory*, John Maynard Keynes wrote that

> . . . the ideas of economists and political philosophers, both when they are right and when they are wrong, are more powerful than is commonly understood. Indeed, the world is ruled by little else. Practical men, who believe themselves to be quite exempt from intellectual influences, are usually the slaves of some defunct economist. Madmen in authority, who hear voices in the air, are distilling their frenzy from some academic scribbler of a few years back.

This is as true today as it was when Keynes wrote it in 1935—except now that academic scribbler is often Keynes himself.

Summary

1. Advocates of active policy view the economy as subject to frequent shocks that will lead to inefficient fluctuations in output and employment unless monetary or fiscal policy responds. Many believe that economic policy has been successful in stabilizing the economy.

2. Advocates of passive policy argue that because monetary and fiscal policies work with long and variable lags, attempts to stabilize the economy are likely to end up being destabilizing. In addition, they believe that our present understanding of the economy is too limited to be useful in formulating successful stabilization policy and that inept policy is a frequent source of economic fluctuations.

3. Advocates of discretionary policy argue that discretion gives more flexibility to policymakers in responding to various unforeseen situations.

4. Advocates of policy rules argue that the political process cannot be trusted. They believe that politicians make frequent mistakes in conducting economic policy and sometimes use economic policy for their own political ends. In addition, advocates of policy rules argue that a commitment to a fixed policy rule is necessary to solve the problem of time inconsistency.

KEY CONCEPTS

Inside and outside lags

Automatic stabilizers

Leading indicators

Lucas critique

Political business cycle

Time inconsistency

Monetarists

QUESTIONS FOR REVIEW

1. What are the inside lag and the outside lag? Which has the longer inside lag—monetary or fiscal policy? Which has the longer outside lag? Why?

2. Why would more accurate economic forecasting make it easier for policymakers to stabilize the economy? Describe two ways economists try to forecast developments in the economy.

3. Describe the Lucas critique.

4. Why is macroeconomic history important for macroeconomic policy?

5. What is meant by the "time inconsistency" of economic policy? Why might policymakers be tempted to renege on an announcement they made earlier? In this situation, what is the advantage of a policy rule?

6. List three policy rules that the Fed might follow. Which of these would you advocate? Why?

7. Give three reasons why requiring a balanced budget might be too restrictive a rule for fiscal policy.

PROBLEMS AND APPLICATIONS

1. Suppose that the tradeoff between unemployment and inflation is determined by the Phillips curve:

$$u = u^n - \alpha(\pi - \pi^e),$$

where u denotes the unemployment rate, u^n the natural rate, π the rate of inflation, and π^e the expected rate of inflation. In addition, suppose that the Democratic party always follows a policy of high money growth and the Republican party always follows a policy of low money growth. What "political business cycle" pattern of inflation and unemployment would you predict under the following conditions?

    a. Every four years, one of the parties takes control based on a random flip of a coin.

    b. The two parties take turns.

2. When cities pass laws limiting the rent landlords can charge on apartments, the laws usually apply to existing buildings and exempt any buildings not yet built. Advocates of rent control argue that this exemption ensures that rent control does not discourage the construction of new housing. Evaluate this argument in light of the time-inconsistency problem.

3. The *cyclically adjusted budget deficit* is the budget deficit corrected for the effects of the business cycle. In other words, it is the budget deficit that the government would be running if unemployment were at the natural rate. (It is also called the *full-employment budget deficit*.) Some economists have proposed the rule that the cyclically adjusted budget deficit always be balanced. Compare this proposal to a strict balanced-budget rule. Which is preferable? What problems do you see with the rule requiring a balanced cyclically adjusted budget?

Time Inconsistency and the Tradeoff Between Inflation and Unemployment

In this appendix, we examine more analytically the time-inconsistency argument for rules rather than discretion. This material is relegated to an appendix because we will need to use some calculus.

Suppose that the Phillips curve describes the relationship between inflation and unemployment. Letting u denote the unemployment rate, u^n the natural rate of unemployment, π the rate of inflation, and π^e the expected rate of inflation, unemployment is determined by

$$u = u^n - \alpha(\pi - \pi^e).$$

Unemployment is low when inflation exceeds expected inflation and high when inflation falls below expected inflation.

For simplicity, suppose also that the Fed chooses the rate of inflation. Of course, more realistically, the Fed controls inflation only imperfectly through its control of the money supply. But for the purposes of illustration, it is useful to assume that the Fed can control inflation perfectly.

The Fed likes low unemployment and low inflation. Suppose that the cost of unemployment and inflation, as perceived by the Fed, can be represented as

$$L(u, \pi) = u + \gamma\pi^2,$$

where the parameter γ represents how much the Fed dislikes inflation relative to unemployment. $L(u, \pi)$ is called the *loss function*. The Fed's objective is to make the loss as small as possible.

Having specified how the economy works and the Fed's objective, let's compare monetary policy made under a fixed rule and under discretion.

First, consider policy under a fixed rule. A rule commits the Fed to a particular level of inflation. As long as private agents understand that the Fed is committed to this rule, the expected level of inflation will be the level the Fed is committed to produce. Since expected inflation equals actual inflation ($\pi^e = \pi$), unemployment will be at its natural rate ($u = u^n$).

What is the optimal rule? Since unemployment is at its natural rate regardless of the level of inflation legislated by the rule, there is no benefit to having any inflation at all. Therefore, the optimal fixed rule requires that the Fed produce zero inflation.

Second, consider discretionary monetary policy. Under discretion, the economy works as follows:

1. Private agents form their expectations of inflation π^e.

2. The Fed chooses the actual level of inflation π.

3. Based on expected and actual inflation, unemployment is determined.

Under this arrangement, the Fed minimizes its loss $L(u, \pi)$ subject to the constraint that the Phillips curve imposes. When making its decision about the rate of inflation, the Fed takes expected inflation as already determined.

To find what outcome we would obtain under discretionary policy, we must examine what level of inflation the Fed would choose. By substituting the Phillips curve into the Fed's loss function, we obtain

$$L(u, \pi) = u^n - \alpha(\pi - \pi^e) + \gamma\pi^2.$$

Notice that the Fed's loss is negatively related to unexpected inflation (the second term in the equation) and positively related to actual inflation (the third term). To find the level of inflation that minimizes this loss, differentiate with respect to π to obtain

$$dL/d\pi = -\alpha + 2\gamma\pi.$$

The loss is minimized when this derivative equals zero. Solving for π, we get

$$\pi = \alpha/(2\gamma).$$

Whatever level of inflation private agents expected, this is the "optimal" level of inflation for the Fed to choose. Of course, rational private agents understand the objective of the Fed and the constraint that the Phillips curve imposes. They therefore expect that the Fed will choose this level of inflation. Expected inflation equals actual inflation $[\pi^e = \pi = \alpha/(2\gamma)]$, and unemployment equals its natural rate ($u = u^n$).

Now compare the outcome under optimal discretion to the outcome under the optimal rule. In both cases, unemployment is at its natural rate. Yet discretionary policy produces more inflation than does policy under the rule. Thus, optimal discretion is worse than the optimal rule, even though the Fed under discretion was attempting to minimize its loss, $L(u, \pi)$.

At first it may seem bizarre that the Fed can achieve a better outcome by being committed to a fixed rule. Why can't the Fed with discretion mimic the Fed committed to a zero-inflation rule? The answer is that the Fed is playing a game against private decisionmakers who have rational expectations. Unless it is committed to a fixed rule of zero inflation, the Fed cannot get private agents to expect zero inflation.

Suppose, for example, that the Fed simply announces that it will follow a zero-inflation policy. Such an announcement by itself cannot be credible. After private agents have formed their expectations of inflation, the Fed has the incentive to renege on its announcement in order to decrease unemployment.

(As we have just seen, once expectations are given, the Fed's optimal policy is to set inflation at $\pi = \alpha/(2\gamma)$, regardless of π^e.) Private agents understand the incentive to renege and therefore do not believe the announcement in the first place.

This theory of monetary policy has an important corollary. Under one circumstance, the Fed with discretion achieves the same outcome as the Fed committed to a fixed rule of zero inflation. If the Fed dislikes inflation much more than it dislikes unemployment (so that γ is very large), inflation under discretion is near zero, since the Fed has little incentive to inflate. This finding provides some guidance to those who have the job of appointing central bankers. An alternative to imposing a fixed rule is to appoint an individual with a fervent distaste for inflation. Perhaps this is why even liberal politicians who are more concerned about unemployment than inflation often appoint conservative central bankers who are more concerned about inflation.

MORE PROBLEMS AND APPLICATIONS

1. In the 1970s in the United States, the inflation rate and the natural rate of unemployment both rose. Let's use this model of time inconsistency to examine this phenomenon. Assume that policy is discretionary.

    a. In the model as developed so far, what happens to the inflation rate when the natural rate of unemployment rises?

    b. Let's now change the model slightly by supposing that the Fed's loss function is quadratic in both inflation and unemployment. That is,

$$L(u, \pi) = u^2 + \gamma\pi^2.$$

Follow steps similar to those in the text to solve for the inflation rate under discretionary policy.

c. Now what happens to the inflation rate when the natural rate of unemployment rises?

d. In 1979, President Jimmy Carter appointed the conservative central banker Paul Volcker to head the Federal Reserve. According to this model, what should have happened to inflation and unemployment?

Chapter 14

Recent Developments in the Theory of Economic Fluctuations

What is the best way to explain short-run fluctuations in output and employment? How should monetary and fiscal policy respond to these fluctuations? These are the central questions of short-run macroeconomics. Unfortunately, there is no consensus on the answers.

As a matter of logic, the output of the economy can fluctuate for two reasons—either because the natural rate of output fluctuates or because the output of the economy has deviated from its natural rate. Many of the disagreements among macroeconomists arise from differing views of the source of short-run fluctuations. Throughout most of this book, we have presumed, as most economists do, that the natural rate of output grows smoothly over time and that short-run fluctuations are deviations from the natural rate. Yet some economists suggest that deviations from the natural rate are relatively unimportant and that most fluctuations should be viewed as changes in the natural, or equilibrium, level of output.

This chapter discusses recent research by economists in both camps. We begin by considering the **theory of real business cycles**. According to this theory, the assumptions that we have used to study the long run apply to the short run as well. That is, this theory assumes that we can explain short-run economic fluctuations while we maintain the assumptions of the classical model. Most important, real-business-cycle theory assumes that prices are fully flexible, even in the short run. Almost all microeconomic analysis is based on the premise that prices adjust to clear markets. Advocates of real-business-cycle theory argue that macroeconomic analysis should be grounded on the same assumption.

Because real-business-cycle theory assumes complete price flexibility, it obeys the classical dichotomy. According to this theory, nominal variables, such as the money supply and the price level, do not influence real variables, such as output and employment. To explain fluctuations in real variables, this theory emphasizes real changes in the economy, such as changes in production technologies, that can alter the economy's natural rate. The "real" in real-business-cycle theory refers to the theory's exclusion of nominal variables in explaining economic fluctuations.

By contrast, a second line of research, called **new Keynesian economics**, is based on the premise that market-clearing models cannot explain short-run economic fluctuations. In *The General Theory*, Keynes urged economists to abandon the classical presumption that wages and prices adjust quickly to equilibrate markets. He emphasized that aggregate demand is a primary determinant of national income in the short run. New Keynesian economists accept these basic conclusions, and so they advocate models with sticky wages and prices.

In their research, new Keynesian economists try to develop more fully the Keynesian approach to economic fluctuations. Many new Keynesians accept the *IS-LM* model as the theory of aggregate demand and, in their research, try to refine the theory of aggregate supply. This work tries to explain how wages and prices behave in the short run by identifying more precisely the market imperfections that make wages and prices sticky and that cause the economy to return only slowly to the natural rate. We discuss this research in the second half of the chapter.

In presenting the work of these two schools of thought, this chapter takes an approach that is more descriptive than analytic. Studying recent theoretical developments in detail would require more mathematics than is appropriate for this book. Yet, even without the formal models, we can discuss the direction of this research and get a sense of the continuing debate.[1]

14-1 The Theory of Real Business Cycles

When we studied the growth of the economy in Chapter 4, we described a relatively smooth process. Output grew as population, capital, and the available technology evolved over time. In the Solow growth model, the economy approaches a steady state in which most variables grow together at a rate determined by the constant rate of technological progress.

But is the process of economic growth necessarily as steady as the Solow model assumes? Perhaps technological progress and economic growth occur unevenly. Perhaps there are shocks to the economy that induce short-run fluctuations in the natural rates of output and employment. To see how this might be so, we consider a famous allegory that economists have borrowed from author Daniel Defoe.

The Economics of Robinson Crusoe

Robinson Crusoe is a sailor stranded on a desert island. Because Crusoe lives alone, his life is simple. Yet he has to make many economic decisions. Considering Crusoe's decisions—and how they change in response to changing circumstances—sheds light on the decisions that people face in larger, more complex economies.

To keep things simple, imagine that Crusoe engages in only a few activities. Crusoe spends some of his time enjoying leisure, perhaps swimming on his island's beaches. He spends the rest of his time working, either catching fish or

---

[1] For a more formal treatment of the issues discussed here, see David Romer, *Advanced Macroeconomics* (New York: McGraw-Hill, 1996).

collecting vines to make into fishing nets. Both forms of work produce a valuable good: fish are Crusoe's consumption, and nets are Crusoe's investment. If we were to compute GDP for Crusoe's island, we would add together the number of fish caught and the number of nets made (weighted by some "price" to reflect Crusoe's relative valuation of these two goods).

Crusoe allocates his time among swimming, fishing, and making nets based on his preferences and the opportunities available to him. It is reasonable to assume that Crusoe optimizes. That is, he chooses the quantities of leisure, consumption, and investment that are best for him given the constraints that nature imposes.

Over time, Crusoe's decisions change as shocks impinge on his life. For example, suppose that one day a big school of fish passes by the island. GDP rises in the Crusoe economy for two reasons. First, Crusoe's productivity rises: with a large school in the water, Crusoe catches more fish per hour of fishing. Second, Crusoe's employment rises. That is, he decides to reduce temporarily his enjoyment of leisure in order to work harder and take advantage of this unusual opportunity to catch fish. The Crusoe economy is booming.

Similarly, suppose that a storm arrives one day. Because the storm makes outdoor activity difficult, productivity falls: each hour spent fishing or making nets yields a smaller output. In response, Crusoe decides to spend less time working and to wait out the storm in his hut. Consumption of fish and investment in nets both fall, so GDP falls as well. The Crusoe economy is in recession.

Suppose that one day Crusoe is attacked by natives. While he is defending himself, Crusoe has less time to enjoy leisure. Thus, the increase in "defense spending" spurs employment in the Crusoe economy. To some extent, Crusoe spends less time fishing for consumption. To a larger extent, he spends less time making nets, since this task is easy to put off for a while. Thus, defense spending crowds out investment. Because Crusoe spends more time at work, GDP (which now includes the value of national defense) rises. The Crusoe economy is experiencing a wartime boom.

What is notable about this story of booms and recessions is its simplicity. *In this story, fluctuations in output, employment, consumption, investment, and productivity are all the natural and desirable response of an individual to the inevitable changes in his environment.* In the Crusoe economy, fluctuations have nothing to do with monetary policy, sticky prices, or any type of market failure.

The theory of real business cycles suggests that fluctuations in our economy are much the same as fluctuations in Robinson Crusoe's. Shocks to our ability to produce goods and services (like the changing weather on Crusoe's island) alter the natural rates of employment and output. These shocks are not necessarily desirable, but they are inevitable. Once the shocks occur, it is desirable for GDP, employment, and other macroeconomic variables to fluctuate in response.

Is this a good theory of short-run fluctuations in modern industrial economies? Economists disagree about the answer to this question. At the heart of the debate are four basic issues:

- The interpretation of the labor market

- The importance of technology shocks
- The neutrality of money
- The flexibility of wages and prices.

Whether you think the parable of Robinson Crusoe is clever or silly, considering these four issues is instructive, for each of them raises fundamental questions about how the economy works.

The Interpretation of the Labor Market

Real-business-cycle theory emphasizes the idea that the quantity of labor supplied at any point in time depends on the incentives that workers face, just as Robinson Crusoe changes his work effort voluntarily in response to changing circumstances. When workers are well rewarded, they are willing to work more hours; when the rewards are less, they are willing to work fewer hours. Sometimes, if the reward for working is sufficiently small, workers choose to forgo working altogether—at least temporarily. This willingness to reallocate hours of work over time is called the **intertemporal substitution of labor**.

To see how intertemporal substitution affects labor supply, consider the following example. A college student finishing her sophomore year has two summer vacations left before graduation. She wishes to work for one of these summers (so she can buy a car after she graduates) and to relax at the beach during the other summer. How should she choose which summer to work?

Let W_1 be her real wage in the first summer and W_2 the real wage she expects in the second summer. To choose which summer to work, the student compares these two wages. Yet, because she can earn interest on money earned earlier, a dollar earned in the first summer is more valuable than a dollar earned in the second summer. Let r be the real interest rate. If the student works in the first summer and saves her earnings, she will have $(1 + r)W_1$ a year later. If she works in the second summer, she will have W_2. The intertemporal relative wage—that is, the earnings from working the first summer relative to the earnings from working the second summer—is

$$\text{Intertemporal Relative Wage} = \frac{(1 + r)W_1}{W_2}.$$

Working the first summer is more attractive if the interest rate is high or if the wage is high relative to the wage expected to prevail in the future.

According to real-business-cycle theory, all workers perform this cost-benefit analysis to decide when to work and when to enjoy leisure. If the wage is temporarily high or if the interest rate is high, it is a good time to work. If the wage is temporarily low or if the interest rate is low, it is a good time to enjoy leisure.

Real-business-cycle theory uses the intertemporal substitution of labor to explain why employment and output fluctuate. Shocks to the economy that cause the interest rate to rise or the wage to be temporarily high cause people to want to work more. The increase in work effort raises employment and production.

Critics of this theory believe that fluctuations in employment do not reflect changes in the amount people want to work. They believe that desired employment is not very sensitive to the real wage and the real interest rate. They point out that the unemployment rate fluctuates substantially over the business cycle. The high unemployment in recessions suggests that the labor market does not clear: if people were voluntarily choosing not to work in recessions, they would not call themselves unemployed. These critics conclude that wages do not adjust to equilibrate labor supply and labor demand, as real-business-cycle models assume.

In reply, advocates of real-business-cycle theory argue that unemployment statistics are difficult to interpret. The mere fact that the unemployment rate is high does not mean that intertemporal substitution of labor is unimportant. Individuals who voluntarily choose not to work may call themselves unemployed so they can collect unemployment-insurance benefits. Or they may call themselves unemployed because they would be willing to work if they were offered the wage they receive in most years.

Case Study *14-1*

Looking for Intertemporal Substitution

Because intertemporal substitution of labor is central to real-business-cycle theory, much research has been aimed at examining whether it is an important determinant of labor supply. This research looks at data on wages and hours to see whether people alter the amount they work in response to small changes in the real wage. If leisure were highly intertemporally substitutable, then individuals expecting increases in the real wage should work little today and much in the future. Those expecting decreases in their real wage should work hard today and enjoy leisure in the future.

Studies of labor supply find that expected changes in the real wage lead to only small changes in hours worked. Individuals appear not to respond to expected real-wage changes by substantially reallocating leisure over time. This evidence suggests that intertemporal substitution is not as important a determinant of labor supply as real-business-cycle theorists claim.

This evidence does not convince everyone, however. One reason is that the data are often far from perfect. For example, to study labor supply, we need data on wages; yet when a person is not working, we do not observe the wage that person could have earned by taking a job. Thus, although these studies of labor supply find little evidence for intertemporal substitution, they do not end the debate over real-business-cycle theory.[2]

---

[2] The classic article emphasizing the role of intertemporal substitution in the labor market is Robert E. Lucas, Jr., and Leonard A. Rapping, "Real Wages, Employment, and Inflation," *Journal of Political Economy* 77 (September/October 1969): 721–754. For some of the empirical work that casts doubt on this hypothesis, see Joseph G. Altonji, "Intertemporal Substitution in Labor Supply: Evidence from Micro Data," *Journal of Political Economy* 94 (June 1986, Part 2): S176–S215; and Laurence Ball, "Intertemporal Substitution and Constraints on Labor Supply: Evidence from Panel Data," *Economic Inquiry* 28 (October 1990): 706–724.

The Importance of Technology Shocks

The Crusoe economy fluctuates because of changes in the weather, which induce Crusoe to alter his work effort. Similarly, real-business-cycle theory assumes that our economy experiences fluctuations in the ability to turn inputs (capital and labor) into output (goods and services) and that these fluctuations in technology cause fluctuations in output and employment. When the available production technology improves, the economy produces more output. Because of intertemporal substitution of labor, the improved technology also leads to greater employment. Real-business-cycle theorists often explain recessions as periods of technological regress. According to these models, output and employment fall during recessions because the available production technology deteriorates, lowering output and reducing the incentive to work.

Critics of real-business-cycle theory are skeptical that the economy experiences large shocks to technology. It is a more common presumption that technological progress occurs gradually. Critics argue that technological regress is especially implausible: the accumulation of technological knowledge may slow down, but it is hard to imagine that it would go in reverse.

Advocates respond by taking a broad view of shocks to technology. They argue that there are many events that, although not literally technological, affect the economy much as technology shocks do. For example, bad weather, the passage of strict environmental regulations, or increases in world oil prices have effects similar to adverse changes in technology: they all reduce our ability to turn capital and labor into goods and services. Whether such events are sufficiently common to explain the frequency and magnitude of business cycles is an open question.

Case Study *14-2*

• • • • • • • • • • • • • •

The Solow Residual and the Business Cycle

To demonstrate the role of technology shocks in generating business cycles, economist Edward Prescott looked at data on the economy's inputs (capital and labor) and its output (GDP). For every year, he computed the **Solow residual**—the percentage change in output minus the percentage change in inputs, where the different inputs are weighted by their factor shares. The Solow residual measures the change in the economy's output of goods and services that cannot be explained by changes in the amounts of capital and labor. Prescott interprets it as a measure of the rate of technological progress.[3]

---

[3] The appendix to Chapter 4 shows that the Solow residual is

$$\frac{\Delta A}{A} = \frac{\Delta Y}{Y} - \alpha \frac{\Delta K}{K} - (1 - \alpha)\frac{\Delta L}{L},$$

where A is total factor productivity, Y output, K capital, L labor, and α capital's share of income.

Figure 14-1 shows the Solow residual and the growth in output for the period 1948 to 1994. Notice that the Solow residual fluctuates substantially. It tells us, for example, that technology worsened in 1982 and improved in 1984. In addition, the Solow residual moves closely with output: in years when output falls, technology worsens. According to Prescott, these large fluctuations in the Solow residual show that technology shocks are an important source of economic fluctuations.

Figure 14-1

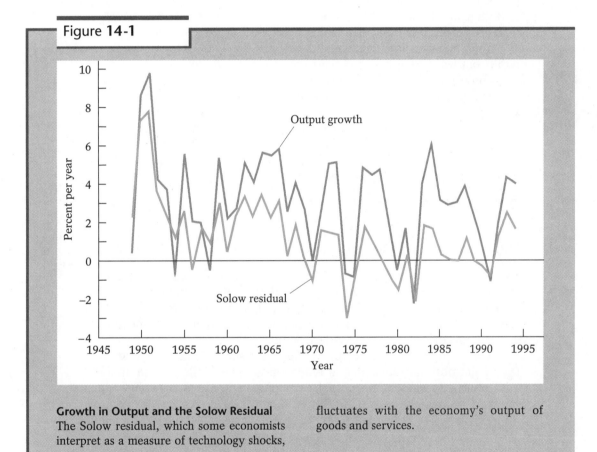

Growth in Output and the Solow Residual
The Solow residual, which some economists interpret as a measure of technology shocks, fluctuates with the economy's output of goods and services.

Source: U.S. Department of Commerce and author's calculations.

Prescott's interpretation of this figure is controversial, however. Many economists believe that the Solow residual does not accurately represent changes in technology over short periods of time. The standard explanation of the cyclical behavior of the Solow residual is that it results from two measurement problems.

First, during recessions, firms may continue to employ workers they do not need, so that they will have these workers on hand when the economy recovers. This phenomenon is called **labor hoarding**. If firms do hoard labor, then labor input is overestimated in recessions, because the hoarded workers are probably not working as hard as usual. Labor hoarding makes the Solow residual more cyclical than the available production technology.

Second, when demand is low, firms may produce things that are not easily measured. In recessions, workers may clean the factory, organize the inventory, get some training, and do other useful tasks that standard measures of output fail to include. If so, then output is underestimated in recessions, which also makes the measured Solow residual more cyclical than technology.

Thus, economists can interpret the cyclical behavior of the Solow residual in different ways. Real-business-cycle theorists point to the low productivity in recessions as evidence for adverse technology shocks. Other economists believe that measured productivity is low in recessions because workers are not working as hard as usual and because more of their output is not measured. Unfortunately, there is no clear evidence on the importance of labor hoarding and the cyclical mismeasurement of output. Therefore, different interpretations of Figure 14-1 persist. This disagreement is one part of the debate between advocates and critics of real-business-cycle theory.[4]

· · · · · · · · · · · · · ·

The Neutrality of Money

Just as money has no role in the Crusoe economy, real-business-cycle theory assumes that money in our economy is neutral. That is, monetary policy is assumed not to affect real variables such as output and employment. Not only does the neutrality of money give real-business-cycle theory its name, but neutrality is also the theory's most radical assumption.

Critics argue that the evidence does not support monetary neutrality. They point out that reductions in money growth and inflation are almost always associated with periods of high unemployment. Monetary policy appears to have a strong influence on the real economy.

Advocates of real-business-cycle theory argue that their critics confuse the direction of causation between money and output. These advocates claim that the money supply is endogenous: fluctuations in output might cause fluctuations in the money supply. For example, when output rises because of a beneficial technology shock, the quantity of money demanded rises. The Federal Reserve may respond by raising the money supply to accommodate the greater demand. This endogenous response of money to economic activity may give the illusion of monetary non-neutrality.[5]

---

[4] For the two sides of this debate, see Edward C. Prescott, "Theory Ahead of Business Cycle Measurement," and Lawrence H. Summers, "Some Skeptical Observations on Real Business Cycle Theory." Both are in *Quarterly Review*, Federal Reserve Bank of Minneapolis (Fall 1986).

[5] Robert G. King and Charles I. Plosser, "Money, Credit, and Prices in a Real Business Cycle," *American Economic Review* 74 (June 1984): 363–380.

Case Study *14-3*

• • • • • • • • • • • •

Testing for Monetary Neutrality

The direction of causation between fluctuations in the money supply and fluctuations in output is hard to establish. The only sure way to determine cause and effect would be to conduct a controlled experiment. Imagine that the Fed set the money supply according to some random process. Every January, the Fed chairman would flip a coin. Heads would mean an expansionary monetary policy for the coming year; tails a contractionary one. After a number of years we would know with confidence the effects of monetary policy. If output and employment usually rose after the coin came up heads and usually fell after it came up tails, then we would conclude that monetary policy has real effects. Yet if the flip of the Fed's coin were unrelated to subsequent economic performance, then we would conclude that real-business-cycle theorists are right about the neutrality of money.

Unfortunately for scientific progress, but fortunately for the economy, economists are not allowed to conduct such experiments. Instead, we must glean what we can from the data that history gives us.

In an important but controversial study, Christina Romer and David Romer proposed one way to study the historical record. The Romers read through the minutes of the meetings of the Federal Reserve's Open Market Committee, which sets monetary policy. From these minutes, they identified dates when the Fed appears to have shifted its policy toward reducing the rate of inflation. These dates, they argue, are the equivalent of the Fed's coin coming up tails. After each of these dates, the economy experienced a decline in output and employment. The Romers interpret this evidence as establishing the non-neutrality of money.[6]

• • • • • • • • • • • •

The Flexibility of Wages and Prices

Real-business-cycle theory assumes that wages and prices adjust quickly to clear markets, just as Crusoe always achieves his optimal level of GDP without any impediment from a market imperfection. Advocates of this theory believe that the market imperfection of sticky wages and prices is not important for understanding economic fluctuations. They also believe that the assumption of flexible prices is superior methodologically to the assumption of sticky prices, because it ties macroeconomic theory more closely to microeconomic theory. Most of microeconomic analysis is based on the assumption that prices adjust to equilibrate supply and demand. Advocates of real-business-cycle theory believe that macroeconomists should base the analysis of economic fluctuations on the same assumption.

6 Christina Romer and David Romer, "Does Monetary Policy Matter? A New Test in the Spirit of Friedman and Schwartz," *NBER Macroeconomics Annual* (1989): 121–170.

What Is New Classical Economics?

Real-business-cycle theory is called **new classical economics** because it uses the assumptions of the classical model—especially flexible prices and monetary neutrality—to study short-run economic fluctuations. Yet real-business-cycle theory is not the only part of macroeconomics that bears the label "new classical." Most economists use the term broadly to describe the many challenges to the Keynesian orthodoxy that prevailed in the 1960s.

According to this broad definition, one can apply the label "new classical" to some of the ideas we discussed in earlier chapters, including rational expectations (Chapter 12), the Lucas critique (Chapter 13), and the problem of time inconsistency (Chapter 13). And, as we shall see, the Ricardian view of government debt (Chapter 16) can be called "new classical." Some economists apply the label "new classical" to any model in which prices are fully flexible in the short run. By this definition, the worker-misperception and imperfect-information models of aggregate supply (Chapter 12) are new classical, even though they violate the classical dichotomy.

Although real-business-cycle theory is widely called "new classical," in some ways the term is a misnomer, for the classical economists themselves never suggested that money was neutral in the short run. For example, David Hume, in his 1752 essay "Of Money," stressed that money was neutral only in the long run:

> In my opinion, it is only in the interval or intermediate situation, between the acquisition of money and the rise in prices, that the increasing quantity of gold or silver is favourable to industry. . . . The farmer or gardener, finding that their commodities are taken off, apply themselves with alacrity to the raising of more. . . . It is easy to trace the money in its progress through the whole commonwealth; where we shall find that it must first quicken the diligence of every individual, before it increases the price of labour.

In claiming that money is neutral in the short run, real-business-cycle theorists take the assumptions of classical economics more seriously than did the classical economists themselves.[7]

Critics point out that many wages and prices are not flexible. They believe that this inflexibility explains both the existence of unemployment and the non-neutrality of money. To explain why prices are sticky, they rely on the various new Keynesian theories that we discuss in the next section.

[7] For a textbook that emphasizes the new classical approach, see Robert J. Barro, *Macroeconomics*, 4th ed. (New York: Wiley, 1993). To read more about real-business-cycle theory, see N. Gregory Mankiw, "Real Business Cycles: A New Keynesian Perspective," *Journal of Economic Perspectives* 3 (Summer 1989): 79–90; Bennett T. McCallum, "Real Business Cycle Models," in R. Barro, ed., *Modern Business Cycle Theory* (Cambridge, Mass.: Harvard University Press, 1989), 16–50; and Charles I. Plosser, "Understanding Real Business Cycles," *Journal of Economic Perspectives* 3 (Summer 1989): 51–77.

14-2 New Keynesian Economics

Most economists are skeptical of the theory of real business cycles and believe that short-run fluctuations in output and employment represent deviations from the economy's natural rate. These deviations occur because wages and prices are slow to adjust to changing economic conditions. As we have discussed in Chapters 8 and 12, this stickiness makes the aggregate supply curve upward sloping rather than vertical. As a result, fluctuations in aggregate demand cause short-run fluctuations in output and employment.

But why exactly are prices sticky? New Keynesian research has attempted to answer this question by examining the microeconomics behind short-run price adjustment. By doing so, it tries to put the traditional theories of fluctuations on a firmer theoretical foundation.

Small Menu Costs and Aggregate-Demand Externalities

One reason prices do not adjust immediately in the short run is that there are costs to price adjustment. To change its prices, a firm may need to send out a new catalog to customers, distribute new price lists to its sales staff, or, in the case of a restaurant, print new menus. These costs of price adjustment, called **menu costs**, lead firms to adjust prices intermittently rather than continuously.

Economists disagree about whether menu costs explain the short-run stickiness of prices. Skeptics point out that menu costs are usually very small. How can small menu costs help to explain recessions, which are very costly for society? Proponents reply that small does not mean inconsequential: even though menu costs are small for the individual firm, they can have large effects on the economy as a whole.

According to proponents of the menu-cost hypothesis, to understand why prices adjust slowly, we must acknowledge that there are externalities to price adjustment: a price reduction by one firm benefits other firms in the economy. When a firm lowers the price it charges, it slightly lowers the average price level and thereby raises real money balances. The increase in real money balances expands aggregate income (by shifting the *LM* curve outward). The economic expansion in turn raises the demand for the products of all firms. This macroeconomic impact of one firm's price adjustment on the demand for all other firms' products is called an **aggregate-demand externality**.

In the presence of this aggregate-demand externality, small menu costs can make prices sticky, and this stickiness can have a large cost to society. Suppose that a firm originally sets its price too high and later must decide whether to cut its price. The firm makes this decision by comparing the benefit of a price cut—higher sales and profit—to the cost of price adjustment. Yet because of the aggregate-demand externality, the benefit to society of the price cut would exceed the benefit to the firm. The firm ignores this externality when making its decision, so it may decide not to pay the menu cost and cut its price even though the price cut is socially desirable. *Hence, sticky prices may be*

*optimal for those setting prices, even though they are undesirable for the econ-
omy as a whole.*[8]

The Staggering of Wages and Prices

Not everyone in the economy sets new wages and prices at the same time. Instead, the adjustment of wages and prices throughout the economy is staggered. *Staggering makes the overall level of wages and prices adjust slowly,
even when individual wages and prices change frequently.*

Consider the following example. Suppose first that price setting is synchronized: every firm adjusts its price on the first day of every month. If the
money supply and aggregate demand rise on May 10, output will be higher
from May 10 to June 1 because prices are fixed during this interval. But on
June 1 all firms will raise their prices in response to the higher demand, ending
the boom.

Now suppose that price setting is staggered: half the firms set prices on
the first of each month and half on the fifteenth. If the money supply rises on
May 10, then half the firms can raise their prices on May 15. But these firms
will probably not raise their prices very much. Because half the firms will not
be changing their prices on the fifteenth, a price increase by any firm will raise
that firm's *relative* price, causing it to lose customers. (By contrast, if all firms
are synchronized, all firms can raise prices together, thus leaving relative
prices unaffected.) If the May 15 price-setters make little adjustment in their
prices, then the other firms will make little adjustment when their turn comes
on June 1, because they also want to avoid relative price changes. And so on.
The price level rises slowly as the result of small price increases on the first and
the fifteenth of each month. Hence, staggering makes the price level sluggish,
because no firm wishes to be the first to post a substantial price increase.

Staggering also affects wage determination. Consider, for example, how a
fall in the money supply works its way through the economy. A smaller money
supply reduces aggregate demand, which in turn requires a proportionate fall in
nominal wages to maintain full employment. Each worker might be willing to
take a lower nominal wage if all other wages were to fall proportionately. But
each worker is reluctant to be the first to take a pay cut, knowing that this
means, at least temporarily, a fall in his or her relative wage. Since the setting
of wages is staggered, the reluctance of each worker to reduce his or her wage
first makes the overall level of wages slow to respond to changes in aggregate
demand. In other words, the staggered setting of individual wages makes the
overall level of wages sticky.[9]

---

[8] For more on this topic, see N. Gregory Mankiw, "Small Menu Costs and Large Business Cycles: A Macroeconomic Model of Monopoly," *Quarterly Journal of Economics* 100 (May 1985): 529–537; George A. Ak-
erlof and Janet L. Yellen, "A Near Rational Model of the Business Cycle, with Wage and Price Inertia,"
Quarterly Journal of Economics 100 (Supplement 1985): 823–838; and Olivier Jean Blanchard and
Nobuhiro Kiyotaki, "Monopolistic Competition and the Effects of Aggregate Demand," *American Economic Review* 77 (September 1987): 647–666.

[9] For more on the effects of staggering, see John Taylor, "Staggered Price Setting in a Macro Model," *Amer-
ican Economic Review* 69 (May 1979): 108–113; and Olivier J. Blanchard, "Price Asynchronization and
Price Level Inertia," in R. Dornbusch and Mario Henrique Simonsen, eds., *Inflation, Debt, and Indexation*
(Cambridge, Mass.: MIT Press, 1983), 3–24.

Recessions as Coordination Failure

Some new Keynesian economists suggest that recessions result from a failure of coordination. In recessions, output is low, workers are unemployed, and factories sit idle. It is possible to imagine allocations of resources in which everyone is better off—for example, the high output and employment of the 1920s is clearly preferable to the low output and employment of the 1930s. If society fails to reach an outcome that is feasible and that everyone prefers, then the members of society have failed to coordinate in some way.

Coordination problems can arise in the setting of wages and prices because those who set them must anticipate the actions of other wage- and price-setters. Union leaders negotiating wages are concerned about the concessions other unions will win. Firms setting prices are mindful of the prices other firms will charge.

To see how a recession could arise as a failure of coordination, consider the following parable. The economy is made up of two firms. After a fall in the money supply, each firm must decide whether to cut its price, based on its goal of maximizing profit. Each firm's profit, however, depends not only on its pricing decision but also on the decision made by the other firm.

The choices facing each firm are listed in Figure 14-2, which shows how the profits of the two firms depend on their actions. If neither firm cuts its price, real money balances are low, a recession ensues, and each firm makes a profit of only $15. If both firms cut their prices, real money balances are high, a recession is avoided, and each firm makes a profit of $30. Although both firms prefer to avoid a recession, neither can do so by its own actions. If one firm cuts its price while the other does not, a recession follows. The firm making the price cut makes only $5, while the other firm makes $15.

Figure 14-2

		Firm 2	
		Cut Price	Keep High Price
Firm 1	Cut Price	Firm 1 makes $30 Firm 2 makes $30	Firm 1 makes $5 Firm 2 makes $15
	Keep High Price	Firm 1 makes $15 Firm 2 makes $5	Firm 1 makes $15 Firm 2 makes $15

Price Setting and Coordination Failure This figure shows a hypothetical "game" between two firms, each of which is deciding whether to cut prices after a fall in the money supply. Each firm must choose a strategy without knowing the strategy the other firm will choose. What outcome would you expect?

The essence of this parable is that each firm's decision influences the set of outcomes available to the other firm. When one firm cuts its price, it improves the position of the other firm, because the other firm can then avoid the recession. This positive impact of one firm's price cut on the other firm's profit opportunities might arise from an aggregate-demand externality.

What outcome should we expect in this economy? On the one hand, if each firm expects the other to cut its price, both will cut prices, resulting in the preferred outcome in which each makes $30. On the other hand, if each firm expects the other to maintain its price, both will maintain their prices, resulting in the inferior solution in which each makes $15. Either of these outcomes is possible: economists say that there are *multiple equilibria*.

The inferior outcome, in which each firm makes $15, is an example of a **coordination failure**. If the two firms could coordinate, they would both cut their price and reach the preferred outcome. In the real world, unlike in our parable, coordination is often difficult because the number of firms setting prices is large. *The moral of the story is that prices can be sticky simply because people expect them to be sticky, even though stickiness is in no one's interest.*[10]

14-3   Conclusion

Recent developments in the theory of economic fluctuations remind us that we do not understand economic fluctuations as well as we would like. Fundamental questions about the economy remain open to dispute. Is the stickiness of wages and prices a key to understanding economic fluctuations? Does monetary policy have real effects?

The way an economist answers these questions influences the way he or she views the role of economic policy. Those economists who believe that wages and prices are sticky often believe that monetary and fiscal policy should be used to try to stabilize the economy. Price stickiness is a type of market imperfection. This imperfection leaves open the possibility that government policies can raise economic well-being.

By contrast, real-business-cycle theorists believe that the government's influence on the economy is limited and that even if the government could stabilize the economy, it should not try. They view the business cycle as the natural and efficient response of the economy to changing technological possibilities. Most real-business-cycle models do not include any type of market imperfection. In these models, the "invisible hand" of the marketplace guides the economy to an optimal allocation of resources.

---

10   For more on coordination failure, see Russell Cooper and Andrew John, "Coordinating Coordination Failures in Keynesian Models," *Quarterly Journal of Economics* 103 (1988): 441–463; and Laurence Ball and David Romer, "Sticky Prices as Coordination Failure," *American Economic Review* 81 (June 1991): 539–552.

These two views of economic fluctuations are a source of frequent and heated debate among economists. Much is at stake, both in economic science and in economic policy. It is this kind of debate that makes macroeconomics an exciting field of study.

Summary

1. The theory of real business cycles is an alternative explanation of economic fluctuations. It applies the assumptions of the classical model, including the flexibility of wages and prices, to the short run. According to this theory, economic fluctuations are the natural and efficient response of the economy to changing economic circumstances.

2. Advocates and critics of real-business-cycle theory disagree about whether employment fluctuations represent intertemporal substitution of labor, whether technology shocks cause most economic fluctuations, whether monetary policy affects real variables, and whether the short-run stickiness of wages and prices is important for understanding economic fluctuations.

3. New Keynesian research has tried to provide a better explanation of aggregate supply by explaining why wages and prices are sticky in the short run. One new Keynesian theory suggests that even small costs of price adjustment can have large macroeconomic effects because of aggregate-demand externalities. Another theory suggests that staggering in price adjustment makes the overall price level more sluggish. A third theory suggests that recessions occur as a type of coordination failure.

KEY CONCEPTS

Real-business-cycle theory

New Keynesian economics

Intertemporal substitution of labor

Solow residual

Labor hoarding

New classical economics

Menu costs

Aggregate-demand externality

Coordination failure

QUESTIONS FOR REVIEW

1. How does real-business-cycle theory explain fluctuations in employment?

2. What are the four central disagreements in the debate over real-business-cycle theory?

3. How does staggering of price adjustment by individual firms affect the adjustment of the overall price level to a monetary contraction?

PROBLEMS AND APPLICATIONS

1. According to real-business-cycle theory, permanent and transitory shocks to technology should have very different effects on the economy. Use the parable of Robinson Crusoe to compare the effects of a transitory shock (good weather expected to last only a few days) and a permanent shock (a beneficial change in weather patterns). Which shock would have a greater effect on Crusoe's work effort? On GDP? Is it possible that one of these shocks might reduce work effort?

2. Suppose that prices are fully flexible and that the output of the economy fluctuates because of shocks to technology, as real-business-cycle theory claims.

   a. If the Federal Reserve holds the money supply constant, what will happen to the price level as output fluctuates?

   b. If the Federal Reserve adjusts the money supply to stabilize the price level, what will happen to the money supply as output fluctuates?

   c. Many economists have observed that fluctuations in the money supply are positively correlated with fluctuations in output. Is this evidence against real-business-cycle theory?

3. Coordination failure is an idea with many applications. Here is one: Andy and Ben are running a business together. If both work hard, the business is a success, and they each earn $100 in profit. If one of them fails to work hard, the business is less successful, and they each earn $70. If neither works hard, the business is even less successful, and they each earn $60. Working hard takes $20 worth of effort.

   a. Set up this "game" as in Figure 14-2.

   b. What outcome would Andy and Ben prefer?

   c. What outcome would occur if each expected his partner to work hard?

   d. What outcome would occur if each expected his partner to be lazy?

   e. Is this a good description of the relationship among partners? Why or why not?

4. (This problem uses basic microeconomics.) The chapter discussed the price-adjustment decisions of firms with menu costs. This problem asks you to consider that issue more analytically in the simple case of a single firm.

   a. Draw a diagram describing a monopoly firm, including a downward-sloping demand curve and a cost curve. (For simplicity, assume that marginal cost is constant, so the cost curve is a horizontal line.) Show the profit-maximizing price and quantity. Show the areas that represent profit and consumer surplus at this optimum.

   b. Now suppose the firm has previously announced a price slightly above the optimum. Show this price and the quantity sold. Show the area representing the lost profit from the excessive price. Show the area representing the lost consumer surplus.

   c. The firm decides whether to cut its price by comparing the extra profit from a lower price to the menu cost. In making this decision, what externality is the firm ignoring? In what sense is the firm's price-adjustment decision inefficient?

Part Four

More on the Microeconomics Behind Macroeconomics

To understand the economy as a whole, we must understand the households and firms that make up the economy. In the next four chapters we look more closely at the behavior of households and firms. These chapters present microeconomic models that help refine our macroeconomic analysis.

Chapter 15 looks at how consumers behave and provides a more thorough explanation of the consumption function. As we see in Chapter 16, different views about consumer behavior can lead to different views about how government debt affects the economy.

Chapter 17 examines the determinants of the three types of investment—business fixed investment, residential investment, and inventory investment. It discusses why investment depends on the interest rate, what might cause the investment function to shift, and why investment fluctuates so much over the business cycle.

Chapter 18 studies the supply and demand for money. It discusses the role of the banking system in determining the money supply, as well as the various theories of the money demand function. The discussion offers new insights into the instruments and problems of monetary policy.

These chapters offer a taste of modern research. Much recent progress in macroeconomics has come from applying microeconomic models. Most often, these models refine, rather than overturn, traditional macroeconomic theory. They are important to learn, for they can enhance our understanding of the economy and economic policies.

Consumption

Chapter 15

Consumption is the sole end and purpose of all production.

Adam Smith

How do households decide how much of their income to consume today and how much to save for the future? This is a microeconomic question because it addresses the behavior of individual decisionmakers. Yet its answer has macroeconomic consequences. As we have seen in previous chapters, households' consumption decisions affect the way the economy as a whole behaves both in the long run and in the short run.

The consumption decision is crucial for long-run analysis because of its role in economic growth. The Solow growth model of Chapter 4 shows that the saving rate is a key determinant of the steady-state capital stock and thus of the level of economic well-being. The saving rate measures how much of its income the present generation is putting aside for its own future and for future generations.

The consumption decision is crucial for short-run analysis because of its role in aggregate demand. Since consumption is two-thirds of GDP, fluctuations in consumption are a key element of booms and recessions. The *IS-LM* model of Chapters 9 and 10 shows that changes in consumer confidence can be a source of shocks to the economy, and that the marginal propensity to consume is a determinant of the fiscal-policy multipliers.

In previous chapters we explained consumption with a function that relates consumption to disposable income: $C = C(Y - T)$. This approximation allowed us to develop simple models for long-run and short-run analysis. But it is too simple to provide a complete explanation of consumer behavior. In this chapter we examine the consumption function in greater detail and develop a more thorough explanation of what determines aggregate consumption.

Since macroeconomics began as a field of study, many economists have written about the theory of consumer behavior and suggested alternative ways of interpreting the data on consumption and income. This chapter presents the views of four prominent economists, roughly in historical order. By examining the theories of consumer behavior developed by John Maynard Keynes, Irving Fisher, Franco Modigliani, and Milton Friedman, this chapter provides an overview of the diverse approaches to explaining consumption.

15-1 John Maynard Keynes and the Consumption Function

We begin our study of consumption with John Maynard Keynes's *General Theory*, which was published in 1936. Keynes made the consumption function central to his theory of economic fluctuations, and it has played a key role in macroeconomic analysis ever since. Let's consider what Keynes thought about the consumption function, and then see what puzzles arose when his ideas were confronted with the data.

Keynes's Conjectures

Today, economists who study consumption rely on sophisticated techniques of data analysis. With the help of computers, they analyze aggregate data on the behavior of the overall economy from the national income accounts and detailed data on the behavior of individual households from surveys. Because Keynes wrote in the 1930s, however, he had neither the advantage of these data nor the computers necessary to analyze such large data sets. Instead of relying on statistical analysis, Keynes made conjectures about the consumption function based on introspection and casual observation.

First and most important, Keynes conjectured that the **marginal propensity to consume**—the amount consumed out of an additional dollar of income—is between zero and one. He wrote that the "fundamental psychological law, upon which we are entitled to depend with great confidence, . . . is that men are disposed, as a rule and on the average, to increase their consumption as their income increases, but not by as much as the increase in their income." The marginal propensity to consume was crucial to Keynes's policy recommendations for how to reduce widespread unemployment. The power of fiscal policy to influence the economy—as expressed by the fiscal-policy multipliers—arises from the feedback between income and consumption.

Second, Keynes posited that the ratio of consumption to income, called the **average propensity to consume**, falls as income rises. He believed that saving was a luxury, so he expected the rich to save a higher proportion of their income than the poor. Although not essential for Keynes's own analysis, the postulate that the average propensity to consume falls as income rises became a central part of early Keynesian economics.

Third, Keynes thought that income is the primary determinant of consumption and that the interest rate does not have an important role. This conjecture stood in stark contrast to the beliefs of the classical economists who preceded him. The classical economists held that a higher interest rate encourages saving and discourages consumption. Keynes admitted that the interest rate could influence consumption as a matter of theory. Yet he wrote that "the main conclusion suggested by experience, I think, is that the short-period influence of the rate of interest on individual spending out of a given income is secondary and relatively unimportant."

On the basis of these three conjectures, the Keynesian consumption function is often written as

$$C = \overline{C} + cY \qquad \overline{C} > 0,\ 0 < c < 1,$$

where C is consumption, Y is disposable income, $\overline{C}$ is a constant sometimes called *autonomous consumption*, and c is the marginal propensity to consume. This consumption function, shown in Figure 15-1, is graphed as a straight line.

Figure 15-1

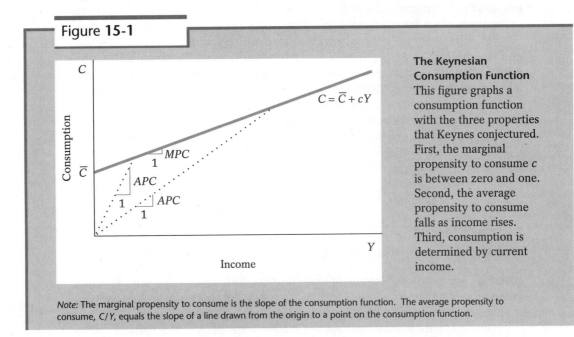

The Keynesian Consumption Function This figure graphs a consumption function with the three properties that Keynes conjectured. First, the marginal propensity to consume c is between zero and one. Second, the average propensity to consume falls as income rises. Third, consumption is determined by current income.

Note: The marginal propensity to consume is the slope of the consumption function. The average propensity to consume, C/Y, equals the slope of a line drawn from the origin to a point on the consumption function.

Notice that this consumption function exhibits the three properties that Keynes posited. It satisfies Keynes's first property because the marginal propensity to consume c is between zero and one, so that higher income leads to higher consumption and also to higher saving. This consumption function satisfies Keynes's second property because the average propensity to consume APC is

$$APC = C/Y = \overline{C}/Y + c.$$

As Y rises, $\overline{C}/Y$ falls, and so the average propensity to consume C/Y falls. And finally, this consumption function satisfies Keynes's third property because the interest rate is not included in this equation as a determinant of consumption.

The Early Empirical Successes

Soon after Keynes proposed the consumption function, economists began collecting and examining data to test his conjectures. The earliest studies indicated that the Keynesian consumption function is a good approximation of how consumers behave.

In some of these studies, researchers surveyed households and collected data on consumption and income. They found that households with higher income consumed more, which confirms that the marginal propensity to consume is greater than zero. They also found that households with higher income saved more, which confirms that the marginal propensity to consume is less than one. In addition, these researchers found that higher-income households saved a larger fraction of their income, which confirms that the average propensity to consume falls as income rises. Thus, these data verified Keynes's conjectures about the marginal and average propensities to consume.

In other studies, researchers examined aggregate data on consumption and income for the period between the two world wars. These data also supported the Keynesian consumption function. In years when income was unusually low, such as during the depths of the Great Depression, both consumption and saving were low, indicating that the marginal propensity to consume is between zero and one. In addition, during those years of low income, the ratio of consumption to income was high, confirming Keynes's second conjecture. Finally, because the correlation between income and consumption was so strong, no other variable appeared to be important for explaining consumption. Thus, the data also confirmed Keynes's third conjecture that income is the primary determinant of how much people choose to consume.

Secular Stagnation, Simon Kuznets, and the Consumption Puzzle

Although the Keynesian consumption function met with early successes, two anomalies soon arose. Both concern Keynes's conjecture that the average propensity to consume falls as income rises.

The first anomaly became apparent after some economists made a dire—and, it turned out, erroneous—prediction during World War II. On the basis of the Keynesian consumption function, these economists reasoned that as incomes in the economy grew over time, households would consume a smaller and smaller fraction of their incomes. They feared that there might not be enough profitable investment projects to absorb all this saving. If so, the low consumption would lead to an inadequate demand for goods and services, resulting in a depression once the wartime demand from the government ceased. In other words, on the basis of the Keynesian consumption function, these economists predicted that the economy would experience what they called *secular stagnation*—a long depression of indefinite duration—unless fiscal policy was used to expand aggregate demand.

Fortunately for the economy, but unfortunately for the Keynesian consumption function, the end of World War II did not throw the country into another depression. Although incomes were much higher after the war than before, these higher incomes did not lead to large increases in the rate of saving. Keynes's conjecture that the average propensity to consume would fall as income rose appeared not to hold.

The second anomaly arose when economist Simon Kuznets constructed new data on consumption and income dating back to 1869. Kuznets assembled these data in the 1940s and would later receive the Nobel Prize for this work. He discovered that the ratio of consumption to income was remarkably stable from decade to decade, despite large increases in income over the period he studied. Again, Keynes's conjecture that the average propensity to consume would fall as income rose appeared not to hold.

The failure of the secular-stagnation hypothesis and the findings of Kuznets both indicated that the average propensity to consume is fairly constant over long periods of time. This fact presented a puzzle that motivated much of the subsequent work on consumption. Economists wanted to know why some studies confirmed Keynes's conjectures and others refuted them. That is, why did Keynes's conjectures hold up well in the studies of household data and in the studies of short time-series, but fail when long time-series were examined?

Figure 15-2 illustrates the puzzle. The evidence suggested that there were two consumption functions. For the household data or for the short time-series, the Keynesian consumption function appeared to work well. Yet for the long time-series, the consumption function appeared to have a constant average propensity to consume. In Figure 15-2, these two relationships between consumption and income are called the short-run and long-run consumption

Figure 15-2

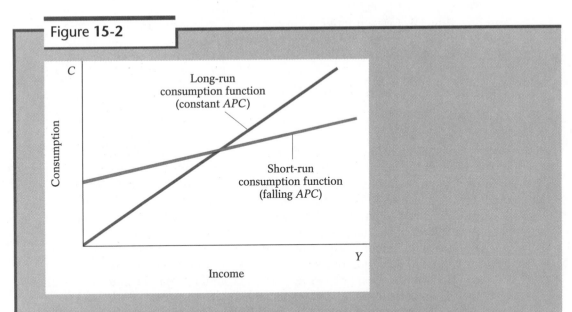

The Consumption Puzzle Studies of household data and short time-series found a relationship between consumption and income similar to the one Keynes conjectured. In the figure, this relationship is called the short-run consumption function. But studies of long time-series found that the average propensity to consume did not vary systematically with income. This relationship is called the long-run consumption function. Notice that the short-run consumption function has a falling average propensity to consume, whereas the long-run consumption function has a constant average propensity to consume.

functions. Economists needed to explain how these two consumption functions could be consistent with each other.

In the 1950s, Franco Modigliani and Milton Friedman each proposed explanations of these seemingly contradictory findings. Both economists later won Nobel Prizes, in part because of their work on consumption. But before we see how Modigliani and Friedman tried to solve the consumption puzzle, we must discuss Irving Fisher's contribution to consumption theory. Both Modigliani's life-cycle hypothesis and Friedman's permanent-income hypothesis rely on the theory of consumer behavior proposed much earlier by Irving Fisher.

15-2   Irving Fisher and Intertemporal Choice

When people decide how much to consume and how much to save, they consider both the present and the future. The more consumption they enjoy today, the less they will be able to enjoy tomorrow. In making this tradeoff, households must look ahead to the income they expect to receive in the future and to the consumption of goods and services they hope to be able to afford.

The economist Irving Fisher developed the model economists use to analyze how rational, forward-looking consumers make intertemporal choices—that is, choices involving different periods of time. Fisher's model shows the constraints consumers face and how they choose consumption and saving.

The Intertemporal Budget Constraint

Most people would prefer to increase the quantity or quality of the goods and services they consume—to wear nicer clothes, eat at better restaurants, or see more movies. The reason people consume less than they desire is that their consumption is constrained by their income. In other words, consumers face a limit on how much they can spend, called a *budget constraint*. When they are deciding how much to consume today versus how much to save for the future, they face an **intertemporal budget constraint**. To understand how people choose their level of consumption, we must examine this constraint.

To keep things simple, we examine the decision facing a consumer who lives for two periods. Period one represents the consumer's youth, and period two represents the consumer's old age. The consumer earns income Y_1 and consumes C_1 in period one, and earns income Y_2 and consumes C_2 in period two. (All variables are real—that is, adjusted for inflation.) Because the consumer has the opportunity to borrow and save, consumption in any single period can be either greater or less than income in that period.

Consider how the consumer's income in the two periods constrains consumption in the two periods. In the first period, saving equals income minus consumption. That is,

$$S = Y_1 - C_1,$$

where S is saving. In the second period, consumption equals the accumulated saving, including the interest earned on that saving, plus second-period income. That is,

$$C_2 = (1 + r)S + Y_2,$$

where r is the real interest rate. For example, if the interest rate is 5 percent, then for every \$1 of saving in period one, the consumer enjoys an extra \$1.05 of consumption in period two. Because there is no third period, the consumer does not save in the second period.

Note that these two equations still apply if the consumer is borrowing rather than saving in the first period. The variable S represents both saving and borrowing. If first-period consumption is less than first-period income, the consumer is saving, and S is greater than zero. If first-period consumption exceeds first-period income, the consumer is borrowing, and S is less than zero. For simplicity, we assume that the interest rate for borrowing is the same as the interest rate for saving.

To derive the consumer's budget constraint, combine the two equations above. Substitute the first equation for S into the second equation to obtain

$$C_2 = (1 + r)(Y_1 - C_1) + Y_2.$$

To make the equation easier to interpret, we must rearrange terms. To place all the consumption terms together, bring $(1 + r)C_1$ from the right-hand side to the left-hand side of the equation to obtain

$$(1 + r)C_1 + C_2 = (1 + r)Y_1 + Y_2.$$

Now divide both sides by $(1 + r)$ to obtain

$$C_1 + \frac{C_2}{1 + r} = Y_1 + \frac{Y_2}{1 + r}.$$

This equation relates consumption in the two periods to income in the two periods. It is the standard way of expressing the consumer's intertemporal budget constraint.

The consumer's budget constraint is easily interpreted. If the interest rate is zero, the budget constraint shows that total consumption in the two periods equals total income in the two periods. In the usual case in which the interest rate is greater than zero, future consumption and future income are discounted by a factor $1 + r$. This **discounting** arises from the interest earned on savings. In essence, because the consumer earns interest on current income that is saved, future income is worth less than current income. Similarly, because future consumption is paid for out of savings that have earned interest, future consumption costs less than current consumption. The factor $1/(1 + r)$ is the price of second-period consumption measured in terms of first-period consumption: it is the amount of first-period consumption that the consumer must forgo to obtain 1 unit of second-period consumption.

Figure 15-3 graphs the consumer's budget constraint. Three points are marked on this figure. At point A, first-period consumption is Y_1 and second-period consumption is Y_2, so there is neither saving nor borrowing between the two periods. At point B, the consumer consumes nothing in the first period and saves all income, so second-period consumption is $(1 + r)Y_1 + Y_2$. At point C, the consumer plans to consume nothing in the second period and borrows as much as possible against second-period income, so first-period consumption is $Y_1 + Y_2/(1 + r)$. Of course, these are only three of the many combinations of first- and second-period consumption that the consumer can choose: all the points on the line from B to C are possible.

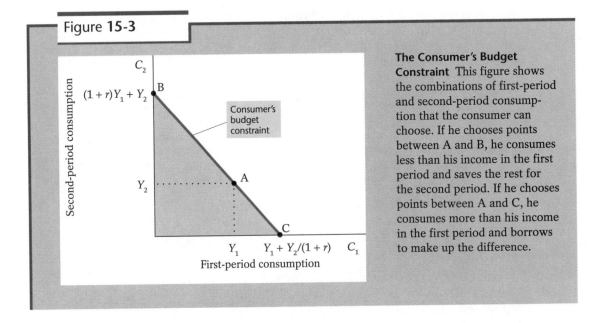

Figure 15-3

The Consumer's Budget Constraint This figure shows the combinations of first-period and second-period consumption that the consumer can choose. If he chooses points between A and B, he consumes less than his income in the first period and saves the rest for the second period. If he chooses points between A and C, he consumes more than his income in the first period and borrows to make up the difference.

The shaded area below the budget constraint shows other combinations of first-period and second-period consumption available to the consumer. The consumer can choose points below the budget constraint because he can discard some of his income. The important points are those on the budget constraint, however. As long as more consumption is preferred to less, the consumer will always choose a point on—rather than below—this budget line.

Consumer Preferences

The consumer's preferences regarding consumption in the two periods can be represented by **indifference curves**. An indifference curve shows the combinations of first-period and second-period consumption that make the consumer equally happy.

Figure 15-4 shows two possible indifference curves. The consumer is indifferent among combinations W, X, and Y, because they are all on the same curve. Not surprisingly, if the consumer's first-period consumption is reduced, say from point W to point X, second-period consumption must increase to keep him equally happy. If first-period consumption is reduced again, from point X to point Y, the amount of extra second-period consumption he requires for compensation is greater.

Figure 15-4

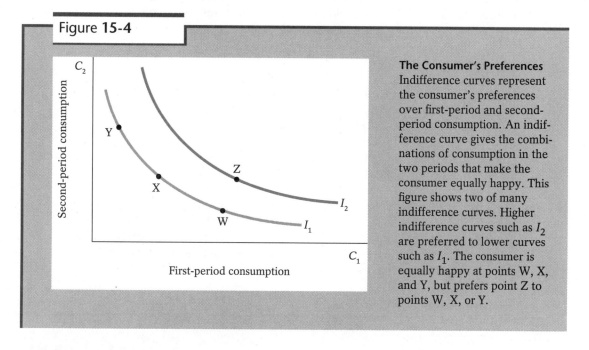

The Consumer's Preferences Indifference curves represent the consumer's preferences over first-period and second-period consumption. An indifference curve gives the combinations of consumption in the two periods that make the consumer equally happy. This figure shows two of many indifference curves. Higher indifference curves such as I_2 are preferred to lower curves such as I_1. The consumer is equally happy at points W, X, and Y, but prefers point Z to points W, X, or Y.

The slope at any point on the indifference curve shows how much second-period consumption the consumer requires in order to be compensated for a 1-unit reduction in first-period consumption. This slope is the **marginal rate of substitution** between first-period consumption and second-period consumption. It tells us the rate at which the consumer is willing to substitute second-period consumption for first-period consumption.

We can see from Figure 15-4 that the marginal rate of substitution depends on the levels of consumption in the two periods. When first-period consumption is high and second-period consumption is low, as at point W, the marginal rate of substitution is low: the consumer requires only a little extra second-period consumption to give up 1 unit of first-period consumption. When first-period consumption is low and second-period consumption is high, as at point Y, the marginal rate of substitution is high: the consumer requires much additional second-period consumption to give up 1 unit of first-period consumption.

The consumer is equally happy at all points on a given indifference curve, but he prefers some indifference curves to others. Because he prefers more consumption to less, higher indifference curves are preferred to lower ones. In Figure 15-4, the consumer prefers the points on curve I_2 to the points on curve I_1.

The set of indifference curves gives a complete ranking of the consumer's preferences. They tell us that the consumer prefers point Z to point W, but that may be obvious because point Z has more consumption in both periods. Yet compare point Z and point Y: point Z has more consumption in period one and less in period two. Which is preferred, Z or Y? Because Z is on a higher indifference curve than Y, we know that the consumer prefers point Z to point Y. Hence, we can use the set of indifference curves to rank any combinations of first-period and second-period consumption.

Optimization

Having discussed the consumer's budget constraint and preferences, we can consider the decision about how much to consume. The consumer would like to end up with the best possible combination of consumption in the two periods—that is, on the highest possible indifference curve. But the budget constraint requires that the consumer also end up on or below the budget line, because the budget line measures the total resources available to him.

Figure 15-5 shows that many indifference curves cross the budget line. The highest indifference curve that the consumer can obtain without violating the budget constraint is the indifference curve that just barely touches the budget line, which is curve I_3 in the figure. The point at which the curve and line touch—point O for "optimum"—is the best combination of consumption in the two periods available to the consumer.

Figure 15-5

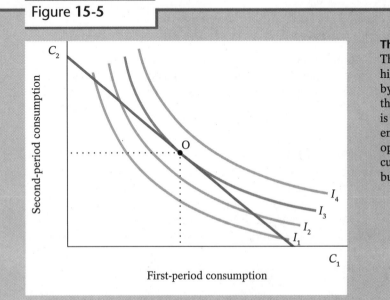

The Consumer's Optimum
The consumer achieves his highest level of satisfaction by choosing the point on the budget constraint that is on the highest indifference curve. At the optimum, the indifference curve is tangent to the budget constraint.

Notice that, at the optimum, the slope of the indifference curve equals the slope of the budget line. The indifference curve is *tangent* to the budget line. The slope of the indifference curve is the marginal rate of substitution *MRS*, and the slope of the budget line is 1 plus the real interest rate. We conclude that at point O,

$$MRS = 1 + r.$$

The consumer chooses consumption in the two periods so that the marginal rate of substitution equals 1 plus the real interest rate.

How Changes in Income Affect Consumption

Now that we have seen how the consumer makes the consumption decision, let's examine how consumption responds to an increase in income. An increase in either Y_1 or Y_2 shifts the budget constraint outward, as in Figure 15-6. The higher budget constraint allows the consumer to choose a better combination of first- and second-period consumption—that is, the consumer can now reach a higher indifference curve.

Notice that in Figure 15-6, the consumer chooses more consumption in both periods. Although not implied by the logic of the model alone, this situation is the most usual. If a consumer wants more of a good when his or her income rises, economists call it a **normal good**. The indifference curves in Figure 15-6 are drawn under the assumption that consumption in period one and consumption in period two are both normal goods.

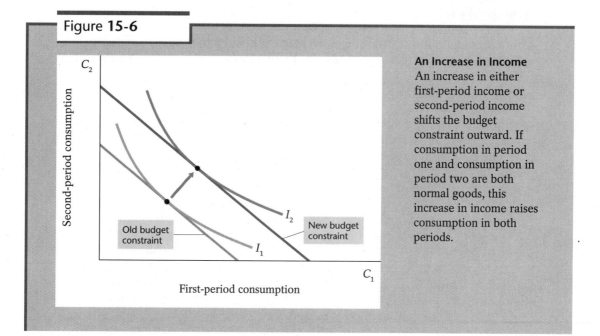

Figure 15-6

An Increase in Income An increase in either first-period income or second-period income shifts the budget constraint outward. If consumption in period one and consumption in period two are both normal goods, this increase in income raises consumption in both periods.

The key conclusion from Figure 15-6 is that regardless of whether the increase in income occurs in the first period or the second period, the consumer spreads it over consumption in both periods. Because the consumer can borrow and lend between periods, the timing of the income is irrelevant to how much is consumed today (except, of course, that future income is discounted by the interest rate). The lesson of this analysis is that consumption depends on the present value of current and future income—that is, on

$$\text{Present Value of Income} = Y_1 + \frac{Y_2}{1 + r}.$$

In contrast to Keynes's consumption function, Fisher's model says that consumption does not depend primarily on current income. Instead, consumption depends on the resources the consumer expects over his lifetime.

How Changes in the Real Interest Rate Affect Consumption

Let's now use Fisher's model to consider how a change in the real interest rate alters the consumer's choices. There are two cases to consider: the case in which the consumer is initially saving and the case in which he is initially borrowing. Here we discuss the saving case, and Problem 1 at the end of the chapter asks you to analyze the borrowing case.

Figure 15-7 shows that an increase in the real interest rate rotates the consumer's budget line around the point (Y_1, Y_2). This change alters the amount of consumption he chooses in both periods. That is, the consumer moves from point A to point B. You can see that, for the indifference curves drawn in this figure, first-period consumption falls and second-period consumption rises.

Economists decompose the impact of an increase in the real interest rate on consumption into two effects: an **income effect** and a **substitution effect**. Textbooks in microeconomics discuss these effects in detail. We summarize them briefly here.

The income effect is the change in consumption that results from the movement to a higher indifference curve. Because the consumer is a saver rather than a borrower, the increase in the interest rate makes him better off. If consumption in period one and consumption in period two are both normal goods, the consumer will want to spread this improvement in his welfare over both periods. This income effect tends to make the consumer choose more consumption in both periods.

The substitution effect is the change in consumption that results from the change in the relative price of consumption in the two periods. In particular, consumption in period two becomes less expensive relative to consumption in period one when the interest rate rises. That is, because the real interest rate earned on saving is higher, the consumer must now give up less first-period consumption to obtain an extra unit of second-period consumption. This substitution effect tends to make the consumer choose more consumption in period two and less consumption in period one.

Figure 15-7

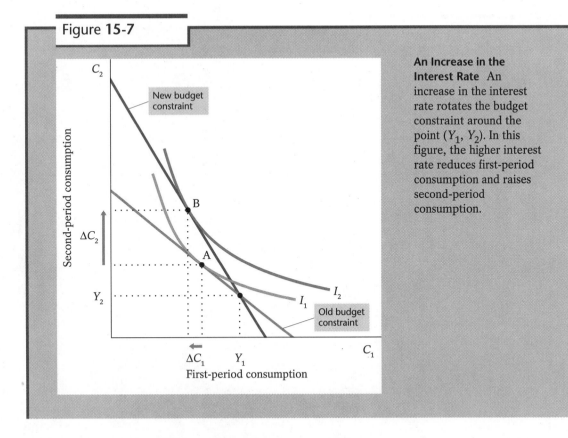

An Increase in the Interest Rate An increase in the interest rate rotates the budget constraint around the point (Y_1, Y_2). In this figure, the higher interest rate reduces first-period consumption and raises second-period consumption.

The consumer's choice depends on both the income effect and the substitution effect. Both effects act to increase the amount of second-period consumption; hence, we can confidently conclude that an increase in the real interest rate raises second-period consumption. But the two effects have opposite impacts on first-period consumption. Hence, the increase in the interest rate could either lower or raise first-period consumption.

Case Study *15-1*

● ● ● ● ● ● ● ● ● ● ● ● ●

Consumption and the Real Interest Rate

Irving Fisher's model shows that, depending on the consumer's preferences, changes in the real interest rate could either raise or lower consumption. In other words, economic theory alone cannot predict how the interest rate influences consumption. Therefore, economists have devoted much energy to examining empirically how the interest rate affects consumption and saving.

Figure 15-8 presents a scatterplot of the personal saving rate and the real interest rate. This figure shows that there is no apparent relationship between

Figure 15-8

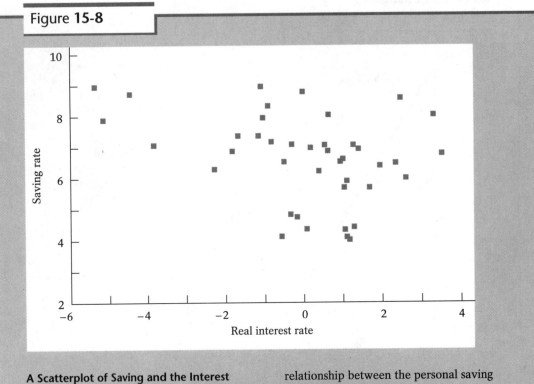

A Scatterplot of Saving and the Interest Rate This figure uses annual data from 1954 to 1994 to examine whether there is any relationship between the personal saving rate and the real interest rate. No relationship is evident.

Note: The personal saving rate is personal disposable income minus consumer spending as a fraction of personal disposable income. The real interest rate is the after-tax interest rate on one-year Treasury notes minus the previous year's inflation rate; this was calculated assuming a tax rate of 30 percent.

Source: U.S. Department of Commerce, U.S. Department of Treasury, and author's calculations.

the two variables. The evidence suggests that saving does not depend on the interest rate. In other words, it appears that the income and substitution effects of higher interest rates approximately cancel each other.

This sort of evidence, however, is not completely persuasive. The task of estimating the sensitivity of saving to the interest rate is complicated by the identification problem discussed in Chapter 3. Nonetheless, more sophisticated examinations of the data usually find that the real interest rate has little effect on consumption and saving. Keynes's conjecture that consumption depends primarily on income and not on the interest rate has held up well in the face of much empirical testing.[1]

---

[1]   For some of the recent research on the relationship between consumption and the real interest rate, see Robert E. Hall, "Intertemporal Substitution and Consumption," *Journal of Political Economy* 96 (April 1988): 339–357; and John Y. Campbell and N. Gregory Mankiw, "Consumption, Income, and Interest Rates: Reinterpreting the Time-Series Evidence," *NBER Macroeconomics Annual* (1989): 185–216.

Constraints on Borrowing

Fisher's model assumes that the consumer can borrow as well as save. The ability to borrow allows current consumption to exceed current income. In essence, when the consumer borrows, he consumes some of his future income today. Yet for many people such borrowing is impossible. For example, a student wishing to enjoy spring break in Florida would probably be unable to finance this vacation with a bank loan. Let's examine how Fisher's analysis changes if the consumer cannot borrow.

The inability to borrow prevents current consumption from exceeding current income. A constraint on borrowing can therefore be expressed as

"What I'd like, basically, is a temporary line of credit just to tide me over the rest of my life."

$$C_1 \leq Y_1.$$

This inequality states that consumption in period one is less than or equal to income in period one. This additional constraint on the consumer is called a **borrowing constraint** or, sometimes, a *liquidity constraint*.

Figure 15-9 shows how this borrowing constraint restricts the consumer's set of choices. The consumer's choice must satisfy both the intertemporal budget constraint and the borrowing constraint. The shaded area represents the

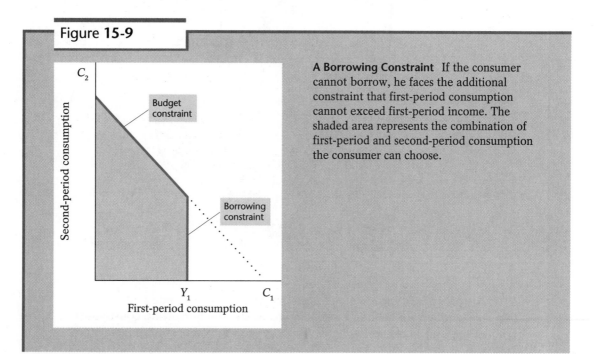

Figure 15-9

A Borrowing Constraint If the consumer cannot borrow, he faces the additional constraint that first-period consumption cannot exceed first-period income. The shaded area represents the combination of first-period and second-period consumption the consumer can choose.

combinations of first-period consumption and second-period consumption that satisfy both constraints.

Figure 15-10 shows how this borrowing constraint affects the consumption decision. There are two possibilities. In panel (a), the consumer wishes to consume less in period one than he earns. The borrowing constraint is not binding in this case and, therefore, does not affect consumption. In panel (b), the consumer would like to consume more in period one than he earns. In this case, the consumer consumes all his first-period income, and the borrowing constraint prevents him from consuming more.

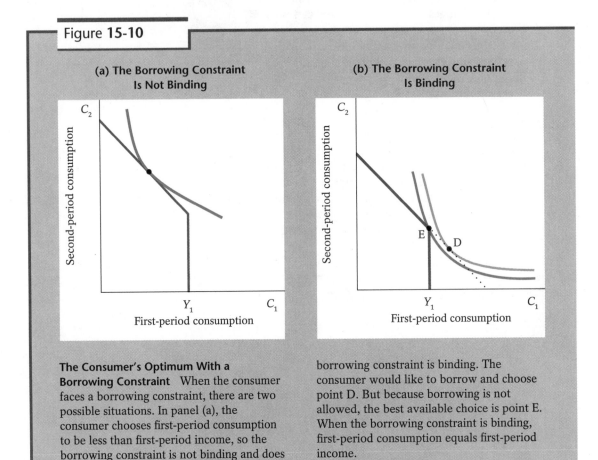

Figure 15-10

(a) The Borrowing Constraint Is Not Binding

(b) The Borrowing Constraint Is Binding

The Consumer's Optimum With a Borrowing Constraint When the consumer faces a borrowing constraint, there are two possible situations. In panel (a), the consumer chooses first-period consumption to be less than first-period income, so the borrowing constraint is not binding and does not affect consumption. In panel (b), the borrowing constraint is binding. The consumer would like to borrow and choose point D. But because borrowing is not allowed, the best available choice is point E. When the borrowing constraint is binding, first-period consumption equals first-period income.

The analysis of borrowing constraints leads us to conclude that there are two consumption functions. For some consumers, the borrowing constraint is not binding, and consumption depends on the present value of lifetime income,

$Y_1 + [Y_2/(1 + r)]$. For other consumers, the borrowing constraint binds, and the consumption function is $C_1 = Y_1$. *Hence, for those consumers who would like to borrow but cannot, consumption depends only on current income.*

Case Study *15-2*

The High Japanese Saving Rate

Japan has one of the world's highest saving rates, and many economists believe that this is one reason for its economic success. The Solow growth model in Chapter 4 shows that, in the long run, the saving rate is a primary determinant of a country's level of income. Because saving is so important for long-run economic performance, economists spend much time studying international differences in saving.

Why do the Japanese consume a much smaller fraction of their income than Americans? One reason is that it is harder for households to borrow in Japan. As Fisher's model shows, a household facing a binding borrowing constraint consumes less than it would without the borrowing constraint. Hence, societies in which borrowing constraints are common will tend to have higher rates of saving.

One reason that households often wish to borrow is to buy a home. In the United States, a person can usually buy a home with a down payment of 10 percent. A homebuyer in Japan cannot borrow nearly this much: down payments of 40 percent are common. Moreover, housing prices are very high in Japan, primarily because land prices are high. A Japanese family must save a great deal in order to eventually afford its own home.

Although constraints on borrowing are part of the explanation of high Japanese saving, there are many other differences between Japan and the United States that contribute to the difference in the saving rates. The Japanese tax system encourages saving by taxing capital income very lightly. In addition, cultural differences may lead to differences in consumer preferences regarding present and future consumption. One prominent Japanese economist writes, "The Japanese are simply *different*. They are more risk averse and more patient. If this is true, the long-run implication is that Japan will absorb all the wealth in the world. I refuse to comment on this explanation."[2]

Many economists believe that a low saving rate is one of the United States' biggest economic problems. As we discussed in Chapter 4, increasing national saving is often a stated goal of economic policy. Keep in mind, however, that policies designed to raise saving have their costs. Homebuyers in the United States would not be happy if they faced the borrowing constraints that are so common in Japan.

---

[2] Fumio Hayashi, "Why Is Japan's Saving Rate So Apparently High?" *NBER Macroeconomics Annual* (1986): 147–210.

15-3 Franco Modigliani and the Life-Cycle Hypothesis

In a series of papers written in the 1950s, Franco Modigliani and his collaborators Albert Ando and Richard Brumberg used Fisher's model of consumer behavior to study the consumption function. One of their goals was to solve the consumption puzzle—that is, to explain the apparently conflicting pieces of evidence that came to light when Keynes's consumption function was brought to the data. According to Fisher's model, consumption depends on a person's lifetime income. Modigliani emphasized that income varies systematically over people's lives and that saving allows consumers to move income from those times in life when income is high to those times when it is low. This interpretation of consumer behavior formed the basis for his **life-cycle hypothesis.**[3]

The Hypothesis

One important reason that income varies over a person's life is retirement. Most people plan to stop working at about age 65, and they expect their incomes to fall when they retire. Yet they do not want a large drop in their standard of living, as measured by their consumption. To maintain consumption after retirement, people must save during their working years. Let's see what this motive for saving implies for the consumption function.

Consider a consumer who expects to live another T years, has wealth of W, and expects to earn income Y until she retires R years from now. What level of consumption will the consumer choose if she wishes to maintain a smooth level of consumption over her life?

The consumer's lifetime resources are composed of initial wealth W and lifetime earnings of $R \times Y$. (For simplicity, we are assuming an interest rate of zero; if the interest rate were greater than zero, we would need to take account of interest earned on savings as well.) The consumer can divide up her lifetime resources among her T remaining years of life. We assume that she wishes to achieve the smoothest possible path of consumption over her lifetime. Therefore, she divides this total of $W + RY$ equally among the T years and each year consumes

$$C = (W + RY)/T.$$

We can write this person's consumption function as

$$C = (1/T)W + (R/T)Y.$$

---

[3] For references to the large body of work on the life-cycle hypothesis, a good place to start is the lecture Modigliani gave when he won the Nobel Prize. Franco Modigliani, "Life Cycle, Individual Thrift, and the Wealth of Nations," *American Economic Review* 76 (June 1986): 297–313.

For example, if the consumer expects to live for 50 more years and work for 30 of them, then $T = 50$ and $R = 30$, so her consumption function is

$$C = 0.02W + 0.6Y.$$

This equation says that consumption depends on both income and wealth. An extra \$1 of income per year raises consumption by \$0.60 per year, and an extra \$1 of wealth raises consumption by \$0.02 per year.

If every individual in the economy plans consumption like this, then the aggregate consumption function is much the same as the individual one. In particular, aggregate consumption depends on both wealth and income. That is, the economy's consumption function is

$$C = \alpha W + \beta Y,$$

where the parameter α is the marginal propensity to consume out of wealth, and the parameter β is the marginal propensity to consume out of income.

Implications

Figure 15-11 graphs the relationship between consumption and income predicted by the life-cycle model. For any given level of wealth, the model yields a conventional consumption function, such as in Figure 15-1. Notice, however, that the intercept of the consumption function αW is not a fixed value but depends on the level of wealth.

Figure 15-11

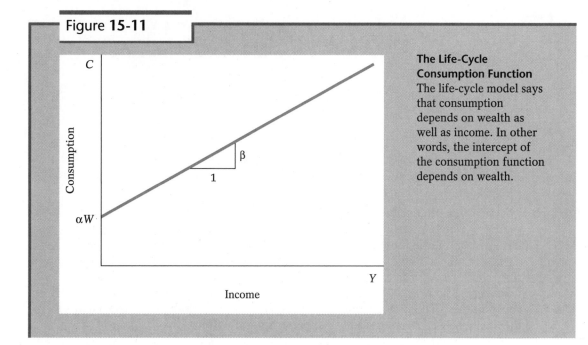

The Life-Cycle Consumption Function The life-cycle model says that consumption depends on wealth as well as income. In other words, the intercept of the consumption function depends on wealth.

This life-cycle model of consumer behavior can solve the consumption puzzle. According to the life-cycle consumption function, the average propensity to consume is

$$C/Y = \alpha(W/Y) + \beta.$$

Because wealth does not vary proportionately with income from person to person or from year to year, we should find that high income corresponds to a low average propensity to consume when looking at data across individuals or over short periods of time. But, over long periods of time, wealth and income grow together, resulting in a constant ratio W/Y and thus a constant average propensity to consume.

Figure 15-12

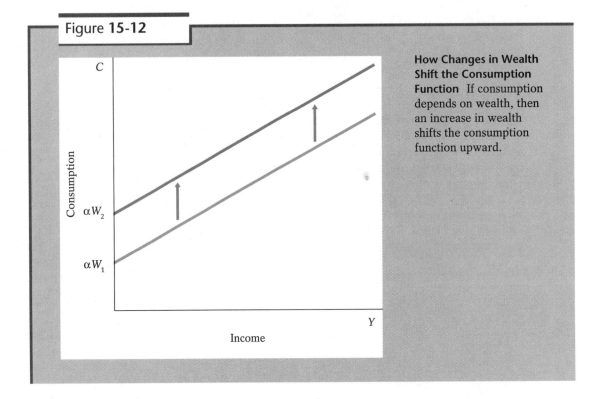

How Changes in Wealth Shift the Consumption Function If consumption depends on wealth, then an increase in wealth shifts the consumption function upward.

To make the same point somewhat differently, consider how the consumption function changes over time. As Figure 15-11 shows, for any given level of wealth, the life-cycle consumption function looks like the one Keynes suggested. But this function holds only in the short run when wealth is constant. In the long run, as wealth increases, the consumption function shifts upward, as in Figure 15-12. This upward shift prevents the average propensity to consume from falling as income increases. In this way, Modigliani reconciled the apparently conflicting studies of the consumption function.

The life-cycle model makes many other predictions as well. Most important, it predicts that saving varies over a person's lifetime. If a person begins adulthood with no wealth, she will accumulate wealth during her working years and then run down her wealth during her retirement years. Figure 15-13 illustrates the consumer's income, consumption, and wealth over her adult life. According to the life-cycle hypothesis, the young who are working save, while the old who are retired dissave.

Figure 15-13

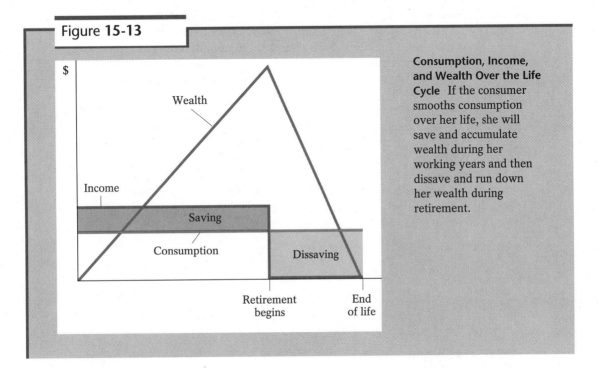

Consumption, Income, and Wealth Over the Life Cycle If the consumer smooths consumption over her life, she will save and accumulate wealth during her working years and then dissave and run down her wealth during retirement.

Case Study *15-3*

• • • • • • • • • • • • •

The Consumption and Saving of the Elderly

Many economists have studied the consumption and saving of the elderly. Their findings present a problem for the life-cycle model. It appears that the elderly do not dissave as much as the model predicts. In other words, the elderly do not run down their wealth as quickly as one would expect if they were trying to smooth their consumption over their remaining years of life.

There are two chief explanations for why the elderly do not dissave to the extent that the model predicts. Each suggests a direction for further research on consumption.

The first explanation is that the elderly are concerned about unpredictable expenses. Additional saving that arises from uncertainty is called **precautionary saving**. One reason for precautionary saving by the elderly is the possibility of living longer than expected and thus having to provide for a longer than average span of retirement. Another reason is the possibility of illness and large medical bills. The elderly may respond to this uncertainty by saving more in order to be better prepared for these contingencies.

The precautionary-saving explanation is not completely persuasive, because the elderly can largely insure against these risks. To protect against uncertainty regarding life span, they can buy annuities from insurance companies. For a fixed fee, annuities offer a stream of income that lasts as long as the recipient lives. Uncertainty about medical expenses should be largely eliminated by Medicare, the government's health insurance plan for the elderly, and by private insurance plans.

The second explanation for the failure of the elderly to dissave is that they may want to leave bequests to their children. Economists have proposed various theories of the parent–child relationship and the bequest motive. In Chapter 16 we discuss some of these theories and their implications for consumption.

Overall, research on the elderly suggests that the simplest life-cycle model cannot fully explain consumer behavior. There is no doubt that providing for retirement is an important motive for saving, but other motives, such as precautionary saving and bequests, appear important as well.[4]

● ● ● ● ● ● ● ● ● ● ● ● ● ●

Case Study *15-4*

● ● ● ● ● ● ● ● ● ● ● ● ●

Social Security and Saving

Government policy affects private saving in many ways. The government encourages retirement saving, for example, by giving preferential tax treatment to income earned in pension plans and other retirement accounts. Such policies are intended to raise national saving in order to promote capital accumulation.

One government program that is often thought to reduce private saving is the Social Security system. Social Security is a transfer system designed to maintain individuals' income in their old age. A payroll tax on the working-age population pays for these transfers to the elderly. This system reduces the need for individuals to save for their own retirement.

To counteract the reduction in national saving attributed to Social Security, many economists have proposed that the Social Security system be re-

---

[4]   To read more about the consumption and saving of the elderly, see Albert Ando and Arthur Kennickell, "How Much (or Little) Life Cycle Saving Is There in Micro Data?" in Rudiger Dornbusch, Stanley Fischer, and John Bossons, eds., *Macroeconomics and Finance: Essays in Honor of Franco Modigliani* (Cambridge, Mass.: MIT Press, 1986); and Michael Hurd, "Research on the Elderly: Economic Status, Retirement, and Consumption and Saving," *Journal of Economic Literature* 28 (June 1990): 565–589.

formed. The system is now *pay as you go*—most of the current tax receipts are paid out to the current elderly population. One suggestion is that Social Security should be *fully funded*. Under this plan, the government would put aside in a trust fund the payments a generation makes when it is young and working; the government would then pay out the principal and accumulated interest to this same generation when it is older and retired. Under a fully funded Social Security system, an increase in public saving would offset the reduction in private saving.

Because the impact of Social Security on national saving is potentially so important, many economists have attempted to estimate the magnitude of this effect. The evidence, however, is mixed. There is, therefore, no consensus about whether Social Security reduces national saving or, if it does, by how much.[5]

● ● ● ● ● ● ● ● ● ● ● ● ● ●

15-4 Milton Friedman and the Permanent-Income Hypothesis

In a book published in 1957, Milton Friedman proposed the **permanent-income hypothesis** to explain consumer behavior. Friedman's permanent-income hypothesis complements Modigliani's life-cycle hypothesis: both use Irving Fisher's theory of the consumer to argue that consumption should not depend on current income alone. But unlike the life-cycle hypothesis, which emphasizes that income follows a regular pattern over a person's lifetime, the permanent-income hypothesis emphasizes that people experience random and temporary changes in their incomes from year to year.[6]

The Hypothesis

Friedman suggested that we view current income Y as the sum of two components, **permanent income** Y^P and **transitory income** Y^T. That is,

$$Y = Y^P + Y^T.$$

Permanent income is the part of income that people expect to persist into the future. Transitory income is the part of income that people do not expect to persist. Put differently, permanent income is average income, and transitory income is the random deviation from that average.

---

5 To get the flavor of the debate, see Martin S. Feldstein, "Social Security, Induced Retirement, and Aggregate Capital Accumulation," *Journal of Political Economy* 82 (September/October 1974): 905–926; Dean R. Leimer and Selig D. Lesnoy, "Social Security and Private Saving: New Time Series Evidence," *Journal of Political Economy* 90 (June 1982): 606–629; and Martin S. Feldstein, "Social Security and Private Saving: Reply," *Journal of Political Economy* 90 (June 1982): 630–642.

6 Milton Friedman, *A Theory of the Consumption Function* (Princeton, N.J.: Princeton University Press, 1957).

To see how we might separate income into these two parts, consider these examples:

- Maria, who has a law degree, earned more this year than John, who is a high-school dropout. Maria's higher income resulted from higher permanent income, because her education will continue to provide her a higher salary.

- Sue, a Florida orange grower, earned less than usual this year because a freeze destroyed her crop. Bill, a California orange grower, earned more than usual because the freeze in Florida drove up the price of oranges. Bill's higher income resulted from higher transitory income, because he is no more likely than Sue to have good weather next year.

These examples show that different forms of income have different degrees of persistence. A good education provides a permanently higher income, whereas good weather provides only transitorily higher income. Although one can imagine intermediate cases, it is useful to keep things simple by supposing that there are only two kinds of income: permanent and transitory.

Friedman reasoned that consumption should depend primarily on permanent income, because consumers use saving and borrowing to smooth consumption in response to transitory changes in income. For example, if a person received a permanent raise of $10,000, his consumption would rise by about as much. Yet if a person won $10,000 in a lottery, he would not consume it all in one year. Instead, he would spread the extra consumption over the rest of his life. Assuming an interest rate of zero and a remaining life span of 50 years, consumption would rise by only $200 per year in response to the $10,000 prize. Thus, consumers spend their permanent income, but they save rather than spend most of their transitory income.

Friedman concluded that we should view the consumption function as approximately

$$C = \alpha Y^P,$$

where α is a constant. The permanent-income hypothesis, as expressed by this equation, states that consumption is proportional to permanent income.

Implications

The permanent-income hypothesis solves the consumption puzzle by suggesting that the standard Keynesian consumption function uses the wrong variable. According to the permanent-income hypothesis, consumption depends on permanent income; yet many studies of the consumption function try to relate consumption to current income. Friedman argued that this *errors-in-variables problem* explains the seemingly contradictory findings.

Let's see what Friedman's hypothesis implies for the average propensity to consume. Divide both sides of his consumption function by Y to obtain

$$APC = C/Y = \alpha Y^P/Y.$$

According to the permanent-income hypothesis, the average propensity to consume depends on the ratio of permanent income to current income. When current income temporarily rises above permanent income, the average propensity to consume temporarily falls; when current income temporarily falls below permanent income, the average propensity to consume temporarily rises.

Now consider the studies of household data. Friedman reasoned that these data reflect a combination of permanent and transitory income. Households with high permanent income have proportionately higher consumption. If all variation in current income came from the permanent component, the average propensity to consume would be the same in all households. But some of the variation in income comes from the transitory component, and households with high transitory income do not have higher consumption. Therefore, researchers find that high-income households have, on average, lower average propensities to consume.

Similarly, consider the studies of time-series data. Friedman reasoned that year-to-year fluctuations in income are dominated by transitory income. Therefore, years of high income should be years of low average propensities to consume. But over long periods of time—say, from decade to decade—the variation in income comes from the permanent component. Hence, in long time-series, one should observe a constant average propensity to consume.

Case Study *15-5*

The 1964 Tax Cut and the 1968 Tax Surcharge

The permanent-income hypothesis can help us to interpret how the economy responds to changes in fiscal policy. According to the *IS-LM* model of Chapters 9 and 10, tax cuts stimulate consumption and raise aggregate demand, and tax increases depress consumption and reduce aggregate demand. The permanent-income hypothesis, however, predicts that consumption responds only to changes in permanent income. Therefore, transitory changes in taxes will have only a negligible effect on consumption and aggregate demand. If a change in taxes is to have a large effect on aggregate demand, it must be permanent.

Two changes in fiscal policy—the tax cut of 1964 and the tax surcharge of 1968—illustrate this principle. The tax cut of 1964 was popular. It was announced to be a major and permanent reduction in tax rates. As we discussed in Chapter 9, this policy change had the intended effect of stimulating the economy.

The tax surcharge of 1968 arose in a very different political climate. It became law because the economic advisors of President Lyndon Johnson believed that the increase in government spending from the Vietnam War had excessively stimulated aggregate demand. To offset this effect, they recommended a tax increase. But Johnson, aware that the war was already unpopular, feared the political repercussions of higher taxes. He finally agreed to a temporary tax surcharge—in essence, a one-year increase in taxes. The tax surcharge did not have the desired effect of reducing aggregate demand. Unemployment continued to fall, and inflation continued to rise.

The lesson to be learned from these episodes is that a full analysis of tax policy must go beyond the simple Keynesian consumption function; it must take into account the distinction between permanent and transitory income. If consumers expect a tax change to be temporary, it will have a smaller impact on consumption and aggregate demand.

● ● ● ● ● ● ● ● ● ● ● ● ●

Rational Expectations and Consumption

The permanent-income hypothesis is founded on Fisher's model of intertemporal choice. It builds on the idea that forward-looking consumers base their consumption decisions not only on their current income but also on the income they expect to receive in the future. Thus, the permanent-income hypothesis highlights that consumption depends on people's expectations.

Recent research on consumption has combined this view of the consumer with the assumption of rational expectations. The rational-expectations assumption states that people use all available information to make optimal forecasts about the future. You might recall from Chapter 12 that this assumption has potentially profound implications for the costs of stopping inflation. It can also have profound implications for consumption.

The economist Robert Hall was the first to derive the implications of rational expectations for consumption. He showed that if the permanent-income hypothesis is correct, and if consumers have rational expectations, then changes in consumption over time should be unpredictable. When changes in a variable are unpredictable, the variable is said to follow a *random walk*. According to Hall, the combination of the permanent-income hypothesis and rational expectations implies that consumption follows a random walk.

Hall reasoned as follows. According to the permanent-income hypothesis, consumers face fluctuating income and try their best to smooth their consumption over time. At any moment, consumers choose consumption based on their current expectations of their lifetime incomes. Over time, they change their consumption because they receive news that causes them to revise their expectations. For example, a person getting an unexpected promotion increases consumption, whereas a person getting an unexpected demotion decreases consumption. In other words, changes in consumption reflect "surprises" about lifetime income. If consumers are optimally using all available information, then these surprises should be unpredictable. Therefore, changes in their consumption should be unpredictable as well.

The evidence shows that the random-walk theorem does not describe the world exactly. That is, changes in aggregate consumption are somewhat predictable. Yet because the degree of predictability is small, some economists view the random-walk theorem—and therefore the rational expectations assumption—as a good approximation to reality.[7]

---

[7]   Robert E. Hall, "Stochastic Implications of the Life Cycle–Permanent Income Hypothesis: Theory and Evidence," *Journal of Political Economy* 86 (April 1978): 971–987.

The rational-expectations approach to consumption has implications not only for forecasting but also for the analysis of economic policies. *If consumers obey the permanent-income hypothesis and have rational expectations, then only unexpected policy changes influence consumption. These policy changes take effect when they change expectations.* For example, suppose that today Congress passes a tax increase to be effective next year. In this case, consumers receive the news about their lifetime incomes when Congress passes the law (or even earlier if the law's passage was predictable). The arrival of this news causes consumers to revise their expectations and reduce their consumption. The following year, when the tax hike goes into effect, consumption is unchanged because no news has arrived.

Hence, if consumers have rational expectations, policymakers influence the economy not only through their actions but also through the public's expectation of their actions. Expectations, however, cannot be observed directly. Therefore, it is often hard to know how and when changes in fiscal policy alter aggregate demand.

Case Study *15-6*

Do Consumers Anticipate Future Income?

The essence of Fisher's model of the consumer—and of almost all subsequent work on consumption—is that consumption today depends not just on income today but also on income in the future. The more consumers expect to earn in the future, the more they consume today.

The model suggests that saving rates should help forecast future income growth. If consumers are saving a low fraction of current income, then they must be optimistic about future income. Conversely, if consumers are saving a high fraction of current income, then they must be pessimistic about future income. If this theory is correct, we should be able to examine data on the saving rate and find that periods of low saving are typically followed by periods of high income growth.[8]

Studies of time-series data on consumption and income support this prediction. The saving rate does tend to rise when recessions are approaching, and booms are often preceded by low saving rates. Consumers do look ahead to their future income when making their consumption decisions.

The evidence is not completely consistent with the theory, however. In particular, saving moves less than predicted. In other words, it appears that future income has a weaker influence on consumption, and current income has a stronger influence, than the permanent-income hypothesis predicts. One

---

[8] *Mathematical note:* To see how this works, let us consider our two-period example. Suppose that the interest rate is zero and that the consumer divides his total resources between the two periods, so that $C_1 = (Y_1 + Y_2)/2$. Then with simple algebraic rearrangement, you can show that $g = -2s$, where $g = (Y_2 - Y_1)/Y_1$ is the growth rate of income between the two periods and $s = (Y_1 - C_1)/Y_1$ is the first-period saving rate. Hence, saving and subsequent growth are negatively related.

possible reason for this behavior is that some consumers may not have rational expectations: they may base their expectations of future income excessively on current income. Another possible reason is that some consumers are borrowing-constrained and therefore base their consumption on current income alone.[9]

• • • • • • • • • • • • • • • •

15-5 Conclusion

In the work of Keynes, Fisher, Modigliani, and Friedman, we have seen a progression of views on consumer behavior. Keynes proposed that consumption depends largely on current income. Since then, economists have argued that consumers understand that they face an intertemporal decision. Consumers look ahead to their future resources and needs, implying a more complex consumption function than the one that Keynes proposed. Keynes suggested a consumption function of the form

$$Consumption = f(Current\ Income).$$

Recent work suggests instead that

$$Consumption = f(Current\ Income,\ Wealth,\ Expected\ Future\ Income,\ Interest\ Rates).$$

In other words, current income is only one determinant of aggregate consumption.

Economists continue to debate the relative importance of these determinants of consumption. There remains disagreement, for example, on the effect of interest rates and the prevalence of borrowing constraints. One reason economists sometimes disagree about the effects of economic policy is that they assume different consumption functions. In the next chapter, we examine the debates about the impact of government debt, which are largely about alternative views of consumer behavior.

Summary

1. Keynes conjectured that the marginal propensity to consume is between zero and one, that the average propensity to consume falls as income rises, and that current income is the primary determinant of consumption. Studies of household data and short time-series confirmed Keynes's conjectures. Yet stud-

---

[9] John Y. Campbell, "Does Saving Anticipate Declining Labor Income?" *Econometrica* 55 (November 1982): 1249–1273; John Y. Campbell and N. Gregory Mankiw, "Consumption, Income, and Interest Rates: Reinterpreting the Time-Series Evidence," *NBER Macroeconomics Annual* (1989): 185–216.

ies of long time-series found no tendency for the average propensity to consume to fall as income rises over time.

2. Recent work on consumption builds on Irving Fisher's model of the consumer. In this model, the consumer faces an intertemporal budget constraint and chooses consumption for the present and the future to achieve the highest level of lifetime satisfaction. As long as the consumer can save and borrow, consumption depends on the consumer's lifetime resources.

3. Modigliani's life-cycle hypothesis emphasizes that income varies somewhat predictably over a person's life and that consumers use saving and borrowing to smooth their consumption over their lifetimes. According to this hypothesis, consumption depends on both income and wealth.

4. Friedman's permanent-income hypothesis emphasizes that individuals experience both permanent and transitory fluctuations in their income. Because consumers can save and borrow, and because they want to smooth their consumption, consumption does not respond much to transitory income. Consumption depends primarily on permanent income.

KEY CONCEPTS

Marginal propensity to consume	Substitution effect
Average propensity to consume	Borrowing constraint
Intertemporal budget constraint	Life-cycle hypothesis
Discounting	Precautionary saving
Indifference curves	Permanent-income hypothesis
Marginal rate of substitution	Permanent income
Normal good	Transitory income
Income effect	

QUESTIONS FOR REVIEW

1. What were Keynes's three conjectures about the consumption function?

2. Describe the evidence that was consistent with Keynes's conjectures and the evidence that was inconsistent with them.

3. How do the life-cycle and permanent-income hypotheses resolve the seemingly contradictory pieces of evidence regarding consumption behavior?

4. Use Fisher's model of consumption to analyze an increase in second-period income. Compare the case in which the consumer faces a binding borrowing constraint and the case in which he does not.

5. Explain why changes in consumption are unpredictable if consumers obey the permanent-income hypothesis and have rational expectations.

PROBLEMS AND APPLICATIONS

1. The chapter uses the Fisher model to discuss a change in the interest rate for a consumer who saves some of his first-period income. Suppose, instead, that the consumer is a borrower. How does that alter the analysis? Discuss the income and substitution effects on consumption in both periods.

2. Jack and Jill both obey the two-period Fisher model of consumption. Jack earns $100 in the first period and $100 in the second period. Jill earns nothing in the first period and $210 in the second period. Both of them can borrow or lend at the interest rate r.

   a. You observe both Jack and Jill consuming $100 in the first period and $100 in the second period. What is the interest rate r?

   b. Suppose the interest rate increases. What will happen to Jack's consumption in the first period? Is Jack better off or worse off than before the interest rate rise?

   c. What will happen to Jill's consumption in the first period when the interest rate increases? Is Jill better off or worse off than before the interest rate increase?

3. The chapter analyzes Fisher's model for the case in which the consumer can save or borrow at an interest rate of r and for the case in which the consumer can save at this rate but cannot borrow at all. Consider now the intermediate case in which the consumer can save at rate r_s and borrow at rate r_b, where $r_s < r_b$.

   a. What is the consumer's budget constraint in the case in which he consumes less than his income in period one?

   b. What is the consumer's budget constraint in the case in which he consumes more than his income in period one?

   c. Graph the two budget constraints and shade the area that represents the combination of first-period and second-period consumption the consumer can choose.

   d. Now add to your graph the consumer's indifference curves. Show three possible outcomes: one in which the consumer saves, one in which he borrows, and one in which he neither saves nor borrows.

   e. What determines first-period consumption in each of the three cases?

4. Explain whether borrowing constraints increase or decrease the potency of fiscal policy to influence aggregate demand in each of the following two cases:

   a. A temporary tax cut.

   b. An announced future tax cut.

5. In the discussion of the life-cycle hypothesis in the text, income is assumed to be constant during the period before retirement. For most people, however, income grows over their lifetimes. How does this growth in income influence the lifetime pattern of consumption and wealth accumulation shown in Figure 15-13 under the following conditions?

   a. Consumers can borrow, so their wealth can be negative.

   b. Consumers face borrowing constraints that prevent their wealth from falling below zero.

Do you consider case (a) or case (b) to be more realistic? Why?

6. Demographers predict that the fraction of the population that is elderly will increase over the next 20 years. What does the life-cycle model predict for the influence of this demographic change on the national saving rate?

7. One study found that the elderly who do not have children dissave at about the same rate as the elderly who do have children. What might this finding imply about the reason the elderly do not dissave as much as the life-cycle model predicts?

Chapter 16

The Debates Over Government Debt

Blessed are the young, for they shall inherit the national debt.

Herbert Hoover

When a government spends more than it collects in taxes, it borrows from the private sector to finance the budget deficit. The accumulation of past borrowing is the government debt. All governments have some debt, although the amount varies substantially from country to country. Table 16-1 shows the amount of government debt for 19 major countries.

Table 16-1	How Indebted Are the World's Governments?
Country	Government Debt as a Percentage of GDP
Belgium	136%
Italy	121
Greece	120
Japan	96
Canada	94
Sweden	86
Netherlands	80
Ireland	79
Finland	73
Portugal	71
Spain	69
Denmark	68
United States	64
Germany	63
Austria	61
France	61
United Kingdom	53
Norway	46
Australia	37

Source: OECD Economic Outlook. Figures are based on estimates of general government gross financial liabilities and GDP for 1996.

Figure **16-1**

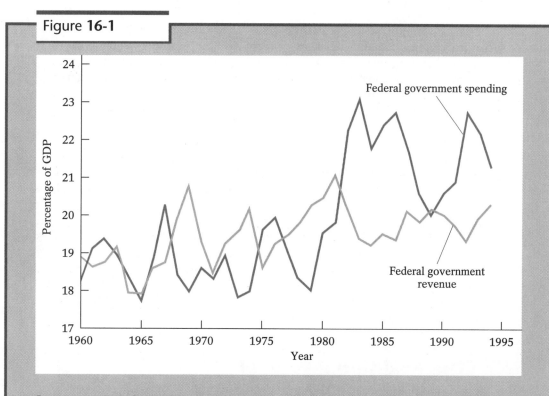

Government Spending and Revenue as a Percentage of GDP This figure shows spending and revenue of the U.S. federal government as a percentage of GDP since 1960. When spending exceeds revenue, the government runs a budget deficit, which it finances by issuing government debt. When revenue exceeds spending, the government runs a budget surplus, which allows it to retire some of the government debt.

Note: These data are corrected for the effects of inflation. As discussed in Section 16-3, only the real interest paid on the debt is counted as spending.

Source: U.S. Department of Treasury, U.S. Department of Commerce, and author's calculations.

Although the debt of the U.S. government is typical by international standards, the rapid rise in the debt over the past two decades is striking. Figure 16-1 shows federal spending and revenue as a percentage of GDP. The difference between these two lines is the budget surplus or budget deficit. The figure shows that in the early 1980s, the federal government began running large budget deficits. In part because of higher spending, and in part because of lower taxes, the government began spending more than it received. As a result, the government debt rose from 34 percent of GDP in 1980 to about twice that level today. Such a large peacetime increase in government debt is unprecedented in U.S. history.

This experience sparked a renewed interest among economists and policymakers in the economic effects of government debt. Some view these large budget deficits as the worst mistake of economic policy since the Great Depression. Others think that the deficits matter very little.

This chapter presents the various views of government debt. Section 16-1 describes the traditional view of government debt, according to which government borrowing reduces national saving and crowds out capital accumulation. This view is held by most economists and has been implicit in the discussion of fiscal policy throughout this textbook.

Section 16-2 discusses an alternative view, called *Ricardian equivalence*, which is held by a small but influential minority of economists. According to the Ricardian view, government debt does not influence saving and capital accumulation. We will see that this debate over government debt arises from disagreements over the theory of consumption. In evaluating whether the traditional or the Ricardian view of government debt is correct, the key question is how fiscal policy affects consumer spending. To analyze the effects of government budget deficits on the economy, we must take a stand on whether consumers are shortsighted or forward-looking, on whether they face borrowing constraints or not, and on other aspects of consumer behavior.

Section 16-3 turns to another set of issues in the debate over government debt. We will see that the budget deficit is not as easy to measure as it might seem. Some economists have argued that traditional measures of the budget deficit are so misleading that they should be completely ignored.

16-1   The Traditional View of Government Debt

You are an economist working for the Congressional Budget Office (CBO). You receive a letter from the chair of the Senate Budget Committee:

> Dear CBO Economist:
>
> Congress is about to consider the president's request to cut all taxes by 20 percent. Before deciding whether to endorse the request, my committee would like your analysis. We see little hope of reducing government spending, so the tax cut would mean an increase in the budget deficit. How would the tax cut and budget deficit affect the economy and the economic well-being of the country?
>
> Sincerely,
> Committee Chair

Before responding to the senator, you open your favorite economics textbook—this one, of course—to see what the models predict for such a change in fiscal policy.

To analyze the long-run effects of this policy change, you turn to the models in Chapters 3 and 4. The model in Chapter 3 shows that a tax cut stimulates consumer spending and reduces national saving. The reduction in saving raises the interest rate, which crowds out investment. The Solow growth model in Chapter 4 shows that lower investment eventually leads to a lower steady-state capital stock and a lower level of output. Because the economy starts with less capital than in the Golden Rule steady state, the reduction in steady-state capital implies lower consumption and reduced economic well-being.

To analyze the short-run effects of the policy change, you turn to the *IS-LM* model in Chapters 9 and 10. This model shows that a tax cut stimulates consumer spending, which implies an expansionary shift in the *IS* curve. If there is no change in monetary policy, the shift in the *IS* curve leads to an expansionary shift in the aggregate demand curve. In the short run, when prices are sticky, the expansion in aggregate demand leads to higher output and lower unemployment. Over time, as prices adjust, the economy returns to the natural rate of output, and the higher aggregate demand results in a higher price level.

To see how international trade affects your analysis, you turn to the open-economy models in Chapters 7 and 11. The model in Chapter 7 shows that reduced national saving causes a trade deficit. Although the inflow of capital from abroad lessens the effect of the fiscal policy change on capital accumulation, the United States becomes indebted to foreign countries. The fiscal policy change also causes the dollar to appreciate, which makes foreign goods cheaper in the United States and domestic goods more expensive abroad. The Mundell-Fleming model in Chapter 11 shows that the appreciation of the dollar and the fall in net exports reduce the short-run expansionary impact of the fiscal change on output and employment.

With all these models in mind, you draft a response:

Dear Senator:

A tax cut financed by government borrowing would have many effects on the economy. The immediate impact of the tax cut would be to stimulate consumer spending. Higher consumer spending affects the economy in both the short run and the long run.

In the short run, higher consumer spending would raise the demand for goods and services and thus raise output and employment. Interest rates would also rise, however, as investors competed for a smaller flow of saving. Higher interest rates would discourage investment and would encourage capital to flow in from abroad. The dollar would rise in value against foreign currencies, and U.S. firms would become less competitive in world markets.

In the long run, the smaller national saving caused by the tax cut would mean a smaller capital stock and a greater foreign debt. Therefore, the output of the nation would be smaller, and a greater share of that output would be owed to foreigners.

The overall effect of the tax cut on economic well-being is hard to judge. Current generations would benefit from higher consumption and higher employment, although inflation would likely be higher as well. Future generations would bear much of the burden of today's budget deficits: they would be born into a nation with a smaller capital stock and a larger foreign debt.

Your faithful servant,
CBO Economist

The senator replies:

Dear CBO Economist:

Thank you for your letter. It made sense to me. But yesterday my committee heard testimony from a prominent economist who called herself a "Ricardian" and who reached quite a different conclusion. She said that a tax cut by itself would not stimulate consumer spending. She concluded that the budget deficit would therefore not have all the effects you listed. What's going on here?

Sincerely,
Committee Chair

After studying the next section, you write back to the senator, explaining in detail the debate over Ricardian equivalence.

16-2 The Ricardian View of Government Debt

Modern theories of consumer behavior emphasize that, because consumers are forward-looking, consumption does not depend on current income alone. The forward-looking consumer is at the heart of Franco Modigliani's life-cycle hypothesis and Milton Friedman's permanent-income hypothesis. The Ricardian view of government debt applies the logic of the forward-looking consumer to analyze the impact of fiscal policy.

The Basic Logic of Ricardian Equivalence

Consider the response of a forward-looking consumer to the tax cut that the Senate Budget Committee is considering. The consumer might reason as follows:

> The government is cutting taxes without any plans to reduce government spending. Does this policy alter my set of opportunities? Am I richer because of this tax cut? Should I consume more?
>
> Maybe not. The government is financing the tax cut by running a budget deficit. At some point in the future, the government will have to raise taxes to pay off the debt and accumulated interest. So the policy really represents a tax cut today coupled with a tax hike in the future. The tax cut merely gives me transitory income that eventually will be taken back. I am not any better off, so I will leave my consumption unchanged.

The forward-looking consumer understands that government borrowing today means higher taxes in the future. A tax cut financed by government debt does not reduce the tax burden; it merely reschedules it. It does not raise the consumer's permanent income and, therefore, does not increase consumption.

One can view this argument another way. Suppose that the government borrows $1,000 from the typical citizen to give that citizen a $1,000 tax cut. In essence, this policy is the same as giving the citizen a $1,000 government bond as a gift. One side of the bond says, "The government owes you, the bondholder, $1,000 plus interest." The other side says, "You, the taxpayer, owe the government $1,000 plus interest." Overall, the gift of a bond from the government to the typical citizen does not make the citizen richer or poorer, because the value of the bond is offset by the value of the future tax liability.

The general principle is that government debt is equivalent to future taxes, and if consumers are sufficiently forward-looking, future taxes are equivalent to current taxes. Hence, financing the government by debt is equivalent to financing it by taxes. This view, called **Ricardian equivalence**, is named after the famous nineteenth-century economist David Ricardo, because he first noted the theoretical argument.[1]

The implication of Ricardian equivalence is that a debt-financed tax cut leaves consumption unaffected. Households save the extra disposable income to pay the future tax liability that the tax cut implies. This increase in private saving just offsets the decrease in public saving. National saving—the sum of private and public saving—remains the same. The tax cut therefore has none of the effects that the traditional analysis predicts.

The logic of Ricardian equivalence does not mean that all changes in fiscal policy are irrelevant. Changes in fiscal policy do influence consumer spending if they influence present or future government purchases. For example, suppose that the government cuts taxes today because it plans to reduce government purchases in the future. If the consumer understands that this tax cut does not require an increase in future taxes, he feels richer and raises his consumption. But note that it is the reduction in government purchases, rather than the reduction in taxes, that stimulates consumption: the announcement of a future reduction in government purchases would raise consumption today even if current taxes were unchanged, because it would imply lower taxes at some time in the future.

The Government Budget Constraint

To better understand the link between government debt and future taxes, it is useful to imagine that the economy lasts for only two periods. Period one represents the present, period two the future. In period one, the government collects taxes T_1 and makes purchases G_1; in period two, it collects taxes T_2 and makes purchases G_2. Because the government can run a budget deficit or a budget surplus, taxes and purchases in any single period need not be closely related.

We want to see how the government's tax receipts in the two periods are related to its purchases in the two periods. In the first period, the budget deficit equals government purchases minus taxes. That is,

$$D = G_1 - T_1,$$

where D is the deficit. The government finances this deficit by selling an equal amount of government bonds. In the second period, the government must collect enough taxes to repay the debt, including the accumulated interest, and to pay for its second-period purchases. Thus,

$$T_2 = (1 + r)D + G_2,$$

where r is the interest rate.

---

[1] Ironically, Ricardo was not a Ricardian. He was skeptical about the theory that now bears his name.

To derive the equation linking taxes and purchases, combine the two equations above. Substitute the first equation for D into the second equation to obtain

$$T_2 = (1 + r)(G_1 - T_1) + G_2.$$

This equation relates purchases in the two periods to taxes in the two periods. To make the equation easier to interpret, we rearrange terms. After a little algebra, we obtain

$$T_1 + \frac{T_2}{1 + r} = G_1 + \frac{G_2}{1 + r}.$$

This equation is the **government budget constraint**. It states that the present value of government purchases must equal the present value of taxes.

The government budget constraint shows how changes in fiscal policy today are linked to changes in fiscal policy in the future. If the government cuts first-period taxes without altering first-period purchases, then it enters the second period owing a debt to the holders of government bonds. This debt forces the government to choose between reducing purchases and raising taxes.

Figure 16-2 uses the Fisher diagram from Chapter 15 to show how a tax cut in period one affects the consumer under the assumption that the government does not alter its purchases in either period. In period one, the govern-

Figure 16-2

A Debt-Financed Tax Cut in the Fisher Diagram A debt-financed tax cut of ΔT raises first-period income. Yet if government purchases are unchanged, then the government budget constraint requires that second-period taxes be raised by $(1 + r)\Delta T$. The consumer's income in the two periods moves from point A to point B. Because the present value of income is unchanged, the budget constraint is unchanged. As a result, the tax cut does not alter the level of consumption in either period. Hence, Ricardian equivalence holds.

ment cuts taxes by ΔT and finances this tax cut by borrowing. In period two, the government must raise taxes by $(1 + r)\Delta T$ to repay its debt and accumulated interest. Thus, the change in fiscal policy raises the consumer's income by ΔT in period one and reduces it by $(1 + r)\Delta T$ in period two. The consumer's set of opportunities is unchanged, however, because the present value of the consumer's lifetime income is the same as before the change in fiscal policy. Therefore, the consumer chooses the same level of consumption as he would have without the tax cut, which implies that private saving rises by the amount of the tax cut. Hence, by combining the government budget constraint and Fisher's model of intertemporal choice, we obtain the Ricardian result that a debt-financed tax cut does not affect consumption.

Consumers and Future Taxes

The essence of the Ricardian view is that when people choose their consumption, they rationally look ahead to the future taxes implied by government debt. But how forward-looking are consumers? Defenders of the traditional view of government debt believe that future taxes do not have as large an influence on current consumption as the Ricardian view assumes. Here are some of their arguments.[2]

Myopia Proponents of the Ricardian view of fiscal policy assume that people are rational when making important decisions such as choosing how much of their income to consume and how much to save. When the government borrows to pay for current spending, rational consumers look ahead to the future taxes required to support this debt. Thus, the Ricardian view presumes that people have substantial knowledge and foresight.

One possible argument for the traditional view of tax cuts is that people are shortsighted, perhaps because they do not fully comprehend the implications of government budget deficits. It is possible that some people follow simple and not fully rational rules of thumb when choosing how much to save. Suppose, for example, that a person acts on the assumption that future taxes will be the same as current taxes. This person will fail to take account of future changes in taxes required by current government policies. A debt-financed tax cut will lead this person to believe that his permanent income has increased, even if it hasn't. The tax cut will therefore lead to higher consumption and lower national saving.

Borrowing Constraints The Ricardian view of government debt is based on the permanent-income hypothesis. This view assumes that consumption does not depend on current income alone, but on permanent income, which includes both current and expected future income. According to the Ricardian view, a debt-financed tax cut increases current income, but it leaves permanent income and consumption unchanged.

---

[2] For a survey of the debate over Ricardian equivalence, see Douglas Bernheim, "Ricardian Equivalence: An Evaluation of Theory and Evidence," *NBER Macroeconomics Annual* (1987): 263–303. See also the symposium on budget deficits in the Spring 1989 issue of the *Journal of Economic Perspectives*.

Advocates of the traditional view of government debt argue that we should not rely on the permanent-income hypothesis because some consumers face borrowing constraints. As we discussed in Chapter 15, a person facing a binding borrowing constraint can consume only his current income. For this person, current income rather than permanent income determines consumption; a debt-financed tax cut raises current income and thus consumption, even though future income is lower. In essence, when the government cuts current taxes and raises future taxes, it is giving taxpayers a loan. For individuals who wanted to obtain a loan but were unable to, the tax cut raises consumption.

Figure 16-3 uses the Fisher diagram to illustrate how a debt-financed tax cut raises consumption for a consumer facing a borrowing constraint. As we saw previously, this change in fiscal policy raises first-period income by ΔT and lowers second-period income by $(1 + r)\Delta T$. But the result is now different. Although the present value of income is the same, the consumer's set of opportu-

Figure 16-3

How a Debt-Financed Tax Cut Relaxes a Borrowing Constraint The consumer here faces two constraints. The budget constraint says that the present value of consumption must not exceed the present value of income. The borrowing constraint says that first-period consumption must not exceed first-period income. A debt-financed tax cut of ΔT raises first-period income by ΔT and reduces second-period income by $(1 + r)\Delta T$. Because the present value of income is unchanged, the budget constraint is unchanged. Yet because first-period income is higher, the borrowing constraint allows a higher level of first-period consumption. The consumer now chooses point B rather than point A. Hence, Ricardian equivalence fails to hold.

nities is larger: the tax cut has loosened the borrowing constraint that prevents first-period consumption from exceeding first-period income. The consumer can now choose point B rather than point A.

You can see that the debate over government debt naturally evolves into a debate over consumer behavior. If many consumers would like to borrow to consume but cannot, then a debt-financed tax cut will stimulate consumption, as the traditional view assumes. Yet if borrowing constraints are unimportant for most consumers and if the permanent-income hypothesis is valid, then consumers are more likely to take into account the future taxes required by government debt.

Case Study *16-1*

● ● ● ● ● ● ● ● ● ● ● ● ●

George Bush's Withholding Experiment

In early 1992, President George Bush pursued a novel policy to deal with the lingering recession in the United States. By executive order, he lowered the amount of income taxes that were being withheld from workers' paychecks. The order did not reduce the amount of taxes that workers owed; it merely delayed payment. The higher take-home pay that workers received during 1992 was to be offset by higher tax payments, or smaller tax refunds, when income taxes were due in April 1993.

What effect would you predict for this policy? According to the logic of Ricardian equivalence, consumers should realize that their lifetime resources were unchanged and, therefore, save the extra take-home pay to meet the upcoming tax liability. Yet George Bush claimed his policy would provide "money people can use to help pay for clothing, college, or to get a new car." That is, he believed that consumers would spend the extra income, thereby stimulating aggregate demand and helping the economy recover from the recession. Bush seemed to be assuming that consumers were shortsighted or faced binding borrowing constraints.

Gauging the actual effects of this policy is difficult with aggregate data, because many other things were happening at the same time. Yet some evidence comes from a survey two economists conducted shortly after the policy was announced. The survey asked people what they would do with the extra income. Fifty-seven percent of the respondents said they would save it, use it to repay debts, or adjust their withholding in order to reverse the effect of Bush's executive order. Forty-three percent said they would spend the extra income. Thus, for this policy change, a majority of the population was planning to act Ricardian. Nonetheless, Bush was partly right: many people planned to spend the extra income, even though they understood that the following year's tax bill would be higher.[3]

● ● ● ● ● ● ● ● ● ● ● ● ●

[3] Matthew D. Shapiro and Joel Slemrod, "Consumer Response to the Timing of Income: Evidence from a Change in Tax Withholding," *American Economic Review* 85 (March 1995): 274–283.

Future Generations   Besides myopia and borrowing constraints, a third argument for the traditional view of government debt is that consumers expect the implied future taxes to fall not on them but on future generations. Suppose, for example, that the government cuts taxes today, issues 30-year bonds to finance the budget deficit, and then raises taxes in 30 years to repay the loan. In this case, the government debt represents a transfer of wealth from the next generation of taxpayers (which faces the tax hike) to the current generation of taxpayers (which gets the tax cut). This transfer raises the lifetime resources of the current generation, so it raises their consumption. In essence, a debt-financed tax cut stimulates consumption because it gives the current generation the opportunity to consume at the expense of the next generation.

Economist Robert Barro has provided a clever rejoinder to this argument to support the Ricardian view. Barro argues that because future generations are the children and grand-

"What's this I hear about you adults mortgaging my future?"

children of the current generation, we should not view them as independent economic actors. Instead, he argues, the appropriate assumption is that current generations care about future generations. This altruism between generations is evidenced by the gifts that many people give their children, often in the form of bequests at the time of their death. The existence of bequests suggests that many people are not eager to take advantage of the opportunity to consume at their children's expense.

According to Barro's analysis, the relevant decisionmaking unit is not the individual, who lives only a finite number of years, but the family, which continues forever. In other words, an individual decides how much to consume based not only on his own income but also on the income of future members of his family. A debt-financed tax cut may raise the income an individual receives in his lifetime, but it does not raise his family's permanent income. Instead of consuming the extra income from the tax cut, the individual saves it and leaves it as a bequest to his children, who will bear the future tax liability.

Again, we see that the debate over government debt is really a debate over consumer behavior. The Ricardian view assumes that consumers have a long time horizon. Barro's analysis of the family implies that the consumer's time horizon, like the government's, is effectively infinite. Yet it is possible that consumers do not look ahead to the tax liabilities of future generations, perhaps because they do not care enough about their children to leave them a bequest. In this case, a debt-financed tax cut can alter consumption by redistributing wealth among generations.[4]

---

[4]   Robert J. Barro, "Are Government Bonds Net Wealth?" *Journal of Political Economy* 81 (1974): 1095–1117.

Case Study *16-2*

• • • • • • • • • • • • •

Why Do Parents Leave Bequests?

The debate over Ricardian equivalence is partly a debate over how different generations are linked to one another. Robert Barro's defense of the Ricardian view is based on the assumption that parents leave their children bequests because they care about them. But is altruism really the reason that parents leave bequests?

One group of economists has suggested that parents use bequests to control their children. Parents often want their children to do certain things for them, such as phoning home regularly and visiting on holidays. Perhaps parents use the implicit threat of disinheritance to induce their children to be more attentive.

To test this "strategic bequest motive," these economists examined data on how often children visit their parents. They found that the more wealthy the parent, the more often the children visit. Even more striking was another result: only wealth that can be left as a bequest induces more frequent visits. Wealth that cannot be bequeathed, such as pension wealth which reverts to the pension company in the event of an early death, does not encourage children to visit. These findings suggest that there may be more to the relationships among generations than mere altruism.[5]

• • • • • • • • • • • • •

Making a Choice

Having considered the traditional and Ricardian views of government debt, you should ask yourself two sets of questions.

First, which view do you agree with? If the government cuts taxes today, runs a budget deficit, and raises taxes in the future, how will the policy affect the economy? Will it stimulate consumption, as the traditional view holds? Or will consumers understand that their permanent income is unchanged and, therefore, offset the budget deficit with higher private saving?

Second, why do you hold the view that you do? If you agree with the traditional view of government debt, what is the reason? Do consumers fail to understand that higher government borrowing today means higher taxes tomorrow? Or do they ignore future taxes, either because they are borrowing-constrained or because future taxes fall on future generations with which they do not feel an economic link? If you hold the Ricardian view, do you believe that consumers have the foresight to see that government borrowing today will result in future taxes levied on them or their descendants? Do you believe that consumers will save the extra income to offset that future tax liability?

---

[5] B. Douglas Bernheim, Andrei Shleifer, and Lawrence H. Summers, "The Strategic Bequest Motive," *Journal of Political Economy* 93 (1985): 1045–1076.

We might hope that the evidence could help us decide between these two views of government debt. Yet when economists examine historical episodes of large budget deficits, the evidence is inconclusive. History can be interpreted in different ways.

Consider, for example, the experience of the 1980s. The large budget deficits, caused partly by the Reagan tax cut of 1981, seem to offer a natural experiment to test the two views of government debt. At first glance, this episode appears decisively to support the traditional view. The large budget deficits coincided with low national saving, high real interest rates, and a large trade deficit. Indeed, advocates of the traditional view of government debt often claim that the experience of the 1980s confirms their position.

Yet those who hold the Ricardian view of government debt interpret these events differently. Perhaps saving was low in the 1980s because people were optimistic about future economic growth—an optimism that was also reflected in a booming stock market. Or perhaps saving was low because people expected that the tax cut would eventually lead not to higher taxes but, as Reagan promised, to lower government spending. Because it is hard to rule out any of these interpretations, both views of government debt survive.

16-3 Is the Budget Deficit Correctly Measured?

Although the debate between the traditional and Ricardian views of government debt is central to the disagreements among economists over fiscal policy, it is not the only source of controversy. Even economists who hold the traditional view that government borrowing has important effects on the economy argue among themselves about how best to evaluate fiscal policy.

Many of the arguments concern the question of how the budget deficit should be measured. Some economists believe that the deficit as currently measured is not a good indicator of the stance of fiscal policy. They believe that the budget deficit does not accurately gauge either the impact of fiscal policy on today's economy or the burden being placed on future generations of taxpayers. In this section we discuss four problems with the usual measure of the budget deficit.

The general principle is that *the government budget deficit should accurately reflect the change in the government's overall indebtedness.* This principle seems simple enough. But its application is not as straightforward as we might expect.

Measurement Problem No. 1: Inflation

The least controversial of the measurement issues is the correction for inflation. Almost all economists agree that the government's indebtedness should be measured in real terms, not in nominal terms. The measured deficit should equal the change in the government's real debt, not the change in its nominal debt.

The budget deficit as commonly measured, however, does not correct for inflation. To see how large an error this induces, consider the following example. Suppose that the real government debt is not changing; in other words, in real terms, the budget is balanced. In this case, the nominal debt must be rising at the rate of inflation. That is,

$$\Delta D/D = \pi,$$

where π is the inflation rate and D is the stock of government debt. This implies

$$\Delta D = \pi D.$$

The government would look at the change in the nominal debt ΔD and would report a budget deficit of πD. Hence, most economists believe that the reported budget deficit is overstated by the amount πD.

We can make the same argument in another way. The deficit is government expenditure minus government revenue. Part of expenditure is the interest paid on the government debt. Expenditure should include only the real interest paid on the debt rD, not the nominal interest paid iD. Because the difference between the nominal interest rate i and the real interest rate r is the inflation rate π, the budget deficit is overstated by πD.

This correction for inflation can be large, especially when inflation is high, and it can often change our evaluation of fiscal policy. For example, in 1979, the federal government reported a budget deficit of $28 billion. Inflation was 8.6 percent, and the government debt held at the beginning of the year by the public (excluding the Federal Reserve) was $495 billion. The deficit was therefore overstated by

$$\pi D = 0.086 \times \$495 \text{ billion}$$
$$= \$43 \text{ billion}.$$

Corrected for inflation, the reported budget deficit of $28 billion turns into a budget surplus of $15 billion! In other words, even though nominal government debt was rising, real government debt was falling.

Measurement Problem No. 2: Capital Assets

Many economists believe that an accurate assessment of the government's budget deficit requires accounting for the government's assets as well as its liabilities. In particular, when measuring the government's overall indebtedness, we should subtract government assets from government debt. Therefore, the budget deficit should be measured as the change in debt minus the change in assets.

Certainly, individuals and firms treat assets and liabilities symmetrically. When a person borrows to buy a house, we do not say that he is running a budget deficit. Instead, we offset the increase in assets (the house) against the increase in debt (the mortgage) and record no change in net wealth. Perhaps we should treat the government's finances the same way.

A budget procedure that accounts for assets as well as liabilities is called **capital budgeting**, because it takes into account changes in capital. For example, suppose that the government sells one of its office buildings or some of its land and uses the proceeds to reduce the government debt. Under current budget procedures, the reported deficit would be lower. Under capital budgeting, the revenue received from the sale would not lower the deficit, because the reduction in debt would be offset by a reduction in assets. Similarly, under capital budgeting, government borrowing to finance the purchase of a capital good would not raise the deficit.

The major difficulty with capital budgeting is that it is hard to decide which government expenditures should count as capital expenditures. For example, should the interstate highway system be counted as an asset of the government? If so, what is its value? What about the stockpile of nuclear weapons? Should spending on education be treated as expenditure on human capital? These difficult questions must be answered if the government is to adopt a capital budget.

Economists and policymakers disagree about whether the federal government should use capital budgeting. (Many state governments already use it.) Opponents of capital budgeting argue that, although the system is superior in principle to the current system, it is too difficult to implement in practice. Proponents of capital budgeting argue that even an imperfect treatment of capital assets would be better than ignoring them altogether.

Measurement Problem No. 3: Uncounted Liabilities

Some economists argue that the measured budget deficit is misleading because it excludes some important government liabilities. For example, consider the pensions of government workers. These workers provide labor services to the government today, but part of their compensation is deferred to the future. In essence, these workers are providing a loan to the government. Their future pension benefits represent a government liability not very different from government debt. Yet the accumulation of this liability is not included as part of the budget deficit.

Similarly, consider the Social Security system. In some ways, the system is like a pension plan. People pay some of their income into the system when young and expect to receive benefits when old. Perhaps accumulated future Social Security benefits should be included in the government's liabilities.

One might argue that Social Security liabilities are different from government debt because the government can change the laws determining Social Security benefits. Yet, in principle, the government could always choose not to repay all of its debt: the government honors its debt only because it chooses to do so. Promises to pay the holders of government debt may not be fundamentally different from promises to pay the future recipients of Social Security.

A particularly difficult form of government liability to measure is the *contingent liability*—the liability that is due only if a specified event occurs. For example, the government guarantees many forms of private credit, such as student loans, mortgages for low- and moderate-income families, and deposits in banks and savings and loan institutions. If the borrower repays the loan, the government pays nothing; if the borrower defaults, the government makes the repayment. When the government provides this guarantee, it undertakes a liability contingent on the borrower's default. Yet this contingent liability is not reflected in the budget deficit, in part because it is not clear what dollar value to attach to it.

Measurement Problem No. 4: The Business Cycle

Many changes in the government's budget deficit occur automatically in response to a fluctuating economy. For example, when the economy goes into a recession, incomes fall, so people pay less in personal income taxes. Profits fall, so corporations pay less in corporate income taxes. More people become eligible for government assistance, such as welfare and unemployment insurance, so government spending rises. Even without any change in the laws governing taxation and spending, the budget deficit increases.

These automatic changes in the deficit are not errors in measurement, for the government truly borrows more when a recession depresses tax revenue and boosts government spending. But these changes do make it more difficult to use the deficit to monitor changes in fiscal policy. That is, the deficit can rise or fall either because the government has changed policy or because the economy has changed direction. For some purposes, it would be good to know which is occurring.

To solve this problem, the government calculates a **cyclically adjusted budget deficit** (sometimes called the *full-employment budget deficit*). The cyclically adjusted deficit is based on estimates of what government spending and tax revenue would be if the economy were operating at its natural rate of output and employment. Many economists argue that the cyclically adjusted deficit better captures the stance of fiscal policy than does the deficit as usually reported.

Whither the Budget Deficit?

Economists differ in the importance they place on these measurement problems. Some believe that the problems are so severe that the measured budget deficit is almost meaningless. Most take these measurement problems seriously but still view the measured budget deficit as a useful indicator of fiscal policy.

The undisputed lesson is that to evaluate fully the course of fiscal policy, economists and policymakers must look at more than just the measured budget deficit. And, in fact, they do. The budget documents prepared annually by the Office of Management and Budget contain much detailed information about the government's finances, including data on capital expenditures and credit programs.

No economic statistic is perfect. Whenever we see a number reported in the media, we need to know what it is measuring and what it is leaving out. This is especially true for the government budget deficit.

Case Study *16-3*

• • • • • • • • • • • • •

Generational Accounting

One harsh critic of the budget deficit is economist Laurence Kotlikoff. Kotlikoff argues that the budget deficit is like the fabled emperor who wore no clothes. Everyone should plainly see the problem, but no one is willing to admit to it. He writes, "On the conceptual level, the budget deficit is intellectually bankrupt. On the practical level, there are so many official deficits that 'balanced budget' has lost any true meaning." He sees an "urgent need to switch from an outdated, misleading, and fundamentally noneconomic measure of fiscal policy, namely the budget deficit, to generational accounting."

Generational accounting, Kotlikoff's new way to gauge fiscal policy, is based on Modigliani's life-cycle theory of consumer behavior. According to this theory, a person's economic well-being depends on his or her lifetime income. This theory suggests that, in evaluating fiscal policy, we should not be concerned with taxes or spending in any single year. Instead, we should look at the taxes paid, and transfers received, by people over their entire lives. Generational accounts measure the impact of fiscal policy on the lifetime incomes of different generations.

Generational accounts tell a very different story than the budget deficit about the history of U.S. fiscal policy. In the early 1980s, the U.S. government cut taxes, beginning a long period of large budget deficits. Most commentators claim that older generations benefited at the expense of younger generations during this period, since the young inherited the government debt. Kotlikoff agrees that these tax cuts raised the burden on the young, but he claims that this standard analysis ignores the impact of many other policy changes. His generational accounts show that the young were hit even harder during the 1950s, 1960s, and 1970s. During these years, the government raised Social Security benefits for the elderly and financed the higher spending by taxing the working-age population. This policy redistributed income away from the young, even though it did not affect the budget deficit. During the 1980s, Social Security reforms reversed this trend, benefiting younger generations.

Despite Kotlikoff's advocacy, generational accounting is not likely to replace the budget deficit. This alternative system also has flaws. For example, to calculate the total tax burden on different generations, one needs to make assumptions about future policy. These assumptions are open to dispute. Nonetheless, generational accounting offers a useful perspective in the debate over fiscal policy.[6]

• • • • • • • • • • • • •

---

[6] Laurence J. Kotlikoff, *Generational Accounting: Knowing Who Pays, and When, for What We Spend* (New York: The Free Press, 1992). For an appraisal of the book, see David M. Cutler, Book Review, *National Tax Journal 56* (March 1993): 61–67. See also the symposium on generational accounting in the Winter 1994 issue of the *Journal of Economic Perspectives*.

16-4   Conclusion

Fiscal policy and government debt have been central in the U.S. political debate over the past decade. When Bill Clinton became president in 1993, he made reducing the budget deficit a high priority of his administration. When the Republicans took control of Congress in 1995, they pushed for even faster deficit reduction than Clinton had advocated.

This chapter has discussed the parallel debate among economists. Economists disagree about how fiscal policy affects the economy and how fiscal policy is best measured. To be sure, these are among the most important and controversial questions facing policymakers today. We can be confident that as long as the U.S. government runs large budget deficits, these debates will continue.

Summary

1. According to the traditional view of government debt, a debt-financed tax cut stimulates consumer spending and lowers national saving. This increase in consumer spending raises aggregate demand and income in the short run but leads to a lower capital stock and lower income in the long run.

2. According to the Ricardian view of government debt, a debt-financed tax cut does not stimulate consumer spending because it does not raise permanent income—it merely reschedules taxes from the present to the future.

3. The debate between the traditional and Ricardian views of government debt is ultimately a debate over how consumers behave. Are consumers rational or shortsighted? Do they face binding borrowing constraints? Are they economically linked to future generations through altruistic bequests? Economists' views of government debt hinge on their answers to these questions.

4. Standard measures of the budget deficit are imperfect measures of fiscal policy for several reasons. In particular, these measures do not correct for the effects of inflation, do not offset changes in liabilities with changes in assets, omit some liabilities altogether, and do not correct for the effects of the business cycle.

KEY CONCEPTS

Ricardian equivalence

Government budget constraint

Capital budgeting

Cyclically adjusted budget deficit

QUESTIONS FOR REVIEW

1. According to the traditional view, how does a debt-financed tax cut affect public saving, private saving, and national saving?

2. According to the Ricardian view, how does a debt-financed tax cut affect public saving, private saving, and national saving?

3. Do you believe the traditional or the Ricardian view of government debt? Why?

4. Describe four problems affecting measurement of the government budget deficit.

PROBLEMS AND APPLICATIONS

1. Draft a letter to the senator described in Section 16-1, explaining and evaluating the Ricardian view of government debt.

2. Chapter 15 discusses various theories of the consumption function: Keynes's three conjectures, the life-cycle hypothesis, and the permanent-income hypothesis. What do these different views about consumption imply for the debate between the traditional and Ricardian views of government debt?

3. The Social Security system levies a tax on workers and pays benefits to the elderly. Suppose that Congress increases both the tax and the benefits. For simplicity, assume that the Congress announces that the increases will last for one year only.

   a. How would this change affect the economy?

   b. Does your answer depend on whether generations are altruistically linked?

4. Evaluate the usefulness of generational accounting from the perspective of someone who believes that generations

are altruistically linked. Now evaluate the usefulness of generational accounting from the perspective of someone who believes that many consumers face binding borrowing constraints.

5. On April 1, 1996, Taco Bell, the fast-food chain, ran a full-page ad in *The New York Times* with this news: "In an effort to help the national debt, Taco Bell is pleased to announce that we have agreed to purchase the Liberty Bell, one of our country's most historic treasures. It will now be called the *Taco Liberty Bell* and will still be accessible to the American public for viewing. We hope our move will prompt other corporations to take similar action to do their part to reduce the country's debt." Would such actions by U.S. corporations actually reduce the national debt as it is now measured? How would your answer change if the U.S. government adopted capital budgeting? Do you think these actions represent a true reduction in the government's indebtedness? Do you think Taco Bell was serious about this plan? (*Hint:* Note the date.)

Chapter 17

Investment

Investment is the most volatile component of GDP. When expenditure on goods and services falls during a recession, much of the decline is usually due to a drop in investment spending. In the severe recession of 1982, for example, real GDP fell $105 billion from its peak in the third quarter of 1981 to its trough in the fourth quarter of 1982. Investment spending over the same period fell $152 billion, accounting for more than the entire fall in spending.

Economists study investment to better understand fluctuations in the economy's output of goods and services. In previous chapters our models of GDP used a simple investment function relating investment to the real interest rate: $I = I(r)$. That function states that an increase in the real interest rate reduces investment. In this chapter we look more closely at the theory behind this investment function.

There are three types of investment spending. **Business fixed investment** includes the equipment and structures that businesses buy to use in production. **Residential investment** includes the new housing that people buy to live in and that landlords buy to rent out. **Inventory investment** includes those goods that businesses put aside in storage, including materials and supplies, work in process, and finished goods. Figure 17-1 plots total investment and its three components in the United States during the past 25 years. You can see that all types of investment fall substantially during recessions, which are shown as shaded areas in the figure.

In this chapter we build models of each type of investment to explain these fluctuations. The models will shed light on the following questions:

- Why is investment negatively related to the interest rate?

- What causes the investment function to shift?

- Why does investment rise during booms and fall during recessions?

At the end of the chapter, we return to these questions and summarize the answers that the models offer.

17-1 Business Fixed Investment

The standard model of business fixed investment is called the **neoclassical model of investment**. The neoclassical model examines the benefits and costs to firms of owning capital goods. The model shows how the level of investment—the addition to the stock of capital—is related to the marginal product of capital, the interest rate, and the tax rules affecting firms.

Figure 17-1

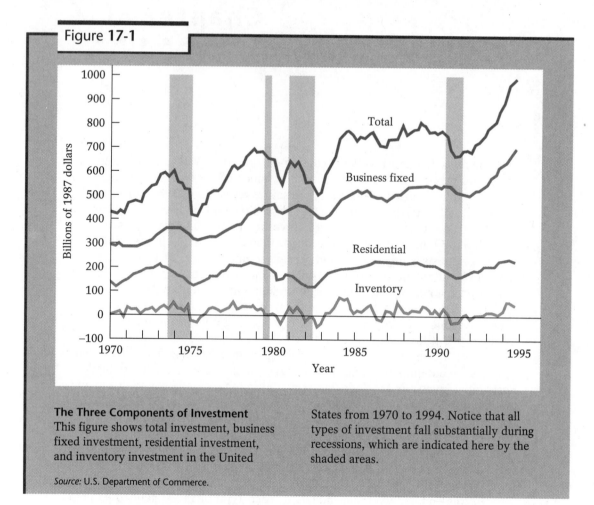

The Three Components of Investment
This figure shows total investment, business fixed investment, residential investment, and inventory investment in the United States from 1970 to 1994. Notice that all types of investment fall substantially during recessions, which are indicated here by the shaded areas.

Source: U.S. Department of Commerce.

To develop the model, imagine that there are two kinds of firms in the economy. *Production firms* produce goods and services using capital that they rent. *Rental firms* make all the investments in the economy; they buy capital and rent it out to the production firms. Of course, most firms in the actual economy perform both functions: they produce goods and services, and they invest in capital for future production. Our analysis is simpler, however, if we separate these two activities by imagining that they take place in different firms.

The Rental Price of Capital

Let's first consider the typical production firm. As we discussed in Chapter 3, this firm decides how much capital to rent by comparing the cost and benefit of each unit of capital. The firm rents capital at a rental rate R and sells its output at a price P; the real cost of a unit of capital to the production firm is R/P. The real benefit of a unit of capital is the marginal product of capital MPK—the extra output produced with one more unit of capital. The marginal product of capital declines as the amount of capital rises: the more capital the firm has, the less an additional unit of capital will add to its production. Chapter 3 concluded that, to maximize profit, the firm rents capital until the marginal product of capital falls to equal the real rental price.

Figure 17-2 shows the equilibrium in the rental market for capital. For the reasons just discussed, the marginal product of capital determines the demand curve. The demand curve slopes downward because the marginal product of capital is low when the level of capital is high. At any point in time, the amount of capital in the economy is fixed, so the supply curve is vertical. The real rental price of capital adjusts to equilibrate supply and demand.

To see what variables influence the equilibrium rental price, let's consider a particular production function. As the appendix to Chapter 3 discusses, many economists consider the Cobb-Douglas production function a good approximation of how the actual economy turns capital and labor into goods and services. The Cobb-Douglas production function is

$$Y = AK^{\alpha}L^{1-\alpha},$$

where Y is output, K capital, L labor, A a parameter measuring the level of technology, and α a parameter between zero and one that measures capital's share of output. The marginal product of capital for the Cobb-Douglas production function is

$$MPK = \alpha A(L/K)^{1-\alpha}.$$

Because the real rental price equals the marginal product of capital in equilibrium, we can write

$$R/P = \alpha A(L/K)^{1-\alpha}.$$

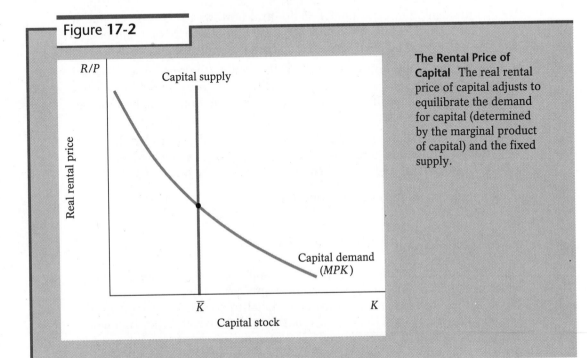

Figure 17-2

The Rental Price of Capital The real rental price of capital adjusts to equilibrate the demand for capital (determined by the marginal product of capital) and the fixed supply.

This expression identifies the variables that determine the real rental price. It shows the following:

- The lower the stock of capital, the higher the real rental price of capital.
- The greater the amount of labor employed, the higher the real rental price of capital.
- The better the technology, the higher the real rental price of capital.

Events that reduce the capital stock (an earthquake), or raise employment (an expansion in aggregate demand), or improve the technology (a scientific discovery) raise the equilibrium real rental price of capital.

The Cost of Capital

Next consider the rental firms. These firms, like car-rental companies, merely buy capital goods and rent them out. Since our goal is to explain the investments made by the rental firms, we begin by considering the benefit and cost of owning capital.

The benefit of owning capital is the revenue from renting it to the production firms. The rental firm receives the real rental price of capital R/P for each unit of capital it owns and rents out.

The cost of owning capital is more complex. For each period of time that it rents out a unit of capital, the rental firm bears three costs:

1. When a rental firm buys a unit of capital and rents it out, it loses the interest it could have earned by depositing the purchase price of the capital in the bank. Or, equivalently, if the firm borrows to buy the capital, it must pay interest on the loan. If P_K is the purchase price of a unit of capital and i is the nominal interest rate, then iP_K is the interest cost.

2. While the rental firm is renting out the capital, the price of capital can change. If the price of capital falls, the firm loses, because the firm's asset has fallen in value. If the price of capital rises, the firm gains, because the firm's asset has risen in value. The cost of this loss or gain is $-\Delta P_K$.

3. While the capital is rented out, it suffers wear and tear, called **depreciation**. If δ is the rate of depreciation—the fraction of value lost per period because of wear and tear—then the dollar cost of depreciation is δP_K.

The total cost of renting out a unit of capital for one period is therefore

$$\text{Cost of Capital} = iP_K - \Delta P_K + \delta P_K$$
$$= P_K(i - \Delta P_K/P_K + \delta).$$

The cost of capital depends on the price of capital, the interest rate, the rate at which capital prices are changing, and the depreciation rate.

For example, consider the cost of capital to a car-rental company. The company buys cars for $10,000 each and rents them out to other businesses. The company faces an interest rate i of 10 percent per year, so the interest cost iP_K is $1,000 per year for each car the company owns. Car prices are rising at

6 percent per year, so, excluding wear and tear, the firm gets a capital gain ΔP_K of $600 per year. Cars depreciate at 20 percent per year, so the loss due to wear and tear δP_K is $2,000 per year. Therefore, the company's cost of capital is

$$\text{Cost of Capital} = \$1,000 - \$600 + \$2,000$$
$$= \$2,400.$$

The cost to the car-rental company of keeping a car in its capital stock is $2,400 per year.

To make the expression for the cost of capital simpler and easier to interpret, we assume that the price of capital goods rises with the prices of other goods. In this case, $\Delta P_K/P_K$ equals the rate of inflation π. Because $i - \pi$ equals the real interest rate r, we can write the cost of capital as

$$\text{Cost of Capital} = P_K(r + \delta).$$

This equation states that the cost of capital depends on the price of capital, the real interest rate, and the depreciation rate.

Finally, we want to express the cost of capital relative to other goods in the economy. The **real cost of capital**—the cost of buying and renting out a unit of capital measured in units of the economy's output—is

$$\text{Real Cost of Capital} = (P_K/P)(r + \delta).$$

This equation states that the real cost of capital depends on the relative price of a capital good P_K/P, the real interest rate r, and the depreciation rate δ.

The Determinants of Investment

Now consider a rental firm's decision about whether to increase or decrease its capital stock. For each unit of capital, the firm earns real revenue R/P and bears the real cost $(P_K/P)(r + \delta)$. The real profit per unit of capital is

$$\text{Profit Rate} = \text{Revenue} - \text{Cost}$$
$$= R/P - (P_K/P)(r + \delta).$$

Because the real rental price in equilibrium equals the marginal product of capital, we can write the profit rate as

$$\text{Profit Rate} = MPK - (P_K/P)(r + \delta).$$

The rental firm makes a profit if the marginal product of capital is greater than the cost of capital. It incurs a loss if the marginal product is less than the cost of capital.

We can now see the economic incentives that lie behind the rental firm's investment decision. The firm's decision regarding its capital stock—that is, whether to add to it or to let it depreciate—depends on whether owning and renting out capital is profitable. The change in the capital stock, called **net investment**, depends on the difference between the marginal product of capital and the cost of capital. *If the marginal product of capital exceeds the cost of capital, firms find it profitable to add to their capital stock. If the marginal product of capital falls short of the cost of capital, they let their capital stock shrink.*

We can also now see that the separation of economic activity between production and rental firms, although useful for clarifying our thinking, is not necessary for our conclusion regarding how firms choose investment. For a firm that both uses and owns capital, the benefit of an extra unit of capital is the marginal product of capital, and the cost is the cost of capital. Like a firm that owns and rents out capital, this firm adds to its capital stock if the marginal product exceeds the cost of capital. Thus, we can write

$$\Delta K = I_n \left[MPK - (P_K/P)(r + \delta) \right],$$

where $I_n(\ )$ is the function showing how much net investment responds to the incentive to invest.

We can now derive the investment function. Total spending on business fixed investment is the sum of net investment and the replacement of depreciated capital. The investment function is

$$I = I_n \left[MPK - (P_K/P)(r + \delta) \right] + \delta K.$$

Business fixed investment depends on the marginal product of capital, the cost of capital, and the amount of depreciation.

This model shows why investment depends on the interest rate. An increase in the real interest rate raises the cost of capital. It therefore reduces the amount of profit from owning capital and reduces the incentive to accumulate more capital. Similarly, a decrease in the real interest rate reduces the cost of capital and stimulates investment. For this reason, the investment schedule relating investment to the interest rate slopes downward, as in Figure 17-3.

Figure 17-3

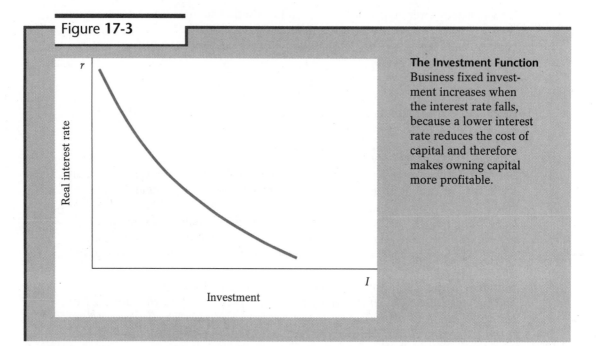

The Investment Function Business fixed investment increases when the interest rate falls, because a lower interest rate reduces the cost of capital and therefore makes owning capital more profitable.

Figure 17-4

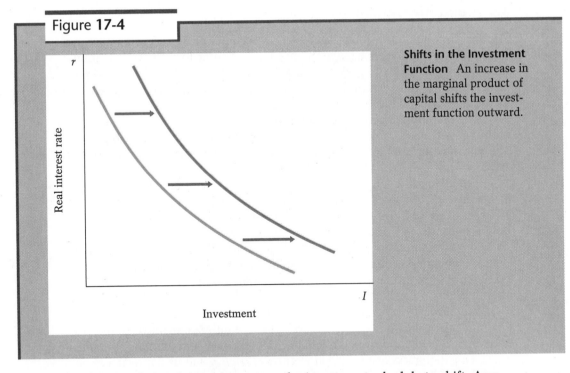

Shifts in the Investment Function An increase in the marginal product of capital shifts the investment function outward.

The model also shows what causes the investment schedule to shift. Any event that raises the marginal product of capital increases the profitability of investment and causes the investment schedule to shift outward, as in Figure 17-4. For example, a technological innovation that increases the production function parameter A raises the marginal product of capital and, for any given interest rate, increases the amount of capital goods that rental firms wish to buy.

Finally, consider what happens as this adjustment of the capital stock continues over time. If the marginal product begins above the cost of capital, the capital stock will rise and the marginal product will fall. If the marginal product of capital begins below the cost of capital, the capital stock will fall and the marginal product will rise. Eventually, as the capital stock adjusts, the marginal product of capital approaches the cost of capital. When the capital stock reaches a steady-state level, we can write

$$MPK = (P_K/P)(r + \delta).$$

Thus, in the long run, the marginal product of capital equals the real cost of capital. The speed of adjustment toward the steady state depends on how quickly firms adjust their capital stock, which in turn depends on how costly it is to build, deliver, and install new capital.[1]

---

[1] Economists often measure capital goods in units such that the price of 1 unit of capital equals the price of 1 unit of other goods and services ($P_K = P$). This was the approach taken implicitly in Chapter 4, for example. In this case, the steady-state condition says that the marginal product of capital net of depreciation, $MPK - \delta$, equals the real interest rate r.

Taxes and Investment

The tax laws influence firms' incentives to accumulate capital in many ways. Sometimes policymakers change the tax laws in order to shift the investment function and influence aggregate demand. Here we consider two of the most important provisions of corporate taxation: the corporate income tax and the investment tax credit.

The **corporate income tax** is a tax on corporate profits. Throughout most of the past 40 years, the corporate tax rate in the United States was 46 percent. The rate was lowered to 34 percent in 1986 and then raised to 35 percent in 1993.

The effect of a corporate income tax on investment depends on how the law defines "profit" for the purpose of taxation. Suppose, first, that the law defined profit as we did above—the rental price of capital minus the cost of capital. In this case, even though firms would be sharing a fraction of their profits with the government, it would still be rational for them to invest if the rental price of capital exceeded the cost of capital, and to disinvest if the rental price fell short of the cost of capital. A tax on profit, measured in this way, would not alter investment incentives.

Yet, because of the tax law's definition of profit, the corporate income tax does affect investment decisions. There are many differences between the law's definition of profit and ours. One major difference is the treatment of depreciation. Our definition of profit deducts the *current* value of depreciation as a cost. That is, it bases depreciation on how much it would cost today to replace worn-out capital. By contrast, under the corporate tax laws, firms deduct depreciation using *historical* cost. That is, the depreciation deduction is based on the price of the capital when it was originally purchased. In periods of inflation, replacement cost is greater than historical cost, so the corporate tax tends to understate the cost of depreciation and overstate profit. As a result, the tax law sees a profit and levies a tax even when economic profit is zero, which makes owning capital less attractive. For this and other reasons, many economists believe that the corporate income tax discourages investment.

The **investment tax credit** is a tax provision that encourages the accumulation of capital. The investment tax credit reduces a firm's taxes by a certain amount for each dollar spent on capital goods. Because a firm recoups part of its expenditure on new capital in lower taxes, the credit reduces the effective purchase price of a unit of capital P_K. Thus, the investment tax credit reduces the cost of capital and raises investment.

Many economists believe that the investment tax credit is an effective way to stimulate investment. In 1985 the investment tax credit was 10 percent. Yet the Tax Reform Act of 1986, which reduced the corporate income tax rate, also eliminated the investment tax credit. When Bill Clinton ran for president in 1992, he campaigned on a platform of reinstituting the investment tax credit. Yet this change in tax law did not occur.[2]

---

[2] To read more about how taxes influence investment, see Robert E. Hall and Dale W. Jorgenson, "Tax Policy and Investment Behavior," *American Economic Review* 57 (June 1967): 391–414.

Case Study *17-1*

● ● ● ● ● ● ● ● ● ● ● ●

The Swedish Investment Funds System

Tax incentives for investment are one tool policymakers can use to control aggregate demand. For example, an increase in the investment tax credit reduces the cost of capital, shifts the investment function outward, and raises aggregate demand. Similarly, a reduction in the tax credit reduces aggregate demand by making investment more costly.

From the mid-1950s to the mid-1970s, the government of Sweden attempted to control aggregate demand by alternately encouraging or discouraging investment. A system called the *investment fund* subsidized investment, much like an investment tax credit does, during periods of recession. When government officials decided that economic growth had slowed, they authorized a temporary investment subsidy. When the officials concluded that the economy had recovered sufficiently, they revoked the subsidy. Eventually, however, Sweden abandoned the use of temporary investment subsidies to control the business cycle, and the subsidy became a permanent feature of Swedish tax policy.

Should investment subsidies be used to combat economic fluctuations? Some economists believe that, for the two decades it was in effect, the Swedish policy reduced the magnitude of the business cycle. Other economists believe that such a policy can have unintended and perverse effects: for example, if the economy begins to slow down, firms may anticipate a future subsidy and delay investment, making the slowdown worse. Because the use of countercyclical investment subsidies could either reduce or amplify the size of economic fluctuations, their overall impact on economic performance is hard to evaluate.[3]

● ● ● ● ● ● ● ● ● ● ● ●

The Stock Market and Tobin's *q*

Many economists see a link between fluctuations in investment and fluctuations in the stock market. The term **stock** refers to the shares in the ownership of corporations, and the **stock market** is the market in which these shares are traded. Stock prices tend to be high when firms have many opportunities for profitable investment, since these profit opportunities mean higher future income for the shareholders. Thus, stock prices reflect the incentives to invest.

---

[3] John B. Taylor, "The Swedish Investment Funds System as a Stabilization Rule," *Brookings Papers on Economic Activity* (1982:1): 57–106.

The Nobel-Prize-winning economist James Tobin proposed that firms base their investment decisions on the following ratio, which is now called **Tobin's** q:

$$q = \frac{\text{Market Value of Installed Capital}}{\text{Replacement Cost of Installed Capital}}.$$

The numerator of Tobin's q is the value of the economy's capital as determined by the stock market. The denominator is the price of the capital if it were purchased today.

Tobin reasoned that net investment should depend on whether q is greater or less than 1. If q is greater than 1, then the stock market values installed capital at more than its replacement cost. In this case, managers can raise the market value of their firms' stock by buying more capital. Conversely, if q is less than 1, the stock market values capital at less than its replacement cost. In this case, managers will not replace capital as it wears out.

Although at first the q theory of investment may appear quite different from the neoclassical model developed above, in fact the two theories are closely related. To see the relationship, note that Tobin's q depends on current and future expected profits from installed capital. If the marginal product of capital exceeds the cost of capital, then firms are earning profit on their installed capital. These profits make the rental firms desirable to own, which raises the market value of these firms' stock, implying a high value of q. Similarly, if the marginal product of capital falls short of the cost of capital, then firms are incurring losses on their installed capital, implying a low market value and a low value of q.

The advantage of Tobin's q as a measure of the incentive to invest is that it reflects the expected future profitability of capital as well as the current profitability. For example, suppose that Congress legislates a reduction in the corporate income tax beginning next year. This expected fall in the corporate tax means greater profits for the owners of capital. These higher expected profits raise the value of stock today, raise Tobin's q, and therefore encourage investment today. Thus, Tobin's q theory of investment emphasizes that investment decisions depend not only on current economic policies, but also on policies expected to prevail in the future.

Tobin's q theory provides a simple way of interpreting the role of the stock market in the economy. Suppose, for example, that you observe a fall in stock prices. Because the replacement cost of capital is fairly stable, a fall in the stock market is usually associated with a fall in Tobin's q. A fall in q reflects investors' pessimism about the current or future profitability of capital. According to q theory, the fall in q will lead to a fall in investment, which could lower aggregate demand. In essence, q theory gives a reason to expect fluctuations in the stock market to be closely tied to fluctuations in output and employment.[4]

---

[4] To read more about the relationship between the neoclassical model of investment and q theory, see Fumio Hayashi, "Tobin's Marginal q and Average q: A Neoclassical Approach," *Econometrica* 50 (January 1982): 213–224; and Lawrence H. Summers, "Taxation and Corporate Investment: A q-theory Approach," *Brookings Papers on Economic Activity* (1981:1): 67–140.

Case Study *17-2*

• • • • • • • • • • • • • • •

The Stock Market as an Economic Indicator

"The stock market has predicted nine out of the last five recessions." So goes Paul Samuelson's famous quip about the stock market's reliability as an economic indicator. The stock market is in fact quite volatile, and it can give false signals about the future of the economy.

Yet one should not ignore the link between the stock market and the economy. Figure 17-5 shows that changes in the stock market often reflect changes in real GDP. This fact is not lost on policymakers, such as those at the Federal Reserve. Indeed, because the stock market often anticipates changes in real GDP, and because data on the stock market are available more quickly than data on GDP, the stock market is a closely watched indicator of economic activity.

Figure 17-5

The Stock Market and the Economy
This figure shows the association between the stock market and real economic activity. Using quarterly data from 1965 to 1994, it presents the percentage change from one year earlier in the Dow Jones Industrial Average and real GDP. The Dow Jones Industrial Average is an index of stock prices of major industrial companies.

Source: U.S. Department of Commerce.

• • • • • • • • • • • • • • •

Financing Constraints

When a firm wants to invest in new capital, such as building a new factory, it often raises the necessary funds in financial markets. This financing may take several forms—obtaining loans from banks, selling bonds to the public, or selling shares in future profits on the stock market. The neoclassical model assumes that if a firm is willing to pay the cost of capital, the financial markets will make the funds available.

Yet sometimes firms face **financing constraints**—limits on the amount they can raise in financial markets. Financing constraints can prevent firms from undertaking profitable investments. When a firm is unable to raise funds in financial markets, the amount it can spend on new capital goods is limited to the amount it is currently earning. Financing constraints influence the investment behavior of firms just as borrowing constraints influence the consumption behavior of households. Borrowing constraints cause households to determine their consumption on the basis of current rather than permanent income; financing constraints cause firms to determine their investment on the basis of their current cash flow rather than expected profitability.

To see the impact of financing constraints, consider the effect of a short recession on investment spending. A recession reduces employment, the rental price of capital, and profits. If firms expect the recession to be short-lived, however, they will want to continue investing, knowing that their investments will be profitable in the future. That is, a short recession will have only a small effect on Tobin's q. For firms that can raise funds in financial markets, the recession should have only a small effect on investment.

Quite the opposite is true for firms that face financing constraints. The fall in current profits restricts the amount that these firms can spend on new capital goods and may prevent them from making profitable investments. Thus, financing constraints make investment more sensitive to current economic conditions.[5]

17-2   Residential Investment

In this section we consider the determinants of residential investment. We begin by presenting a simple model of the housing market. Residential investment includes the purchase of new housing both by people who plan to live in it themselves and by landlords who plan to rent it to others. To keep things simple, however, it is useful to imagine that all housing is owner-occupied.

The Stock Equilibrium and the Flow Supply

There are two parts to the model. First, the market for the existing stock of houses determines the equilibrium housing price. Second, the housing price determines the flow of residential investment.

[5] For empirical work supporting the importance of these financing constraints, see Steven M. Fazzari, R. Glenn Hubbard, and Bruce C. Petersen, "Financing Constraints and Corporate Investment," *Brookings Papers on Economic Activity* (1988:1): 141–195.

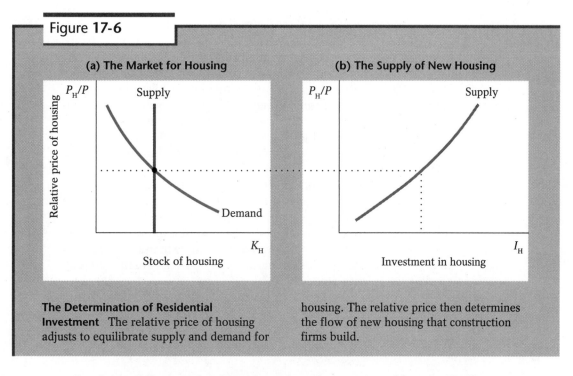

Figure 17-6

(a) The Market for Housing

Relative price of housing

P_H/P

Supply

Demand

K_H

Stock of housing

(b) The Supply of New Housing

P_H/P

Supply

I_H

Investment in housing

The Determination of Residential Investment The relative price of housing adjusts to equilibrate supply and demand for

housing. The relative price then determines the flow of new housing that construction firms build.

Panel (a) of Figure 17-6 shows how the relative price of housing P_H/P is determined by the supply and demand for the existing stock of houses. At any point in time, the supply of houses is fixed. We represent this stock with a vertical supply curve. The demand curve for houses slopes downward, because high prices cause people to live in smaller houses, to share residences, or sometimes even to become homeless. The price of housing adjusts to equilibrate supply and demand.

Panel (b) of Figure 17-6 shows how the relative price of housing determines the supply of new houses. Construction firms buy materials and hire labor to build houses, and then sell the houses at the market price. Their costs depend on the overall price level P, and their revenue depends on the price of houses P_H. The higher the relative price of housing, the greater the incentive to build houses, and the more houses are built. The flow of new houses—residential investment—therefore depends on the equilibrium price set in the market for existing houses.

This model of residential investment is similar to the q theory of business fixed investment. According to q theory, business fixed investment depends on the market price of installed capital relative to its replacement cost; this relative price, in turn, depends on the expected profits from owning installed capital. According to this model of the housing market, residential investment depends on the relative price of housing. The relative price of housing, in turn, depends on the demand for housing, which depends on the imputed rent that individuals expect to receive from their housing. Hence, the relative price of housing plays much the same role for residential investment as Tobin's q does for business fixed investment.

Changes in Housing Demand

When the demand for housing shifts, the equilibrium price of housing changes, and this change in turn affects residential investment. The demand curve for housing can shift for various reasons. An economic boom raises national income and therefore the demand for housing. A large increase in the population, perhaps because of immigration, also raises the demand for housing. Panel (a) of Figure 17-7 shows that an expansionary shift in demand raises the equilibrium price. Panel (b) shows that the increase in the housing price increases residential investment.

   One important determinant of housing demand is the real interest rate. Many people take out loans—mortgages—to buy their homes; the interest rate is the cost of the loan. Even the few people who do not have to borrow to purchase a home will respond to the interest rate, because the interest rate is the opportunity cost of holding their wealth in housing rather than putting it in a bank. A reduction in the interest rate therefore raises housing demand, housing prices, and residential investment.

Figure 17-7

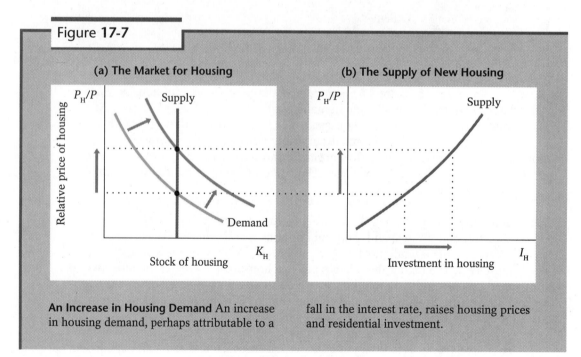

(a) The Market for Housing

(b) The Supply of New Housing

An Increase in Housing Demand An increase in housing demand, perhaps attributable to a fall in the interest rate, raises housing prices and residential investment.

The Tax Treatment of Housing

Just as the tax laws affect the accumulation of business fixed investment, they also affect the accumulation of residential investment. In this case, however, their effects are nearly the opposite. Rather than discouraging investment, as the corporate income tax does for businesses, the personal income tax encourages households to invest in housing.

What Price House Can You Afford?

When someone takes out a mortgage to buy a house, the bank often places a ceiling on the size of the loan. That ceiling depends on the person's income and the market interest rate. A typical bank requirement is that the monthly mortgage payment—including both interest and repayment of principal—not exceed 28 percent of the borrower's monthly income.

Table 17-1 shows how the interest rate affects the loan ceiling. The home-buyer in the example has an income of $30,000 and is applying for a 30-year mortgage. The bank is assumed to use the standard 28 percent limit on the size of the loan.

As you can see, if the home-buyer is up against the borrowing limit, as many are, small changes in the interest rate can have a large influence on the amount he or she can spend on a house. An increase in the interest rate from 8 to 10 percent reduces the maximum loan from $95,398 to $79,766—a fall of 16 percent. An increase in the interest rate therefore reduces housing demand, which in turn depresses housing prices and residential investment.

It is noteworthy—and a bit puzzling—that banks make this calculation using the nominal rather than the real interest rate. The real interest rate measures the true cost of borrowing to buy a house, because the price of the house will normally rise at the overall rate of inflation. Yet bank rules use nominal interest rates when computing mortgage eligibility. Because of these bank rules, residential investment depends on nominal as well as real interest rates.

Table 17-1

How High Interest Rates Reduce Mortgage Eligibility and Housing Demand

Assumptions: 30-year mortgage
$30,000 annual income
28 percent limit on mortgage payment

Interest Rate	Maximum Possible Loan
5%	$130,397
6	116,754
7	105,215
8	95,398
9	86,997
10	79,766
11	73,504
12	68,053

One can view a homeowner as a landlord with himself as a tenant. But he is a landlord with a special tax treatment. The U.S. income tax does not require him to pay tax on the imputed rent (the rent he "pays" himself), yet it allows him to deduct mortgage interest. In essence, when computing his taxable income, he can subtract part of the cost of owning a home, but he does not have to add any of the benefit.

The size of this subsidy to homeownership depends on the rate of inflation. The reason is that the tax law allows homeowners to deduct their *nominal* interest payments. Because the nominal interest rate on mortgages rises when inflation rises, the value of this subsidy is higher at higher rates of inflation. When inflation and nominal interest rates rose substantially in the 1970s, the tax benefits of homeownership rose as well. When inflation and nominal interest rates fell in the 1980s and early 1990s, the tax benefits became smaller.

Many economists have criticized the tax treatment of homeownership. They believe that, because of this subsidy, the United States invests too much in housing compared to other forms of capital. They advocate reducing the subsidy, perhaps by eliminating the deductibility of mortgage interest. This idea received attention during the presidential campaign of 1996. The "flat tax" proposal advocated by Republican primary candidate Steve Forbes eliminated the mortgage-interest deduction and used the extra revenue to lower tax rates.

17-3   Inventory Investment

Inventory investment—the goods that businesses put aside in storage—is at the same time negligible and of great significance. It is one of the smallest components of spending, averaging about 1 percent of GDP. Yet its remarkable volatility makes it central to the study of economic fluctuations. In recessions, firms stop replenishing their inventory as goods are sold, and inventory investment becomes negative. In a typical recession, more than half the fall in spending comes from a decline in inventory investment.

Reasons for Holding Inventories

Inventories serve many purposes. Before presenting a model to explain fluctuations in inventory investment, let's discuss some of the motives firms have for holding inventories.

One use of inventories is to smooth the level of production over time. Consider a firm that experiences temporary booms and busts in sales. Rather than adjusting production to match the fluctuations in sales, the firm may find it cheaper to produce goods at a steady rate. When sales are low, the firm produces more than it sells and puts the extra goods into inventory. When sales are high, the firm produces less than it sells and takes goods out of inventory. This motive for holding inventories is called **production smoothing**.

A second reason for holding inventories is that they may allow a firm to operate more efficiently. Retail stores, for example, can sell merchandise more effectively if they have goods on hand to show to customers. Manufacturing firms keep inventories of spare parts in order to reduce the time that the assembly line is shut down when a machine breaks. In some ways, we can view **inventories as a factor of production**: the larger the stock of inventories a firm holds, the more output it can produce.

A third reason for holding inventories is to avoid running out of goods when sales are unexpectedly high. Firms often have to make production decisions before knowing the level of customer demand. For example, a publisher must decide how many copies of a new book to print before knowing whether the book will be popular. If demand exceeds production and there are no inventories, the good will be out of stock for a period, and the firm will lose sales and profit. Inventories can prevent this from happening. This motive for holding inventories is called **stock-out avoidance**.

A fourth explanation of inventories is dictated by the production process. Many goods require a number of steps in production and, therefore, take time to produce. When a product is only partly completed, its components are counted as part of a firm's inventory. These inventories are called **work in process**.

Case Study *17-3*

● ● ● ● ● ● ● ● ● ● ● ● ●

Seasonal Fluctuations and Production Smoothing

Economists have spent much time studying data on production, sales, and inventories to test alternative theories of inventory holding. Much of this research examines whether the production-smoothing theory accurately describes the behavior of firms. Contrary to what many economists expected, most of the evidence suggests that firms do not use inventories to smooth production over time.

The clearest evidence against production smoothing comes from industries with seasonal fluctuations in demand. In many industries, sales fluctuate regularly over the course of a year. For example, the toy industry sells more of its output in December than in January. One might expect that firms would build up inventories in times of low sales and draw them down in times of high sales.

Yet, in most industries, firms do not use inventories to smooth production over the year. Instead, the seasonal pattern in production closely matches the seasonal pattern in sales. The evidence from seasonal fluctuations suggests that, in most industries, firms see little benefit to smoothing production.[6]

● ● ● ● ● ● ● ● ● ● ● ● ●

---

[6] Jeffrey A. Miron and Stephen P. Zeldes, "Seasonality, Cost Shocks, and the Production Smoothing Model of Inventories," *Econometrica* 56 (July 1988): 877–908.

The Accelerator Model of Inventories

Because there are many motives for holding inventories, there are many models of inventory investment. One simple model that explains the data well, without endorsing a particular motive, is the **accelerator model**. This model was developed about half a century ago, and it is sometimes applied to all types of investment. Here we apply it to the type for which it works best—inventory investment.

The accelerator model of inventories assumes that firms hold a stock of inventories that is proportional to the firms' level of output. There are various reasons for this assumption. When output is high, manufacturing firms need more materials and supplies on hand, and they have more goods in the process of being completed. When the economy is booming, retail firms want to have more merchandise on the shelves to show customers. Thus, if N is the economy's stock of inventories and Y is output, then

$$N = \beta Y,$$

where β is a parameter reflecting how much inventory firms wish to hold as a proportion of output.

Inventory investment I is the change in the stock of inventories ΔN. Therefore,

$$I = \Delta N = \beta \Delta Y.$$

The accelerator model predicts that inventory investment is proportional to the change in output. When output rises, firms want to hold a larger stock of inventory, so inventory investment is high. When output falls, firms want to hold a smaller stock of inventory, so they allow their inventory to run down, and inventory investment is negative.

We can now see how the model earned its name. Because the variable Y is the rate at which firms are producing goods, ΔY is the "acceleration" of production. The model says that inventory investment depends on whether the economy is speeding up or slowing down.

Case Study *17-4*

• • • • • • • • • • • • • •

The Evidence for the Accelerator Model

To see how well the accelerator model fits the data, look at Figure 17-8. This figure is a scatterplot of annual data from the national income accounts for the United States. On the horizontal axis is the change in real GDP. On the vertical axis is real inventory investment.

The positive association between the change in GDP and inventory investment supports the prediction of the accelerator model. The line drawn

Figure 17-8

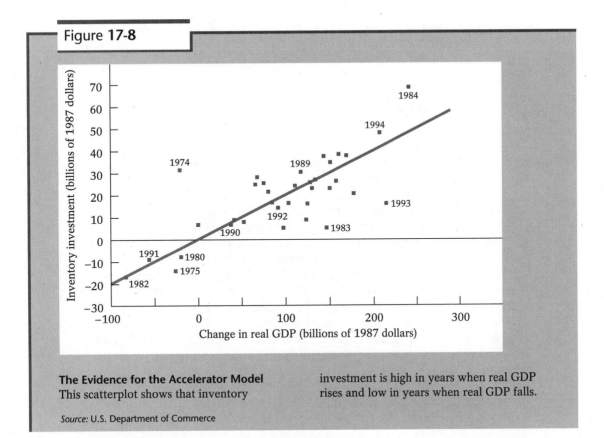

The Evidence for the Accelerator Model
This scatterplot shows that inventory investment is high in years when real GDP rises and low in years when real GDP falls.

Source: U.S. Department of Commerce

through these points shows the following relationship:

$$I = 0.2\Delta Y.$$

For every $1 that GDP rises, there is $0.20 of inventory investment.

• • • • • • • • • • • • • •

Inventories and the Real Interest Rate

Like other components of investment, inventory investment depends on the real interest rate. When a firm holds a good in inventory and sells it tomorrow rather than selling it today, it gives up the interest it could have earned between today and tomorrow. Thus, the real interest rate measures the opportunity cost of holding inventories.

When the real interest rate rises, holding inventories becomes more costly, so rational firms try to reduce their stock. Therefore, an increase in the real interest rate depresses inventory investment. For example, in the 1980s many firms adopted "just-in-time" production plans, which were designed to reduce the amount of inventory by producing goods just before sale. The high real interest rates that prevailed during most of this decade are one possible explanation for this change in business strategy.

17-4 Conclusion

The purpose of this chapter has been to examine the determinants of investment in more detail. Looking back on the various models of investment, we can see three themes.

First, all types of investment spending are inversely related to the real interest rate. A higher interest rate raises the cost of capital to firms that invest in plant and equipment, raises the cost of borrowing to homebuyers, and raises the cost of holding inventories. Thus, the models of investment developed here justify the investment function we have used throughout this book.

Second, there are various causes of shifts in the investment function. An improvement in the available technology raises the marginal product of capital and raises business fixed investment. An increase in the population raises the demand for housing and raises residential investment. Most important, various economic policies, such as changes in the investment tax credit and the corporate income tax, alter the incentives to invest and thus shift the investment function.

Third, it is natural to expect investment to be volatile over the business cycle, because investment spending depends on the output of the economy as well as on the interest rate. In the neoclassical model of business fixed investment, higher employment raises the marginal product of capital and the incentive to invest. Higher output also raises firms' profits and, thereby, relaxes the financing constraints that some firms face. In addition, higher income raises the demand for houses, in turn raising housing prices and residential investment. Higher output raises the stock of inventories firms wish to hold, stimulating inventory investment. Our models predict that an economic boom should stimulate investment and a recession should depress it. This is exactly what we observe.

Summary

1. The marginal product of capital determines the real rental price of capital. The real interest rate, the depreciation rate, and the relative price of capital goods determine the cost of capital. According to the neoclassical model, firms invest if the rental price is greater than the cost of capital, and they disinvest if the rental price is less than the cost of capital.

2. Various parts of the federal tax code influence the incentive to invest. The corporate income tax discourages investment, and the investment tax credit—which has now been repealed in the United States—encourages it.

3. An alternative way of expressing the neoclassical model is to state that investment depends on Tobin's q, the ratio of the market value of installed capital to its replacement cost. This ratio reflects the current and expected future profitability of capital.

4. In contrast to the assumption of the neoclassical model, firms cannot always raise funds to finance investment. Financing constraints make investment sensitive to firms' current cash flow.

5. Residential investment depends on the relative price of housing. Housing prices in turn depend on the demand for housing and the fixed supply. An increase in housing demand, perhaps attributable to a fall in the interest rate, raises housing prices and residential investment.

6. Firms have various motives for holding inventories of goods: smoothing production, using them as a factor of production, avoiding stock-outs, and storing work in process. One model of inventory investment that works well without endorsing a particular motive is the accelerator model. According to this model, the stock of inventories depends on the level of GDP, and inventory investment depends on the change in GDP.

KEY CONCEPTS

Business fixed investment

Residential investment

Inventory investment

Neoclassical model of investment

Depreciation

Real cost of capital

Net investment

Corporate income tax

Investment tax credit

Stock

Stock market

Tobin's q

Financing constraints

Production smoothing

Inventories as a factor of production

Stock-out avoidance

Work in process

Accelerator model

QUESTIONS FOR REVIEW

1. In the neoclassical model of business fixed investment, under what conditions will firms find it profitable to add to their capital stock?

2. What is Tobin's q, and what does it have to do with investment?

3. Explain why an increase in the interest rate reduces the amount of residential investment.

4. List four reasons firms might hold inventories.

PROBLEMS AND APPLICATIONS

1. Use the neoclassical model of investment to explain the impact of each of the following on the rental price of capital, the cost of capital, and investment:

   a. Anti-inflationary monetary policy raises the real interest rate.

   b. An earthquake destroys part of the capital stock.

   c. Immigration of foreign workers increases the size of the labor force.

2. Suppose that the government levies a tax on oil companies equal to a proportion of the value of the company's oil reserves. (The government assures the firms that the tax is for one time only.) According to the neoclassical model, what effect will the tax have on business fixed investment by these firms? What if these firms face financing constraints?

3. The *IS-LM* model developed in Chapters 9 and 10 assumes that investment depends only on the interest rate. Yet our theories of investment suggest that investment might also depend on national income: higher income might induce firms to invest more.

   a. Explain why investment might depend on national income.

   b. Suppose that investment is determined by

   $$I = \bar{I} + aY,$$

   where a is a constant between zero and one. With investment set this way, what are the fiscal-policy multipliers in the Keynesian cross model? Explain.

   c. Suppose that investment depends on both income and the interest rate. That is, the investment function is

   $$I = \bar{I} + aY - br,$$

   where a is a constant between zero and one, and b is a constant greater than zero. Use the *IS-LM* model to consider the short-run impact of an increase in government purchases on national income Y, the interest rate r, consumption C, and investment I. How might this investment function alter the conclusions implied by the basic *IS-LM* model?

4. When the stock market crashes, as it did in October 1929 and October 1987, how should the Federal Reserve respond? Why?

5. It is an election year, and the economy is in a recession. The opposition candidate campaigns on a platform of passing an investment tax credit, which would be effective next year after she takes office. What impact does this campaign promise have on economic conditions during the current year?

6. The United States experienced a large increase in the number of births in the 1950s. People in this baby-boom generation reached adulthood and started forming their own households in the 1970s.

   a. Use the model of residential investment to predict the impact of this event on housing prices and residential investment.

   b. For the years 1970 and 1980, compute the real price of housing, measured as the residential investment deflator divided by the GDP deflator. What do you find? Is this finding consistent with the model? (*Hint*: A good source of data is the *Economic Report of the President*, which is published annually.)

7. The U.S. tax laws encourage investment in housing and discourage investment in business capital. What are the long-run effects of this policy? (*Hint*: Think about the labor market.)

Chapter 18 . . . .

Money Supply and Money Demand

There have been three great inventions since the beginning of time:
fire, the wheel, and central banking.

Will Rogers

The supply and demand for money are crucial to many issues in macroeconomics. In Chapter 6, we discussed how economists use the term "money," how the central bank controls the quantity of money, and how monetary policy affects prices and interest rates in the long run when prices are flexible. In Chapters 9 and 10, we saw that the money market is a key element of the *IS-LM* model, which describes the economy in the short run when prices are sticky.

This chapter examines money supply and money demand more closely. In Section 18-1 we see that the banking system plays a key role in determining the money supply, and we discuss various policy instruments that the central bank can use to alter the money supply. In Section 18-2 we consider the motives behind money demand, and we analyze the household's decision about how much money to hold. In Section 18-3 we discuss how recent changes in the financial system have blurred the distinction between money and other assets and how this development complicates the conduct of monetary policy.

18-1 Money Supply

Chapter 6 introduced the concept of "money supply" in a highly simplified manner. In that chapter we defined the quantity of money as the number of dollars held by the public, and we assumed that the Federal Reserve controls the supply of money by increasing or decreasing the number of dollars in circulation through open-market operations. Although this explanation is acceptable as a first approximation, it is not complete. This is because it omits the role of the banking system in determining the money supply. We now present a more complete explanation.

In this section we see that the money supply is determined not only by Fed policy, but also by the behavior of households which hold money and of banks in which money is held. We begin by recalling that the money supply includes both currency in the hands of the public and the deposits at banks that households can use on demand for transactions, such as checking accounts. That is, letting M denote the money supply, C currency, and D demand deposits, we can write

$$\text{Money Supply} = \text{Currency} + \text{Demand Deposits}$$
$$M = C + D.$$

To understand the money supply, we must understand the interaction between currency and demand deposits and how Fed policy influences these two components of the money supply.

100-Percent-Reserve Banking

We begin by imagining a world without banks. In such a world, all money takes the form of currency, and the quantity of money is simply the amount of currency that the public holds. For this discussion, suppose that there is $1,000 of currency in the economy.

Now introduce banks. At first, suppose that banks accept deposits but do not make loans. The only purpose of the banks is to provide a safe place for depositors to keep their money.

The deposits that banks have received but have not lent out are called **reserves**. Some reserves are held in the vaults of local banks throughout the country, but most are held at a central bank, such as the Federal Reserve. In our hypothetical economy, all deposits are held as reserves: banks simply accept deposits, place the money in reserve, and leave the money there until the depositor makes a withdrawal or writes a check against the balance. This system is called **100-percent-reserve banking**.

Suppose that households deposit the economy's entire $1,000 in Firstbank. Figure 18-1 shows Firstbank's **balance sheet**—its accounting statement of assets and liabilities. The bank's assets are the $1,000 it holds as reserves; the bank's liabilities are the $1,000 it owes to depositors. Unlike banks in our economy, this bank is not making loans, so it will not earn profit from its assets. The bank presumably charges depositors a small fee to cover its costs.

What is the money supply in this economy? Before the creation of Firstbank, the money supply was the $1,000 of currency. After the creation of First-

Figure 18-1

Firstbank's Balance Sheet	
Assets	Liabilities
Reserves $1,000	Deposits $1,000

A Balance Sheet Under 100-Percent-Reserve Banking A bank's balance sheet shows its assets and liabilities. Under 100-percent-reserve banking, banks hold all deposits as reserves. Here the $1,000 of reserves exactly balances the $1,000 of deposits.

bank, the money supply is the $1,000 of demand deposits. A dollar deposited in a bank reduces currency by one dollar and raises deposits by one dollar, so the money supply remains the same. *If banks hold 100 percent of deposits in reserve, the banking system does not affect the supply of money.*

Fractional-Reserve Banking

Now imagine that banks start to use some of their deposits to make loans—for example, to families who are buying houses or to firms that are investing in new plants and equipment. The advantage to banks is that they can charge interest on the loans. The banks must keep some reserves on hand so that reserves are available whenever depositors want to make withdrawals. But as long as the amount of new deposits approximately equals the amount of withdrawals, a bank need not keep all its deposits in reserve. Thus, bankers have an incentive to make loans. When they do so, we have **fractional-reserve banking**, a system under which banks keep only a fraction of their deposits in reserve.

Panel (a) of Figure 18-2 shows the balance sheet of Firstbank after it makes a loan. This balance sheet assumes that the *reserve–deposit ratio*—the fraction of deposits kept in reserve—is 20 percent. Firstbank keeps $200 of the $1,000 in deposits in reserve and lends out the remaining $800.

Figure 18-2

(a) Firstbank's Balance Sheet

Assets		Liabilities	
Reserves	$200	Deposits	$1,000
Loans	$800		

(b) Secondbank's Balance Sheet

Assets		Liabilities	
Reserves	$160	Deposits	$800
Loans	$640		

Balance Sheets Under Fractional-Reserve Banking When banks can use deposits to make loans, they create money. Here the $1,000 of reserves initially deposited in Firstbank leads to a much greater quantity of deposits.

(c) Thirdbank's Balance Sheet

Assets		Liabilities	
Reserves	$128	Deposits	$640
Loans	$512		

Notice that Firstbank increases the supply of money by $800 when it makes this loan. Before the loan is made, the money supply is $1,000, equaling the deposits in Firstbank. After the loan is made, the money supply is $1,800: the depositor still has a demand deposit of $1,000, but now the borrower holds $800 in currency. *Thus, in a system of fractional-reserve banking, banks create money.*

The creation of money does not stop with Firstbank. If the borrower deposits the $800 in another bank (or if the borrower uses the $800 to pay someone who then deposits it), the process of money creation continues. Panel (b) of Figure 18-2 shows the balance sheet of Secondbank. Secondbank receives the $800 in deposits, keeps 20 percent, or $160, in reserve, and then loans out $640. Thus, Secondbank creates $640 of money. If this $640 is eventually deposited in Thirdbank, this bank keeps 20 percent, or $128, in reserve and loans out $512, and so on. With each deposit and loan, more money is created.

Although this process of money creation can continue forever, it does not create an infinite amount of money. Letting rr denote the reserve–deposit ratio, the amount of money that the original $1,000 creates is

$$
\begin{aligned}
\text{Original Deposit} &= \$1,000 \\
\text{Firstbank Lending} &= (1 - rr) \times \$1,000 \\
\text{Secondbank Lending} &= (1 - rr)^2 \times \$1,000 \\
\text{Thirdbank Lending} &= (1 - rr)^3 \times \$1,000 \\
&\quad\ \ \vdots \\
\hline
\text{Total Money Supply} &= [1 + (1 - rr) + (1 - rr)^2 \\
&\quad + (1 - rr)^3 + \ldots] \times \$1,000 \\
&= (1/rr) \times \$1,000
\end{aligned}
$$

Each $1 of reserves generates $(1/rr)$ of money. In our example, $rr = 0.2$, so the original $1,000 generates $5,000 of money.[1]

The banking system's ability to create money is the primary difference between banks and other financial institutions. As we first discussed in Chapter 3, financial markets have the important function of transferring the economy's resources from those households that wish to save some of their income for the future to those households and firms that wish to borrow to buy investment goods to be used in future production. The process of transferring funds from savers to borrowers is called **financial intermediation**. Many institutions in the economy act as financial intermediaries: the most prominent examples are the stock market, the bond market, and the banking system. Yet, of these financial institutions, only banks have the legal authority to create assets that are part of the money supply, such as checking accounts. Therefore, banks are the only financial institutions that directly influence the money supply.

Note that although the system of fractional-reserve banking creates money, it does not create wealth. When a bank loans out some of its reserves, it gives borrowers the ability to make transactions and therefore increases the supply of money. The borrowers are also undertaking a debt obligation to the bank, however, so the loan does not make them wealthier. In other words, the creation of money by the banking system increases the economy's liquidity, not its wealth.

---

[1] *Mathematical Note:* The last step in the derivation of the total money supply uses the algebraic result for the sum of an infinite geometric series (which we used previously in computing the multiplier in Chapter 9). According to this result, if x is a number between -1 and 1, then

$$1 + x + x^2 + x^3 + \ldots = 1/(1 - x).$$

In this application, $x = (1 - rr)$.

A Model of the Money Supply

Now that we have seen how banks create money, let's examine in more detail what determines the money supply. Here we present a model of the money supply under fractional-reserve banking. The model has three exogenous variables:

- The **monetary base** B is the total number of dollars held by the public as currency C and by the banks as reserves R. It is directly controlled by the Federal Reserve.

- The **reserve–deposit ratio** rr is the fraction of deposits that banks hold in reserve. It is determined by the business policies of banks and the laws regulating banks.

- The **currency–deposit ratio** cr is the amount of currency C people hold as a fraction of their holdings of demand deposits D. It reflects the preferences of households about the form of money they wish to hold.

Our model shows how the money supply depends on the monetary base, the reserve–deposit ratio, and the currency–deposit ratio. It allows us to examine how Fed policy and the choices of banks and households influence the money supply.

We begin with the definitions of the money supply and the monetary base:

$$M = C + D,$$
$$B = C + R.$$

The first equation states that the money supply is the sum of currency and demand deposits. The second equation states that the monetary base is the sum of currency and bank reserves. To solve for the money supply as a function of the three exogenous variables, we begin by dividing the first equation by the second to obtain

$$\frac{M}{B} = \frac{C + D}{C + R}.$$

Then divide both the top and bottom of the expression on the right by D.

$$\frac{M}{B} = \frac{C/D + 1}{C/D + R/D}.$$

Note that C/D is the currency–deposit ratio cr, and that R/D is the reserve–deposit ratio rr. Making these substitutions, and bringing the B from the left to the right side of the equation, we obtain

$$M = \frac{cr + 1}{cr + rr} \times B.$$

This equation shows how the money supply depends on the three exogenous variables.

We can now see that the money supply is proportional to the monetary base. The factor of proportionality, $(cr + 1)/(cr + rr)$, is denoted m and is called the **money multiplier**. We can write

$$M = m \times B.$$

Each dollar of the monetary base produces m dollars of money. Because the monetary base has a multiplied effect on the money supply, the monetary base is sometimes called **high-powered money**.

Here's a numerical example that approximately describes the U.S. economy today. Suppose that the monetary base B is $400 billion, the reserve–deposit ratio rr is 0.1, and the currency–deposit ratio cr is 0.4. In this case, the money multiplier is

$$m = \frac{0.4 + 1}{0.4 + 0.1} = 2.8,$$

and the money supply is

$$M = 2.8 \times \$400 \text{ billion} = \$1,120 \text{ billion}.$$

Each dollar of the monetary base generates 2.8 dollars of money, so the total money supply is $1,120 billion.

We can now see how changes in the three exogenous variables—B, rr, and cr—cause the money supply to change.

1. The money supply is proportional to the monetary base. Thus, an increase in the monetary base increases the money supply by the same percentage.

2. The lower the reserve–deposit ratio, the more loans banks make, and the more money banks create from every dollar of reserves. Thus, a decrease in the reserve–deposit ratio raises the money multiplier and the money supply.

3. The lower the currency–deposit ratio, the fewer dollars of the monetary base the public holds as currency, the more base dollars banks hold as reserves, and the more money banks can create. Thus, a decrease in the currency–deposit ratio raises the money multiplier and the money supply.

With this model in mind, we can discuss the ways in which the Fed influences the money supply.

The Three Instruments of Monetary Policy

In previous chapters we made the simplifying assumption that the Federal Reserve controls the money supply directly. In fact, the Fed controls the money supply indirectly by altering either the monetary base or the reserve–deposit ratio. To do this, the Fed has at its disposal three instruments of monetary policy: open-market operations, reserve requirements, and the discount rate.

Open-market operations are the purchases and sales of government bonds by the Fed. When the Fed buys bonds from the public, the dollars it pays for the bonds increase the monetary base and thereby increase the money supply. When the Fed sells bonds to the public, the dollars it receives reduce the monetary base and thus decrease the money supply. Open-market operations are the policy instrument that the Fed uses most often. In fact, the Fed conducts open-market operations in New York bond markets almost every weekday.

Reserve requirements are Fed regulations that impose on banks a minimum reserve–deposit ratio. An increase in reserve requirements raises the reserve–deposit ratio and thus lowers the money multiplier and the money supply. Changes in reserve requirements are the least frequently used of the Fed's three policy instruments.

The **discount rate** is the interest rate that the Fed charges when it makes loans to banks. Banks borrow from the Fed when they find themselves with too few reserves to meet reserve requirements. The lower the discount rate, the cheaper are borrowed reserves, and the more banks borrow at the Fed's discount window. Hence, a reduction in the discount rate raises the monetary base and the money supply.

Although these three instruments—open-market operations, reserve requirements, and the discount rate—give the Fed substantial power to influence the money supply, the Fed cannot control the money supply perfectly. Bank discretion in conducting business can cause the money supply to change in ways the Fed did not anticipate. For example, banks may choose to hold **excess reserves**—that is, reserves above the reserve requirement. The higher the amount of excess reserves, the higher the reserve–deposit ratio, and the lower the money supply. As another example, the Fed cannot precisely control the amount banks borrow from the discount window. The less banks borrow, the smaller the monetary base, and the smaller the money supply. Hence, the money supply sometimes moves in ways the Fed does not intend.

Case Study *18-1*

● ● ● ● ● ● ● ● ● ● ● ● ● ●

Bank Failures and the Money Supply in the 1930s

Between August 1929 and March 1933, the money supply fell 28 percent. As we discussed in Chapter 10, some economists believe that this large decline in the money supply was the primary cause of the Great Depression. But we did not discuss why the money supply fell so dramatically.

The three variables that determine the money supply—the monetary base, the reserve–deposit ratio, and the currency–deposit ratio—are shown in Table 18-1 for 1929 and 1933. You can see that the fall in the money supply cannot be attributed to a fall in the monetary base: in fact, the monetary base rose 18 percent over this period. Instead, the money supply fell because the money multiplier fell 38 percent. The money multiplier fell because the currency–deposit and reserve–deposit ratios both rose substantially.

Table 18-1		
The Money Supply and Its Determinants: 1929 and 1933		
	August 1929	March 1933
Money Supply	26.5	19.0
Currency	3.9	5.5
Demand deposits	22.6	13.5
Monetary Base	7.1	8.4
Currency	3.9	5.5
Reserves	3.2	2.9
Money Multiplier	3.7	2.3
Reserve–deposit ratio	0.14	0.21
Currency–deposit ratio	0.17	0.41

Source: Adapted from Milton Friedman and Anna Schwartz, *A Monetary History of the United States, 1867–1960* (Princeton, N.J.: Princeton University Press, 1963), Appendix A.

Most economists attribute the fall in the money multiplier to the large number of bank failures in the early 1930s. From 1930 to 1933, more than 9,000 banks suspended operations, often defaulting on their depositors. The bank failures caused the money supply to fall by altering the behavior of both depositors and bankers.

Bank failures raised the currency–deposit ratio by reducing public confidence in the banking system. People feared that bank failures would continue, and they began to view currency as a more desirable form of money than demand deposits. When they withdrew their deposits, they drained the banks of reserves. The process of money creation reversed itself, as banks responded to lower reserves by reducing their outstanding balance of loans.

In addition, the bank failures raised the reserve–deposit ratio by making bankers more cautious. Having just observed many bank runs, bankers became apprehensive about operating with a small amount of reserves. They therefore increased their holdings of reserves to well above the legal minimum. Just as households responded to the banking crisis by holding more currency relative to deposits, bankers responded by holding more reserves relative to loans. Together these changes caused a large fall in the money multiplier.

Although it is easy to explain why the money supply fell, it is more difficult to decide whether to blame the Federal Reserve. One might argue that the monetary base did not fall, so the Fed should not be blamed. Critics of Fed policy during this period make two arguments. First, they claim that the Fed should have taken a more vigorous role in preventing bank failures by acting as a *lender of last resort* when banks needed cash during bank runs. This would have helped maintain confidence in the banking system and prevented the large fall in the money multiplier. Second, they point out that the Fed could have responded to the fall in the money multiplier by increasing the monetary base even more than it did. Either of these actions would likely have prevented such a large fall in the money supply, which in turn might have reduced the severity of the Great Depression.

Since the 1930s, many policies have been put into place that make such a large and sudden fall in the money multiplier less likely today. Most important, the system of federal deposit insurance maintains public confidence in the banking system and thus prevents large swings in the currency–deposit ratio. Deposit insurance, however, can be a costly policy: in the late 1980s and early 1990s, the federal government incurred the large expense of bailing out many insolvent savings and loan institutions. Yet deposit insurance does help stabilize the banking system and the money supply.

18-2 Money Demand

We now turn to the other side of the money market and examine what determines money demand. In previous chapters, we used simple money demand functions. We started with the quantity theory, which assumes that the demand for real balances is proportional to income. That is, the quantity theory assumes

$$(M/P)^d = kY,$$

where k is a constant. We then considered a more general and realistic money demand function that assumes the demand for real balances depends on both the interest rate and income:

$$(M/P)^d = L(i, Y).$$

We used this money demand function when we discussed the link between money and prices in Chapter 6 and when we developed the *IS-LM* model in Chapters 9 and 10.

The purpose of studying money demand in more detail is to gain insight into the money demand function. Just as studies of the consumption function rely on microeconomic models of the consumption decision, studies of the money demand function rely on microeconomic models of the money demand decision. In this section we first discuss in broad terms the different ways to model money demand. We then develop one prominent model.

Recall that money serves three functions: it is a unit of account, a store of value, and a medium of exchange. The first function—money as a unit of account—does not by itself generate any demand for money, because one can quote prices in dollars without holding any. By contrast, money can serve its other two functions only if people hold it. Theories of money demand emphasize the role of money either as a store of value or as a medium of exchange.

Portfolio Theories of Money Demand

Theories of money demand that emphasize the role of money as a store of value are called **portfolio theories**. According to these theories, people hold money as part of their portfolio of assets. The key insight is that money offers a different combination of risk and return than other assets. In particular, money offers a safe (nominal) return, whereas the prices of stocks and bonds may rise or fall. Thus, some economists have suggested that households choose to hold money as part of their optimal portfolio.[2]

Portfolio theories predict that the demand for money should depend on the risk and return offered by money and by the various assets households can hold instead of money. In addition, money demand should depend on total wealth, because wealth measures the size of the portfolio to be allocated among money and the alternative assets. For example, we might write the money demand function as

$$(M/P)^d = L(r_s, r_b, \pi^e, W),$$

where r_s is the expected real return on stock, r_b is the expected real return on bonds, π^e is the expected inflation rate, and W is real wealth. An increase in r_s or r_b reduces money demand, because other assets become more attractive. An increase in π^e also reduces money demand, because money becomes less attractive. (Recall that $-\pi^e$ is the expected real return to holding money.) An increase in W raises money demand, because higher wealth means a larger portfolio.

From the standpoint of portfolio theories, we can view our money demand function, $L(i, Y)$, as a useful simplification. First, it uses real income Y as a proxy for real wealth W. Second, the only return variable it includes is the nominal interest rate, which is the sum of the real return on bonds and expected inflation (that is, $i = r_b + \pi^e$). According to portfolio theories, however, the money demand function should include the expected returns on other assets as well.

Are portfolio theories useful for studying money demand? The answer depends on which measure of money we are considering. The most narrow measures of money, such as $M1$, include only currency and checking accounts. These forms of money earn zero or very low rates of interest. There are other assets—such as savings accounts, Treasury bills, certificates of deposit, and money market mutual funds—that earn higher rates of interest and have the same risk characteristics as currency and checking accounts. Economists say that money ($M1$) is a **dominated asset**: as a store of value, it exists alongside other assets that are always better. Thus, it is not optimal for people to hold money as part of their portfolio, and portfolio theories cannot explain the demand for these dominated forms of money.

Portfolio theories are more plausible as theories of money demand if we adopt a broad measure of money. The broad measures include many of those assets that dominate currency and checking accounts. $M2$, for example, includes savings accounts and money market mutual funds. When we examine why people hold assets in the form of $M2$, rather than bonds or stock, the portfolio considerations of risk and return may be paramount. Hence, although the portfolio approach to money demand may not be plausible when applied to $M1$, it may be a good theory to explain the demand for $M2$ or $M3$.

[2] James Tobin, "Liquidity Preference as Behavior Toward Risk," *Review of Economic Studies* 25 (February 1958): 65–86.

Case Study *18-2*

● ● ● ● ● ● ● ● ● ● ● ● ● ● ●

Currency and the Underground Economy

How much currency are you holding right now in your wallet? How many $100 bills?

In the United States today, the amount of currency per person exceeds $1,000. About half of that is in $100 bills. Most people find this fact surprising, because they hold much smaller amounts and in smaller denominations.

Some of this currency is used by people in the underground economy—that is, by those engaged in illegal activity such as the drug trade and by those trying to hide income in order to evade taxes. People whose wealth was earned illegally may have fewer options for investing their portfolio, because by holding wealth in banks, bonds, or stock, they assume a greater risk of detection. For criminals, currency may not be a dominated asset: it may be the best store of value available.

Some economists point to the large amount of currency in the underground economy as one reason that some inflation may be desirable. Recall that inflation is a tax on the holders of money, because inflation erodes the real value of money. A drug dealer holding $20,000 in cash pays an inflation tax of $2,000 per year when the inflation rate is 10 percent. The inflation tax may be the only tax those in the underground economy cannot evade.

● ● ● ● ● ● ● ● ● ● ● ● ● ● ●

Transactions Theories of Money Demand

Theories of money demand that emphasize the role of money as a medium of exchange are called **transactions theories**. These theories acknowledge that money is a dominated asset and stress that people hold money, unlike other assets, to make purchases. These theories best explain why people hold narrow measures of money, such as currency and checking accounts, as opposed to holding assets that dominate them, such as savings accounts or Treasury bills.

Transactions theories of money demand take many forms, depending on how one models the process of obtaining money and making transactions. All these theories assume that money has the cost of earning a low rate of return and the benefit of making transactions more convenient. People decide how much money to hold by trading off these costs and benefits.

To see how transactions theories explain the money demand function, let's develop one prominent model of this type. The **Baumol-Tobin model** was developed in the 1950s by economists William Baumol and James Tobin, and it remains a leading theory of money demand.[3]

---

[3]   William Baumol, "The Transactions Demand for Cash: An Inventory Theoretic Approach," *Quarterly Journal of Economics* 66 (November 1952): 545–556; James Tobin, "The Interest Elasticity of the Transactions Demand for Cash," *Review of Economics and Statistics* (August 1956): 241–247.

The Baumol-Tobin Model of Cash Management

The Baumol-Tobin model analyzes the costs and benefits of holding money. The benefit of holding money is convenience: people hold money to avoid making a trip to the bank every time they wish to buy something. The cost of this convenience is the forgone interest they would have received had they left the money deposited in a savings account that paid interest.

To see how people trade off these benefits and costs, consider a person who plans to spend Y dollars gradually over the course of a year. (For simplicity, assume that the price level is constant, so real spending is constant over the year.) How much money should he hold in the process of spending this amount? That is, what is the optimal size of average cash balances?

Consider the possibilities. He could withdraw the Y dollars at the beginning of the year and gradually spend the money. Panel (a) of Figure 18-3 shows his money holdings over the course of the year under this plan. His money holdings begin the year at Y and end the year at zero, averaging $Y/2$ over the year.

Figure 18-3

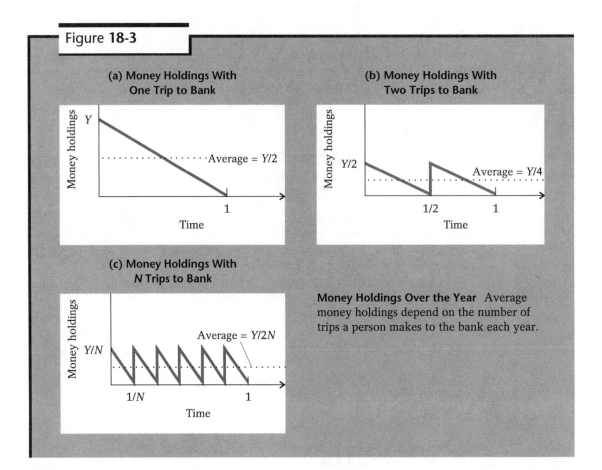

(a) Money Holdings With One Trip to Bank

(b) Money Holdings With Two Trips to Bank

(c) Money Holdings With N Trips to Bank

Money Holdings Over the Year Average money holdings depend on the number of trips a person makes to the bank each year.

A second possible plan is to make two trips to the bank. In this case, he withdraws $Y/2$ dollars at the beginning of the year, gradually spends this amount over the first half of the year, and then makes another trip to withdraw $Y/2$ for the second half of the year. Panel (b) of Figure 18-3 shows that money holdings over the year vary between $Y/2$ and zero, averaging $Y/4$. This plan has the advantage that less money is held on average, so the individual forgoes less interest, but it has the disadvantage of requiring two trips to the bank rather than one.

More generally, suppose the individual makes N trips to the bank over the course of the year. On each trip, he withdraws Y/N dollars; he then spends the money gradually over the following $1/N$th of the year. Panel (c) of Figure 18-3 shows that money holdings vary between Y/N and zero, averaging $Y/(2N)$.

The question is, what is the optimal choice of N? The greater N is, the less money the individual holds on average and the less interest he forgoes. But as N increases, so does the inconvenience of making frequent trips to the bank.

Suppose that the cost of going to the bank is some fixed amount F. F represents the value of the time spent traveling to and from the bank and waiting in line to make the withdrawal. For example, if a trip to the bank takes 15 minutes and a person's wage is $12 per hour, then F is $3. Also, let i denote the interest rate; because money does not bear interest, i measures the opportunity cost of holding money.

Now we can analyze the optimal choice of N, which determines money demand. For any N, the average amount of money held is $Y/(2N)$, so the forgone interest is $iY/(2N)$. Because F is the cost per trip to the bank, the total cost of making trips to the bank is FN. The total cost the individual bears is the sum of the forgone interest and the cost of trips to the bank:

$$\text{Total Cost} = \text{Forgone Interest} + \text{Cost of Trips}$$
$$= \quad iY/(2N) \quad + \quad FN.$$

The larger the number of trips N, the smaller the forgone interest, and the larger the cost of going to the bank.

Figure 18-4 shows how total cost depends on N. There is one value of N that minimizes total cost. The optimal value of N, denoted N^*, is[4]

$$N^* = \sqrt{\frac{iY}{2F}}.$$

[4] *Mathematical Note:* Deriving this expression for the optimal choice of N requires simple calculus. Differentiate total cost C with respect to N to obtain

$$dC/dN = -iYN^{-2}/2 + F.$$

At the optimum, $dC/dN = 0$, which yields the formula for N^*.

Figure 18-4

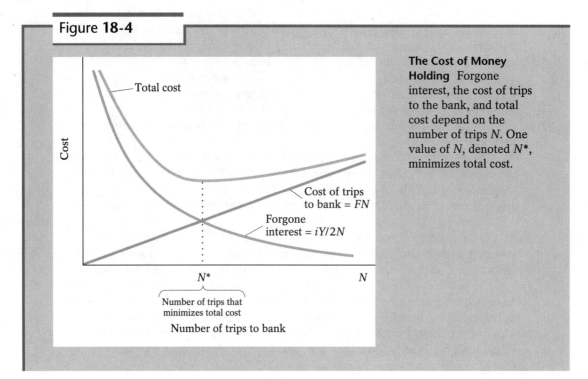

The Cost of Money Holding Forgone interest, the cost of trips to the bank, and total cost depend on the number of trips N. One value of N, denoted N^*, minimizes total cost.

Average money holding is

$$\text{Average Money Holding} = Y/(2N^*)$$

$$= \sqrt{\frac{YF}{2i}}.$$

This expression shows that the individual holds more money if the fixed cost of going to the bank F is higher, if expenditure Y is higher, or if the interest rate i is lower.

So far, we have been interpreting the Baumol-Tobin model as a model of the demand for currency. That is, we have used it to explain the amount of money held outside of banks. Yet one can interpret the model more broadly. Imagine a person who holds a portfolio of monetary assets (currency and checking accounts) and nonmonetary assets (stocks and bonds). Monetary assets are used for transactions but offer a low rate of return. Let i be the difference in the return between monetary and nonmonetary assets, and let F be the cost of transferring nonmonetary assets into monetary assets, such as a brokerage fee. The decision about how often to pay the brokerage fee is analogous to the decision about how often to make a trip to the bank. Therefore, the Baumol-Tobin model describes this person's demand for monetary assets. By showing that money demand depends positively on expenditure Y and negatively on the interest rate i, the model provides a microeconomic justification for the money demand function, $L(i, Y)$, that is used throughout this book.

Case Study *18-3*

● ● ● ● ● ● ● ● ● ● ● ● ● ●

Empirical Studies of Money Demand

Many economists have studied the data on money, income, and interest rates to learn more about the money demand function. One purpose of these studies is to estimate how money demand responds to changes in income and the interest rate. The sensitivity of money demand to these two variables determines the slope of the *LM* curve; it thus influences how monetary and fiscal policy affect the economy.

Another purpose of the empirical studies is to test the theories of money demand. The Baumol-Tobin model, for example, makes precise predictions for how income and interest rates influence money demand. The model's square-root formula implies that the income elasticity of money demand is 1/2: a 10 percent increase in income should lead to a 5 percent increase in the demand for real balances. It also says that the interest elasticity of money demand is 1/2: a 10 percent increase in the interest rate (say, from 10 percent to 11 percent) should lead to a 5 percent decrease in the demand for real balances.

Most empirical studies of money demand do not confirm these predictions. They find that the income elasticity of money demand is larger than 1/2 and that the interest elasticity is smaller than 1/2. Thus, although the Baumol-Tobin model may capture part of the story behind the money demand function, it is not completely correct.

One possible explanation for the failure of the Baumol-Tobin model is that some people may have less discretion over their money holdings than the model assumes. For example, consider a person who must go to the bank once a week to deposit her paycheck; while at the bank, she takes advantage of her visit to withdraw the currency needed for the coming week. For this person, the number of trips to the bank, N, does not respond to changes in expenditure or the interest rate. Because N is fixed, average money holdings ($Y/2N$) are proportional to expenditure and insensitive to the interest rate.

Now imagine that the world is populated with two sorts of people. Some obey the Baumol-Tobin model, so they have income and interest elasticities of 1/2. The others have a fixed N, so they have an income elasticity of 1 and an interest elasticity of zero. In this case, the overall demand for money looks like a weighted average of the demands of the two groups. The income elasticity will be between 1/2 and 1, and the interest elasticity will be between 1/2 and zero, as the empirical studies find.[5]

● ● ● ● ● ● ● ● ● ● ● ● ● ●

5 To learn more about the empirical studies of money demand, see Stephen M. Goldfeld and Daniel E. Sichel, "The Demand for Money," *Handbook of Monetary Economics*, volume 1 (Amsterdam: North-Holland, 1990): 299–356; and David Laidler, *The Demand for Money: Theories and Evidence*, 3rd ed. (New York: Harper & Row, 1985).

18-3 Financial Innovation and the Rise of Near Money

Traditional macroeconomic analysis groups assets into two categories: those used as a medium of exchange as well as a store of value (currency, checking accounts) and those used only as a store of value (stocks, bonds, savings accounts). The first category of assets is called "money." In this chapter we discussed its supply and demand.

Although the distinction between monetary and nonmonetary assets remains a useful theoretical tool, in recent years it has become more difficult to use in practice. In part because of deregulation of banks and other financial institutions, and in part because of improved computer technology, the past decade has seen rapid financial innovation. Monetary assets such as checking accounts once paid no interest; today they earn market interest rates and are comparable to nonmonetary assets as stores of value. Nonmonetary assets such as stocks and bonds were once inconvenient to buy and sell; today mutual funds allow depositors to hold stocks and bonds and to make withdrawals simply by writing checks from their accounts. These nonmonetary assets that have acquired some of the liquidity of money are called **near money**.

The existence of near money complicates monetary policy by making the demand for money unstable. Since money and near money are close substitutes, households can easily switch their assets from one form to the other. Such changes can occur for minor reasons and do not necessarily reflect changes in spending. Thus, the velocity of money becomes unstable, and the quantity of money gives faulty signals about aggregate demand.

One response to this problem is to use a broad definition of money that includes near money. Yet, since there is a continuum of assets in the world with varying characteristics, it is not clear how to choose a subset to label "money." Moreover, if we adopt a broad definition of money, the Fed's ability to control this quantity may be limited, since many forms of near money have no reserve requirement.

The instability in money demand caused by near money has been an important practical problem for the Federal Reserve. In the early 1990s, different measures of the quantity of money gave conflicting signals: some measures of money grew quickly, while others grew slowly. In 1993, Fed Chairman Alan Greenspan announced that the Fed would pay less attention to short-run fluctuations in monetary aggregates. Under the new policy, the Fed would use the instruments of monetary policy to set interest rates at a level it believed to be consistent with low inflation and continued growth. Only time will tell whether this new policy yields greater macroeconomic stability.

Case Study *18-4*

●　●　●　●　●　●　●　●　●　●　●　●

John Taylor's (and Alan Greenspan's?) Monetary Rule

If you wanted to set interest rates to achieve stable prices while avoiding large fluctuations in output and employment, how would you do it? This is exactly the question that Alan Greenspan and the other governors of the Federal Reserve must ask themselves every day. The short-term policy instrument that the Fed now sets is the federal funds rate—the short-term interest rate at which banks make loans to one another. Whenever the Federal Open Market Committee meets, it chooses a target for the federal funds rate. The Fed's bond traders are then told to conduct open-market operations in order to hit the desired target.

The hard part of the Fed's job is choosing the target for the federal funds rate. Two guidelines are clear. First, when inflation heats up, the federal funds rate should rise. An increase in the interest rate will mean a smaller money supply and, eventually, lower investment, lower output, higher unemployment, and reduced inflation. Second, when real economic activity slows—as reflected in real GDP or unemployment—the federal funds rate should fall. A decrease in the interest rate will mean a larger money supply and, eventually, higher investment, higher output, and lower unemployment.

The Fed needs to go beyond these general guidelines, however, and decide how much to respond to changes in inflation and real economic activity. To help it make this decision, economist John Taylor has proposed a simple rule for the federal funds rate:

$$\text{Nominal Federal Funds Rate} = \text{Inflation} + 2.0 + 0.5\,(\text{Inflation} - 2.0)$$
$$- 0.5\,(\text{GDP gap}).$$

The GDP gap is the percentage shortfall of real GDP from an estimate of its natural rate.

Taylor's rule has the real federal funds rate—the nominal rate minus inflation—responding to inflation and the GDP gap. According to this rule, the real federal funds rate equals 2 percent when inflation is 2 percent and GDP is at its natural rate. For each percentage point by which inflation rises above 2 percent, the real federal funds rate rises by 0.5 percent. For each percentage point by which real GDP falls below its natural rate, the real federal funds rate falls by 0.5 percent. If GDP rises above its natural rate, so that the GDP gap is negative, the real federal funds rate rises accordingly.

Taylor's rule for monetary policy is not only simple and reasonable, but it also resembles actual Fed behavior in recent years. Figure 18-5 shows the

Figure 18-5

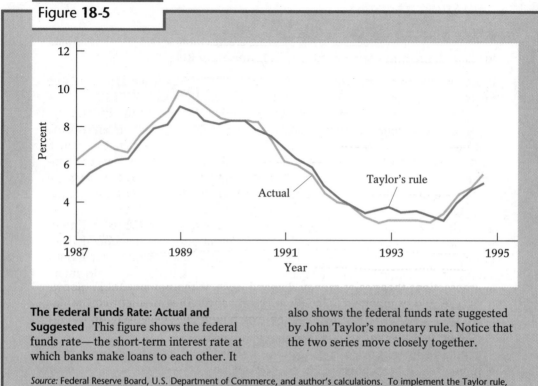

The Federal Funds Rate: Actual and Suggested This figure shows the federal funds rate—the short-term interest rate at which banks make loans to each other. It also shows the federal funds rate suggested by John Taylor's monetary rule. Notice that the two series move closely together.

Source: Federal Reserve Board, U.S. Department of Commerce, and author's calculations. To implement the Taylor rule, the inflation rate is measured as the percentage change in the GDP deflator over the previous four quarters, and the GDP gap is measured as twice the deviation of the unemployment rate from 6 percent.

actual federal funds rate and the target rate as determined by Taylor's proposed rule. Notice how closely together the two series move. John Taylor's monetary rule may be more than an academic suggestion. It may be the rule that Alan Greenspan and his colleagues are (perhaps unconsciously) following.[6]

18-4 Conclusion

Money is at the heart of much macroeconomic analysis. Models of money supply and money demand can help shed light on the long-run determinants of the price level and the short-run causes of economic fluctuations. The rise of near money in recent years has shown that there is still much to be learned. Building reliable microeconomic models of money and near money remains a central challenge for macroeconomists.

[6] John B. Taylor, "The Inflation/Output Variability Tradeoff Revisited," in *Goals, Guidelines, and Constraints Facing Monetary Policymakers* (Federal Reserve Bank of Boston, 1994).

Summary

1. The system of fractional-reserve banking creates money, because each dollar of reserves generates many dollars of demand deposits.

2. The supply of money depends on the monetary base, the reserve–deposit ratio, and the currency–deposit ratio. An increase in the monetary base leads to a proportionate increase in the money supply. A decrease in the reserve–deposit ratio or in the currency–deposit ratio increases the money multiplier and thus the money supply.

3. The Federal Reserve changes the money supply using three policy instruments. It can increase the monetary base by making an open-market purchase of bonds or by lowering the discount rate. It can reduce the reserve–deposit ratio by relaxing reserve requirements.

4. Portfolio theories of money demand stress the role of money as a store of value. They predict that the demand for money depends on the risk and return on money and alternative assets.

5. Transactions theories of money demand, such as the Baumol-Tobin model, stress the role of money as a medium of exchange. They predict that the demand for money depends positively on expenditure and negatively on the interest rate.

6. Financial innovation has led to the creation of assets with many of the attributes of money. These near monies make the demand for money less stable, which complicates the conduct of monetary policy.

KEY CONCEPTS

Reserves	Excess reserves
100-percent-reserve banking	Portfolio theories
Balance sheet	Dominated asset
Fractional-reserve banking	Transactions theories
Financial intermediation	Baumol-Tobin model
Monetary base	Near money
Reserve–deposit ratio	
Currency–deposit ratio	
Money multiplier	
High-powered money	
Open-market operations	
Reserve requirements	
Discount rate	

QUESTIONS FOR REVIEW

1. Explain how banks create money.

2. What are the three ways in which the Federal Reserve can influence the money supply?

3. Why might a banking crisis lead to a fall in the money supply?

4. Explain the difference between portfolio and transactions theories of money demand.

5. According to the Baumol-Tobin model, what determines how often people go to the bank? What does this decision have to do with money demand?

6. In what way does the existence of near money complicate the conduct of monetary policy?

PROBLEMS AND APPLICATIONS

1. The money supply fell during the years 1929 to 1933 because both the currency–deposit ratio and the reserve–deposit ratio increased. Use the model of the money supply and the data in Table 18-1 to answer the following hypothetical questions about this episode.

   a. What would have happened to the money supply if the currency–deposit ratio had risen but the reserve–deposit ratio had remained the same?

   b. What would have happened to the money supply if the reserve–deposit ratio had risen but the currency–deposit ratio had remained the same?

   c. Which of the two changes was more responsible for the fall in the money supply?

2. To increase tax revenue, the U.S. government in 1932 imposed a two-cent tax on checks written on deposits in bank accounts. (In today's dollars, this tax was about 25 cents per check.)

   a. How do you think the check tax affected the currency–deposit ratio? Explain.

   b. Use the model of the money supply under fractional-reserve banking to discuss how this tax affected the money supply.

   c. Now use the *IS-LM* model to discuss the impact of this tax on the economy. Was the check tax a good policy to implement in the middle of the Great Depression?

3. Suppose that an epidemic of street crime sweeps the country, making it more likely that your wallet will be stolen. Using the Baumol-Tobin model, explain (in words, not equations) how this crime wave will affect the optimal frequency of trips to the bank and the demand for money.

4. Let's see what the Baumol-Tobin model says about how often you should go to the bank to withdraw cash.

   a. How much do you buy per year with currency (versus checks or credit cards)? This is your value of Y.

   b. How long does it take you to go to the bank? What is your hourly wage? Use these two figures to compute your value of F.

   c. What interest rate do you earn on the money you leave in your bank account? This is your value of i. (Be sure to write i in decimal form—that is, 6 percent should be expressed 0.06.)

   d. According to the Baumol-Tobin model, how many times should you go to the bank each year, and how much should you withdraw each time?

e. In practice, how often do you go to the bank, and how much do you withdraw?

f. Compare the predictions of the Baumol-Tobin model to your behavior. Does the model describe how you actually behave? If not, why not? How would you change the model to make it a better description of your behavior?

5. In Chapter 6, we defined the velocity of money as the ratio of nominal expenditure to the quantity of money. Let's now use the Baumol-Tobin model to examine what determines velocity.

a. Recalling that average money holdings equal $Y/(2N)$, write velocity as a function of the number of trips to the bank N. Explain your result.

b. Use the formula for the optimal number of trips to express velocity as a function of expenditure Y, the interest rate i, and the cost of a trip to the bank F.

c. What happens to velocity when the interest rate rises? Explain.

d. What happens to velocity when the price level rises? Explain.

e. As the economy grows, what should happen to the velocity of money? (*Hint:* Think about how economic growth will influence Y and F.)

f. Suppose now that the number of trips to the bank is fixed rather than discretionary. What does this assumption imply about velocity?

What We Know, What We Don't

If all economists were laid end to end, they would not reach a conclusion.

George Bernard Shaw

The theory of economics does not furnish a body of settled conclusions immediately applicable to policy. It is a method rather than a doctrine, an apparatus of the mind, which helps its possessor to draw correct conclusions.

John Maynard Keynes

The first chapter of this book states that the purpose of macroeconomics is to understand economic events and to improve economic policy. Now that we have developed and used many of the most important models in the macroeconomist's toolbox, we can assess whether macroeconomists have achieved these goals.

Any fair assessment of macroeconomics today must admit that the science is incomplete. There are some principles that almost all macroeconomists accept and on which we can rely when trying to analyze events or formulate policies. Yet there are also many questions about the economy that remain open to debate. In this last chapter we briefly review the central lessons of macroeconomics, and we discuss the most pressing unresolved questions.

The Four Most Important Lessons of Macroeconomics

We begin with four lessons that have recurred throughout this book and that most economists today would endorse. Each lesson tells us how policy can influence a key economic variable—output, inflation, or unemployment—either in the long run or in the short run.

Lesson No. 1: In the long run, a country's capacity to produce goods and services determines the standard of living of its citizens.

Of all the measures of economic performance introduced in Chapter 2 and used throughout this book, the one that best measures economic well-being is GDP. Real GDP measures the economy's total output of goods and services and, therefore, a country's ability to satisfy the needs and desires of its citizens. Perhaps the most important question in macroeconomics is what determines the level and the growth of GDP.

The models in Chapters 3 and 4 identify the long-run determinants of GDP. In the long run, GDP depends on the factors of production—capital and labor—and on the technology for turning capital and labor into output. GDP grows when the factors of production increase or when the available technology improves.

This lesson has an obvious but important corollary: public policy can raise GDP in the long run only by improving the productive capability of the economy. There are many ways in which policymakers can attempt to do this. Policies that raise national saving—either through higher public saving or higher private saving—eventually lead to a larger capital stock. Policies that raise the efficiency of labor—such as those that improve education or increase technological progress—lead to a more productive use of capital and labor. All these policies raise the economy's output of goods and services and, thereby, the standard of living. It is less clear, however, which is the best way to raise the economy's productive capability.

Lesson No. 2: In the short run, aggregate demand influences the amount of goods and services that a country produces.

Although the economy's ability to *supply* goods and services is the sole determinant of GDP in the long run, in the short run GDP depends also on the aggregate *demand* for goods and services. Aggregate demand is of key importance because prices are sticky in the short run. The *IS-LM* model developed in Chapters 9 and 10 shows what causes changes in aggregate demand and, therefore, short-run fluctuations in GDP.

Because aggregate demand influences output in the short run, all the variables that affect aggregate demand can influence economic fluctuations. Monetary policy, fiscal policy, and shocks to the money and goods markets are often responsible for year-to-year changes in output and employment. Since aggregate demand is crucial to short-run fluctuations, policymakers monitor the economy closely. Before making any change in monetary or fiscal policy, they want to know whether the economy is booming or heading into a recession.

Lesson No. 3: In the long run, the rate of money growth determines the rate of inflation, but it does not affect the rate of unemployment.

In addition to GDP, inflation and unemployment are among the most closely watched measures of economic performance. Chapter 2 discussed how these two variables are measured, and subsequent chapters developed models to explain how they are determined.

The long-run analysis of Chapter 6 stresses that growth in the money supply is the ultimate determinant of inflation. That is, in the long run, a currency loses real value over time if and only if the central bank prints more and more of it. This lesson can explain the decade-to-decade variation in the inflation rate that we have observed in the United States, as well as the far more dramatic hyperinflations that various countries have experienced from time to time.

We have also seen many of the long-run effects of high money growth and high inflation. In Chapter 6 we saw that, according to the Fisher effect, high inflation raises the nominal interest rate (so that the real interest rate remains unaffected). In Chapter 7 we saw that high inflation leads to a depreciation of the currency in the market for foreign exchange.

The long-run determinants of unemployment are very different. According to the classical dichotomy—the irrelevance of nominal variables in the determination of real variables—growth in the money supply does not affect unemployment in the long run. As we saw in Chapter 5, the natural rate of unemployment is determined by the rates of job separation and job finding, which in turn are determined by the process of job search and by the rigidity of the real wage.

Thus, we concluded that persistent inflation and persistent unemployment are unrelated problems. To combat inflation in the long run, policymakers must reduce the growth in the money supply. To combat unemployment, they must alter the structure of labor markets. In the long run, there is no tradeoff between inflation and unemployment.

Lesson No. 4: In the short run, policymakers who control monetary and fiscal policy face a tradeoff between inflation and unemployment.

Although inflation and unemployment are not related in the long run, in the short run there is a tradeoff between these two variables, which is illustrated by the short-run Phillips curve. As we discussed in Chapter 12, policymakers can use monetary and fiscal policies to expand aggregate demand, which lowers unemployment and raises inflation. Or they can use these policies to contract aggregate demand, which raises unemployment and lowers inflation.

Policymakers face a fixed tradeoff between inflation and unemployment only in the short run. Over time, the short-run Phillips curve shifts for two reasons. First, supply shocks, such as changes in the price of oil, change the short-run tradeoff; an adverse supply shock offers policymakers the difficult choice between higher inflation or higher unemployment. Second, when people change their expectations of inflation, the short-run tradeoff between inflation and unemployment changes. The adjustment of expectations ensures that the tradeoff exists only in the short run. That is, only in the short run does unemployment deviate from its natural rate, and only in the short run does monetary policy have real effects. In the long run, the classical model of Chapters 3 through 7 describes the world.

The Four Most Important Unresolved Questions of Macroeconomics

So far, we have been discussing some of the broad lessons about which most economists would agree. We now turn to four questions about which there is continuing debate. Some of the disagreements concern the validity of alternative economic theories; others concern the ways in which economic theory should be applied to economic policy.

Question No. 1: How should policymakers try to raise the economy's natural rate of output?

The economy's natural rate of output depends on the amount of capital, the amount of labor, and the level of technology. Any policy designed to raise output in the long run must aim to increase the amount of capital, improve the use of labor, or enhance the available technology. There is, however, no simple and costless way to achieve these goals.

The Solow growth model of Chapter 4 shows that increasing the amount of capital requires raising the economy's rate of saving and investment. Therefore, many economists advocate policies to raise national saving. Yet the Solow model also shows that raising the capital stock requires a period of reduced consumption for current generations. Some argue that policymakers should not encourage current generations to make this sacrifice, because technological progress will ensure that future generations are better off than current generations. Moreover, even those who advocate increased saving and investment disagree about how to encourage additional saving and whether the investment should be in privately owned plants and equipment or in public infrastructure, such as roads and schools.

To improve the economy's use of its labor force, most policymakers would like to lower the natural rate of unemployment. Yet, as we discussed in Chapter 5, this is not an easy task. Reducing unemployment-insurance benefits would decrease the amount of frictional unemployment, and reducing the minimum wage would decrease the amount of wait unemployment. Yet these policies do not command a consensus among economists, because they would also hurt some of those members of society most in need.

Raising the rate of technological progress is, according to some economists, the most important objective for public policy. The Solow growth model shows that persistent growth in living standards ultimately requires continuing technological progress. This conclusion suggests that the worldwide slowdown in productivity growth that began in the early 1970s may be the worst economic development of the past half century. Economists have not been successful at explaining this slowdown, and policymakers have not been successful at finding ways to reverse it.

Question No. 2: Should policymakers try to stabilize the economy?

The model of aggregate supply and aggregate demand developed in Chapters 8 through 12 shows how various shocks to the economy cause economic fluctuations and how monetary and fiscal policy can influence these fluctuations. Some economists believe that policymakers should use this analysis in an attempt to stabilize the economy. They believe that monetary and fiscal policy should try to offset shocks in order to keep output and employment close to their natural rates.

Yet, as we discussed in Chapter 13, others are skeptical about our ability to stabilize the economy. These economists cite the long and variable lags inherent in economic policymaking, the poor record of economic forecasting, and our still-limited understanding of the economy. They conclude that the best policy is a passive one. In addition, many economists believe that policymakers are all too often opportunistic or follow time-inconsistent policies. They conclude that policymakers should not have discretion over monetary and fiscal policy but should be committed to following a fixed policy rule.

A related question is whether the benefits of economic stabilization—assuming stabilization could be achieved—would be large or small. Without any change in the natural rate of unemployment, stabilization policy can only reduce the magnitude of fluctuations around the natural rate. Thus, successful stabilization policy would eliminate booms as well as recessions. Some economists have suggested that the average gain from stabilization would be small.

Finally, not all economists endorse the model of economic fluctuations developed in Chapters 8 through 12, which assumes sticky prices and monetary nonneutrality. According to real-business-cycle theory, which we discussed in Chapter 14, economic fluctuations are the optimal response of the economy to changing technology. Advocates of this approach believe that policymakers should not stabilize the economy, even if it were possible.

Question No. 3: How costly is inflation, and how costly is reducing inflation?

Whenever prices are rising, policymakers confront the question of whether to pursue policies to reduce the rate of inflation. To make this decision, they must compare the cost of allowing inflation to continue to the cost of reducing it. Yet economists cannot offer accurate estimates of either of these two costs.

The cost of inflation is a topic on which economists and laymen often disagree. When inflation reached 10 percent per year in the late 1970s, opinion polls showed that the public viewed inflation as a major economic problem. Yet, as we discussed in Chapter 6, when economists try to identify the social costs of inflation, they can point only to shoeleather costs, menu costs, the costs of a nonindexed tax system, and so on. These costs become large when countries experience hyperinflation, but they seem relatively minor at the moderate rates of inflation experienced in most major economies. Some economists believe that the public confuses inflation with other economic problems that coincide with inflation. For example, growth in productivity and real wages slowed in the 1970s; some laymen might have viewed inflation as the cause of the slowdown in real wages. Yet it is also possible that economists are mistaken: perhaps inflation is in fact very costly, and we have yet to figure out why.

The cost of reducing inflation is a topic on which economists often disagree among themselves. As we discussed in Chapter 12, the standard view—as described by the short-run Phillips curve—is that reducing inflation requires a period of low output and high unemployment. According to this view, the cost of reducing inflation is measured by the sacrifice ratio, which is the number of percentage points of a year's GDP that must be forgone to reduce inflation by 1 percentage point.

Some economists think that the cost of reducing inflation can be much smaller than standard estimates of the sacrifice ratio indicate. According to the rational-expectations approach discussed in Chapter 12, if a disinflationary policy is announced in advance and is credible, people will adjust their expectations quickly, so the disinflation need not cause a recession. According to the real-business-cycle models discussed in Chapter 14, prices are flexible and money is neutral, so disinflationary monetary policy will not affect the economy's output of goods and services.

Other economists believe that the cost of reducing inflation is much larger than standard estimates of the sacrifice ratio indicate. The theories of hysteresis discussed in Chapter 12 suggest that a recession caused by disinflationary policy could raise the natural rate of unemployment. If so, then the cost of reducing inflation is not merely a temporary recession but a persistently higher level of unemployment.

Because the costs of inflation and disinflation remain open to debate, economists sometimes offer conflicting advice to policymakers. Perhaps with further research, we can reach a consensus on the benefits of low inflation and the best way to achieve that goal.

Question No. 4: How big a problem are government budget deficits?

In recent years, large budget deficits have been a primary topic of debate among policymakers in the United States and Europe. In January 1993, in his first address on the state of the union, President Bill Clinton made reducing the deficit a central goal of his administration. Then, when the Republicans took control of Congress in 1995, they argued for even faster deficit reduction than the President had advocated. As we discussed in Chapter 16, the budget deficit is a topic about which economists often disagree.

Most of the models in this book, and most economists, take the traditional view of government debt. According to this view, a budget deficit leads to lower national saving, lower investment, and a trade deficit. In the long run, it leads to a smaller steady-state capital stock and a larger foreign debt. Those who hold the traditional view conclude that budget deficits place a burden on future generations.

Yet not all economists agree with this assessment. Advocates of the Ricardian view of government debt are skeptical. They stress that a budget deficit merely represents a substitution of future taxes for current taxes. As long as consumers are forward-looking, as the theories of consumption presented in Chapter 15 assume, they will save today to meet their or their children's future tax liability. These economists believe that budget deficits have only a minor effect on the economy.

Still other economists believe that the budget deficit is an imperfect measure of fiscal policy. They agree that the government's choices regarding taxes and spending have great influence on the welfare of different generations. Yet, according to these economists, the budget deficit does not fully capture the generational impacts of fiscal decisions.

Conclusion

Economists and policymakers must deal with ambiguity. The current state of macroeconomics offers many insights, but it also leaves many questions open. The challenge for economists is to find answers to these questions and to expand our knowledge. The challenge for policymakers is to use the knowledge we now have to improve economic performance. Both challenges are formidable, but neither is insuperable.

Glossary

Accelerator model: The model according to which investment depends on the change in output.

Accommodating policy: A policy that yields to the effect of a shock and thereby prevents the shock from being disruptive; for example, a policy that raises aggregate demand in response to an adverse supply shock, sustaining the effect of the shock on prices and keeping output at the natural rate.

Accounting profit: The amount of revenue remaining for the owners of a firm after all the factors of production except capital have been compensated. (Cf. economic profit, profit.)

Acyclical: Moving in no consistent direction over the business cycle. (Cf. countercyclical, procyclical.)

Adaptive expectations: An approach that assumes that people form their expectation of a variable based on recently observed values of the variable. (Cf. rational expectations.)

Adverse selection: An unfavorable sorting of individuals by their own choices; for example, in efficiency-wage theory, when a wage cut induces good workers to quit and bad workers to remain with the firm.

Aggregate: Total for the whole economy.

Aggregate demand curve: The negative relationship between the price level and the aggregate quantity of output demanded that arises from the interaction between the goods market and the money market.

Aggregate demand externality: The macroeconomic impact of one firm's price adjustment on the demand for all other firms' products.

Aggregate supply curve: The relationship between the price level and the aggregate quantity of output firms produce.

Animal spirits: Exogenous and perhaps self-fulfilling waves of optimism and pessimism about the state of the economy which, according to some economists, influence the level of investment.

Appreciation: A rise in the value of a currency relative to other currencies in the market for foreign exchange. (Cf. depreciation.)

Arbitrage: The act of buying an item in one market and selling it at a higher price in another market in order to profit from the price differential in the two markets.

Automatic stabilizer: A policy that reduces the amplitude of economic fluctuations without regular and deliberate changes in economic policy; for example, an income tax system which automatically reduces taxes when income falls.

Average propensity to consume (APC): The ratio of consumption to income (C/Y).

Balance sheet: An accounting statement that shows assets and liabilities.

Balanced budget: A budget in which receipts equal expenditures.

Baumol-Tobin model: A model of money demand positing that people choose optimal money holdings by comparing the opportunity cost of the forgone interest from holding money and the benefit of making less frequent trips to the bank.

Bond: A document representing an interest-bearing debt of the issuer, usually a corporation or the government.

Borrowing constraint: A restriction on the amount a person can borrow from financial institutions, limiting that person's ability to spend his or her future income today; also called a liquidity constraint.

Budget constraint: The limit that income places on expenditure. (Cf. intertemporal budget constraint.)

Budget deficit: A shortfall of receipts from expenditure.

Budget surplus: An excess of receipts over expenditure.

Business cycle: Economy-wide fluctuations in output, incomes, and employment.

Business fixed investment: Equipment and structures that businesses buy for use in future production.

Capital: 1. The stock of equipment and structures used in production. 2. The funds to finance the accumulation of equipment and structures.

Capital budgeting: An accounting procedure that measures both assets and liabilities.

Central bank: The institution responsible for the conduct of monetary policy, such as the Federal Reserve in the United States.

Classical dichotomy: The theoretical separation of real and nominal variables in the classical model, which implies that nominal variables do not influence real variables. (Cf. neutrality of money.)

Classical model: A model of the economy derived from the ideas of the classical, or pre-Keynesian, economists; a model based on the assumptions that wages and prices adjust to clear markets and that monetary policy does not influence real variables. (Cf. Keynesian model.)

Closed economy: An economy that does not engage in international trade. (Cf. open economy.)

Cobb-Douglas production function: A production function of the form $F(K, L) = AK^\alpha L^{1-\alpha}$, where K is capital, L is labor, and A and α are parameters.

Commodity money: Money that is intrinsically useful and would be valued even if it did not serve as money. (Cf. fiat money, money.)

Competition: A situation in which there are many individuals or firms so that the actions of any one of them do not influence market prices.

Constant returns to scale: A property of a production function whereby a proportionate increase in all factors of production leads to an increase in output of the same proportion.

Consumer price index (CPI): A measure of the overall level of prices that shows the cost of a fixed basket of consumer goods relative to the cost of the same basket in a base year.

Consumption: Goods and services purchased by consumers.

Consumption function: A relationship showing the determinants of consumption; for example, a relationship between consumption and disposable income, $C = C(Y - T)$.

Contractionary policy: Policy that reduces aggregate demand, real income, and employment. (Cf. expansionary policy.)

Coordination failure: A situation in which decisionmakers reach an outcome that is inferior for all of them because of their inability to jointly choose strategies that would result in a preferred outcome.

Corporate income tax: The tax levied on the accounting profit of corporations.

Cost of capital: The amount forgone by holding a unit of capital for one period, including interest, depreciation, and the gain or loss from the change in the price of capital.

Cost-push inflation: Inflation resulting from shocks to aggregate supply. (Cf. demand-pull inflation.)

Countercyclical: Moving in the opposite direction from output, incomes, and employment over the business cycle; rising during recessions and falling during recoveries. (Cf. acyclical, procyclical.)

CPI: *See* consumer price index.

Crowding out: The reduction in investment that results when expansionary fiscal policy raises the interest rate.

Currency: The sum of outstanding paper money and coins.

Cyclical unemployment: The unemployment associated with short-run economic fluctuations; the deviation of the unemployment rate from the natural rate.

Cyclically adjusted budget deficit: The budget deficit adjusted for the influence of the business cycle on government spending and tax revenue; the budget deficit that would occur if the economy's production and employment were at their natural rates. Also called the full-employment budget deficit.

Debt-deflation: A theory according to which an unexpected fall in the price level redistributes real wealth from debtors to creditors and, therefore, reduces total spending in the economy.

Deflation: A decrease in the overall level of prices. (Cf. disinflation, inflation.)

Deflator: *See* GDP deflator.

Demand deposits: Assets that are held in banks and can be used on demand to make transactions, such as checking accounts.

Demand-pull inflation: Inflation resulting from shocks to aggregate demand. (Cf. cost-push inflation.)

Depreciation: 1. The reduction in the capital stock that occurs over time because of aging and use. 2. A fall in the value of a currency relative to other currencies in the market for foreign exchange. (Cf. appreciation.)

Depression: A very severe recession.

Devaluation: An action by the central bank to decrease the value of a currency under a system of fixed exchange rates. (Cf. revaluation.)

Diminishing marginal product: A characteristic of a production function whereby the marginal product of a factor falls as the amount of the factor increases while all other factors are held constant.

Discount rate: The interest rate that the Fed charges when it makes loans to banks.

Discounting: The reduction in value of future expenditure and receipts, compared to current expenditure and receipts, resulting from the presence of a positive interest rate.

Discouraged workers: Individuals who have left the labor force because they believe that there is little hope of finding a job.

Disinflation: A reduction in the rate at which prices are rising. (Cf. deflation, inflation.)

Disposable income: Income remaining after the payment of taxes.

Dominated asset: An asset that offers an inferior return compared to another asset in all possible realizations of future uncertainty.

Double coincidence of wants: A situation in which two individuals each have precisely the good that the other wants.

Economic profit: The amount of revenue remaining for the owners of a firm after all the factors of production have been compensated. (Cf. accounting profit, profit.)

Efficiency of labor: A variable in the Solow growth model that measures the health, education, skills, and knowledge of the labor force.

Efficiency units of labor: A measure of the labor force that incorporates both the number of workers and the efficiency of each worker.

Efficiency-wage theories: Theories of real-wage rigidity and unemployment according to which firms raise labor productivity and profits by keeping real wages above the equilibrium level.

Elasticity: The percent change in a variable caused by a 1 percent change in another variable.

Endogenous variable: A variable that is explained by a particular model; a variable whose value is determined by the model's solution. (Cf. exogenous variable.)

Equilibrium: A state of balance between opposing forces, such as the balance of supply and demand in a market.

Euler's theorem: The mathematical result economists use to show that economic profit must be zero if the production function has constant returns to scale and if factors are paid their marginal products.

Ex ante **real interest rate**: The real interest rate anticipated when a loan is made; the nominal interest rate minus expected inflation. (Cf. *ex post* real interest rate.)

Ex post **real interest rate**: The real interest rate actually realized; the nominal interest rate minus actual inflation. (Cf. *ex ante* real interest rate.)

Excess reserves: Reserves held by banks above the amount mandated by reserve requirements.

Exchange rate: The rate at which a country makes exchanges in world markets. (Cf. nominal exchange rate, real exchange rate.)

Exchange-rate union: A group of countries that agree to limit exchange-rate fluctuations among their currencies.

Exogenous variable: A variable that a particular model takes as given; a variable whose value is independent of the model's solution. (Cf. endogenous variable.)

Expansionary policy: Policy that raises aggregate demand, real income, and employment. (Cf. contractionary policy.)

Exports: Goods and services sold to other countries.

Factor of production: An input used to produce goods and services; for example, capital or labor.

Factor price: The amount paid for one unit of a factor of production.

Factor share: The proportion of total income being paid to a factor of production.

Federal Reserve (the Fed): The central bank of the United States.

Fiat money: Money that is not intrinsically useful and is valued only because it is used as money. (Cf. commodity money, money.)

Financial intermediation: The process by which resources are allocated from those individuals who wish to save some of their income for future consumption to those individuals and firms who wish to borrow to buy investment goods for future production.

Financing constraint: A limit on the quantity of funds a firm can raise—such as through borrowing—in order to buy capital.

Fiscal policy: The government's choice regarding levels of spending and taxation.

Fisher effect: The one-for-one influence of expected inflation on the nominal interest rate.

Fisher equation: The equation stating that the nominal interest rate is the sum of the real interest rate and expected inflation ($i = r + \pi^e$).

Fixed exchange rate: An exchange rate that is set by the central bank's willingness to buy and sell the domestic currency for foreign currencies at a predetermined price. (Cf. floating exchange rate.)

Flexible prices: Prices that adjust quickly to equilibrate supply and demand. (Cf. sticky prices.)

Floating exchange rate: An exchange rate that the central bank allows to change in response to changing economic conditions and economic policies. (Cf. fixed exchange rate.)

Flow: A variable measured as a quantity per unit of time. (Cf. stock.)

Fractional-reserve banking: A system in which banks keep only some of their deposits on reserve. (Cf. 100-percent-reserve banking.)

Frictional unemployment: The unemployment that results because it takes time for workers to search for the jobs that best suit their skills and tastes. (Cf. wait unemployment.)

Full-employment budget deficit: *See* cyclically adjusted budget deficit.

GDP: *See* gross domestic product.

GDP deflator: The ratio of nominal GDP to real GDP; a measure of the overall level of prices that shows the cost of the currently produced basket of goods relative to the cost of that basket in a base year.

General equilibrium: The simultaneous equilibrium of all the markets in the economy.

GNP: *See* gross national product.

Gold standard: A monetary system in which gold serves as money or in which all money is convertible into gold.

Golden rule: The saving rate in the Solow growth model that leads to the steady state in which consumption per worker (or consumption per efficiency unit of labor) is maximized.

Government purchases: Goods and services bought by the government. (Cf. transfer payments.)

Government-purchases multiplier: The change in aggregate income resulting from a one-dollar change in government purchases.

Gross domestic product (GDP): The total income earned domestically, including the income earned by foreign-owned factors of production; the total expenditure on domestically produced goods and services.

Gross national product (GNP): The total income of all residents of a nation, including the income from factors of production used abroad; the total expenditure on the nation's output of goods and services.

High-powered money: The sum of currency and bank reserves; also called the monetary base.

Hyperinflation: Extremely high inflation.

Hysteresis: The long-lasting influence of history, such as on the natural rate of unemployment.

Identification problem: The difficulty of isolating a particular relationship in data when two or more variables are related in more than one way.

Imperfect-information model: The model of aggregate supply emphasizing that individuals do not always know the overall price level because they cannot observe the prices of all goods and services in the economy.

Import quota: A legal limit on the amount of a good that can be imported.

Imports: Goods and services bought from other countries.

Imputed value: An estimate of the value of a good or service that is not sold in the marketplace and therefore does not have a market price.

Income effect: The change in consumption of a good resulting from a movement to a higher or lower indifference curve, holding the relative price constant. (Cf. substitution effect.)

Index of leading indicators: *See* leading indicators.

Indifference curves: A graphical representation of preferences that shows different combinations of goods producing the same level of satisfaction.

Inflation: An increase in the overall level of prices. (Cf. deflation, disinflation.)

Inflation tax: The revenue raised by the government through the creation of money; seigniorage.

Inside lag: The time between a shock hitting the economy and the policy action taken to respond to the shock. (Cf. outside lag.)

Insiders: Workers who are already employed and therefore have an influence on wage bargaining. (Cf. outsiders.)

Interest rate: The market price at which resources are transferred between the present and the future; the return to saving and the cost of borrowing.

Intermediation: *See* financial intermediation.

Intertemporal budget constraint: The budget constraint applying to expenditure and income in more than one period of time. (Cf. budget constraint.)

Intertemporal substitution of labor: The willingness of people to trade off working in one period for working in future periods.

Inventory investment: The change in the quantity of goods that firms hold in storage, including materials and supplies, work in process, and finished goods.

Investment: Goods purchased by individuals and firms to add to their stock of capital.

Investment tax credit: A provision of the corporate income tax that reduces a firm's tax when it buys new capital goods.

IS curve: The negative relationship between the interest rate and the level of income that arises in the market for goods and services. (Cf. *IS-LM* model, *LM* curve.)

IS-LM model: A model of aggregate demand that shows what determines aggregate income for a given price level by analyzing the interaction between the goods market and the money market. (Cf. *IS* curve, *LM* curve.)

Keynesian cross: A simple model of income determination, based on the ideas in Keynes's *General Theory*, which shows how changes in spending can have a multiplied effect on aggregate income.

Keynesian model: A model derived from the ideas of Keynes's *General Theory*; a model based on the assumptions that wages and prices do not adjust to clear markets and that aggregate demand determines the economy's output and employment. (Cf. classical model.)

Labor-augmenting technological progress: Advances in productive capability that raise the efficiency of labor.

Labor force: Those in the population who have a job or are looking for a job.

Labor-force participation rate: The percent of the adult population in the labor force.

Labor hoarding: The phenomenon of firms employing workers whom they do not need when the demand for their products is low, so that they will still have these workers when demand recovers.

Large open economy: An open economy that can influence its domestic interest rate; an economy that, by virtue of its size, can have a substantial impact on world markets and, in particular, on the world interest rate. (Cf. small open economy.)

Laspeyres price index: A measure of the level of prices based on a fixed basket of goods. (Cf. Paasche price index.)

Leading indicators: Economic variables that fluctuate in advance of the economy's output and thus signal the direction of economic fluctuations.

Life-cycle hypothesis: The theory of consumption that emphasizes the role of saving and borrowing as transferring resources from those times in life when income is high to those times in life when income is low, such as from working years to retirement.

Liquid: Readily convertible into the medium of exchange; easily used to make transactions.

Liquidity constraint: A restriction on the amount a person can borrow from a financial institution, which limits the person's ability to spend his future income today; also called a borrowing constraint.

Liquidity-preference theory: A simple model of the interest rate, based on the ideas in Keynes's *General Theory*, which says that the interest rate adjusts to equilibrate the supply and demand for real money balances.

LM curve: The positive relationship between the interest rate and the level of income (while holding the price level fixed) that arises in the market for real money balances. (Cf. *IS-LM* model, *IS* curve.)

Loanable funds: The flow of resources available to finance capital accumulation.

Lucas critique: The argument that traditional policy analysis does not adequately take into account the impact of policy changes on people's expectations.

M1, M2, M3: Various measures of the stock of money, where larger numbers signify a broader definition of money.

Macroeconometric model: A model that uses data and statistical techniques to describe the economy quantitatively, rather than just qualitatively.

Macroeconomics: The study of the economy as a whole. (Cf. microeconomics.)

Marginal product of capital (*MPK*): The amount of extra output produced when the capital input is increased by one unit.

Marginal product of labor (*MPL*): The amount of extra output produced when the labor input is increased by one unit.

Marginal propensity to consume (*MPC*): The increase in consumption resulting from a one-dollar increase in disposable income.

Marginal rate of substitution (*MRS*): The rate at which a consumer is willing to give up some of one good in exchange for more of another; the slope of the indifference curve.

Market-clearing model: A model that assumes that prices freely adjust to equilibrate supply and demand.

Medium of exchange: The item widely accepted in transactions for goods and services; one of the functions of money. (Cf. store of value, unit of account.)

Menu cost: The cost of changing a price.

Microeconomics: The study of individual markets and decisionmakers. (Cf. macroeconomics.)

Model: A simplified representation of reality, often using diagrams or equations, that shows how variables interact.

Monetarism: The doctrine according to which changes in the money supply are the primary cause of economic fluctuations, implying that a stable money supply would lead to a stable economy.

Monetary base: The sum of currency and bank reserves; also called high-powered money.

Monetary neutrality: *See* neutrality of money.

Monetary policy: The central bank's choice regarding the supply of money.

Monetary transmission mechanism: The process by which changes in the money supply influence the amount that households and firms wish to spend on goods and services.

Money: The stock of assets used for transactions. (Cf. commodity money, fiat money.)

Money demand function: A function showing the determinants of the demand for real money balances; for example, $(M/P)^d = L(i, Y)$.

Money multiplier: The increase in the money supply resulting from a one-dollar increase in the monetary base.

Moral hazard: The possibility of dishonest behavior in situations in which behavior is imperfectly monitored; for example, in efficiency-wage theory, the possibility that low-wage workers may shirk their responsibilities and risk getting caught and fired.

Multiplier: *See* government-purchases multiplier, money multiplier, or tax multiplier.

Mundell-Fleming model: The *IS-LM* model for a small open economy.

Mundell-Tobin effect: The fall in the real interest rate that results when an increase in expected inflation raises the nominal interest rate, lowers real money balances and real wealth, and thereby reduces consumption and raises saving.

National income accounting: The accounting system that measures GDP and many other related statistics.

National income accounts identity: The equation showing that GDP is the sum of consumption, investment, government purchases, and net exports.

National saving: A nation's income minus consumption and government purchases; the sum of private and public saving.

Natural rate of unemployment: The steady-state rate of unemployment; the rate of unemployment toward which the economy gravitates in the long run.

Natural-rate hypothesis: The premise that fluctuations in aggregate demand influence output, employment, and unemployment only in the short run, and that in the long run these variables return to the levels implied by the classical model.

Near money: Assets that are almost as useful as money for engaging in transactions and, therefore, are close substitutes for money.

Neoclassical model of investment: The theory according to which investment depends on the deviation of the marginal product of capital from the cost of capital.

Net exports: Exports minus imports.

Net foreign investment: The net flow of funds being invested abroad; domestic saving minus domestic investment.

Net investment: The amount of investment after the replacement of depreciated capital; the change in the capital stock.

Neutrality of money: The property that a change in the money supply does not influence real variables. (Cf. classical dichotomy.)

New classical economics: The school of thought according to which economic fluctuations can be explained while maintaining the assumptions of the classical model. (Cf. new Keynesian economics.)

New Keynesian economics: The school of thought according to which economic fluctuations can be explained only by admitting a role for some microeconomic imperfection, such as sticky wages or prices. (Cf. new classical economics.)

Nominal: Measured in current dollars; not adjusted for inflation. (Cf. real.)

Nominal exchange rate: The rate at which one country's currency trades for another country's currency. (Cf. exchange rate, real exchange rate.)

Nominal interest rate: The return to saving and the cost of borrowing without adjustment for inflation. (Cf. real interest rate.)

Normal good: A good that a consumer demands in greater quantity when his or her income rises.

Okun's law: The negative relationship between unemployment and real GDP, according to which a decrease in unemployment of one percentage point is associated with additional growth in real GDP of approximately two percent.

100-percent-reserve banking: A system in which banks keep all deposits on reserve. (Cf. fractional-reserve banking.)

Open economy: An economy in which people can freely engage in international trade in goods and capital. (Cf. closed economy.)

Open-market operations: The purchase or sale of government bonds by the central bank for the purpose of increasing or decreasing the money supply.

Outside lag: The time between a policy action and its influence on the economy. (Cf. inside lag.)

Outsiders: Workers who are not employed and therefore have no influence on wage bargaining. (Cf. insiders.)

Paasche price index: A measure of the level of prices based on a changing basket of goods. (Cf. Laspeyres price index.)

Permanent income: Income that people expect to persist into the future; normal income. (Cf. transitory income.)

Permanent-income hypothesis: The theory of consumption according to which people choose consumption based on their permanent income, and use saving and borrowing to smooth consumption in response to transitory variations in income.

Phillips curve: A negative relationship between inflation and unemployment; in its modern form, a relationship among inflation, cyclical unemployment, expected inflation, and supply shocks, derived from the short-run aggregate supply curve.

Pigou effect: The increase in consumer spending that results when a fall in the price level raises real money balances and, thereby, consumers' wealth.

Political business cycle: The fluctuations in output and employment resulting from the manipulation of the economy for electoral gain.

Portfolio theories of money demand: Theories that explain how much money people choose to hold and that stress the role of money as a store of value. (Cf. transactions theories of money demand.)

Precautionary saving: The extra saving that results from uncertainty regarding, for example, longevity or future income.

Present value: The amount today that is equivalent to an amount to be received in the future, taking into account the interest that could be earned over the interval of time.

Private saving: Disposable income minus consumption.

Procyclical: Moving in the same direction as output, incomes, and employment over the business cycle; falling during recessions and rising during recoveries. (Cf. acyclical, countercyclical.)

Production function: The mathematical relationship showing how the quantities of the factors of production determine the quantity of goods and services produced; for example, $Y = F(K, L)$.

Production smoothing: The motive for holding inventories according to which a firm can reduce its costs by keeping the amount of output it produces steady and allowing its stock of inventories to respond to fluctuating sales.

Profit: The income of firm owners; firm revenue minus firm costs. (Cf. accounting profit, economic profit.)

Public saving: Government receipts minus government spending; the budget surplus.

Purchasing-power parity: The doctrine according to which goods must sell for the same price in every country, implying that the nominal exchange rate reflects differences in price levels.

q-theory of investment: The theory according to which expenditure on capital goods depends on the ratio of the market value of installed capital to its replacement cost.

Quantity equation: The identity stating that the product of the money supply and the velocity of money equals nominal expenditure ($MV = PY$); coupled with the assumption of stable velocity, an explanation of nominal expenditure called the quantity theory of money.

Quantity theory of money: The doctrine emphasizing that changes in the quantity of money lead to changes in nominal expenditure.

Quota: *See* import quota.

Random walk: The path of a variable whose changes over time are unpredictable.

Rational expectations: An approach that assumes that people optimally use all available information—including information about current and prospective policies—to forecast the future. (Cf. adaptive expectations.)

Real: Measured in constant dollars; adjusted for inflation. (Cf. nominal.)

Real-business-cycle theory: The theory according to which economic fluctuations can be explained by real changes in the economy (such as changes in technology) and without any role for nominal variables (such as the money supply).

Real exchange rate: The rate at which one country's goods trade for another country's goods. (Cf. exchange rate, nominal exchange rate.)

Real interest rate: The return to saving and the cost of borrowing after adjustment for inflation. (Cf. nominal interest rate.)

Real money balances: The quantity of money expressed in terms of the quantity of goods and services it can buy; the quantity of money divided by the price level (M/P).

Recession: A sustained period of falling real income.

Rental price of capital: The amount paid to rent one unit of capital.

Reserve requirements: Regulations imposed on banks by the central bank that specify a minimum reserve–deposit ratio.

Reserves: The money that banks have received from depositors but have not used to make loans.

Residential investment: New housing bought by people to live in and by landlords to rent out.

Revaluation: An action undertaken by the central bank to raise the value of a currency under a system of fixed exchange rates. (Cf. devaluation.)

Ricardian equivalence: The theory according to which forward-looking consumers fully anticipate the future taxes implied by government debt, so that government borrowing today coupled with a tax increase in the future to repay the debt has the same effect on the economy as a tax increase today.

Sacrifice ratio: The number of percentage points of a year's real GDP that must be forgone to reduce inflation by one percentage point.

Saving: *See* national saving, private saving, and public saving.

Seasonal adjustment: The removal of the regular fluctuations in an economic variable that occur as a function of the time of year.

Sectoral shift: A change in the composition of demand among industries or regions.

Seigniorage: The revenue raised by the government through the creation of money; the inflation tax.

Shock: An exogenous change in an economic relationship, such as the aggregate demand or aggregate supply curve.

Shoeleather cost: The cost of inflation from reducing real money balances, such as the inconvenience of needing to make more frequent trips to the bank.

Small open economy: An open economy that takes its interest rate as given by world financial markets; an economy that, by virtue of its size, has a negligible impact on world markets and, in particular, on the world interest rate. (Cf. large open economy.)

Solow growth model: A model showing how saving, population growth, and technological progress determine the level of and growth in the standard of living.

Solow residual: The growth in total factor productivity, measured as the percentage change in output minus the percentage change in inputs, where the inputs are weighted by their factor shares. (Cf. total factor productivity.)

Stabilization policy: Public policy aimed at keeping output and employment at their natural-rate levels.

Stagflation: A situation of falling output and rising prices; combination of stagnation and inflation.

Steady state: A condition in which key variables are not changing.

Sticky prices: Prices that adjust sluggishly and, therefore, do not always equilibrate supply and demand. (Cf. flexible prices.)

Sticky-price model: The model of aggregate supply emphasizing the slow adjustment of the prices of goods and services.

Sticky-wage model: The model of aggregate supply emphasizing the slow adjustment of nominal wages.

Stock: 1. A variable measured as a quantity at a point in time. (Cf. flow.) 2. Shares of ownership in a corporation.

Stock market: A market in which shares of ownership in corporations are bought and sold.

Stock-out avoidance: The motive for holding inventories according to which firms keep extra goods on hand to prevent running out if sales are unexpectedly high.

Store of value: A way of transferring purchasing power from the present to the future; one of the functions of money. (Cf. medium of exchange, unit of account.)

Substitution effect: The change in consumption of a good resulting from a movement along an indifference curve because of a change in the relative price. (Cf. income effect.)

Tariff: A tax on imported goods.

Tax multiplier: The change in aggregate income resulting from a one-dollar change in taxes.

Time inconsistency: The tendency of policymakers to announce policies in advance in order to influence the expectations of private decisionmakers, and then to follow different policies after those expectations have been formed and acted upon.

Tobin's q: The ratio of the market value of installed capital to its replacement cost.

Total factor productivity: A measure of the level of technology; the amount of output per unit of input, where different inputs are combined on the basis of their factor shares. (Cf. Solow residual.)

Trade balance: The receipts from exports minus the payments for imports.

Transactions theories of money demand: Theories that explain how much money people choose to hold and that stress the role of money as a medium of exchange. (Cf. portfolio theories of money demand.)

Transfer payments: Payments from the government to individuals that are not in exchange for goods and services, such as Social Security payments. (Cf. government purchases.)

Transitory income: Income that people do not expect to persist into the future; current income minus normal income. (Cf. permanent income.)

Underground economy: Economic transactions that are hidden in order to evade taxes or conceal illegal activity.

Unemployment insurance: A government program under which unemployed workers can collect benefits for a certain period of time after losing their jobs.

Unemployment rate: The percentage of those in the labor force who do not have jobs.

Unit of account: The measure in which prices and other accounting records are recorded; one of the functions of money. (Cf. medium of exchange, store of value.)

Value-added: The value of a firm's output minus the value of the intermediate goods the firm purchased.

Velocity of money: The ratio of nominal expenditure to the money supply; the rate at which money changes hands.

Wage: The amount paid for one unit of labor.

Wage rigidity: The failure of wages to adjust to equilibrate labor supply and labor demand.

Wait unemployment: The unemployment resulting from wage rigidity and job rationing. (Cf. frictional unemployment.)

Work in process: Goods in inventory that are in the process of being completed.

Worker-misperception model: The model of aggregate supply emphasizing that workers sometimes perceive incorrectly the overall level of prices.

World interest rate: The interest rate prevailing in world financial markets.

Index